M000117739

The Common Language Infrastructure Annotated Standard

Microsoft .NET Development Series

John Montgomery, *Series Advisor*
Don Box, *Series Advisor*
Martin Heller, *Series Editor*

The **Microsoft .NET Development Series** is supported and developed by the leaders and experts of Microsoft development technologies including Microsoft architects and DevelopMentor instructors. The books in this series provide a core resource of information and understanding every developer needs in order to write effective applications and managed code. Learn from the leaders how to maximize your use of the .NET Framework and its programming languages.

Titles in the Series

Brad Abrams, *.NET Framework Standard Library Annotated Reference Volume 1*, 0-321-15489-4

Keith Ballinger, *.NET Web Services: Architecture and Implementation*, 0-321-11359-4

Don Box with Chris Sells, *Essential .NET, Volume 1: The Common Language Runtime*, 0-201-73411-7

Mahesh Chand, *Graphics Programming with GDI+*, 0-321-16077-0

Anders Hejlsberg, Scott Wiltamuth, Peter Golde, *The C# Programming Language*, 0-321-15491-6

Alex Homer, Dave Sussman, Mark Fussell, *A First Look at ADO.NET and System.Xml v. 2.0*, 0-321-22839-1

Alex Homer, Dave Sussman, Rob Howard, *A First Look at ASP.NET v. 2.0*, 0-321-22896-0

James S. Miller and Susann Ragsdale, *The Common Language Infrastructure Annotated Standard*, 0-321-15493-2

Fritz Onion, *Essential ASP.NET with Examples in C#*, 0-201-76040-1

Fritz Onion, *Essential ASP.NET with Examples in Visual Basic .NET*, 0-201-76039-8

Ted Pattison and Dr. Joe Hummel, *Building Applications and Components with Visual Basic .NET*, 0-201-73495-8

Chris Sells, *Windows Forms Programming in C#*, 0-321-11620-8

Chris Sells and Justin Gehtland, *Windows Forms Programming in Visual Basic .NET*, 0-321-12519-3

Damien Watkins, Mark Hammond, Brad Abrams, *Programming in the .NET Environment*, 0-201-77018-0

Shawn Wildermuth, *Pragmatic ADO.NET: Data Access for the Internet World*, 0-201-74568-2

www.awprofessional.com/msdotnetseries/

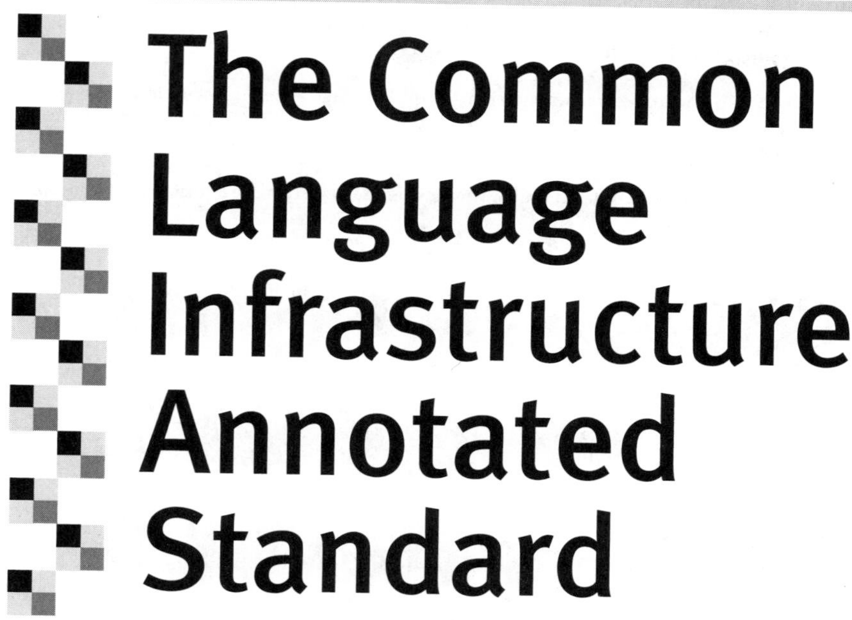

The Common Language Infrastructure Annotated Standard

Jim Miller
Susann Ragsdale

Addison-Wesley

Boston • San Francisco • New York • Toronto • Montreal
London • Munich • Paris • Madrid
Capetown • Sydney • Tokyo • Singapore • Mexico City

The publisher offers discounts on this book when ordered in quantity for special sales. For more information, please contact:

U.S. Corporate and Government Sales
(800) 382-3419
corpsales@pearsontechgroup.com

For sales outside of the U.S., please contact:

International Sales
(317 581-3793)
international@pearsontechgroup.com

Visit Addison-Wesley on the Web:
www.awprofessional.com

Library of Congress Cataloging-in-Publication Data

Miller, James S., 1954–
The common language infrastructure annotated standard / James S. Miller, Susann Ragsdale.
p. cm.
Includes bibliographical references and index.
ISBN 0-321-15493-2 (alk. paper)
1. Programming languages (Electronic computers) 2. Microsoft .NET Framework I. Ragsdale, Susann. II. Title.

QA76.7.M52 2003
005.13—dc22

2003062765

ISBN 0-321-15493-2
Text printed on recycled paper
1 2 3 4 5 6 7 8 9 10—CRW—0706050403
First printing, October 2003

This book is dedicated to the hundreds of members of the Microsoft Common Language Runtime and Compact Framework teams. Special thanks are due to MikeToutonghi, whose vision and drive took us from a dream to a reality, and to Barbara Miller, whose support and willingness to pull up twenty-five years of roots and move across a continent made it possible for me to join that team.

Contents

Tables

Foreword

When looking at the Common Language Runtime (CLR) in historical context, it's hard not to marvel at how far the platform has advanced from the circa-1990s world of COM it replaces.

Yes, there are a number of technological advances that occurred (such as ubiquitous and extensible type information, virtualized execution, first-class support for opaque structure and behavior) as we moved from COM to the CLR. The one advance over the COM era that I am personally very excited about is the fact that the core architecture of the abstract model (Common Language Infrastructure often called the CLI) was written down and published concurrently with the shipping of the DLLs and configuration scripts necessary to make the platform real.

COM suffered immensely from the fact that the product team lacked the resources to finish the COM specification (to this day, the COM specification is only available in draft form as a collection of Word files downloadable over the Web). The fact that the CLR product team had the foresight to maintain a readable, objective, and direct document that describes the contract between the CLR and your program is a concrete feature that is at least as important as fast garbage collection or a version-aware loader.[1] When Jim Miller asked me to write the foreword for the printed and annotated version of that document, I was flattered beyond words and immediately accepted.

There have been (and will continue to be) countless books and primers published on writing programs that run in the CLR. However, there is no single book that is more vital to the professional developer than the one you are holding in your hands, because it describes in direct yet readable terms the basic physics of what makes your programs actually work.

I caution you not to mistake this book with an "internals" book—internals books by necessity tend to focus on release-specific details that are likely to change from version to version

1. That Microsoft was able to shepherd that document through ECMA and ISO without losing precision or clarity is an accomplishment in itself.

(roughly 20 percent of my own CLR book will be rendered obsolete or inaccurate by the next release of the CLR). In contrast, the book you are holding focuses only on the semantics and structure of the contract between your code and an abstract execution engine whose implementation can and will change as often as is necessary.

I encourage you to read this book twice—once now and then again after you've written CLR-based programs for six months or more. I personally find that each time I read the original CLI specification, I gain new insights into how my programs work and how I can better take advantage of the capabilities and features of the Common Language Runtime. I'm certain you will too.

Don Box
Architect, Microsoft Corporation

Preface

This book, *The Common Language Infrastructure Annotated Standard*, annotates and amplifies the Common Language Infrastructure (CLI) Standard. It describes the CLI and its parts, and contains all of the information required to understand and implement a Virtual Execution System (VES) or design a compiler that generates portable code and runs on top of a VES.

This book is indispensable for anyone who wants to understand the CLI Standard. By necessity, standards follow a specific set of guidelines, including non-repetition of information. The result is a good standard, but it can be difficult to read and easily understand.

The annotations in this book came directly from the authors of the original specification (primarily Jim Miller) and from the highly talented ECMA technical committee that is responsible for standardizing that specification. The many annotations explain and expand on the original standard, clarifying it, connecting the dots, and supplying many more cross-references to make the system understandable.

This book is intended for four audiences:

- Language and tool designers
- Developers of libraries
- Those interested in developing or understanding a Virtual Execution System
- Programmers, who will use primarily the Base Class Libraries, published in companion volumes to this one, and entitled the *.NET Framework Standard Library Annotated Reference*

About This Book

Along with the complete text of the CLI Standard, except for the portion describing the class libraries, this book contains some other information that may be of help.

Chapter 1 is an overview of CLI and describes, in context, where to go in this book to find specific technical areas.

Chapter 2 contains the annotated Partition I of this standard, an architectural overview and recommended to anyone who needs to understand the CLI. It also contains the specifications for the Common Language Specification (CLS), the restrictions on the CLI for anyone writing code that may be used across languages.

Chapter 3 is the part of the standard describing the semantics of metadata, with annotations. It contains the first 20 sections of Partition II, and uses an assembly language, ilasm, to describe these semantics.

Chapter 4 contains information that is not in the standard. It is an overview of the second half of Partition II, and describes how to find different areas of information. It also provides some information on the PE (Portable Executable) file format for managed files and its relation to the layout of metadata.

Chapter 5 contains the annotated second half of Partition II of the standard, sections 21–24, which describes the file format as it relates to managed files, and the physical metadata layout.

Chapter 6 is Partition III of the standard, which consists primarily of a detailed description of the Common Intermediate Language (CIL) instruction set. In addition, this chapter includes an annotated section important to both language designers and developers of Virtual Execution Systems that describes the effect of various numeric operations between types.

Chapter 7 is the annotated Partition IV, which is an overview of the CLI libraries, also describing what is, and is not, required for a conforming CLI implementation. In the International Standard, this Partition contains the Base Class Libraries in XML format. In this series, however, these are published in companion volumes entitled the *.NET Framework Standard Library Annotated Reference*.

Chapter 8 is the annotated Partition V, which is a set of annexes to the standard. These include sample programs in ilasm with corresponding annotations containing approximate high-level language examples for the same programs, implementation information for a version of ilasm, library design guidelines, and other information of interest to CLI implementers.

The Appendix in this book reprints the *Microsoft Portable Executable and Object File Format Specification*. This specification includes a good deal of information on the file format that is specific to Microsoft products and hence not standardized. This information allows you to see how the file format for managed code, described in Chapter 5, relates to the existing Microsoft Windows file format. It also helps clarify why the file format for managed code is more complicated than would be necessary if one were designing a portable format strictly for CIL. For those designing a Microsoft Windows–compatible implementation of the VES, it describes how to handle unmanaged code.

Goals of the Standard and of This Book

The goal of any standard is to set out what must be done to comply with the standard, not to tell you how to implement it. The information makes it possible to guarantee that if you write a program and compile it on one implementation of the VES, it will also run on another implementation, unless the program violates the rules. It specifies both what is needed for portability and the limits of portability. It also specifies the rules for creating a Virtual Execution System (VES).

It was not a goal of this standard to describe why decisions were made. However, many of the annotations in this book attempt to provide some of that context, to make the system more coherent.

Another important part of the International Standard is an implementation of a set of libraries that work on all compliant implementations and are language-independent, called the Base Class Libraries. These libraries are described in detail in companion volumes to this one, entitled the *.NET Framework Standard Library Annotated Reference.*

Where Did the Standard Come From?

This standard started with a band of troublemakers (as most big ideas do), this time at Microsoft. They had a vision of a multi-language standard that would allow programmers to use whichever language best fit the programming task for any module. Furthermore, they believed that these modules should not only work together correctly, but it should be possible to run them on any operating system without rewriting or recompiling.

This idea faced a lot of opposition in a company whose different divisions had invested huge amounts of time and effort in different programming models; no group wanted to give up its special model. Good technology finally prevailed, however, and the .NET concept, with the development of the Common Language Runtime, gained acceptance.

Language groups within Microsoft were involved in early design talks, and by 1999 the talks had expanded to include language developers from outside Microsoft. Many of these discussions were contentious, but they resulted, eventually, in the CTS and the CLS. More significantly, all of Microsoft's Visual Studio languages did what was necessary to comply with the rules. All of the languages had to make significant changes to their initial designs. The Visual Basic team, in fact, did a complete redesign of the language. Another thing that laid the foundation for creating a standard is that the group at Microsoft started partnerships very early in the process with language and system developers around the world, to ensure that it would really work as a standard, not just an in-house flash in the pan.

Early on, the development team recognized that the concept of the CLI made sense only if it was in wide use, and the best way to do that was to turn it into a standard that was freely available. So, in 2000, long before the release of Microsoft's Common Language Runtime, Jim Miller, a senior architect of the CLI, went to a meeting of ECMA International, an international industry association for the standardization of information and communications systems, to talk about creating a standard. At that time, it was informally agreed that the CLI should be submitted.

About a year later, after Hewlett-Packard and Intel had joined Microsoft as co-sponsors, a meeting of the ECMA Technical Committee TC39 in Bristol, England, was presented with three documents—(1) what is now Partition I of this book, (2) a document containing information for compiler designers (now the first half of Partition II), and (3) an XML version of the documentation of the Base Class Libraries. Other companies, such as Fujitsu, who was interested in developing a compliant COBOL, had also joined the effort. The copyright was turned over to ECMA, and standardization really began.

At this writing, Microsoft has shipped as product five implementations of the CLI (or a large subset thereof). Of those, three are completely independent implementations, sharing no code at all. These are:

1. The Common Language Runtime, and derived from that is the Shared Source CLI (commonly known as Rotor).
2. The .NET Compact Framework, and derived from that code base is a CLI being used for the Microsoft TV platform, called the Microsoft .NET Compact Framework TV Edition.
3. A minimal CLI, called the Smart Personal Objects Technology (SPOT), being used for very small devices, like watches.

Other CLIs are under development by other companies, such as the Mono project by Ximian, an open-source project called the DotGNU Portable.NET, and one developed as a research project at Intel Corporation.

Where Is the Standard Headed?

This book is based on these ECMA and ISO standards:

- ECMA: Standard ECMA-335, 2nd Edition, December 2002.
- ISO: ISO/IEC 23271:2003(E), Information Technology—Common Language Infrastructure (CLI).

But standards are living documents. The ECMA technical committee that is responsible for the technical content of the CLI standard is working to refine and improve the standard. The committee's plan is to create an ECMA edition 3, and then submit it to ISO. Some of the topics under discussion for possible inclusion in a future standard are the following:

- Generics
- Extended threading
- Exception reordering/runtime check disablement
- Debugging enhancements
- Extensible metadata

Generics seem to be the next step in the object-oriented community, and they are likely to be included in a future version of the standard. In the current version, it is not possible to transmit debug information to another debugger, and this change is currently under discussion. Also under discussion are some enhancements that would make it easier to extend the metadata.

Although the CLI standard does not embrace all one might expect in a platform (such as the inclusion of a windowing library or a graphics library), it is felt that these still evolve too rapidly to be standardized. The standard permits anyone to develop these because it lays out the basis for library development.

Acknowledgments

We would like to acknowledge, gratefully, the contributions of the members of ECMA TC39/TG3, who contributed significantly toward the development of the standard and helped with this book. Special thanks to Michał Cierniak, Senior Researcher, Intel Corporation; Dr. Nigel Perry, University of Canterbury; Arch D. Robison, Principal Engineer, Intel Corporation; and Emmanuel Stapf, Head of Compiler Technology Division, Eiffel Software; both for lending their time and expertise to the standard and for contributing significantly to this book.

It is important to acknowledge the enormous effort also put into the standard by other members of the committee generally, and in particular:

- Carol Thompson, Software Architect, and Eric Eidt, of Hewlett-Packard Corporation
- Jim Hogg of Microsoft Corporation, for significant authoring and editing on Partitions I and II of the standard
- Basim Kadhim of Fujitsu, Erik Eidt of Hewlett-Packard Corporation, and Emmanuel Stapf for significant contributions in refining the CLS
- Professor Christine Mingins and Dr. Damien Watkins of Monash University, Melbourne Australia, for their contributions to the glossary
- Toshiaki Kurokawa, CSK Fellow, for facilitating work in the ISO fast track process
- Joel Marcy of Intel Corporation (also TC39 Chair and TG3 Convener) and Sam Ruby of IBM for all their work in convening the standards committee
- For bringing their expertise in the process of standardization to this effort, Jan van den Beld, Secretary General of ECMA, Rex Jaeschke, Tom Plum of Plum Hall, and Mike Deese

We would also like to thank Brad Abrams, Lead Program Manager; Lisa Supinski, Documentation Manager; and Sheridan Harrison—all of the Common Language Runtime,

Microsoft Corporation—for working with us, and for the tremendous amount of effort that went into producing the class library part of the standard.

And finally, we would like to thank Don Box, Jeff Richter, and John Montgomery for encouraging us and making it possible to write this book, and the Common Language Runtime team for making the technology real in the first place.

1. Introduction to the Common Language Infrastructure

The Common Language Infrastructure (CLI) is an International Standard that is the basis for creating execution and development environments in which languages and libraries work together seamlessly. The CLI specifies a *virtual execution system* that insulates CLI-compliant programs from the underlying operating system. Where virtual execution systems are developed for different operating systems, programs written with CLI-compliant languages can be run in these different systems without recompiling, or worse, rewriting.

Programming with CLI-compliant languages ultimately gives the programmer a simple but rich development model, allowing development in multiple languages, promoting code reuse across languages, and removing most of the plumbing required in traditional programming. The CLI makes it possible for modules to be self-registering, to run in remote processes, to handle versioning, to deal with errors through exception handling, and more.

This book, by amplifying the standard, provides a blueprint for creating the infrastructure for this simpler programming model across languages and across platforms. Because the theme of the CLI is broad reach, it also includes provisions for running modules compiled by existing languages into "native code"—machine code targeted at a specific system. This is called **unmanaged code**, as opposed to the managed code that is CLI-compliant.

This book also describes what is required of languages to be CLI-compliant, and what library developers need to do to ensure that their libraries are accessible to any programmer writing in any CLI-compliant language. In addition, it provides the guidelines for implementing a virtual execution system, which insulates executables from the underlying operating system.

This chapter is an overview of the CLI and attempts to provide a key to understanding the standard. In addition, throughout the specification, annotations explain many of the details—either clarifying what is written in the specification or explaining the origins of some of its elements.

Components of the CLI

It is most important at the beginning to understand the basic elements of the CLI and how they are related. These elements are

- Common Language Infrastructure (CLI)
- Common Type System (CTS)
- Common Language Specification (CLS)
- Virtual Execution System (VES), which executes managed code and lies between the code and the native operating system

Figure 1-1 shows how these elements are related. Together, these aspects of the CLI form a unifying specification for designing, developing, deploying, and executing distributed components and applications.

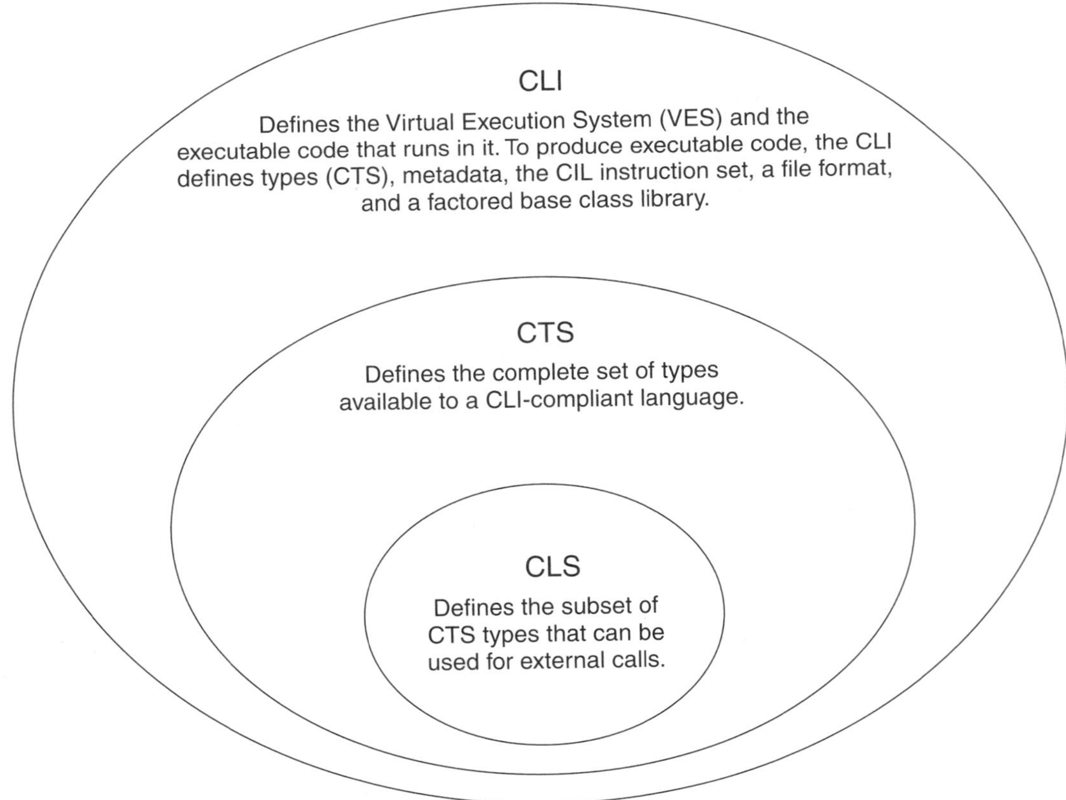

Figure 1-1 Relationship of the CLI, the CTS, and the CLS

Each programming language that complies with the CLI uses a subset of the Common Type System that is appropriate for that language. Language-based tools communicate with each other and with the Virtual Execution System using metadata to define and reference the types used to construct the application. When a constructor is called to create an instance of an object, the VES uses the metadata to create instances of types, and to provide data type information to other parts of the infrastructure (remoting services, assembly downloading, security, etc.).

Languages and programming environments that do target the CLI—there are currently more than 20, and the list is growing—produce what is called **managed code** and **managed data**. The key to these is **metadata**—information associated with the code and data that describes the data, identifies the locations of references to objects, and gives the VES enough information to handle most of the overhead associated with older programming models. This overhead includes handling exceptions and security, and providing information to tools that can ensure memory safety. It may also include running on remote systems by creating proxies for the programmer, as well as managing object lifetime (called **garbage collection**).

Among the things the CLI specifies are the following:

- The Common Type System
- The Common Language Specification for publicly available calls
- Metadata
- Portable file format for managed code
- The Common Intermediate Language (CIL) instruction set
- Basic requirements of a Virtual Execution System
- A programming framework built on top of all of this

The CLI also bridges the managed and unmanaged worlds. The CLI describes how, in the same program, managed modules can be run with unmanaged modules compiled in native code (machine code, specific to a given system). This interoperation is also crucial to describing how modules can communicate though the VES with the underlying operating systems.

The Common Type System

Ultimately, all programs are built from data types. At the core of every language are built-in data types, ways of combining them to form new types, and ways of naming the new types so that they can be used like the built-in types.

Data types are more than just the contents of the bits that the data occupy. They are also the methods that can be used to manipulate them. In value-oriented programming, "type" usually means data representation. In object-oriented programming, it usually refers to behavior rather than to representation. The CTS combines these notions, so "type" means both of these things: two entities have the same type if and only if they have both compatible representations and compatible behaviors. Thus, in the CTS, if a type is derived from a base type, instances of the derived type may be substituted for instances of the base type because both the representation and the behavior should be compatible.

The idea of the Common Type System is that compatible types allow language interoperation. If you can read the contract provided by any type and use its operations, you can build data structures and use your control structures to manipulate them.

The CTS presents a set of rules for types. As long as you follow those rules, you can define as many of those types as you like—in effect, the types are extensible, but the type system is not. For example, you can define any object or value type you like, as long as it follows the rules, but you cannot, for example, define a CTS-compliant type that uses multiple inheritance, which is outside of the type system.

The Common Type System was designed for broad reach: for object-oriented, procedural, and functional languages, generally in that order. It provides a rich set of types and operations. Although many languages have types that they have found useful that are not in the CTS, the advantages of language integration usually outweigh the disadvantages. Out of 20 languages that carefully investigated the CTS, at the time of this writing 15 have chosen to implement it.

The CTS is described in detail in section 8 of Partition I (Chapter 2 of this book).

The Common Language Specification

The Common Language Specification (CLS) is a subset of the Common Type System (CTS). It is a set of types that may be used in external calls in code that is intended to be portable. All of the standardized framework (described in Partition IV, including the Base Class Library, XML Library, Network Library, Reflection Library, and Extended Numerics Library) are intended to be used on any system running a compliant VES, and in any CLS-compliant language. Therefore, the framework follows the CLS rules, and all (well, almost all) the types it defines are CLS-compliant to ensure the broadest possible use. In the few cases in which types or methods are not CLS-compliant, they are labeled as such (that's one of the CLS rules), and they are intended for use by compilers and language runtimes rather than direct use by programmers.

Figure 1-2 shows the relationship of languages, the Common Type System, and the Common Language Specification. It illustrates examples of how two compliant languages,

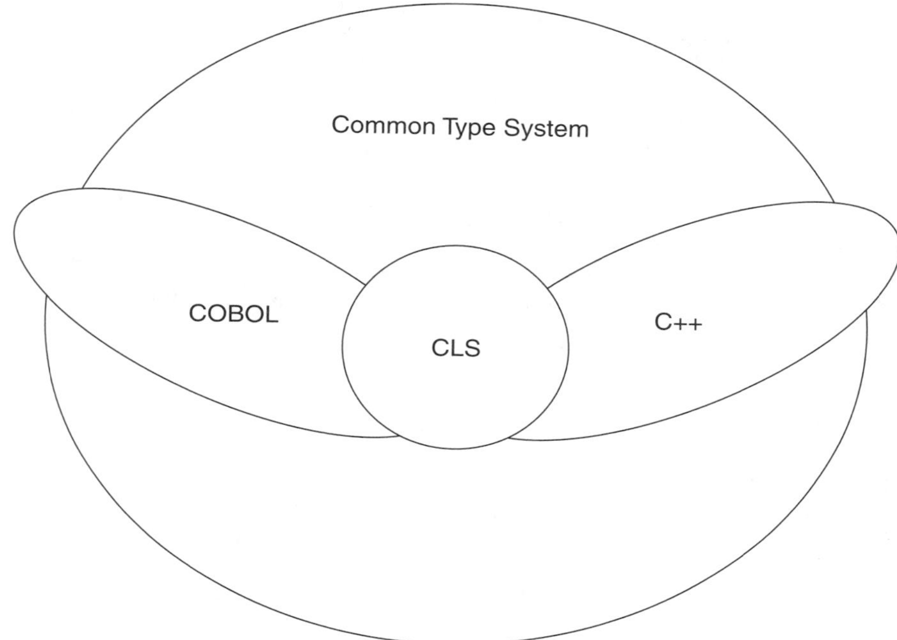

Figure 1-2 Relationship of Languages, the CTS, and the CLS

Fujitsu COBOL, and Microsoft Managed C++, use the CTS and CLS. One of the things it shows is that some aspects of both languages are not CTS compliant. It also shows that the Common Type System is too big for any single language.

The CLS is actually a set of restrictions on the CTS. The CLS defines not only the types allowed in external calls, but the rules for using them, depending on the goal of the user. There are three categories of those who might wish to comply with the CLS: frameworks, extenders, and consumers. **Frameworks** are libraries that are intended to be language- and system-independent. Extenders and consumers are both targeted at language developers. **Consumers** intend their languages only to use frameworks supplied by others. **Extenders** intend to extend their language—define types based on base types, define language-based libraries, etc.

Information on the CLS is contained in Partition I (Chapter 2 of this book), in the following sections:

- Section 7 is a discussion of frameworks, consumers, and extenders.
- Section 8 describes CLS rules in the context of the CTS discussion because the CLS is a subset, with restrictions, of the CTS.

- Section 10 explains name and type rules for the CLS.
- Section 11 is a list of the CLS rules only.

Metadata

Along with the Common Type System, metadata is at the heart of the CLI. CLI-compliant compilers generate metadata and store it with the code in the executable file according to the file format specified in Partition II, sections 21–24 (Chapter 5 of this book). Metadata describes the code by describing the types that the code defines and the types that the code references externally. There is enough information stored in the metadata to (among other things):

- Manage code execution (load, execute, manage memory, and inspect execution state)
- Install code, resolve implementation versions, and perform other administrative functions
- Enable cross-language operation

Metadata provides information to tools like debuggers and verifiers, and it permits communication between tools. Among the information the metadata contains is the following:

- A description of the deployment unit (the assembly), called the **manifest**
- Descriptions of all of the types in each module
- Signatures of all methods in each module
- Custom attributes in each module

Figure 1-3 shows some of the possible users of metadata.

One of the services of the CLI that uses metadata is called **reflection**. In the CLI, a reflection object represents a type, describes it, and is an in-memory representation of the type—but is not an instance of the type. Reflection allows you to discover all of the information contained in metadata about a type, including the name of the type, its fields, its methods, whether it is public or private, any attributes attached to it, and more.

Metadata simplifies the job of developing designers, debuggers, profilers, type browsers, and other tools by making the information they need easily available without making them walk the code to find it. Metadata is the key that enables cross-language programming. When a compiler reads a module compiled in a different language, it reads the metadata, thus allowing seamless interoperation, much as a traditional compiler might read a "header file" describing the other module; but by reading the metadata directly from the module, there's no possibility of reading the wrong header file and there is no need to generate a separate header file to describe your own code.

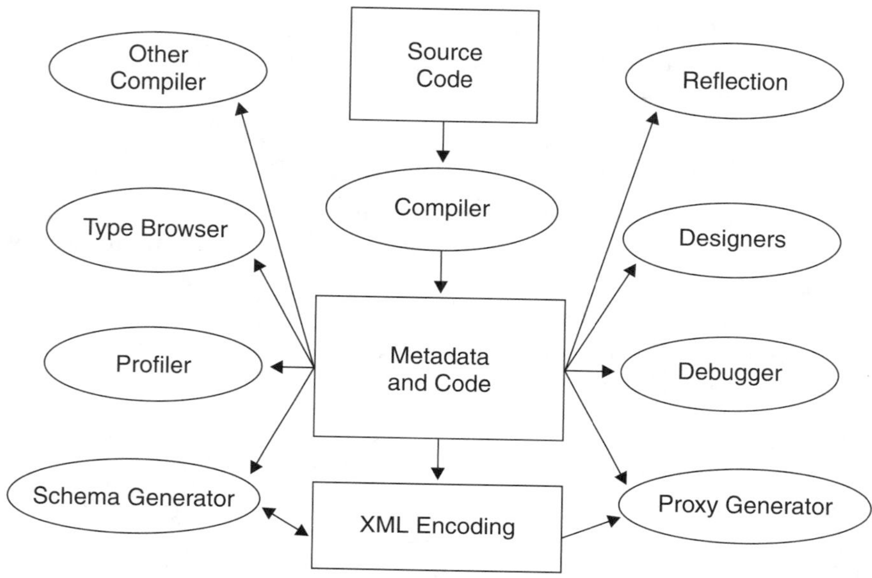

Figure 1-3 Users of Metadata

Custom attributes were designed as part of the CLI to allow extensibility without requiring languages to continue to add new keywords. Custom attributes include markers for CLS compliance, security, debugging, and many language- and tool-specific attributes. Some custom attributes are defined by the CLI, but they can also be defined by a compiler or by the tools that use the attribute. Languages that identify as distinct types what the VES sees simply as 32-bit integers—for example, C++, which distinguishes **int** from **long** even when both are 32-bit—would create a custom attribute that would identify the different types to the compiler.

Custom attributes are essential to tools. In a programming environment with designers, you might create a new button object. A custom attribute would tell the designer that this object is a button, and at runtime the designer would list it as one of the available buttons.

If the VES that you're using includes a proxy generator, you could make an object available externally to a Web service by putting in a custom attribute telling the proxy generator to create a proxy for the object, and another attribute telling the Web service that the proxy should be included. Metadata stores custom attributes, making them readily available to any tool.

Section 9 of Partition I (Chapter 2 of this book) is a discussion of the architecture of metadata. Sections 1–20 of Partition II (Chapter 3 of this book) define an assembly language based on the CIL, using it to define the semantics of metadata.

Execution and Deployment Models

Assemblies are the unit of deployment for one or more modules. They are not a packaging mechanism and are not intended to be an "application," although an application will consist of one or more assemblies. An assembly is defined by a **manifest**, which is metadata that lists all of the files included and directly referenced in the assembly, what types are exported and imported by the assembly, versioning information, and security permissions that apply to the whole assembly.

Although the compilers capture the versioning and security information, it is the implementation of the VES that allows users to set policies that determine which versions are to be used, and how security is implemented. An assembly has a security boundary that grants the entire assembly some level of security permission; e.g., the entire assembly may write to a certain part of the disk, and methods can demand proof that everyone in the call chain has permission to perform a given operation.

The notion of "application" is not part of this standard. It is up to the implementer to determine how applications relate to assemblies. The standard does, however, encompass the idea of an **application domain**.

A process may have more than one application domain. Assemblies are loaded into application domains. Information about the available classes, the associated code, and the static variables is housed in that application domain.

The execution model is that compilers generate the Common Intermediate Language (CIL). How and when the CIL is compiled to machine code are not specified as part of the standard, and those determinations rest with the implementation of the VES. The most frequently used model is just-in-time (JIT) compilers that generate native code as it is needed. Install-time compilers are another option, and it is also possible to implement an interpreter, rather than a compiler, for the CIL. Native unmanaged code would go directly to the VES. Figure 1-4 illustrates the execution model.

Chapter 6 of this book contains Partition III, which includes a complete reference to CIL instructions.

Metadata and the File Format

The file format specified by the CLI is an extension of the standard PE (Portable Executable) file. The information required to write a PE file for managed code, and the logical and

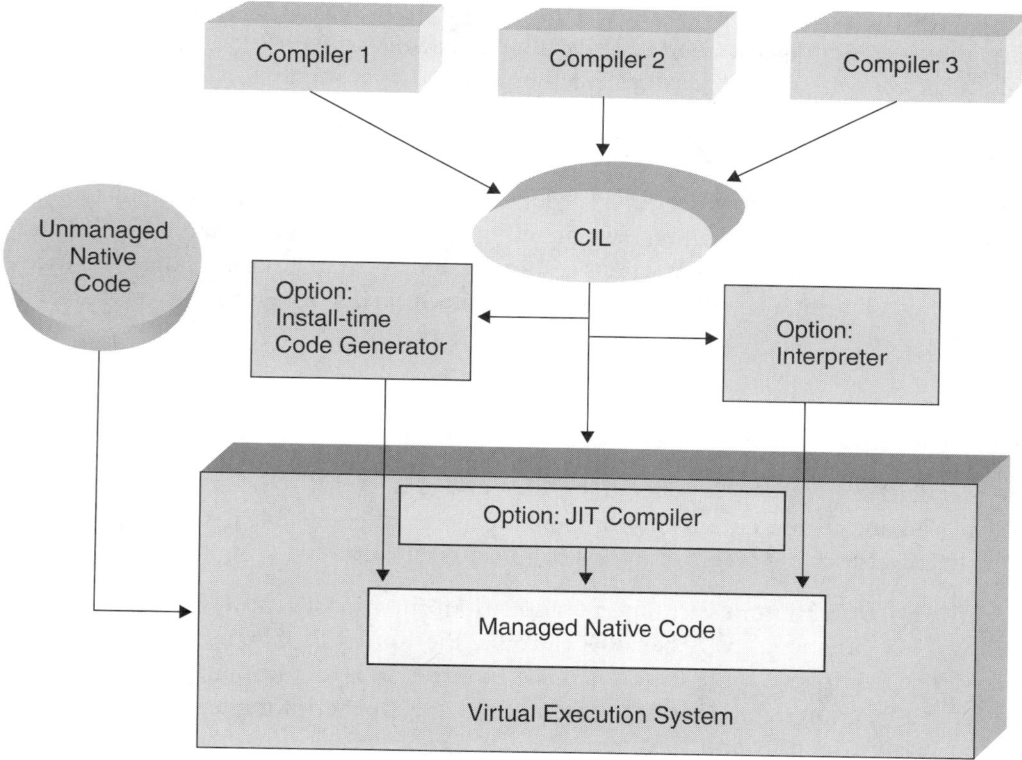

Figure 1-4 Execution Model

physical layout of metadata within a file, are described in detail in Chapter 5 of this book, which covers sections 21–24 of Partition II. Chapter 4 of this book provides a road map to the very dense, but important, information in those sections. Chapter 4 also contains a detailed diagram of the metadata tables and an annotated dump of a very small managed PE file, as well as a map of the metadata.

The Virtual Execution System

The Virtual Execution System (VES) provides an environment for executing managed code. It provides direct support for a set of built-in data types, and it defines a hypothetical machine with an associated machine model and state, a set of control flow constructs, and an exception handling model. To a large extent, the purpose of the VES is to provide the support required to execute the Common Intermediate Language instruction set, described in Partition III (Chapter 6 of this book).

Understanding the VES is important not only to those interested in implementing a VES, but to compiler designers. Compiler designers need to know what the VES does and does not do. This book clearly lays out those lines. Although there is information on the VES throughout the standard, section 12 of Partition I, and all of its subsections, contains important information on the VES, as does Partition III. The early sections of Partition IV (Chapter 7 of this book) are valuable for VES developers because they explain what must be implemented if a staged development is required.

For VES developers, there is a suggested order for reading the standard. If you understand the basic notion of a Virtual Execution System and managed code, read Partition III (Chapter 6) first, because it describes the instructions of the CIL, which are at the heart of the VES. Then go back and read Partition I, and try to fill in the architectural details. Finally, go on to the other sections.

The Standard Framework

The Standard Framework adheres to the CLS, and is intended to be cross-language. Both the libraries and the execution environment are factored: being able to use certain libraries requires corresponding pieces of the execution environment.

A **profile** is a set of libraries, grouped together to form a consistent whole that provides a fixed level of functionality. A basic CLI profile, the Kernel Profile, includes the C# class library. The Compact Profile includes those libraries and, in addition, libraries for XML and reflection, enough for scripting languages like ECMAScript (better known under the product names "JScript" and "JavaScript").

Optional libraries include floating point numbers, decimal arithmetic, and multidimensional arrays.

Each library specifies the available types and how they are grouped into assemblies, the set of CLI features that support that library, and any modifications in the library to types defined in other libraries, such as the addition of methods and interfaces to types defined in other libraries and additional exceptions that may be thrown by this library. A **framework**, a term used extensively in this standard, consists of simply the available type definitions, without the additional supporting information.

The Standard Framework is published in a companion to this book, entitled the *.NET Framework Standard Library Annotated Reference.*

2. Partition I: Concepts and Architecture

1 Scope

This International Standard defines the Common Language Infrastructure (CLI) in which applications written in multiple high-level languages may be executed in different system environments without the need to rewrite the applications to take into consideration the unique characteristics of those environments. This International Standard consists of the following parts:

- Partition I: Concepts and Architecture – Describes the overall architecture of the CLI, and provides the normative description of the Common Type System (CTS), the Virtual Execution System (VES), and the Common Language Specification (CLS). It also provides a non-normative description of the metadata and a comprehensive set of abbreviations, acronyms, and definitions, which are included by reference into all other Partitions.
- Partition II: Metadata Definition and Semantics – Provides the normative description of the metadata: its physical layout (as a file format), its logical contents (as a set of tables and their relationships), and its semantics (as seen from a hypothetical assembler, ilasm).
- Partition III: CIL Instruction Set – Describes, in detail, the Common Intermediate Language (CIL) instruction set.
- Partition IV: Profiles and Libraries – Provides an overview of the CLI Libraries and a specification of their factoring into Profiles and Libraries. A companion document, considered to be part of this Partition but distributed in XML format, provides details of each class, value type, and interface in the CLI Libraries.

ANNOTATION: These libraries are also published in a companion to this book, entitled the *.NET Framework Standard Library Annotated Reference*. References in the original International Standard to specific classes in Partition IV, which contained that information in XML format, have been changed to references to the *.NET Framework Standard Library Annotated Reference.*

- Partition V: Annexes – Contains some sample programs written in CIL Assembly Language (ilasm), information about a particular implementation of an assembler, a machine-readable description of the CIL instruction set which may be used to derive parts of the grammar used by this assembler as well as other tools that manipulate CIL, and a set of guidelines used in the design of the libraries of Partition IV.

2 Conformance

A system claiming conformance to this International Standard shall implement all the mandatory requirements of this standard, and shall specify the profile (see Partition IV) that it implements. The minimal implementation is the Kernel Profile (see Partition IV). A conforming implementation may also include additional functionality that does not prevent running code written to rely solely on the profile as specified in this standard. For example, it may provide additional classes, new methods on existing classes, or a new interface on a standardized class, but it shall not add methods or properties to interfaces specified in this standard.

A compiler that generates Common Intermediate Language (CIL, see Partition III) and claims conformance to this International Standard shall produce output files in the format specified in this standard and the CIL it generates shall be valid CIL as specified in this standard. Such a compiler may also claim that it generates *verifiable* code, in which case the CIL it generates shall be verifiable as specified in this standard.

3 References

ANNOTATION: In the International Standard, this section contains references used in the standard. In this book, the references are at the end of the volume.

---

4 Conventions

The remainder of this section contains only informative text.

4.1 Organization

The divisions of this International Standard are organized using a hierarchy. At the top level is the *Partition*. The next level is the *Chapter*, followed by *section* then *clause*. Divisions within a clause are also referred to as clauses rather than subclauses. Partitions are numbered using Roman numerals. All other divisions are numbered using Arabic digits, with their place in the hierarchy indicated by nested numbers. For example, Partition II, 14.4.3.2 refers to clause 2 in clause 3 in section 4 in Chapter 14 in Partition II.

ANNOTATION: To avoid confusion with the use of the term "Chapter," the hierarchical designation used in the International Standard is not used in this book. In this book, only the book chapters are referred to as "Chapter." Sections within partitions are all called "sections," but they are given the full numeric designation—for example, "see Partition I, section 12.4.2.3."

4.2 Informative Text

This International Standard is intended to be used by implementers, academics, and application programmers. As such, it contains explanatory material that, strictly speaking, is not necessary in a formal specification.

Examples are provided to illustrate possible forms of the constructions described. References are used to refer to related sections. Notes are provided to give advice or guidance to implementers or programmers. Annexes provide additional information.

Except for whole sections that are identified as being informative, informative text that is contained within normative sections is identified as follows:

The beginning and end of informative text is marked as shown in this chapter, using pairs of narrow horizontal rules. Some informative passages span pages between opening and closing indicators.

4.3 Hyperlinks

The text of this standard contains numerous hyperlinks that are intended to allow a person viewing it electronically to be able to transfer to the referenced sections. Such hyperlinks are displayed with a double underline, and, depending on the rendered format, may be colored; for example: "see Partition IV," "see section 8.7," "see Chapter 22," and "see clause 7.5.3." Some tables also contain hyperlinked section number references, such as 5.10 and 6.7.

ANNOTATION: The hyperlinks in the International Standard are replaced with full references to Partition and section in this book.

End informative text

5 Glossary

ANNOTATION: In the International Standard, this section contains the glossary. In this book the glossary is printed at the end of the volume.

6 Overview of the Common Language Infrastructure

The Common Language Infrastructure (CLI) provides a specification for executable code and the execution environment (the Virtual Execution System, or VES) in which it runs. Executable code is presented to the VES as **modules**. A module is a single file containing executable content in the format specified in Partition II, sections 21–24.

The remainder of this section and its subsections contain only informative text.

At the center of the Common Language Infrastructure (CLI) is a unified type system, the Common Type System (CTS), that is shared by compilers, tools, and the CLI itself. It is the model that defines the rules the CLI follows when declaring, using, and managing types. The CTS establishes a framework that enables cross-language integration, type safety, and high performance code execution. This section describes the architecture of CLI by describing the CTS.

The following four areas are covered in this section:

- **The Common Type System.** See Partition I, section 8. The Common Type System (CTS) provides a rich type system that supports the types and operations found in many programming languages. The Common Type System is intended to support the complete implementation of a wide range of programming languages.

- **Metadata.** See Partition I, section 9. The CLI uses metadata to describe and reference the types defined by the Common Type System. Metadata is stored ("persisted") in a way that is independent of any particular programming language. Thus, metadata provides a common interchange mechanism for use between tools that manipulate programs (compilers, debuggers, etc.) as well as between these tools and the Virtual Execution System.
- **The Common Language Specification.** See Partition I, section 10. The Common Language Specification is an agreement between language designers and framework (class library) designers. It specifies a subset of the Common Type System and a set of usage conventions. Languages provide their users the greatest ability to access frameworks by implementing at least those parts of the CTS that are part of the CLS. Similarly, frameworks will be most widely used if their publicly exposed aspects (classes, interfaces, methods, fields, etc.) use only types that are part of the CLS and adhere to the CLS conventions.
- **The Virtual Execution System.** See Partition I, section 12. The Virtual Execution System (VES) implements and enforces the CTS model. The VES is responsible for loading and running programs written for the CLI. It provides the services needed to execute managed code and data, using the metadata to connect separately generated modules together at runtime (late binding).

Together, these aspects of the CLI form a unifying framework for designing, developing, deploying, and executing distributed components and applications. The appropriate subset of the Common Type System is available from each programming language that targets the CLI. Language-based tools communicate with each other and with the Virtual Execution System using metadata to define and reference the types used to construct the application. The Virtual Execution System uses the metadata to create instances of the types as needed and to provide data type information to other parts of the infrastructure (such as remoting services, assembly downloading, security, etc.).

ANNOTATION: This Common Language Infrastructure standard describes the requirements to which languages and implementations of the Virtual Execution System (VES) must adhere to be in compliance. Although it does not, of course, prescribe implementations, it does define the outcome of the design. The CLI specifies a file format and an instruction set, and it describes how programs written with that file format, using that instruction set, are supposed to work. Implementations of the VES are responsible for making them work. The CLI defines for compilers what they must produce to work with a VES, and what they are required to consume from others. To describe the semantics of the file format, this standard also defines a compiler called the **IL assembler** (**ilasm**), although it is intended, of course, to be illustrative.

End informative text

6.1 Relationship to Type Safety

Type safety is usually discussed in terms of what it does (e.g., guaranteeing encapsulation between different objects) or in terms of what it prevents (e.g., memory corruption by writing where one shouldn't). However, from the point of view of the Common Type System, type safety guarantees that:

- **References are what they say they are** – Every reference is typed and the object or value referenced also has a type, and they are assignment compatible (see Partition I, section 8.7).
- **Identities are who they say they are** – There is no way to corrupt or spoof an object, and by implication a user or security domain. The access to an object is through accessible functions and fields. An object may still be designed in such a way that security is compromised. However, a local analysis of the class, its methods, and the things it uses, as opposed to a global analysis of all uses of a class, is sufficient to assess the vulnerabilities.
- **Only appropriate operations can be invoked** – The reference type defines the accessible functions and fields. This includes limiting visibility based on where the reference is—e.g., protected fields only visible in subclasses.

The Common Type System promotes type safety; e.g., everything is typed. Type safety can be optionally enforced. The hard problem is determining if an implementation conforms to a typesafe declaration. Since the declarations are carried along as metadata with the compiled form of the program, a compiler from the Common Intermediate Language (CIL) to native code (see Partition I, section 8.8) can type-check the implementations.

6.2 Relationship to Managed Metadata-Driven Execution

Metadata describes code by describing the types that the code defines and the types that it references externally. The compiler produces the metadata when the code is produced. Enough information is stored in the metadata to:

- **Manage code execution** – not just load and execute, but also memory management and execution state inspection.
- **Administer the code** – Installation, resolution, and other services.

- **Reference types in the code** – Importing into other languages and tools as well as scripting and automation support.

The Common Type System assumes that the execution environment is metadata-driven. Using metadata allows the CLI to support:

- **Multiple execution models** – The metadata also allows the execution environment to deal with a mixture of interpreted, JITted, native and legacy code and still present uniform services to tools like debuggers or profilers, consistent exception handling and unwinding, reliable code access security, and efficient memory management.
- **Auto support for services** – Since the metadata is available at execution time, the execution environment and the base libraries can automatically supply support for reflection, automation, serialization, remote objects, and interoperability with existing unmanaged native code with little or no effort on the part of the programmer.
- **Better optimization** – Using metadata references instead of physical offsets, layouts, and sizes allows the CLI to optimize the physical layouts of members and dispatch tables. In addition, this allows the generated code to be optimized to match the particular CPU or environment.
- **Reduced binding brittleness** – Using metadata references reduces version-to-version brittleness by replacing compile-time object layout with load-time layout and binding by name.
- **Flexible deployment resolution** – Since we can have metadata for both the reference and the definition of a type, more robust and flexible deployment and resolution mechanisms are possible. Resolution means that by looking in the appropriate set of places it is possible to find the implementation that best satisfies these requirements for use in this context. There are five elements of information in the foregoing: two items are made available via metadata (requirements and context); the others come from application packaging and deployment (where to look, how to find an implementation, and how to decide the best match).

6.2.1 *Managed Code*

Managed code is simply code that provides enough information to allow the CLI to provide a set of core services, including

- Given an address inside the code for a method, locate the metadata describing the method
- Walk the stack
- Handle exceptions
- Store and retrieve security information

This standard specifies a particular instruction set, the Common Intermediate Language (CIL, see Partition III), and a file format (see Partition II, sections 21–24) for storing and transmitting managed code.

6.2.2 *Managed Data*

Managed data is data that is allocated and released automatically by the CLI, through a process called **garbage collection**.

6.2.3 *Summary*

The Common Type System is about integration between languages: using another language's objects as if they were one's own.

The objective of the CLI is to make it easier to write components and applications from any language. It does this by defining a standard set of types, making all components fully self-describing, and providing a high performance common execution environment. This ensures that all CLI-compliant system services and components will be accessible to all CLI-aware languages and tools. In addition, this simplifies deployment of components and applications that use them, all in a way that allows compilers and other tools to leverage the high performance execution environment. The Common Type System covers, at a high level, the concepts and interactions that make all of this possible.

The discussion is broken down into four areas:

- Type System – What types are and how to define them.
- Metadata – How types are described and how those descriptions are stored.
- Common Language Specification – Restrictions required for language interoperability.
- Virtual Execution System – How code is executed and types are instantiated, interact, and die.

ANNOTATION: The discussion of the Common Type System starts in section 8, rather than in section 7, which follows. Section 7 introduces the Common Language Specification, which is the set of restrictions on the CTS that ensure interoperability among languages.

End informative text

7 Common Language Specification (CLS)

ANNOTATION: This section briefly introduces the CLS, the set of restrictions on the CTS (Common Type System) that ensure interoperability among languages. It is important to remember that the CLS rules apply only to items that are visible outside of their defining assembly, with **public**, **family**, or **family-or-assembly** accessibility.

The CLS rules themselves are presented in the context of the discussion of the CTS, primarily in Partition I, section 8. This context is very important to understanding each of the rules, although Partition I, section 11 is simply a list of the CLS rules, provided as a convenient reference. Partition I, section 10 provides the name and type rules for the CLS and is also very important for understanding the CLS.

There are expected to be three categories of implementers of the CLS: frameworks, consumers, and extenders. Each CLS rule in this standard is described in terms of how it affects implementers in each of these three categories. This section mainly describes these categories, discusses CLS compliance, and explains how to mark CLS compliance.

7.1 Introduction

The Common Language Specification (CLS) is a set of rules intended to promote language interoperability. These rules shall be followed in order to conform to the CLS. They are described in greater detail in subsequent chapters and are summarized in Partition I, section 11. CLS conformance is a characteristic of types that are generated for execution on a CLI implementation. Such types must conform to the CLI specification, in addition to the CLS rules. These additional rules apply only to types that are visible in assemblies other than those in which they are defined, and to the members (fields, methods, properties, events, and nested types) that are accessible outside the assembly (i.e., those that have an accessibility of **public**, **family**, or **family-or-assembly**).

NOTE

A library consisting of CLS-compliant code is herein referred to as a "framework." Compilers that generate code for the CLI may be designed to make use of such libraries, but not to be able to produce or extend such library code. These compilers are referred to as "consumers." Compilers that are designed to both produce and extend frameworks are referred to as "extenders." In the description of each CLS rule, additional informative text is provided to assist the reader in understanding the rule's implication for each of these situations.

ANNOTATION: The Common Type System was designed for reach—to allow as many programming languages as possible to support all of their types. Equally important was to ensure interoperation among languages, which meant that all complying languages and framework developers had to agree on a subset of the CTS for all publicly exposed types.

Framework developers need to ensure that all complying languages can fully use their libraries, and that those libraries are full-featured. The process of coming to an agreement was not an easy one, because the agreement required compromise from all parties. In most cases, languages had to add elements not previously supported and accept that some features that their programmers liked were not interoperable with other languages. Framework developers had to write libraries with a limited set of types, so all conforming languages could use the libraries.

Framework developers need to be language-agnostic because generally the goal is for the framework to be usable by any compliant language, and the restrictions described in the CLS ensure this. The other two categories described, consumers and extenders, are usually language-centered.

In general, language designers need to add features to their languages to adhere to the rules of the CLS, and to ensure language access to frameworks. Consumer languages have a small set of requirements because they will simply use the frameworks. Extender languages, however, must implement more of the CLS to allow them to extend existing frameworks. Section 7.2 below lists some of the requirements of each of these three.

7.2 Views of CLS Compliance

This section and its subsections contain only informative text.

The CLS is a set of rules that apply to generated assemblies. Because the CLS is designed to support interoperability for libraries and the high-level programming languages used to write them, it is often useful to think of the CLS rules from the perspective of the high-level source code and tools, such as compilers, that are used in the process of generating assemblies. For this reason, informative notes are added to the description of CLS rules to assist the reader in understanding the rule's implications for several different classes of tools and users. The different viewpoints used in the description are called **framework**, **consumer**, and **extender** and are described here.

7.2.1 *CLS Framework*

A library consisting of CLS-compliant code is herein referred to as a "framework." Frameworks (libraries) are designed for use by a wide range of programming languages and tools, including both CLS consumer and extender languages. By adhering to the rules of the CLS, authors of libraries ensure that the libraries will be usable by a larger class of tools than if they chose not to adhere to the CLS rules. The following are some additional guidelines that CLS-compliant frameworks should follow:

- Avoid the use of names commonly used as keywords in programming languages.
- Should not expect users of the framework to be able to author nested types.
- Should assume that implementations of methods of the same name and signature on different interfaces are independent.
- Should not rely on initialization of value types to be performed automatically based on specified initializer values.

7.2.2 *CLS Consumer*

A CLS consumer is a language or tool that is designed to allow access to all of the features supplied by CLS-compliant frameworks (libraries), but not necessarily be able to produce them. The following is a partial list of things CLS consumer tools are expected to be able to do:

- Support calling any CLS-compliant method or delegate.
- Have a mechanism for calling methods that have names that are keywords in the language.
- Support calling distinct methods supported by a type that have the same name and signature, but implement different interfaces.
- Create an instance of any CLS-compliant type.
- Read and modify any CLS-compliant field.
- Access nested types.
- Access any CLS-compliant property. This does not require any special support other than the ability to call the getter and setter methods of the property.
- Access any CLS-compliant event. This does not require any special support other than the ability to call methods defined for the event.

The following is a list of things CLS consumer tools need not support:

- Creation of new types or interfaces.

- Initialization metadata (see Partition II) on fields and parameters other than static literal fields. Note that consumers may choose to use initialization metadata, but may also safely ignore such metadata on anything other than static literal fields.

7.2.3 *CLS Extender*

A CLS extender is a language or tool that is designed to allow programmers to both use and extend CLS-compliant frameworks. CLS extenders support a superset of the behavior supported by a CLS consumer; i.e., everything that applies to a CLS consumer also applies to CLS extenders. In addition to the requirements of a consumer, extenders are expected to be able to:

- Define new CLS-compliant types that extend any (non-sealed) CLS-compliant base class.
- Have some mechanism for defining types with names that are keywords in the language.
- Provide independent implementations for all methods of all interfaces supported by a type. That is, it is not sufficient for an extender to require a single code body to implement all interface methods of the same name and signature.
- Implement any CLS-compliant interface.
- Place any CLS-compliant custom attribute on all appropriate elements of metadata.

Extenders need not support the following:

- Definition of new CLS-compliant interfaces
- Definition of nested types

The Common Language Specification is designed to be large enough that it is properly expressive and small enough that all languages can reasonably accommodate it.

End informative text

7.3 CLS Compliance

ANNOTATION: Whenever no CLS rule is specified, the CTS specifications apply to the CLS with no change.

As these rules are introduced in detail, they are described in a common format. For an example, see the first rule below. The first paragraph specifies the rule itself. This is then followed by an informative description of the implications of the rule from the three different viewpoints as described above.

The CLS defines language interoperability rules, which apply only to "externally visible" items. The CLS unit of that language interoperability is the assembly—that is, within a single assembly there are no restrictions as to the programming techniques that are used. Thus, the CLS rules apply only to items that are visible (see Partition I, section 8.5.3) outside of their defining assembly and have **public**, **family**, or **family-or-assembly** accessibility (see Partition I, section 8.5.3.2).

CLS Rule 1: CLS rules apply only to those parts of a type that are accessible or visible outside of the defining assembly.

NOTE

CLS (consumer): No impact.

CLS (extender): When checking CLS compliance at compile time, be sure to apply the rules only to information that will be exposed outside the assembly.

CLS (framework): CLS rules do not apply to internal implementation within an assembly. A type is CLS-compliant if all its publicly accessible parts (those classes, interfaces, methods, fields, properties, and events that are available to code executing in another assembly) either

- have signatures composed only of CLS-compliant types, or
- are specifically marked as not CLS-compliant

Any construct that would make it impossible to rapidly verify code is excluded from the CLS. This allows all CLS-compliant languages to produce verifiable code if they so choose.

7.3.1 *Marking Items as CLS-Compliant*

The CLS specifies how to mark externally visible parts of an assembly to indicate whether or not they comply with the CLS requirements. This is done using the custom attribute mechanism (see Partition I, section 9.7 and Partition II). The class `System.CLSCompliantAttribute` (see the *.NET Framework Standard Library Annotated Reference*) indicates which types and type members are CLS-compliant. It also can be attached to an assembly, to specify the default value for all top-level types it contains.

The constructor for `System.CLSCompliantAttribute` takes a Boolean argument indicating whether the item with which it is associated is or is not CLS-compliant. This allows any item (assembly, type, or type member) to be explicitly marked as CLS-compliant or not.

The rules for determining CLS compliance are:

- When an assembly does not carry an explicit `System.CLSCompliantAttribute`, it shall be assumed to carry `System.CLSCompliantAttribute(false)`.
- By default, a type inherits the CLS-compliance attribute of its enclosing type (for nested types) or acquires the value attached to its assembly (for top-level types). It may be marked as either CLS-compliant or not CLS-compliant by attaching the `System.CLSCompliantAttribute` attribute.
- By default, other members (methods, fields, properties, and events) inherit the CLS compliance of their type. They may be marked as not CLS-compliant by attaching the attribute `System.CLSCompliantAttribute(false)`.

CLS Rule 2: Members of non-CLS-compliant types shall not be marked CLS-compliant.

NOTE

CLS (consumer): May ignore any member that is not CLS-compliant using the above rules.

CLS (extender): Should encourage correct labeling of newly authored assemblies, classes, interfaces, and methods. Compile-time enforcement of the CLS rules is strongly encouraged.

CLS (framework): Shall correctly label all publicly exposed members as to their CLS compliance. The rules specified here may be used to minimize the number of markers required (for example, label the entire assembly if all types and members are compliant or if there are only a few exceptions that need to be marked).

8 Common Type System

Types describe values and specify a contract (see Partition 1, section 8.6) that all values of that type shall support. Because the CTS supports Object-Oriented Programming (OOP) as well as functional and procedural programming languages, it deals with two kinds of entities: Objects and Values. Values are simple bit patterns for things like integers and floats; each value has a type that describes both the storage that it occupies and the meanings of the bits in its representation, and also the operations that may be performed on that representation. Values are intended for representing the corresponding simple types in programming languages like C, and also for representing non-objects in languages like C++ and Java.

Objects have rather more to them than do values. Each object is self-typing; that is, its type is explicitly stored in its representation. It has an identity that distinguishes it from all other objects, and it has slots that store other entities (which may be either objects or values). While the contents of its slots may be changed, the identity of an object never changes.

There are several kinds of Objects and Values, as shown in Figure 2-1.

8.1 Relationship to Object-Oriented Programming

This section contains only informative text.

The term **type** is often used in the world of value-oriented programming to mean data representation. In the object-oriented world it usually refers to behavior rather than to representation. In the CTS, type is used to mean both of these things: two entities have the same type if and only if they have both compatible representations and behaviors. Thus, in the CTS, if one type is derived from a base type, then instances of the derived type may be substituted for instances of the base type because **both** the representation and the behavior are compatible.

In the CTS, unlike some OOP languages, two objects that have fundamentally different representations have different types. Some OOP languages use a different notion of type. They consider two objects to have the same type if they respond in the same way to the same set of messages. This notion is captured in the CTS by saying that the objects implement the same interface.

Similarly, some OOP languages (e.g., Smalltalk) consider message passing to be the fundamental model of computation. In the CTS, this corresponds to calling virtual methods (see Partition I, section 8.4.4), where the signature of the virtual method plays the role of the message.

The CTS itself does not directly capture the notion of "typeless programming." That is, there is no way to call a non-static method without knowing the type of the object. Nevertheless, typeless programming can be implemented based on the facilities provided by the reflection package (see the *.NET Framework Standard Library Annotated Reference*) if it is implemented.

ANNOTATION: Subclass is an OOP and computer science idea that approximates what a subtype is. Subtype is a mathematical idea that is very well defined but, as is

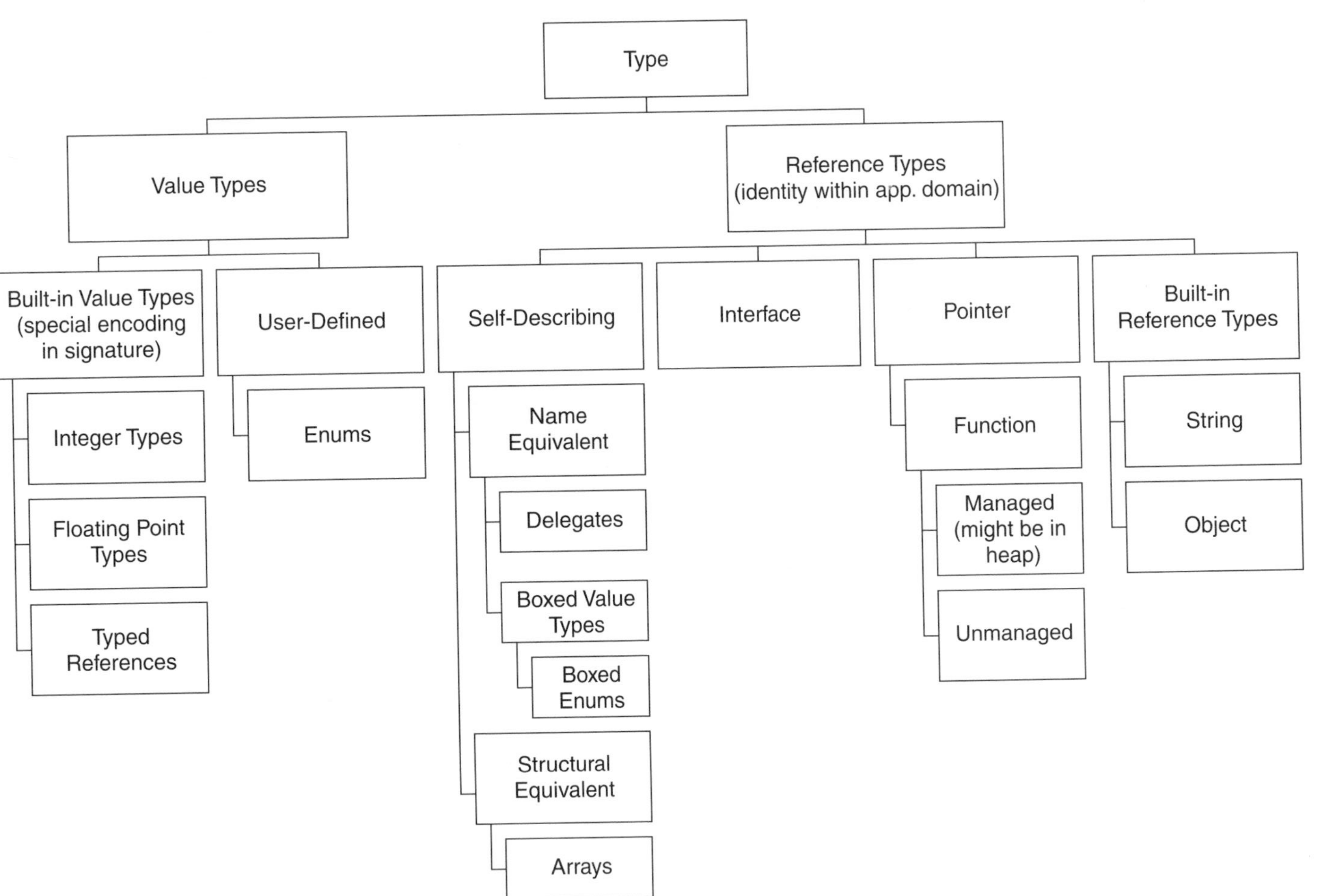

Figure 2-1 Type System

true for many mathematical definitions, is too complicated for most programming languages. Instead, the idea of subclass is used.

Subclass means that there is an inheritance relationship—that the subclass inherits from its parent class. If A is a subclass of B, then although it is true that A is a subtype of B, the inverse is not necessarily true—it is possible for a subtype of something not to be its subclass.

End informative text

8.2 Values and Types

Types describe values. All places where values are stored, passed, or operated upon have a type—e.g., all variables, parameters, evaluation stack locations, and method results. The type defines the allowable values and the allowable operations supported by the values of the type. All operators and functions have expected types for each of the values accessed or used.

A value can be of more than one type. A value that supports many interfaces is an example of a value that is of more than one type, as is a value that inherits from another.

8.2.1 *Value Types and Reference Types*

There are two kinds of types: **Value Types** and **Reference Types**.

- Value Types – Value Types describe values that are represented as sequences of bits.
- Reference Types – Reference Types describe values that are represented as the location of a sequence of bits. There are four kinds of Reference Types:
  - An **object type** is a reference type of a self-describing value (see Partition I, section 8.2.3). Some object types (e.g., abstract classes) are only a partial description of a value.
  - An **interface type** is always a partial description of a value, potentially supported by many object types.
  - A **pointer type** is a compile-time description of a value whose representation is a machine address of a location.
  - Built-in types.

ANNOTATION: Instances of value types are on the heap if they are boxed, a field of a class, or an element of an array. Instances of value types are on the stack if they are return values to methods, arguments of methods, local variables of methods, or fields of value types used in those ways. Instances of reference types are always allocated on the heap.

The definitions of built-in types must be supplied by the Virtual Execution System. The primary built-in types are value types, mainly the built-in numeric integer types, floating point types, and arrays. Also built into the VES is knowledge of some reference types: the base object type (`System.Object`), delegates, strings, and pointers.

8.2.2 *Built-in Types*

The data types in Table 2-1 are an integral part of the CTS and are supported directly by the Virtual Execution System (VES). They have special encoding in the persisted metadata:

ANNOTATION: Unlike all other types, built-in types do not require an explicit definition—they need only be named in a signature. The VES must supply the definition when the type is named. Array and pointer definitions are also built into the VES.

With regard to the numeric types in Table 2-1, long discussions among language designers and CLI designers resulted in a decision to support only one type per length—either signed or unsigned, not both. Notably, supporting `unsigned int8`, while not supporting `signed int8`, even though all other numeric types are signed, was controversial. Another decision was that `char` is distinct from the other numeric types, so it remains in the CLS.

Although there was general agreement that for most sizes, signed integers were generally more useful than unsigned integers, some parties, led by the C# designers, felt that unsigned bytes were more useful than signed bytes. Their reasoning was that bytes tend not to be used as signed values, and in fact, having to deal with signed bytes can cause certain programming problems. Bytes tend to be part of a larger structure, so values from 0 to 255 make more sense (the low byte of something is not given a negative value on its own). In arrays, the use of bytes is very limited, and if used at all, they would be unsigned bytes.

Some common errors result if programmers are forced to use signed bytes. If bytes were signed, programmers might have to mask the signed byte parameters to force them to be positive. Most programmers expect byte values to range from 0 to 255, not from –1 to –127, and omitting the mask might permit a negative value, thus producing a subtle bug. Another common problem could arise in building up a short from bytes; if the low byte is negative, it produces the wrong answer.

Table 2-1 Special Encoding

Name in CIL Assembler (see Partition II)	CLS Type?	Name in Class Library (see the *.NET Framework Standard Library Annotated Reference*)	Description
`bool`	Yes	`System.Boolean`	True/false value
`char`	Yes	`System.Char`	Unicode 16-bit char
`object`	Yes	`System.Object`	Object or boxed value type
`string`	Yes	`System.String`	Unicode string
`float32`	Yes	`System.Single`	IEC 60559:1989 32-bit float
`float64`	Yes	`System.Double`	IEC 60559:1989 64-bit float
`int8`	No	`System.SByte`	Signed 8-bit integer
`int16`	Yes	`System.Int16`	Signed 16-bit integer
`int32`	Yes	`System.Int32`	Signed 32-bit integer
`int64`	Yes	`System.Int64`	Signed 64-bit integer
`native int`	Yes	`System.IntPtr`	Signed integer, native size
`native unsigned int`	No	`System.UIntPtr`	Unsigned integer, native size
`typedref`	No	`System.TypedReference`	Pointer plus runtime type
`unsigned int8`	Yes	`System.Byte`	Unsigned 8-bit integer
`unsigned int16`	No	`System.UInt16`	Unsigned 16-bit integer
`unsigned int32`	No	`System.UInt32`	Unsigned 32-bit integer
`unsigned int64`	No	`System.UInt64`	Unsigned 64-bit integer

So although on the surface it may seem inconsistent to choose all signed integers except the unsigned byte for the CLS, it was, in the end, felt to be the more useful choice.

ANNOTATION: For a discussion of offset to string data, refer to the annotation in Partition IV, section 5.2.

8.2.3 *Classes, Interfaces, and Objects*

Every value has an **exact type** that **fully describes** the value. A type fully describes a value if it unambiguously defines the value's representation and the operations defined on the value.

For a Value Type, defining the representation entails describing the sequence of bits that make up the value's representation. For a Reference Type, defining the representation entails describing the location and the sequence of bits that make up the value's representation.

A **method** describes an operation that may be performed on values of an exact type. Defining the set of operations allowed on values of an exact type entails specifying named methods for each operation.

Some types are only a partial description—e.g., **interface types**. Interface types describe a subset of the operations and none of the representation, and hence, cannot be an exact type of any value. Hence, while a value has only one exact type, it may also be a value of many other types as well. Furthermore, since the exact type fully describes the value, it also fully specifies all of the other types that a value of the exact type can have.

While it is true that every value has an exact type, it is not always possible to determine the exact type by inspecting the representation of the value. In particular, it is *never* possible to determine the exact type of a value of a Value Type. Consider two of the built-in Value Types, 32-bit signed and unsigned integers. While each type is a full specification of their respective values—i.e., an exact type—there is no way to derive that exact type from a value's particular 32-bit sequence.

For some values, called **objects**, it *is* always possible to determine the exact type from the value. Exact types of objects are also called **object types**. Objects are values of Reference Types, but not all Reference Types describe objects. Consider a value that is a pointer to a 32-bit integer, a kind of Reference Type. There is no way to discover the type of the value by examining the pointer bits, hence it is not an object. Now consider the built-in CTS Reference Type `System.String` (see the *.NET Framework Standard Library Annotated Reference*).

The exact type of a value of this type is always determinable by examining the value, hence values of type `System.String` are objects and `System.String` is an object type.

ANNOTATION: Unlike classes, interfaces prescribe a set of behaviors (a contract), but cannot provide the implementations for those behaviors. Abstract classes can do that as well but need not provide the implementation, although they may.

People in the Object-Oriented (OO) community talk about the **shape** and the **behavior** of objects. The shape is determined by the fields the object will have in memory. The behavior is determined by the methods, events, properties, and interfaces that are available on the object.

Interfaces are simply a contract and may not have implementations associated with the interface type, other than implementations of static methods and definitions of static fields. Interfaces contribute to the behavior of an object that implements them, but they can never contribute to the shape because they are never allowed to define new fields. Their static fields determine only the shape of the interface itself, not the shape of the object. Static fields and static method implementations are not associated with instances of the interface. So interfaces contribute to behavior, not shape.

The **exact type** of an object instance is the most specific type of which it is an instance. For example, the exact type of the string "abc" is its parent type, `System.String`, rather than `System.Object`, because it is also, of course, an instance of an object. It has all of the behaviors of that type, and exactly its shape without anything additional.

Bordering on the realm of metaphysics, all objects have types. Some objects actually represent types, and their type is `System.Type`. Reflection has a method that returns the type of any object. If you want to explore the metaphysics of this notion, refer to *The Art of the Metaobject Protocol*, by Gregor Kiczales (MIT Press, 1991). In the CLI, you can determine the exact type of an object through use of the Reflection classes in the Base Class Library.

8.2.4 *Boxing and Unboxing of Values*

For every Value Type, the CTS defines a corresponding Reference Type called the **boxed type**. The reverse is not true: Reference Types do not in general have a corresponding Value Type. The representation of a value of a boxed type (a **boxed value**) is a location where a value of the Value Type may be stored. A boxed type is an object type, and a boxed value is an object.

2. Concepts and Architecture

All Value Types have an operation called **box**. Boxing a value of any Value Type produces its boxed value—i.e., a value of the corresponding boxed type containing a bit copy of the original value. All boxed types have an operation called **unbox**. Unboxing results in a managed pointer to the bit representation of the value.

Notice that interfaces and inheritance are defined only on Reference Types. Thus, while a Value Type definition (see Partition I, section 8.9.7) can specify both interfaces that shall be implemented by the Value Type and the class (`System.ValueType` or `System.Enum`) from which it inherits, these apply only to boxed values.

CLS Rule 3: The CLS does not include boxed value types.

NOTE

In lieu of boxed types, use `System.Object`, `System.ValueType` or `System.Enum`, as appropriate. (See the *.NET Framework Standard Library Annotated Reference*.)

CLS (consumer): Need not import boxed value types.

CLS (extender): Need not provide syntax for defining or using boxed value types.

CLS (framework): Shall not use boxed value types in their publicly exposed aspects.

ANNOTATION: The CLI specifies that when a value type is defined, the VES creates a corresponding boxed type, which is a reference type. It is important to reiterate that the **unbox** operation does not literally remove the box. It does not take away the type header or pointer—it simply provides a managed pointer to the value within the box. There is, of course, no corresponding creation of a value type when a reference type is defined.

When a programmer allocates a value type as a local variable, the VES allocates space for it and can zero that space if you set the zero init flag. To have verifiable code, that is a requirement. The "zero init flag"— the **.local init** directive in assembler syntax, and the **CorILMethod_InitLocals** flag in the file format—is described in Partition II, section 24.4.4.

A value type describes a layout in memory, plus the operations on it. The operations on it are also available through the corresponding boxed type. Some of the operations might involve changing the fields. When a value type is passed on a call, a copy is passed, so any operations on the call do not affect the original value. But since a boxed type is an object, it is always passed by reference, which means the caller is given a managed pointer to the original value. In that case, any changes to the value would change the original value. This is a potential problem.

Another issue is that it is not currently possible to create an array in which all of the entries must be the same boxed value type. For example, if you have Date/Time value types, you can create an array of those, but not an array of boxed Date/Time values.

8.2.5 *Identity and Equality of Values*

There are two binary operators defined on all pairs of values, **identity** and **equality**, that return a Boolean result. Both of these operators are mathematical **equivalence** operators; i.e., they are:

- Reflexive – `a op a` is true.
- Symmetric – `a op b` is true if and only if `b op a` is true.
- Transitive – if `a op b` is true and `b op c` is true, then `a op c` is true.

In addition, identity always implies equality, but not the reverse; i.e., the equality operator need not be the same as the identity operator as long as two identical values are also equal values.

To understand the difference between these operations, consider three variables whose type is `System.String`, where the arrow is intended to mean "is a reference to":

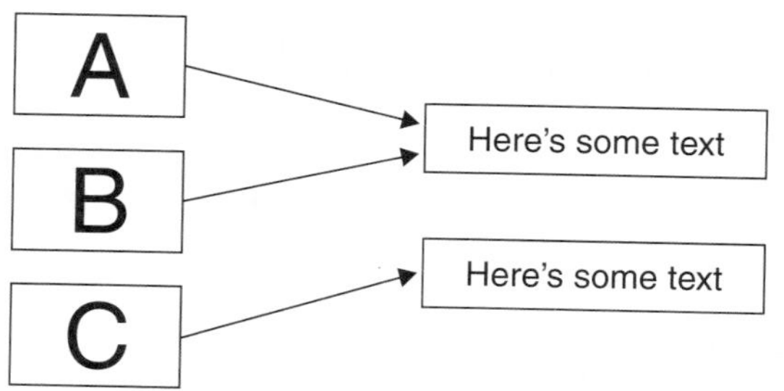

The values of the variables are **identical** if the locations of the sequences of characters are the same—i.e., there is in fact only one string in memory. The values stored in the variables are **equal** if the sequences of characters are the same. Thus, the values of variables A and B are identical, the values of variables A and C as well as B and C are not identical, and the values of all three of A, B, and C are equal.

ANNOTATION: The statements at the beginning of this section:

> There are two binary operators defined on all pairs of values, **identity** and **equality**, that return a Boolean result. Both of these operators are mathematical **equivalence** operators.

are mathematical truisms. From the point of view of computer science, these statements are perhaps a little optimistic. They certainly should be true, but will be true only if the programmers implementing the equality operator (i.e., overriding `object.=`) follow these guidelines.

8.2.5.1 Identity

The identity operator is defined by the CTS as follows.

- If the values have different exact types, then they are not identical.
- Otherwise, if their exact type is a Value Type, then they are identical if and only if the bit sequences of the values are the same, bit by bit.
- Otherwise, if their exact type is a Reference Type, then they are identical if and only if the locations of the values are the same.

Identity is implemented on `System.Object` via the `ReferenceEquals` method.

8.2.5.2 Equality

For value types, the equality operator is part of the definition of the exact type. Definitions of equality should obey the following rules:

- Equality should be an equivalence operator, as defined above.
- Identity should imply equality, as stated earlier.
- If either (or both) operand is a boxed value, equality should be computed by
  - First unboxing any boxed operand(s), and then
  - Applying the usual rules for equality on the resulting values.

Equality is implemented on `System.Object` via the `Equals` method.

NOTE

Although two floating point NaNs are defined by IEC 60559:1989 to always compare as unequal, the contract for `System.Object.Equals` requires that overrides must satisfy the requirements for an equivalence operator. Therefore, `System.Double.Equals` and `System.Single.Equals` return **True** when comparing two NaNs, while the equality operator returns False in that case, as required by the standard.

ANNOTATION: "NaN" stands for "not a number" and is a value returned on overflow conditions.

8.3 Locations

Values are stored in **locations**. A location can hold a single value at a time. All locations are typed. The type of the location embodies the requirements that shall be met by values that are stored in the location. Examples of locations are local variables and parameters.

More importantly, the type of the location specifies the restrictions on usage of any value that is loaded from the location. For example, a location can hold values of potentially many exact types as long as all of the values are assignment compatible with the type of the location (see below). All values loaded from a location are treated as if they are of the type of the location. Only operations valid for the type of the location may be invoked even if the exact type of the value stored in the location is capable of additional operations.

8.3.1 *Assignment Compatible Locations*

A value may be stored in a location only if one of the types of the value is **assignment compatible** with the type of the location. A type is always assignment compatible with itself. Assignment compatibility can often be determined at compile time, in which case there is no need for testing at runtime. Assignment compatibility is described in detail in Partition I, section 8.7.

8.3.2 *Coercion*

Sometimes it is desirable to take a value of a type that is *not* assignment compatible with a location and convert the value to a type that *is* assignment compatible. This is accomplished through **coercion** of the value. Coercion takes a value of a particular type and a desired type and attempts to create a value of the desired type that has equivalent meaning to the original value. Coercion can result in representation changes as well as type changes, hence coercion does not necessarily preserve the identity of two objects.

There are two kinds of coercion: **widening**, which never loses information, and **narrowing**, in which information may be lost. An example of a widening coercion would be coercing a value that is a 32-bit signed integer to a value that is a 64-bit signed integer. An example of a narrowing coercion is the reverse: coercing a 64-bit signed integer to a 32-bit signed integer. Programming languages often implement widening coercions as **implicit conversions**, whereas narrowing coercions usually require an **explicit conversion**.

Some widening coercion is built directly into the VES operations on the built-in types (see Partition I, section 12.1). All other coercion shall be explicitly requested. For the built-in types, the CTS provides operations to perform widening coercions with no runtime checks and narrowing coercions with runtime checks.

8.3.3 *Casting*

Since a value can be of more than one type, a use of the value needs to clearly identify which of its types is being used. Since values are read from locations that are typed, the type of the value which is used is the type of the location from which the value was read. If a different type is to be used, the value is **cast** to one of its other types. Casting is usually a compile-time operation, but if the compiler cannot statically know that the value is of the target type, a runtime cast check is done. Unlike coercion, a cast never changes the actual type of an object, nor does it change the representation. Casting preserves the identity of objects.

For example, a runtime check may be needed when casting a value read from a location that is typed as holding values of a particular interface. Since an interface is an incomplete description of the value, casting that value to be of a different interface type will usually result in a runtime cast check.

8.4 Type Members

As stated above, the type defines the allowable values and the allowable operations supported by the values of the type. If the allowable values of the type have a substructure, that substructure is described via fields or array elements of the type. If there are operations that are part of the type, those operations are described via methods on the type. Fields, array elements, and methods are called **members** of the type. Properties and events are also members of the type.

8.4.1 *Fields, Array Elements, and Values*

The representation of a value (except for those of built-in types) can be subdivided into sub-values. These sub-values are either named, in which case they are called **fields**, or they are accessed by an indexing expression, in which case they are called **array elements**. Types that describe values composed of array elements are **array types**. Types that describe values composed of fields are **compound types**. A value cannot contain both fields and array elements, although a field of a compound type may be an array type and an array element may be a compound type.

Array elements and fields are typed, and these types never change. All of the array elements shall have the same type. Each field of a compound type may have a different type.

8.4.2 *Methods*

A type may associate operations with the type or with each instance of the type. Such operations are called methods. A method is named and has a signature (see Partition I, section 8.6.1) that specifies the allowable types for all of its arguments and for its return value, if any.

A method that is associated only with the type itself (as opposed to a particular instance of the type) is called a static method (see Partition I, section 8.4.3).

A method that is associated with an instance of the type is either an instance method or a virtual method (see Partition I, section 8.4.4). When they are invoked, instance and virtual methods are passed the instance on which this invocation is to operate (known as **this** or a **this pointer**).

The fundamental difference between an instance method and a virtual method is in how the implementation is located. An instance method is invoked by specifying a class and the instance method within that class. The object passed as **this** may be **null** (a special value indicating that no instance is being specified) or an instance of any type that inherits (see Partition I, section 8.9.8) from the class that defines the method. A virtual method may also be called in this manner. This occurs, for example, when an implementation of a virtual method wishes to call the implementation supplied by its parent class. The CTS allows **this** to be **null** inside the body of a virtual method.

> **RATIONALE**
>
> Allowing a virtual method to be called with a non-virtual call eliminates the need for a "call super" instruction and allows version changes between virtual and non-virtual methods. It requires CIL generators to insert explicit tests for a null pointer if they don't want the null **this** pointer to propagate to called methods.

A virtual or instance method may also be called by a different mechanism, a **virtual call**. Any type that inherits from a type that defines a virtual method may provide its own implementation of that method (this is known as **overriding**, see Partition I, section 8.10.4). It is the exact type of the object (determined at runtime) that is used to decide which of the implementations to invoke.

ANNOTATION: There are three kinds of methods: **static methods**, **virtual methods**, and **instance methods**. Static methods are the same as functions or procedures in Pascal or C—these are traditional functions with arguments, and reside in a class without being part of an object. Where you would put them in a class hierarchy depends on where users might be most likely to look for them, and on the other methods to which you want the static method to have access. Putting a static method in a class gives it access to the private data and methods of that class, and to family methods and data of all its parent classes.

Both virtual and instance methods are tied to an object. In addition to their other arguments, they get, implicitly from the VES, a **this** pointer (seen by the system as argument 0, although not specified by the programmer), which is an instance of the class in which they reside. Whereas static methods are just in a class, virtual methods are actually a part of the object itself. Virtual methods provide an implementation available to their children, but the children can also override it with their own implementation.

Instance methods include a definition of the method that cannot be changed, although it can be called by a child. Their location in a class is essentially for convenience, although they also have a **this** pointer. Any subclass can call them, but the method definition is provided with the instance methods themselves, and the child cannot change it in any way. Instance methods are a way of packaging useful code that child classes might want to use.

The CLI allows the programmer to call virtual or instance methods in one of two ways, which determine the source of the method implementation that will be used. You can make either a virtual call or an instance call on a virtual or instance method. The similarity of terms can be confusing, but it is important to understand the distinction. An instance call is made using the CIL call instruction (see Partition III, section 3.19). A virtual call is made with the CIL callvirt instruction (see Partition III, section 4.2).

For a virtual method, this determines the source of the implementation of the method that will be used. Because these methods get the same arguments regardless of how they are marked, the VES does not require that all virtual methods be called with a virtual call.

A virtual call takes the implementation that belongs to the exact object type associated with the virtual method at runtime. Instance calls, on the other hand, are not associated with an object but with a class, and an instance call uses the implementation of the method on the class indicated statically in the method signature in the metadata. Instance calls let the compiler determine the implementation, while virtual calls determine the implementation at runtime, based on the location of the **this** pointer.

For example, suppose there is an instance call to the virtual method Bob on class A (using the **call** instruction). In this case, Bob will always get class A's implementation, no matter where the **this** pointer is. A virtual call (using the **callvirt** instruction), on the other hand, will take the implementation from wherever the **this** pointer is—if it is in subclass B, Bob gets subclass B's implementation.

For more information, see Partition II, section 14.2.

An important point to remember is that each specific call to a virtual method can be labeled as either a virtual or an instance call. In a virtual call, because the object determines the implementation, the **this** pointer cannot be null—a null **this** pointer would require the VES to return an exception. Because instance calls call the virtual method's implementation in the class, the **this** pointer can be null. Some programming languages insert null checks at the beginning of virtual methods, to guarantee that the **this** pointer is not null, no matter how the virtual method is called.

A virtual call on an instance method (using **callvirt**) is generally used to ensure that the **this** pointer is not null, and then to make an instance call on that method.

8.4.3 *Static Fields and Static Methods*

Types may declare locations that are associated with the type rather than any particular value of the type. Such locations are **static fields** of the type. As such, static fields declare a location that is shared by all values of the type. Just like non-static (instance) fields, a static field is typed and that type never changes. Static fields are always restricted to a single application domain basis (see Partition I, section 12.5), but they may also be allocated on a per-thread basis.

Similarly, types may also declare methods that are associated with the type rather than with values of the type. Such methods are **static methods** of the type. Since an invocation of a static method does not have an associated value on which the static method operates, there is no **this** pointer available within a static method.

8.4.4 *Virtual Methods*

An object type may declare any of its methods as **virtual**. Unlike other methods, each exact type that implements the type may provide its own implementation of a virtual method. A virtual method may be invoked through the ordinary method call mechanism that uses the static type, method name, and types of parameters to choose an implementation, in which case the **this** pointer may be **null**. In addition, however, a virtual method may be invoked by a special mechanism (a **virtual call**) that chooses the implementation based on the dynamically detected type of the instance used to make the virtual call rather than the type statically known at compile time. Virtual methods may be marked **final** (see Partition I, section 8.10.2).

8.5 Naming

Names are given to entities of the type system so that they can be referred to by other parts of the type system or by the implementations of the types. Types, fields, methods, properties, and events have names. With respect to the type system, values, locals, and parameters do not have names. An entity of the type system is given a single name; e.g., there is only one name for a type.

8.5.1 *Valid Names*

All comparisons [of CLI names] are done on a byte-by-byte (i.e., case-sensitive, locale-independent, also known as code-point comparison) basis. Where names are used to access built-in VES-supplied functionality (for example, the class initialization method) there is always an accompanying indication on the definition so as not to build in any set of reserved names.

CLS Rule 4: Assemblies shall follow Annex 7 of Technical Report 15 of the Unicode Standard 3.0 (ISBN 0-201-61633-5) governing the set of characters permitted to start and be included in identifiers, available on-line at http://www.unicode.org/unicode/reports/tr15/tr15-18.html. Identifiers shall be in the canonical format defined by Unicode Normalization Form C. For CLS purposes, two identifiers are the same if their lowercase mappings (as specified by the Unicode locale-insensitive, 1-1 lowercase mappings) are the same. That is, for two identifiers to be considered different under the CLS they shall differ in more than simply their case. However, in order to override an inherited definition the CLI requires the precise encoding of the original declaration be used.

NOTE

CLS (consumer): Need not consume types that violate CLS rule 4, but shall have a mechanism to allow access to named items that use one of its own keywords as the name.

CLS (extender): Need not create types that violate CLS rule 4. Shall provide a mechanism for defining new names that obey these rules but are the same as a keyword in the language.

CLS (framework): Shall not export types that violate CLS rule 4. Should avoid the use of names that are commonly used as keywords in programming languages (see Partition V, Annex D).

ANNOTATION: One of the challenges in trying to make different languages work together is resolving the differences in valid names. The areas of difference are:

- Case sensitivity
- Variables from another language that may be keywords in your language
- The characters that may be parts of identifiers

To resolve these areas of difference, the CLS rules require that compilers remember the case of names, and not permit externally visible names to have case-only differences. In addition, every language must have a means of identifying variables that are keywords in that language. The CLS also had to standardize on what characters could be part of identifiers, and Annex 7 of Technical Report 15 of the Unicode Standard was chosen.

Another issue is screen representation versus file encoding. The standard does not address the source code file format used as input to a compiler, but rather only the format of the runnable binary files produced by the compiler. This covers all cases except the class of characters that have two different 16-bit representations. These include characters, which include accents as part of the character. Unicode Normalization Form C, which specifies which representation to use, was chosen. For more information, see Partition I, section 10.2.

8.5.2 *Assemblies and Scoping*

Generally, names are not unique. Names are collected into groupings called **scopes**. Within a scope, a name may refer to multiple entities as long as they are of different **kinds** (methods, fields, nested types, properties, and events) or have different signatures.

CLS Rule 5: All names introduced in a CLS-compliant scope shall be distinct independent of kind, except where the names are identical and resolved via overloading. That is, while the CTS allows a single type to use the same name for a method and a field, the CLS does not.

CLS Rule 6: Fields and nested types shall be distinct by identifier comparison alone, even though the CTS allows distinct signatures to be distinguished. Methods, properties, and events that have the same name (by identifier comparison) shall differ by more than just the return type, except as specified in CLS Rule 39.

> **NOTE**
>
> **CLS (consumer):** Need not consume types that violate these rules after ignoring any members that are marked as not CLS-compliant.
>
> **CLS (extender):** Need not provide syntax for defining types that violate these rules.
>
> **CLS (framework):** Shall not mark types as CLS-compliant if they violate these rules unless they mark sufficient offending items within the type as not CLS-compliant so that the remaining members do not conflict with one another.

A named entity has its name in exactly one scope. Hence, to identify a named entity, both a scope and a name need to be supplied. The scope is said to **qualify** the name. Types provide a scope for the names in the type; hence types qualify the names in the type. For example, consider a compound type `Point` that has a field named `x`. The name "field `x`" by itself does not uniquely identify the named field, but the **qualified name** "field `x` in type `Point`" does.

ANNOTATION: The full qualification of a name is more complex and includes the unique identification of the assembly in which it resides.

Since types are named, the names of types are also grouped into scopes. To fully identify a type, the type name shall be qualified by the scope that includes the type name. Type names are scoped by the **assembly** that contains the implementation of the type. An assembly is a configured set of loadable code modules and other resources that together implement a unit of functionality. The type name is said to be in the **assembly scope** of the assembly that implements the type. Assemblies themselves have names that form the basis of the CTS naming hierarchy.

The **type definition**:

- Defines a name for the type being defined—i.e., the **type name**—and specifies a scope in which that name will be found.
- Defines a **member scope** in which the names of the different kinds of members (fields, methods, events, and properties) are bound. The tuple of (member name, member kind, and member signature) is unique within a member scope of a type.
- Implicitly assigns the type to the assembly scope of the assembly that contains the type definition.

[8.5.2a Enumeration Types]

ANNOTATION: This section was inadvertently not given its own heading in the International Standard. To avoid renumbering sections, this section is given the number 8.5.2a in this book.

The CTS supports an **enum** (also known as an **enumeration type**), an alternate name for an existing type. For purposes of matching signatures an enum shall not be the same as the underlying type. Instances of an enum, however, shall be assignment compatible with the underlying type and vice versa. That is: no cast (see Partition I, section 8.3.3) or coercion (see Partition I, section 8.3.2) is required to convert from the enum to the underlying type, nor are they required from the underlying type to the enum. An enum is considerably more restricted than a true type:

- It shall have exactly one instance field, and the type of that field defines the underlying type of the enumeration.
- It shall not have any methods of its own.
- It shall derive from `System.Enum` (see the *.NET Framework Standard Library Annotated Reference*).
- It shall not implement any interfaces of its own.
- It shall not have any properties or events of its own.
- It shall not have any static fields unless they are literal (see Partition I, section 8.6.1).

The underlying type shall be a built-in integer type. Enums shall derive from `System.Enum`, hence they are value types. Like all value types, they shall be sealed (see Partition I, section 8.9.8.2).

CLS Rule 7: The underlying type of an enum shall be a built-in CLS integer type.

CLS Rule 8: There are two distinct kinds of enums, indicated by the presence or absence of the `System.FlagsAttribute` (see the *.NET Framework Standard Library Annotated Reference)* custom attribute. One represents named integer values; the other, named bit flags that can be combined to generate an unnamed value. The value of an enum is not limited to the specified values.

CLS Rule 9: Literal static fields (see Partition I, section 8.6.1) of an enum shall have the type of the enum itself.

2. Concepts and Architecture

> **NOTE**
>
> **CLS (consumer):** Shall accept definition of enums that follow these rules, but need not distinguish flags from named values.
>
> **CLS (extender):** Same as consumer. Extender languages are encouraged to allow the authoring of enums, but need not do so.
>
> **CLS (framework):** Shall not expose enums that violate these rules, and shall not assume that enums have only the specified values (even for enums that are named values).

8.5.3 *Visibility, Accessibility, and Security*

To refer to a named entity in a scope, both the scope and the name in the scope shall be **visible** (see Partition I, section 8.5.3.1). Visibility is determined by the relationship between the entity that contains the reference (the **referent**) and the entity that contains the name being referenced. Consider the following pseudo-code:

```
class A
{ int32 IntInsideA;
}
class B inherits from A
{ void method X(int32, int32)
  { IntInsideA := 15;
  }
}
```

If we consider the reference to the field `IntInsideA` in `class A`:

- We call class B the **referent** because it has a method that refers to that field,
- We call `IntInsideA` in `class A` the **referenced entity**.

There are two fundamental questions that need to be answered in order to decide whether the referent is allowed to access the referenced entity. The first is whether the name of the referenced entity is **visible** to the referent. If it is visible, then there is a separate question of whether the referent is **accessible (see Partition I,** section 8.5.3.2).

Access to a member of a type is permitted only if all three of the following conditions are met:

- The type is visible.
- The member is accessible.
- All relevant security demands (see Partition I, section 8.5.3.3) have been granted.

8.5.3.1 Visibility of Types

Only type names, not member names, have controlled visibility. Type names fall into one of the following three categories

- **Exported** from the assembly in which they are defined. While a type may be marked to *allow* it to be exported from the assembly, it is the configuration of the assembly that decides whether the type name *is* made available.
- **Not exported** outside the assembly in which they are defined.
- Nested within another type. In this case, the type itself has the visibility of the type inside of which it is nested (its **enclosing type**). See Partition I, section 8.5.3.4.

8.5.3.2 Accessibility of Members

A type scopes all of its members, and it also specifies the accessibility rules for its members. Except where noted, accessibility is decided based only on the statically visible type of the member being referenced and the type and assembly that is making the reference. The CTS supports seven different rules for accessibility:

- **Compiler-Controlled** – accessible only through use of a definition, not a reference, hence only accessible from within a single compilation unit and under the control of the compiler.
- **Private** – accessible only to referents in the implementation of the exact type that defines the member.
- **Family** – accessible to referents that support the same type—i.e., an exact type and all of the types that inherit from it. For verifiable code (see Partition I, section 8.8), there is an additional requirement that may require a runtime check: the reference shall be made through an item whose exact type supports the exact type of the referent. That is, the item whose member is being accessed shall inherit from the type performing the access.
- **Assembly** – accessible only to referents in the same assembly that contains the implementation of the type.
- **Family-and-Assembly** – accessible only to referents that qualify for both Family and Assembly access.
- **Family-or-Assembly** – accessible only to referents that qualify for either Family or Assembly access.
- **Public** – accessible to all referents.

ANNOTATION: Not all languages support all of the possible accessibility rules. Languages support what they believe their users will need. For example, originally C#

had only four accessibility levels: **public**, **internal** (assembly), **protected** (family), and **private**. The designers believed that was enough because a protected member could call an internal member. However, they received feedback from the framework developers that some members should be accessible only from within the assembly or by descendants outside, which is the family-or-assembly level. So C# implemented it, calling it **protected internal**. But the designers stood firm on not implementing family-and-assembly because they did not see it as useful. They still believe that assembly is usually enough—it may have a few more permissions than necessary, but they feel that programmers usually just want to control access within the assembly.

In general, a member of a type can have any one of these accessibility rules assigned to it. There are two exceptions, however:

1. Members defined by an interface shall be public.
2. When a type defines a virtual method that overrides an inherited definition, the accessibility shall either be identical in the two definitions or the overriding definition shall permit more access than the original definition. For example, it is possible to override an **assembly virtual** method with a new implementation that is **public virtual**, but not with one that is **family virtual**. In the case of overriding a definition derived from another assembly, it is not considered restricting access if the base definition has **family-or-assembly** access and the override has only **family** access.

RATIONALE

Languages including C++ allow this "widening" of access. Restricting access would provide an incorrect illusion of security since simply casting an object to the base class (which occurs implicitly on method call) would allow the method to be called despite the restricted accessibility. To prevent overriding a virtual method, use **final** (see Partition I, section 8.10.2) rather than relying on limited accessibility.

CLS Rule 10: Accessibility shall not be changed when overriding inherited methods, except when overriding a method inherited from a different assembly with accessibility **family-or-assembly**. In this case the override shall have accessibility **family**.

> **NOTE**
>
> **CLS (consumer):** Need not accept types that widen access to inherited virtual methods.
>
> **CLS (extender):** Need not provide syntax to widen access to inherited virtual methods.
>
> **CLS (frameworks):** Shall not rely on the ability to widen access to a virtual method, either in the exposed portion of the framework or by users of the framework.

8.5.3.3 Security Permissions

Access to members is also controlled by security demands that may be attached to an assembly, type, method, property, or event. Security demands are not part of a type contract (see Partition I, section 8.6), and hence are not inherited. There are two kinds of demands:

- An **inheritance demand.** When attached to a type, it requires that any type that wishes to inherit from this type shall have the specified security permission. When attached to a non-final virtual method, it requires that any type that wishes to override this method shall have the specified permission. It shall not be attached to any other member.
- A **reference demand.** Any attempt to resolve a reference to the marked item shall have specified security permission.

Only one demand of each kind may be attached to any item. Attaching a security demand to an assembly implies that it is attached to all types in the assembly unless another demand of the same kind is attached to the type. Similarly, a demand attached to a type implies the same demand for all members of the type unless another demand of the same kind is attached to the member. For additional information, see Declarative Security in Partition II, section 19, and the classes in the `System.Security` namespace in the *.NET Framework Standard Library Annotated Reference.*

8.5.3.4 Nested Types

A type (called a nested type) can be a member of an enclosing type. A nested type has the same visibility as the enclosing type and has an accessibility as would any other member of the enclosing type. This accessibility determines which other types may make references to the nested type. That is, for a class to define a field or array element of a nested type, have a method that takes a nested type as a parameter or returns one as value, etc., the nested type shall be both visible and accessible to the referencing type. A nested type is part of the enclosing type, so its methods have access to all members of its enclosing type, as well as family access to members of the type from which it inherits (see Partition I, section 8.9.8).

The names of nested types are scoped by their enclosing type, not their assembly (only top-level types are scoped by their assembly). There is no requirement that the names of nested types be unique within an assembly.

8.6 Contracts

Contracts are named. They are the shared assumptions on a set of **signatures** (see Partition I, section 8.6.1) between all implementers and all users of the contract. The signatures are the part of the contract that can be checked and enforced.

ANNOTATION: The standard does not specify structural equivalence, other than for arrays. A type named **point (real** *x*, **real** *y*) and a type **rect (real** *x*, **real** *y*) are not the same, despite having the same signatures. Some languages, such as C++, in its use of type templates, do use structural equivalence.

Contracts are not types; rather they specify requirements on the implementation of types. Types state which contracts they abide by—i.e., which contracts all implementations of the type shall support. An implementation of a type can be verified to check that the enforceable parts of a contract, the named signatures, have been implemented. The kinds of contracts are:

- **Class contract** – A class contract is specified with a class definition. Hence, a class definition defines both the class contract and the **class type**. The name of the class contract and the name of the class type are the same. A class contract specifies the representation of the values of the class type. Additionally, a class contract specifies the other contracts that the class type supports—e.g., which interfaces, methods, properties, and events shall be implemented. A class contract, and hence the class type, can be supported by other class types as well. A class type that supports the class contract of another class type is said to **inherit** from that class type.
- **Interface contract** – An interface contract is specified with an interface definition. Hence, an interface definition defines both the interface contract and the **interface type**. The name of the interface contract and the name of the interface type are the same. Many types can support an interface contract. Like a class contract, interface contracts specify which other contracts the interface supports—e.g., which interfaces, methods, properties, and events shall be implemented.

NOTE

An interface type can never fully describe the representation of a value. Therefore an interface type can never support a class contract, and hence can never be a class type or an exact type.

- **Method contract –** A method contract is specified with a method definition. A method contract is a named operation that specifies the contract between the implementation(s) of the method and the callers of the method. A method contract is always part of a type contract (class, value type, or interface), and describes how a particular named operation is implemented. The method contract specifies the contracts that each parameter to the method shall support and the contracts that the return value shall support, if there is a return value.
- **Property contract –** A property contract is specified with a property definition. There is an extensible set of operations for handling a named value, which includes a standard pair for reading the value and changing the value [typically get and set]. A property contract specifies method contracts for the subset of these operations that shall be implemented by any type that supports the property contract. A type can support many property contracts, but any given property contract can be supported by exactly one type. Hence, property definitions are a part of the type definition of the type that supports the property.
- **Event contract –** An event contract is specified with an event definition. There is an extensible set of operations for managing a named event, which includes three standard methods (register interest in an event, revoke interest in an event, fire the event). An event contract specifies method contracts for all of the operations that shall be implemented by any type that supports the event contract. A type can support many event contracts, but any given event contract can be supported by exactly one type. Hence, event definitions are a part of the type definition of the type that supports the event.

8.6.1 *Signatures*

Signatures are the part of a contract that can be checked and automatically enforced. Signatures are formed by adding constraints to types and other signatures. A constraint is a limitation on the use of or allowed operations on a value or location. Example constraints would be whether a location may be overwritten with a different value or whether a value may ever be changed.

All locations have signatures, as do all values. Assignment compatibility requires that the signature of the value, including constraints, is compatible with the signature of the location, including constraints. There are four fundamental kinds of signatures: type signatures, location signatures, parameter signatures, and method signatures.

CLS Rule 11: All types appearing in a signature shall be CLS-compliant.

CLS Rule 12: The visibility and accessibility of types and members shall be such that types in the signature of any member shall be visible and accessible whenever the member itself is visible and accessible. For example, a public method that is visible outside its assembly shall not have an argument whose type is visible only within the assembly.

NOTE

CLS (consumer): Need not accept types whose members violate these rules.

CLS (extender): Need not provide syntax to violate these rules.

CLS (framework): Shall not violate this rule in its exposed types and their members.

The following sections describe the various kinds of signatures. These descriptions are cumulative: the simplest signature is a type signature; a location signature is a type signature plus (optionally) some additional attributes; and so forth.

ANNOTATION: Signatures store both **constraints** and **modifiers**. Both have similar functions, but constraints are defined by the standard, and modifiers are defined by implementers. Both are stored in the signatures in the metadata, in compact form. They are distinct from attributes, which are much more complex. Modifiers are often referred to as custom modifiers, and they can be designated either optional or required (**modopt** or **modreq**, respectively, as described in Partition II, section 7.1.1).

8.6.1.1 Type Signatures

Type signatures define the constraints on a value and its usage. A type, by itself, is a valid type signature. The type signature of a value cannot be determined by examining the value or even by knowing the class type of the value. The type signature of a value is derived from the location signature (see below) of the location from which the value is loaded. Normally the type signature of a value is the type in the location signature from which the value is loaded.

ANNOTATION: Currently there are no constraints that can be placed on types, although at one point in the design, it was possible to designate a type as constant. At present, only location constraints, described in the next section, are possible. Type signatures are standardized to allow the possibility of introducing type constraints in the future.

RATIONALE

The distinction between a Type Signature and a Location Signature (below) is not currently useful. It is made because certain constraints, such as "constant," are constraints on values, not locations. Future versions of this standard, or non-standard extensions, may introduce type constraints, thus making the distinction meaningful.

8.6.1.2 Location Signatures

All locations are typed. This means that all locations have a **location signature**, which defines constraints on the location, its usage, and on the usage of the values stored in the location. Any valid type signature is a valid location signature. Hence, a location signature contains a type and may additionally contain the constant constraint. The location signature may also contain **location constraints** that give further restrictions on the uses of the location. The location constraints are:

- The **init-only constraint** promises (hence, requires) that once the location has been initialized, its contents never change. Namely, the contents are initialized before any access, and after initialization, no value may be stored in the location. The contents are always identical to the initialized value (see Partition I, section 8.2.3). This constraint, while logically applicable to any location, shall only be placed on fields (static or instance) of compound types.
- The **literal constraint** promises that the value of the location is actually a fixed value of a built-in type. The value is specified as part of the constraint. Compilers are required to replace all references to the location with its value, and the VES therefore need not allocate space for the location. This constraint, while logically applicable to any location, shall only be placed on static fields of compound types. Fields that are so marked are not permitted to be referenced from CIL (they shall be inlined to their constant value at compile time), but are available using Reflection and tools that directly deal with the metadata.

CLS Rule 13: The value of a literal static is specified through the use of field initialization metadata (see Partition II). A CLS-compliant literal must have a value specified in field initialization metadata that is of exactly the same type as the literal (or of the underlying type, if that literal is an **enum**).

NOTE

CLS (consumer): Must be able to read field initialization metadata for static literal fields and inline the value specified when referenced. Consumers may assume that the type of the field initialization metadata is exactly the same as the type of the literal field; i.e., a consumer tool need not implement conversions of the values.

CLS (extender): Must avoid producing field initialization metadata for static literal fields in which the type of the field initialization metadata does not exactly match the type of the field.

CLS (framework): Should avoid the use of syntax specifying a value of a literal that requires conversion of the value. Note that compilers may do the conversion themselves before persisting the field initialization metadata resulting in a CLS-compliant framework, but frameworks are encouraged not to rely on such implicit conversions.

NOTE

It might seem reasonable to provide a **volatile constraint** on a location that would require that the value stored in the location not be cached between accesses. Instead, CIL includes a **volatile.** prefix to certain instructions to specify that the value neither be cached nor computed using an existing cache. Such a constraint may be encoded using a custom attribute (see Partition I, section 9.7), although this standard does not specify such an attribute.

ANNOTATION: Specifiying **volatile** as a prefix rather than as a constraint provides more flexibility. It allows greater code optimization than a constraint, which would apply to all variables or types so labeled. CLS rule 13 tells how to specify the value of literal statics. Although you can reflect on a literal static, it is not possible to go in with a tool, such as a debugger, and change its value.

ANNOTATION: Some programming languages, such as C and C++, support the notion of passing explicit pointers. Others, such as Pascal, support the notion of passing a variable by reference. Still other languages, such as Eiffel and Lisp, do not support the notion at all. Microsoft received significant opposition to the inclusion of the managed pointer in the CLI, and more importantly, to putting it in the CLS, and therefore in libraries.

The decision to include it was largely so that library routines such as atomic increment, atomic decrement, volatile reference, etc., could be provided in a language-independent manner. Without managed pointers or a similar mechanism, these could not be written in libraries, but would have had to be added directly to programming languages. I feel strongly that language-independent access to these kinds of facilities is essential in a modern programming world.

– Jim Miller

8.6.1.3 Local Signatures

A **local signature** specifies the contract on a local variable allocated during the running of a method. A local signature contains a full location signature, plus it may specify one additional constraint:

The **byref** constraint states that the content of the corresponding location is a **managed pointer**. A managed pointer may point to a local variable, parameter, field of a compound type, or element of an array. However, when a call crosses a remoting boundary (see Partition I, section 12.5) a conforming implementation may use a copy-in/copy-out mechanism instead of a managed pointer. Thus programs shall not rely on the aliasing behavior of true pointers.

In addition, there is one special local signature. The **typed reference** local variable signature states that the local will contain both a managed pointer to a location and a runtime representation of the type that may be stored at that location. A typed reference signature is similar to a byref constraint, but while the byref specifies the type as part of the byref constraint (and hence as part of the type description), a typed reference provides the type information dynamically. A typed reference is a full signature in itself and cannot be combined with other constraints. In particular, it is not possible to specify a **byref** whose type is **typed reference**.

The typed reference signature is actually represented as a built-in value type, like the integer and floating point types. In the Base Class Library (see **.NET Framework Standard Library Annotated Reference)** the type is known as `System.TypedReference`, and in the assembly language used in Partition II it is designated by the keyword **typedref**. This type shall only be used for parameters and local variables. It shall not be boxed, nor shall it be used as the type of a field, element of an array, return value, etc.

ANNOTATION: The typed reference is a reference to a memory location in which only a specified type can be stored. Although it is an elegant idea based on a notion from Visual Basic 6, most languages do not currently support it (including the current version of Visual Basic), because it requires special syntax and there some restrictions on what can be done with it, as described above.

Typed references are not required in the Kernel Profile (see Partition IV, section 4), so it is possible that some VES implementations will not support them.

CLS Rule 14: Typed references are not CLS-compliant.

NOTE

CLS (consumer): There is no need to accept this type.

CLS (extender): There is no need to provide syntax to define this type or to extend interfaces or classes that use this type.

CLS (framework): This type shall not appear in exposed members.

8.6.1.4 Parameter Signatures

Parameter signatures define constraints on how an individual value is passed as part of a method invocation. Parameter signatures are declared by method definitions. Any valid local signature is a valid parameter signature.

8.6.1.5 Method Signatures

Method signatures are composed of

- A calling convention,
- A list of zero or more parameter signatures, one for each parameter of the method,
- And a type signature for the result value if one is produced.

Method signatures are declared by method definitions. Only one constraint can be added to a method signature in addition to those of parameter signatures:

- The **varargs** constraint may be included to indicate that all arguments past this point are optional. When it appears, the calling convention shall be one that supports variable[-length] argument lists.

Method signatures are used in two different ways. They are used as part of a method definition and as a description of a calling site when calling through a function pointer. In this latter case, the method signature indicates

- The calling convention (which may include platform-specific calling conventions)
- The type of all the argument values that are being passed,

- If needed, a varargs marker indicating where the fixed parameter list ends and the variable parameter list begins

When used as part of a method definition, the varargs constraint is represented by the choice of calling convention.

ANNOTATION: Because of the special handling required for the **varargs** constraint, many languages choose not to support this option. In addition, the varargs library is not in the Kernel Profile, so it is not required of a base VES implementation.

CLS Rule 15: The varargs constraint is not part of the CLS, and the only calling convention supported by the CLS is the standard managed calling convention.

NOTE

CLS (consumer): There is no need to accept methods with variable[-length] argument lists or unmanaged calling conventions.

CLS (extender): There is no need to provide syntax to declare varargs methods or unmanaged calling conventions.

CLS (framework): Neither varargs methods nor methods with unmanaged calling conventions may be exposed externally.

8.7 Assignment Compatibility

The constraints in the type signature and the location signature affect assignment compatibility of a value to a location. Assignment compatibility of a value (described by a type signature) to a location (described by a location signature) is defined as follows:

One of the types supported by the exact type of the value is the same as the type in the location signature.

This allows, for example, an instance of a class that inherits from a base class (hence supports the base class's type contract) to be stored into a location whose type is that of the base class.

8.8 Type Safety and Verification

Since types specify contracts, it is important to know whether a given implementation lives up to these contracts. An implementation that lives up to the enforceable part of the contract (the named signatures) is said to be **typesafe**. An important part of the contract deals with restrictions on the visibility and accessibility of named items as well as the mapping of names to implementations and locations in memory.

ANNOTATION: As Figure 2-2 shows, not all CTS programs will be memory-safe, and not all memory-safe programs will be verifiable.

In trying to define a platform for many languages, a primary goal is to ensure code that is safe. Although the standard talks about type safety, in the area of verification it is, strictly speaking, memory safety that verifiers ensure.

Type safety is a well-defined mathematical concept that says that the only operations on the type are those that the type was designed to support. The verifier does not require that. For example, it is not typesafe to take a long and cast it to a 32-bit int. Because you have lost information, it is not strictly typesafe. But it does not damage memory, and most languages allow you to do it—as do verifiers (such as Microsoft's PEVerify) constructed using the verification algorithm and rules described in Partition III. However, the verifier enforces type safety according to a much smaller type system than the entire range specified by the Common Type System (CTS), and it guarantees memory safety.

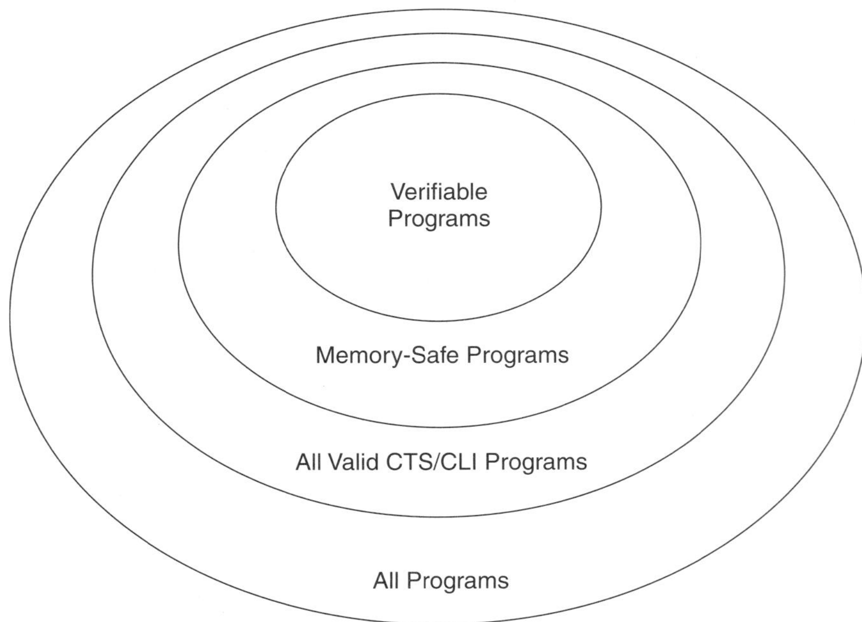

Figure 2-2 Type Safety and Programs

However, plenty of programs are safe but not verifiable. For example, C and C++ are both capable of doing many operations in memory that are not verifiable. They must therefore rely on standard testing techniques to be sure the code is safe. In contrast, Eiffel has its own constructs that are perfectly safe—it has a strong development environment that ensures safety.

Typesafe implementations only store values described by a type signature in a location that is assignment compatible with the location signature of the location (see Partiton I, section 8.6.1). Typesafe implementations never apply an operation to a value that is not defined by the exact type of the value. Typesafe implementations only access locations that are both visible and accessible to them. In a typesafe implementation, the exact type of a value cannot change.

Verification is a mechanical process of examining an implementation and asserting that it is typesafe. Verification is said to succeed if the process proves that an implementation is typesafe. Verification is said to fail if that process does not prove the type safety of an implementation. Verification is necessarily conservative: it may report failure for a typesafe implementation, but it never reports success for an implementation that is not typesafe. For example, most verification processes report implementations that do pointer-based arithmetic as failing verification, even if the implementation is in fact typesafe.

There are many different processes that can be the basis of verification. The simplest possible process simply says that all implementations are not typesafe. While correct and efficient, this is clearly not particularly useful. By spending more resources (time and space), a process can correctly identify more typesafe implementations. It has been proven, however, that no mechanical process can in finite time and with no errors correctly identify all implementations as either typesafe or not typesafe. The choice of a particular verification process is thus a matter of engineering, based on the resources available to make the decision and the importance of detecting the type safety of different programming constructs.

8.9 Type Definers

Type definers construct a new type from existing types. **Implicit types** (e.g., built-in types, arrays, and pointers, including function pointers) are defined when they are used. The mention of an implicit type in a signature is in and of itself a complete definition of the type. Implicit types allow the VES to manufacture instances with a standard set of members, interfaces, etc. Implicit types need not have user-supplied names.

All other types shall be explicitly defined using an explicit type definition. The explicit type definers are:

- Interface definitions – used to define interface types

- Class definitions – used to define:
  - Object types
  - Value types and their associated boxed types

> **NOTE**
>
> While class definitions always define class types, not all class types require a class definition. Array types and pointer types, which are implicitly defined, are also class types. See Partition I, section 8.2.3.
>
> Similarly, not all types defined by a class definition are object types. Array types, explicitly defined object types, and boxed types are object types. Pointer types, function pointer types, and value types are not object types. See Partition I, section 8.2.3.

8.9.1 *Array Types*

An **array type** shall be defined by specifying the element type of the array, the **rank** (number of dimensions) of the array, and the upper and lower bounds of each dimension of the array. Hence, no separate definition of the array type is needed. The bounds (as well as indices into the array) shall be signed integers. While the actual bounds for each dimension are known at runtime, the signature may specify the information that is known at compile time: no bounds, a lower bound, or both an upper and lower bound.

Array elements shall be laid out within the array object in row-major order; i.e., the elements associated with the rightmost array dimension shall be laid out contiguously from lowest to highest index. The actual storage allocated for each array element may include platform-specific padding.

Values of an array type are objects; hence an array type is a kind of object type (see Partition I, section 8.2.3). Array objects are defined by the CTS to be a repetition of locations where values of the array element type are stored. The number of repeated values is determined by the rank and bounds of the array.

Only type signatures, not location signatures, are allowed as array element types.

Exact array types are created automatically by the VES when they are required. Hence, the operations on an array type are defined by the CTS. These generally are: allocating the array based on size and lower bound information, indexing the array to read and write a value, computing the address of an element of the array (a managed pointer), and querying for the rank, bounds, and the total number of values stored in the array.

ANNOTATION: Arrays are seen by the system as objects and are one of the implicit types—declaring the type, rank, and bounds alone causes the VES to define the array. Other implicit types are the built-in numeric types, pointers, the base object type, delegates, and strings. The compiler sees only the reference to the array, and the VES constructs the objects. This makes the methods associated with `System.Array` (the **Get**, **Set**, and **Address** methods) available as well.

In deciding how to define arrays for this standard, there were several difficult questions to answer during the design of the CLI: whether arrays should be covariant or invariant, the allowed dimensions for an array, and the allowed array bounds.

If covariant arrays are supported, anywhere you have an array of a given type you can have an array of any subclass of that type. Invariant arrays mean that an array of a subclass of a type is not a subclass of an array of the type. The following short program will illustrate the difference between covariant and invariant.

```
class Vehicle { …. }
class Car : Vehicle { … }
void M(Vehicle[] MyVehicles)
{ Vehicle V = new Vehicle();
  Car C = new Car();
  MyVehicles[0] = V;
  MyVehicles[1] = C;
}

void Main()
{ Car[] MyCars = new Car[2];
  M(MyCars);
}
```

`main()` makes an array of cars, and passes it into `M`. The code inside of `M` is legal code for both covariant and invariant arrays. The issue is whether `main()` is legal. With invariant arrays, the call to `M` in `main()` is not verifiable, and in fact, the compiler should return an error because an array of `Car` is not a subclass of an array of `Vehicle`.

The covariant approach is that anywhere you have an array of any subclass of that type, you can have an array of that type's subclass—anywhere you have an array of Vehicles, you can have an array of Cars. The problem is that in order to do it, and still make `M` legal, at runtime the assignments of `V` and `C` into the array must be checked to see if they are legal. In a covariant system, the assignment of `C` turns out to be legal, but there is no way to know that prior to runtime. The assignment of `V` is not legal, because instead of an array of Vehicles, `main()` supplied an array of Cars, so Vehicles cannot be in that array.

In a system that requires invariant arrays, storing into an array would not require any type checking at runtime, but it would not have let us write this program. With covariant arrays, this program is legal, but the penalty is that anytime you store into an array, or take the address of an element of an array, a type check is required.

The decision to support covariant arrays was primarily to allow Java to run on the VES. The covariant design is not thought to be the best design in general, but it was chosen in the interest of broad reach.

The dimensionality of allowed arrays was also an issue. The decision was made to support multi-dimensional arrays, but not to support zero-dimensional arrays (allowed currently only in APL).

Array bounds were another question. The options were always 0 for lower, always 1 for lower, or user specifies both upper and lower bounds. Here the CTS and the CLS took different paths. The CTS supports all of these (lower bounds specified arbitrarily by the programmer).

CLS Rule 16: Arrays shall have elements with a CLS-compliant type, and all dimensions of the array shall have lower bounds of zero. Only the fact that an item is an array and the element type of the array shall be required to distinguish between overloads. When overloading is based on two or more array types, the element types shall be named types.

NOTE

So-called "jagged arrays" are CLS-compliant, but when overloading multiple array types they are one-dimensional, zero-based arrays of type `System.Array`.

CLS (consumer): There is no need to support arrays of non-CLS types, even when dealing with instances of `System.Array`. Overload resolution need not be aware of the full complexity of array types. Programmers should have access to the Get, Set, and Address methods on instances of `System.Array` if there is no language syntax for the full range of array types.

CLS (extender): There is no need to provide syntax to define non-CLS types of arrays or to extend interfaces or classes that use non-CLS array types. Shall provide access to the type `System.Array`, but may assume that all instances will have a CLS-compliant type. While the full array signature must be used to override an inherited method that has an array parameter, the full complexity of array types need not be made visible to programmers. Programmers should have access to the Get, Set, and Address methods on instances of `System.Array` if there is no language syntax for the full range of array types.

CLS (framework): Non-CLS array types shall not appear in exposed members. Where possible, use only one-dimensional, zero-based arrays (vectors) of simple named types, since these are supported in the widest range of programming languages. Overloading on array types should be avoided, and when used shall obey the restrictions.

ANNOTATION: The CLS has one rule (rule 16) for arrays, which implies three things:

1. The type of the element must be CLS-compliant.
2. The only arrays supported for interlanguage use must have lower bounds of zero.
3. Overloading a method based on arrays is severely restricted.

Imagine a method named "Ralph." The following overloadings of `Ralph` are legal:

`void Ralph()`
`void Ralph(int)`—differs by arity (number of arguments)
`void Ralph(float)`—differs by simple type
`void Ralph(int[])`
`void Ralph(float[])`—arrays differ by type of element

The following are not legal:

`void Ralph(int *[])`—element type doesn't have a name
`void Ralph(int[][])`—element type doesn't have a name
`void Ralph(int[,])`—array has same element type
`void Ralph(int[1,])`—array has same element type

C and Java do not support multi-dimensional arrays, just arrays of arrays (called jagged arrays). For purposes of overloading, however, these look like one-dimensional arrays with a zero-based index, and the element type is called `System.Array`. Therefore, you cannot define a jagged array of integers and a jagged array of floating point numbers and overload on that distinction:

`void Ralph(int [][])`—C/Java jagged array of integers
`void Ralph(float [][])`—C/Java jagged array of floats

Neither of these has a simple name for the element type of the array—the first is `int[]`, the second is `float[]`.

Array types form a hierarchy, with all array types inheriting from the type `System.Array`. This is an abstract class (see Partition I, section 8.9.6.2) that represents all

2. Concepts and Architecture

arrays regardless of the type of their elements, their rank, or their upper and lower bounds. The VES creates one array type for each distinguishable array type. In general, array types are only distinguished by the type of their elements and their rank. The VES, however, treats single-dimensional, zero-based arrays (also known as **vectors**) specially. Vectors are also distinguished by the type of their elements, but a vector is distinct from a single-dimensional array of the same element type that has a non-zero lower bound. Zero-dimensional arrays are not supported.

ANNOTATION: The only language that supports zero-dimensional arrays is APL. Although there was discussion about supporting them in the CLI, it was felt, in the end, that the difficulties entailed in supporting it outweighed the benefits.

Consider the examples in Table 2-2, using the syntax of CIL as described in Partition II:

ANNOTATION: The CLI supports multi-dimensional arrays. The specification requires that the arrays be laid out in memory as dense arrays in a row-major form (see Partition I, section 8.9.1). Figure 2-3(a) shows a row-major layout for a two-dimensional array with three rows and two columns.

Row-major array layout was chosen because many existing applications assume that layout. During the discussions of the standard, it was noted that a future standard may add new array types whose layout is not specified and can be chose by the implementation to fit a given application best. That new array element would make

Table 2-2 Array Examples

Static Specification of Type	Actual Type Constructed	Allowed in CLS?
`int32[]`	vector of int32	Yes
`int32[0..5]`	vector of int32	Yes
`int32[1..5]`	array, rank 1, of int32	No
`int32[,]`	array, rank 2, of int32	Yes
`int32[0..3, 0..5]`	array, rank 2, of int32	Yes
`int32[0.., 0..]`	array, rank 2, of int32	Yes
`int32[1.., 0..]`	array, rank 2, of int32	No

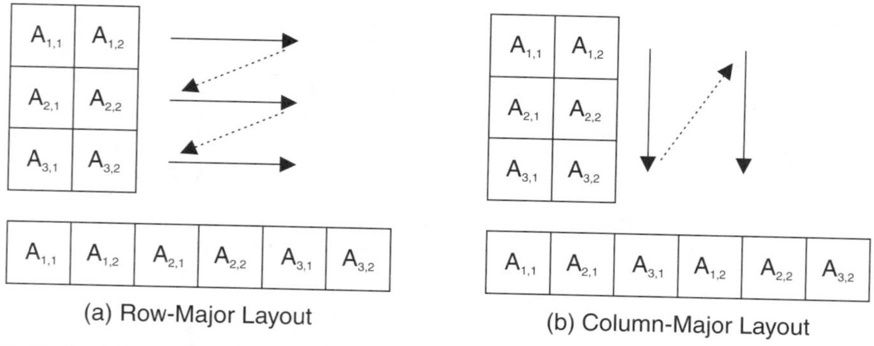

Figure 2-3 Typical Array Layouts in Memory

pointer arithmetic on pointers to array elements meaningless and would allow access only through standard member functions like these that are declared in `System.Array`.

In the future, the VES might choose a layout different from the default row-major format for a couple of reasons:

- Other layouts may provide better performance by providing better spatial locality and exploiting processor caches more efficiently; e.g., a column-major layout may be beneficial in some circumstances; see Figure 2-3(b).
- Sparse arrays (i.e., arrays in which the majority of elements are zero) may be represented in a way that uses less memory and makes operations on larger data sets possible.

The VES might choose a different array layout at the time the array is created, or it might even remap an existing array by changing its layout to react to newly available information about the application behavior.

A decision about an array layout can be made completely automatically by the use of compiler analysis or by instrumentation of the runtime behavior, or it may be decided with the programmer's help by allowing an annotation or an extra argument in the array constructor.

– Michał Cierniak, Intel Corporation

8.9.2 *Unmanaged Pointer Types*

An unmanaged pointer type (also known simply as a "pointer type") is defined by specifying a location signature for the location the pointer references. Any signature of a pointer type includes this location signature. Hence, no separate definition of the pointer type is needed.

While pointer types are Reference Types, values of a pointer type are not objects (see Partition I, section 8.2.3), and hence it is not possible, given a value of a pointer type, to determine its exact type. The CTS provides two typesafe operations on pointer types: one to load the value from the location referenced by the pointer and the other to store an assignment compatible value into that location. The CTS also provides three operations on pointer types (byte-based address arithmetic): adding and subtracting integers from pointers, and subtracting one pointer from another. The results of the first two operations are pointers to the same type signature as the original pointer. See Partition III for details.

CLS Rule 17: Unmanaged pointer types are not CLS-compliant.

NOTE

CLS (consumer): There is no need to support unmanaged pointer types.

CLS (extender): There is no need to provide syntax to define or access unmanaged pointer types.

CLS (framework): Unmanaged pointer types shall not be externally exposed.

ANNOTATION: Unmanaged pointers are specified by the CTS because it is important to have tools that deal with both managed and unmanaged code.

Not described in this part of Partition I (other than a brief mention in the discussion of the byref constraint in section 8.6.1.3) is another important type: **managed pointers**. Managed pointers, strictly speaking, are not a data type, but a modifier to a data type. An object reference points to the start of an object or array, while a managed pointer points to the interior of an object—to one of its fields. Because it is managed, you have access to the field to which it points, even if the object moves. Managed pointers are allowed only in local variables, parameters to methods, and the return value of a method.

A managed pointer can also point to a value type. When the value type is boxed, making it an object, it points to the value in the interior of the object on the heap. But a managed pointer can also point directly to a value type on the stack.

In C# the managed pointer surfaces as an **out** parameter, but it is not possible to have a variable of that type. You would not declare a variable named x of type managed pointer to integer. It is instead a parameter passing convention. You would have a parameter named x, which is an **out** parameter to an integer. Historically, this is the same thing that Pascal called a **var** parameter. In Visual Basic it was called a **byref** rather than a **byval** parameter.

When a managed pointer is treated as an **out** parameter, its definition as a modifier (constraint) makes sense. But for many other languages, and their exposure of managed pointers, it makes more sense to think of it as a type with restrictions. Managed pointers are allowed only in local variables, parameters to methods, and the return value of a method. Returning a managed pointer is not, however, verifiable.

If you are writing unmanaged code and want to deal with managed data, there are three options: (1) pass a managed pointer to a pinned object on the heap, (2) pass an unmanaged pointer to a value on the stack, or (3) pass an instance of the `System.Runtime.InteropServices.GCHandle` structure, where the handle was created as "pinned" to a value on the heap. It is strongly recommended that you avoid the first of these options.

For more information on managed pointers, see Partition II, section 13.4.2, and Partition III, section 1.1.4.2.

8.9.3 *Delegates*

Delegates are the object-oriented equivalent of function pointers. Unlike function pointers, delegates are object-oriented, typesafe, and secure. Delegates are created by defining a class that derives from the base type `System.Delegate` (see the *.NET Framework Standard Library Annotated Reference*). Each delegate type shall provide a method named **Invoke** with appropriate parameters, and each instance of a delegate forwards calls to its **Invoke** method to a compatible static or instance method on a particular object. The object and method to which it delegates are chosen when the delegate instance is created.

In addition to an instance constructor and an **Invoke** method, delegates may optionally have two additional methods: **BeginInvoke** and **EndInvoke**. These are used for asynchronous calls.

While, for the most part, delegates appear to be simply another kind of user-defined class, they are tightly controlled. The implementations of the methods are provided by the VES, not user code. The only additional members that may be defined on delegate types are static or instance methods.

ANNOTATION: Delegates are a good object-oriented model for what is a function pointer in the unmanaged world. Delegates are themselves objects with two private fields, one of which is an object, and the other of which is the method that can be called on that object. They can also contain no object and a static method.

Delegates can be single-cast or multicast. The simplest form of delegate—single-cast—corresponds to a simple function pointer in the non-OO world.

Multicast delegates call all of the single-cast delegates.

One of the advantages of delegates is that they can be called asynchronously, unlike function pointers. Calling a delegate asynchronously means that another thread makes the actual call, and the original caller can check back later for the result.

Delegates may also point to multiple functions. In this case, calling the delegate means that all of the functions get called, and there are methods that allow you to set or change the order in which they are called. Thus, a programmer can write code that will call functions in a given order, rearrange it, and catch all the exceptions.

But delegates are particularly nice for the event model (publish and subscribe). It is possible to provide a delegate that is not intended to call a function but allows other objects to add themselves to it, and to notify them that a particular event, such as a left-hand mouse click, has occurred. When the event occurs, the delegate publishes the event to all subscribers.

There is support for events in the metadata, but not directly in the VES. Whatever syntax compilers use for events, underneath they are just calling the delegate associated with it.

Although the VES builds in support for delegates by providing the class `System.Delegate`, delegates are slightly different from the other built-in types because you must declare the delegate class. However, because `System.Delegate` is an abstract class, you cannot make instances of it. Therefore, you need another class, which inherits from `System.Delegate`, that can have an instance made from it.

To declare a delegate, it is only necessary to declare a subclass of the wrapper that programming languages provide for `System.Delegate`, which then provides the values (such as arguments to the **Invoke** method and the return type value). The VES then creates the delegate, and builds everything else in. Programmers just see the **Invoke**, **GetInvoke**, and **EndInvoke** methods. When a delegate is declared, it can't have any fields, properties, or enumerations; it can have only these methods.

For more detailed information on declaring delegates, and on the delegate methods, see Partition II, section 13.6.

8.9.4 *Interface Type Definition*

An **interface definition** defines an interface type. An interface type is a named group of methods, locations, and other contracts that shall be implemented by any object type that supports the interface contract of the same name. An interface definition is always an incomplete description of a value, and as such can never define a class type or an exact type, nor can it be an object type.

Zero or more object types can support an interface type, and only object types can support an interface type. An interface type may require that objects that support it shall also support other (specified) interface types. An object type that supports the named interface contract shall provide a complete implementation of the methods, locations, and other contracts specified (but not implemented by) the interface type. Hence, a value of an object type is also a value of all of the interface types the object type supports. Support for an interface contract is declared, never inferred; i.e., the existence of implementations of the methods, locations, and other contracts required by the interface type does not imply support of the interface contract.

ANNOTATION: Interfaces specify a set of method contracts. To provide an interface, an object must implement its methods—there is no implementation of the methods associated with the interface itself. An interface, in itself, may also include static field or static method definitions with implementations, but it may not include any non-static method implementations (although CLS-compliant interfaces may define neither static fields nor static methods). Therefore, while an interface contributes to the behavior of an object, it does not contribute to its shape (static fields and methods are not associated with instances of the interface within an object).

Interfaces often specify other interfaces within their contract. An object using an interface must implement all other interfaces specified within that interface as well. This is not, however, inheritance in the way that a class may inherit its implementations from a parent class, because no implementations are associated with any of the interfaces directly. Instead, when writing a class that uses an interface that specifies one or more other interfaces, that class must implement all of those interfaces for the contract to be fulfilled.

CLS Rule 18: CLS-compliant interfaces shall not require the definition of non-CLS-compliant methods in order to implement them.

NOTE

CLS (consumer): There is no need to deal with such interfaces.

CLS (extender): Need not provide a mechanism for defining such interfaces..

CLS (framework): Shall not expose any non-CLS-compliant methods on interfaces it defines for external use.

Interfaces types are necessarily incomplete, since they say nothing about the representation of the values of the interface type. For this reason, an interface type definition shall not provide field definitions for values of the interface type (i.e., instance fields), although it may declare static fields (see Partition I, section 8.4.3).

Similarly, an interface type definition shall not provide implementations for any methods on the values of its type. However, an interface type definition may and usually does define method contracts (method name and method signature) that shall be implemented by supporting types. An interface type definition may define and implement static methods (see Partition I, section 8.4.3), since static methods are associated with the interface type itself rather than with any value of the type.

Interfaces may have static or virtual methods, but shall not have instance methods.

CLS Rule 19: CLS-compliant interfaces shall not define static methods, nor shall they define fields.

NOTE

CLS-compliant interfaces may define properties, events, and virtual methods.

CLS (consumer): Need not accept interfaces that violate these rules.

CLS (extender): Need not provide syntax to author interfaces that violate these rules.

CLS (framework): Shall not externally expose interfaces that violate these rules. Where static methods, instance methods, or fields are required, a separate class may be defined that provides them.

Interface types may also define event and property contracts that shall be implemented by object types that support the interface. Since event and property contracts reduce to sets of method contracts (see Partition I, section 8.6), the above rules for method definitions apply. For more information, see Partition I, sections 8.11.4 and 8.11.3.

Interface type definitions may specify other interface contracts that implementations of the interface type are required to support. See Partition I, section 8.9.8.3 for specifics.

An interface type is given a visibility attribute, as described in Partition I, section 8.5.3, that controls from where the interface type may be referenced. An interface type definition is separate from any object type definition that supports the interface type. Hence, it is possible, and often desirable, to have a different visibility for the interface type and the implementing object type. However, since accessibility attributes are relative to the implementing type rather than the interface itself, all members of an interface shall have public accessibility, and no security permissions may be attached to members or to the interface itself.

8.9.5 *Class Type Definition*

All types other than interfaces, and those types for which a definition is automatically supplied by the CTS, are defined by **class definitions**. A **class type** is a complete specification of the representation of the values of the class type and all of the contracts (class, interface, method, property, and event) that are supported by the class type. Hence, a class type is an exact type. A class definition, unless it specifies that the class is an **abstract object type**, not only defines the class type; it also provides implementations for all of the contracts supported by the class type.

A class definition, and hence the implementation of the class type, always resides in some assembly. An assembly is a configured set of loadable code modules and other resources that together implement a unit of functionality.

> **NOTE**
>
> While class definitions always define class types, not all class types require a class definition. Array types and pointer types, which are implicitly defined, are also class types. See Partition I, section 8.2.3.

An explicit class definition is used to define:

- An object type (see Partition I, section 8.2.3).
- A value type and its associated boxed type (see Partition I, section 8.2.4).

An explicit class definition:

- Names the class type.
- Implicitly assigns the class type name to a scope—i.e., the assembly that contains the class definition, (see Partition I, section 8.5.2).
- Defines the class contract of the same name (see Partition I, section 8.6).
- Defines the representations and valid operations of all values of the class type using member definitions for the fields, methods, properties, and events (see Partition I, section 8.11).
- Defines the static members of the class type (see Partition I, section 8.11).
- Specifies any other interface and class contracts also supported by the class type.

- Supplies implementations for member and interface contracts supported by the class type.
- Explicitly declares a visibility for the type, either public or assembly (see Partition I, section 8.5.3).
- May optionally specify a method to be called to initialize the type.

ANNOTATION: "Class types" is a general term that includes both object types and value types. All class types require definitions, except for the built-in types—those types that the VES initializes upon their declaration in code. The built-in object types are arrays and pointers. The built-in value types are the numeric types (integers and floating point values).

Class definitions usually have both shape and behavior—types and fields and the methods that manipulate them—but they may have just one or the other.

One potential source of confusion is the terminology. Whereas **class type** is used in this standard as the general term for both object and value types, many of the conforming languages, such as C#, Visual Basic.NET, and Java, use **class** as the keyword for an object type, and **struct** or **structure** to designate a value type. Even more confusing, C++ uses the keyword **class** for a value type.

Another potential confusion in terminology is that C# and Visual Basic.NET both use the keyword **object**, but only to refer to the single class `System.Object`, the object root.

The semantics of when, and what triggers execution of such type initialization methods, is as follows:

1. A type may have a type-initializer method, or not.
2. A type may be specified as having a relaxed semantic for its type-initializer method (for convenience below, we call this relaxed semantic **BeforeFieldInit**).
3. If marked **BeforeFieldInit**, then the type's initializer method is executed at, or sometime before, first access to any static field defined for that type
4. If *not* marked **BeforeFieldInit** then that type's initializer method is executed at (i.e., is triggered by):
   - First access to any static or instance field of that type, or
   - First invocation of any static, instance, or virtual method of that type

5. Execution of any type's initializer method will *not* trigger automatic execution of any initializer methods defined by its base type, nor of any interfaces that the type implements

> **NOTE**
>
> **BeforeFieldInit** behavior is intended for initialization code with no interesting side-effects, where exact timing does not matter. Also, under **BeforeFieldInit** semantics, type initializers are allowed to be executed *at or before* first access to any static field of that Type—at the discretion of the CLI.
>
> If a language wishes to provide more rigid behavior—e.g., type initialization automatically triggers execution of parent initializers, in a top-to-bottom order, then it can do so by either:
>
> - defining hidden static fields and code in each class constructor that touches the hidden static field of its parent and/or interfaces it implements, or
> - by making explicit calls to `System.Runtime.CompilerServices.RuntimeHelpers.RunClassConstructor` (see the *.NET Framework Standard Library Annotated Reference).*

ANNOTATION: The CLI specifies two ways to initialize types: one with strict rules and guarantees built into it, and the other more flexible and with much higher performance. Type initialization is done with a call to a class constructor (**.cctor**). This is distinct from an object constructor (**.ctor**). An object constructor, which sets up the shape of an object, must be called on all CLI objects, but a call to a class constructor (type initialization) is optional. Object construction does not set up the static data in a class, because that is not part of the shape of the object, so most class constructors are called to set up the static fields, although they may do many other things, such as ensuring that another class has been loaded, setting up global variables, etc.

There has been an argument in the programming community about when type initialization should occur. One point of view calls for strict rules, saying that types should be initialized at the first access to any static or instance field of a type, or at the first invocation of a static, instance, or virtual method. These rules provide repeatable behavior in all cases, and some languages, like Java, initialize types according to those rules, so the CLI supports that.

There is, however, a performance cost to doing it that way, especially in JIT-compiled systems. So the CLI offers a more relaxed way to initialize types, with the **BeforeFieldInit** bit. When this bit is set, the VES will call the class constructor at the first access to the static fields of a type. In this case, instance fields and virtual methods do not make a difference. These rules were chosen as a result of analyzing a large body of code in several different languages, and determining that what most programmers mainly need is the assurance that their static data is initialized before they use it.

The rules for **BeforeFieldInit** initialization provide high performance, but they do not provide a strong, repeatable guarantee of initialization.

In some languages, as in C#, both of these behaviors are available depending on how you write your program. If you write the code for the initializer in your program, you get the strict semantics for exactly when that initializer is called. If you just use the syntax that specifies the values for static fields, C# uses the more relaxed initialization, guaranteeing that static fields are set up before you call them.

Type initialization is also discussed in Partition II, section 9.5.3 and its subsections.

8.9.6 *Object Type Definitions*

All objects are instances of an **object type**. The object type of an object is set when the object is created, and it is immutable. The object type describes the physical structure of the instance and the operations that are allowed on it. All instances of the same object type have the same structure and the same allowable operations. Object types are explicitly declared by a class type definition, with the exception of Array types, which are intrinsically provided by the VES.

8.9.6.1 Scope and Visibility

Since object type definitions are class type definitions, object type definitions implicitly specify the scope of the name of [the] object type to be the assembly that contains the object type definition, see Partition I, section 8.5.2. Similarly, object type definitions shall also explicitly state the visibility attribute of the object type (either **public** or **assembly**); see Partition I, section 8.5.3.

8.9.6.2 Concreteness

An object type may be marked as **abstract** by the object type definition. An object type that is not marked **abstract** is by definition **concrete**. Only object types may be declared as abstract. Only an abstract object type is allowed to define method contracts for which the type or the VES does not also provide the implementation. Such method contracts are called abstract methods (see Partition I, section 8.11). All methods on an abstract class need not be abstract.

It is an error to attempt to create an instance of an abstract object type, whether or not the type has abstract methods. An object type that derives from an abstract object type may be concrete if it provides implementations for any abstract methods in the base object type and is not itself marked as abstract. Instances may be made of such a concrete derived class. Locations may have an abstract type, and instances of a concrete type that derives from the abstract type may be stored in them.

ANNOTATION: Concreteness is about whether you can make an instance of the class. If you define a class and provide definitions for all of its methods, and its marked abstract, you still can't make an instance of it. An abstract class cannot be made concrete, therefore. An instance can be made only from a subclass of an abstract class. Therefore, an abstract type is never the exact type of anything. Any instance of a class must have implementations for all methods, and it cannot be marked abstract.

8.9.6.3 Type Members

Object type definitions include member definitions for all of the members of the type. Briefly, members of a type include fields into which values are stored, methods that may be invoked, properties that are available, and events that may be raised. Each member of a type may have attributes as described in Partition I, section 8.4.

- Fields of an object type specify the representation of values of the object type by specifying the component pieces from which it is composed (see Partition I, section 8.4.1). Static fields specify fields associated with the object type itself (see Partition I, section 8.4.3). The fields of an object type are named and they are typed via location signatures. The names of the members of the type are scoped to the type (see Partition I, section 8.5.2). Fields are declared using a field definition (see Partition I, section 8.11.2).
- Methods of an object type specify operations on values of the type (see Partition I, section 8.4.2). Static methods specify operations on the type itself (see Partition I, section 8.4.3). Methods are named, and they have a method signature. The names of methods are scoped to the type (see Partition I, section 8.5.2). Methods are declared using a method definition (see Partition I, section 8.11.1).
- Properties of an object type specify named values that are accessible via methods that read and write the value. The name of the property is the grouping of the methods; the methods themselves are also named and typed via method signatures. The names of properties are scoped to the type (see Partition I, section 8.5.2). Properties are declared using a property definition (see Partition I, section 8.11.3).
- Events of an object type specify named state transitions in which subscribers may register/unregister interest via accessor methods. When the state changes, the subscribers are notified of the state transition. The name of the event is the grouping of the accessor methods; the methods themselves are also named and typed via method signatures. The names of events are scoped to the type (see Partition I, section 8.5.2). Events are declared using an event definition (see Partition I, section 8.11.4).

ANNOTATION: There is no direct support in the VES for properties and events, except for reflection. At compile time, the compilers specify the methods that perform the property and event functions. As a result, properties and events do not affect VES behavior or shape at all.

8.9.6.4 Supporting Interface Contracts

Object type definitions may declare that they support zero or more interface contracts. Declaring support for an interface contract places a requirement on the implementation of the object type to fully implement that interface contract. Implementing an interface contract always reduces to implementing the required set of methods—i.e., the methods required by the interface type.

The different types that the object type implements—i.e., the object type and any implemented interface types—are each a separate logical grouping of named members. If a class `Foo` implements an interface `IFoo` and `IFoo` declares a member method `int a()` and the class also declares a member method `int a()`, there are two members, one in the `IFoo` interface type and one in the `Foo` class type. An implementation of `Foo` will provide an implementation for both, potentially shared.

Similarly, if a class implements two interfaces, `IFoo` and `IBar`, each of which defines a method `int a()`, the class will supply two method implementations, one for each interface, although they may share the actual code of the implementation.

CLS Rule 20: CLS-compliant classes, value types, and interfaces shall not require the implementation of non-CLS-compliant interfaces.

NOTE

CLS (consumer): Need not accept classes, value types or interfaces that violate this rule.

CLS (extender): Need not provide syntax to author classes, value types, or interfaces that violate this rule.

CLS (framework): Shall not externally expose classes, value types, or interfaces that violate this rule.

8.9.6.5 Supporting Class Contracts

Object type definitions may declare support for one other class contract. Declaring support for another class contract is synonymous with object type inheritance (see Partition I, section 8.9.8.1).

ANNOTATION: Supporting class contracts means that with the exception of `System.Object` itself, all objects have one unique parent type. If a parent implements a method, the child must implement it, although it may do so by doing nothing, and using the parent implementation. By default, the child is given the same implementation as the parent.

8.9.6.6 Constructors

New values of an object type are created via **constructors**. Constructors shall be instance methods, defined via a special form of method contract, which defines the method contract as a constructor for a particular object type. The constructors for an object type are part of the object type definition. While the CTS and VES ensure that only a properly defined constructor is used to make new values of an object type, the ultimate correctness of a newly constructed object is dependent on the implementation of the constructor itself.

Object types shall define at least one constructor method, but that method need not be public. Creating a new value of an object type by invoking a constructor involves the following steps in order:

1. Space for the new value is allocated in managed memory.
2. VES data structures of the new value are initialized, and user-visible memory is zeroed.
3. The specified constructor for the object type is invoked.

Inside the constructor, the object type may do any initialization it chooses (possibly none).

CLS Rule 21: An object constructor shall call some class constructor of its base class before any access occurs to inherited instance data. This does not apply to value types, which need not have constructors.

CLS Rule 22: An object constructor shall not be called except as part of the creation of an object, and an object shall not be initialized twice.

> **NOTE**
>
> **CLS (consumer):** Shall provide syntax for choosing the constructor to be called when an object is created.
>
> **CLS (extender):** Shall provide syntax for defining constructor methods with different signatures. May issue a compiler error if the constructor does not obey these rules.
>
> **CLS (framework):** May assume that object creation includes a call to one of the constructors, and that no object is initialized twice. `System.MemberwiseClone` (see the *.NET Framework Standard Library Annotated Reference*) and deserialization (including object remoting) may not run constructors.

ANNOTATION: This section discusses object instance constructors (**.ctor**), not class constructors (**.cctor**), which are discussed in Partition I, section 8.9.5. The CLS, in rules 21 and 22, imposes rules on the constructors that are not imposed by the CLI.

ANNOTATION: The CLI requires that the CIL use the name **.ctor** for instance constructors, and **.cctor** for type initializers. Further, to be verifiable, a class constructor must call one of the constructors defined in its parent. Not all languages were enthusiastic about these aspects of the CLI. Among the less enthusiastic were developers of the Eiffel development team. This annotation expresses the Eiffel viewpoint.

Verifiability rules say that to be verifiable, a **.ctor** constructor should call one of the constructors defined in its parent. The only purpose of this rule is to force a descendant class to initialize fields defined in parent classes. It is basically a lack of trust from the underlying machinery toward the library designer/developer. And it is true, it is very easy to forget to initialize a field. There is also the security aspect and the notion of private fields, which only the parent that is defining them knows how to initialize, as they are not accessible from descendant classes.

However, this is a problem for languages that do not support either this restriction or descendant hiding.

Such is the case with Eiffel. Eiffel does not impose such restrictions because it has the Design by Contract methodology. This methodology enables a parent class to define a behavior. Therefore, if a descendant class does not satisfy this behavior, it is rejected. In the end, it is equivalent to the above CLI design decision, but in Eiffel the library designer/developer is free to reach this goal the way he wants.

Another issue is the requirement of the name **.ctor** for constructors. Because of this name restriction, it is not possible to create two different instances from the same object—for example, **point(real** *a*, **real** *b*) could be written to produce either polar or Cartesian coordinates, depending on how it was constructed. In Eiffel, a constructor is just a normal routine used for construction purposes. With named constructors, you could have `make_polar` and `make_cartesian` as two constructors, each taking two real numbers as arguments. Moreover, having them will make it easier for a language such as Eiffel to map to the CLR model.

– Emmanuel Stapf

Microsoft's CLR Architect team agreed that the ability to have independent names for the constructors of objects would have been a better design. Unfortunately, after months of study, it was not possible to find a solution that encompassed the Eiffel design, along with C#, C++, and Java designs.

– Jim Miller

8.9.6.7 Finalizers

A class definition that creates an object type may supply an instance method to be called when an instance of the class is no longer accessible. The class `System.GC` (see the *.NET Framework Standard Library Annotated Referencen*) provides limited control over the behavior of finalizers through the methods `SuppressFinalize` and `ReRegisterForFinalize`. Conforming implementations of the CLI may specify and provide additional mechanisms that affect the behavior of finalizers.

A conforming implementation of the CLI shall not automatically call a finalizer twice for the same object unless

- There has been an intervening call to `ReRegisterForFinalize` (not followed by a call to `SuppressFinalize`), or
- The program has invoked an implementation-specific mechanism that is clearly specified to produce an alteration to this behavior.

RATIONALE

Programmers expect that finalizers are run precisely once on any given object unless they take an explicit action to cause the finalizer to be run multiple times.

It is legal to define a finalizer for a Value Type. That finalizer, however, will only be run for *boxed* instances of that Value Type.

ANNOTATION: Finalizers are typically called by the garbage collector (assuming that the VES implements a garbage collector) to close down any allocated resources used by an object when that object goes away. File handles and database connections are the kind of resource you would want to shut down with a finalizer. However, it is more efficient to close out the resource in code when it is no longer needed, because it is expensive to have the GC do it through a finalizer.

Implementation-Specific (Microsoft): In the first release of the Microsoft Common Language Runtime, the behavior of finalizers for Value Types is undefined.

NOTE

Since programmers may depend on finalizers to be called, the CLI should make every effort to ensure that finalizers are called, before it shuts down, for all objects that have not been exempted from finalization by a call to `SuppressFinalize`. The implementation should specify any conditions under which this behavior cannot be guaranteed.

NOTE

Since resources may become exhausted if finalizers are not called expeditiously, the CLI should ensure that finalizers are called soon after the instance becomes inaccessible. While relying on memory pressure to trigger finalization is acceptable, implementers should consider the use of additional metrics.

8.9.7 *Value Type Definition*

Not all types defined by a class definition are object types (see Partition I, section 8.2.3); in particular, value types are not object types, but they are defined using a class definition. A class definition for a value type defines both the (unboxed) value type and the associated boxed type (see Partition I, section 8.2.4). The members of the class definition define the representation of both:

1. When a non-static method (i.e., an instance or virtual method) is called on the value type, its **this** pointer is a managed reference to the instance, whereas when the method is called on the associated boxed type, the **this** pointer is an object reference.

Instance methods on value types receive a **this** pointer that is a managed pointer to the unboxed type whereas virtual methods (including those on interfaces implemented by the value type) receive an instance of the boxed type.

2. Value types do not support interface contracts, but their associated boxed types do.
3. A value type does not inherit; rather the base type specified in the class definition defines the base type of the boxed type.
4. The base type of a boxed type shall not have any fields.
5. Unlike object types, instances of value types do not require a constructor to be called when an instance is created. Instead, the verification rules require that verifiable code initialize instances to zero (null for object fields).

ANNOTATION: A class definition for a value causes the VES to define its associated boxed type. The boxed type always inherits from either `System.ValueType` or `System.Enum`. They must be sealed, so they cannot have subclasses and do not form a hierarchy. Their shape is fixed.

During the design of the CLI, there was considerable discussion about whether value types should have constructors. There are implementation difficulties, however. You can declare a value type on the stack, and value types can also appear through interactions with unmanaged code in ways that objects can't. When they come from unmanaged code, there is no way to ensure that the constructor has been run. In the end it was decided that it would have been impossible to enforce the construction semantics, so it would be impossible to verify.

However, although value types do not require constructors, they do require initializers to be verifiable.

8.9.8 *Type Inheritance*

Inheritance of types is another way of saying that the derived type guarantees support for all of the type contracts of the base type. In addition, the derived type usually provides additional functionality or specialized behavior. A type inherits from a base type by implementing the type contract of the base type. An interface type inherits from zero or more other interfaces[, although interface inheritance is not the same as class inheritance. For more information, see Partition I, section 8.9.8.3]. Value types do not inherit, although the associated boxed type is an object type and hence inherits from other types.

The derived class type shall support all of the supported interface contracts, class contracts, event contracts, method contracts, and property contracts of its base type. In addition, all of the locations defined by the base type are also defined in the derived type. The inheritance rules [when followed] guarantee that code that was compiled to work with a value of a base type will still work when passed a value of the derived type. Because of this, a derived type also inherits the implementations of the base type. The derived type may extend, override, and/or hide these implementations.

ANNOTATION: Inheritance rules are described in this section and its subsections. In the International Standard, sections 8.9.8.1–8.9.8.3 are actually numbered (erroneously) 8.9.9–8.9.11. These sections are, in fact, subsections of 8.9.8 and have been renumbered here accordingly. No other subsequent section numbers have been affected.

ANNOTATION: "Derived from" does not equate to "inherits from" in the CLI.

As stated in Partition I, section 8.9.8.2, "value types do not inherit, although the associated boxed type is an object type and hence inherits [from its superclasses]."

The terms "is derived from" and "inherits from" are usually interchangeable; in the CLI, however, they are not interchangeable for value types. (Note: "inherits from" and "is a subclass of" are equivalent terms; also "derived from" and "extends" are equivalent.) The difference affects *assignment compatibility*.

In the CLI, every type (except `System.Object`) is derived from a base type. This is represented in IL by the **extends** keyword. For example, the following IL fragment defines three types: `ObjectA`, `ObjectB`, and `ValueC`:

```
.class ObjectA extends [mscorlib]System.Object { … }
.class ObjectB extends ObjectA { … }
.class ValueC extends [mscorlib]System.ValueType { … }
```

In the CLI type system, the following relations hold:

Type	Derived From	Inherits From
`ObjectB`	`ObjectA`	`ObjectA`
`ValueC`	`System.ValueType`	none

So although object type and value type definitions are syntactically the same, they are *semantically* different. In the CLI type system, `ValueC` *is derived from* `System.ValueType`.

The consequence of the above is that values of type `ObjectB` are *assignment compatible* with variables of type `ObjectA`. However, values of type `ValueC` are not *assignment compatible* with variables of `System.ValueType`, but those of the corresponding (unnamed) boxed value type are.

Unfortunately, `System.Reflection` treats value types as though they were the corresponding boxed value types, so the results can be misleading. Here's a C# example:

```
using System;
namespace DerivedDemo
{
   class ObjectA { int FieldA; };
   class ObjectB : ObjectA { int FieldB; };

   struct ValueC { int FieldC; }

   class Examine
   {
      static void SubclassExample()
      {  Type tObjectA = System.Type.GetType("DerivedDemo.ObjectA");
         Type tObjectB = System.Type.GetType("DerivedDemo.ObjectB");

         bool isObjectAssignable = tObjectA.IsAssignableFrom(tObjectB);
         bool isObjectSubclass = tObjectB.IsSubclassOf(tObjectA);

         Type tValueC = System.Type.GetType("DerivedDemo.ValueC");
         Type baseValueC = System.Type.GetType("System.ValueType");

         bool isValueAssignable = baseValueC.IsAssignableFrom(tValueC);
         bool isValueSubclass = tValueC.IsSubclassOf(baseValueC);

         ...
      }
   }
}
```

Here the variable `tValueC` represents the type of the value type `ValueC`. In the code fragment, however, all the Boolean variables are set to the value **true,** yet according to the CLI type system the last two should be **false**. The last two *are* **true** for the boxed version of `ValueC`. This difference between `System.Reflection` and the CLI type system means, for instance, that the `IsAssignableFrom` method may return **true** for a given value/variable pair, yet the `stind.ref` instruction (see Partition III, section 3.62) will fail verification for the same pair.

– Nigel Perry

8.9.8.1 Object Type Inheritance

With the sole exception of `System.Object`, which does not inherit from any other object type, all object types shall either explicitly or implicitly declare support for (inherit from) exactly one other object type. The graph of the inherits relation shall form a singly rooted tree with `System.Object` at the base; i.e., all object types eventually inherit from the type `System.Object`.

An object type declares it shall not be used as a base type (be inherited from) by declaring that it is a **sealed** type.

CLS Rule 23: `System.Object` is CLS-compliant. Any other CLS-compliant class shall inherit from a CLS-compliant class.

Arrays are object types and as such inherit from other object types. Since array object types are manufactured by the VES, the inheritance of arrays is fixed. See Partition I, section 8.9.1.

ANNOTATION: Many languages strongly urged the Microsoft design team to provide support for multiple inheritance, but the design team rejected the idea for two reasons. The first is that there are three different models of multiple inheritance found in languages. They are not compatible, and in the opinion of the team, no single model was superior to the others. The second reason is that, at the time of this writing, there is no implementation of multiple inheritance in a system that supports dynamic loading that does not sacrifice performance. The feeling of the Microsoft design team was that languages that require multiple inheritance could support it with no performance cost at compile time. The team was unwilling to impose the performance cost on all languages.

– Jim Miller

8.9.8.2 Value Type Inheritance

Value Types, in their unboxed form, do not inherit from any type. Boxed value types shall inherit directly from `System.ValueType` unless they are enumerations, in which case they shall inherit from `System.Enum`. Boxed value types shall be sealed.

Logically, the boxed type corresponding to a value type

- Is an object type.
- Will specify which object type is its base type—i.e., the object type from which it inherits.
- Will have a base type that has no fields defined.
- Will be **sealed** to avoid dealing with the complications of value slicing

The more restrictive rules specified here allow for more efficient implementation without severely compromising functionality.

8.9.8.3 Interface Type Inheritance

Interface types may inherit from multiple interface types; i.e., an interface contract may list other interface contracts that shall also be supported. Any type that implements support for an interface type shall also implement support for all of the inherited interface types. This is different from object type inheritance in two ways.

- Object types form a single inheritance tree; interface types do not.
- Object type inheritance specifies how implementations are inherited; interface type inheritance does not, since interfaces do not define implementation. Interface type inheritance specifies additional contracts that an implementing object type shall support.

To highlight the last difference, consider an interface, `IFoo`, that has a single method. An interface, `IBar`, which inherits from it is requiring that any object type that supports `IBar` also support `IFoo`. It does not say anything about which methods `IBar` itself will have.

8.10 Member Inheritance

Only object types may inherit implementations, hence only object types may inherit members (see Partition I, section 8.9.8). Interface types, while they do inherit from other interface types, only inherit the requirement to implement method contracts, never fields or method implementations.

ANNOTATION: Members are methods, fields, properties, events, and nested types.

---

2. Concepts and Architecture

8.10.1 *Field Inheritance*

A derived object type inherits all of the non-static fields of its base object type. This allows instances of the derived type to be used wherever instances of the base type are expected (the shapes, or layouts, of the instances will be the same). Static fields are not inherited. Just because a field exists does not mean that it may be read or written. The type visibility, field accessibility, and security attributes of the field definition (see Partition I, section 8.5.3) determine if a field is accessible to the derived object type.

8.10.2 *Method Inheritance*

A derived object type inherits all of the instance and virtual methods of its base object type. It does not inherit constructors or static methods. Just because a method exists does not mean that it may be invoked. It shall be accessible via the typed reference that is being used by the referencing code. The type visibility, method accessibility, and security attributes of the method definition (see Partition I, section 8.5.3) determine if a method is accessible to the derived object type.

A derived object type may hide a non-virtual (i.e., static or instance) method of its base type by providing a new method definition with the same name or same name and signature. Either method may still be invoked, subject to method accessibility rules, since the type that contains the method always qualifies a method reference.

Virtual methods may be marked as **final**, in which case they shall not be overridden in a derived object type. This ensures that the implementation of the method is available, by a virtual call, on any object that supports the contract of the base class that supplied the final implementation. If a virtual method is not final, it is possible to demand a security permission in order to override the virtual method, so that the ability to provide an implementation can be limited to classes that have particular permissions. When a derived type overrides a virtual method, it may specify a new accessibility for the virtual method, but the accessibility in the derived class shall permit at least as much access as the access granted to the method it is overriding. See Partition I, section 8.5.3.

ANNOTATION: Two of the important points in this section should perhaps be emphasized. The first is that methods can be marked as final, which is a feature not available in all systems. The second is that although accessibility may be widened on a method in a subtype, making a method accessible to more things than the base type method, accessibility may not be narrowed.

The accessibility issue was decided after considerable discussion. Although narrowing accessibility would lead you to assume that you are guaranteed that the implementation will not be called, this is not necessarily the case. If you cast the object to the base type and call the virtual method, a virtual call would get you the method without an error because the base type says it's public. Programming languages can implement accessibility as they choose, but the standard does not enforce it.

8.10.3 *Property and Event Inheritance*

Properties and events are fundamentally constructs of the metadata intended for use by tools that target the CLI and are not directly supported by the VES itself. It is, therefore, the job of the source language compiler and the Reflection Library (see the *.NET Framework Standard Library Annotated Reference*) to determine rules for name hiding, inheritance, and so forth. The source compiler shall generate CIL that directly accesses the methods named by the events and properties, not the events or properties themselves.

8.10.4 *Hiding, Overriding, and Layout*

There are two separate issues involved in inheritance. The first is which contracts a type shall implement and hence which member names and signatures it shall provide. The second is the layout of the instance so that an instance of a derived type can be substituted for an instance of any of its base types. Only the non-static fields and the virtual methods that are part of the derived type affect the layout of an object.

The CTS provides independent control over both the names that are visible from a base type (**hiding**) and the sharing of layout slots in the derived class (**overriding**). Hiding is controlled by marking a member in the derived class as either **hide by name** or **hide by name-and-signature**. Hiding is always performed based on the kind of member; that is, derived field names may hide base field names, but not method names, property names, or event names. If a derived member is marked **hide by name**, then members of the same kind in the base class with the same name are not visible in the derived class; if the member is marked **hide by name-and-signature** then only a member of the same kind with exactly the same name and type (for fields) or method signature (for methods) is hidden in the derived class. Implementation of the distinction between these two forms of hiding is provided entirely by source language compilers and the Reflection Library; it has no direct impact on the VES itself.

For example:

```
class Base
{ field  int32          A;
  field  System.String  A;
  method int32          A();
  method int32          A(int32);
}
class Derived inherits from Base
{ field  int32 A;
  hidebysig method int32 A();
}
```

Table 2-3 Member Names

Kind of Member	Type / Signature of Member	Name of Member
`Field`	`int32`	`A`
`Method`	`() -> int32`	`A`
`Method`	`(int32) -> int32`	`A`

The member names available in type `Derived` are listed above in Table 2-3.:

While hiding applies to all members of a type, overriding deals with object layout and is applicable only to instance fields and virtual methods. The CTS provides two forms of member overriding, **new slot** and **expect existing slot**. A member of a derived type that is marked as a new slot will always get a new slot in the object's layout, guaranteeing that the base field or method is available in the object by using a qualified reference that combines the name of the base type with the name of the member and its type or signature. A member of a derived type that is marked as **expect existing slot** will reuse (i.e., share or override) a slot that corresponds to a member of the same kind (field or method), name, and type if one already exists from the base type; if no such slot exists, a new slot is allocated and used.

The general algorithm that is used for determining the names in a type and the layout of objects of the type is roughly as follows:

- Flatten the inherited names (using the **hide by name** or **hide by name-and-signature** rule), *ignoring* accessibility rules.
- For each new member that is marked "expect existing slot," look to see if an exact match on kind (i.e., field or method), name, and signature exists and use that slot if it is found; otherwise allocate a new slot.
- After doing this for all new members, add these new member-kind/name/signatures to the list of members of this type.
- Finally, remove any inherited names that match the new members based on the **hide by name** or **hide by name-and-signature** rules.

ANNOTATION: There is further discussion of hiding in Partition II, section 8.3. That discussion explains that a conforming implementation of the CLI treats all references as though the names were marked **hide by name-and-signature**, and then tells compilers how to get the effect of **hide by name**. The notion of hiding is a compile-time feature, not a runtime feature.

Overriding concerns behavior. It determines which implementation of a method is expected to be used. In a child class, a method with a given name and signature is supposed to be fulfilling the same contract as the corresponding method in the base class. But circumstances can change. Suppose you create a child class from a base class named `Automobile`. To that child class, you add a virtual method named `Speed`. Any class that inherits from your class would, of course, implement the contract of your `Speed` method.

But in the next version the base class is updated, and a method named `Speed` is added to it—a method that does not have the same function as your method of the same name. This presents a name conflict. The **newslot** directive prevents a virtual method from being overridden, even if there is another one with the same name in the base type. The advice to compilers is that at compile time, if there is a definition of a new virtual method not seen above in the hierarchy (and so not being inherited), set the **newslot** bit, which guarantees that no matter what, this method will be seen as a newly introduced virtual method. If the parent class later adds something of the same name, the child's same-name-but-different-contract definition will not be used to implement the parent method.

Without the **newslot** directive, it is assumed that you were aware of a preceding method in the hierarchy that you are implementing, and your implementation will be used for that method.

Languages choose the way they deal with this. Java, for example, has a specific rule that would forbid setting the **newslot** directive.

8.11 Member Definitions

Object type definitions, interface type definitions, and value type definitions may include member definitions. Field definitions define the representation of values of the type by specifying the substructure of the value. Method definitions define operations on values of the type and operations on the type itself (static methods). Property and event definitions may only be defined on object types. Property and events define named groups of accessor method definitions that implement the named event or property behavior. Nested type declarations define types whose names are scoped by the enclosing type and whose instances have full access to all members of the enclosing class.

Depending on the kind of type definition, there are restrictions on the member definitions allowed.

8.11.1 *Method Definitions*

Method definitions are composed of a name, a method signature, and optionally an implementation of the method. The method signature defines the calling convention, type of the parameters to the method, and the return type of the method (see Partition I, section 8.6.1). The implementation is the code to execute when the method is invoked. A value type or object type may define only one method of a given name and signature. However, a derived object type may have methods that are of the same name and signature as its base object type. See Partition I, sections 8.10.2 and 8.10.4.

The name of the method is scoped to the type (see Partition I, section 8.5.2). Methods may be given accessibility attributes (see Partition I, section 8.5.3). Methods may only be invoked with arguments that are assignment compatible with the parameter types of the method signature. The return value of the method shall also be assignment compatible with the location in which it is stored.

Methods may be marked as **static**, indicating that the method is not an operation on values of the type but rather an operation associated with the type as a whole. Methods not marked as static define the valid operations on a value of a type. When a non-static method is invoked, a particular value of the type, referred to as **this** or the **this pointer**, is passed as an implicit parameter.

A method definition that does not include a method implementation shall be marked as **abstract.** All non-static methods of an interface definition are abstract. Abstract method definitions are only allowed in object types that are marked as abstract.

A non-static method definition in an object type may be marked as **virtual**, indicating that an alternate implementation may be provided in derived types. All non-static method definitions in interface definitions shall be virtual methods. A virtual method may be marked as **final**, indicating that derived object types are not allowed to override the method implementation.

ANNOTATION: Whereas non-static methods define valid operations on a value of the type, static methods are operations on the type as a whole. Non-static methods—both instance and virtual methods—pass an implicit **this** pointer, which is a reference to the object being called. The programmer does not deal with the implicit **this** pointer at all. When compilers compile to the Common Intermediate Language (CIL), the **this** pointer becomes argument 0. The compiler must generate code to figure out which object is being called, and the VES is responsible for making it appear as argument 0. On a virtual call, the VES transfers the **this** pointer.

For more information, see Partition I, section 8.4.2.

8.11.2 *Field Definitions*

Field definitions are composed of a name and a location signature. The location signature defines the type of the field and the accessing constraints (see Partition I, section 8.6.1). A value type or object type may define only one field of a given name and type. However, a derived object type may have fields that are of the same name and type as its base object type. See Partition I, sections 8.10.1 and 8.10.4.

The name of the field is scoped to the type (see Partition I, section 8.5.2). Fields may be given accessibility attributes (see Partition I, section 8.5.3). Fields may only store values that are assignment compatible with the type of the field (see Partition I, section 8.3.1).

Fields may be marked as **static**, indicating that the field is not part of values of the type but rather a location associated with the type as a whole. Locations for the static fields are created when the type is loaded and initialized when the type is initialized.

Fields not marked as static define the representation of a value of a type by defining the substructure of the value (see Partition I, section 8.4.1). Locations for such fields are created within every value of the type whenever a new value is constructed. They are initialized during construction of the new value. A non-static field of a given name is always located at the same place within every value of the type.

ANNOTATION: The last sentence of the previous paragraph may be misleading. It was intended to say that the goal of inheritance is to allow the value of a subtype to be used wherever the value of the parent type is used. There is an implementation issue that says that the simplest way to do subtyping (subclassing) is to create subtypes that have the same shape as the parent initially, with additions at the end. But this is not a requirement of the standard.

A field that is marked **serializable** is to be serialized as part of the persistent state of a value of the type. This standard does not specify the mechanism by which this is accomplished.

ANNOTATION: The standard completely specifies the file format, and the **serializable** bit is in the file format, although serialization was not standardized. Implementing serialization would allow such things as remoting, interactive Web services, saving data in persistent format, etc.

8.11.3 *Property Definitions*

A property definition defines a named value and the methods that access the value. A property definition defines the accessing contracts on that value. Hence, the property definition specifies which accessing methods exist and their respective method contracts. An implementation of a type that declares support for a property contract shall implement the accessing methods required by the property contract. The implementation of the accessing methods defines how the value is retrieved and stored.

A property definition is always part of either an interface definition or a class definition. The name and value of a property definition is scoped to the object type or the interface type that includes the property definition. While all of the attributes of a member may be applied to a property (accessibility, static, etc.), these are not enforced by the CTS. Instead, the CTS requires that the method contracts that comprise the property shall match the method implementations, as with any other method contract. There are no CIL instructions associated with properties, just metadata.

By convention, properties define a **getter** method (for accessing the current value of the property) and optionally a **setter** method (for modifying the current value of the property). The CTS places no restrictions on the set of methods associated with a property, their names, or their usage.

CLS Rule 24: The methods that implement the `getter` and `setter` methods of a property shall be marked **SpecialName** in the metadata.

CLS Rule 25: The accessibility of a property and of its accessors shall be identical.

CLS Rule 26: A property and its accessors shall all be static, all be virtual, or all be instance.

CLS Rule 27: The type of a property shall be the return type of the `getter` and the type of the last argument of the `setter`. The types of the parameters of the property shall be the types of the parameters to the `getter` and the types of all but the final parameter of the `setter`. All of these types shall be CLS-compliant, and shall not be managed pointers (i.e., shall not be passed by reference).

CLS Rule 28: Properties shall adhere to a specific naming pattern. See Partition I, section 10.4. The `SpecialName` attribute referred to in CLS rule 24 shall be ignored in appropriate name comparisons and shall adhere to identifier rules.

> **NOTE**
>
> **CLS (consumer):** Shall ignore the `SpecialName` bit in appropriate name comparisons and shall adhere to identifier rules. Otherwise, no direct support other than the usual access to the methods that define the property.
>
> **CLS (extender):** Shall ignore the `SpecialName` bit in appropriate name comparisons and shall adhere to identifier rules. Otherwise, no direct support other than the usual access to the methods that define the property. In particular, an extender need not be able to define properties.
>
> **CLS (framework):** Shall design understanding that not all CLS languages will access the property using special syntax.

8.11.4 *Event Definitions*

The CTS supports events in precisely the same way that it supports properties (see Partition I, section 8.11.3). The conventional methods, however, are different and include means for subscribing and unsubscribing to events as well as for firing the event.

> **CLS Rule 29:** The methods that implement an event shall be marked `SpecialName` in the metadata.
>
> **CLS Rule 30:** The accessibility of an event and of its accessors shall be identical.
>
> **CLS Rule 31:** The `add` and `remove` methods for an event shall both either be present or absent.
>
> **CLS Rule 32:** The `add` and `remove` methods for an event shall each take one parameter whose type defines the type of the event and that shall be derived from `System.Delegate`.
>
> **CLS Rule 33:** Events shall adhere to a specific naming pattern. See Partition I, section 10.4. The `SpecialName` attribute referred to in CLS rule 29 shall be ignored in appropriate name comparisons and shall adhere to identifier rules.
>
> **NOTE**
>
> **CLS (consumer):** Shall ignore the `SpecialName` bit in appropriate name comparisons and shall adhere to identifier rules. Otherwise, no direct support other than the usual access to the methods that define the event.

CLS (extender): Shall ignore the `SpecialName` bit in appropriate name comparisons and shall adhere to identifier rules. Otherwise, no direct support other than the usual access to the methods that define the event. In particular, an extender need not be able to define events.

CLS (framework): Shall design based on the understanding that not all CLS languages will access the event using special syntax.

8.11.5 *Nested Type Definitions*

A nested type definition is identical to a top-level type definition, with one exception: a top-level type has a visibility attribute, while the visibility of a nested type is the same as the visibility of the enclosing type. See Partition I, section 8.5.3.

ANNOTATION: The previous statement is not accurate. The visibility of top-level types and the accessibility of nested types are specified using three bits in the `TypeDef` flags, specified in Partition II, section 22.1.14, Flags for Types (TypeAttributes). For top-level types, the only legal values of these three bits are 0 (`NotPublic`, sometimes called internal) or 1 (`Public`). For nested types, they must be 2 through 7, indicating one of six possible accessibility values.

9 Metadata

This section and its subsections contain only informative text, with the exception of the CLS rules introduced here and repeated in Partition I, section 11. The metadata format is specified in Partition II.

New types—value types and reference types—are introduced into the CTS via type declarations expressed in **metadata**. In addition, metadata is a structured way to represent all information that the CLI uses to locate and load classes, lay out instances in memory, resolve method invocations, translate CIL to native code, enforce security, and set up runtime context boundaries. Every CLI PE/COFF module (see Partition II) carries a compact metadata binary that is emitted into the module by the CLI-enabled development tool or compiler.

Each CLI-enabled language will expose a language-appropriate syntax for declaring types and members and for annotating them with attributes that express which services they require of the infrastructure. Type imports are also handled in a language-appropriate way, and it is the development tool or compiler that consumes the metadata to expose the types that the developer sees.

Note that the typical component or application developer will not need to be aware of the rules for emitting and consuming CLI metadata. While it may help a developer to understand the structure of metadata, the rules outlined in this section are primarily of interest to tool builders and compiler writers.

9.1 Components and Assemblies

Each CLI component carries the metadata for declarations, implementations, and references specific to that component. Therefore, the component-specific metadata is referred to as **component metadata**, and the resulting component is said to be **self-describing**. In object models such as COM or CORBA, this information is represented by a combination of typelibs, IDL files, DLLRegisterServer, and a myriad of custom files in disparate formats and separate from the actual executable file. In contrast, the metadata is a fundamental part of a CLI component.

Collections of CLI components and other files are packaged together for deployment into **assemblies**, discussed in more detail in a later section [Partition II, section 6]. An assembly is a logical unit of functionality that serves as the primary unit of reuse in the CLI. Assemblies establish a name scope for types.

Types declared and implemented in individual components are exported for use by other implementations via the assembly in which the component participates. All references to a type are scoped by the identity of the assembly in whose context the type is being used. The CLI provides services to locate a referenced assembly and request resolution of the type reference. It is this mechanism that provides an isolation scope for applications: the assembly alone controls its composition.

9.2 Accessing Metadata

Metadata is emitted into and read from a CLI module using either direct access to the file format as described in Partition II or through the Reflection Library. It is possible to create a tool that verifies a CLI module, including the metadata, during development, based on the specifications supplied in Partition III and Partition II.

When a class is loaded at runtime, the CLI loader imports the metadata into its own in-memory data structures, which can be browsed via the CLI Reflection services. The Reflection services should be considered as similar to a compiler; they automatically walk the inheritance hierarchy to obtain information about inherited methods and fields, they have rules about hiding by name or name-and-signature, rules about inheritance of methods and properties, and so forth.

ANNOTATION: Reflection is mentioned in many places in this part of the standard but is not discussed at length. That is because it is a set of services implemented in the Base Class Library (see the *.NET Framework Standard Library Annotated Reference*), rather than a part of the CTS or VES, which is the focus of this book, and of the standard, except for the XML description of the Base Class Library in Partition IV. The importance of Reflection, however, as described in the preceding paragraph, cannot be overstated.

9.2.1 *Metadata Tokens*

A metadata token is an implementation-dependent encoding mechanism. Partition II describes the manner in which metadata tokens are embedded in various sections of a CLI PE/COFF module. Metadata tokens are embedded in CIL and native code to encode method invocations and field accesses at call sites; the token is used by various infrastructure services to retrieve information from metadata about the reference and the type on which it was scoped in order to resolve the reference.

A metadata token is a typed identifier of a metadata object (type declaration, member declaration, etc.). Given a token, its type can be determined and it is possible to retrieve the specific metadata attributes for that metadata object. However, a metadata token is not a persistent identifier. Rather it is scoped to a specific metadata binary. A metadata token is represented as an index into a metadata data structure, so access is fast and direct.

9.2.2 *Member Signatures in Metadata*

Every location—including fields, parameters, method return values, and properties—has a type, and a specification for its type is carried in metadata.

A value type describes values that are represented as a sequence of bits. A reference type describes values that are represented as the location of a sequence of bits. The CLI provides an explicit set of built-in types, each of which has a default runtime form as either a value type or a reference type. The metadata APIs may be used to declare additional types, and part of the type specification of a variable encodes the identity of the type as well as which form (value or reference) the type is to take at runtime.

Metadata tokens representing encoded types are passed to CIL instructions that accept a type (**newobj**, **newarray**, **ldtoken**). See the CIL instruction set specification in Partition III.

These encoded type metadata tokens are also embedded in member signatures. To optimize runtime binding of field accesses and method invocations, the type and location signatures associated with fields and methods are encoded into member signatures in metadata. A member signature embodies all of the contract information that is used to decide whether a reference to a member succeeds or fails.

9.3 Unmanaged Code

It is possible to pass data from CLI managed code to unmanaged code. This always involves a transition from managed to unmanaged code, which has some runtime cost, but data can often be transferred without copying. When data must be reformatted the VES provides a reasonable specification of default behavior, but it is possible to use metadata to explicitly require other forms of **marshalling** (i.e., reformatted copying). The metadata also allows access to unmanaged methods through implementation-specific pre-existing mechanisms.

ANNOTATION: One of the major design features of the CLI is to make it possible to describe pre-existing native code data structures, and enable calling to and from native code. There is very little description of this in the standard because the standard focuses on producing and running managed code.

However, an important part of the standard is making provision for dealing with unmanaged code. Metadata is one of those places. Metadata can describe data structures for native code, and methods that are implemented in native code. For example, metadata can describe what appears to be a managed method, the actual implementation of which is unmanaged. The marshalling information is carried in the metadata, to tell you how to marshal to and from that method. The mechanism used to call unmanaged code is **PInvoke** (Partition II, section 14.5.2).

Although native interoperation services are part of the standard, operating systems are likely to implement extensions that allow CLI implementations access to platform-specific data types. For example, Microsoft has in its Common Language Runtime implementation of the CLI a number of extensions for a pre-existing wider set of data types, and a full COM interoperation implementation.

9.4 Method Implementation Metadata

For each method for which an implementation is supplied in the current CLI module, the tool or compiler will emit information used by the CIL-to-native-code compilers, the CLI loader, and other infrastructure services. This information includes:

- Whether the code is managed or unmanaged.
- Whether the implementation is in native code or CIL (note that all CIL code is managed).

- The location of the method body in the current module, as an address relative to the start of the module file in which it is located (a **Relative Virtual Address**, or **RVA**). Or, alternatively, the RVA is encoded as 0 and other metadata is used to tell the infrastructure where the method implementation will be found, including:
  - An implementation to be located via the CLI Interoperability Services.
  - Forwarding calls through an imported global static method.

ANNOTATION: For more information on the RVA, see Chapter 4 of this book, and Partition II, section 21.

9.5 Class Layout

In the general case, the CLI loader is free to lay out the instances of a class in any way it chooses, consistent with the rules of the CTS. However, there are times when a tool or compiler needs more control over the layout. In the metadata, a class is marked with an attribute indicating whether its layout rule is:

- **autolayout**: A class marked "autolayout" indicates that the loader is free to lay out the class in any way it sees fit; any layout information that may have been specified is ignored. This is the default.
- **layoutsequential**: A class marked "layoutsequential" guides the loader to preserve field order as emitted, but otherwise the specific offsets are calculated based on the CLI type of the field; these may be shifted by explicit offset, padding, and/or alignment information.
- **explicitlayout**: A class marked "explicitlayout" causes the loader to ignore field sequence and to use the explicit layout rules provided, in the form of field offsets and/or overall class size or alignment. There are restrictions on legal layouts, specified in Partition II.

It is also possible to specify an overall size for a class. This enables a tool or compiler to emit a value type specification where only the size of the type is supplied. This is useful in declaring CLI built-in types (such as 32-bit integer). It is also useful in situations where the data type of a member of a structured value type does not have a representation in CLI metadata (e.g., C++ bit fields). In the latter case, as long as the tool or compiler controls the layout, and CLI doesn't need to know the details or play a role in the layout, this is sufficient. Note that this means that the VES can move bits around but can't marshal across machines—the emitting tool or compiler will need to handle the marshalling.

Optionally, a developer may specify a packing size for a class. This is layout information that is not often used, but it allows a developer to control the alignment of the fields. It is not an alignment specification, per se, but rather serves as a modifier that places a ceiling on all alignments. Typical values are 1, 2, 4, 8, or 16.

For the full specification of class layout attributes, see the classes in `System.Runtime.InteropServices` in the *.NET Framework Standard Library Annotated Reference*.

ANNOTATION: The published standard refers to descriptions of the standardized framework as a reference to Partition IV. This is because the International Standard contains the complete standardized descriptions of the framework in XML as a part of Partition IV. This book refers to the *.NET Framework Standard Library Annotated Reference* in these cases.

9.6 Assemblies: Name Scopes for Types

An assembly is a collection of resources that are built to work together to deliver a cohesive set of functionality. An assembly carries all of the rules necessary to ensure that cohesion. It is the unit of access to resources in the CLI.

Externally, an assembly is a collection of exported resources, including types. Resources are exported by name. Internally, an assembly is a collection of public (exported) and private (internal to the assembly) resources. It is the assembly that determines which resources are to be exposed outside of the assembly and which resources are accessible only within the current assembly scope. It is the assembly that controls how a reference to a resource, public or private, is mapped onto the bits that implement the resource. For types in particular, the assembly may also supply runtime configuration information. A CLI module can be thought of as a packaging of type declarations and implementations, where the packaging decisions may change under the covers without affecting clients of the assembly.

The identity of a type is its assembly scope and its declared name. A type defined identically in two different assemblies is considered two different types.

ANNOTATION: The previous paragraph is accurate, but only for defined types. The identity of types that are created by the VES from a reference, such as arrays and pointers, is tied to the assembly in which the underlying type (array of <type>, or pointer to <type>) is defined, not the assembly in which they are referenced.

Although giving every type a unique identity in itself would be very cumbersome, we can get close, by tying the type's identity to the identity of the assembly. The assembly's identity consists of the name of the assembly, the public key used to sign the assembly, the version number of the assembly, and the culture for which that assembly was specialized. That is generally enough to uniquely identify the assembly. On agreement that the assembly is uniquely identified, we have uniquely identified the types within it because the CLI specifies that there cannot be two types of the same name within one assembly. For example, a subtype cannot have the same name as its parent type within the same assembly.

Assembly Dependencies: An assembly may depend on other assemblies. This happens when implementations in the scope of one assembly reference resources that are scoped in or owned by another assembly.

- All references to other assemblies are resolved under the control of the current assembly scope. This gives an assembly an opportunity to control how a reference to another assembly is mapped onto a particular version (or other characteristic) of that referenced assembly (although that target assembly has sole control over how the referenced resource is resolved to an implementation).
- It is always possible to determine which assembly scope a particular implementation is running in. All requests originating from that assembly scope are resolved relative to that scope.

From a deployment perspective, an assembly may be deployed by itself, with the assumption that any other referenced assemblies will be available in the deployed environment. Or, it may be deployed with its dependent assemblies.

Manifests: Every assembly has a manifest that declares what files make up the assembly, what types are exported, and what other assemblies are required to resolve type references within the assembly. Just as CLI components are self-describing via metadata in the CLI component, so are assemblies self-describing via their manifests. When a single file makes up an assembly, it contains both the metadata describing the types defined in the assembly and the metadata describing the assembly itself. When an assembly contains more than one file with metadata, each of the files describes the types defined in the file, if any, and one of these files also contains the metadata describing the assembly (including the names of the other files, their cryptographic hashes, and the types they export outside of the assembly).

Applications: Assemblies introduce isolation semantics for applications. An application is simply an assembly that has an external entry point that triggers (or causes a hosting environment such as a browser to trigger) the creation of a new Application Domain. This entry point is effectively the root of a tree of request invocations and resolutions. Some applications are a single, self-contained assembly. Others require the availability of other assemblies to provide needed resources. In either case, when a request is resolved to a module to load, the module is loaded into the same Application Domain from which the request originated. It is possible to monitor or stop an application via the Application Domain.

References: A reference to a type always qualifies a type name with the assembly scope within which the reference is to be resolved; that is, an assembly establishes the name scope of available resources. However, rather than establishing relationships between individual modules and referenced assemblies, every reference is resolved through the current assembly. This allows each assembly to have absolute control over how references are resolved. See Partition II.

9.7 Metadata Extensibility

CLI metadata is extensible. There are three reasons this is important:

- The Common Language Specification (CLS) is a specification for conventions that languages and tools agree to support in a uniform way for better language integration. The CLS constrains parts of the CTS model, and the CLS introduces higher-level abstractions that are layered over the CTS. It is important that the metadata be able to capture these sorts of development-time abstractions that are used by tools even though they are not recognized or supported explicitly by the CLI.
- It should be possible to represent language-specific abstractions in metadata that are neither CLI nor CLS language abstractions. For example, it should be possible, over time, to enable languages like C++ to not require separate header files or IDL files in order to use types, methods, and data members exported by compiled modules.
- It should be possible, in member signatures, to encode types and type modifiers that are used in language-specific overloading—for example, to allow C++ to distinguish **int** from **long** even on 32-bit machines where both map to the underlying type **int32**.

This extensibility comes in the following forms:

- Every metadata object can carry custom attributes, and the metadata APIs provide a way to declare, enumerate, and retrieve custom attributes. Custom attributes may be identified by a simple name, where the value encoding is opaque and known only to the specific tool, language, or service that defined it. Or, custom attributes may be identified by a type reference, where the structure of the attribute is self-describing (via data members declared on the type) and any tool including the CLI Reflection services may browse the value encoding.

CLS Rule 34: The CLS only allows a subset of the encodings of custom attributes. The only types that shall appear in these encodings are (see the *.NET Framework Standard Library Annotated Reference*): `System.Type`, `System.String`, `System.Char`, `System.Boolean`, `System.Byte`, `System.Int16`, `System.Int32`, `System.Int64`, `System.Single`, `System.Double`, and any enumeration type based on a CLS-compliant base integer type.

NOTE

CLS (consumer): Shall be able to read attributes encoded using the restricted scheme.

CLS (extender): Must meet all requirements for CLS consumer and be able to author new classes and new attributes. Shall be able to attach attributes based on existing attribute classes to any metadata that is emitted. Shall implement the rules for the `System.AttributeUsageAttribute` (see the *.NET Framework Standard Library Annotated Reference*).

CLS (framework): Shall externally expose only attributes that are encoded within the CLS rules and following the conventions specified for `System.AttributeUsageAttribute`.

- In addition to CTS type extensibility, it is possible to emit custom modifiers into member signatures (see Types in Partition II, section 7.1). The CLI will honor these modifiers for purposes of method overloading and hiding, as well as for binding, but will not enforce any of the language-specific semantics. These modifiers can reference the return type or any parameter of a method, or the type of a field. They come in two kinds: **required modifiers** that anyone using the member must understand in order to correctly use it, and **optional modifiers** that may be ignored if the modifier is not understood.

CLS Rule 35: The CLS does not allow publicly visible required modifiers (**modreq**; see Partition II, section 7.1.1), but does allow optional modifiers (**modopt**; see Partition II, section 7.1.1) they do not understand.

NOTE

CLS (consumer): Shall be able to read metadata containing optional modifiers and correctly copy signatures that include them. May ignore these modifiers in type matching and overload resolution. May ignore types that become ambiguous when the optional modifiers are ignored, or that use required modifiers.

CLS (extender): Shall be able to author overrides for inherited methods with signatures that include optional modifiers. Consequently, an extender must be able to copy such modifiers from metadata that it imports. There is no requirement to support required modifiers, nor to author new methods that have any kind of modifier in their signature.

CLS (framework): Shall not use required modifiers in externally visible signatures unless they are marked as not CLS-compliant. Shall not expose two members on a class that differ only by the use of optional modifiers in their signature unless only one is marked CLS-compliant.

ANNOTATION: It would be good to briefly describe the difference between attributes and modifiers. Metadata is partly represented as a series of tables (in the database sense), that describe different parts of the program—defined types, referenced types, and type members. Custom attributes can be attached to any of these. Custom attributes have an encoding that lets the programmer define an object, and the custom attribute looks to the user like a call to a constructor for that object.

Another part of the metadata is an area concerned with space-efficient encoding of a lot of data in a few bytes. These are called "signatures." Signatures are used to describe the types of arguments or the types of fields. You might want to put attributes on the information in signatures as well, but there is not enough space. Instead, there is a special compacted form called "modifier" (CLI-specified modifiers are called constraints). Modifiers have a much simpler structure than attributes, and they are not objects. Usually a modifier is just a type name.

For more information on custom attributes, see Partition II, section 20 and its subsections.

9.8 Globals, Imports, and Exports

The CTS does not have the notion of **global statics**: all statics are associated with a particular class. Nonetheless, the metadata is designed to support languages that rely on static data that is stored directly in a PE/COFF file and accessed by its relative virtual address. In addition, while access to managed data and managed functions is mediated entirely through the metadata itself, the metadata provides a mechanism for accessing unmanaged data and unmanaged code.

ANNOTATION: Even though the CTS does not have the notion of global statics, the CLI supports languages that support global statics by creating a special class named **<module>**, into which it puts what are defined in a language as global static fields and global static methods. There are special rules for how that module is treated, described in Partition II, section 9.8.

CLS Rule 36: Global static fields and methods are not CLS-compliant.

NOTE

CLS (consumer): Need not support global static fields or methods.

CLS (extender): Need not author global static fields or methods.

CLS (framework): Shall not define global static fields or methods.

9.9 Scoped Statics

The CTS does not include a model for file- or function-scoped static functions or data members. However, there are times when a compiler needs a metadata token to emit into CIL for a scoped function or data member. The metadata allows members to be marked so that they are never visible/accessible outside of the PE/COFF file in which they are declared and for which the compiler guarantees to enforce all access rules.

ANNOTATION: The accessibility referred to in the final sentence of the previous paragraph is compiler-controlled. For more information, see Partition I, section 8.5.3.2.

End informative text

10 Name and Type Rules for the Common Language Specification

ANNOTATION: This section provides the context and detailed information for a number of CLS rules, that generally is not contained elsewhere, as well as CLS rules 37–41 and their context. The following major section (section 11, Collected CLS Rules) is just a list of the CLS rules listed earlier in the standard, without their context, and is intended as a reference only.

10.1 Identifiers

Languages that are either case-sensitive or case-insensitive can support the CLS. Since its rules apply only to items exposed to other languages, **private** members or types that aren't exported from an assembly may use any names they choose. For interoperation, however, there are some restrictions.

In order to make tools work well with a case-sensitive language, it is important that the exact case of identifiers be maintained. At the same time, when dealing with non-English languages encoded in Unicode, there may be more than one way to represent precisely the same identifier that includes combining characters. The CLS requires that identifiers obey the restrictions of the appropriate Unicode standard and persist them in Canonical form C, which preserves case but forces combining characters into a standard representation. See CLS Rule 4, in Partition I, section 8.5.1.

At the same time, it is important that externally visible names not conflict with one another when used from a case-insensitive programming language. As a result, all identifier comparisons shall be done internally to CLS-compliant tools using the Canonical form KC, which first transforms characters to their case-canonical representation. See CLS Rule 4, in Partition I, section 8.5.1.

When a compiler for a CLS-compliant language supports interoperability with a non-CLS-compliant language, it must be aware that the CTS and VES perform all comparisons using code-point (i.e., byte-by-byte) comparison. Thus, even though the CLS requires that persisted identifiers be in Canonical form C, references to non-CLS identifiers will have to be persisted using whatever encoding the non-CLS language chose to use. It is a language design issue, not covered by the CTS or the CLS, precisely how this should be handled.

ANNOTATION: For more information, see the annotation in Partition I, section 8.5.1.

2. Concepts and Architecture

10.2 Overloading

> **NOTE**
> The CTS, while it describes inheritance, object layout, name hiding, and overriding of virtual methods, does not discuss overloading at all. While this is surprising, it arises from the fact that overloading is entirely handled by compilers that target the CTS and not the type system itself. In the metadata, all references to types and type members are fully resolved and include the precise signature that is intended. This choice was made since every programming language has its own set of rules for coercing types and the VES does not provide a means for expressing those rules.

Following the rules of the CTS, it is possible for duplicate names to be defined in the same scope as long as they differ in either kind (field, method, etc.) or signature. The CLS imposes a stronger restriction for overloading methods. Within a single scope, a given name may refer to any number of methods provided they differ in any of the following:

- Number of parameters
- Type of each argument

Notice that the signature includes more information but CLS-compliant languages need not produce or consume classes that differ only by that additional information (see Partition II for the complete list of information carried in a signature):

- Calling convention
- Custom modifiers
- Return type
- Whether a parameter is passed by value, or whether it is passed by reference (i.e., as a managed pointer or by-ref)

There is one exception to this rule. For the special names `op_Implicit` and `op_Explicit` described in Partition I, section 10.3.3 methods may be provided that differ only by their return type. These are marked specially and may be ignored by compilers that don't support operator overloading.

Properties shall not be overloaded by type (that is, by the return type of their `getter` method), but they may be overloaded with different numbers or types of indices (that is, by the number and types of the parameters of its **getter** method). The overloading rules for properties are identical to the method overloading rules.

CLS Rule 37: Only properties and methods may be overloaded.

CLS Rule 38: Properties, instance methods, and virtual methods may be overloaded based only on the number and types of their parameters, except the conversion operators named **op_Implicit** and **op_Explicit**, which may also be overloaded based on their return type.

NOTE

CLS (consumer): May assume that only properties and methods are overloaded, and need not support overloading based on return type unless providing special syntax for operator overloading. If return type overloading isn't supported, then the **op_Implicit** and **op_Explicit** may be ignored, since the functionality shall be provided in some other way by a CLS-compliant framework.

CLS (extender): Should not permit the authoring of overloads other than those specified here. It is not necessary to support operator overloading at all, hence it is possible to entirely avoid support for overloading on return type.

CLS (framework): Shall not publicly expose overloading except as specified here. Frameworks authors should bear in mind that many programming languages, including Object-Oriented languages, do not support overloading and will expose overloaded methods or properties through mangled names. Most languages support neither operator overloading nor overloading based on return type, so **op_Implicit** and **op_Explicit** shall always be augmented with some alternative way to gain the same functionality.

ANNOTATION: Not all languages support overloading. A strong opponent is Eiffel. Emmanuel Stapf, a member of the ECMA technical committee responsible for this standard and a senior software engineer for Eiffel, has contributed the following argument for why overloading should not have been part of the standard:

Those who believe that object-oriented languages should not support overloading have adopted the principle that different things should have different names. The key, they believe, to simplicity is a one-to-one mapping. To keep its specification as simple as possible, Eiffel does not support overloading.

An example of how overloading can cause problems is taken from the `Point` class. You can represent a `Point` instance with either polar coordinates or Cartesian coordinates. The values for both kinds of coordinates are real numbers. Suppose you then use a simple constructor:

```
.ctor (Single, Single)
```

With this constructor, you can create instances of `Point` in only one of the coordinate systems.

Inheritance and Overloading

Overloading also does not work well with inheritance. A simple example illustrates this.

Class `A` has the method `void f(X x)`.

Class `B`, inheriting from `A`, provides a new implementation for `f`.

Class `Y` inherits from class `X`.

```
A a;
B b;
X x;
Y y;
a = b;
x = y;
a.f(x);
a.f(y);
b.f(x);
b.f(y);
```

In this example there is not much ambiguity. But suppose, in `B`, that you add the following new overloaded definition of `f`:

```
void f (Y y);
```

Doing so breaks the previous code. Before the new overloaded definition, all calls resolved in calling the version of void f(X x) defined in B. Now some calls resolve into void f(X x) and some into void f(Y y). It is not clear which ones resolve to which.

Variance and Overloading

Although the CLI supports only no-variant redefinition of routines, some other languages support either covariant redefinition or contravariant redefinition. Overloading works well with no-variant definition but does not work well with covariant or contravariant languages. Following is an example of a covariant case:

Class `A` has the method `void f(X x)`.

Class `B` has `void f(Y y)`.

Class `Y` inherits from class `X`.

Suppose that in class `B` you want to covariantly redefine `void f(X x)` to be `void f(Y y)`. If you allow overloading you cannot do that, because you will end up with two routines with the same signature. This is not allowed. Therefore you need to rename the `void f(Y y)` initially present in `B` to something else, removing overloading altogether.

Eiffel's argument comes down to three ideas about variant redefinition:

1. Not all languages support it.
2. It has inherent limitations.
3. Its lack of one-to-one mapping results in a lack of simplicity in the programming model.

These arguments are well expressed in an article by Bertrand Meyer, published in the October/November 2001 issue of the *Journal of Object-Oriented Programming*: http://www.inf.ethz.ch/personal/meyer/publications/joop/overloading.pdf.

—*Emmanuel Stapf*

10.3 Operator Overloading

CLS-compliant consumer and extender tools are under no obligation to allow defining of operator overloading. CLS-compliant consumer and extender tools do not have to provide a special mechanism to call these methods.

NOTE

This topic is addressed by the CLS so that

- languages that do provide operator overloading can describe their rules in a way that other languages can understand, and
- languages that do not provide operator overloading can still access the underlying functionality without the addition of special syntax.

Operator overloading is described by using the names specified below, and by setting a special bit in the metadata (**SpecialName**) so that they do not collide with the user's namespace. A CLS-compliant producer tool shall provide some means for setting this bit. If these names are used, they shall have precisely the semantics described here.

ANNOTATION: From the point of view of language design, operator overloading is a very interesting piece of the design space. Adding operator overloading gives a great deal of convenience to the programmer. At the same time, it is the single greatest source of confusion in most of the programming languages that have it. When you are dealing with someone else's code, where an operator like "+" has been redefined but you are not aware of it, you encounter cases in which it no longer means what you intuitively understand.

In designing the CLI, however, the decision was made not to restrict operator overloading. Because most languages do not include operator overloading, these languages had to agree to provide another way to do whatever would have been done through operator overloading. To do that, a standardized set of operator overloads are given names. If you're using a language that does not have operator overloading, you can use those names to get the same behavior. In languages that overload operators, these names are not used. In languages that do not overload operators, standard operators are not customizable or extendable, but other functionality is available with the names in Table 2-4, which is a very large list, containing operations from multiple languages.

Adding the conversion operators was very contentious because it required the inclusion of the odd codicil to CLS rule 38. Rule 38 says:

> Properties, instance methods, and virtual methods may be overloaded based only on the number and types of their parameters, *except the conversion operators named* **op_Implicit** *and* **op_Explicit**, *which may also be overloaded based on their return type.*

Everyone agreed unanimously that overloading the return type is a bad idea, but in this case there was no alternative to getting the needed functionality.

10.3.1 *Unary Operators*

Unary operators take one argument, perform some operation on it, and return the result. They are represented as static methods on the class that defines the type of their one operand or their return type. Table 2-4, Unary Operator Names, shows the names that are defined.

10.3.2 *Binary Operators*

Binary operators take two arguments, perform some operation, and return a value. They are represented as static methods on the class that defines the type of one of their two operands or the return type. Table 2-5, Binary Operator Names, shows the names that are defined.

10.3.3 *Conversion Operators*

Conversion operators are unary operations that allow conversion from one type to another. The operator method shall be defined as a static method on either the operand or return type. There are two types of conversions:

- An implicit (**widening**) coercion shall not lose any magnitude or precision. These should be provided using a method named `op_Implicit`.
- An explicit (**narrowing**) coercion may lose magnitude or precision. These should be provided using a method named `op_Explicit`.

Table 2-4 Unary Operator Names

Name	ISO/IEC 14882:1998 C++ Operator Symbol
`op_Decrement`	Similar to `--`[1]
`op_Increment`	Similar to `++`[1]
`op_UnaryNegation`	`-` (unary)
`op_UnaryPlus`	`+` (unary)
`op_LogicalNot`	`!`
`op_True`[2]	Not defined
`op_False`[2]	Not defined
`op_AddressOf`	`&` (unary)
`op_OnesComplement`	`~`
`op_PointerDereference`	`*` (unary)

1. From a pure C++ point of view, the way one must write these functions for the CLI differs in one very important aspect. In C++, these methods must increment or decrement their operand directly, whereas, in CLI, they must not; instead, they simply return the value of their operand +/- 1, as appropriate, without modifying their operand. The operand must be incremented or decremented by the compiler that generates the code for the ++/-- operator, separate from the call to these methods.
2. The `op_True` and `op_False` operators do not exist in C++. They are provided to support tri-state Boolean types, such as those used in database languages.

Table 2-5 Binary Operator Names

Name	C++ Operator Symbol
`op_Addition`	+ (binary)
`op_Subtraction`	- (binary)
`op_Multiply`	* (binary)
`op_Division`	/
`op_Modulus`	%
`op_ExclusiveOr`	^
`op_BitwiseAnd`	& (binary)
`op_BitwiseOr`	|
`op_LogicalAnd`	&&
`op_LogicalOr`	||
`op_Assign`	=
`op_LeftShift`	<<
`op_RightShift`	>>
`op_SignedRightShift`	Not defined
`op_UnsignedRightShift`	Not defined
`op_Equality`	==
`op_GreaterThan`	>
`op_LessThan`	<
`op_Inequality`	!=
`op_GreaterThanOrEqual`	
`op_LessThanOrEqual`	<=
`op_UnsignedRightShiftAssignment`	Not defined

Table 2-5 Binary Operator Names *(continued)*

Name	C++ Operator Symbol
op_MemberSelection	->
op_RightShiftAssignment	>>=
op_MultiplicationAssignment	*=
op_PointerToMemberSelection	->*
op_SubtractionAssignment	-=
op_ExclusiveOrAssignment	^=
op_LeftShiftAssignment	<<=
op_ModulusAssignment	%=
op_AdditionAssignment	+=
op_BitwiseAndAssignment	&=
op_BitwiseOrAssignment	|=
op_Comma	,
op_DivisionAssignment	/=

NOTE

Conversions provide functionality that can't be generated in other ways, and many languages will not support the use of the conversion operators through special syntax. Therefore, CLS rules require that the same functionality be made available through an alternate mechanism. Using the more common ToXxx (where Xxx is the target type) and FromYyy (where Yyy is the name of the source type) naming pattern is recommended.

Because these operations may exist on the class of their operand type (so-called "from" conversions) and would therefore differ on their return type only, the CLS specifically allows that these two operators be overloaded based on their return type. The CLS, however, also requires that if this form of overloading is used then the language shall provide an alternate means for providing the same functionality since not all CLS languages will implement operators with special syntax.

CLS Rule 39: If either `op_Implicit` or `op_Explicit` is provided, an alternate means of providing the coercion *shall* be provided.

NOTE

CLS (consumer): Where appropriate to the language design, use the existence of `op_Implicit` and/or `op_Explicit` in choosing method overloads and generating automatic coercions.

CLS (extender): Where appropriate to the language design, implement user-defined implicit or explicit coercion operators using the corresponding `op_Implicit`, `op_Explicit`, `ToXxx`, and/or `FromXxx` methods.

CLS (framework): If coercion operations are supported, they shall be provided as `FromXxx` and `ToXxx`, and optionally `op_Implicit` and `op_Explicit` as well. CLS frameworks are encouraged to provide such coercion operations.

ANNOTATION: The most contentious discussion during the development of the standard on overloading operators focused on conversion operators, because it required the inclusion of the odd codicil to CLS rule 38. No one was happy with it because although all agreed that overloading should not be allowed based on the return type of a method, it ended up being allowed in this one case. There was no other way to get the needed functionality.

10.4 Naming Patterns

See also Partition V[, Annex D.1, Naming Guidelines].

While the CTS does not dictate the naming of properties or events, the CLS does specify a pattern to be observed.

For Events:

An individual event is created by choosing or defining a delegate type that is used to signal the event. Then, three methods are created with names based on the name of the event and with a fixed signature. For the examples below we define an event named `Click` that uses a delegate type named `EventHandler`.

```
EventAdd, used to add a handler for an event
        Pattern: void add_<EventName> (<DelegateType> handler)
        Example: void add_Click (EventHandler handler);
EventRemove, used to remove a handler for an event
        Pattern: void remove_<EventName> (<DelegateType> handler)
        Example: void remove_Click (EventHandler handler);
EventRaise, used to signal that an event has occurred
        Pattern: void family raise_<EventName> (Event e)
```

For Properties:

An individual property is created by deciding on the type returned by its getter method and the types of the getter's parameters (if any). Then, two methods are created with names based on the name of the property and these types. For the examples below we define two properties: `Name` takes no parameters and returns a `System.String`, while `Item` takes a `System.Object` parameter and returns a `System.Object`. Item is referred to as an indexed property, meaning that it takes parameters and thus may appear to the user as though it were an array with indices.

```
PropertyGet, used to read the value of the property
        Pattern: <PropType> get_<PropName> (<Indices>)
        Example: System.String get_Name ();
        Example: System.Object get_Item (System.Object key);
PropertySet, used to modify the value of the property
        Pattern: void set_<PropName> (<Indices>, <PropType>)
        Example: void set_Name (System.String name);
        Example: void set_Item (System.Object key, System.Object value);
```

10.5 Exceptions

The CLI supports an exception handling model, which is introduced in Partition I, section 12.4.2. CLS-compliant frameworks may define and throw externally visible exceptions, but there are restrictions on the types of objects thrown:

CLS Rule 40: Objects that are thrown shall be of type `System.Exception` or inherit from it. Nonetheless, CLS-compliant methods are not required to block the propagation of other types of exceptions.

NOTE

CLS (consumer): Need not support throwing or catching of objects that are not of the specified type.

2. Concepts and Architecture

> **CLS (extender):** Must support throwing of objects of type `System.Exception` or a type inheriting from it. Need not support throwing of objects of other types.
>
> **CLS (framework):** Shall not publicly expose thrown objects that are not of type `System.Exception` or a type inheriting from it.

10.6 Custom Attributes

In order to allow languages to provide a consistent view of custom attributes across language boundaries, the Base Class Library provides support for the following rules defined by the CLS:

> **CLS Rule 41:** Attributes shall be of type `System.Attribute`, or inherit from it.
>
> **NOTE**
>
> **CLS (consumer):** Need not support attributes that are not of the specified type.
>
> **CLS (extender):** Must support the authoring of custom attributes.
>
> **CLS (framework):** Shall not publicly expose attributes that are not of type `System.Attribute` or a type inheriting from it.

The use of a particular attribute class may be restricted in various ways by placing an attribute on the attribute class. The `System.AttributeUsageAttribute` is used to specify these restrictions. The restrictions supported by the `System.AttributeUsageAttribute` are:

- What kinds of constructs (types, methods, assemblies, etc.) may have the attribute applied to them. By default, instances of an attribute class can be applied to any construct. This is specified by setting the value of the `ValidOn` property of `System.AttributeUsageAttribute`. Several constructs may be combined.
- Multiple instances of the attribute class may be applied to a given piece of metadata. By default, only one instance of any given attribute class can be applied to a single metadata item. The `AllowMultiple` property of the attribute is used to specify the desired value.
- Do not inherit the attribute when applied to a type. By default, any attribute attached to a type should be inherited to types that derive from it. If multiple instances of the attribute class are allowed, the inheritance performs a union of the attributes inherited from the parent and those explicitly applied to the child type. If multiple instances are

not allowed, then an attribute of that type applied directly to the child overrides the attribute supplied by the parent. This is specified by setting the `Inherited` property of `System.AttributeUsageAttribute` to the desired value.

> **NOTE**
> Since these are CLS rules and not part of the CTS itself, tools are required to specify explicitly the custom attributes they intend to apply to any given metadata item. That is, compilers or other tools that generate metadata must implement the `AllowMultiple` and `Inherit` rules. The CLI does not supply attributes automatically. The usage of attributes in the CLI is further described in Partition II.

11 Collected CLS Rules

The complete set of CLS rules are collected here for reference. Recall that these rules apply only to "externally visible" items—types that are visible outside of their own assembly and members of those types that have `public`, `family`, or `family-or-assembly` accessibility. Furthermore, items may be explicitly marked as CLS-compliant or not using the `System.CLSCompliantAttribute`. The CLS rules apply only to items that are marked as CLS-compliant.

1. CLS rules apply only to those parts of a type that are accessible or visible outside of the defining assembly (see Partition I, section 7.3).
2. Members of non-CLS-compliant types shall not be marked CLS-compliant (see Partition I, section 7.3.1).
3. The CLS does not include boxed value types (see Partition I, section 8.2.4).
4. Assemblies shall follow Annex 7 of Technical Report 15 of the Unicode Standard 3.0 (ISBN 0-201-61633-5) governing the set of characters permitted to start and be included in identifiers, available on-line at http://www.unicode.org/unicode/reports/tr15/tr15-18.html. For CLS purposes, two identifiers are the same if their lowercase mappings (as specified by the Unicode locale-insensitive, 1-1 lowercase mappings) are the same. That is, for two identifiers to be considered different under the CLS, they shall differ in more than simply their case. However, in order to override an inherited definition, the CLI requires the precise encoding of the original declaration be used (see Partition I, section 8.5.1).
5. All names introduced in a CLS-compliant scope shall be distinct independent of kind, except where the names are identical and resolved via overloading. That is, while the

CTS allows a single type to use the same name for a method and a field, the CLS does not (see Partition I, section 8.5.2).

6. Fields and nested types shall be distinct by identifier comparison alone, even though the CTS allows distinct signatures to be distinguished. Methods, properties, and events that have the same name (by identifier comparison) shall differ by more than just the return type, except as specified in CLS Rule 39 (see Partition I, section 8.5.2).
7. The underlying type of an enum shall be a built-in CLS integer type (see Partition I, section 8.5.2).
8. There are two distinct kinds of enums, indicated by the presence or absence of the `System.FlagsAttribute` custom attribute. One represents named integer values, the other named bit flags that can be combined to generate an unnamed value. The value of an enum is not limited to the specified values (see Partition I, section 8.5.2).
9. Literal static fields of an enum shall have the type of the enum itself (see Partition I, section 8.5.2).
10. Accessibility shall not be changed when overriding inherited methods, except when overriding a method inherited from a different assembly with accessibility family-or-assembly. In this case the override shall have accessibility family (see Partition I, section 8.5.3.2).
11. All types appearing in a signature shall be CLS-compliant (see Partition I, section 8.6.1).
12. The visibility and accessibility of types and members shall be such that types in the signature of any member shall be visible and accessible whenever the member itself is visible and accessible. For example, a public method that is visible outside its assembly shall not have an argument whose type is visible only within the assembly (see Partition I, section 8.6.1).
13. The value of a literal static is specified through the use of field initialization metadata (see Partition II). A CLS-compliant literal must have a value specified in field initialization metadata that is of exactly the same type as the literal (or of the underlying type, if that literal is an **enum**) (see Partition I, section 8.6.1.2).
14. Typed references are not CLS-compliant (see Partition I, section 8.6.1.3).
15. The varargs constraint is not part of the CLS, and the only calling convention supported by the CLS is the standard managed calling convention (see Partition I, section 8.6.1.5).
16. Arrays shall have elements with a CLS-compliant type, and all dimensions of the array shall have lower bounds of zero. Only the fact that an item is an array and the element type of the array shall be required to distinguish between overloads. When overloading is based on two or more array types, the element types shall be named types (see Partition I, section 8.9.1).
17. Unmanaged pointer types are not CLS-compliant (see Partition I, section 8.9.2).

18. CLS-compliant interfaces shall not require the definition of non-CLS-compliant methods in order to implement them (see Partition I, section 8.9.4).
19. CLS-compliant interfaces shall not define static methods, nor shall they define fields (see Partition I, section 8.9.4).
20. CLS-compliant classes, value types, and interfaces shall not require the implementation of non-CLS-compliant interfaces (see Partition I, section 8.9.6.4).
21. An object constructor shall call some class constructor of its base class before any access occurs to inherited instance data. This does not apply to value types, which need not have constructors (see Partition I, section 8.9.6.6).
22. An object constructor shall not be called except as part of the creation of an object, and an object shall not be initialized twice (see Partition I, section 8.9.6.6).
23. `System.Object` is CLS-compliant. Any other CLS-compliant class shall inherit from a CLS-compliant class (see Partition I, section 8.9.8.1).
24. The methods that implement the `getter` and `setter` methods of a property shall be marked SpecialName in the metadata (see Partition II) (see Partition I, section 8.11.3).
25. The accessibility of a property and of its accessors shall be identical (see Partition I, section 8.11.3).
26. A property and its accessors shall all be static, all be virtual, or all be instance (see Partition I, section 8.11.3).
27. The type of a property shall be the return type of the `getter` and the type of the last argument of the `setter`. The types of the parameters of the property shall be the types of the parameters to the `getter` and the types of all but the final parameter of the `setter`. All of these types shall be CLS-compliant and shall not be managed pointers (i.e., shall not be passed by reference) (see Partition I, section 8.11.3).
28. Properties shall adhere to a specific naming pattern. See Partition I, section 10.4. The SpecialName attribute referred to in CLS rule 24 shall be ignored in appropriate name comparisons and shall adhere to identifier rules (see Partition I, section 8.11.3).
29. The methods that implement an event shall be marked SpecialName in the metadata (see Partition II) (see Partition I, section 8.11.4).
30. The accessibility of an event and of its accessors shall be identical (see Partition I, section 8.11.4).
31. The `add` and `remove` methods for an event shall both either be present or absent (see Partition I, section 8.11.4).
32. The `add` and `remove` methods for an event shall each take one parameter whose type defines the type of the event and that shall be derived from `System.Delegate` (see Partition I, section 8.11.4).

33. Events shall adhere to a specific naming pattern. See Partition I, section 10.4. The SpecialName attribute referred to in CLS rule 29 shall be ignored in appropriate name comparisons and shall adhere to identifier rules (see Partition I, section 8.11.4).

34. The CLS only allows a subset of the encodings of custom attributes. The only types that shall appear in these encodings are: `System.Type`, `System.String`, `System.Char`, `System.Boolean`, `System.Byte`, `System.Int16`, `System.Int32`, `System.Int64`, `System.Single`, `System.Double`, and any enumeration type based on a CLS-compliant base integer type (see Partition I, section 9.7).

35. The CLS does not allow publicly visible required modifiers (modreq; see Partition II), but does allow optional modifiers (modopt; see Partition II) they do not understand (see Partition I, section 9.7).

36. Global static fields and methods are not CLS-compliant (see Partition I, section 9.8).

37. Only properties and methods may be overloaded (see Partition I, section 10.2).

38. Properties, instance methods, and virtual methods may be overloaded based only on the number and types of their parameters, except the conversion operators named `op_Implicit` and `op_Explicit`, which may also be overloaded based on their return type (see Partition I, section 10.2).

39. If either `op_Implicit` or `op_Explicit` is overloaded on its return type, an alternate means of providing the coercion *shall* be provided (see Partition I, section 10.3.3).

40. Objects that are thrown shall be of type `System.Exception` or inherit from it (see Partition I, section 10.5). Nonetheless, CLS-compliant methods are not required to block the propagation of other types of exceptions.

41. Attributes shall be of type `System.Attribute`, or inherit from it (see Partition I, section 10.6).

12 Virtual Execution System

The Virtual Execution System (VES) provides an environment for executing managed code. It provides direct support for a set of built-in data types, defines a hypothetical machine with an associated machine model and state, a set of control flow constructs, and an exception handling model. To a large extent, the purpose of the VES is to provide the support required to execute the Common Intermediate Language instruction set (see Partition III).

12.1 Supported Data Types

The CLI directly supports the data types shown in Table 2-6, Data Types Directly Supported by the CLI Instruction Set. That is, these data types can be manipulated using the CIL instruction set (see Partition III).

Table 2-6 Data Types Directly Supported by the CLI Instruction Set

Data Type	Description
int8	8-bit 2's complement signed value
unsigned int8	8-bit unsigned binary value
int16	16-bit 2's complement signed value
unsigned int16	16-bit unsigned binary value
int32	32-bit 2's complement signed value
unsigned int32	32-bit unsigned binary value
int64	64-bit 2's complement signed value
unsigned int64	64-bit unsigned binary value
float32	32-bit IEC 60559:1989 floating point value
float64	64-bit IEC 60559:1989 floating point value
native int	native size 2's complement signed value
native unsigned int	native size unsigned binary value, also unmanaged pointer
F	native size floating point number (internal to VES, not user visible)
O	native size object reference to managed memory
&	native size managed pointer (may point into managed memory)

The CLI model uses an evaluation stack. Instructions that copy values from memory to the evaluation stack are "loads"; instructions that copy values from the stack back to memory are "stores." The full set of data types in Table 2-6, Data Types Directly Supported by the CLI Instruction Set, can be represented in memory. However, the CLI supports only a subset of these types in its operations upon values stored on its evaluation stack—int32, int64, native int. In addition, the CLI supports an internal data type to represent floating point values on the internal evaluation stack. The size of the **internal data** type is implementation-dependent. For further information on the treatment of floating point values on the evaluation stack, see Partition I, section 12.1.3 and Partition III. Short numeric values (int8, int16, unsigned int8, unsigned int16) are widened when loaded (memory-to-stack) and narrowed when stored (stack-to-memory). This reflects a computer model that assumes, for numeric and object references, [that] memory cells are 1, 2, 4, or 8 bytes wide but stack locations are either 4 or 8 bytes wide. User-defined value types may appear in memory locations or on the stack and have no size limitation; the only built-in operations on them are those that compute their address and copy them between the stack and memory.

The only CIL instructions with special support for short numeric values (rather than support for simply the 4- or 8-byte integral values) are:

- Load and store instructions to/from memory: **ldelem, ldind, stind, stelem**
- Data conversion: **conv, conv.ovf**
- Array creation: **newarr**

The signed integer (int8, int16, int32, int64, and native int) and the respective unsigned integer (unsigned int8, unsigned int16, unsigned int32, unsigned int64, and native unsigned int) types differ only in how the bits of the integer are interpreted. For those operations where an unsigned integer is treated differently from a signed integer (e.g., comparisons or arithmetic with overflow) there are separate instructions for treating an integer as unsigned (e.g., **cgt.un** and **add.ovf.u**).

This instruction set design simplifies CIL-to-native-code (e.g., JIT) compilers and interpreters of CIL by allowing them to internally track a smaller number of data types. See Partition I, section 12.3.2.1.

As described below, CIL instructions do not specify their operand types. Instead, the CLI keeps track of operand types based on data flow and aided by a stack consistency requirement described below. For example, the single **add** instruction will add two integers or two floats from the stack.

ANNOTATION: Which data types are supported, and what that means, depends on the point of view. Viewed from programming languages, each language has its own type system. From the point of view of the CLI, there is a full-fledged type system, the CTS, that includes user-defined types, all the built-in types, etc.

Then there is a type system that is used by the internals of the JIT and the one actually implemented by the VES, which is much reduced and really only knows about the size of integers (not whether they are signed or unsigned), a floating point type, objects, and pointers. The verifier sees a more expanded type system than that, but still restricted. Finally there's the one described in Partition I, section 12.1, which is what the CIL instructions can make of the base type system in the VES, which includes both signed and unsigned arithmetic.

If you are implementing a VES, you concentrate on the basics, and that's what the JIT understands. But this section describes the types that can be supported with the instruction set using normal programming techniques. This topic is of particular interest to compiler writers, who have to implement the types of their language on top of what the VES provides.

12.1.1 *Native Size: native int, native unsigned int, O, and &*

The native-size, or generic, types (native int, native unsigned int, O, and &) are a mechanism in the CLI for deferring the choice of a value's size. These data types exist as CIL types. But the CLI maps each to the native size for a specific processor. (For example, data type I would map to int32 on a Pentium processor, but to int64 on an IA64 processor). So, the choice of size is deferred until JIT compilation or runtime, when the CLI has been initialized and the architecture is known. This implies that field and stack frame offsets are also not known at compile time. For languages like Visual Basic, where field offsets are not computed early anyway, this is not a hardship. In languages like C or C++, where sizes must be known when source code is compiled, a conservative assumption that they occupy 8 bytes is sometimes acceptable (for example, when laying out compile-time storage).

12.1.1.1 Unmanaged Pointers as Type Native Unsigned Int

RATIONALE

For languages like C, when compiling all the way to native code, where the size of a pointer is known at compile time and there are no managed objects, the fixed-size unsigned integer types (unsigned int32 or unsigned int64) may serve as pointers. However, choosing pointer size at compile time has its disadvantages. If pointers were chosen to be 32-bit quantities at compile time, the code would be restricted to 4 gigabytes of address space, even if it were run on a 64-bit machine. Moreover, a 64-bit CLI would need to take special care so those pointers passed back to 32-bit code would always fit in 32 bits. If pointers were chosen at compile time to be 64 bits, the code would run on a 32-bit machine, but pointers in every data structure would be twice as large as necessary on that CLI.

For other languages, where the size of a data type need not be known at compile time, it is desirable to defer the choice of pointer size from compile time to CLI initialization time. In that way, the same CIL code can handle large address spaces for those applications that need them, while also being able to reap the size benefit of 32-bit pointers for those applications that do not need a large address space.

The native unsigned int type is used to represent unmanaged pointers with the VES. The metadata allows unmanaged pointers to be represented in a strongly typed manner, but these types are translated into type native unsigned int for use by the VES.

12.1.1.2 Managed Pointer Types: O and &

The **O** data type represents an object reference that is managed by the CLI. As such, the number of specified operations is severely limited. In particular, references shall only be used on operations that indicate that they operate on reference types (e.g., **ceq** and **ldind.ref**), or on operations whose metadata indicates that references are allowed (e.g., **call**, **ldsfld**, and **stfld**).

The **&** data type (managed pointer) is similar to the **O** type but points to the interior of an object. That is, a managed pointer is allowed to point to a field within an object or an element within an array, rather than to point to the "start" of object or array.

ANNOTATION: The previous paragraph is accurate but not complete. A managed pointer can also point directly to a value type. It can point to the entire value type on the stack when it is not associated with an object, or it can point, after an unbox operation, to the value type within the boxed object.

Object references (**O**) and managed pointers (**&**) may be changed during garbage collection, since the data to which they refer may be moved.

> **NOTE**
> In summary, object references, or **O** types, refer to the "outside" of an object, or to an object as a whole. But managed pointers, or **&** types, refer to the interior of an object. The **&** types are sometimes called "by-ref types" in source languages, since passing a field of an object by reference is represented in the VES by using an **&** type to represent the type of the parameter.

In order to allow managed pointers to be used more flexibly, they are also permitted to point to areas that aren't under the control of the CLI garbage collector, such as the evaluation stack, static variables, and unmanaged memory. This allows them to be used in many of the same ways that unmanaged pointers (**U**) are used. Verification restrictions guarantee that, if all code is verifiable, a managed pointer to a value on the evaluation stack doesn't outlast the life of the location to which it points.

12.1.1.3 Portability: Storing Pointers in Memory

Several instructions, including **calli**, **cpblk**, **initblk**, **ldind.***, and **stind.***, expect an address on the top of the stack. If this address is derived from a pointer stored in memory, there is an important portability consideration.

1. Code that stores pointers in a native sized integer or pointer location (types **native int**, **O**, **native unsigned int**, or **&**) is always fully portable.
2. Code that stores pointers in an 8-byte integer (type **int64** or **unsigned int64**) *can* be portable. But this requires that a **conv.ovf.u** instruction be used to convert the pointer from its memory format before its use as a pointer. This may cause a runtime exception if run on a 32-bit machine.
3. Code that uses any smaller integer type to store a pointer in memory (**int8**, **unsigned int8**, **int16**, **unsigned int16**, **int32**, **unsigned int32**) is *never* portable, even though the use of an unsigned int32 or int32 will work correctly on a 32-bit machine.

ANNOTATION: This section is directed to compiler writers, or those writing an IL assembly language. If you expect to generate code that works correctly on all machines, it is important to follow these rules.

12.1.2 *Handling of Short Integer Data Types*

The CLI defines an evaluation stack that contains either 4-byte or 8-byte integers, but a memory model that encompasses in addition 1-byte and 2-byte integers. To be more precise, the following rules are part of the CLI model:

- Loading from 1-byte or 2-byte locations (arguments, locals, fields, statics, pointers) expands to 4-byte values. For locations with a known type (e.g., local variables) the type being accessed determines whether the load sign-extends (signed locations) or zero-extends (unsigned locations). For pointer dereference (**ldind.***), the instruction itself identifies the type of the location (e.g., **ldind.u1** indicates an unsigned location, while **ldind.i1** indicates a signed location).
- Storing into a 1-byte or 2-byte location truncates to fit and will not generate an overflow error. Specific instructions (**conv.ovf.***) can be used to test for overflow before storing.
- Calling a method assigns values from the evaluation stack to the arguments for the method, hence it truncates just as any other store would when the actual argument is larger than the formal argument.
- Returning from a method assigns a value to an invisible return variable, so it also truncates as a store would when the type of the value returned is larger than the return type of the method. Since the value of this return variable is then placed on the evaluation

stack, it is then sign-extended or zero-extended as any other load would be. Note that this truncation followed by extending is *not* identical to simply leaving the computed value unchanged.

It is the responsibility of any translator from CIL to native machine instructions to make sure that these rules are faithfully modeled through the native conventions of the target machine. The CLI does not specify, for example, whether truncation of short integer arguments occurs at the call site or in the target method.

ANNOTATION: This section brings out a subtle and important point. It is important to understand when sign extensions and truncations happen automatically without notification. If you are implementing a VES, you have to ensure that these truncations happen. If you are writing an IL assembler or a compiler, you have to know they are happening. For complete information on this, see the tables in Partition III, section 1.5.

12.1.3 *Handling of Floating Point Data Types*

Floating point calculations shall be handled as described in IEC 60559:1989. This standard describes encoding of floating point numbers, definitions of the basic operations and conversion, rounding control, and exception handling.

The standard defines special values, **NaN** (not a number), **+infinity**, and –**infinity**. These values are returned on overflow conditions. A general principle is that operations that have a value in the limit return an appropriate infinity while those that have no limiting value return **NaN**, but see the standard for details.

NOTE

The following examples show the most commonly encountered cases.

X **rem** 0 = **NaN**
0 * **+infinity** = 0 * **-infinity** = **NaN**
(X / 0) = **+infinity**, if X>0
 NaN, if X=0
 -infinity, if X < 0
NaN op X = X op **NaN** = **NaN** for all operations
(**+infinity**) + (**+infinity**) = (**+infinity**)
X / (**+infinity**) = 0
X mod (**-infinity**) = -X
(**+infinity**) – (**+infinity**) = NaN

> **NOTE**
>
> This standard does not specify the behavior of arithmetic operations on denormalized floating point numbers, nor does it specify when or whether such representations should be created. This is in keeping with IEC 60559:1989. In addition, this standard does not specify how to access the exact bit pattern of NaNs that are created, nor the behavior when converting a NaN between 32-bit and 64-bit representation. All of this behavior is deliberately left implementation-specific.

For purposes of comparison, infinite values act like a number of the correct sign but with a very large magnitude when compared with finite values. **NaN** is "unordered" for comparisons (see **clt**, **clt.un**).

While the IEC 60559:1989 standard also allows for exceptions to be thrown under unusual conditions (such as overflow and invalid operand), the CLI does not generate these exceptions. Instead, the CLI uses the **NaN**, **+infinity**, and **–infinity** return values and provides the instruction **ckfinite** to allow users to generate an exception if a result is **NaN**, **+infinity**, or **–infinity**.

The rounding mode defined in IEC 60559:1989 shall be set by the CLI to "round to the nearest number," and neither the CIL nor the class library provide a mechanism for modifying this setting. Conforming implementations of the CLI need not be resilient to external interference with this setting. That is, they need not restore the mode prior to performing floating point operations, but rather may rely on it having been set as part of their initialization.

ANNOTATION: There is an important point in the preceding paragraph: you must do your computation using the specified rounding mode (round to nearest). This is a requirement, not an option. Some scientific computations that require other rounding modes cannot be accommodated in the VES, and these operations need to be done in native code using **PInvoke**.

For conversion to integers, the default operation supplied by the CIL is "truncate toward zero." There are class libraries supplied to allow floating point numbers to be converted to integers using any of the other three traditional operations (**round** to nearest integer, **floor** (truncate towards **–infinity**), **ceiling** (truncate toward **+infinity**)).

Storage locations for floating point numbers (statics, array elements, and fields of classes) are of fixed size. The supported storage sizes are **float32** and **float64**. Everywhere else (on the evaluation stack, as arguments, as return types, and as local variables) floating point numbers are represented using an internal floating point type. In each such instance, the nominal type of the variable or expression is either R4 or R8, but its value may be represented internally with additional range and/or precision. The size of the internal floating point representation is implementation-dependent, may vary, and shall have precision at least as great as that of the variable or expression being represented. An implicit widening conversion to the internal representation from **float32** or **float64** is performed when those types are loaded from storage. The internal representation is typically the native size for the hardware, or as required for efficient implementation of an operation. The internal representation shall have the following characteristics:

- The internal representation shall have precision and range greater than or equal to the nominal type.
- Conversions to and from the internal representation shall preserve value.

NOTE

This implies that an implicit widening conversion from **float32** (or **float64**) to the internal representation, followed by an explicit conversion from the internal representation to **float32** (or **float64**), will result in a value that is identical to the original **float32** (or **float64**) value.

RATIONALE

This design allows the CLI to choose a platform-specific high performance representation for floating point numbers until they are placed in storage locations. For example, it may be able to leave floating point variables in hardware registers that provide more precision than a user has requested. At the same time, CIL generators can force operations to respect language-specific rules for representations through the use of conversion instructions.

When a floating point value whose internal representation has greater range and/or precision than its nominal type is put in a storage location, it is automatically coerced to the type of the storage location. This may involve a loss of precision or the creation of an out-of-range value (NaN, +infinity, or –infinity). However, the value may be retained in the internal representation for future use, if it is reloaded from the storage location without having been modified. It is the responsibility of the compiler to ensure that the retained value is still valid at the time of a subsequent load, taking into account the effects of aliasing and other execution threads (see Partition I, section 12.6). This freedom to carry extra precision is not permitted, however, following the execution of an explicit conversion (conv.r4 or conv.r8), at which time the internal representation must be exactly representable in the associated type.

NOTE

To detect values that cannot be converted to a particular storage type, a conversion instruction (**conv.r4**, or **conv.r8**) may be used, followed by a check for a non-finite value using **ckfinite**. To detect underflow when converting to a particular storage type, a comparison to zero is required before and after the conversion.

NOTE

The use of an internal representation that is wider than **float32** or **float64** may cause differences in computational results when a developer makes seemingly unrelated modifications to their code, the result of which may be that a value is spilled from the internal representation (e.g., in a register) to a location on the stack.

ANNOTATION: The above specification allows a compliant implementation to avoid rounding to the precision of the target type on intermediate computations, and thus permits the use of wider precision hardware registers, as well as the application of optimizing transformations that result in the same or greater precision, such as contractions. Where exactly reproducible precision is required by a language or application (e.g., the Kahan Summation Formula), explicit conversions may be used. Reproducible precision does not guarantee reproducible behavior. Implementations with extra precision may round twice: once for the floating point operation, and once for the explicit conversion. Implementations without extra precision effectively round only once. In rare cases, rounding twice versus rounding once can yield results differing by one unit of least precision.

For example, consider adding two **float64** values via the sequence **add conv.r8**. If the internal floating point type has the same precision as float64, the add instruction rounds to **float64**, and the **conv.r8** has no effect. If the internal floating point type has greater precision, then both instructions might round. Rounding twice can yield a different result from rounding once. Here's a simple example of the principle in decimal: Consider the value $1.49. If rounded to dimes, it's $1.50, and rounding $1.50 to dollars yields $2.00 (by the usual round-to-even rule). But rounding $1.49 directly to dollars yields $1.00.

– Arch Robison

It is left to the implementation of the CLI whether to support precise floating point computations.

ANNOTATION: To those not familiar with floating point arithmetic, a word of caution. It is very easy to underestimate the subtlety of small implementation decisions that have profound effects. People writing the standard strongly advise you to hire a professional floating point expert if you are worried about such things, because novices can make mistakes that ultimately crash space shuttles.

12.1.4 *CIL Instructions and Numeric Types*

This section contains only informative text.

Most CIL instructions that deal with numbers take their operands from the evaluation stack (see Partition I, section 12.3.2.1), and these inputs have an associated type that is known to the VES. As a result, a single operation like **add** can have inputs of any numeric data type, although not all instructions can deal with all combinations of operand types. Binary operations other than addition and subtraction require that both operands be of the same type. Addition and subtraction allow an integer to be added to or subtracted from a managed pointer (types **&** and **O**). Details are specified in Partition II.

Instructions fall into the following categories:

Numeric: These instructions deal with both integers and floating point numbers, and consider integers to be signed. Simple arithmetic, conditional branch, and comparison instructions fit in this category.

Integer: These instructions deal only with integers. Bit operations and unsigned integer division/remainder fit in this category.

Floating point: These instructions deal only with floating point numbers.

Specific: These instructions deal with integer and/or floating point numbers, but have variants that deal specially with different sizes and unsigned integers. Integer operations with overflow detection, data conversion instructions, and operations that transfer data between the evaluation stack and other parts of memory (see Partition I, section 12.3.2) fit into this category.

Unsigned/unordered: There are special comparison and branch instructions that treat integers as unsigned and consider unordered floating point numbers specially (as in "branch if greater than or unordered"):

Load constant: The load constant (**ldc.***) instructions are used to load constants of type int32, int64, float32, or float64. Native size constants (type native int) shall be created by conversion from int32 (conversion from int64 would not be portable) using **conv.i** or **conv.u.** Table 2-7, CIL Instructions by Numeric Category, shows the CIL instructions that

Table 2-7 CIL Instructions by Numeric Category

Instruction	Category
add	Numeric
add.ovf.*	Specific
and	Integer
beq[.s]	Numeric
bge[.s]	Numeric
bge.un[.s]	Unsigned/ unordered
bgt[.s]	Numeric
bgt.un[.s]	Unsigned/ unordered
ble[.s]	Numeric
ble.un[.s]	Unsigned/ unordered
blt[.s]	Numeric
blt.un[.s]	Unsigned/ unordered
bne.un[.s]	Unsigned/ unordered
ceq	Numeric
cgt	Numeric
cgt.un	Unsigned/ unordered
ckfinite	Floating point
clt	Numeric
clt.un	Unsigned/ unordered
conv.*	Specific
conv.ovf.*	Specific
div	Numeric
div.un	Integer
ldc.*	Load constant
ldelem.*	Specific
ldind.*	Specific
mul	Numeric
mul.ovf.*	Specific
neg	Integer
newarr.*	Specific
not	Integer
or	Integer
rem	Numeric
rem.un	Integer
shl	Integer
shr	Integer
shr.un	Specific
stelem.*	Specific
stind.*	Specific
sub	Numeric
sub.ovf.*	Specific
xor	Integer

deal with numeric values, along with the category to which they belong. Instructions that end in ".*" indicate all variants of the instruction (based on size of data and whether the data is treated as signed or unsigned).

End informative text

12.1.5 *CIL Instructions and Pointer Types*

This section contains only informative text.

> **RATIONALE**
> Some implementations of the CLI will require the ability to track pointers to objects and to collect objects that are no longer reachable (thus providing memory management by "garbage collection"). This process moves objects in order to reduce the working set and thus will modify all pointers to those objects as they move. For this to work correctly, pointers to objects may only be used in certain ways. The **O** (object reference) and **&** (managed pointer) datatypes are the formalization of these restrictions.

The use of object references is tightly restricted in the CIL. They are used almost exclusively with the "virtual object system" instructions, which are specifically designed to deal with objects. In addition, a few of the base instructions of the CIL handle object references. In particular, object references can be:

1. Loaded onto the evaluation stack to be passed as arguments to methods (**ldloc**, **ldarg**), and stored from the stack to their home locations (**stloc, starg**)
2. Duplicated or popped off the evaluation stack (**dup**, **pop**)
3. Tested for equality with one another, but not other data types (**beq**, **beq.s**, **bne**, **bne.s**, **ceq**)
4. Loaded from / stored into unmanaged memory, in type unmanaged code only (**ldind.ref**, **stind.ref**)
5. Created as a null reference (**ldnull**)
6. Returned as a value (**ret**)

Managed pointers have several additional base operations.

1. Addition and subtraction of integers, in units of *bytes*, returning a managed pointer (**add**, **add.ovf.u**, **sub**, **sub.ovf.u**)
2. Subtraction of two managed pointers to elements of the same array, returning the number of *bytes* between them (**sub**, **sub.ovf.u**)
3. Unsigned comparison and conditional branches based on two managed pointers (**bge.un**, **bge.un.s**, **bgt.un**, **bgt.un.s**, **ble.un**, **ble.un.s**, **blt.un**, **blt.un.s**, **cgt.un**, **clt.un**)

Arithmetic operations upon managed pointers are intended *only* for use on pointers to elements of the same array. Other uses of arithmetic on managed pointers is unspecified.

RATIONALE

Since the memory manager runs asynchronously with respect to programs and updates managed pointers, both the distance between distinct objects and their relative position can change.

End informative text

12.1.6 *Aggregate Data*

This section contains only informative text.

The CLI supports *aggregate data*, that is, data items that have sub-components (arrays, structures, or object instances) but are passed by copying the value. The sub-components can include references to managed memory. Aggregate data is represented using a *value type*, which can be instantiated in two different ways:

- **Boxed**: as an Object, carrying full type information at runtime, and typically allocated on the heap by the CLI memory manager.
- **Unboxed**: as a "value type instance" that does *not* carry type information at runtime and that is never allocated directly on the heap. It can be part of a larger structure on the heap—a field of a class, a field of a boxed value type, or an element of an array. Or it can be in the local variables or incoming arguments array (see Partition I, section 12.3.2). Or it can be allocated as a static variable or static member of a class or a static member of another value type.

Because value type instances, specified as method arguments, are copied on method call, they do not have "identity" in the sense that Objects (boxed instances of classes) have.

12.1.6.1 Homes for Values

The **home** of a data value is where it is stored for possible reuse. The CLI directly supports the following home locations:

- An incoming **argument**
- A **local variable** of a method
- An instance **field** of an object or value type
- A **static** field of a class, interface, or module
- An **array element**

For each home location, there is a means to compute (at runtime) the address of the home location and a means to determine (at JIT compile time) the type of a home location. These are summarized in Table 2-8, Address and Type of Home Locations.

In addition to homes, built-in values can exist in two additional ways (i.e., without homes):

1. As constant values (typically embedded in the CIL instruction stream using **ldc.*** instructions)
2. As an intermediate value on the evaluation stack, when returned by a method or CIL instruction

Table 2-8 Address and Type of Home Locations

Type of Home	Runtime Address Computation	JITtime Type Determination
Argument	ldarga for by-value arguments or ldarg for by-reference arguments	Method signature
Local Variable	ldloca for by-value locals or ldloc for by-reference locals	Locals signature in method header
Field	ldflda	Type of field in the class, interface, or module
Static	ldsflda	Type of field in the class, interface, or module
Array Element	ldelema for single-dimensional zero-based arrays or call the instance method Address	Element type of array

12.1.6.2 Operations on Value Type Instances

Value type instances can be created (see Partition I, section 12.1.6.2.1), passed as arguments (see Partition I, section 12.1.6.2.3), returned as values (see Partition I, section 12.1.6.2.3), and stored into and extracted from locals, fields, and elements of arrays (i.e., copied). Like classes, value types may have both static and non-static members (methods and fields). But, because they carry no type information at runtime, value type instances are not substitutable for items of type Object; in this respect, they act like the built-in types int, long, and so forth. There are two operations, box and unbox (see Partition I, sections 8.2.4 and 12.1.6.2.5), that convert between value type instances and Objects.

12.1.6.2.1 Initializing Instances of Value Types

There are three options for initializing the home of a value type instance. You can zero it by loading the address of the home (see Table 2-8, Address and Type of Home Locations) and using the **initobj** instruction (for local variables this is also accomplished by setting the **zero initialize** bit in the method's header). You can call a user-defined constructor by loading the address of the home (see Table 2-8, Address and Type of Home Locations) and then calling the constructor directly. Or you can copy an existing instance into the home, as described in Partition I, section 12.1.6.2.

ANNOTATION: The "zero init flag" syntax is the **.local init** directive in the assembler syntax, and the flag **CorILMethod_InitLocals** in the file format (see Partition II, section 24.4.4).

12.1.6.2.2 Loading and Storing Instances of Value Types

There are two ways to load a value type onto the evaluation stack:

- Directly load the value from a home that has the appropriate type, using an **ldarg**, **ldloc**, **ldfld**, or **ldsfld** instruction.
- Compute the address of the value type, then use an **ldobj** instruction.

Similarly, there are two ways to store a value type from the evaluation stack:

- Directly store the value into a home of the appropriate type, using a **starg**, **stloc**, **stfld**, or **stsfld** instruction.
- Compute the address of the value type, then use a **stobj** instruction.

12.1.6.2.3 Passing and Returning Value Types

Value types are treated just as any other value would be treated:

- **To pass a value type by value**, simply load it onto the stack as you would any other argument: use **ldloc**, **ldarg**, etc., or call a method that returns a value type. To access a value type parameter that has been passed by value, use the **ldarga** instruction to compute its address or the **ldarg** instruction to load the value onto the evaluation stack.

- **To pass a value type by reference**, load the address of the value type as you normally would (see Table 2-8, Address and Type of Home Locations). To access a value type parameter that has been passed by reference, use the **ldarg** instruction to load the address of the value type and then the **ldobj** instruction to load the value type onto the evaluation stack.
- **To return a value type**, just load the value onto an otherwise empty evaluation stack and then issue a **ret** instruction.

12.1.6.2.4 ***Calling Methods***

Static methods on value types are handled no differently from static methods on an ordinary class: use a **call** instruction with a metadata token specifying the value type as the class of the method. Non-static methods (i.e., instance and virtual methods) are supported on value types, but they are given special treatment. A non-static method on a class (rather than a value type) expects a **this** pointer that is an instance of that class. This makes sense for classes, since they have identity and the **this** pointer represents that identity. Value types, however, have identity only when boxed. To address this issue, the **this** pointer on a non-static method of a value type is a by-ref parameter of the value type rather than an ordinary by-value parameter.

A non-static method on a value type may be called in the following ways:

- Given an unboxed instance of a value type, the compiler will know the exact type of the object statically. The **call** instruction can be used to invoke the function, passing as the first parameter (the **this** pointer) the address of the instance. The metadata token used with the **call** instruction shall specify the value type itself as the class of the method.
- Given a boxed instance of a value type, there are three cases to consider:
  - Instance or virtual methods introduced on the value type itself: unbox the instance and call the method directly using the value type as the class of the method.
  - Virtual methods inherited from a parent class: use the **callvirt** instruction and specify the method on the `System.Object`, `System.ValueType`, or `System.Enum` class as appropriate.
  - Virtual methods on interfaces implemented by the value type: use the **callvirt** instruction and specify the method on the interface type.

12.1.6.2.5 ***Boxing and Unboxing***

Box and **unbox** are conceptually equivalent to (and may be seen in higher-level languages as) casting between a value type instance and `System.Object`. Because they change data representations, however, boxing and unboxing are like the widening and narrowing of various sizes of integers (the **conv** and **conv.ovf** instructions) rather than the casting of reference types (the **isinst** and **castclass** instructions). The **box** instruction is a widening (always typesafe) operation that converts a value type instance to `System.Object` by making a copy of the instance and embedding it in a newly allocated object. **Unbox** is a narrowing (runtime exception may be generated) operation that converts a `System.Object` (whose runtime type is a value type) to a value type instance. This is done by computing the address of the embedded value type instance without making a copy of the instance.

12.1.6.2.6 Castclass and Isinst on Value Types

Casting to and from value type instances isn't permitted (the equivalent operations are **box** and **unbox**). When boxed, however, it is possible to use the **isinst** instruction to see whether a value of type `System.Object` is the boxed representation of a particular class.

12.1.6.3 Opaque Classes

Some languages provide multi-byte data structures whose contents are manipulated directly by address arithmetic and indirection operations. To support this feature, the CLI allows value types to be created with a specified size but no information about their data members. Instances of these "opaque classes" are handled in precisely the same way as instances of any other class, but the **ldfld**, **stfld**, **ldflda**, **ldsfld**, and **stsfld** instructions shall not be used to access their contents.

ANNOTATION: Opaque classes were included to support languages like C, C++, and COBOL, which have multi-byte data types, where the individual fields are not intended to be seen by other languages. So you may pass a lump of data, or the address of a lump of data, but the actual content is intended only for the language that defined it.

End informative text

12.2 Module Information

Partition II[, section 24 and its subsections] provides details of the CLI PE file format. The CLI relies on the following information about each method defined in a PE file:

- The *instructions* composing the method body, including all exception handlers.
- The *signature* of the method, which specifies the return type and the number, order, parameter passing convention, and built-in data type of each of the arguments. It also

specifies the native calling convention (this does *not* affect the CIL virtual calling convention, just the native code).

- The *exception handling array*. This array holds information delineating the ranges over which exceptions are filtered and caught. See Partition II and Partition I, section 12.4.2.
- The size of the evaluation stack that the method will require.
- The size of the locals array that the method will require.

ANNOTATION: The size of the evaluation stack is not the number of machine words, or bytes needed, but the number of pushes of objects or data on the stack. The size of the locals array is not in bytes, but the number of locals.

The JIT compiler is free to discover that not all the locals are actually needed, and not to allocate space for them, or to overlap that space with the evaluation stack where appropriate. The actual size at runtime bears no relation to these numbers, which are for JIT compilers or interpreters, to allow them to size their data structures.

- A "zero init flag" that indicates whether the local variables and memory pool should be initialized by the CLI (see also **localloc**).
- Type of each local variable in the form of a signature of the local variable array (called the "locals signature").

In addition, the file format is capable of indicating the degree of portability of the file. There is one kind of restriction that may be described:

- Restriction to a specific (32-bit) native size for integers.

By stating which restrictions are placed on executing the code, the CLI class loader can prevent non-portable code from running on an architecture that it cannot support.

ANNOTATION: The "zero init flag" syntax is the **.local init** directive in the assembler syntax, and the flag **CorILMethod_InitLocals** in the file format (see Partition II, section 24.4.4).

12.3 Machine State

One of the design goals of the CLI is to hide the details of a method call frame from the CIL code generator. This allows the VES (and not the CIL code generator) to choose the most efficient calling convention and stack layout. To achieve this abstraction, the call frame is integrated into the CLI. The machine state definitions below reflect these design choices, where machine state consists primarily of global state and method state.

12.3.1 *The Global State*

The CLI manages multiple concurrent threads of control (not necessarily the same as the threads provided by a host operating system), multiple managed heaps, and a shared memory address space.

> **NOTE**
>
> A thread of control can be thought of, somewhat simplistically, as a singly linked list of *method states*, where a new state is created and linked back to the current state by a method call instruction—the traditional model of a stack-based calling sequence. Notice that this model of the thread of control doesn't correctly explain the operation of **tail.**, **jmp**, or **throw** instructions.

Figure 2-4, Machine State Model, illustrates the machine state model, which includes threads of control, method states, and multiple heaps in a shared address space. Method state, shown separately in Figure 2-5, Method State, is an abstraction of the stack frame. Arguments and local variables are part of the method state, but they can contain Object References that refer to data stored in any of the managed heaps. In general, arguments and local variables are only visible to the executing thread, while instance and static fields and array elements may be visible to multiple threads, and modification of such values is considered a side-effect.

12.3.2 *Method State*

Method state describes the environment within which a method executes. (In conventional compiler terminology, it corresponds to a superset of the information captured in the "invocation stack frame.") The CLI method state consists of the following items:

- An instruction pointer (**IP**). This points to the next CIL instruction to be executed by the CLI in the present method.
- An *evaluation stack*. The stack is empty upon method entry. Its contents are entirely local to the method and are preserved across call instructions (that's to say, if this method calls another, once that other method returns, our evaluation stack contents are "still there.") The evaluation stack is not addressable. At all times it is possible to deduce which one of a reduced set of types is stored in any stack location at a specific point in the CIL instruction stream (see Partition I, section 12.3.2.1).

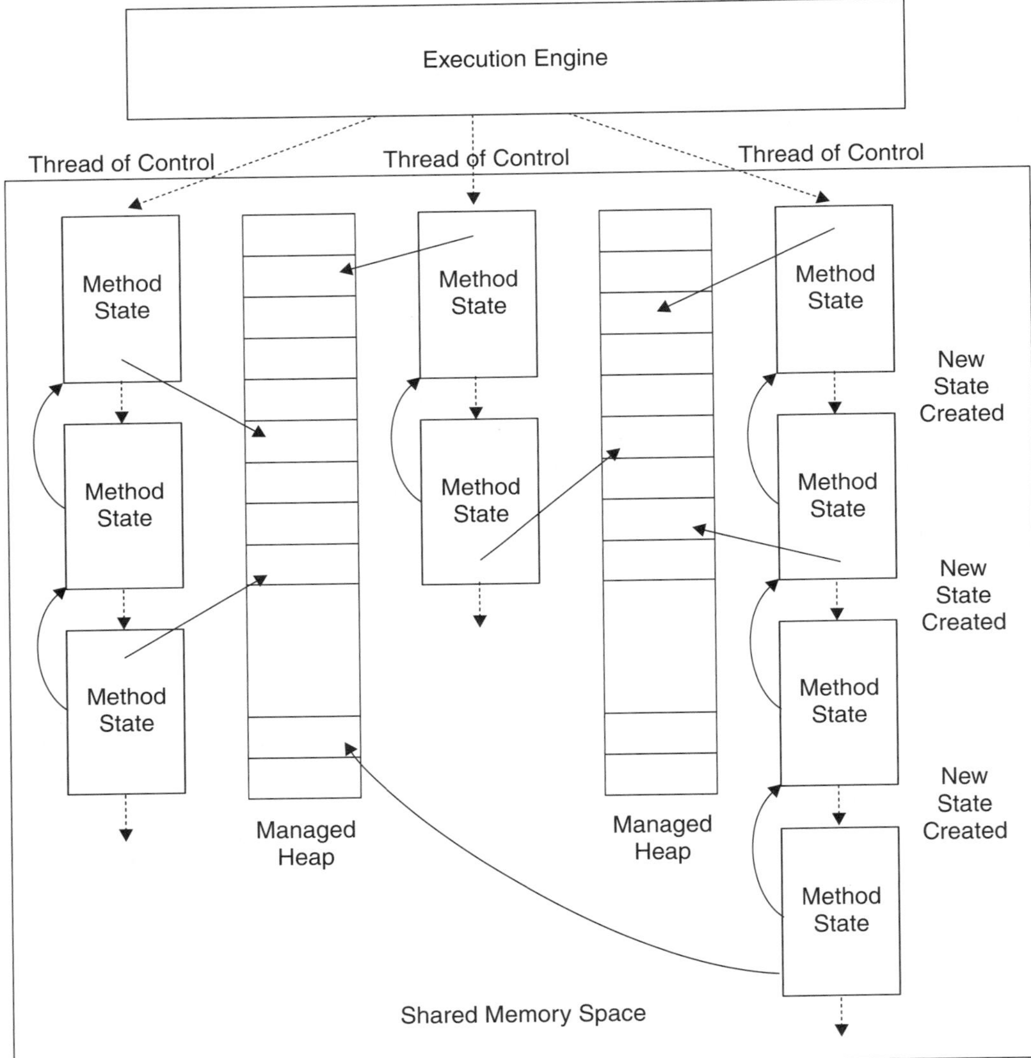

Figure 2-4 Machine State Model

- A *local variable array* (starting at index 0). Values of local variables are preserved across calls (in the same sense as for the evaluation stack). A local variable may hold any data type. However, a particular slot shall be used in a type-consistent way (where the type system is the one described in Partition I, section 12.3.2.1). Local variables are initialized to 0 before entry if the initialize flag for the method is set (see Partition II, section 12.2). The address of an individual local variable may be taken using the **ldloca** instruction.

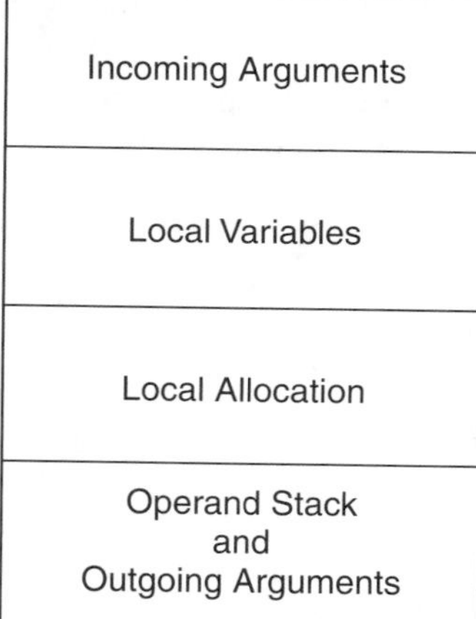

Figure 2-5 Method State

ANNOTATION: The ilasm syntax for initializing local variables to 0 is the **.local init** directive (see Partition II, section 12.2). In the file format it is the flag **CorILMethod_InitLocals**, described in Partition II, section 24.4.4.

- An *argument array.* The values of the current method's incoming arguments (starting at index 0). These can be read and written by logical index. The address of an argument can be taken using the **ldarga** instruction. The address of an argument is also implicitly taken by the **arglist** instruction for use in conjunction with typesafe iteration through variable-length argument lists.
- A *methodInfo* handle. This contains read-only information about the method. In particular it holds the signature of the method, the types of its local variables, and data about its exception handlers.
- A *local memory pool.* The CLI includes instructions for dynamic allocation of objects from the local memory pool (**localloc**). Memory allocated in the local memory pool is *addressable.* The memory allocated in the local memory pool is reclaimed upon method context termination.
- A *return state* handle. This handle is used to restore the method state on return from the current method. Typically, this would be the state of the method's caller. This corresponds to what in conventional compiler terminology would be the *dynamic link.*
- A *security descriptor.* This descriptor is not directly accessible to managed code but is used by the CLI security system to record security overrides (**assert**, **permit-only**, and **deny**).

The four areas of the method state—incoming arguments array, local variables array, local memory pool, and evaluation stack—are specified as if logically distinct areas. A conforming implementation of the CLI may map these areas into one contiguous array of memory, held as a conventional stack frame on the underlying target architecture, or use any other equivalent representation technique.

12.3.2.1 The Evaluation Stack

Associated with each method state is an evaluation stack. Most CLI instructions retrieve their arguments from the evaluation stack and place their return values on the stack. Arguments to other methods and their return values are also placed on the evaluation stack. When a procedure call is made, the arguments to the called methods become the incoming arguments array (see Partition I, section 12.3.2.2) to the method. This may require a memory copy, or simply a sharing of these two areas by the two methods.

The evaluation stack is made up of slots that can hold any data type, including an unboxed instance of a value type. The type state of the stack (the stack depth and types of each element on the stack) at any given point in a program shall be identical for all possible control flow paths. For example, a program that loops an unknown number of times and pushes a new element on the stack at each iteration would be prohibited.

While the CLI, in general, supports the full set of types described in Partition I, section 12.1, the CLI treats the evaluation stack in a special way. While some JIT compilers may track the types on the stack in more detail, the CLI only requires that values be one of:

- int64, an 8-byte signed integer
- int32, a 4-byte signed integer
- native int, a signed integer of either 4 or 8 bytes, whichever is more convenient for the target architecture
- F, a floating point value (float32, float64, or other representation supported by the underlying hardware)
- &, a managed pointer
- O, an object reference
- *, a "transient pointer," which may be used only within the body of a single method, that points to a value known to be in unmanaged memory (see Partition III for more details. * types are generated internally within the CLI; they are not created by the user).

ANNOTATION: Transient pointers affect only those writing for CIL or an assembly language. They are not visible in higher-level languages. A transient pointer is a legitimate managed pointer to a managed data type, but the data is known to be stored in a place where it cannot be moved by the garbage collector. This means that transient pointers can be passed to unmanaged code, which needs absolute memory addresses that won't move.

- A user-defined value type

The other types are synthesized through a combination of techniques:

- Shorter integer types in other memory locations are zero-extended or sign-extended when loaded onto the evaluation stack; these values are truncated when stored back to their home location.
- Special instructions perform numeric conversions, with or without overflow detection, between different sizes and between signed and unsigned integers.
- Special instructions treat an integer on the stack as though it were unsigned.
- Instructions that create pointers which are guaranteed not to point into the memory manager's heaps (e.g., **ldloca**, **ldarga**, and **ldsflda**) produce transient pointers (type *) that may be used wherever a managed pointer (type &) or unmanaged pointer (type **native unsigned int**) is expected.
- When a method is called, an unmanaged pointer (type **native unsigned int** or *) is permitted to match a parameter that requires a managed pointer (type &). The reverse, however, is *not* permitted, since it would allow a managed pointer to be "lost" by the memory manager.
- A managed pointer (type &) may be explicitly converted to an unmanaged pointer (type **native unsigned int**), although this is not verifiable and may produce a runtime exception.

ANNOTATION: Managed pointers can be converted to unmanaged pointers. If the managed pointer points into the stack or unmanaged memory, it is safe to turn it into an unmanaged pointer. But if it is pointing into the garbage collector heap, it is not legal and will produce a runtime exception.

12.3.2.2 Local Variables and Arguments

Part of each method state is an array that holds local variables and an array that holds arguments. Like the evaluation stack, each element of these arrays can hold any single data type or an instance of a value type. Both arrays start at 0 (that is, the first argument or local variable is numbered 0). The address of a local variable can be computed using the **ldloca** instruction, and the address of an argument using the **ldarga** instruction.

Associated with each method is metadata that specifies:

- Whether the local variables and memory pool memory will be initialized when the method is entered

---

ANNOTATION: The ilasm syntax for initializing local variables to 0 is the **.local init** directive (see Partition II, section 12.2). In the file format it is the flag **CorILMethod_InitLocals**, described in Partition II, section 24.4.4.

- The type of each argument and the length of the argument array (but see below for variable[-length] argument lists)
- The type of each local variable and the length of the local variable array

The VES inserts padding as appropriate for the target architecture. That is, on some 64-bit architectures all local variables may be 64-bit aligned, while on others they may be 8-, 16-, or 32-bit aligned. The CIL generator shall make no assumptions about the offsets of local variables within the array. In fact, the VES is free to reorder the elements in the local variable array, and different JITters may choose to order them in different ways.

12.3.2.3 Variable[-Length] Argument Lists

The CLI works in conjunction with the class library to implement methods that accept argument lists of unknown length and type ("varargs methods"). Access to these arguments is through a typesafe iterator in the [Base] Class Library, called `System.ArgIterator` (see the *.NET Framework Standard Library Annotated Reference*).

The CIL includes one instruction provided specifically to support the argument iterator, **arglist**. This instruction may be used only within a method that is declared to take a variable number of arguments. It returns a value that is needed by the constructor for a `System.ArgIterator` object. Basically, the value created by **arglist** provides access both to the address of the argument list that was passed to the method and a runtime data structure that specifies the number and type of the arguments that were provided. This is sufficient for the class library to implement the user-visible iteration mechanism.

From the CLI point of view, varargs methods have an array of arguments like other methods. But only the initial portion of the array has a fixed set of types, and only these may be accessed directly using the **ldarg**, **starg**, and **ldarga** instructions. The argument iterator allows access to both this initial segment and the remaining entries in the array.

ANNOTATION: Support for variable-length argument lists is not part of the minimum requirement for implementing the CLI, so a given implementation may not support it. The library support for it, `System.ArgIterator`, is not standardized.

12.3.2.4 Local Memory Pool

Part of each method state is a local memory pool. Memory can be explicitly allocated from the local memory pool using the **localloc** instruction. All memory in the local memory pool is reclaimed on method exit, and that is the only way local memory pool memory is reclaimed (there is no instruction provided to *free* local memory that was allocated during this method invocation). The local memory pool is used to allocate objects whose type or size is not known at compile time and which the programmer does not wish to allocate in the managed heap.

Because the local memory pool cannot be shrunk during the lifetime of the method, a language implementation cannot use the local memory pool for general-purpose memory allocation.

ANNOTATION: Support for the local memory pool is not part of the minimum requirement for implementing the CLI. Therefore, the **localloc** instruction may not be available in your implementation.

12.4 Control Flow

The CIL instruction set provides a rich set of instructions to alter the normal flow of control from one CIL instruction to the next.

- **Conditional and Unconditional Branch** instructions for use within a method, provided the transfer doesn't cross a protected region boundary (see Partition I, section 12.4.2).
- **Method call** instructions to compute new arguments, [and to] transfer them and control to a known or computed destination method (see Partition I, section 12.4.1).
- **Tail call** prefix to indicate that a method should relinquish its stack frame before executing a method call (see Partition I, section 12.4.1).
- **Return** from a method, returning a value if necessary.
- **Method jump** instructions to transfer the current method's arguments to a known or computed destination method (see Partition I, section 12.4.1).

- **Exception-related** instructions (see Partition I, section 12.4.2). These include instructions to initiate an exception, transfer control out of a protected region, and end a filter, catch clause, or finally clause.

While the CLI supports control transfers within a method, there are several restrictions that shall be observed:

1. Control transfer is never permitted to enter a catch handler or finally clause (see Partition I, section 12.4.2) except through the exception handling mechanism.
2. Control transfer out of a protected region (see Partition I, section 12.4.2) is only permitted through an exception instruction (**leave**, **endfilter**, **endcatch**, or **endfinally**).
3. The evaluation stack shall be empty after the return value is popped by a **ret** instruction.
4. Each slot on the stack shall have the same data type at any given point within the method body, regardless of the control flow that allows execution to arrive there.
5. In order for the JIT compilers to efficiently track the data types stored on the stack, the stack shall normally be empty at the instruction following an unconditional control transfer instruction (**br**, **br.s**, **ret**, **jmp**, **throw**, **endfilter**, **endcatch**, or **endfinally**). The stack may be non-empty at such an instruction only if at some earlier location within the method there has been a forward branch to that instruction.
6. Control is not permitted to simply "fall through" the end of a method. All paths shall terminate with one of these instructions: **ret**, **throw**, **jmp**, or (**tail.** followed by **call**, **calli**, or **callvirt**).

ANNOTATION: Points 1 and 2 in the preceding list are described more fully in Partition I, section 12.4.2. Points 3 and 4 are common restrictions on virtual machines, although they are unusual in hardware. Point 5, concerning method jump instructions, is fairly tricky from the point of view of a compiler, and too easily overlooked. It says that there are certain rotations of loops that you cannot perform. After an unconditional jump, the VES assumes that the evaluation stack is empty unless there has been a forward branch to that location. For generating portable code this is important because not all JITs enforce this constraint. Although it is possible to write a compiler that does not follow this rule, such a compiler would run on only some implementations of the VES.

ANNOTATION: Support for exception filters is not part of the minimum requirement for implementing the CLI. Therefore, the **endfilter** instruction may not be available in your implementation.

12.4.1 *Method Calls*

Instructions emitted by the CIL code generator contain sufficient information for different implementations of the CLI to use different native calling conventions. All method calls initialize the method state areas (see Partition I, section 12.3.2) as follows:

1. The incoming arguments array is set by the caller to the desired values.
2. The local variables array always has **null** for Object types and for fields within value types that hold objects. In addition, if the "zero init flag" is set in the method header, then the local variables array is initialized to 0 for all integer types and 0.0 for all floating point types. ValueTypes are not initialized by the CLI, but verified code will supply a call to an initializer as part of the method's entry point code.

ANNOTATION: The last sentence of number 2 above is not accurate. To be verifiable, the zero init flag must be set. The ilasm syntax for setting this is the **.local init** directive (see Partition II, section 12.2). In the file format it is the flag **CorILMethod_InitLocals**, described in Partition II, section 24.4.4.

- 3.The evaluation stack is empty.

12.4.1.1 Call Site Descriptors

Call sites specify additional information that enables an interpreter or JIT compiler to synthesize any native calling convention. All CIL calling instructions (**call, calli,** and **callvirt**) include a description of the call site. This description can take one of two forms. The simpler form, used with the **calli** instruction, is a "call site description" (represented as a metadata token for a stand-alone call signature) that provides:

- The number of arguments being passed
- The data type of each argument
- The order in which they have been placed on the call stack
- The native calling convention to be used

The more complicated form, used for the **call** and **callvirt** instructions, is a "method reference" (a metadata **methodref** token) that augments the call site description with an identifier for the target of the call instruction.

ANNOTATION: Many see the **call** instruction as simpler than the **calli** instruction, although the reverse is true from the point of view of the call site descriptor. The **calli** instruction actually provides less information, which is what is meant by simpler here. In the **calli** instruction, the destination address is computed at runtime, so that information is not part of the call. It carries all of the other information—the number of arguments, the type of each argument, the order of arguments, the calling convention. With **call** and **callvirt** you also know the destination of the call.

12.4.1.2 Calling Instructions

The CIL has three call instructions that are used to transfer new argument values to a destination method. Under normal circumstances, the called method will terminate and return control to the calling method.

- **call** is designed to be used when the destination address is fixed at the time the CIL is generated. In this case, a method reference is placed directly in the instruction. This is comparable to a direct call to a static function in C. It may be used to call static or instance methods or the (statically known) superclass method within an instance method body.
- **calli** is designed for use when the destination address is calculated at runtime. A method pointer is passed on the stack, and the instruction contains only the call site description.
- **callvirt** uses the exact type of an object (known only at runtime) to determine the method to be called. The instruction includes a method reference, but the particular method isn't computed until the call actually occurs. This allows an instance of a subclass to be supplied and the method appropriate for that subclass to be invoked. The **callvirt** instruction is used both for instance methods and methods on interfaces.

In addition, each of these instructions may be immediately preceded by a `tail.` instruction prefix. This specifies that the calling method terminates with this method call (and returns whatever value is returned by the called method). The `tail.` prefix instructs the JIT compiler to discard the caller's method state prior to making the call (if the call is from untrusted code to trusted code, the frame cannot be fully discarded for security reasons). When the called method executes a **ret** instruction, control returns not to the calling method but rather to wherever that method would itself have returned (typically, to the caller's caller). Notice that the `tail.` instruction shortens the lifetime of the caller's frame so it is unsafe to pass managed pointers (type &) as arguments.

Finally, there is an instruction that indicates an optimization of the `tail.` case, which is the **jmp** instruction, followed by a **methodref** or **methoddef** token, and indicates that the current method's state should be discarded, its arguments should be transferred intact to the destination method, and control should be transferred to the destination. The signature of the calling method shall exactly match the signature of the destination method.

12.4.1.3 Computed Destinations

The destination of a method call may be either encoded directly in the CIL instruction stream (the **call** and **jmp** instructions) or computed (the **callvirt** and **calli** instructions). The destination address for a **callvirt** instruction is automatically computed by the CLI based on the method token and the value of the first argument (the **this** pointer). The method token shall refer to a virtual method on a class that is a direct ancestor of the class of the first argument. The CLI computes the correct destination by locating the nearest ancestor of the first argument's class that supplies an implementation of the desired method.

> **NOTE**
> The implementation can be assumed to be more efficient than the linear search implied here.

For the **calli** instruction the CIL code is responsible for computing a destination address and pushing it on the stack. This is typically done through the use of a **ldftn** or **ldvirtfn** instruction at some earlier time. The **ldftn** instruction includes a metadata token in the CIL stream that specifies a method, and the instruction pushes the address of that method. The **ldvirtfn** instruction takes a metadata token for a virtual method in the CIL stream and an object on the stack. It performs the same computation described above for the **callvirt** instruction but pushes the resulting destination on the stack rather than calling the method.

The **calli** instruction includes a call site description that includes information about the native calling convention that should be used to invoke the method. Correct CIL code shall specify a calling convention specified in the **calli** instruction that matches the calling convention for the method that is being called.

12.4.1.4 Virtual Calling Convention

The CIL provides a "virtual calling convention" that is converted by the JIT into a native calling convention. The JIT determines the optimal native calling convention for the target architecture. This allows the native calling convention to differ from machine to machine, including details of register usage, local variable homes, copying conventions for large call-by-value objects (as well as deciding, based on the target machine, what is considered "large"). This also allows the JIT to reorder the values placed on the CIL virtual stack to match the location and order of arguments passed in the native calling convention.

The CLI uses a single uniform calling convention for all method calls. It is the responsibility of the JITters to convert this into the appropriate native calling convention. The contents of the stack at the time of a call instruction (call, calli, or callvirt—any of which may be preceded by `tail.`) are as follows:

1. If the method being called is an instance method (class or interface) or a virtual method, the **this** pointer is the first object on the stack at the time of the call instruction. For methods on Objects (including boxed value types), the **this** pointer is of type O (object reference). For methods on value types, the **this** pointer is provided as a by-ref parameter; that is, the value is a pointer (managed, &, or unmanaged, *, or native int) to the instance.
2. The remaining arguments appear on the stack in left-to-right order (that is, the lexically leftmost argument is the first push on the stack, immediately following the **this** pointer, if any). Partition I, section 12.4.1.5 describes how each of the three parameter passing conventions (by-value, by-reference, and typed reference) should be implemented.

ANNOTATION: The main thrust of this section is that the calling convention of CIL has nothing to do with the calling convention of the underlying native system.

Although JIT (just-in-time) compilation is not required by this standard, it is commonly used, and it relates directly to this discussion of calling convention. Most implementations do use it, however. The assumption is that source language compilers produce CIL (the Common Intermediate Language) only. If the implementation does not have a JIT compiler, it may have an interpreter.

12.4.1.5 Parameter Passing

The CLI supports three kinds of parameter passing, all indicated in metadata as part of the signature of the method. Each parameter to a method has its own passing convention (e.g., the first parameter may be passed by value while all others are passed by ref). Parameters shall be passed in one of the following ways (see detailed descriptions below):

- **By-value** parameters, where the **value** of an object is passed from the caller to the callee.
- **By-ref** parameters, where the **address** of the data is passed from the caller to the callee, and the type of the parameter is therefore a managed or unmanaged pointer.
- **Typed reference** parameters, where a runtime representation of the data type is passed along with the address of the data, and the type of the parameter is therefore one specially supplied for this purpose.

It is the responsibility of the CIL generator to follow these conventions. Verification checks that the types of parameters match the types of values passed, but is otherwise unaware of the details of the calling convention.

12.4.1.5.1 *By-Value Parameters*

For built-in types (integers, floats, etc.) the caller copies the value onto the stack before the call. For objects, the object reference (type **O**) is pushed on the stack. For managed pointers (type **&**) or unmanaged pointers (type **native unsigned int**), the address is passed from the caller to the callee. For value types, see the protocol in Partition I, section 12.1.6.2.

12.4.1.5.2 *By-Ref Parameters*

By-ref parameters are the equivalent of C++ reference parameters or Pascal **var** parameters: instead of passing as an argument the value of a variable, field, or array element, its address is passed instead; and any assignment to the corresponding parameter actually modifies the corresponding caller's variable, field, or array element. Much of this work is done by the higher-level language, which hides from the user the need to compute addresses to pass a value and the use of indirection to reference or update values.

Passing a value by reference requires that the value have a home (see Partition I, section 12.1.6.1), and it is the address of this home that is passed. Constants, and intermediate values on the evaluation stack, cannot be passed as by-ref parameters because they have no home.

The CLI provides instructions to support by-ref parameters:

- Calculate addresses of home locations (see Table 2-8, Address and Type of Home Locations).
- Load and store built-in data types through these address pointers (**ldind.***, **stind.***, **ldfld,** etc.).
- Ccopy value types (**ldobj** and **cpobj**).

Some addresses (e.g., local variables and arguments) have lifetimes tied to that method invocation. These shall not be referenced outside their lifetimes, and so they should not be stored in locations that last beyond their lifetime. The CIL does not (and cannot) enforce this restriction, so the CIL generator shall enforce this restriction or the resulting CIL will not work correctly. For code to be verifiable (see Partition I, section 8.8), by-ref parameters may **only** be passed to other methods or referenced via the appropriate **stind** or **ldind** instructions.

12.4.1.5.3 *Typed Reference Parameters*

By-ref parameters and value types are sufficient to support statically typed languages (C++, Pascal, etc.). They also support dynamically typed languages that pay a performance penalty to box value types before passing them to polymorphic methods (Lisp, Scheme, Smalltalk, etc.). Unfortunately, they are not sufficient to support languages like Visual Basic that require by-reference passing of unboxed data to methods that are not statically restricted as to the type of data they accept. These languages require a way of passing *both* the address of the home of the data *and* the static type of the home. This is exactly the information that would be provided if the data were boxed, but without the heap allocation required of a box operation.

Typed reference parameters address this requirement. A typed reference parameter is very similar to a standard by-ref parameter, but the static data type is passed as well as the address of the data. Like by-ref parameters, the argument corresponding to a typed reference parameter will have a home.

> **NOTE**
> If it were not for the fact that verification and the memory manager need to be aware of the data type and the corresponding address, a by-ref parameter could be implemented as a standard value type with two fields: the address of the data and the type of the data.

Like a regular by-ref parameter, a typed reference parameter can refer to a home that is on the stack, and that home will have a lifetime limited by the call stack. Thus, the CIL generator shall apply appropriate checks on the lifetime of by-ref parameters; and verification imposes the same restrictions on the use of typed reference parameters as it does on by-ref parameters (see Partition I, section 12.4.1.5.2).

A typed reference is passed by either creating a new typed reference (using the **mkrefany** instruction) or by copying an existing typed reference. Given a typed reference argument, the address to which it refers can be extracted using the **refanyval** instruction; the type to which it refers can be extracted using the **refanytype** instruction.

ANNOTATION: The typed reference is not required in all CLI implementations, so a given implementation may not support it. It resides in the Vararg Library, which is excluded from the Kernel Profile.

12.4.1.5.4 ***Parameter Interactions***

A given parameter may be passed using any one of the parameter passing conventions: by-value, by-ref, or typed reference. No combination of these is allowed for a single parameter, although a method may have different parameters with different calling mechanisms.

A parameter that has been passed in as typed reference shall not be passed on as by-ref or by-value without a runtime type check and (in the case of by-value) a copy.

A by-ref parameter may be passed on as a typed reference by attaching the static type. Table 2-9, Parameter Passing Conventions, illustrates the parameter passing convention used for each data type.

Table 2-9 Parameter Passing Conventions

Type of Data	Pass By	How Data Is Sent
Built-in value type (int, float, etc.)	Value	Copied to called method, type statically known at both sides
	Reference	Address sent to called method, type statically known at both sides
	Typed reference	Address sent along with type information to called method
User-defined value type	Value	Called method receives a copy; type statically known at both sides
	Reference	Address sent to called method, type statically known at both sides
	Typed reference	Address sent along with type information to called method
Object	Value	Reference to data sent to called method, type statically known and class available from reference
	Reference	Address of reference sent to called method, type statically known and class available from reference
	Typed reference	Address of reference sent to called method along with static type information, class (i.e., dynamic type) available from reference

12.4.2 *Exception Handling*

Exception handling is supported in the CLI through exception objects and protected blocks of code. When an exception occurs, an object is created to represent the exception. All exception objects are instances of some class (i.e., they can be boxed value types, but not pointers, unboxed value types, etc.). Users may create their own exception classes, typically by subclassing `System.Exception` (see the *.NET Framework Standard Library Annotated Reference*).

There are four kinds of handlers for protected blocks. A single protected block shall have exactly one handler associated with it:

- A **finally handler** that shall be executed whenever the block exits, regardless of whether that occurs by normal control flow or by an unhandled exception.

- A **fault handler** that shall be executed if an exception occurs, but not on completion of normal control flow.
- A **type-filtered handler** that handles any exception of a specified class or any of its subclasses.
- A **user-filtered handler** that runs a user-specified set of CIL instructions to determine whether the exception should be ignored (i.e., execution should resume), handled by the associated handler, or passed on to the next protected block.

Protected regions, the type of the associated handler, and the location of the associated handler and (if needed) user-supplied filter code are described through an Exception Handler Table associated with each method. The exact format of the Exception Handler Table is specified in detail in Partition II. Details of the exception handling mechanism are also specified in Partition II, section 18.

ANNOTATION: Filtered exception handling is not required in the Kernel Profile, so a given implementation of the VES may not support it and its associated instructions.

12.4.2.1 Exceptions Thrown by the CLI

CLI instructions can throw the following exceptions as part of executing individual instructions. The documentation for each instruction lists all the exceptions the instruction can throw (except for the general-purpose **ExecutionEngineException** described below that may be generated by all instructions).

Base Instructions (see Partition III[, section 3])

- ArithmeticException
- DivideByZeroException
- ExecutionEngineException
- InvalidAddressException
- OverflowException
- SecurityException
- StackOverflowException

Object Model Instructions (see Partition III[, section 4])

- TypeLoadException
- IndexOutOfRangeException
- InvalidAddressException

- InvalidCastException
- MissingFieldException
- MissingMethodException
- NullReferenceException
- OutOfMemoryException
- SecurityException
- StackOverflowException

The `ExecutionEngineException` is special. It can be thrown by any instruction and indicates an unexpected inconsistency in the CLI. Running exclusively verified code can never cause this exception to be thrown by a conforming implementation of the CLI. However, unverified code (even though that code is conforming CIL) can cause this exception to be thrown if it corrupts memory. Any attempt to execute non-conforming CIL or non-conforming file formats can cause completely unspecified behavior: a conforming implementation of the CLI need not make any provision for these cases.

There are no exceptions for things like "MetaDataTokenNotFound." CIL verification (see Partition V) will detect this inconsistency before the instruction is executed, leading to a verification violation. If the CIL is not verified, this type of inconsistency shall raise the generic ExecutionEngineException.

Exceptions can also be thrown by the CLI, as well as by user code, using the **throw** instruction. The handing of an exception is identical, regardless of the source.

12.4.2.2 Subclassing of Exceptions

Certain types of exceptions thrown by the CLI may be subclassed to provide more information to the user. The specification of CIL instructions in Partition III describes what types of exceptions should be thrown by the runtime environment when an abnormal situation occurs. Each of these descriptions allows a conforming implementation to throw an object of the type described or an object of a subclass of that type.

> **NOTE**
>
> For instance, the specification of the `ckfinite` instruction requires that an exception of type `ArithmeticException` or a subclass of `ArithmeticException` be thrown by the CLI. A conforming implementation may simply throw an exception of type `ArithmeticException`, but it may also choose to provide more information to the programmer by throwing an exception of type `NotFiniteNumberException` with the offending number.

12.4.2.3 Resolution Exceptions

CIL allows types to reference, among other things, interfaces, classes, methods, and fields. Resolution errors occur when references are not found or are mismatched. Resolution exceptions can be generated by references from CIL instructions, references to base classes, to implemented interfaces, and by references from signatures of fields, methods, and other class members.

To allow scalability with respect to optimization, detection of resolution exceptions is given latitude such that it may occur as early as install time and as late as execution time.

The latest opportunity to check for resolution exceptions from all references except CIL instructions is as part of initialization of the type that is doing the referencing (see Partition II). If such a resolution exception is detected, the static initializer for that type, if present, shall not be executed.

The latest opportunity to check for resolution exceptions in CIL instructions is as part of the first execution of the associated CIL instruction. When an implementation chooses to perform resolution exception checking in CIL instructions as late as possible, these exceptions, if they occur, shall be thrown prior to any other non-resolution exception that the VES may throw for that CIL instruction. Once a CIL instruction has passed the point of throwing resolution errors (it has completed without exception, or has completed by throwing a non-resolution exception), subsequent executions of that instruction shall no longer throw resolution exceptions.

If an implementation chooses to detect some resolution errors, from any references, earlier than the latest opportunity for that kind of reference, it is not required to detect all resolution exceptions early.

An implementation that detects resolution errors early is allowed to prevent a class from being installed, loaded, or initialized as a result of resolution exceptions detected in the class itself or in the transitive closure of types from following references of any kind.

For example, each of the following represents a permitted scenario. An installation program can throw resolution exceptions (thus failing the installation) as a result of checking CIL instructions for resolution errors in the set of items being installed. An implementation is allowed to fail to load a class as a result of checking CIL instructions in a referenced class for resolution errors. An implementation is permitted to load and initialize a class that has resolution errors in its CIL instructions.

The following exceptions are among those considered resolution exceptions:

- `BadImageFormatException`
- `EntryPointNotFoundException`
- `MissingFieldException`

- `MissingMemberException`
- `MissingMethodException`
- `NotSupportedException`
- `TypeLoadException`
- `TypeUnloadedException`

For example, when a referenced class cannot be found, a `TypeLoadException` is thrown. When a referenced method (whose class is found) cannot be found, a `MissingMethodException` is thrown. If a matching method being used consistently is accessible but violates declared security policy, a `SecurityException` is thrown.

ANNOTATION: It is possible for a program compiled to IL to reference a type, or members of types, that do not actually exist at runtime. A few situations lead to this problem. One is that in a language that is not statically typed, such as Lisp or Perl, you may not know at runtime whether the type will exist. In cases where the type does not exist at runtime through programmer error, there will be a resolution exception. In a statically typed language, a resolution exception can occur when parts of a program are deployed independently and some parts of the program are not deployed when needed. For example, if a main program is written to assume a certain set of libraries but the program is run without installing the libraries, a resolution exception results.

12.4.2.4 Timing of Exceptions

Certain types of exceptions thrown by CIL instructions may be detected before the instruction is executed. In these cases, the specific time of the throw is not precisely defined, but the exception should be thrown no later than the instruction is executed. That relaxation of the timing of exceptions is provided so that an implementation may choose to detect and throw an exception before any code is run—e.g., at the time of CIL-to-native-code conversion.

There is a distinction between the time of detecting the error condition and throwing the associated exception. An error condition may be detected early (e.g., at JIT time), but the condition may be signaled later (e.g., at the execution time of the offending instruction) by throwing an exception.

The following exceptions are among those that may be thrown early by the runtime:

- `MissingFieldException`
- `MissingMethodException`

- `SecurityException`
- `TypeLoadException`

12.4.2.5 Overview of Exception Handling

See the Exception Handling specification in Partition II, section 18 for details.

Each method in an executable has associated with it a (possibly empty) array of exception handling information. Each entry in the array describes a protected block, its filter, and its handler (which may be a **catch** handler, a **filter** handler, a **finally** handler, or a **fault** handler). When an exception occurs, the CLI searches the array for the first protected block

- That protects a region including the current instruction pointer *and*
- That is a catch handler block *and*
- Whose filter wishes to handle the exception

If a match is not found in the current method, the calling method is searched, and so on. If no match is found, the CLI will dump a stack trace and abort the program.

> **NOTE**
> A debugger can intervene and treat this situation like a breakpoint, before performing any stack unwinding, so that the stack is still available for inspection through the debugger.

If a match is found, the CLI walks the stack back to the point just located, but this time calling the **finally** and **fault** handlers. It then starts the corresponding exception handler. Stack frames are discarded either as this second walk occurs or after the handler completes, depending on information in the exception handler array entry associated with the handling block.

Some things to notice are:

- The ordering of the exception clauses in the Exception Handler Table is important. If handlers are nested, the most deeply nested try blocks shall come before the try blocks that enclose them.
- Exception handlers may access the local variables and the local memory pool of the routine that catches the exception, but any intermediate results on the evaluation stack at the time the exception was thrown are lost.

- An exception object describing the exception is automatically created by the CLI and pushed onto the evaluation stack as the first item upon entry of a filter or catch clause.
- Execution cannot be resumed at the location of the exception, except with a **user-filtered handler**.

12.4.2.6 CIL Support for Exceptions

The CIL has special instructions to:

- **Throw** and **rethrow** a user-defined exception.
- **Leave** a protected block and execute the appropriate **finally** clauses within a method, without throwing an exception. This is also used to exit a **catch** clause. Notice that leaving a protected block does *not* cause the fault clauses to be called.
- End a user-supplied filter clause (**endfilter**) and return a value indicating whether to handle the exception.
- End a finally clause (**endfinally**) and continue unwinding the stack.

12.4.2.7 Lexical Nesting of Protected Blocks

A protected region (also called a "try block") is described by two addresses: the **trystart** is the address of the first instruction to be protected, and [the] **tryend** is the address immediately following the last instruction to be protected. A handler region is described by two addresses: the **handlerstart** is the address of the first instruction of the handler, and the **handlerend** is the address immediately following the last instruction of the handler.

There are three kinds of handlers: catch, finally, and fault. A single exception entry consists of

- Optional: a type token (the type of exception to be handled) or **filterstart** (the address of the first instruction of the user-supplied filter code)
- Required: **protected region**
- Required: **handler region**

Every method has associated with it a set of exception entries, called the **exception set**.

If an exception entry contains a **filterstart**, then **filterstart < handlerstart**. The **filter region** starts at the instruction specified by **filterstart** and contains all instructions up to (but not including) that specified by **handlerstart**. If there is no **filterstart**, then the filter region is empty (hence does not overlap with any region).

No two regions (protected region, handler region, filter region) of a single exception entry may overlap with one another.

For every pair of exception entries in an exception set, one of the following must be true:

- They **nest**: all three regions of one entry must be within a single region of the other entry.
- They are **disjoint**: all six regions of the two entries are pairwise disjoint (no addresses overlap).
- They **mutually protect**: the protected regions are the same, and the other regions are pairwise disjoint.

The encoding of an exception entry in the file format (see Partition II) guarantees that only a catch handler (not a fault handler or finally handler) can have a filter region.

ANNOTATION: Sections 12.4.2.7 and 12.4.2.8 of Partition I have been rewritten more times than any other sections of this standard, because the edge cases of exception handling are incredibly complicated. There continues to be disagreement (on the edge cases) about what is meant by these two sections.

– Jim Miller

12.4.2.8 Control Flow Restrictions on Protected Blocks

The following restrictions govern control flow into, out of, and between **try** blocks and their associated handlers.

1. CIL code shall not enter a **filter**, **catch**, **fault,** or **finally** block except through the CLI exception handling mechanism.
2. There are only two ways to enter a **try** block from outside its lexical body:
   a. **Branching to or falling into the try block's first instruction**. The branch may be made using a conditional branch, an unconditional branch, or a **leave** instruction.
   b. **Using a leave instruction from that try's catch block.** In this case, correct CIL code may branch to any instruction within the **try** block, not just its first instruction, so long as that branch target is not protected by yet another **try**, nested within the first.
3. Upon entry to a **try** block, the evaluation stack shall be empty.
4. The only ways CIL code may leave a try, filter, catch, finally, or fault block are as follows:
   a. **throw** from any of them.
   b. **leave** from the body of a **try** or **catch** (in this case the destination of the **leave** shall have an empty evaluation stack and the **leave** instruction has the side-effect of emptying the evaluation stack).

c. **endfilter** may appear only as the lexically last instruction of a **filter** block, and it shall always be present (even if it is immediately preceded by a **throw** or other unconditional control flow). If reached, the evaluation stack shall contain an **int32** when the **endfilter** is executed, and the value is used to determine how exception handling should proceed.

d. **endfinally** from anywhere within a **finally or fault, with the side-effect of emptying the evaluation stack.**

e. **rethrow from within a catch block, with the side-effect of emptying the evaluation stack.**

5. When the try block is exited with a **leave** instruction, the evaluation stack shall be empty.
6. When a catch or filter clause is exited with a leave instruction, the evaluation stack shall be empty. This involves popping, from the evaluation stack, the exception object that was automatically pushed onto the stack.
7. CIL code shall not exit any try, filter, catch, finally, or fault block using a **ret** instruction.
8. The `localloc` instruction cannot occur within an exception block: **filter**, **catch**, **finally**, or **fault**.

ANNOTATION: The edge cases have continued to make it difficult to write these sections precisely. If you have a try block for the catch handler, and inside that catch handler there is another try block and a catch handler, the question is whether one can go from the inner catch to the outer try, and the answer is almost always yes. There are some rules that restrict that. For example, you can't leave from a filter. Those are the kinds of edge cases that have made these sections difficult to write.

Another point that has resulted in confusion in the edge cases is number 5 of the preceding list: "When the try block is exited with a **leave** instruction, the evaluation stack shall be empty." My understanding is that the intent was to state that the**leave** instruction *causes* the evaluation stack to be empty, rather than the alternate reading that you need to empty the evaluation stack.

–Jim Miller

12.5 Proxies and Remoting

A **remoting boundary** exists if it is not possible to share the identity of an object directly across the boundary. For example, if two objects exist on physically separate machines that do not share a common address space, then a remoting boundary will exist between them. There are other administrative mechanisms for creating remoting boundaries.

The VES provides a mechanism, called the **application domain**, to isolate applications running in the same operating system process from one another. Types loaded into one application domain are distinct from the same type loaded into another application domain, and instances of objects shall not be directly shared from one application domain to another. Hence, the application domain itself forms a remoting boundary.

The VES implements remoting boundaries based on the concept of a **proxy**. A proxy is an object that exists on one side of the boundary and represents an object on the other side. The proxy forwards references to instance fields and methods to the actual object for interpretation. Proxies do not forward references to static fields or calls to static methods.

The implementation of proxies is provided automatically for instances of types that derive from **System.MarshalByRefObject** (see the *.NET Framework Standard Library Annotated Reference*).

12.6 Memory Model and Optimizations

12.6.1 *The Memory Store*

By "memory store" we mean the regular process memory that the CLI operates within. Conceptually, this store is simply an array of bytes. The index into this array is the address of a data object. The CLI accesses data objects in the memory store via the **ldind.*** and **stind.*** instructions.

12.6.2 *Alignment*

Built-in datatypes shall be *properly aligned*, which is defined as follows:

- 1-byte, 2-byte, and 4-byte data is properly aligned when it is stored at a 1-byte, 2-byte, or 4-byte boundary, respectively.
- 8-byte data is properly aligned when it is stored on the same boundary required by the underlying hardware for atomic access to a **native int**.

Thus, **int16** and **unsigned int16** start on even address; **int32**, **unsigned int32**, and **float32** start on an address divisible by 4; and **int64**, **unsigned int64**, and **float64** start on an address divisible by 4 or 8, depending on the target architecture. The native size types (**native int**, **native unsigned int**, and **&**) are always naturally aligned (4 bytes or 8 bytes, depending on architecture). When generated externally, these should also be aligned to their natural size, although portable code may use 8-byte alignment to guarantee architecture independence. It is strongly recommended that **float64** be aligned on an 8-byte boundary, even when the size of **native int** is 32 bits.

There is a special prefix instruction, **unaligned.**, that may immediately precede a **ldind**, **stind**, **initblk**, or **cpblk** instruction. This prefix indicates that the data may have arbitrary alignment; the JIT is required to generate code that correctly performs the effect of the instructions regardless of the actual alignment. Otherwise, if the data is not properly aligned and no **unaligned.** prefix has been specified, executing the instruction may generate unaligned memory faults or incorrect data.

ANNOTATION: Compiler writers can assume, and VES writers must ensure, that by default, data is aligned. The design point of the CLI is that compilers have to give a heads up to the JIT if data might be unaligned, with the **unaligned.** prefix. Otherwise, the VES, by default, aligns data.

12.6.3 *Byte Ordering*

For data types larger than 1 byte, the byte ordering is dependent on the target CPU. Code that depends on byte ordering may not run on all platforms. The PE file format (see Partition I, section 12.2) allows the file to be marked to indicate that it depends on a particular type ordering.

12.6.4 *Optimization*

Conforming implementations of the CLI are free to execute programs using any technology that guarantees, within a single thread of execution, that side-effects and exceptions generated by a thread are visible in the order specified by the CIL. For this purpose volatile operations (including volatile reads) constitute side-effects. Volatile operations are specified in Partition I, section 12.6.7. There are no ordering guarantees relative to exceptions injected into a thread by another thread (such exceptions are sometimes called "asynchronous exceptions"—e.g., **System.Threading.ThreadAbortException**).

ANNOTATION: The parenthetical comment in the second sentence of this section above—"including volatile reads"—was intended to be interpreted within the context of the preceding comment "within a single thread of execution." Although that is not a sufficiently strong guarantee to allow I/O drivers to be written using **volatile**, it restricts a compiler from CIL to native code. It is likely that the next edition of the standard will make this clear.

–Jim Miller

RATIONALE

An optimizing compiler is free to reorder side-effects and synchronous exceptions to the extent that this reordering does not change any observable program behavior.

> **NOTE**
>
> An implementation of the CLI is permitted to use an optimizing compiler—for example, to convert CIL to native machine code, provided the compiler maintains (within each single thread of execution) the same order of side-effects and synchronous exceptions.
>
> This is a stronger condition than ISO C++ (which permits reordering between a pair of sequence points) or ISO Scheme (which permits reordering of arguments to functions).

12.6.5 *Locks and Threads*

The logical abstraction of a thread of control is captured by an instance of the `System.Threading.Thread` object in the class library. Classes beginning with the string "System.Threading" (see the *.NET Framework Standard Library Annotated Reference*) provide much of the user-visible support for this abstraction.

To create consistency across threads of execution, the CLI provides the following mechanisms:

1. **Synchronized methods**. A lock that is visible across threads controls entry to the body of a synchronized method. For instance and virtual methods the lock is associated with the **this** pointer. For static methods the lock is associated with the type to which the method belongs. The lock is taken by the logical thread (see `System.Threading.Thread` in the *.NET Framework Standard Library Annotated Reference*) and may be entered any number of times by the same thread; entry by other threads is prohibited while the first thread is still holding the lock. The CLI shall release the lock when control exits (by any means) the method invocation that first acquired the lock.
2. **Explicit locks and monitors.** These are provided in the class library (see `System.Threading.Monitor`). Many of the methods in the `System.Threading.Monitor` class accept an `Object` as argument, allowing direct access to the same lock that is used by synchronized methods. While the CLI is responsible for ensuring correct protocol when this lock is only used by synchronized methods, the user must accept this responsibility when using explicit monitors on these same objects.
3. **Volatile reads and writes.** The CIL includes a prefix, `volatile.`, that specifies that the subsequent operation is to be performed with the cross-thread visibility constraints described in Partition I, section 12.6.7. In addition, the class library provides methods to perform explicit volatile reads (`System.Thread.VolatileRead`) and writes (`System.Thread.VolatileWrite`), as well as barrier synchronization (`System.Thread.MemoryBarrier`).

4. **Built-in atomic reads and writes.** All reads and writes of certain properly aligned data types are guaranteed to occur atomically. See Partition I, section 12.6.6.
5. **Explicit atomic operations.** The class library provides a variety of atomic operations in the `System.Threading.Interlocked` class.

Acquiring a lock (`System.Threading.Monitor.Enter` or entering a synchronized method) shall implicitly perform a volatile read operation, and releasing a lock (`System.Threading.Monitor.Exit` or leaving a synchronized method) shall implicitly perform a volatile write operation. See Partition I, section 12.6.7.

12.6.6 *Atomic Reads and Writes*

A conforming CLI shall guarantee that read and write access to *properly aligned* memory locations no larger than the native word size (the size of type **native int**) is atomic (see Partition I, section 12.6.2). Atomic writes shall alter no bits other than those written. Unless explicit layout control (see Partition II, Controlling Instance Layout [section 9.7]) is used to alter the default behavior, data elements no larger than the natural word size (the size of a **native int**) shall be properly aligned. Object references shall be treated as though they are stored in the native word size.

> **NOTE**
>
> There is no guarantee about atomic update (read-modify-write) of memory, except for methods provided for that purpose as part of the class library (see the *.NET Framework Standard Library Annotated Reference*). An atomic write of a "small data item" (an item no larger than the native word size) *is* required to do an atomic read/write/modify on hardware that does not support direct writes to small data items.

> **NOTE**
>
> There is no guaranteed atomic access to 8-byte data when the size of a **native int** is 32 bits, even though some implementations may perform atomic operations when the data is aligned on an 8-byte boundary.

12.6.7 *Volatile Reads and Writes*

The **volatile.** prefix on certain instructions shall guarantee cross-thread memory ordering rules. They do not provide atomicity, other than that guaranteed by the specification of Partition I, section 12.6.6.

2. Concepts and Architecture

A volatile read has "acquire semantics," meaning that the read is guaranteed to occur prior to any references to memory that occur after the read instruction in the CIL instruction sequence. A volatile write has "release semantics," meaning that the write is guaranteed to happen after any memory references prior to the write instruction in the CIL instruction sequence.

A conforming implementation of the CLI shall guarantee this semantics of volatile operations. This ensures that all threads will observe volatile writes performed by any other thread in the order they were performed. But a conforming implementation is *not* required to provide a single total ordering of volatile writes as seen from all threads of execution.

ANNOTATION: Microsoft expects to enforce a stronger restriction on its implementations and has proposed that the next edition of the standard also impose that restriction. This restriction says that writes may not be reordered with respect to other writes, independent of whether the writes are volatile. In the proposed model, writes could never be reordered with respect to other writes, and **volatile.** prefix would, in addition, restrict the reorder of writes relative to reads, as described in this section.

An optimizing compiler that converts CIL to native code shall not remove any volatile operation, nor may it coalesce multiple volatile operations into a single operation.

> **RATIONALE**
>
> One traditional use of volatile operations is to model hardware registers that are visible through direct memory access. In these cases, removing or coalescing the operations may change the behavior of the program.

> **NOTE**
>
> An optimizing compiler from CIL to native code is permitted to reorder code, provided that it guarantees both the single-thread semantics described in Partition I, section 12.6 and the cross-thread semantics of volatile operations.

12.6.8 *Other Memory Model Issues*

All memory allocated for static variables (other than those assigned RVAs within a PE file; see Partition II) and objects shall be zeroed before they are made visible to any user code.

A conforming implementation of the CLI shall ensure that, even in a multi-threaded environment and without proper user synchronization, objects are allocated in a manner that prevents unauthorized memory access and prevents illegal operations from occurring. In particular, on multi-processor memory systems where explicit synchronization is required to ensure that all relevant data structures are visible (for example, vtable pointers) the VES shall be responsible for either enforcing this synchronization automatically or for converting errors due to lack of synchronization into non-fatal, non-corrupting, user-visible exceptions.

It is explicitly *not* a requirement that a conforming implementation of the CLI guarantee that all state updates performed within a constructor be uniformly visible before the constructor completes. CIL generators may ensure this requirement themselves by inserting appropriate calls to the memory barrier or volatile write instructions.

COMMON LANGUAGE INFRASTRUCTURE (CLI)

3. Partition IIA: Metadata Semantics

1 Scope

This specification provides the normative description of the metadata: its physical layout (as a file format), its logical contents (as a set of tables and their relationships), and its semantics (as seen from a hypothetical assembler, ilasm).

2 Overview

This document focuses on the structure and semantics of metadata. The semantics of metadata, which dictate much of the operation of the VES, are described using the syntax of ilasm, an assembler language for CIL. The ilasm syntax itself is considered a normative part of this International Standard. This constitutes Partition II, sections 5 through 20. A complete syntax for ilasm is included in Partition V. The structure [of metadata] (both logical and physical) is covered in Partition II, sections 21 through 24.

RATIONALE

An assembly language is really just syntax for specifying the metadata in a file and the CIL instructions in that file. Specifying ilasm provides a means of interchanging programs written directly for the CLI without the use of a higher-level language and also provides a convenient way to express examples.

The semantics of the metadata also can be described independently of the actual format in which the metadata is stored. This point is important because the storage format as specified in Partition II, sections 21 through 24 is engineered to be efficient for both storage space and access time, but this comes at the cost of the simplicity desirable for describing its semantics.

ANNOTATION: In this book, Partition II of the standard has been divided into two separate chapters. The first 20 sections of the Partition describe the semantics of metadata, using the **ilasm** assembler, and that is a single chapter in this book. The final four sections of Partition II—sections 21–24—describe in detail the file format, the physical layout of metadata, and its logical format as well. There was some debate in the ECMA committee responsible for this standard about turning these into two partitions after the first version of the standard, but it was felt to be too much work for too little gain.

It is worth emphasizing that although the ilasm language described in this standard is considered a normative part of the standard, it is standardized just to provide a means of describing the semantics of metadata. It does not dictate the syntax that you might use in developing an ilasm assembly language, although it would certainly make development easier if used as a basis for an ilasm language. This is why you will see several notes in this Partition that refer to the development of "a complete assembler." For example, one note in section 5.2 says, "A complete assembler may also provide syntax for infinities and NaNs."

---

3 Validation and Verification

Validation refers to a set of tests that can be performed on any file to check that the file format, metadata, and CIL are self-consistent. These tests are intended to ensure that the file conforms to the mandatory requirements of this specification. The behavior of conforming implementations of the CLI when presented with non-conforming files is unspecified.

Verification refers to a check of both CIL and its related metadata to ensure that the CIL code sequences do not permit any access to memory outside the program's logical address space. In conjunction with the validation tests, verification ensures that the program cannot access memory or other resources to which it is not granted access.

ANNOTATION: **Verification** is performed on a valid CLI file to ensure that its operation is memory safe. By contrast, **validation** determines whether the bits of a CIL (Common Intermediate Language) file conform to the CLI standard, or whether the file is, in terms of the CLI, nonsense. As stated, Partition III specifies the rules for creating valid and verifiable CIL from source code. It also lists, as informative material, rules that can be used in the design of a validating tool and, in fact, are used in the Microsoft implementation. These rules are listed as informative rather than normative (part of the standard) because it was felt that they could all be derived from the rules for valid use of CIL instructions. Nevertheless, these informative rules make it much easier to create a validation tool.

Although this discussion states that the goal of verification is type safety, it is more accurate to say that the goal of verification is memory safety. The type system used with the verifier is not the user's type system but a simpler one. For example, the verifier's type system does not distinguish signed from unsigned types. The verifier enforces type safety according to a much smaller type system, one designed to guarantee memory safety.

Partition III specifies the rules for both valid and verifiable use of CIL instructions. Partition III also provides an informative description of rules for validating the internal consistency of metadata (the rules follow, albeit indirectly, from the specification in this Partition), as well as containing a normative description of the verification algorithm. A mathematical proof of soundness of the underlying type system is possible, and provides the basis for the verification requirements. Aside from these rules this standard does *not* specify:

- At what time (if ever) such an algorithm should be performed
- What a conforming implementation should do in case of failure of verification

The graph in Figure 3-1 makes this relationship clearer (see next paragraph for a description).

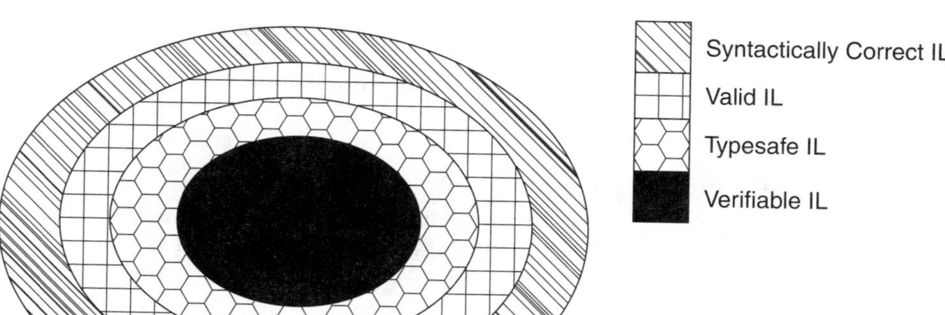

Figure 3-1 Relationship between Valid and Verifiable CIL

In Figure 3-1 the outer circle contains all code permitted by the ilasm syntax. The next circle represents all code that is valid CIL. The dotted inner circle represents all typesafe code. Finally, the black innermost circle contains all code that is verifiable. (The difference between typesafe code and verifiable code is one of *provability*: code which passes the VES verification algorithm is, by definition, *verifiable*; but that simple algorithm rejects certain code, even though a deeper analysis would reveal it as genuinely typesafe). Note that even if a program follows the syntax described in Partition V, the code may still not be valid, because valid code shall adhere to restrictions presented in this document and in Partition III.

Verification is a very stringent test. There are many programs that will pass validation but will fail verification. The VES cannot guarantee that these programs do not access memory or resources to which they are not granted access. Nonetheless, they may have been correctly constructed so that they do not access these resources. It is thus a matter of trust, rather than mathematical proof, whether it is safe to run these programs. A conforming implementation of the CLI may allow *unverifiable code* (valid code that does not pass verification) to be executed, although this may be subject to administrative trust controls that are not part of this standard. A conforming implementation of the CLI shall allow the execution of verifiable code, although this may be subject to additional implementation-specified trust controls.

4 Introductory Examples

This section and its subsections contain only informative text.

Before diving into the details, it is useful to see an introductory sample program to get a feeling for the ilasm assembly language. The next section shows the famous Hello World program, this time in the ilasm assembly language.

4.1 Hello World Example

This section gives a simple example to illustrate the general feel of ilasm. Below is code that prints the well-known "Hello world!" salutation. The salutation is written by calling `WriteLine`, a static method found in the class `System.Console` that is part of the assembly `mscorlib` (see the *.NET Framework Standard Library Annotated Reference*.

```
Example (informative):
.assembly extern mscorlib {}
.assembly hello {}
.method static public void main() cil managed
{ .entrypoint
```

```
    .maxstack 1
    ldstr "Hello world!"
    call void [mscorlib]System.Console::WriteLine(class System.String)
    ret
}
```

The **.assembly extern** declaration references an external assembly, mscorlib, which defines `System.Console`. The **.assembly** declaration in the second line declares the name of the assembly for this program. (Assemblies are the deployment unit for executable content for the CLI.) The **.method** declaration defines the global method `main`. The body of the method is enclosed in braces. The first line in the body indicates that this method is the entry point for the assembly (**.entrypoint**), and the second line in the body specifies that it requires at most one stack slot (**.maxstack**).

The method contains only three instructions. The **ldstr** instruction pushes the string constant `"Hello world!"` onto the stack, and the **call** instruction invokes `System.Console::WriteLine`, passing the string as its only argument (note that string literals in CIL are instances of the standard class `System.String`). As shown, call instructions shall include the full signature of the called method. Finally, the last instruction returns (**ret**) from `main`.

ANNOTATION: There is a common misunderstanding that **maxstack** refers to how much stack space is needed when the program runs. Instead, it is the maximum number of virtual machine slots needed in a particular method. When the method is converted to assembly, more or fewer actual machine words may be needed. A single virtual slot can hold an entire value type, which could be 100 words long—actual size is not a part of the virtual slot. Maxstack is there primarily for verifiers, and has no real effect on running the program. This information about virtual slots is needed when a verifier simulates a program, to tell the verifier how much space to allocate to represent that stack when it simulates this program.

4.2 Examples

This document contains integrated examples for most features of the CLI metadata. Many sections conclude with an example showing a typical use of the feature. All these examples are written using the ilasm assembly language. In addition, Partition V contains a longer example of a program written in the ilasm assembly language. All examples are, of course, informative only.

End informative text

---

5 General Syntax

This section describes aspects of the ilasm syntax that are common to many parts of the grammar. The term "ASCII" refers to the American Standard Code for Information Interchange, a standard 7-bit code that was proposed by ANSI in 1963, and finalized in 1968. The ASCII repertoire of Unicode is the set of 128 Unicode characters from U+0000 to U+007F.

5.1 General Syntax Notation

This document uses a modified form of the BNF syntax notation. The following is a brief summary of this notation.

Bold items are terminals. Items placed in angle brackets (e.g., <int64>) are names of syntax classes and shall be replaced by actual instances of the class. Items placed in square brackets (e.g., [<float>]) are optional, and any item followed by * can appear zero or more times. The character "|" means that the items on either side of it are acceptable. The options are sorted in alphabetical order (to be more specific: in ASCII order, ignoring "<" for syntax classes, and case-insensitive). If a rule starts with an optional term, the optional term is *not* considered for sorting purposes.

ilasm is a case-sensitive language. All terminals shall be used with the same case as specified in this reference.

Example (informative):

A grammar such as

```
<top> ::= <int32> | float <float> |
          floats [<float> [, <float>]*] | else <QSTRING>
```

would consider the following all to be legal:

```
12
float 3
float -4.3e7
floats
floats 2.4
floats 2.4, 3.7
else "Something \t weird"
```

but all of the following to be illegal:

```
else 3
3, 4
float 4.3, 2.4
float else
stuff
```

5.2 Terminals

The basic syntax classes used in the grammar are used to describe syntactic constraints on the input intended to convey logical restrictions on the information encoded in the metadata.

The syntactic constraints described in this section are informative only. The semantic constraints (e.g., "shall be represented in 32 bits") are normative.

`<int32>` is either a decimal number or "0x" followed by a hexadecimal number, and shall be represented in 32 bits.

`<int64>` is either a decimal number or "0x" followed by a hexadecimal number, and shall be represented in 64 bits.

`<hexbyte>` is a 2-digit hexadecimal number that fits into one byte.

`<realnumber>` is any syntactic representation for a floating point number that is distinct from that for all other terminal nodes. In this document, a period (.) is used to separate the integer and fractional parts, and "e" or "E" separates the mantissa from the exponent. Either (but not both) may be omitted.

> **NOTE**
> A complete assembler may also provide syntax for infinities and NaNs.

`<QSTRING>` is a string surrounded by double quote (") marks. Within the quoted string the character "\" can be used as an escape character, with "\t" for a tab character, "\n" for a new line character, or followed by three octal digits in order to insert an arbitrary byte into the string. The "+" operator can be used to concatenate string literals. This way, a long string can be broken across multiple lines by using "+" and a new string on each line. An alternative is using "\" as the last character in a line, in which case the line break is not entered into the generated string. Any white characters (space, line feed, carriage return, and tab) between the "\" and the first character on the next line are ignored. See also examples below.

> **NOTE**
> A complete assembler will need to deal with the full set of issues required to support Unicode encodings, see Partition I (especially CLS Rule 4, in section 8.5.1).

<SQSTRING> is similar to <QSTRING>, with the difference that it is surrounded by single quote (') marks instead of double quote marks.

<ID> is a contiguous string of characters which starts with either an alphabetic character or one of "_", "$", "@", or "?" and is followed by any number of alphanumeric characters or any of "_", "$", "@", or "?". An <ID> is used in only two ways:

- As a label of a CIL instruction
- As an <id> which can either be an <ID> or an <SQSTRING>, so that special characters can be included.

Example (informative):

The following examples show breaking of strings:

```
    ldstr "Hello " + "World " +
    "from CIL!"
```

and

```
    ldstr "Hello World\
         \040from CIL!"
```

become both "Hello World from CIL!".

5.3 Identifiers

Identifiers are used to name entities. Simple identifiers are just equivalent to an <ID>. However, the ilasm syntax allows the use of any identifier that can be formed using the Unicode character set (see Partition I, section 10.1). To achieve this, an identifier is placed within single quotation marks. This is summarized in the following grammar.

<id> ::=
<ID>
| <SQSTRING>

Keywords may only be used as identifiers if they appear in single quotes (see Partition V for a list of all keywords).

Several <id>'s may be combined to form a larger <id>. The <id>'s are separated by a dot (.). An <id> formed in this way is called a <dottedname>.

<dottedname> ::= <id> [. <id>]*

RATIONALE

<dottedname> is provided for convenience, since "." can be included in an <id> using the <SQSTRING> syntax. <dottedname> is used in the grammar where "." is considered a common character (e.g., fully qualified type names).

ANNOTATION

Implementation-Specific (Microsoft): Names that end with `$PST` followed by a hexadecimal number have a special meaning. The assembler will automatically truncate the part starting with `$PST`, to support compiler-controlled accessibility, described in Partition I, section 8.5.3.2. Also the first release of the Microsoft CLR limits the length of identifiers; see Partition II, section 21 for details.

Examples (informative):

The following shows some simple identifiers:

```
A
Test
$Test
@Foo?
?_X_
```

The following shows identifiers in single quotes:

```
'Weird Identifier'
'Odd\102Char'
'Embedded\nReturn'
```

The following shows dotted names:

```
System.Console
A.B.C
'My Project'.'My Component'.'My Name'
```

5.4 Labels and Lists of Labels

Labels are provided as a programming convenience; they represent a number that is encoded in the metadata. The value represented by a label is typically an offset in bytes from the beginning of the current method, although the precise encoding differs depending on where in the logical metadata structure or CIL stream the label occurs. For details of how labels are encoded in the metadata, see Partition II, sections 21–24; for their encoding in CIL instructions, see Partition III.

A simple label is a special name that represents an address. Syntactically, a label is equivalent to an <id>. Thus, labels may be also single quoted and may contain Unicode characters.

A list of labels is comma separated, and can be any combination of these simple labels:

```
<labeloroffset> ::= <id>
<labels> ::= <labeloroffset> [, <labeloroffset>]*
```

RATIONALE

In a real assembler, the syntax for <labeloroffset> might allow the direct specification of a number rather than requiring symbolic labels.

ANNOTATION

Implementation-Specific (Microsoft): The following syntax is also supported, for round-tripping purposes:

```
<labeloroffset> ::= <int32> | <label>
```

ilasm distinguishes between two kinds of labels: code labels and data labels. Code labels are followed by a colon (":") and represent the address of an instruction to be executed. Code labels appear before an instruction and they represent the address of the instruction that immediately follows the label. A particular code label name may not be declared more than once in a method.

In contrast to code labels, data labels specify the location of a piece of data and do not include the colon character. The data label may not be used as a code label, and a code label may not be used as a data label. A particular code label name may not be declared more than once in a module.

```
<codeLabel> ::= <id> :
<dataLabel> ::= <id>
```

```
Example (informative):

The following defines a code label, ldstr_label, that represents the address of
the ldstr instruction:

ldstr_label:        ldstr   "A label"
```

5.5 Lists of Hex Bytes

A list of bytes consists simply of one or more hex bytes. Hex bytes are pairs of characters 0–9, a–f, and A–F.

```
<bytes> ::= <hexbyte> [<hexbyte>*]
```

5.6 Floating Point Numbers

There are two different ways to specify a floating point number:

1. Use the dot (".") for the decimal point and "e" or "E" in front of the exponent. Both the decimal point and the exponent are optional.
2. Indicate that the floating point value is derived from an integer using the keyword **float32** or **float64** and indicating the integer in parentheses.

```
<float64> ::=
  float32 ( <int32> )
| float64 ( <int64> )
| <realnumber>
```

```
Example (informative):

5.5

1.1e10

float64(128)        // note: this converts the integer 128 to its fp value
```

5.7 Source Line Information

The metadata does not encode information about the lexical scope of variables or the mapping from source line numbers to CIL instructions. Nonetheless, it is useful to specify an assembler syntax for providing this information for use in creating alternate encodings of the information.

ANNOTATION: See Partition I, section 9.7 for more information on attributes and modifiers.

Implementation-Specific (Microsoft): Source line information is stored in the PDB (Portable Debug) file associated with each module.

.line takes a line number, an optional column number (preceded by a colon), and a single-quoted string that specifies the name of the file the line number is referring to:

```
<externSourceDecl> ::= .line <int32> [ : <int32> ]  [<SQSTRING>]
```

ANNOTATION

Implementation-Specific (Microsoft): For compatibility reasons, ilasm allows the following:

```
<externSourceDecl> ::= … | #line <int32> <QSTRING>
```

Notice that this requires the file name and that it shall be double quoted, not single quoted as with **.line.**

5.8 File Names

Some grammar elements require that a file name be supplied. A file name is like any other name where "." is considered a normal constituent character. The specific syntax for file names follows the specifications of the underlying operating system.

`<filename> ::=`	Section in Partition II
`<dottedname>`	5.3

5.9 Attributes and Metadata

Attributes of types and their members attach descriptive information to their definition. The most common attributes are predefined and have a specific encoding in the metadata associated with them (see Partition II, section 22). In addition, the metadata provides a way of attaching user-defined attributes to metadata, using several different encodings.

From a syntactic point of view, there are several ways for specifying attributes in ilasm:

- Using special syntax built into ilasm. For example the keyword **private** in a `<classAttr>` specifies that the visibility attribute on a type should be set to allow access only within the defining assembly.
- Using a general-purpose syntax in ilasm. The non-terminal `<customDecl>` describes this grammar (see Partition II, section 20). For some attributes, called **pseudo custom attributes**, this grammar actually results in setting special encodings within the metadata (see Partition II, section 20.2.1).
- Some attributes are required to be set based on the settings of other attributes or information within the metadata and are not visible from the syntax of ilasm at all. These attributes are called **hidden attributes**.
- Security attributes are treated specially. There is special syntax in ilasm that allows the XML representing security attributes to be described directly (see Partition II, section 19). While all other attributes defined either in the standard library or by user-provided extension are encoded in the metadata using one common mechanism described in Partition II, section 21.10, security attributes (distinguished by the fact that they inherit, directly or indirectly from `System.Security.Permissions.SecurityAttribute`; see the *.NET Framework Standard Library Annotated Reference*) shall be encoded as described in Partition II, 21.11.

5.10 ilasm Source Files

An input to ilasm is a sequence of declarations, defined as follows:

`<ILFile> ::=`	Section in Partition II
`<decl>*`	5.10

The complete grammar for a top-level declaration is shown below. The following sections will concentrate on the various parts of this grammar.

`<decl> ::=`	Section in Partition II
`.assembly <dottedname> { <asmDecl>* }`	6.2
`| .assembly extern <dottedname> { <asmRefDecl>* }`	6.3
`| .class <classHead> { <classMember>* }`	9

<decl> ::=	Section in Partition II
| **.class extern** <exportAttr> <dottedname> { <externClassDecl>* }	6.7
| **.corflags** <int32>	6.2
| **.custom** <customDecl>	20
| **.data** <datadecl>	15.3.1
| **.field** <fieldDecl>	15
| **.file** [**nometadata**] <filename> [**.hash** = (<bytes>)] [**.entrypoint**]	6.2.3
| **.mresource** [**public** | **private**] <dottedname> [(<QSTRING>)] { <manResDecl>* }	6.2.2
| **.method** <methodHead> { <methodBodyItem>* }	14
| **.module** [<filename>]	6.4
| **.module extern** <filename>	6.5
| **.subsystem** <int32>	6.2
| **.vtfixup** <vtfixupDecl>	14.5.1
| <externSourceDecl>	5.7
| <securityDecl>	19

ANNOTATION

Implementation-Specific (Microsoft): The grammar for declarations also includes the following. These are described in a separate product specification.

<decl> ::=
.file alignment <int32>
| .imagebase <int64>
| **.language** <languageDecl>

```
| .namespace <id>
| ...
```

6 Assemblies, Manifests, and Modules

Assemblies and modules are grouping constructs, each playing a different role in the CLI.

An **assembly** is a set of one or more files deployed as a unit. An assembly always contains a **manifest** that specifies (see Partition II, section 6.1):

- Version, name, culture, and security requirements for the assembly.
- Which other files, if any, belong to the assembly, along with a cryptographic hash of each file. The manifest itself resides in the metadata part of a file, and that file is always part of the assembly.
- Which of the types defined in other files of the assembly are to be exported from the assembly. Types defined in the same file as the manifest are exported based on attributes of the type itself.
- Optionally, a digital signature for the manifest itself and the public key used to compute it.

A *module* is a single file containing executable content in the format specified here. If the module contains a manifest, then it also specifies the modules (including itself) that constitute the assembly. An assembly shall contain only one manifest among all its constituent files. For an assembly to be executed (rather than dynamically loaded) the manifest shall reside in the module that contains the entry point.

While some programming languages introduce the concept of a *namespace*, there is no support in the CLI for this concept. Type names are always specified by their full name relative to the assembly in which they are defined.

ANNOTATION: The CLI uses the term "namespace" simply to define a way to organize classes in the class library. It also allows some compression of the space required to store names. The metadata encodes names in two parts:

namespace. name

3. Metadata Semantics

and the namespace string does not need to be duplicated for each name. There is no internal support in the CLI other than that, and there are no operations on a namespace. That is what is meant by the phrase in the last paragraph, ". . . there is no support in the CLI for this concept."

6.1 Overview of Modules, Assemblies, and Files

This section contains informative text only.

Figure 3-2 should clarify the various forms of references.

Eight files are shown in the picture. The name of each file is shown below the file. Files that declare a module have an additional border around them and have names beginning with "M." The other two files have a name beginning with "F." These files may be resource files, like bitmaps, or other files that do not contain CIL code.

Files M1 and M4 declare an assembly in addition to the module declaration—namely, assemblies A and B, respectively. The assembly declaration in M1 and M4 references other modules, shown with straight lines. Assembly A references M2 and M3. Assembly B references M3 and M5. Thus, both assemblies reference M3.

Usually, a module belongs only to one assembly, but it is possible to share it across assemblies. When assembly A is loaded at runtime, an instance of M3 will be loaded for it. When assembly B is loaded into the same application domain, possibly simultaneously with assembly A, M3 will be shared for both assemblies. Both assemblies also reference F2, for which similar rules apply.

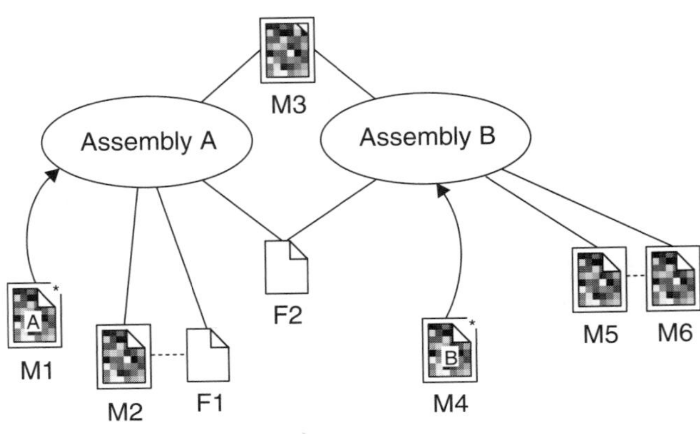

Figure 3-2 References

The module M2 references F1, shown by dotted lines. As a consequence, F1 will be loaded as part of assembly A when A is executed. Thus, the file reference shall also appear with the assembly declaration. Similarly, M5 references another module, M6, which becomes part of B when B is executed. It follows that assembly B shall also have a module reference to M6.

End informative text

6.2 Defining an Assembly

ANNOTATION: It is worth emphasizing that the notion of an assembly is just a manifest plus the modules that it specifies, including the module in which the manifest resides. The manifest can be in a separate module but is typically in the main module. The discussion here describes how you would create a manifest in ilasm using the **.assembly** and other directives.

An assembly is specified as a module that contains a manifest in the metadata; see Partition II, section 21.2. The information for the manifest is created from the following portions of the grammar:

`<decl> ::=`	Section in Partition II
`.assembly <dottedname> { <asmDecl>* }`	6.2
`| .assembly extern <dottedname> { <asmRefDecl>* }`	6.3
`| .corflags <int32>`	6.2
`| .file [nometadata] <filename> .hash = ( <bytes> ) [.entrypoint ]`	6.2.3
`| .module extern <filename>`	6.5
`| .mresource [public | private] <dottedname> [( <QSTRING> )] { <manResDecl>* }`	6.2.2
`| .subsystem <int32>`	6.2
`| ...`	

The **.assembly** directive declares the manifest and specifies to which assembly the current module belongs. A module shall contain at most one **.assembly** directive. The `<dottedname>` specifies the name of the assembly.

> **NOTE**
> Since some platforms treat names in a case-insensitive manner, two assemblies that have names that differ only in case should not be declared.

ANNOTATION: The identity of the assembly is important because that is what distinguishes it from other assemblies. It is not just the <dottedname> that it is given, but also a version number, language, and a public key, along with its security permissions. While it is possible to put in 0 instead of a public key, there is the possibility of name collisions, particularly if the assembly is to be made widely available. When a public key is specified, it is called "strong-named." Although the standard specifies the information that can be put into the name, it does not specify how that information should be evaluated. For example, it is up to the developer of a VES to determine what to do when the version requested is not available.

The **.corflags** directive sets a field in the CLI header of the output PE file [the COMIMAGE_FLAGS_ILONLY flag] (see Partition II, section 24.3.3.1). A conforming implementation of the CLI shall expect it to be 1. For backward compatibility, the three least significant bits are reserved. Future versions of this standard may provide definitions for values between 8 and 65,535. Experimental and non-standard uses should thus use values greater than 65,535.

The **.subsystem** directive is used only when the assembly is directly executed (as opposed to used as a library for another program). It specifies the kind of application environment required for the program, by storing the specified value in the PE file header (see Partition II, section 24.2.2). While a full 32-bit integer may be supplied, a conforming implementation of the CLI need only respect two possible values:

If the value is 2, the program should be run using whatever conventions are appropriate for an application that has a graphical user interface.

If the value is 3, the program should be run using whatever conventions are appropriate for an application that has a direct console attached.

ANNOTATION

Implementation-Specific (Microsoft):

```
<decl> ::= … | .file alignment <int32> | .imagebase <int64>
```

The **.file alignment** directive sets the file **alignment** field in the PE header of the output file. Legal values are multiples of 512. (Different sections of the PE file are aligned, on disk, at the specified value (in bytes).)

The **.imagebase** directive sets the **imagebase** field in the PE header of the output file. This value specifies the virtual address at which this PE file will be loaded into the process.

See Partition II, section 24.2.3.2.

```
Example (informative):
.assembly CountDown
{ .hash algorithm 32772
  .ver 1:0:0:0
}
.file Counter.dll .hash = (BA D9 7D 77 31 1C 85 4C 26 9C 49 E7 02 BE E7 52 3A CB
17 AF)
```

6.2.1 *Information about the Assembly (<asmDecl>)*

The following grammar shows the information that can be specified about an assembly.

`<asmDecl> ::=`	Description	Section in Partition II
`.custom <customDecl>`	Custom attributes	20
`.hash algorithm <int32>`	Hash algorithm used in the **.file** directive	6.2.1.1
`| .culture <QSTRING>`	Culture for which this assembly is built	6.2.1.2
`| .publickey = ( <bytes> )`	The originator's public key	6.2.1.3
`| .ver <int32> : <int32> : <int32> : <int32>`	Major version, minor version, revision, and build	6.2.1.4
`| <securityDecl>`	Permissions needed, desired, or prohibited	19

6.2.1.1 Hash Algorithm

```
<asmDecl> ::= .hash algorithm <int32> | ...
```

When an assembly consists of more than one file (see Partition II, section 6.2.3), the manifest for the assembly specifies both the name of the file and the cryptographic hash of the contents of the file. The algorithm used to compute the hash can be specified, and shall be the same for all files included in the assembly. All values are reserved for future use, and conforming implementations of the CLI shall use the SHA1 hash function and shall specify this algorithm by using a value of 32772 (0x8004).

> **RATIONALE**
> SHA1 was chosen as the best widely available technology at the time of standardization (see Partition I). A single algorithm is chosen, since all conforming implementations of the CLI would be required to implement all algorithms to ensure portability of executable images.

6.2.1.2 Culture

```
<asmDecl> ::= .culture <QSTRING> | ...
```

When present, this indicates that the assembly has been customized for a specific culture. The strings that shall be used here are those specified in the *.NET Framework Standard Library Annotated Reference* as acceptable with the class `System.Globalization.CultureInfo`. When used for comparison between an assembly reference and an assembly definition, these strings shall be compared in a case-insensitive manner.

ANNOTATION

Implementation-Specific (Microsoft): The product version of ilasm and ildasm use **.locale** rather than **.culture**.

> **NOTE**
> The culture names follow the IETF RFC1766 names. The format is "<language>-<country/region>", where <language> is a lowercase two-letter code in ISO 639-1. <country/region> is an uppercase two-letter code in ISO 3166.

6.2.1.3 Originator's Public Key

```
<asmDecl> ::= .publickey = ( <bytes> ) | ...
```

The CLI metadata allows the producer of an assembly to compute a cryptographic hash of the assembly (using the SHA1 hash function) and then encrypt it using the RSA algorithm and a public/private key pair of the producer's choosing. The results of this (an "SHA1/RSA digital signature") can then be stored in the metadata along with the public part of the key pair required by the RSA algorithm. The **.publickey** directive is used to specify the public key that was used to compute the signature. To calculate the hash, the signature is zeroed, the hash calculated, then the result stored into the signature.

A reference to an assembly (see Partition II, section 6.3) captures some of this information at compile time. At runtime, the information contained in the assembly reference can be combined with the information from the manifest of the assembly located at runtime to ensure that the same private key was used to create both the assembly seen when the reference was created (compile time) and when it is resolved (runtime).

6.2.1.4 Version Numbers

```
<asmDecl> ::= .ver <int32> : <int32> : <int32> : <int32> | ...
```

The version number of the assembly is specified as four 32-bit integers. This version number shall be captured at compile time and used as part of all references to the assembly within the compiled module. This standard places no other requirements on the use of the version numbers.

All standardized assemblies shall have the last two 32-bit integers set to 0. This standard places no other requirement on the use of the version numbers, although individual implementers are urged to avoid setting both of the last two 32-bit integers to 0 to avoid a possible collision with future standards.

Future versions of this standard shall change one or both of the first two 32-bit integers specified for a standardized assembly if any additional functionality is added or any additional features of the virtual machine are required to implement it. Furthermore, this standard shall change one or both of the first two 32-bit integers specified for the **mscorlib** assembly so that its version number may be used (if desired) to distinguish between different versions of the Virtual Execution system required to run programs conforming to that version of the standard.

NOTE

A conforming implementation may ignore version numbers entirely, or it may require that they match precisely when binding a reference, or any other behavior deemed appropriate. By convention:

The first of these is considered the major version number, and assemblies with the same name but different major versions are not interchangeable. This would be appropriate, for example, for a major rewrite of a product where backward compatibility cannot be assumed.

The second of these is considered the minor version number, and assemblies with the same name and major version but different minor versions indicate significant enhancements but with intention to be backward compatible. This would be appropriate, for example, on a "point release" of a product or a fully backward compatible new version of a product.

The third of these is considered the revision number, and assemblies with the same name, major and minor version number, but different revisions are intended to be fully interchangeable. This would be appropriate, for example, to fix a security hole in a previously released assembly.

The fourth of these is considered the build number, and assemblies that differ only by build number are intended to represent a recompilation from the same source. This would be appropriate, for example, because of processor, platform, or compiler changes.

6.2.2 *Manifest Resources*

A **manifest resource** is simply a named item of data associated with an assembly. A manifest resource is introduced using the **.mresource** directive, which adds the manifest resource to the assembly manifest begun by a preceding **.assembly** declaration.

ANNOTATION: Manifest resources are named items of data in a file that is part of the manifest. Both the file and how to access the data of interest in the file are specified in the manifest. This is distinct from specifying a file to be used as a whole, as described in the section following this one. A file used as a whole is often documentation, as opposed to the data within a file that is a manifest resource.

<decl> ::=	Section in Partition II
.mresource [**public** | **private**] <dottedname> { <manResDecl>* }	5.10
| ...	

If the manifest resource is declared public, it is exported from the assembly. If it is declared private, it is not exported and hence only available from within the assembly. The <dotted-name> is the name of the resource, and the optional quoted string is a description of the resource.

<manResDecl> ::=	Description	Section in Partition II
.assembly extern <dottedname>	Manifest resource is in external assembly with name <dottedname>.	6.3
| **.custom** <customDecl>	Custom attribute.	20
| **.file** <dottedname> **at** <int32>	Manifest resource is in file <dotted-name> at byte offset <int32>.	

For a resource stored in a file that is not a module (for example, an attached text file), the file shall be declared in the manifest using a separate (top-level) **.file** declaration (see Partition II, section 6.2.3) and the byte offset shall be zero. Similarly, a resource that is defined in another assembly is referenced using **.assembly extern,** which requires that the assembly has been defined in a separate (top-level) **.assembly extern** directive (see Partition II, section 6.3).

6.2.3 *Files in the Assembly*

Assemblies may be associated with other files—e.g., documentation and other files that are used during execution. The declaration **.file** is used to add a reference to such a file to the manifest of the assembly (see Partition II, section 21.19).

<decl> ::=	Section in Partition II
.file [**nometadata**] <filename> **.hash** = (<bytes>) [**.entrypoint**]	5.10
| ...	

The attribute **nometadata** is specified if the file is not a module according to this specification. Files that are marked as **nometadata** may have any format; they are considered pure data files.

The <bytes> after the **.hash** specify a hash value computed for the file. The VES shall recompute this hash value prior to accessing this file and shall generate an exception if it does not match. The algorithm used to calculate this hash value is specified with **.hash algorithm** (see Partition II, section 6.2.1.1).

If specified, the **.entrypoint** directive indicates that the entry point of a multi-module assembly is contained in this file.

ANNOTATION

Implementation-Specific (Microsoft): If the hash value is not specified, it will be automatically computed by the assembly linker **al** when an assembly file is created using **al**. Even though the hash value is optional in the grammar for ilasm, it is required at runtime.

6.3 Referencing Assemblies

```
<asmRefDecl> ::= .assembly extern <dottedname> [ as <dottedname> ]
                 { <asmRefDecl>* }
```

An assembly mediates all accesses from the files that it contains to other assemblies. This is done through the metadata by requiring that the manifest for the executing assembly contain a declaration for any assembly referenced by the executing code. The syntax **.assembly extern** as a top-level declaration is used for this purpose. The optional **as** clause provides an alias which allows ilasm to address external assemblies that have the same name, but that differ in version, culture, etc.

The dotted name used in **.assembly extern** shall exactly match the name of the assembly as declared with the **.assembly** directive in a case-sensitive manner. (So, even though an assembly might be stored within a file, within a file system that is case-blind, the names stored internally within metadata are case-sensitive, and shall match exactly.)

ANNOTATION: A complete program often consists of more than one assembly. In that case, the other assembly or assemblies that a given assembly might use are specified in the manifest. In ilasm, it is done with the **.assembly extern** directive.

Implementation-Specific (Microsoft): The assembly mscorlib contains many of the types and methods in the Base Class Library. For convenience, ilasm automatically inserts a **.assembly extern** *mscorlib* declaration if required.

<asmRefDecl> ::=	Description	Section in Partition II
.hash = (<bytes>)	Hash of referenced assembly	6.2.3
| **.custom** <customDecl>	Custom attributes	20
| **.culture** <QSTRING>	Culture of the referenced assembly	6.2.1.2
| **.publickeytoken** = (<bytes>)	The low 8 bytes of the SHA1 hash of the originator's public key	6.3
| **.publickey** = (<bytes>)	The originator's full public key	6.2.1.3
| **.ver** <int32> : <int32> : <int32> : <int32>	Major version, minor version, revision, and build	6.2.1.4

These declarations are the same as those for **.assembly** declarations (Partition II, section 6.2.1), except for the addition of **.publickeytoken.** This declaration is used to store the low 8 bytes of the SHA1 hash of the originator's public key in the assembly reference, rather than the full public key.

An assembly reference can store either a full public key or an 8-byte "publickeytoken." Either can be used to validate that the same private key used to sign the assembly at compile time signed the assembly used at runtime. Neither is required to be present, and while both can be stored, this is not useful.

A conforming implementation of the CLI need not perform this validation, but it is permitted to do so, and it may refuse to load an assembly for which the validation fails. A conforming implementation of the CLI may also refuse to permit access to an assembly unless the assembly reference contains either the public key or the public key token. A conforming implementation of the CLI shall make the same access decision independent of whether a public key or a token is used.

RATIONALE

The full public key is cryptographically safer, but requires more storage space in the assembly reference.

```
Example (informative):
.assembly extern MyComponents
{ .publickey = (BB AA BB EE 11 22 33 00)
  .hash = (2A 71 E9 47 F5 15 E6 07 35 E4 CB E3 B4 A1 D3 7F 7F A0 9C 24)
  .ver 2:10:2002:0
}
```

6.4 Declaring Modules

All CIL files are modules and are referenced by a logical name carried in the metadata rather than their file name. See Partition II, section 21.27.

<decl> ::=	Section in Partition II
| .module <filename>	5.10
| ...	

```
Example (informative):
.module CountDown.exe
```

ANNOTATION

Implementation-Specific (Microsoft): If the **.module** directive is missing, ilasm will automatically add a **.module** directive and set the module name to be the file name, including its extension in capital letters. For example, if the file is called "foo" and compiled into an executable, the module name will become "Foo.EXE."

Note that ilasm also generates a required GUID to uniquely identify this instance of the module and emits that into the Mvid metadata field: see Partition II, section 21.27.

6.5 Referencing Modules

When an item is in the current assembly but part of a different module than the one containing the manifest, the defining module shall be declared in the manifest of the assembly using the **.module extern** directive. The name used in the **.module extern** directive of the referencing assembly shall exactly match the name used in the **.module** directive (see Partition II, section 6.4) of the defining module. See Partition II, section 21.28.

<decl> ::=	Section in Partition II
| **.module extern** <filename>	5.10
| ...	

```
Example (informative):
.module extern Counter.dll
```

6.6 Declarations inside a Module or Assembly

Declarations inside a module or assembly are specified by the following grammar. More information on each option can be found in the corresponding section.

<decl> ::=	Section in Partition II
| **.class** <classHead> { <classMember>* }	9
| **.custom** <customDecl>	20
| **.data** <datadecl>	15.3.1
| **.field** <fieldDecl>	15
| **.method** <methodHead> { <methodBodyItem>* }	14
| <externSourceDecl>	5.7
| <securityDecl>	19
| ...	

6.7 Exported Type Definitions

The manifest module, of which there can only be one per assembly, includes the **.assembly** statement. To export a type defined in any other module of an assembly requires an entry in the assembly's manifest. The following grammar is used to construct such an entry in the manifest:

<decl> ::=	Section in Partition II
`.class extern <exportAttr> <dottedname> { <externClassDecl>* }`	[21.14]

<externClassDecl> ::=	Section in Partition II

`.file <dottedname>`
`| .class extern <dottedname>`
`| .custom <customDecl>`
	20

The <exportAttr> value shall be either **public** or **nested public** and shall match the visibility of the type.

For example, suppose an assembly consists of two modules: A.EXE and B.DLL. A.EXE contains the manifest. A public class "Foo" is defined in B.DLL. In order to export it—that is, to make it visible by, and usable from, other assemblies –a **.class extern** statement shall be included in A.EXE.

Conversely, a public class "Bar" defined in A.EXE does not need any **.class extern** statement.

> **RATIONALE**
> Tools should be able to retrieve a single module, the manifest module, to determine the complete set of types defined by the assembly. Therefore, information from other modules within the assembly is replicated in the manifest module. By convention, the manifest module is also known as the assembly.

7 Types and Signatures

The metadata provides mechanisms to both *define* types and *reference* types. Partition II, section 9 describes the metadata associated with a type definition, regardless of whether the type is an interface, class, or a value type.

The mechanism used to reference types is divided into two parts. The first is the creation of a logical description of user-defined types that are referenced but (typically) not defined in the current module. These are stored in a logical table in the metadata (see Partition II, section 21.35).

The second is a *signature* that encodes one or more type references, along with a variety of modifiers. The grammar non-terminal `<type>` describes an individual entry in a signature. The encoding of a signature is specified in Partition II, section 22.1.15.

ANNOTATION: Type definitions are the heart of the CLI. There are built-in types, for which the VES must create a definition on declaration; class types, which are defined with one of the base library classes; global methods, which are methods that are not part of a class; managed and unmanaged pointers; and arrays. Like built-in types, both kinds of pointers and arrays are defined by the VES upon declaration, without a specific definition. The grammar also allows both optional and required modifiers to types.

7.1 Types

The following grammar completely specifies all built-in types, including pointer types of the CLI system. It also shows the syntax for user-defined types that can be defined in the CLI system:

`<type> ::=`	Description	Section in Partition II
bool	Boolean.	7.2
| **boxed** `<typeReference>`	Boxed user-defined value type.	
| **char**	16-bit Unicode code point.	7.2
| **class** `<typeReference>`	User-defined reference type.	7.3
| **float32**	32-bit floating point number.	7.2
| **float64**	64-bit floating point number.	7.2
| **int8**	Signed 8-bit integer.	7.2
| **int16**	Signed 16-bit integer.	7.2
| **int32**	Signed 32-bit integer.	7.2
| **int64**	Signed 64-bit integer.	7.2

<type> ::=	Description	Section in Partition II
| **method** <callConv> <type> * (<parameters>)	Method pointer.	13.5
| **native int**	Signed integer whose size varies depending on platform (32- or 64-bit).	7.2
| **native unsigned int**	Unsigned integer whose size varies depending on platform (32- or 64-bit).	7.2
| **object**	See `System.Object` in the *.NET Framework Standard Library Annotated Reference.*	[7.2]
| **string**	See `System.String` in the *.NET Framework Standard Library Annotated Reference.*	[7.2]
| <type> **&**	Managed pointer to ‹type›. ‹type› shall not be a managed pointer type or **typedref.**	13.4
| <type> *****	Unmanaged pointer to ‹type›.	13.4
| <type> **[** [<bound> [,<bound>]*] **]**	Array of ‹type› with optional rank (number of dimensions) and bounds.	13.1 and 13.2
| <type> **modopt** (<typeReference>)	Custom modifier that may be ignored by the caller.	7.1.1
| <type> **modreq** (<typeReference>)	Custom modifier that the caller shall understand.	7.1.1
| <type> **pinned**	For local variables only. The garbage collector shall not move the referenced value.	7.1.2
| **typedref**	Typed reference, created by **mkrefany** and used by **refanytype** or **refanyval.**	7.2

<type> ::=	Description	Section in Partition II
| **valuetype** <typeReference>	User-defined value type (unboxed).	12.1
| **unsigned int8**	Unsigned 8-bit integers.	7.2
| **unsigned int16**	Unsigned 16-bit integers.	7.2
| **unsigned int32**	Unsigned 32-bit integers.	7.2
| **unsigned int64**	Unsigned 64-bit integers.	7.2
| **void**	No type. Only allowed as a return type or as part of **void** *.	

In several situations the grammar permits the use of a slightly simpler mechanism for specifying types, by just allowing type names (e.g., "System.GC") to be used instead of the full algebra (e.g., "class System.GC"). These are called **type specifications**:

<typeSpec> ::=	Section in Partition II
[[.module] <dottedname>]	7.3
| <typeReference>	7.3
| <type>	7.1

ANNOTATION: The <typedref> is an elegant construct not currently used by any languages. It requires that both the reference to an address and its data type will be passed. It is an artifact of **paramvalues**, which were part of earlier versions of Microsoft Visual Basic. Although no longer available in Visual Basic, it would be useful in a language with dynamic types, or languages with variable-length argument lists.

7.1.1 *modreq and modopt*

Custom modifiers, defined using **modreq** ("required modifier") and **modopt** ("optional modifier"), are similar to custom attributes (see Partition II, section 20) except that modifiers are part of a signature rather than attached to a declaration. Each modifer associates a type reference with an item in the signature.

The CLI itself shall treat required and optional modifiers in the same manner. Two signatures that differ only by the addition of a custom modifier (required or optional) shall not be considered to match. Custom modifiers have no other effect on the operation of the VES.

RATIONALE

The distinction between required and optional modifiers is important to tools other than the CLI that deal with the metadata, typically compilers and program analyzers. A required modifier indicates that there is a special semantics to the modified item that should not be ignored, while an optional modifier can simply be ignored.

For example, the concept of const in the C programming language can be modelled with an optional modifier, since the caller of a method that has a constant parameter need not treat it in any special way. On the other hand, a parameter that shall be copy constructed in C++ shall be marked with a required custom attribute, since it is the caller who makes the copy.

ANNOTATION: The **modopt** construct tells the compiler that there is more information about the type, but the information is compiler-specific, and it will have no effect on compilers that do not recognize the modifer. The **modreq** modifer, on the other hand, requires any compiler to recognize the modifer. If it does not, the compiler cannot use the parameter and must return an error.

7.1.2 *pinned*

The signature encoding for **pinned** shall appear only in signatures that describe local variables (see Partition II, section 14.4.1.3). While a method with a pinned local variable is executing, the VES shall not relocate the object to which the local refers. That is, if the implementation of the CLI uses a garbage collector that moves objects, the collector shall not move objects that are referenced by an active pinned local variable.

RATIONALE

If unmanaged pointers are used to dereference managed objects, these objects shall be pinned. This happens, for example, when a managed object is passed to a method designed to operate with unmanaged data.

ANNOTATION: Pinning is necessary to enable unmanaged code (code that does not deal with the garbage collector) to work with managed objects. Managed references (<type>&) are tied to objects, so if the object moves by virtue of a garbage collector, the reference moves with it. In contrast, an unmanaged reference (unmanaged pointer) is tied to a specific address. If the object to which it points moves, the reference stays, and unpredictable results follow. Pinning allows the programmer to fix the object to which the reference points. This is generally used for machine assembly language or C and C++ programs that have been compiled for CLI execution.

Other than dealing with unmanaged programs, pinning is not generally used, because a garbage collector must move things around the pinned object. This would make the garbage collector slower, make holes in memory, etc.

7.2 Built-in Types

The CLI built-in types have corresponding value types defined in the Base Class Library. They shall be referenced in signatures only using their special encodings (i.e., not using the general-purpose **valuetype** `<typeReference>` syntax). Partition I [section 8.2.2] specifies the built-in types.

ANNOTATION: Built-in types must be defined by the VES upon their declaration, and they do not require the specific definition required of most types. The built-in numeric types (which are value types) are shown in the following table, copied here from Partition I, section 8.2.2:

Name in CIL Assembler	CLS Type?	Name in Class Library (see the *.NET Framework Standard Library Annotated Reference*)	Description
`bool`	Yes	`System.Boolean`	True/false value
`char`	Yes	`System.Char`	Unicode 16-bit char
`object`	Yes	`System.Object`	Object or boxed value type
`string`	Yes	`System.String`	Unicode string
`float32`	Yes	`System.Single`	IEC 60559:1989 32-bit float

3. Metadata Semantics

Name in CIL Assembler	CLS Type?	Name in Class Library (see the *.NET Framework Standard Library Annotated Reference*)	Description
`float64`	Yes	`System.Double`	IEC 60559:1989 64-bit float
`int8`	No	`System.SByte`	Signed 8-bit integer
`int16`	Yes	`System.Int16`	Signed 16-bit integer
`int32`	Yes	`System.Int32`	Signed 32-bit integer
`int64`	Yes	`System.Int64`	Signed 64-bit integer
`native int`	Yes	`System.IntPtr`	Signed integer, native size
`native unsigned int`	No	`System.UIntPtr`	Unsigned integer, native size
`typedref`	No	`System.TypedReference`	Pointer plus runtime type
`unsigned int8`	Yes	`System.Byte`	Unsigned 8-bit integer
`unsigned int16`	No	`System.UInt16`	Unsigned 16-bit integer
`unsigned int32`	No	`System.UInt32`	Unsigned 32-bit integer
`unsigned int64`	No	`System.UInt64`	Unsigned 64-bit integer

7.3 References to User-Defined Types (‹typeReference›)

User-defined types are referenced either using their full name and a resolution scope or (if one is available in the same module) a type definition (see Partition II, section 9).

A `<typeReference>` is used to capture the full name and resolution scope.

```
<typeReference> ::=
   [<resolutionScope>] <dottedname> [/ <dottedname>]*
```

<resolutionScope> ::=
[.module <filename> **]**
| **[** <assemblyRefName> **]**

<assemblyRefName> ::=	Section in Partition II
<dottedname>	5.3

The following resolution scopes are specified for un-nested types:

- **Current module (and, hence, assembly)**. This is the most common case and is the default if no resolution scope is specified. The type shall be resolved to a definition only if the definition occurs in the same module as the reference.

> **NOTE**
> A type reference that refers to a type in the same module and assembly is better represented using a type definition. Where this is not possible (for example, when referencing a nested type that has **compilercontrolled** accessibility) or convenient (for example, in some one-pass compilers), a type reference is equivalent and may be used.

- **Different module, current assembly**. The resolution scope shall be a module reference syntactically reprented using the notation `[.module <filename>]`. The type shall be resolved to a definition only if the referenced module (see Partition II, section 6.4) and type (see Partition II, section 6.7) have been declared by the current assembly and hence have entries in the assembly's manifest. Note that in this case the manifest is not physically stored with the referencing module.
- **Different assembly**. The resolution scope shall be an assembly reference syntactically represented using the notation `[<assemblyRefName>]`. The referenced assembly shall be declared in the manifest for the current assembly (see Partition II, section 6.3), the type shall be declared in the referenced assembly's manifest, and the type shall be marked as exported from that assembly (see Partition II, sections 6.7 and 9.1.1).

- For nested types, the resolution scope is always the enclosing type (see Partition II, section 9.6). This is indicated syntactically by using a slash ("/") to separate the enclosing type name from the nested type's name.

  Example (informative):

  The proper way to refer to a type defined in the Base Class Library. The name of the type is `System.Console`, and it is found in the assembly named *mscorlib*.

  ```
  .assembly extern mscorlib { }
  .class [mscorlib]System.Console
  ```

  A reference to the type named `C.D` in the module named *x* in the current assembly.

  ```
  .module extern x
  .class [.module x]C.D
  ```

  A reference to the type named `C` nested inside of the type named `Foo.Bar` in another assembly, named *MyAssembly*.

  ```
  .assembly extern MyAssembly { }
  .class [MyAssembly]Foo.Bar/C
  ```

7.4 Native Data Types

Some implementations of the CLI will be hosted on top of existing operating systems or runtime platforms that specify data types required to perform certain functions. The metadata allows interaction with these **native data types** by specifying how the built-in and user-defined types of the CLI are to be marshalled to and from native data types. This marshalling information can be specified (using the keyword **marshal**) for

- The return type of a method, indicating that a native data type is actually returned and shall be marshalled back into the specified CLI data type
- A parameter to a method, indicating that the CLI data type provided by the caller shall be marshalled into the specified native data type (if the parameter is passed by reference, the updated value shall be marshalled back from the native data type into the CLI data type when the call is completed)
- A field of a user-defined type, indicating that any attempt to pass the object in which it occurs to platform methods shall make a copy of the object, replacing the field by the specified native data type (if the object is passed by reference, then the updated value shall be marshalled back when the call is completed)

The following table lists all native types supported by the CLI and provides a description for each of them. A more complete description can be found in the *.NET Framework Standard Library Annotated Reference* in the definition of the enum `System.Runtime.Interopservices.UnmanagedType`, which provides the actual values used to encode the types. All encoding values from 0 through 63 are reserved for backward compatibility with existing implementations of the CLI. Values 64 through 127 are reserved for future use in this and related standards.

`<nativeType> ::=`	Description	Name in Class Library
`[ ]`	Native array. Type and size are determined at runtime from the actual marshalled array.	LPArray
`| bool`	Boolean. 4-byte integer value where a non-zero value represents TRUE and 0 represents FALSE.	Bool
`| float32`	32-bit floating point number.	FLOAT32
`| float64`	64-bit floating point number.	FLOAT64
`| [unsigned] int`	Signed or unsigned integer, sized to hold a pointer on the platform.	SysUInt or SysInt
`| [unsigned] int8`	Signed or unsigned 8-bit integer.	unsigned int8 or int8
`| [unsigned] int16`	Signed or unsigned 16-bit integer.	unsigned int16 or int16
`| [unsigned] int32`	Signed or unsigned 32-bit integer.	unsigned int32 or int32
`| [unsigned] int64`	Signed or unsigned 64-bit integer.	unsigned int64 or int64
`| lpstr`	A pointer to a null terminated array of ANSI characters. Code page is implementation specific.	LPStr
`| lptstr`	A pointer to a null terminated array of platform characters (ANSI or Unicode). Code page and character encoding are implementation-specific.	LPTStr
`| lpvoid`	An untyped pointer; platform specifies size.	LPVoid
`| lpwstr`	A pointer to a null terminated array of Unicode characters. Character encoding is implementation-specific.	LPWStr

`<nativeType> ::=`	Description	Name in Class Library
`| method`	A function pointer.	FunctionPtr
`| <nativeType> [ ]`	Array of <nativeType>. The length is determined at runtime by the size of the actual marshalled array.	LPArray
`| <nativeType> [ <int32> ]`	Array of <nativeType> of length <int32>.	LPArray
`| <nativeType> [ + <int32> ]`	Array of <nativeType> with runtime-supplied element size. The int32 specifies a parameter to the current method (counting from parameter number 0) that, at runtime, will contain the size of an element of the array in bytes. Can only be applied to methods, not fields.	LPArray
`| <nativeType> [ <int32> + <int32> ]`	Array of <nativeType> with runtime-supplied element size. The first int32 specifies the number of elements in the array. The second int32 specifies which parameter to the current method (counting from parameter number 1) will specify the additional number of elements in the array. Can only be applied to methods, not fields.	LPArray

ANNOTATION

Implementation-Specific (Microsoft): The Microsoft implementation supports a richer set of types to describe marshalling between Windows native types and COM. These additional options are listed in the following table:

`<nativeType> ::=`	Description	Name in Class Library
`| as any`	Determines the type of an object at runtime and marshals the object as that type.	AsAny
`| byvalstr`	A string in a fixed-length buffer.	VBByRefStr

<nativeType> ::=	Description	Name in Class Library
| **custom** (<QSTRING>, <QSTRING>)	Custom marshaller. The first string is the name of the marshalling class, using the string conventions of Reflection.Emit to specify the assembly and/or module. The second is an arbitrary string passed to the marshaller at runtime to identify the form of marshalling required.	CustomMarshaler
| **fixed array** [<int32>]	A fixed-size array of length <int32> bytes.	ByValArray
| **fixed sysstring** [<int32>]	A fixed-size system string of length <int32>. This can only be applied to fields, and a separate attribute specifies the encoding of the string.	ByValTStr
| **lpstruct**	A pointer to a C-style structure. Used to marshal managed formatted types.	LPStruct
| **struct**	A C-style structure, used to marshal managed formatted types.	Struct

Example (informative):

```
.method int32 M1( int32 marshal(int32), bool[] marshal(bool[5]) )
```

Method M1 takes two arguments: an int32, and an array of five bools

++++++++++

```
.method int32 M2( int32 marshal(int32), bool[] marshal(bool[+1]) )
```

Method M2 takes two arguments: an int32, and an array of bools: the number of elements in that array is given by the value of the first parameter

++++++++++

```
.method int32 M3( int32 marshal(int32), bool[] marshal(bool[7+1]) )
```

Method M3 takes two arguments: an int32, and an array of bools: the number of elements in that array is given as 7 plus the value of the first parameter

8 Visibility, Accessibility, and Hiding

Partition I, section 8.5.3 specifies visibility and accessibility. In addition to these attributes, the metadata stores information about method name hiding. **Hiding** controls which method names inherited from a base type are available for compile-time name binding.

ANNOTATION: Most programming languages do not distinguish between visibilitiy and accessibility, hence it is a confusing concept. **Visibility** concerns only top-level types—it determines whether or not they are visible outside their assembly or module. Those are the only two possibilities that make any sense for a top-level type, because generally it is always visible inside its own assembly and its subclasses can see it. The **accessibility** modes apply to nested types, fields, properties, and events, and determine who has access to them—everyone, no one, another assembly, or subclasses.

Hiding is a much more complicated issue. It is supported by the VES for the use of compilers but has no impact on the VES itself. Languages use it at compile time to determine whether a parent implementation can be seen in a subclass. However, languages have chosen two different approaches, and it is important for cross-language interoperability to know which model a language uses.

For example, suppose a parent class has a method **F(*int*)**, and a subclass with a method **F(*string*)**. For languages like C++, which hide by name, the parent, **F(*int*)** would not be visible, because it has the same method name, **F**, as the child. However, in languages like Java and C#, which hide by name-and-signature, both would be visible, because the signatures do not match. If there were an **F(*int*)** in the subclass, it would supersede the parent **F**, because both name and signature match.

For hiding, compilers are supposed to follow the rules of the language from which they get the module, even if their own rules differ.

8.1 Visibility of Top-Level Types and Accessibility of Nested Types

Visibility is attached only to top-level types, and there are only two possibilities: visible to types within the same assembly, or visible to types regardless of assembly. For nested types (i.e., types that are members of another type), the nested type has an *accessibility* that further refines the set of methods that can reference the type. A nested type may have any of the seven accessibility modes (see Partition I, section 8.5.3.2), but has no direct visibility attribute of its own, using the visibility of its enclosing type instead.

Because the visibility of a top-level type controls the visibility of the names of all of its members, a nested type cannot be more visible than the type in which it is nested. That is, if the enclosing type is visible only within an assembly, then a nested type with public accessibility is still only available within the assembly. By contrast, a nested type that has assembly accessibility is restricted to use within the assembly even if the enclosing type is visible outside the assembly.

To make the encoding of all types consistent and compact, the visibility of a top-level type and the accessibility of a nested type are encoded using the same mechanism in the logical model of Partition II, section 22.1. 14.

8.2 Accessibility

Accessibility is encoded directly in the metadata. See, for example, Partition II, section 21.24.

ANNOTATION: The available accessibility modes are compiler-controlled, private, family, assembly, family-and-assembly, family-or-assembly, and public. For much more information on these, see Partition I, section 8.5.3.2.

8.3 Hiding

Hiding is a compile-time concept that applies to individual methods of a type. The CTS specifies two mechanisms for hiding, specified by a single bit:

- *hide-by-name*, meaning that the introduction of a name in a given type hides all inherited members of the same kind (method or field) with the same name.
- *hide-by-name-and-sig*, meaning that the introduction of a name in a given type hides any inherited member of the same kind but with precisely the same type (for fields) or signature (for methods, properties, and events).

There is no runtime support for hiding. A conforming implementation of the CLI treats all references as though the names were marked hide-by-name-and-sig. Compilers that desire the effect of hide-by-name can do so by marking method definitions with the `newslot` attribute (see Partition II, section 14.4.2.3) and correctly choosing the type used to resolve a method reference (see Partition II, section 14.1.3).

9 Defining Types

Types (i.e., classes, value types, and interfaces) may be defined at the top level of a module:

<decl> ::=	Section in Partition II
.class <classHead> { <classMember>* }	5.10
| ...	

The logical metadata table created by this declaration is specified in Partition II, section 21.34.

> **RATIONALE**
> For historical reasons, many of the syntactic classes used for defining types incorrectly use "class" instead of "type" in their name. All classes are types, but "types" is a broader term encompassing value types, and interfaces.

9.1 Type Header (<classHead>)

A type header consists of

- Any number of type attributes
- A name (an <id>)
- A base type (or parent type), which defaults to `System.Object`
- An optional list of interfaces whose contract this type and all its descendant types shall satisfy

<classHead> ::=
<classAttr>* <id> [**extends** <typeReference>] [**implements** <typeReference> [, <typeReference>]*]

The **extends** keyword defines the *base type* of a type. A type shall extend from exactly one other type. If no type is specified, ilasm will add an **extends** clause to make the type inherit from `System.Object`.

The **implements** keyword defines the *interfaces* of a type. By listing an interface here, a type declares that all of its concrete implementations will support the contract of that interface, including providing implementations of any virtual methods the interface declares. See also Partition II, sections 10 and 11.

```
Example (informative):
.class private auto autochar CounterTextBox
   extends [System.Windows.Forms]System.Windows.Forms.TextBox
   implements [.module Counter]CountDisplay
{ // body of the class
}
```

This code declares the class CounterTextBox, which extends the class System.Windows.Forms.TextBox in the assembly System.Windows.Forms and implements the interface CountDisplay in the module *Counter* of the current assembly. The attributes **private**, **auto**, and **autochar** are described in the following sections.

A type can have any number of custom attributes attached. Custom attributes are attached as described in Partition II, section 20. The other (predefined) attributes of a type may be grouped into attributes that specify visibility, type layout information, type semantics information, inheritance rules, interoperation information, and information on special handling. The following subsections provide additional information on each group of predefined attributes.

<classAttr> ::=	Description	Section in Partition II
abstract	Type is **abstract.**	9.1.4
| ansi	Marshal strings to platform as **ANSI**.	9.1.5
| auto	Auto layout of type.	9.1.2
| autochar	Marshal strings to platform based on platform.	9.1.5
| beforefieldinit	Calling static methods does not initialize type.	9.1.6
| explicit	Layout of fields is provided explicitly.	9.1.2
| interface	Interface declaration.	9.1.3
| nested assembly	Assembly accessibility for nested type.	9.1.1
| nested famandassem	Family-and-assembly accessibility for nested type.	9.1.1
| nested family	Family accessibility for nested type.	9.1.1
| nested famorassem	Family-or-assembly accessibility for nested type.	9.1.1
| nested private	Private accessibility for nested type.	9.1.1

<classAttr> ::=	Description	Section in Partition II
| **nested public**	Public accessibility for nested type.	9.1.1
| **private**	Private visibility of top-level type.	9.1.1
| **public**	Public visibility of top-level type.	9.1.1
| **rtspecialname**	Special treatment by runtime.	9.1.6
| **sealed**	The type cannot be subclassed.	9.1.4
| **sequential**	The type is laid out sequentially.	9.1.2
| **serializable**	Type may be serialized.	9.1.6
| **specialname**	Special treatment by tools.	9.1.6
| **unicode**	Marshal strings to platform as Unicode.	9.1.5

ANNOTATION

Implementation-Specific (Microsoft): The above grammar also includes

```
<classAttr> ::= import
```

to indicate that the type is imported from a COM type library.

9.1.1 *Visibility and Accessibility Attributes*

<classAttr> ::= ...
| **nested assembly**
| **nested famandassem**
| **nested family**
| **nested famorassem**
| **nested private**
| **nested public**

| **private**
| **public**

See Partition I [section 8.5.3]. A type that is not nested inside another shall have exactly one visibility (private or public) and shall not have an accessiblity. Nested types shall have no visibility, but instead shall have exactly one of the accessibility attributes (nested assembly, nested famandassem, nested family, nested famorassem, nested private, or nested public). The default visibility for top-level types is private. The default accessibility for nested types is nested private.

9.1.2 *Type Layout Attributes*

<classAttr> ::= ...
| **auto**
| **explicit**
| **sequential**

The type layout specifies how the fields of an instance of a type are arranged. A given type shall have only one layout attribute specified. By convention, ilasm supplies auto if no layout attribute is specified.

auto: The layout shall be done by the CLI, with no user-supplied constraints.

explicit: The layout of the fields is explicitly provided (see Partition II, section 9.7).

sequential: The CLI shall lay out the fields in sequential order, based on the order of the fields in the logical metadata table (see Partition II, section 21.15).

> **RATIONALE**
> The default **auto** layout should provide the best layout for the platform on which the code is executing. **sequential** layout is intended to instruct the CLI to match layout rules commonly followed by languages like C and C++ on an individual platform, where this is possible while still guaranteeing verifiable layout. **explicit** layout allows the CIL generator to specify the precise layout semantics.

9.1.3 *Type Semantics Attributes*

<classAttr> ::= ...
| **interface**

The type semantic attributes specify whether an interface, class, or value type shall be defined. The interface attribute specifies an interface. If this attribute is not present and the definition extends (directly or indirectly) `System.ValueType`, a value type shall be defined (see Partition II, section 12). Otherwise, a class shall be defined (see Partition II, section 10).

Note that the runtime size of a value type shall not exceed 1 MByte (0x100000 bytes)

ANNOTATION

Implementation-Specific (Microsoft): The current implementation allows 0x3F0000 bytes, but this size may be reduced in future.

9.1.4 *Inheritance Attributes*

<classAttr> ::= ...
| **abstract**
| **sealed**

Attributes that specify special semantics are **abstract** and **sealed**. These attributes may be used together.

abstract specifies that this type shall not be instantiated. If a type contains **abstract** methods, the type shall be declared as an **abstract** type.

sealed specifies that a type shall not have subclasses. All value types shall be sealed.

RATIONALE

Virtual methods of sealed types are effectively instance methods, since they cannot be overridden. Framework authors should use sealed classes sparingly, since they do not provide a convenient building block for user extensibility. Sealed classes may be necessary when the implementation of a set of virtual methods for a single class (typically inherited from different interfaces) becomes interdependent or depends critically on implementation details not visible to potential subclasses.

A type that is both **abstract** and **sealed** should have only static members, and serves as what some languages call a namespace.

9.1.5 *Interoperation Attributes*

```
<classAttr> ::= ...
| ansi
| autochar
| unicode
```

These attributes are for interoperation with unmanaged code. They specify the default behavior to be used when calling a method (static, instance, or virtual) on the class that has an argument or return type of `System.String` and does not itself specify marshalling behavior. Only one value shall be specified for any type, and the default value is **ansi**.

ansi specifies that marshalling shall be to and from **ANSI** strings.

unicode specifies that marshalling shall be to and from Unicode strings.

autochar specifies either **ANSI** or Unicode behavior, depending on the platform on which the CLI is running.

ANNOTATION: Although in the managed world there is only one type of string, in the unmanaged world there are two standards—ANSI and Unicode—so it is important to specify what the native code uses as the string standard. Typically, this specification is done per class, but it can be done per parameter.

9.1.6 *Special Handling Attributes*

```
<classAttr> ::= ...
| beforefieldinit
```

| **serializable**
| **specialname**
| **rtspecialname**

These attributes may be combined in any way.

beforefieldinit instructs the CLI that it need not initialize the type before a static method is called. See Partition II, section 9.5.3.

ANNOTATION

Implementation-Specific (Microsoft): The **serializable** bit is in the file format and so is listed here, but its use is not standardized. Its presence does allow an implementation of serialization, enabling remoting, interactive Web services, saving data in persistent format, etc. In the Microsoft CLI implementation—the Common Language Runtime—**serializable** indicates that the fields of the type may be serialized into a data stream by the CLR serializer.

---

specialname indicates that the name of this item may have special significance to tools other than the CLI. See, for example, Partition I, sections 8.11.3 and 8.11.4.

rtspecialname indicates that the name of this item has special significance to the CLI. There are no currently defined special type names; this is for future use. Any item marked **rtspecialname** shall also be marked **specialname**.

RATIONALE

If an item is treated specially by the CLI, then tools should also be made aware of that. The converse is not true.

9.2 Body of a Type Definition

A type may contain any number of further declarations. The directives **.event**, **.field**, **.method**, and **.property** are used to declare members of a type. The directive **.class** inside a type declaration is used to create a nested type, which is discussed in further detail in Partition II, section 9.6.

<table>
<tr><th><classMember> ::=</th><th>Description</th><th>Section in Partition II</th></tr>
<tr><td>.class <classHead> { <classMember>* }</td><td>Defines a nested type.</td><td>9</td></tr>
<tr><td>| .custom <customDecl></td><td>Custom attribute.</td><td>20</td></tr>
<tr><td>| .data <datadecl></td><td>Defines static data associated with the type.</td><td>15.3</td></tr>
<tr><td>| .event <eventHead> { <eventMember>* }</td><td>Declares an event.</td><td>17</td></tr>
<tr><td>| .field <fieldDecl></td><td>Declares a field belonging to the type.</td><td>15</td></tr>
<tr><td>| .method <methodHead> { <methodBodyItem>* }</td><td>Declares a method of the type.</td><td>14</td></tr>
<tr><td>| .override <typeSpec> :: <methodName> with <callConv> <type> <typeSpec> :: <methodName> (<parameters>)</td><td>Specifies that the first method is overridden by the definition of the second method.</td><td>9.3.2</td></tr>
<tr><td>| .pack <int32></td><td>Used for explicit layout of fields.</td><td>9.7</td></tr>
<tr><td>| .property <propHead> { <propMember>* }</td><td>Declares a property of the type.</td><td>16</td></tr>
<tr><td>| .size <int32></td><td>Used for explicit layout of fields.</td><td>9.7</td></tr>
<tr><td>| <externSourceDecl></td><td>.line</td><td>5.7</td></tr>
<tr><td>| <securityDecl></td><td>.permission or .capability</td><td>19</td></tr>
</table>

9.3 Introducing and Overriding Virtual Methods

A virtual method of a base type is overridden by providing a direct implementation of the method (using a method definition; see Partition II, section 14.4) and not specifying it to be **newslot** (see Partition II, section 14.4.2.3). An existing method body may also be used to implement a given virtual declaration using the **.override** directive (see Partition II, section 9.3.2).

9.3.1 *Introducing a Virtual Method*

A virtual method is introduced in the inheritance hierarchy by defining a virtual method (see Partition II, section 14.4). The versioning semantics differ depending on whether or not the definition is marked as **newslot** (see Partition II, section 14.4.2.3):

If the definition is marked **newslot,** then the definition *always* creates a new virtual method, even if a base class provides a matching virtual method. Any reference to the virtual method created before the new virtual function was defined will continue to refer to the original definition.

If the definition is not marked **newslot**, then it creates a new virtual method only if there is no virtual method of the same name and signature inherited from a base class. If the inheritance hierarchy changes so that the definition matches an inherited virtual function, the definition will be treated as a new implementation of the inherited function.

ANNOTATION: The **newslot** and **.override** directives were introduced to improve versioning behavior. The **newslot** directive says that the marked method is a new contract, even if there is another method of the same name above it in the hierarchy.

Because CLI programmers have access to libraries and code from many external sources, name conflicts are possible, especially when implementing multiple interfaces. The **.override** directive makes it possible to avoid name conflicts. It is most often used when a class implements two interfaces, each of which has a method of the same name. Because a class cannot have two methods of the same name, the **.override** directive allows a programmer to specify that his implementation, with his name, is to override the specified interface method. The **.override** directive is used by C# to implement what it calls private implementations of an interface.

To make the VES easier to build, the **.override** directive requires that the implementation be provided in the same class as the **.override** directive. It is not possible to refer to an implementation that exists elsewhere.

For more information on newslot, hiding, and overriding, see Partition I, section 8.10.4.

9.3.2 *The .override Directive*

The **.override** directive specifies that a virtual method should be implemented (overridden), in this type, by a virtual method with a different name but with the same signature. It can be used to provide an implementation for a virtual method inherited from a base class or a virtual method specified in an interface implemented by this type. The

.override directive specifies a Method Implementation (MethodImpl) in the metadata (see Partition II, section 14.1.4).

<classMember> ::=	Section in Partition II
.override <typeSpec> :: <methodName> **with** <callConv> <type> <typeSpec> :: <methodName> (<parameters>)	9.2
| ...	

The first `<typeSpec> :: <methodName>` pair specifies the virtual method that is being overridden. It shall reference either an inherited virtual method or a virtual method on an interface that the current type implements. The remaining information specifies the virtual method that provides the implementation.

While the syntax specified here and the actual metadata format (see Partition II, section 21.25) allows any virtual method to be used to provide an implementation, a conforming program shall provide a virtual method actually implemented directly on the type containing the **.override** directive.

RATIONALE

The metadata is designed to be more expressive than can be expected of all implementations of the VES.

Example (informative):

The following example shows a typical use of the **.override** directive. A method implementation is provided for a method declared in an interface (see Partition II, section 11).

```
.class interface I
{ .method public virtual abstract void m() cil managed {}
}
.class C implements I
{ .method virtual public void m2()
  { // body of m2
  }
  .override I::m with instance void C::m2()
}
```

> The **.override** directive specifies that the C::m2 body shall provide the implementation or be used to implement I::m on objects of class C.

9.3.3 *Accessibility and Overriding*

If a type overrides an inherited method, it may *widen*, but it shall not *narrow*, the accessibility of that method. As a principle, if a client of a type is allowed to access a method of that type, then it should also be able to access that method (identified by name and signature) in any derived type. Table 3-1 specifies *narrow* and *widen* in this context—a "Yes" denotes that the subclass can apply that accessibility, a "No" denotes it is illegal.

Table 3-1 Legal Widening of Access to a Virtual Method

Subclass	Base Type Accessibility					
	private	family	assembly	famandassem	famorassem	public
private	Yes	No	No	No	No	No
family	Yes	Yes	No	No	If not in same assembly	No
assembly	Yes	No	Same assembly	No	No	No
famandassem	Yes	No	No	Same assembly	No	No
famorassem	Yes	Yes	Same assembly	Yes	Same assembly	No
public	Yes	Yes	Yes	Yes	Yes	Yes

> **NOTE**
>
> A method may be overridden even if it may not be accessed by the subclass.
>
> If a method has assembly accessibility, then it [the version in the subclass] shall have public accessibility if it is being overridden by a method in a different assembly. A similar rule applies to famandassem, where also famorassem is allowed outside the assembly. In both cases assembly or famandassem, respectively, may be used inside the same assembly.

A special rule applies to **famorassem**, as shown in Table 3-1. This is the only case where the accessibility is apparently narrowed by the subclass. A **famorassem** method may be overridden with **family** accessibility by a type in another assembly.

> **RATIONALE**
>
> Because there is no way to specify "family or specific other assembly" it is not possible to specify that the accessibility should be unchanged. To avoid narrowing access, it would be necessary to specify an accessibility of public, which would force widening of access even when it is not desired. As a compromise, the minor narrowing of "family" alone is permitted.

9.4 Method Implementation Requirements

A type (**concrete** or **abstract**) *may* provide

- Implementations for instance, static, and virtual methods that it introduces
- Implementations for methods declared in interfaces that it has specified it will implement, or that its base type has specified it will implement
- Alternative implementations for virtual methods inherited from its parent
- Implementations for virtual methods inherited from an **abstract** base type that did not provide an implementation

A concrete (i.e., non-abstract) type *shall* provide, either directly or by inheritance, an implementation for

- All methods declared by the type itself
- All virtual methods of interfaces implemented by the type
- All virtual methods that the type inherits from its base type

9.5 Special Members

There are three special members, all methods, that can be defined as part of a type: instance constructors, instance finalizers, and type initializers.

9.5.1 *Instance Constructors*

Instance constructors initialize an instance of a type. An instance constructor is called when an instance of a type is created by the **newobj** instruction (see Partition III [section 4.20]). Instance constructors shall be instance (not static or virtual) methods; they shall be named **.ctor** and marked both **rtspecialname** and **specialname** (see Partition II, section

14.4.2.6). Instance constructors may take parameters, but shall not return a value. Instance constructors may be overloaded (i.e., a type may have several instance constructors). Each instance constructor shall have a unique signature. Unlike other methods, instance constructors may write into fields of the type that are marked with the **initonly** attribute (see Partition II, section 15.1.2).

Example (informative):

The following shows the definition of an instance constructor that does not take any parameters:

```
.class X {
.method public rtspecialname specialname instance void .ctor() cil managed
  { .maxstack 1
  // call super constructor
  ldarg.0            // load this pointer
  call instance void [mscorlib]System.Object::.ctor()
  // do other initialization work
  ret
  }
}
```

ANNOTATION: During the design of the CLI, there was an alternate design proposed with no notion of constructors. The Eiffel language (and design environment) does this, for example. In this alternate design, the programmer must assume that all objects can exist in an uninitialized state, where all their fields are known to be null. In this model, programmers must actively test to see whether an object has been initialized before using it.

In contrast, the adopted model requires that one of an object's constructors has been called by the time the constructor is finished executing, so the constructor can put the object into a non-null self-consistent state. This means that programmers do not have to use defensive test techniques.

9.5.2 *Instance Finalizers*

The behavior of finalizers is specified in Partition I, section 8.9.6.7. The finalize method for a particular type is specified by overriding the virtual method `Finalize` in `System.Object`.

9.5.3 *Type Initializers*

Types may contain special methods called **type initializers** to initialize the type itself.

All types (classes, interfaces, and value types) may have a type initializer. This method shall be static, take no parameters, return no value, be marked with **rtspecialname** and **specialname** (see Partition II, section 14.4.2.6), and be named **.cctor**.

Like instance initializers, type initializers may write into static fields of their type that are marked with the **initonly** attribute (see Partition II, section 15.1.2).

> **NOTE**
>
> Type initializers are often simple methods that initialize the type's static fields from stored constants or via simple computations. There are, however, no limitations on what code is permitted in a type initializer.

9.5.3.1 Type Initialization Guarantees

The CLI shall provide the following guarantees regarding type initialization (but see also Partition II, sections 9.5.3.2 and 9.5.3.3):

1. When type initializers are executed is specified in Partition I, section 8.9.5.
2. A type initializer shall run exactly once for any given type, unless explicitly called by user code.
3. No method other than those called directly or indirectly from the type initializer will be able to access members of a type before its initializer completes execution.

9.5.3.2 Relaxed Guarantees

A type can be marked with the attribute **beforefieldinit** (see Partition II, section 9.1.6) to indicate that all the guarantees specified in Partition II, section 9.5.3.1 are not required. In particular, the final requirement of guarantee 1 need not be provided: the type initializer need not run before a static method is called or referenced.

> **RATIONALE**
>
> When code can be executed in multiple application domains, it becomes particularly expensive to ensure this final guarantee. At the same time, examination of large bodies of managed code have shown that this final guarantee is rarely required, since type initializers are almost always simple methods for initializing static fields. Leaving it up to the CIL generator (and hence, possibly, to the programmer) to decide whether this guarantee is required therefore provides efficiency when it is desired at the cost of consistency guarantees.

9.5.3.3 Races and Deadlocks

In addition to the type initialization guarantees specified in Partition II, section 9.5.3.1, the CLI shall ensure two further guarantees for code that is called from a type initializer:

1. Static variables of a type are in a known state prior to any access whatsoever.
2. Type initialization alone shall not create a deadlock unless some code called from a type initializer (directly or indirectly) explicitly invokes blocking operations.

RATIONALE

Consider the following two class definitions:

```
.class public A extends [mscorlib]System.Object
{ .field static public class A a
  .field static public class B b

  .method public static rtspecialname specialname void .cctor ()
  { ldnull              // b=null
    stsfld class B A::b
ldsfld class A B::a     // a=B.a
    stsfld class A A::a
    ret
  }
}

.class public B extends [mscorlib]System.Object
{ .field static public class A a
  .field static public class B b

  .method public static rtspecialname specialname void .cctor ()
  { ldnull              // a=null
    stsfld class A B::a
    ldsfld class B A::b // b=A.b
    stfld class B B::b
    ret
  }
}
```

After loading these two classes, an attempt to reference any of the static fields causes a problem, since the type initializer for each of A and B requires that the type initializer of the other be invoked first. Requiring that no access to a type be permitted until its initializer has completed would create a deadlock situation. Instead, the CLI provides a weaker guarantee: the initializer will have started to run, but it need not have completed. But this alone would allow the full uninitialized state of a type to be visible, which would make it difficult to guarantee repeatable results.

There are similar, but more complex, problems when type initialization takes place in a multi-threaded system. In these cases, for example, two separate threads might start attempting to access static variables of separate types (A and B), and then each would have to wait for the other to complete initialization.

A rough outline of the algorithm is as follows:

1. At class load time (hence prior to initialization time), store zero or null into all static fields of the type.

2. If the type is initialized, you are done.

2.1. If the type is not yet initialized, try to take an initialization lock.

2.2. If successful, record this thread as responsible for initializing the type and proceed to step 2.3.

2.2.1. If not, see whether this thread or any thread waiting for this thread to complete already holds the lock.

2.2.2. If so, return, since blocking would create a deadlock. This thread will now see an incompletely initialized state for the type, but no deadlock will arise.

2.2.3. If not, block until the type is initialized then return.

2.3 Initialize the parent type and then all interfaces implemented by this type.

2.4 Execute the type initialization code for this type.

2.5 Mark the type as initialized, release the initialization lock, awaken any threads waiting for this type to be initialized, and return.

9.6 Nested Types

Nested types are specified in Partition I, section 8.5.3.4. Interfaces may be nested inside of classes and value types, but classes and value types shall not be nested inside of interfaces. For information about the logical tables associated with nested types, see Partition II, section 21.29.

> **NOTE**
>
> A nested type is not associated with an instance of its enclosing type. The nested type has its own base type and may be instantiated independent of the enclosing type. This means that the instance members of the enclosing type are not accessible using the **this** pointer of the nested type.
>
> A nested type may access any members of its enclosing type, including private members, as long as the member is static or the nested type has a reference to an instance of the enclosing type. Thus, by using nested types a type may give access to its private members to another type.
>
> On the other side, the enclosing type may not access any private or family members of the nested type. Only members with assembly, famorassem, or public accessibility can be accessed by the enclosing type.

Example (informative):

The following example shows a class declared inside another class. Both classes declare a field. The nested class may access both fields, while the enclosing class does not have access to the field b.

```
.class private auto autochar CounterTextBox
    extends [System.Windows.Forms]System.Windows.Forms.TextBox
    implements [.module Counter]IcountDisplay
{ .field static private int32 a
  /* Nested class. Declares the NegativeNumberException */
  .class nested assembly NonPositiveNumberException extends
[mscorlib]System.Exception
  { .field static private int32 b
    // body of nested class
  } // end of nested class NegativeNumberException
}
```

ANNOTATION: It is interesting to contrast the CLI's nested type with Java's inner classes, which share access to an instance of the class that encloses them. In the CLI, nested classes are little more than a naming convenience; the name of the nested class is scoped to the parent class. The only additional property of CLI nested types is that, like any member of the outer class, members of the nested class have access to the private fields of the enclosing type.

9.7 Controlling Instance Layout

The CLI supports both sequential and explicit layout control (see Partition II, section 9.1.2). For explicit layout it is also necessary to specify the precise layout of an instance (see also Partition II, sections 21.18 and 21.16).

```
<fieldDecl> ::=
  [[ <int32> ]] <fieldAttr>* <type> <id>
```

The optional int32 specified in brackets at the beginning of the declaration specifies the byte offset from the beginning of the instance of the type. This form of explicit layout control shall not be used with global fields specified using the **at** notation (see Partition II, section 15.3.2).

Offset values shall be 0 or greater; they cannot be negative. It is possible to overlap fields in this way, even though it is not recommended. The field may be accessed using pointer arithmetic and **ldind** to load the field indirectly or **stind** to store the field indirectly (see Partition III [sections 3.42 and 3.62]). See Partition II, sections 21.18 and 21.16 for encoding of this information. For explicit layout, every field shall be assigned an offset.

The **.pack** directive specifies that fields should be placed within the runtime object at addresses which are a multiple of the specified number, or at natural alignment for that field type, whichever is *smaller*. For example, **.pack** 2 would allow 32-bit-wide fields to be started on even addresses—whereas without any **.pack** directive, they would be naturally aligned—that is to say, placed on addresses that are a multiple of 4. The integer following **.pack** shall be one of 0, 1, 2, 4, 8, 16, 32, 64 or 128. (A value of zero indicates that the pack size used should match the default for the current platform). The **.pack** directive shall not be supplied for any type with explicit layout control.

The directive **.size** specifies that a memory block of the specified amount of bytes shall be allocated for an instance of the type. For example, **.size** 32 would create a block of 32 bytes for the instance. The value specified shall be greater than or equal to the calculated size of the class, based upon its field sizes and any **.pack** directive. Note that if this directive applies to a value type, then the size shall be less than 1 MByte.

> **NOTE**
>
> Metadata that controls instance layout is not a "hint," it is an integral part of the VES that shall be supported by all conforming implementations of the CLI.

ANNOTATION: The purpose of the **.pack** directive is to allow managed data to match the layout of pre-existing unmanaged data types.

Normally the **.size** directive is more useful for value types, but in COM interop it is also useful for classes.

Example (informative):

The following class uses sequential layout of its fields:

```
.class sequential public SequentialClass
{ .field public int32 a                    // store at offset 0 bytes
  .field public int32 b                    // store at offset 4 bytes
}
```

The following class uses explicit layout of its fields:

```
.class explicit public ExplicitClass
{ .field [0] public int32 a                // store at offset 0 bytes
  .field [6] public int32 b                // store at offset 6 bytes
}
```

The following value type uses **.pack** to pack its fields together:

```
.class value sealed public MyClass extends [mscorlib]System.ValueType
{ .pack 2
  .field  public int8  a                   // store at offset 0 bytes
  .field  public int32 b                   // store at offset 2 bytes (not 4)
}
```

The following class specifies a contiguous block of 16 bytes:

```
.class public BlobClass
{ .size          16
}
```

9.8 Global Fields and Methods

In addition to types with static members, many languages have the notion of data and methods that are not part of a type at all. These are referred to as *global* fields and methods.

It is simplest to understand global fields and methods in the CLI by imagining that they are simply members of an invisible **abstract** public class. In fact, the CLI defines such a special class, named "`<Module>`", that does not have a base type and does not implement any interfaces. The only noticeable difference is in how definitions of this special class are treated when multiple modules are combined together, as is done by a class loader. This process is known as **metadata merging**.

For an ordinary type, if the metadata merges two definitions of the same type, it simply discards one definition on the assumption they are equivalent and that any anomaly will be discovered when the type is used. For the special class that holds global members, however, members are unioned across all modules at merge time. If the same name appears to be defined for cross-module use in multiple modules, then there is an error. In detail:

- If no member of the same kind (field or method), name, and signature exists, then add this member to the output class.
- If there are duplicates and no more than one has an accessibility other than **compiler-controlled**, then add them all in the output class.
- If there are duplicates and two or more have an accessibility other than **compiler-controlled,** an error has occurred.

ANNOTATION: The **compilercontrolled** accessibility means that the item so marked is accessible only from within a single compilation unit and under the control of the compiler. This is because it is defined as accessible only through use of a definition, not a reference.

---

10 Semantics of Classes

Classes, as specified in Partition I, sections 8.2.3 and 8.9.5, define types in an inheritance hierarchy. A class (except for the built-in class `System.Object`) shall declare exactly one parent class. A class shall declare zero or more interfaces that it implements (see Partition II, section 11). A concrete class may be instantiated to create an object, but an **abstract** class (see Partition II, section 9.1.4) shall not be instantiated. A class may define fields (static or instance), methods (static, instance, or virtual), events, properties, and nested types (classes, value types, or interfaces).

Instances of a class (objects) are created only by explicitly using the **newobj** instruction (see Partition III [section 4.20]). When a variable or field that has a class as its type is created (for example, by calling a method that has a local variable of a class type), the value shall initially be null, a special value that is assignment compatible with all class types even though it is not an instance of any particular class.

11 Semantics of Interfaces

Interfaces, as specified in Partition I, section 8.9.4, define a contract that other types may implement. Interfaces may have static fields and methods, but they shall not have instance fields or methods. Interfaces may define virtual methods, but only if they are **abstract** (see Partition I, section 8.9.4 and Partition II, section 14.4.2.4).

> **RATIONALE**
>
> Interfaces cannot define instance fields for the same reason that the CLI does not support multiple inheritance of base types: in the presence of dynamic loading of data types there is no known implementation technique that is both efficient when used and has no cost when not used. By contrast, providing static fields and methods need not affect the layout of instances and therefore does not raise these issues.

Interfaces may be nested inside any type (interface, class, or value type). Classes and value types shall not be nested inside of interfaces.

11.1 Implementing Interfaces

Classes and value types shall *implement* zero or more interfaces. Implementing an interface implies that all concrete instances of the class or value type shall provide an implementation for each **abstract** virtual method declared in the interface. In order to implement an interface, a class or value type shall either explicitly declare that it does so (using the **implements** attribute in its type definition, see Partition II, section 9.1) or shall be derived from a base class that implements the interface.

> **NOTE**
>
> An **abstract** class (since it cannot be instantiated) need not provide implementations of the virtual methods of interfaces it implements, but any concrete class derived from it shall provide the implementation.
>
> Merely providing implementations for all of the **abstract** methods of an interface is not sufficient to have a type implement that interface. Conceptually, this represents the fact that an interface represents a contract that may have more requirements than are captured in the set of **abstract** methods. From an implementation point of view, this allows the layout of types to be constrained only by those interfaces that are explicitly declared.

Interfaces shall declare that they require the implementation of zero or more other interfaces. If one interface, A, declares that it requires the implementation of another interface, B, then A implicitly declares that it requires the implementation of all interfaces required by B. If a class or value type declares that it implements A, then all concrete instances shall provide implementations of the virtual methods declared in A and all of the interfaces A requires.

Example (informative):

The following class implements the interface IStartStopEventSource defined in the module Counter.

```
.class private auto autochar StartStopButton
    extends [System.Windows.Forms]System.Windows.Forms.Button
    implements [.module Counter]IstartStopEventSource
{ // body of class
}
```

11.2 Implementing Virtual Methods on Interfaces

Classes that implement an interface (see Partition II, section 11.1) are required to provide implementations for the **abstract** virtual methods defined by the interface. There are three mechanisms for providing this implementation:

- Directly specifying an implementation, using the same name and signature as appear in the interface
- Inheritance of an existing implementation from the base type
- Use of an explicit `MethodImpl` (see Partition II, section 14.1.4)

The Virtual Execution System shall determine the appropriate implementation of a virtual method to be used for an interface **abstract** method using the following algorithm.

- If the parent class implements the interface, start with the same virtual methods that it provides; otherwise create an interface that has empty slots for all virtual functions.
- If this class explicitly specifies that it implements the interface
  - If the class defines any **public virtual newslot** functions whose name and signature match a virtual method on the interface, then use these new virtual methods to implement the corresponding interface method.
- If there are any virtual methods in the interface that still have empty slots, see if there are any **public virtual** methods available on this class (directly or inherited), and use these to implement the corresponding methods on the interface.

- Apply all `MethodImpls` that are specified for this class, thereby placing explicitly specified virtual methods into the interface in preference to those inherited or chosen by name matching.
- If the current class is not **abstract** and there are any interface methods that still have empty slots, then the program is not valid.

RATIONALE

Interfaces can be thought of as specifying, primarily, a set of virtual methods that shall be implemented by any class that implements the interface. The class specifies a mapping from its own virtual methods to those of the interface. Thus it is virtual methods, not specific implementations of those methods, that are associated with interfaces. Overriding a virtual method on a class with a specific implementation will thus affect not only the virtual method named in the class, but also any interface virtual methods to which that same virtual method has been mapped.

ANNOTATION: Interface definitions contain only static methods and declarations of abstract virtual methods, so the interface definition never provides implementations of virtual methods. Instead, classes that implement the interface must always implement these virtual methods. This section describes the algorithm to determine which implementation to use for virtual interface methods when there is more than one implementation for any or all of the interface methods.

One subtle point is worth mentioning. After the first part of the algorithm, in which the machine fills the interface slots with the parent's implementation (if any), it then looks to see if the child class has any public virtual method implementations for a given name and signature—*but only if the child says it is implementing it.* The child would do so by declaring the method in its type declaration, as specified in Partition II, sections 9.1 and 9.1.3. If the child class does not explicitly say it is implementing the interface, then the parent implementation is used.

Most programming languages, with the exception of C#, make no distinction between whether a class explicitly says that it implements an interface, or simply derives from a class that implements the interface. A complete understanding of this algorithm gives great flexibility to compiler writers. If you really understand this algorithm, you can use it to implement several different ways of populating interfaces.

---

12 Semantics of Value Types

In contrast to classes, value types (see Partition I, section 8.2.4) are not accessed by using a reference but are stored directly in the location of that type.

> **RATIONALE**
>
> Value types are used to describe the type of small data items. They can be compared to **struct** (as opposed to pointers to struct) types in C++. Compared to reference types, value types are accessed faster, since there is no additional indirection involved. As elements of arrays they do not require allocating memory for the pointers as well as for the data itself. Typical value types are complex numbers, geometric points, or dates.

Like other types, value types may have fields (static or instance), methods (static, instance, or virtual), properties, events, and nested types. A value type may be converted into a corresponding reference type (its **boxed form**, a class automatically created for this purpose by the VES when a value type is defined) by a process called **boxing**. A boxed value type may be converted back into its value type representation, the **unboxed form**, by a process called **unboxing**. Value types shall be sealed, and they shall have a base type of either `System.ValueType` or `System.Enum` (see the *.NET Framework Standard Library Annotated Reference*). Value types shall implement zero or more interfaces, but this has meaning only in their boxed form (see Partition II, section 12.3).

Unboxed value types are not considered subtypes of another type, and it is not valid to use the **isinst** instruction (see Partition III [section 4.6]) on unboxed value types. The **isinst** instruction may be used for boxed value types. Unboxed value types shall not be assigned the value *null* and they shall not be compared to *null*.

Value types support layout control in the same way as reference types do (see Partition II, section 9.7). This is especially important when values are imported from native code.

12.1 Referencing Value Types

The unboxed form of a value type shall be referred to by using the **valuetype** keyword followed by a type reference. The boxed form of a value type shall be referred to by using the **boxed** keyword followed by a type reference.

```
<valueTypeReference> ::=
    boxed <typeReference> |
  valuetype <typeReference>
```

ANNOTATION

Implementation-Specific (Microsoft): For historical reasons, "**value class**" may be used instead of "**valuetype,**" although the latter is preferred. Microsoft's Common Language Runtime does not support direct references to boxed value types; they should be treated as **object** instead.

12.2 Initializing Value Types

Like classes, value types may have both instance constructors (see Partition II, section 9.5.1) and type initializers (see Partition II, section 9.5.3). Unlike classes that are automatically initialized to null, however, the following rules constitute the only guarantee about the initialization of (unboxed) value types:

- Static variables shall be initialized to zero when a type is loaded (see Partition II, section 9.5.3.3), hence statics whose type is a value type are zero-initialized when the type is loaded.
- Local variables shall be initialized to zero if the appropriate bit in the method header (see Partition II, section 9.5.3.3) is set.
- Arrays shall be zero-initialized.
- Instances of classes (i.e., objects) shall be zero-initialized prior to calling their instance constructor.

ANNOTATION: To initialize locals to zero, the assembler syntax is the **.local init** directive, described in Partition II, 14.4.1.3; and in the file format it is the flag **CorILMethod_InitLocals**, described in Partition II, section 24.4.4.

RATIONALE

Guaranteeing automatic initialization of unboxed value types is both difficult and expensive, especially on platforms that support thread-local storage and allow threads to be created outside of the CLI and then passed to the CLI for management.

NOTE

Boxed value types are classes and follow the rules for classes.

The instruction **initobj** (see Partition III [section 4.5]) performs zero-initialization under program control. If a value type has a constructor, an instance of its unboxed type can be created as is done with classes. The **newobj** instruction (see Partition III [section 4.20]) is used along with the initializer and its parameters to allocate and initialize the instance. The instance of the value type will be allocated on the stack. The Base Class Library provides the method `System.Array.Initialize` (see the *.NET Framework Standard Library Annotated Reference*) to zero all instances in an array of unboxed value types.

Example (informative):

The following code declares and initializes three value type variables. The first variable is zero-initialized, the second is initialized by calling an instance constructor, and the third by creating the object on the stack and storing it into the local.

```
.assembly Test { }
.assembly extern System.Drawing {
  .ver 1:0:3102:0
  .publickeytoken = (b03f5f7f11d50a3a)
}
.method public static void Start()
{ .maxstack 3
  .entrypoint
  .locals init (valuetype [System.Drawing]System.Drawing.Size Zero,
          valuetype [System.Drawing]System.Drawing.Size Init,
          valuetype [System.Drawing]System.Drawing.Size Store)
  // Zero-initialize the local named Zero
  ldloca Zero              // load address of local variable
  initobj valuetype [System.Drawing]System.Drawing.Size
  // Call the initializer on the local named Init
  ldloca Init              // load address of local variable
  ldc.i4 425               // load argument 1 (width)
  ldc.i4 300               // load argument 2 (height)
  call instance void [System.Drawing]System.Drawing.Size::.ctor(int32, int32)

  // Create a new instance on the stack and store into Store. Note that
  // stobj is used here - but one could equally well use stloc, stfld, etc.
  ldloca Store
  ldc.i4 425               // load argument 1 (width)
  ldc.i4 300               // load argument 2 (height)
```

```
    newobj instance void [System.Drawing]System.Drawing.Size::.ctor(int32, int32)
    stobj valuetype [System.Drawing]System.Drawing.Size
    ret
}
```

12.3 Methods of Value Types

Value types may have static, instance, and virtual methods. Static methods of value types are defined and called the same way as static methods of class types. As with classes, both instance and virtual methods of a boxed or unboxed value type may be called using the **call** instruction. The **callvirt** instruction shall not be used with unboxed value types (see Partition I, section 8.4.2), but it may be used on boxed value types.

ANNOTATION: Partition I, section 8.4.2 discusses virtual calls (the **callvirt** instruction, although it is not referred to by that name in that section). However, the statement in the last sentence in the previous paragraph is inaccurate. The **callvirt** instruction can be used with unboxed value types as well as boxed value types.

Instance and virtual methods of classes shall be coded to expect a reference to an instance of the class as the **this** pointer. By contrast, instance and virtual methods of value types shall be coded to expect a managed pointer (see Partition I, section 8.2.4) to an unboxed instance of the value type. The CLI shall convert a boxed value type into a managed pointer to the unboxed value type when a boxed value type is passed as the **this** pointer to a virtual method whose implementation is provided by the unboxed value type.

> **NOTE**
>
> This operation is the same as unboxing the instance, since the **unbox** instruction (see Partition III [section 4.30]) is defined to return a managed pointer to the value type that shares memory with the original boxed instance.
>
> The following diagrams may help understand the relationship between the boxed and unboxed representations of a value type.

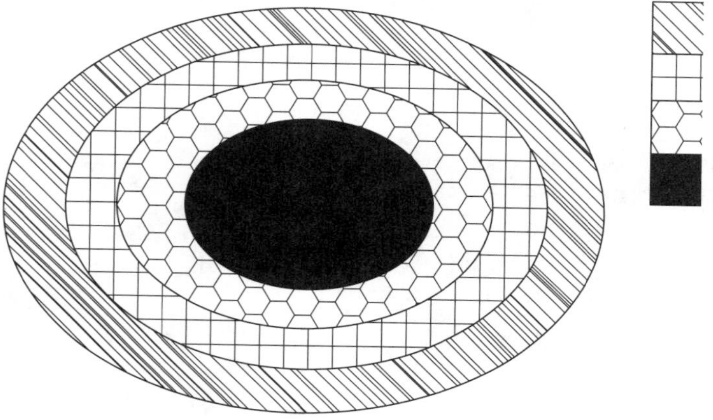

RATIONALE

An important use of instance methods on value types is to change internal state of the instance. This cannot be done if an instance of the unboxed value type is used for the **this** pointer, since it would be operating on a copy of the value, not the original value: unboxed value types are copied when they are passed as arguments.

Virtual methods are used to allow multiple types to share implementation code, and this requires that all classes that implement the virtual method share a common representation defined by the class that first introduces the method. Since value types can (and in the Base Class Library do) implement interfaces and virtual methods defined on `System.Object`, it is important that the virtual method be callable using a boxed value type so it can be manipulated as would any other type that implements the interface. This leads to the requirement that the VES automatically unbox value types on virtual calls.

[Table 3-2 shows the type of the **this** pointer supplied, depending on the type of the instance method, and whether the **call** or **callvirt** instruction is used.]

Table 3-2 Type of *this*, Given CIL Instruction and Declaring Type of Instance Method

	Value Type (Boxed or Unboxed)	Interface	Class Type
call	managed pointer to value type	illegal	object reference
callvirt	managed pointer to value type	object reference	object reference

Example (informative):

The following converts an integer of the value type int32 into a string. Recall that int32 corresponds to the unboxed value type System.Int32 defined in the Base Class Library. Suppose the integer is declared as:

```
.locals init (int32 x)
```

Then the call is made as shown below:

```
ldloca x                  // load managed pointer to local variable
call instance string
     valuetype [mscorlib]System.Int32::ToString()
```

However, if System.Object (a class) is used as the type reference rather than System.Int32 (a value type), the value of x shall be boxed before the call is made, and the code becomes:

```
ldloc x
box valuetype [mscorlib]System.Int32
callvirt instance string [mscorlib]System.Object::ToString()
```

13 Semantics of Special Types

Special Types are those that are referenced from CIL, but for which no definition is supplied: the VES supplies the definitions automatically based on information available from the reference.

ANNOTATION: There are two kinds of special types: (1) those for which no definition is necessary because the VES produces the implementation upon declaration, and (2) those for which the user provides a definition and the VES provides the implementation.

Pointers, vectors, and arrays fall into the first category. In fact, there is no definition of either in the libraries. The VES just creates these upon declaration.

Built-in numeric types are a rather special case of this category. In the Base Class Library is a set of types that define these numeric types and the methods for operating on them. However, the VES requires that signatures encode these types with special values, rather than using the name of the type. For example, in a signature, a compiler must emit `ELEMENT_TYPE_I4`, numeric value 8, rather than `ELEMENT_TYPE CLASS`, followed by a reference to `System.Int32` (see Partition II, section 22.1.15).

This does not mean that a programmer cannot specify the class library type (e.g., `System.Int32`) in a type definition, and some recommend this as a programming practice because that designation is required to access the methods. It does, however, mean that it is the responsibility of the compiler to emit *only* the built-in type in the signatures.

In addition to the built-in numeric types, the following types do not require a definition in code, and they must be defined by the VES:

- Vectors
- Arrays
- Pointer types
- Unmanaged pointers
- Managed pointers
- Method pointers

The following special types, which fall into the second category, must be defined in code, but the implementation is provided by the VES:

- Enums
- Delegates

13.1 Vectors

```
<type> ::= ...
      | <type> [ ]
```

Vectors are single-dimension arrays with a zero lower bound. They have direct support in CIL instructions (**newarr**, **ldelem**, **stelem**, and **ldelema**; see Partition III [sections 4.19, 4.7, 4.25, and 4.8, respectively]). The CIL Framework also provides methods that deal with multi-dimensional arrays, or single-dimension arrays with a non-zero lower bound (see Partition II, section 13.2). Two vectors are the same type if their element types are the same, regardless of their actual upper bounds.

Vectors have a fixed size and element type, determined when they are created. All CIL instructions shall respect these values. That is, they shall reliably detect attempts to index beyond the end of the vector, attempts to store the incorrect type of data into an element of a vector, and attempts to take addresses of elements of a vector with an incorrect data type. See Partition III.

Example (informative):

Declaring a vector of Strings:

```
.field string[] errorStrings
```

Declaring a vector of function pointers:

```
.field method instance void*(int32) [] myVec
```

Create a vector of 4 strings, and store it into the field *errorStrings*. The four strings lie at *errorStrings*[0] through *errorStrings*[3]:

```
ldc.i4.4
newarr        string
stfld         string[] CountDownForm::errorStrings
```

Store the string "First" into *errorStrings*[0]:

```
ldfld string[] CountDownForm::errorStrings
ldc.i4.0
ldstr "First"
stelem
```

Vectors are subtypes of `System.Array`, an **abstract** class predefined by the CLI. It provides several methods that can be applied to all vectors. See the *.NET Framework Standard Library Annotated Reference*.

13.2 Arrays

While vectors (see Partition II, section 13.1) have direct support through CIL instructions, all other arrays are supported by the VES by creating subtypes of the **abstract** class `System.Arrray` (see the *.NET Framework Standard Library Annotated Reference*).

```
<type> ::= ...
  | <type> [ [<bound> [,<bound>]*] ]
```

The *rank* of an array is the number of dimensions. The CLI does not support arrays with rank 0. The type of an array (other than a vector) shall be determined by the type of its elements and the number of dimensions.

<bound> ::=	Description
...\	Lower and upper bounds unspecified. In the case of multi-dimensional arrays, the ellipsis may be omitted.
| <int32>	Zero lower bound, <int32> upper bound.
| <int32> ...	Lower bound only specified.
| <int32> ... <int32>	Both bounds specified.

The fundamental operations provided by the CIL instruction set for vectors are provided by methods on the class created by the VES.

The VES shall provide two constructors for arrays. One takes a sequence of numbers giving the number of elements in each dimension (a lower bound of zero is assumed). The second takes twice as many arguments: a sequence of lower bounds, one for each dimension, followed by a sequence of lengths, one for each dimension (where length is the number of elements required).

ANNOTATION: The last sentence of the previous paragraph is not accurate. It states that the declaration is:

<type> [*lower_bound1*, *lower_bound2*, *element_number1*, *element_number2*]

This is not correct. Instead, it is:

<type> [*lower_bound1*, *element_number1*, *lower_bound2*, *element_number2*]

In addition to array constructors, the VES shall provide the instance methods `Get`, `Set`, and `Address` to access specific elements and compute their addresses. These methods take a number for each dimension, to specify the target element. In addition, `Set` takes an additional final argument specifying the value to store into the target element.

Example (informative):

Creates an array, MyArray, of strings with two dimensions, with indexes 5..10 and 3..7. Stores the string "One" into MyArray[5, 3], retrieves it, and prints it out. Then computes the address of MyArray[5, 4], stores "Test" into it, retrieves it, and prints it out.

```
.assembly Test { }

.assembly extern mscorlib { }

.method public static void Start()
{ .maxstack 5
```

```
.entrypoint
.locals (class [mscorlib]System.String[,] myArray)
ldc.i4.5          // load lower bound for dim 1
ldc.i4.6          // load (upper bound - lower bound + 1) for dim 1
ldc.i4.3          // load lower bound for dim 2
ldc.i4.5          // load (upper bound - lower bound + 1) for dim 2
newobj instance void string[,]::.ctor(int32,
          int32, int32, int32)
stloc  myArray
ldloc myArray
ldc.i4.5
ldc.i4.3
ldstr "One"
call instance void string[,]::Set(int32, int32, string)
ldloc myArray
ldc.i4.5
ldc.i4.3
call instance string string[,]::Get(int32, int32)
call void [mscorlib]System.Console::WriteLine(string)
ldloc myArray
ldc.i4.5
ldc.i4.4
call instance string & string[,]::Address(int32, int32)
ldstr "Test"
stind.ref
ldloc myArray
ldc.i4.5
ldc.i4.4
call instance string string[,]::Get(int32, int32)
call void [mscorlib]System.Console::WriteLine(string)
ret
}
```

The following text is informative.

While the elements of multi-dimensional arrays can be thought of as laid out in contiguous memory, arrays of arrays are different—each dimension (except the last) holds an array reference. The following picture illustrates the difference:

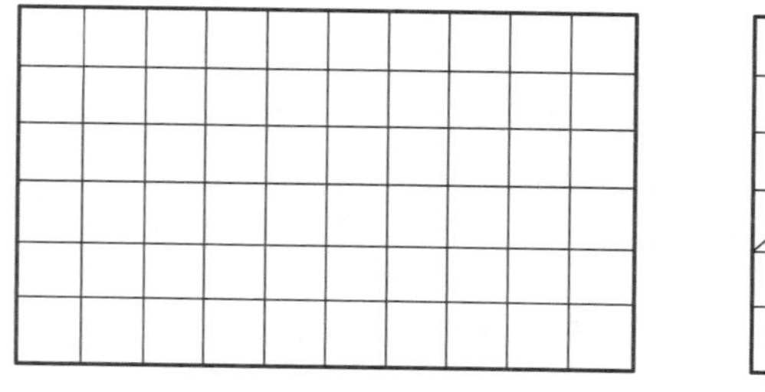

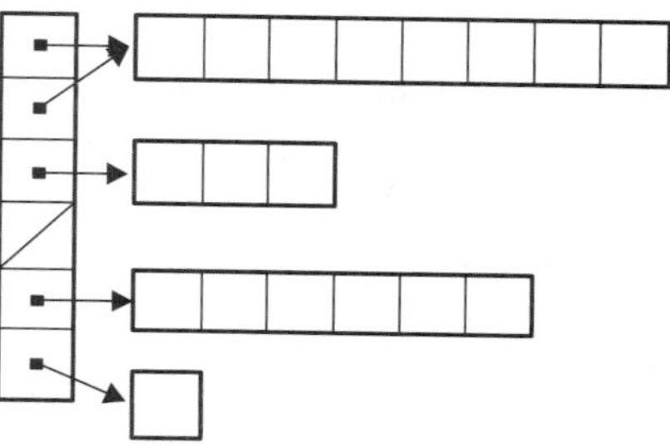

On the left is a [6, 10] rectangular array. On the right is not one, but a total of five arrays. The vertical array is an array of arrays, and references the four horizontal arrays. Note how the first and second elements of the vertical array both reference the same horizontal array.

Note that all dimensions of a multi-dimensional array shall be of the same size. But in an array of arrays, it is possible to reference arrays of different sizes. For example, the figure on the right shows the vertical array referencing arrays of lengths 8, 8, 3, null, 6, and 1.

There is no special support for these so-called "jagged arrays" in either the CIL instruction set or the VES. They are simply vectors whose elements are themselves either the base elements or (recursively) jagged arrays.

End of informative text

13.3 Enums

An **enum**, short for "enumeration," defines a set of symbols that all have the same type. A type shall be an enum if and only if it has an immediate base type of `System.Enum`. Since `System.Enum` itself has an immediate base type of `System.ValueType` (see the *.NET Framework Standard Library Annotated Reference*), enums are value types (see Partition II, section 12). The symbols of an enum are represented by an *underlying* type: one of { **`bool`**, **`char`**, **`int8`**, **`unsigned int8`**, **`int16`**, **`unsigned int16`**, **`int32`**, **`unsigned int32`**, **`int64`**, **`unsigned int64`**, **`float32`**, **`float64`**, **`native int`**, **`unsigned native int`** }.

> **NOTE**
> The CLI does *not* provide a guarantee that values of the enum type are integers corresponding to one of the symbols (unlike Pascal). In fact, the CLS (see Partition I, section 11, Collected CLS Rules) defines a convention for using enums to represent bit flags which can be combined to form integral value that are not named by the enum type itself.

Enums obey additional restrictions beyond those on other value types. Enums shall contain only fields as members (they shall not even define type initializers or instance constructors); they shall not implement any interfaces; they shall have auto field layout (see Partition II, section 9.1.2); they shall have exactly one instance field, and it shall be of the underlying type of the enum; all other fields shall be static and literal (see Partition II, section 15.1); and they shall not be initialized with the **initobj** instruction.

> **RATIONALE**
> These restrictions allow a very efficient implementation of enums.

The single, required, instance field stores the value of an instance of the enum. The static literal fields of an enum declare the mapping of the symbols of the enum to the underlying values. All of these fields shall have the type of the enum and shall have field init metadata that assigns them a value (see Partition II, section 15.2).

For binding purposes (e.g., for locating a method definition from the method reference used to call it), enums shall be distinct from their underlying type. For all other purposes, including verification and execution of code, an unboxed enum freely interconverts with its underlying type. Enums can be boxed (see Partition II, section 12) to a corresponding boxed instance type, but this type is *not* the same as the boxed type of the underlying type, so boxing does not lose the original type of the enum.

Example (informative):

Declare an enum type, then create a local variable of that type. Store a constant of the underlying type into the enum (showing automatic coercion from the underlying type to the enum type). Load the enum back and print it as the underlying type (showing automatic coercion back). Finally, load the address of the enum and extract the contents of the instance field and print that out as well.

```
.assembly Test { }
.assembly extern mscorlib { }
```

```
.class sealed public ErrorCodes extends [mscorlib]System.Enum
{ .field public unsigned int8 MyValue
  .field public static literal valuetype ErrorCodes no_error = int8(0)
  .field public static literal valuetype ErrorCodes format_error =
          int8(1)
  .field public static literal valuetype ErrorCodes overflow_error =
          int8(2)
  .field public static literal valuetype ErrorCodes nonpositive_error =
          int8(3)
}
.method public static void Start()
{ .maxstack 5
  .entrypoint
  .locals init (valuetype ErrorCodes errorCode)
  ldc.i4.1             // load 1 (= format_error)
  stloc errorCode      // store in local, note conversion to enum
  ldloc errorCode
  call void [mscorlib]System.Console::WriteLine(int32)
  ldloca errorCode     // address of enum
  ldfld unsigned int8 valuetype ErrorCodes::MyValue
  call void [mscorlib]System.Console::WriteLine(int32)
  ret
}
```

13.4 Pointer Types

`<type> ::= ...`	Section in Partition II
`| <type> &`	13.4.2
`| <type> *`	13.4.1

A *pointer type* shall be defined by specifying a signature that includes the type for the location it points at. A *pointer* may be **managed** (reported to the CLI garbage collector, denoted by **&**; see Partition II, section 13.4.2) or **unmanaged** (not reported, denoted by *; see Partition II, section 13.4.1).

Pointers may contain the address of a field (of an object or value type) or an element of an array. *Pointers* differ from object references in that they do not point to an entire type instance, but rather to the *interior* of an instance. The CLI provides two typesafe operations on pointers:

- *Loading* the value from the location referenced by the pointer
- *Storing* an assignment compatible value into the location referenced by the pointer

For pointers into the same array or object (see Partition I, section 8.9.2), the following arithmetic operations are supported:

- Adding an integer value to a pointer, where that value is interpreted as a number of bytes, results in a pointer of the same kind.
- Subtracting an integer value (number of bytes) from a pointer results in a pointer of the same kind. Note that subtracting a pointer from an integer value is not permitted.
- Two pointers, regardless of kind, can be subtracted from one another, producing an integer value that specifies the number of bytes between the addresses they reference.

The following is informative text.

Pointers are compatible with unsigned int32 on 32-bit architectures, and with unsigned int64 on 64-bit architectures. They are best considered as unsigned int, whose size varies depending upon the runtime machine architecture.

The CIL instruction set (see Partition III) contains instructions to compute addresses of fields, local variables, arguments, and elements of vectors [and arrays]:

Instruction	Description
`ldarga`	Load address of argument.
`ldelema`	Load address of vector element.
`ldflda`	Load address of field.
`ldloca`	Load address of local variable.
`ldsflda`	Load address of static field.

Once a pointer is loaded onto the stack, the **ldind** class of instructions may be used to load the data item to which it points. Similarly, the **stind** class of instructions can be used to store data into the location.

Note that the CLI will throw an `InvalidOperationException` for an **ldflda** instruction if the address is not within the current application domain. This situation arises typically only from the use of objects with a base type of `System.MarshalByRefObject` (see the *.NET Framework Standard Library Annotated Reference*).

13.4.1 *Unmanaged Pointers*

Unmanaged pointers (*) are the traditional pointers used in languages like C and C++. There are no restrictions on their use, although for the most part they result in code that cannot be verified. While it is perfectly legal to mark locations that contain unmanaged pointers as though they were unsigned integers (and this is, in fact, how they are treated by the VES), it is often better to mark them as unmanaged pointers to a specific type of data. This is done by using * in a signature for a return value, local variable, or an argument or by using a pointer type for a field or array element.

- Unmanaged pointers are not reported to the garbage collector and can be used in any way that an integer can be used.
- Verifiable code cannot dereference unmanaged pointers.
- Unverified code can pass an unmanaged pointer to a method that expects a managed pointer. This is safe only if one of the following is true:
    a. The unmanaged pointer refers to memory that is not in memory used by the CLI for storing instances of objects ("garbage-collected memory" or "managed memory").
    b. The unmanaged pointer contains the address of a field within an object.
    c. The unmanaged pointer contains the address of an element within an array.
    d. The unmanaged pointer contains the address where the element following the last element in an array would be located

13.4.2 *Managed Pointers*

Managed pointers (&) may point to an instance of a value type, a field of an object, a field of a value type, an element of an array, or the address where an element just past the end of an array would be stored (for pointer indexes into managed arrays). Managed pointers cannot be *null*, and they shall be reported to the garbage collector even if they do not point to managed memory.

Managed pointers are specified by using **&** in a signature for a return value, local variable, or an argument, or by using a by-ref type for a field or array element.

- Managed pointers can be passed as arguments, stored in local variables, and returned as values.
- If a parameter is passed by reference, the corresponding argument is a managed pointer.

- Managed pointers cannot be stored in static variables, array elements, or fields of objects or value types.
- Managed pointers are *not* interchangeable with object references.
- A managed pointer cannot point to another managed pointer, but it can point to an object reference or a value type.
- A managed pointer can point to a local variable, or a method argument
- Managed pointers that do not point to managed memory can be converted (using **conv.u** or **conv.ovf.u**) into unmanaged pointers, but this is not verifiable.
  - Unverified code that erroneously converts a managed pointer into an unmanaged pointer can seriously compromise the integrity of the CLI. See Partition III, section 1.1.4.2 (Managed Pointers (type **&**)) for more details [see also Partition I, section 8.9.2].

End informative text

13.5 Method Pointers

```
<type> ::= ...
  | method <callConv> <type> * ( <parameters> )
```

Variables of type **method** pointer shall store the address of the entry point to a method with compatible signature. A pointer to a static or instance method is obtained with the **ldftn** instruction, while a pointer to a virtual method is obtained with the **ldvirtftn** instruction. A method may be called by using a **method** pointer with the **calli** instruction. See Partition III for the specification of these instructions.

> **NOTE**
>
> Like other pointers, method pointers are compatible with unsigned int64 on 64-bit architectures [and] with unsigned int32 and on 32-bit architectures. The preferred usage, however, is **unsigned native int**, which works on both 32- and 64-bit architectures.

3. Metadata Semantics

Example (informative):

Call a method using a pointer. The method MakeDecision::Decide returns a method pointer to either AddOne or Negate, alternating on each call. The main program calls MakeDecision::Decide three times and after each call uses a CALLI instruction to call the method specified. The output printed is "-1 2 -1", indicating successful alternating calls.

```
.assembly Test { }
.assembly extern mscorlib { }
.method public static int32 AddOne(int32 Input)
{ .maxstack 5
  ldarg Input
  ldc.i4.1
  add
  ret
}
.method public static int32 Negate(int32 Input)
{ .maxstack 5
  ldarg Input
  neg
  ret
}
.class value sealed public MakeDecision extends [mscorlib]System.ValueType
{ .field static bool Oscillate
  .method public static method int32 *(int32) Decide()
  { ldsfld bool valuetype MakeDecision::Oscillate
    dup
    not
    stsfld bool valuetype MakeDecision::Oscillate
    brfalse NegateIt
    ldftn int32 AddOne(int32)
    ret
NegateIt:
    ldftn int32 Negate(int32)
    ret
  }
}
```

```
.method public static void Start()
{ .maxstack 2
  .entrypoint

  ldc.i4.1
  call method int32 *(int32) valuetype MakeDecision::Decide()
  calli int32(int32)
  call  void [mscorlib]System.Console::WriteLine(int32)

  ldc.i4.1
  call method int32 *(int32) valuetype MakeDecision::Decide()
  calli int32(int32)
  call  void [mscorlib]System.Console::WriteLine(int32)

  ldc.i4.1
  call method int32 *(int32) valuetype MakeDecision::Decide()
  calli int32(int32)
  call  void [mscorlib]System.Console::WriteLine(int32)

  ret
}
```

13.6 Delegates

Delegates (see Partition I, section 8.9.3) are the object-oriented equivalent of function pointers. Unlike function pointers, delegates are object-oriented, typesafe, and secure. Delegates are reference types and are declared in the form of Classes. Delegates shall have an immediate base type of `System.MulticastDelegate`, which in turn has an immediate base type of `System.Delegate` (see the *.NET Framework Standard Library Annotated Reference*).

Delegates shall be declared sealed, and the only members a delegate shall have are either two or four methods as specified here. These methods shall be declared **runtime** and **managed** (see Partition II, section 14.4.3). They shall not have a body, since it shall be automatically created by the VES. Other methods available on delegates are inherited from the classes `System.Delegate` and `System.MulticastDelegate` in the Base Class Library (see the *.NET Framework Standard Library Annotated Reference*).

> **RATIONALE**
>
> A better design would be to simply have delegate classes derive directly from `System.Delegate`. Unfortunately, backward compatibility with an existing CLI does not permit this design.

The instance constructor (named **.ctor** and marked **specialname** and **rtspecialname**; see Partition II, section 9.5.1) shall take exactly two parameters. The first parameter shall be of type `System.Object`, and the second parameter shall be of type `System.IntPtr`. When actually called (via a **newobj** instruction; see Partition III), the first argument shall be an instance of the class (or one of its subclasses) that defines the target method, and the second argument shall be a method pointer to the method to be called.

The `Invoke` method shall be **virtual** and have the same signature (return type, parameter types, calling convention, and modifiers; see Partition II, section 7.1) as the target method. When actually called, the arguments passed shall match the types specified in this signature.

The `BeginInvoke` method (see Partition II, section 13.6.2.1), if present, shall be **virtual** and have a signature related to, but not the same as, that of the `Invoke` method. There are two differences in the signature. First, the return type shall be `System.IAsyncResult` (see the *.NET Framework Standard Library Annotated Reference*). Second, there shall be two additional parameters that follow those of `Invoke`: the first of type `System.AsyncCallback` and the second of type `System.Object`.

The `EndInvoke` method (see Partition II, section 13.6.2.2) shall be **virtual** and have the same return type as the `Invoke` method. It shall take as parameters exactly those parameters of `Invoke` that are managed pointers, in the same order they occur in the signature for `Invoke`. In addition, there shall be an additional parameter of type `System.IAsyncResult`.

Example (informative):

The following example declares a delegate used to call functions that take a single integer and return void. It provides all four methods so it can be called either synchronously or asynchronously. Because there are no parameters that are passed by reference (i.e., as managed pointers), there are no additional arguments to EndInvoke.

```
.assembly Test { }

.assembly extern mscorlib { }

.class private sealed StartStopEventHandler

       extends [mscorlib]System.MulticastDelegate

 { .method public specialname rtspecialname instance

           void .ctor(object Instance, native int Method)

                 runtime managed {}

   .method public virtual void Invoke(int32 action) runtime managed {}

   .method public virtual

      class [mscorlib]System.IAsyncResult
```

3. Metadata Semantics

```
            BeginInvoke(int32 action,
                        class [mscorlib]System.AsyncCallback callback,
                        object Instance) runtime managed {}
    .method public virtual
        void EndInvoke(class [mscorlib]System.IAsyncResult result)
        runtime managed {}
}
```

As with any class, an instance is created using the **newobj** instruction in conjunction with the instance constructor. The first argument to the constructor shall be the object on which the method is to be called, or it shall be null if the method is a static method. The second argument shall be a method pointer to a method on the corresponding class and with a signature that matches that of the delegate class being instantiated.

ANNOTATION

Implementation-Specific (Microsoft): The Microsoft implementation of the CLI allows programmers to add more methods to a delegate, on the condition that they provide an implementation for those methods (i.e., the methods cannot be marked **runtime**). Note that such use makes the resulting assembly non-portable.

13.6.1 *Synchronous Calls to Delegates*

The synchronous mode of calling delegates corresponds to regular method calls and is performed by calling the virtual method named `Invoke` on the delegate. The delegate itself is the first argument to this call (it serves as the **this** pointer), followed by the other arguments as specified in the signature. When this call is made, the caller shall block until the called method returns. The called method shall be executed on the same thread as the caller.

Example (informative):

Continuing the previous example, define a class Test that declares a method, onStartStop, appropriate for use as the target for the delegate.

```
.class public Test
{ .field public int32 MyData
  .method public void onStartStop(int32 action)
  { ret        // put your code here
  }
  .method public specialname rtspecialname
          instance void .ctor(int32 Data)
```

3. Metadata Semantics

```
    { ret        // call parent constructor, store state, etc.
    }
}
```

Then define a main program. This one constructs an instance of Test and then a delegate that targets the onStartStop method of that instance. Finally, call the delegate.

```
.method public static void Start()
{ .maxstack 3
  .entrypoint
  .locals (class StartStopEventHandler DelegateOne,
           class Test InstanceOne)
  // Create instance of Test class
  ldc.i4.1
  newobj instance void Test::.ctor(int32)
  stloc InstanceOne
  // Create delegate to onStartStop method of that class
  ldloc InstanceOne
  ldftn instance void Test::onStartStop(int32)
  newobj void StartStopEventHandler::.ctor(object, native int)
  stloc DelegateOne
  // Invoke the delegate, passing 100 as an argument
  ldloc DelegateOne
  ldc.i4 100
  callvirt instance void StartStopEventHandler::Invoke(int32)
  ret
}
  // Note that the example above creates a delegate to a non-virtual
  // function. If onStartStop had instead been a virtual function, use
  // the following code sequence instead:
  ldloc InstanceOne
  dup
  ldvirtftn instance void Test::onStartStop(int32)
  newobj void StartStopEventHandler::.ctor(object, native int)
  stloc DelegateOne
  // Invoke the delegate, passing 100 as an argument
  ldloc DelegateOne
```

> **NOTE**
> The code sequence above shall use **dup**—not **ldloc**—InstanceOne twice. The **dup** code sequence is easily recognized as typesafe, whereas alternatives would require more complex analysis. Verifiability of code is discussed in Partition III, section 1.8.

13.6.2 *Asynchronous Calls to Delegates*

In the asynchronous mode, the call is dispatched, and the caller shall continue execution without waiting for the method to return. The called method shall be executed on a separate thread.

To call delegates asynchronously, the `BeginInvoke` and `EndInvoke` methods are used.

> **NOTE**
> If the caller thread terminates before the callee completes, the callee thread is unaffected. The callee thread continues execution and terminates silently.

> **NOTE**
> The callee may throw exceptions. Any unhandled exception propagates to the caller via the `EndInvoke` method.

13.6.2.1 The BeginInvoke Method

An asynchronous call to a delegate shall begin by making a virtual call to the `BeginInvoke` method. `BeginInvoke` is similar to the `Invoke` method (see Partition II, section 13.6.1), but has two differences:

- It has two additional parameters, appended to the list, of type `System.AsyncCallback` and `System.Object`
- The return type of the method is `System.IAsyncResult`

Although the `BeginInvoke` method therefore includes parameters that represent return values, these values are not updated by this method. The results instead are obtained from the `EndInvoke` method (see below).

Unlike a synchronous call, an asynchronous call shall provide a way for the caller to determine when the call has been completed. The CLI provides two such mechanisms. The first is through the result returned from the call. This object, an instance of the interface `System.IAsyncResult`, can be used to wait for the result to be computed, it can be queried for the current status of the method call, and it contains the `System.Object` value that was passed to the call to `BeginInvoke`. See the *.NET Framework Standard Library Annotated Reference*.

The second mechanism is through the `System.AsyncCallback` delegate passed to `BeginInvoke`. The VES shall call this delegate when the value is computed or an exception has been raised indicating that the result will not be available. The value passed to this callback is the same value passed to the call to `BeginInvoke`. A value of null may be passed for `System.AsyncCallback` to indicate that the VES need not provide the callback.

RATIONALE

This model supports both a polling approach (by checking the status of the returned `System.IAsyncResult`) and an event-driven approach (by supplying a `System.AsyncCallback`) to asynchronous calls.

A synchronous call returns information both through its return value and through output parameters. Output parameters are represented in the CLI as parameters with managed pointer type. Both the returned value and the values of the output parameters are not available until the VES signals that the asynchronous call has completed successfully. They are retrieved by calling the `EndInvoke` method on the delegate that began the asynchronous call.

13.6.2.2 The EndInvoke Method

The `EndInvoke` method can be called at any time after `BeginInvoke`. It shall suspend the thread that calls it until the asynchronous call completes. If the call completes successfully, `EndInvoke` will return the value that would have been returned, had the call been made synchronously, and its managed pointer arguments will point to values that would have been returned to the out parameters of the synchronous call.

`EndInvoke` requires as parameters the value returned by the originating call to `BeginInvoke` (so that different calls to the same delegate can be distinguished, since they may execute concurrently), as well as any managed pointers that were passed as arguments (so their return values can be provided).

14 Defining, Referencing, and Calling Methods

Methods may be defined at the global level (outside of any type):

```
<decl> ::= ...
    | .method <methodHead>  { <methodBodyItem>* }
```

as well as inside a type:

```
<classMember> ::= ...
    | .method <methodHead>  { <methodBodyItem>* }
```

14.1 Method Descriptors

There are four constructs in ilasm connected with methods. These correspond with different metadata constructs, as described in Partition II, section 21.

14.1.1 *Method Declarations*

A *MethodDecl*, or method declaration, supplies the method name and signature (parameter and return types), but not its body. That is, a method declaration provides a <methodHead> but no <methodBodyItem>'s. These are used at call sites to specify the call target (**call** or **callvirt** instructions; see Partition III) or to declare an **abstract** method. A *MethodDecl* has no direct logical couterpart in the metadata; it can be either a *Method* or a *MethodRef*.

14.1.2 *Method Definitions*

A *Method*, or method definition, supplies the method name, attributes, signature, and body. That is, a method definition provides a <methodHead>, as well as one or more <methodBodyItem>'s. The body includes the method's CIL instructions, exception handlers, local variable information, and additional runtime or custom metadata about the method. See Partition II, section 14.

14.1.3 *Method References*

A *MethodRef*, or method reference, is a reference to a method. It is used when a method is called whose definition lies in another module or assembly. A *MethodRef* shall be resolved by the VES into a *Method* before the method is called at runtime. If a matching *Method* cannot be found, the VES shall throw a `System.MissingMethodException`. See Partition II, section 21.23.

14.1.4 *Method Implementations*

A *MethodImpl*, or method implementation, supplies the executable body for an existing virtual method. It associates a *Method* (representing the body) with a *MethodDecl* or *Method* (representing the virtual method). A *MethodImpl* is used to provide an implementation for an inherited virtual method or a virtual method from an interface when the default mechanism (matching by name and signature) would not provide the correct result. See Partition II, section 21.25.

14.2 Static, Instance, and Virtual Methods

Static methods are methods that are associated with a type, not with its instances.

Instance methods are associated with an instance of a type: within the body of an instance method it is possible to reference the particular instance on which the method is operating (via the ***this*** *pointer*). It follows that instance methods may only be defined in classes or value types, but not in interfaces or outside of a type (globally). However, notice that

1. Instance methods on classes (including boxed value types) have a **this** pointer [which is implicit] that is by default an object reference to the class on which the method is defined.
2. Instance methods on (unboxed) value types have a **this** pointer that is by default a managed pointer to an instance of the type on which the method is defined.
3. There is a special encoding (denoted by the syntactic item **explicit** in the calling convention; see Partition II, section 14.3) to specify the type of the **this** pointer, overriding the default values specified here.
4. The **this** pointer may be null.

Virtual methods are associated with an instance of a type in much the same way as for instance methods. However, unlike instance methods, it is possible to call a virtual method in such a way that the implementation of the method shall be chosen at runtime by the VES, depending upon the type of object used for the **this** pointer. The particular *Method* that implements a virtual method is determined dynamically at runtime (a *virtual call*) when invoked via the **callvirt** instruction, while the binding is decided at compile time when invoked via the **call** instruction (see Partition III).

ANNOTATION: It is important to distinguish between virtual and instance methods, and virtual (**callvirt**) and instance (**call**) calls. Both kinds of methods can be called with either kind of call. For a more complete discussion of this topic, see Partition I, section 8.4.2.

With virtual calls (only) the notion of inheritance becomes important. A subclass may *override* a virtual method inherited from its base classes, providing a new implementation of the method. The method attribute **newslot** specifies that the CLI shall not override the virtual method definition of the base type, but shall treat the new definition as an independent virtual method definition.

Abstract virtual methods (which shall only be defined in **abstract** classes or interfaces) shall be called only with a **callvirt** instruction. Similarly, the address of an **abstract** virtual method shall be computed with the **ldvirtftn** instruction, and the **ldftn** instruction shall not be used.

> **RATIONALE**
>
> With a concrete virtual method there is always an implementation available from the class that contains the definition; thus there is no need at runtime to have an instance of a class available. **Abstract** virtual methods, however, receive their implementation only from a subtype or a class that implements the appropriate interface, hence an instance of a class that actually implements the method is required.

14.3 Calling Convention

```
<callConv> ::= [instance [explicit]] [<callKind>]
```

A calling convention specifies how a method expects its arguments to be passed from the caller to the called method. It consists of two parts; the first deals with the existence and type of the **this** pointer, while the second relates to the mechanism for transporting the arguments.

If the attribute **instance** is present, it indicates that a **this** pointer shall be passed to the method. It shall be used for both instance and virtual methods.

> **ANNOTATION**
>
> **Implementation-Specific (Microsoft):** For simplicity, the assembler automatically sets or clears the instance bit in the calling convention for a method definition based on the method attributes **static** and **virtual**. In a method reference, however, the instance bit shall be specified directly because the information about static or virtual is not captured in a reference.

Normally, a parameter list (which always follows the calling convention) does *not* provide information about the type of the **this** pointer, since this can be deduced from other information. When the combination **instance explicit** is specified, however, the first type in the subsequent parameter list specifies the type of the **this** pointer, and subsequent entries specify the types of the parameters themselves.

`<callKind> ::=`
`default`
`| unmanaged cdecl`
`| unmanaged fastcall`
`| unmanaged stdcall`
`| unmanaged thiscall`
`| vararg`

ANNOTATION: For more information, see sections 22.2.1, 22.2.2, and 22.2.3 in Partition II.

Managed code shall have only the **default** or **vararg** calling kind. **default** shall be used in all cases except when a method accepts an arbitrary number of arguments, in which case **vararg** shall be used.

When dealing with methods implemented outside the CLI, it is important to be able to specify the calling convention required. For this reason there are 16 possible encodings of the calling kind. Two are used for the managed calling kinds. Four are reserved with defined meaning across many platforms:

- **unmanaged cdecl** is the calling convention used by standard C.
- **unmanaged stdcall** specifies a standard C++ call.
- **unmanaged fastcall** is a special optimized C++ calling convention.
- **unmanaged thiscall** is a C++ call that passes a **this** pointer to the method.

Four more are reserved for existing calling conventions, but their use is not portable. Four more are reserved for future standardization, and two are available for non-standard experimental use.

(By "portable" is meant a feature that is available on all conforming implementations of the CLI.)

14.4 Defining Methods

```
<methodHead> ::=

  <methAttr>* [<callConv>] [<paramAttr>*] <type>
              [marshal ( [<nativeType>] )]
              <methodName> ( <parameters> ) <implAttr>*
```

The method head (see also Partition II, section 14) consists of

- The calling convention (`<callConv>`; see Partition II, section 14.3)
- Any number of predefined method attributes (`<paramAttr>`; see Partition II, section 14.4.2)
- A return type with optional attributes
- Optional marshalling information (see Partition II, section 7.4)
- A method name
- A signature
- And any number of implementation attributes (`<implAttr>`; see Partition II, section 14.4.3)

Methods that do not have a return value shall use void as the return type.

```
<methodName> ::=

  .cctor
| .ctor
| <dottedname>
```

Method names are either simple names or the special names used for instance constructors and type initializers.

ANNOTATION: Both **.ctor**, the object instance constructor name, and **.cctor**, the type initializer (also called a class constructor), are required names and cannot be changed.

<parameters> ::= [<param> [, <param>]*]
<param> ::=
...
| [<paramAttr>*] <type> [**marshal** ([<nativeType>])] [<id>]

The <id>, if present, is the name of the parameter. A parameter may be referenced either by using its name or the zero-based index of the parameter. In CIL instructions it is always encoded using the zero-based index (the name is for ease of use in ilasm).

Note that, in contrast to calling a vararg method, the definition of a vararg method does*not* include any ellipsis ("**...**").

<paramAttr> ::=
[in]
| **[opt]**
| **[out]**

The parameter attributes shall be attached to the parameters (see Partition II, section 21.30) and hence are not part of a method signature.

> **NOTE**
> Unlike parameter attributes, custom modifiers (**modopt** and **modreq**) *are* part of the signature. Thus, modifiers form part of the method's contract, while parameter attributes are not.

`in` and `out` shall only be attached to parameters of pointer (managed or unmanaged) type. They specify whether the parameter is intended to supply input to the method, return a value from the method, or both. If neither is specified, `in` is assumed. The CLI itself does not enforce the semantics of these bits, although they may be used to optimize performance, especially in scenarios where the call site and the method are in different application domains, processes, or computers.

opt specifies that this parameter is intended to be optional from an end-user point of view. The value to be supplied is stored using the **.param** syntax (see Partition II, section 14.4.1.4).

ANNOTATION: "The value to be supplied," in the previous paragraph, is the <fieldinit> value.

14.4.1 *Method Body*

The method body shall contain the instructions of a program. However, it may also contain labels, additional syntactic forms, and many directives that provide additional information to ilasm and are helpful in the compilation of methods of some languages.

<methodBodyItem> ::=	Description	Section in Partition II
.custom <customDecl>	Definition of custom attributes.	20
| **.data** <datadecl>	Emits data to the data section.	15.3
| **.emitbyte** <unsigned int8>	Emits a byte to the code section of the method.	14.4.1.1
| **.entrypoint**	Specifies that this method is the entry point to the application (only one such method is allowed).	14.4.1.2
| **.locals** [init] (<localsSignature>)	Defines a set of local variables for this method.	14.4.1.3
| **.maxstack** <int32>	int32 specifies the maximum number of elements on the evaluation stack during the execution of the method.	14.4.1, [4.1]
| **.override** <typeSpec>::<methodName>	**Use current method as the implementation for the method specified.**	9.3.2
| **.param** [<int32>] [= <fieldInit>]	Store a constant <fieldInit> value for parameter <int32>.	14.4.1.4
| <externSourceDecl>	**.line** or **#line**	5.7
| <instr>	An instruction.	See Partition V [Annex C]

<methodBodyItem> ::=	Description	Section in Partition II
| <id> :	A label.	5.4
| <scopeBlock>	Lexical scope of local variables.	14.4.4
| <securityDecl>	**.permission** or **.permissionset**	19
| <sehBlock>	An exception block.	18

14.4.1.1 .emitbyte

```
<methodBodyItem> ::= ...
    | .emitbyte <unsigned int8>
```

Emits an unsigned 8-bit value directly into the CIL stream of the method. The value is emitted at the position where the directive appears.

> **NOTE**
> The **.emitbyte** directive is used for generating tests. It is not required in generating regular programs.

14.4.1.2 .entrypoint

```
<methodBodyItem> ::= ...
    | .entrypoint
```

The **.entrypoint** directive marks the current method, which shall be static, as the entry point to an application. The VES shall call this method to start the application. An executable shall have exactly one entry point method. This entry point method may be a global method or may appear inside a type. (The effect of the directive is to place the metadata token for this method into the CLI header of the PE file.)

The entry point method shall accept either no arguments or a vector of strings. If it accepts a vector of strings, the strings shall represent the arguments to the executable, with index 0 containing the first argument. The mechanism for specifying these arguments is platform-specific and is not specified here.

The return type of the entry point method shall be void, int32, or unsigned int32. If an int32 or unsigned int32 is returned, the executable may return an exit code to the host environment. A value of 0 shall indicate that the application terminated ordinarily.

The accessibility of the entry point method shall not prevent its use in starting execution. Once started, the VES shall treat the entry point as it would any other method.

Example (informative):

The following example prints the first argument and returns successfully to the operating system:

```
.method public static int32 MyEntry(string[] s) CIL managed
{ .entrypoint
  .maxstack 2
  ldarg.0                          // load and print the first argument
  ldc.i4.0
  ldelem.ref
  call void [mscorlib]System.Console::WriteLine(string)
  ldc.i4.0                         // return success
  ret
}
```

ANNOTATION: If you have a managed entry point, the entry point token is either the method that is the entry point or, if the entry point method is in another file, a file token for that file. That file must have the entry point. For more information on entry points, refer to Partition II, section 24.3.3, which describes the **EntryPointToken** field in the CLI header of the PE file.

14.4.1.3 .locals

The **.locals** statement declares local variables (see Partition I [section 12.3.2.2]) for the current method.

<methodBodyItem> ::= ...
| **.locals** [**init**] (<localsSignature>)
<localsSignature> ::= <local> [, <local>]*
<local> ::= <type> [<id>]

The <id>, if present, is the name of the local.

If **init** is specified, the variables are initialized to their default values according to their type. Reference types are initialized to *null*, and value types are zeroed out.

> **NOTE**
> Verifiable methods shall include the **init** keyword. See Partition III [section 1.8].

ANNOTATION: In the file format, the <localsSignature> is formatted as a LocalVarSig, described in Partition II, section 22.2.6. The flag to set for initializing locals to zero is **CorILMethod_InitLocals**, described in Partition II, section 24.4.4.

Implementation-Specific (Microsoft): ilasm allows nested local variable scopes to be provided and allows locals in nested scopes to share the same location as those in the outer scope. The information about local names, scoping, and overlapping of scoped locals is persisted to the PDB (debugger symbol) file rather than the PE file itself.

```
<local> ::= [[<int32>]] <type> [<id>]
```

The integer in brackets that precedes the <type>, if present, specifies the local number (starting with 0) being described. This allows nested locals to reuse the same location as a local in the outer scope. It is not legal to overlap two local variables unless they have the same type. When no explicit index is specified, the next unused index is chosen. That is, two locals never share an index unless the index is given explicitly.

If **init** is used, all local variables will be initialized to their default values, even variables in another **.locals** directive in the same method, which does not have the **init** directive.

14.4.1.4 .param

```
<methodBodyItem> ::= ...
  | .param [ <int32> ] [= <fieldInit>]
```

[The **.param** directive] stores in the metadata a constant value associated with method parameter number <int32> (see Partition II, section 21.9). While the CLI requires that a value be supplied for the parameter, some tools may use the presence of this attribute to indicate that the tool rather than the user is intended to supply the value of the parameter. Unlike CIL instructions, **.param** uses index 0 to specify the return value of the method, index 1 is the first parameter of the method, and so forth.

NOTE

The CLI attaches no semantic whatsoever to these values—it is entirely up to compilers to implement any semantic they wish (e.g., so-called "default argument values").

ANNOTATION: Partition II, section 21.9 discusses the layout of the Constant table in metadata.

This section requires a little clarification. It means that the CLI requires that when a method is called, all parameters must have values. Some compilers supply default values. In this case, the compiler can extract a value from the <fieldinit> value at compile time, and generate code to pass it to the CLI at runtime.

14.4.2 *Predefined Attributes on Methods*

`<methAttr> ::=`	Description	Section in Partition II
`abstract`	The method is **abstract** (shall also be virtual).	14.4.2.4
`| assembly`	Assembly accessibility.	14.4.2.1
`| compilercontrolled`	Compiler-controlled accessibility.	14.4.2.1
`| famandassem`	Family-and-assembly accessibility.	14.4.2.1
`| family`	Family accessibility.	14.4.2.1
`| famorassem`	Family-or-assembly accessibility.	14.4.2.1
`| final`	This virtual method cannot be overridden by subclasses.	14.4.2.2

`<methAttr> ::=`	Description	Section in Partition II
`| hidebysig`	Hide by signature. Ignored by the runtime.	14.4.2.2
`| newslot`	Specifies that this method shall get a new slot in the virtual method table.	14.4.2.3
`| pinvokeimpl ( <QSTRING> [as <QSTRING>] <pinvAttr>* )`	**Method is actually implemented in native code on the underlying platform.**	14.4.2.5
`| private`	Private accessibility.	14.4.2.1
`| public`	Public accessibility.	14.4.2.1
`| rtspecialname`	The method name needs to be treated in a special way by the runtime.	14.4.2.6
`| specialname`	The method name needs to be treated in a special way by some tool.	14.4.2.6
`| static`	Method is static.	14.4.2.2
`| virtual`	Method is virtual.	14.4.2.2

ANNOTATION: For the metadata MethodAttributes that correspond to these ilasm attributes, refer to Partition II, section 22.1.9.

For more information on **newslot**, refer to Partition I, section 8.10.4, and Partition II, section 9.3.1.

Implementation-Specific (Microsoft): The following syntax is supported:

```
<methAttr> ::= … | unmanagedexp | reqsecobj
```

unmanagedexp indicates that the method is exported to unmanaged code using COM interop; **reqsecobj** indicates that the method calls another method with security attributes.

Note that in the first release of Microsoft's CLR, ilasm does not recognize the **compilercontrolled** keyword. Instead, use **privatescope**.

The following combinations of predefined attributes are illegal:

- **static** combined with any of **final**, **virtual**, or **newslot**
- **abstract** combined with any of **final** or **pinvokeimpl**
- **compilercontrolled** combined with any of **virtual**, **final**, **specialname**, or **rtspecialname**

14.4.2.1 Accessibility Information

`<methAttr> ::= ...`
`| assembly`
`| compilercontrolled`
`| famandassem`
`| family`
`| famorassem`
`| private`
`| public`

Only one of these attributes shall be applied to a given method. See Partition I, section 8.5.3 and its subsections.

14.4.2.2 Method Contract Attributes

`<methAttr> ::= ...`
`| final`
`| hidebysig`
`| static`
`| virtual`

These attributes may be combined, except a method shall not be both **static** and **virtual**; only **virtual** methods may be **final;** and abstract methods shall not be **final**.

final methods shall not be overridden by subclasses of this type.

hidebysig is supplied for the use of tools and is ignored by the VES. It specifies that the declared method hides all methods of the parent types that have a matching method signature; when omitted, the method should hide all methods of the same name, regardless of the signature.

> **RATIONALE**
> Some languages use a hide-by-name semantic (C++) while others use a hide-by-name-and-signature semantic (C#, Java).

Static and **virtual** are described in Partition II, section 14.2.

14.4.2.3 Overriding Behavior

```
<methAttr> ::= ...
  | newslot
```

newslot shall only be used with virtual methods. See Partition II, section 9.3.

14.4.2.4 Method Attributes

```
<methAttr> ::= ...
  | abstract
```

abstract shall only be used with virtual methods that are not final. It specifies that an implementation of the method is not provided but shall be provided by a subclass. Abstract methods shall only appear in **abstract** types (see Partition II, section 9.1.4).

14.4.2.5 Interoperation Attributes

```
<methAttr> ::= ...
  | pinvokeimpl ( <QSTRING> [as <QSTRING>] <pinvAttr>* )
```

See Partition II, sections 14.5.2 and 21.20.

14.4.2.6 Special Handling Attributes

<methAttr> ::= ...
| **rtspecialname**
| **specialname**

The attribute **rtspecialname** specifies that the method name shall be treated in a special way by the runtime. Examples of special names are **.ctor** (object constructor) and **.cctor** (type initializer).

specialname indicates that the name of this method has special meaning to some tools.

14.4.3 *Implementation Attributes of Methods*

<implAttr> ::=	Description	Section in Partition II
cil	The method contains standard CIL code.	14.4.3.1
| forwardref	The body of this method is not specified with this declaration.	14.4.3.3
| internalcall	Denotes [that] the method body is provided by the CLI itself.	14.4.3.3
| managed	The method is a managed method.	14.4.3.2
| native	The method contains native code.	14.4.3.1
| noinlining	The runtime shall not expand the method inline.	14.4.3.3
| runtime	The body of the method is not defined but produced by the runtime.	14.4.3.1
| synchronized	The method shall be executed in a single threaded fashion.	14.4.3.3
| unmanaged	Specifies that the method is unmanaged.	14.4.3.2

ANNOTATION: The <forwardref> attribute is not used by the VES. It is intended for use by compilers to communicate with their linkers. At runtime, there must be no forward reference.

Implementation-Specific (Microsoft): The following syntax is accepted:

```
<implAttr> ::= … | preservesig
```

`preservesig` specifies the method signature is mangled to return HRESULT, with the return value as a parameter.

14.4.3.1 Code Implementation Attributes

```
<implAttr> ::= ...
    | cil
    | native
    | runtime
```

These attributes are exclusive; they specify the type of code the method contains.

cil specifies that the method body consists of CIL code. Unless the method is declared **abstract**, the body of the method shall be provided if **cil** is used.

native specifies that a method was implemented using native code, tied to a specific processor for which it was generated. Native methods shall not have a body but instead refer to a native method that declares the body. Typically, the PInvoke functionality (see Partition II, section 14.5.2) of the CLI is used to refer to a native method.

runtime specifies that the implementation of the method is automatically provided by the runtime and is primarily used for the method of delegates (see Partition II, section 13.6).

14.4.3.2 Managed or Unmanaged

```
<implAttr> ::= ...
    | managed
    | unmanaged
```

These shall not be combined. Methods implemented using CIL are managed. Unmanaged is used primarily with PInvoke (see Partition II, section 14.5.2).

14.4.3.3 Implementation Information

<implAttr> ::= ...
| **forwardref**
| **internalcall**
| **noinlining**
| **synchronized**

These attributes may be combined.

forwardref specifies that the body of the method is provided elsewhere. This attribute shall not be present when an assembly is loaded by the VES. It is used for tools (like a static linker) that will combine separately compiled modules and resolve the forward reference.

internalcall specifies that the method body is provided by this CLI (and is typically used by low-level methods in a system library). It shall not be applied to methods that are intended for use across implementations of the CLI.

ANNOTATION

Implementation-Specific (Microsoft): internalcall allows the lowest-level parts of the Base Class Library to wrap unmanaged code built into Microsoft's Common Language Runtime.

noinlining specifies that the body of this method should not be included in the code of any caller methods, by a CIL-to-native-code compiler; it shall be kept as a separate routine. **noinlining** specifies that the runtime shall not inline this method. Inlining refers to the process of replacing the call instruction with the body of the called method. This may be done by the runtime for optimization purposes.

RATIONALE

Specifying that a method not be inlined ensures that it remains "visible" for debugging (e.g., displaying stack traces) and profiling. It also provides a mechanism for the programmer to override the default heuristics a CIL-to-native-code compiler uses for inlining.

synchronized specifies that the whole body of the method shall be single-threaded. If this method is an instance or virtual method, a lock on the object shall be obtained before the method is entered. If this method is a static method, a lock on the type shall be obtained before the method is entered. If a lock cannot be obtained, the requesting thread shall not proceed until it is granted the lock. This may cause deadlocks. The lock is released when the method exits, through either a normal return or an exception. Exiting a synchronized method using a **tail.** call shall be implemented as though the **tail.** had not been specified.

14.4.4 *Scope Blocks*

```
<scopeBlock> ::= { <methodBodyItem>* }
```

A **scopeBlock** is used to group elements of a method body together. For example, it is used to designate the code sequence that constitutes the body of an exception handler.

ANNOTATION:

Implementation-Specific (Microsoft): Scope blocks are syntactic sugar and primarily serve readability and debugging purposes.

```
<scopeBlock> ::= { <methodBodyItem>* }
```

A scope block defines the scope in which a local variable is accessible by its name. Scope blocks may be nested, such that a reference of a local variable will first be resolved in the innermost scope block, then at the next level, and so on until the topmost level of the method is reached. A declaration in an inner scope block hides declarations in the outer layers.

If duplicate declarations are used, the reference will be resolved to the first occurrence. Even though valid CIL, duplicate declarations are not recommended.

Scoping does not affect the lifetime of a local variable. All local variables are created (and if specified, initialized) when the method is entered. They stay alive until the method has finished executing.

The scoping does not affect the accessibility of a local variable by its zero-based index. All local variables are accessible from anywhere within the method by their index.

The index is assigned to a local variable in the order of declaration. Scoping is ignored for indexing purposes. Thus, each local variable is assigned the next available index starting at the top of the method. This behavior can be altered by specifying an explicit index, as described by a `<localsSignature>` as shown in Partition II, section 14.4.1.3.

14.4.5 *vararg Methods*

vararg methods accept a variable number of arguments. They shall use the **vararg** calling convention (see Partition II, section 14.3).

At each call site, a method reference shall be used to describe the types of the actual arguments that are passed. The fixed part of the argument list shall be separated from the additional arguments with an ellipsis (see Partition I, section 12.3.2.3).

The **vararg** arguments shall be accessed by obtaining a handle to the argument list using the CIL instruction **arglist** (see Partition III [section 3.4]). The handle may be used to create an instance of the value type `System.ArgIterator`, which provides a typesafe mechanism for accessing the arguments (see the *.NET Framework Standard Library Annotated Reference*).

Example (informative):

The following example shows how a **vararg** method is declared and how the first **vararg** argument is accessed, assuming that at least one additional argument was passed to the method:

```
.method public static vararg void MyMethod(int32 required) {
    .maxstack 3
    .locals init (valuetype System.ArgIterator it, int32 x)
    ldloca it                                // initialize the iterator
    initobj        valuetype System.ArgIterator
    ldloca it
    arglist                                  // obtain the argument handle
    call    instance void System.ArgIterator::.ctor(valuetype
System.RuntimeArgumentHandle)                // call constructor of iterator
    /* argument value will be stored in x when retrieved, so load
     address of x */
    ldloca x
    ldloca it
    // retrieve the argument, the argument for required does not matter
    call    instance typedref System.ArgIterator::GetNextArg()
    call    object System.TypedReference::ToObject(typedref)     // retrieve the
object
```

```
    castclass System.Int32              // cast and unbox
    unbox   int32
    cpobj   int32                       // copy the value into x
    // first vararg argument is stored in x
    ret
}
```

ANNOTATION: Support for variable-length argument lists is not part of the minimum requirement for implementing the CLI. The library support for it, `System.ArgIterator`, is not standardized.

14.5 Unmanaged Methods

In addition to supporting managed code and managed data, the CLI provides facilities for accessing pre-existing native code from the underlying platform, known as **unmanaged code**. These facilities are, by necessity, platform-dependent and hence are only partially specified here.

This standard specifies:

- A mechanism in the file format for providing function pointers to managed code that can be called from unmanaged code (see Partition II, section 14.5.1).
- A mechanism for marking certain method definitions as being implemented in unmanaged code (called **platform invoke**; see Partition II, section 14.5.2).
- A mechanism for marking call sites used with method pointers to indicate that the call is to an unmanaged method (see Partition II, section 14.5.3).
- A small set of predefined data types that can be passed (marshalled) using these mechanisms on all implementations of the CLI (see Partition II, section 14.5.5). The set of types is extensible through the use of custom attributes and modifiers, but these extensions are platform-specific.

14.5.1 *Method Transition Thunks*

NOTE

This mechanism is not part of the Kernel Profile, so it may not be present in all conforming implementations of the CLI. See Partition IV.

In order to call from unmanaged code into managed code, some platforms require a specific transition sequence to be performed. In addition, some platforms require that the representation of data types be converted (data marshalling). Both of these problems are solved by the **.vtfixup** directive. This directive may appear several times only at the top level of a CIL assembly file, as shown by the following grammar:

`<decl> ::=`	Section in Partition II
`.vtfixup` `<vtfixupDecl>`	5.10
`| ...`	

The **.vtfixup** directive declares that at a certain memory location there is a table that contains metadata tokens referring to methods that shall be converted into method pointers. The CLI will do this conversion automatically when the file is loaded into memory for execution. The declaration specifies the number of entries in the table, what kind of method pointer is required, the width of an entry in the table, and the location of the table:

`<vtfixupDecl> ::=`
`[ <int32> ] <vtfixupAttr>*` **`at`** `<dataLabel>`

`<vtfixupAttr> ::=`
`fromunmanaged`
`|` **`int32`**
`|` **`int64`**

The attributes **int32** and **int64** are mutually exclusive, and **int32** is the default. These attributes specify the width of each slot in the table. Each slot contains a 32-bit metadata token (zero-padded if the table has 64-bit slots), and the CLI converts it into a method pointer of the same width as the slot.

If **fromunmanaged** is specified, the CLI will generate a thunk that will convert the unmanaged method call to a managed call, call the method, and return the result to the unmanaged environment. The thunk will also perform data marshalling in the platform-specific manner described for *platform invoke.*

The ilasm syntax does not specify a mechanism for creating the table of tokens, but a compiler may simply emit the tokens as byte literals into a block specified using the **.data** directive.

14.5.2 *Platform Invoke*

Methods defined in native code may be invoked using the *platform invoke* (also known as PInvoke or p/invoke) functionality of the CLI. Platform invoke will switch from managed to unmanaged state and back, and also handle necessary data marshalling. Methods that need to be called using PInvoke are marked as **pinvokeimpl**. In addition, the methods shall have the implementation attributes **native** and **unmanaged** (see Partition II, section 14.4.2.5).

<methAttr> ::=	Description	Section in Partition II
pinvokeimpl (<QSTRING> [**as** <QSTRING>] <pinvAttr>*)	Implemented in native code	14.4.2
| ...		

The first quoted string is a platform-specific description indicating where the implementation of the method is located (for example, on Microsoft Windows this would be the name of the DLL that implements the method). The second (optional) string is the name of the method as it exists on that platform, since the platform may use name-mangling rules that force the name as it appears to a managed program to differ from the name as seen in the native implementation (this is common, for example, when the native code is generated by a C++ compiler).

Only static methods, defined at global scope (i.e., outside of any type), may be marked **pinvokeimpl**. A method declared with **pinvokeimpl** shall not have a body specified as part of the definition.

<pinvAttr> ::=	Description (platform-specific, suggestion only)
ansi	**ANSI** character set.
| **autochar**	Determine character set automatically.
| **cdecl**	Standard C style call.
| **fastcall**	C style fastcall.

<pinvAttr> ::=	Description (platform-specific, suggestion only)
| `stdcall`	Standard C++ style call.
| `thiscall`	The method accepts an implicit **this** pointer.
| `unicode`	Unicode character set.
| `platformapi`	Use call convention appropriate to target platform.

ANNOTATION

Implementation-Specific (Microsoft): In the first release, **platformapi** is not recognized by Microsoft ilasm. Instead use **winapi**.

The attributes **ansi**, **autochar**, and **unicode** are mutually exclusive. They govern how strings will be marshalled for calls to this method: **ansi** indicates that the native code will receive (and possibly return) a platform-specific representation that corresponds to a string encoded in the **ANSI** character set (typically this would match the representation of a C or C++ string constant); **autochar** indicates a platform-specific representation that is "natural" for the underlying platform; and **unicode** indicates a platform-specific representation that corresponds to a string encoded for use with Unicode methods on that platform.

The attributes **cdecl**, **fastcall**, **stdcall**, **thiscall**, and **platformapi** are mutually exclusive. They are platform-specific and specify the calling conventions for native code.

ANNOTATION

Implementation-Specific (Microsoft): In addition, the Microsoft implementation of the CLI on Microsoft Windows supports the following attributes:

- **lasterr** to indicate that the native method supports C-style last error querying.
- **nomangle** to indicate that the name in the DLL should be used precisely as specified, rather than attempting to add A (for "ascii") or W ("widechar") to find platform-specific variants based on the type of string marshalling requested.

Example (informative):

The following shows the declaration of the method MessageBeep located in the Microsoft Windows DLL user32.dll:

```
.method public static pinvokeimpl("user32.dll" stdcall) int8
MessageBeep(unsigned int32) native unmanaged {}
```

14.5.3 *Via Function Pointers*

Unmanaged functions can also be called via function pointers. There is no difference between calling managed or unmanaged functions with pointers. However, the unmanaged function needs to be declared with **pinvokeimpl** as described in Partition II, section 14.5.2. Calling managed methods with function pointers is described in Partition II, section 13.5.

[14.5.4 COM Interop]

ANNOTATION

Implementation-Specific (Microsoft): Unmanaged COM operates primarily by publishing uniquely identified interfaces and then sharing them between implementers (traditionally called "servers") and users (traditionally called "clients") of a given interface. It supports a rich set of types for use across the interface, and the interface itself can supply named constants and static methods, but it does not supply instance fields, instance methods, or virtual methods.

The CLI provides mechanisms useful to both implementers and users of existing classical COM interfaces. The goal is to permit programmers to deal with managed data types (thus eliminating the need for explicit memory management) while at the same time allowing interoperability with existing unmanaged servers and clients. COM interop does not support the use of global functions (i.e., methods that are not part of a managed type), static functions, or parameterized constructors.

Given an existing classical COM interface definition as a type library, the **tlbimp** tool produces a file that contains the metadata describing that interface. The types it exposes in the metadata are managed counterparts of the unmanaged types in the original interface.

Implementers of an *existing* classical COM interface can import the metadata produced by tlbimp and then write managed types that provide the implementation of the methods required by that interface. The metadata specifies the use of managed data types in many places, and the CLI provides automatic marshalling (i.e., copying with reformatting) of data between the managed and unmanaged data types.

Implementers of a new service can simply write a managed program whose publicly visible types adhere to a simple set of rules. They can then run the **tlbexp** tool to produce a type library for classical COM users. This set of rules guarantees that the data types exposed to the classical COM user are unmanaged types that can be marshalled automatically by the CLI.

Implementers need to run the **RegAsm** tool to register their implementation with classical COM for location and activation purposes—if they wish to expose managed services to unmanaged code.

Users of *existing* classical COM interfaces simply import the metadata produced by tlbimp. They can then reference the (managed) types defined there, and the CLI uses the assembly mechanism and activation information to locate and instantiate instances of objects implementing the interface. Their code is the same whether the implementation of the interfaces is provided using classical COM (unmanaged) code or the CLI (managed) code: the interfaces they see use managed data types and hence do not need explicit memory management.

For some existing classical COM interfaces, the CLI provides an implementation of the interface. In some cases the VES allows the user to specify all or parts of the implementation; for others it provides the entire implementation.

14.5.5 *Data Type Marshalling*

While data type marshaling is necessarily platform-dependent, this standard specifies a minimum set of data types that shall be supported by all conforming implementations of the CLI. Additional data types may be supported in an implementation-dependent manner, using custom attributes and/or custom modifiers to specify any special handling required on the particular implementation.

The following data types shall be marshalled by all conforming implementations of the CLI; the native data type to which they conform is implementation-specific:

- All integer data types (**int8**, **int16**, **unsigned int8**, **bool**, **char**, etc.), including the **native** integer types.
- Enumerations, as their underlying data type.
- All floating point data types (**float32** and **float64**), if they are supported by the CLI implementation for managed code.
- The type **string**.
- Unmanaged pointers to any of the above types.

In addition, the following types shall be supported for marshalling from managed code to unmanaged code, but need not be supported in the reverse direction (i.e., as return types when calling unmanaged methods or as parameters when calling from unmanaged methods into managed methods):

- One-dimensional zero-based arrays of any of the above.
- Delegates (the mechanism for calling from unmanaged code into a delegate is platform-specific; it should not be assumed that marshalling a delegate will produce a function pointer that can be used directly from unmanaged code).

Finally, the type *GCHandle* can be used to marshal an object to unmanaged code. The unmanaged code receives a platform-specific data type that can be used as an "opaque handle" to a specific object.

ANNOTATION: You can pass a delegate from managed code to unmanaged code. The delegate is then marshalled into a form that the unmanaged code can use to call the method specified by the delegate.

What is returned, however, is not guaranteed to be a function pointer. Basically, it is up to the platform to determine what that returned "something" is. It may be a function pointer, or it might be implemented as a call to something else, to which the function (the thing returned plus the arguments) is passed. It is up to the VES implementation to determine how to do it. Rotor, a publicly available VES implementation, does it one way; the Microsoft Common Language Runtime does it another. Other VES implementations may have yet another way to implement it.

[14.5.6 *Managed Native Calling Conventions (x86)*]

ANNOTATION

Implementation-Specific (Microsoft): This section is intended for an advanced audience. It describes the details of a native method call from managed code on the x86 architecture. The information provided in this section may be important for optimization purposes. This section is not important for further understanding of the CLI and may be skipped.

There are two managed native calling conventions used on the x86. They are described here for completeness and because knowledge of these conventions allows an unsafe mechanism for bypassing the overhead of a transition from managed to unmanaged code.

[14.5.6.1 Standard 80x86 Calling Convention]

ANNOTATION

Implementation-Specific (Microsoft): The standard native calling convention is a variation on the fastcall convention used by Visual C++. It differs primarily in the order in which arguments are pushed onto the stack.

The only values that can be passed in registers are managed and unmanaged pointers, object references, and the built-in integer types int8, unsigned int8, int16, unsigned int16, int32, unsigned int32, native int, and native unsigned int. Enums are passed as their underlying type. All floating point values and 8-byte integer values are passed on the stack. When the return type is a value type that cannot be passed in a register, the caller shall create a buffer to hold the result and pass the address of this buffer as a hidden parameter.

Arguments are passed in left-to-right order, starting with the **this** pointer (for instance and virtual methods), followed by the return buffer pointer if needed, followed by the user-specified argument values. The first of these that can be placed in a register is put into ECX, the next in EDX, and all subsequent arguments are passed on the stack.

The return value is handled as follows:

Floating point values are returned on the top of the hardware floating point (FP) stack.

Integers up to 32 bits long are returned in EAX.

64-bit integers are passed, with EAX holding the least significant 32 bits and EDX holding the most significant 32 bits.

All other cases require the use of a return buffer, through which the value is returned.

In addition, it is guaranteed that if a return buffer is used, a value is stored there only upon ordinary exit from the method. The buffer is not allowed to be used for temporary storage within the method, and its contents will be unaltered if an exception occurs while the method is executing.

Example (informative):

```
static System.Int32 f(int32 x)
```

The incoming argument (x) is placed in ECX; the return value is in EAX.

```
static float64 f(int32 x, int32 y, int32 z)
```

x is passed in ECX, y in EDX, z on the top of stack; the return value is on the top of the FP stack.

```
static float64 f(int32 x, float64 y, float64 z)
```

x is passed in ECX, y on the top of the stack (not the FP stack), z in EDX; the return value is on the top of the FP stack.

```
virtual float64 f(int32 x, int64 y, int64 z)
```

this is passed in ECX, x in EDX; y is pushed on the stack, and then z is pushed on the stack (hence z is on top of the stack); the return value is on the top of the FP stack.

```
virtual int64 f(int32 x, float64 y, float64 z)
```

this is passed in ECX, x in EDX; y is pushed on the stack, and then z is pushed on the stack (hence z is on top of the stack); the return value is in EDX/EAX.

```
virtual [mscorlib]System.Guid f(int32 x, float64 y, float64 z)
```

Because `System.Guid` is a value type, the **this** pointer is passed in ECX, a pointer to the return buffer is passed in EDX, x is pushed, then y, and then z (hence z is on top of the stack); the return value is stored in the return buffer.

[14.5.6.2 Varargs x86 Calling Convention]

ANNOTATION

Implementation-Specific (Microsoft): All user-specified arguments are passed on the stack, pushed in left-to-right order. Following the last argument (hence on top of the stack upon entry to the method body), a special *cookie* is passed that provides information about the types of the arguments that have been pushed.

As with the standard calling convention, the **this** pointer and a return buffer (if either is needed) are passed in ECX and/or EDX.

Values are returned in the same way as for the standard calling convention.

[14.5.6.3 Fast Calls to Unmanaged Code]

ANNOTATION

Implementation-Specific (Microsoft): Transitions from managed to unmanaged code require a small amount of overhead to allow exceptions and garbage collection to correctly determine the execution context. On an x86 processor, under the best circumstances, these transitions take approximately five instructions per call or return from managed to unmanaged code. In addition, any method that includes calls with transitions incurs an eight-instruction overhead spread across the calling method's prolog and epilog.

This overhead can become a factor in performance of certain applications. For use in unverifiable code only, there is a mechanism to call from managed code to unmanaged code without the overhead of a transition. Such so-called "fast native calls" are accomplished by the use of a **calli** instruction that indicates that the destination is managed, even though the code address to which it refers is unmanaged. This can be arranged, for example, by initializing a variable of type *function pointer* in unmanaged code.

Clearly, this mechanism shall be tightly constrained, because the transition is essential if there is any possibility of a garbage collection or exception occurring while in the unmanaged code. The following restrictions apply to the use of this mechanism:

1. The unmanaged code shall follow one of the two managed calling conventions (regular or vararg) that are specified below. In version 1 of the Microsoft CLR, only the regular calling convention is supported for fast native calls.
2. The unmanaged code shall not execute for any extended time, because garbage collection cannot begin while this code is executing. It is wise to keep this code under 100 instructions long in all control flow paths.
3. The unmanaged code shall not throw an exception (managed or unmanaged), including access violations, etc. Page faults are not considered an exception for this purpose.
4. The unmanaged code shall not call back into managed code.
5. The unmanaged code shall not trigger garbage collection (this usually follows from the restriction on calling back to managed code).
6. The unmanaged code shall not block. That is, it shall not call any OS-provided routine that might block the thread (synchronous I/O, explicit acquisition of locks, etc.) Again, page faults are not a problem for this purpose.
7. The managed code that calls the unmanaged method shall not have a long, tight loop in which it makes the call. The total time for the loop to execute should remain under 100 instructions, or the loop should include at least one call to a managed method. More technically, the method including the call shall produce "fully interruptible native code." In future versions, there may be a way to indicate this as a requirement on a method.

NOTE

Restrictions 2 through 6 apply not only to the unmanaged code called directly, but to anything it may call.

15 Defining and Referencing Fields

Fields are typed memory locations that store the data of a program. The CLI allows the declaration of both instance and static fields. While static fields are associated with a type and shared across all instances of that type, instance fields are associated with a particular instance of that type. When instantiated, the instance has its own copy of that field.

The CLI also supports global fields, which are fields declared outside of any type definition. Global fields shall be static.

A field is defined by the **.field** directive (see Partition II, section 21.15).

```
<field> ::= .field <fieldDecl>
```

```
<fieldDecl> ::=
  [[ <int32> ]] <fieldAttr>* <type> <id> [= <fieldInit> | at <dataLabel>]
```

The <fieldDecl> has the following parts:

- An optional integer specifying the byte offset of the field within an instance (see Partition II, section 9.7). If present, the type containing this field shall have the explicit layout attribute. An offset shall not be supplied for global or static fields.
- Any number of field attributes (see Partition II, section 15.2)
- Type
- Name
- Optionally either a <fieldInit> form or a data label

Global fields shall have a data label associated with them. This specifies where, in the PE file, the data for that field is located. Static fields of a type may, but do not need to, be assigned a data label.

Example (informative):

```
.field private class [.module Counter.dll]Counter counter
```

15.1 Attributes of Fields

Attributes of a field specify information about accessibility, contract information, [and] interoperation attributes, as well as information on special handling.

The following subsections contain additional information on each group of predefined attributes of a field.

<fieldAttr> ::=	Description	Section in Partition II
`assembly`	Assembly accessibility.	15.1.1
| `famandassem`	Family-and-assembly accessibility.	15.1.1
| `family`	Family accessibility.	15.1.1
| `famorassem`	Family-or-assembly accessibility.	15.1.1
| `initonly`	Marks a constant field.	15.1.2
| `literal`	Specifies a metadata field. No memory is allocated at runtime for this field.	15.1.2
| `marshal(<nativeType>)`	Marshalling information.	15.1.3
| `notserialized`	Field is not serialized with other fields of the type.	15.1.2
| `private`	Private accessibility.	15.1.1
| `compilercontrolled`	Compiler-controlled accessibility.	15.1.1
| `public`	Public accessibility.	15.1.1
| `rtspecialname`	Special treatment by runtime.	15.1.4
| `specialname`	Special name for other tools.	15.1.4
| `static`	Static field.	15.1.2

15.1.1 *Accessibility Information*

The accessibility attributes are **assembly**, **famandassem**, **family**, **famorassem**, **private**, **compilercontrolled,** and **public**. These attributes are mutually exclusive.

Accessibility attributes are described in Partition II, section 8.2.

15.1.2 *Field Contract Attributes*

Field contract attributes are **initonly**, **literal**, **static,** and **notserialized**. These attributes may be combined. Only static fields may be literal. The default is an instance field that may be serialized.

static specifies that the field is associated with the type itself rather than with an instance of the type. Static fields can be accessed without having an instance of a type—e.g., by static methods. As a consequence, a static field is shared, within an application domain, between all instances of a type, and any modification of this field will affect all instances. If **static** is not specified, an **instance** field is created.

initonly marks fields which are constant after they are initialized. These fields may only be mutated inside a constructor. If the field is a static field, then it may be mutated only inside the type initializer of the type in which it was declared. If it is an instance field, then it may be mutated only in one of the instance constructors of the type in which it was defined. It may not be mutated in any other method or in any other constructor, including constructors of subclasses.

> **NOTE**
> The VES need not check whether **initonly** fields are mutated outside the constructors. The VES need not report any errors if a method changes the value of a constant. However, such code is not valid and is not verifiable.

ANNOTATION: The standard completely specifies the file format, and the **serializable** bit is in the file format, although serialization was not standardized. Implementing serialization would allow such things as remoting, interactive Web services, saving data in persistent format, etc.

Implementation-Specific (Microsoft): notserialized specifies that this field is not serialized when an instance of this type is serialized. It has no meaning on global or static fields, or if the type does not have the **serializable** attribute.

---

literal specifies that this field represents a constant value; they [literal fields] shall be assigned a value. In contrast to **initonly** fields, **literal** fields do not exist at runtime. There is no memory allocated for them. **literal** fields become part of the metadata but cannot be accessed by the code. **literal** fields are assigned a value by using the *<fieldInit>* syntax (see Partition II, section 15.2).

> **NOTE**
> It is the responsibility of tools generating CIL to replace source code references to the literal with its actual value. Hence changing the value of a literal requires recompilation of any code that references the literal. Literal values are, thus, not version-resilient.

3. Metadata Semantics

15.1.3 *Interoperation Attributes*

There is one attribute for interoperation with pre-existing native applications; it is platform-specific and shall not be used in code intended to run on multiple implementations of the CLI. The attribute is **marshal** and specifies that the field's contents should be converted to and from a specified native data type when passed to unmanaged code. Every conforming implementation of the CLI will have default marshalling rules, as well as restrictions on what automatic conversions can be specified using the **marshal** attribute. See also Partition II, section 14.5.5.

> **NOTE**
> Marshaling of user-defined types is not required of all implementations of the CLI. It is specified in this standard so that implementations which choose to provide it will allow control over its behavior in a consistent manner. While this is not sufficient to guarantee portability of code that uses this feature, it does increase the likelihood that such code will be portable.

15.1.4 *Other Attributes*

The attribute **rtspecialname** indicates that the field name shall be treated in a special way by the runtime.

> **RATIONALE**
> There are currently no field names that are required to be marked with **rtspecialname**. It is provided for extensions, future standardization, and to increase consistency between the declaration of fields and methods (instance and type initializer methods shall be marked with this attribute).

The attribute **specialname** indicates that the field name has special meaning to tools other than the runtime, typically because it marks a name that has meaning for the Common Language Specification (CLS; see Partition I, sections 8.11.3 and 8.11.4).

15.2 Field Init Metadata

The <fieldInit> metadata can be optionally added to a field declaration. The use of this feature may not be combined with a data label.

The <fieldInit> information is stored in metadata, and this information can be queried from metadata. But the CLI does not use this information to automatically initialize the corresponding fields. The field initializer is typically used with **literal** fields (see Partition II, section 15.1.2) or parameters with default values. See Partition II, section 21.9.

The following table lists the options for a field initializer. Note that while both the type and the field initializer are stored in metadata, there is no requirement that they match. (Any importing compiler is responsible for coercing the stored value to the target field type). The description column in the table below provides additional information.

`<fieldInit> ::=`	Description
bool (**true** | **false**)	Boolean value, encoded as true or false.
| **bytearray** (<bytes>)	String of bytes, stored without conversion. May be padded with one zero byte to make the total byte-count an even number.
| **char** (<int32>)	16-bit unsigned integer (Unicode character).
| **float32** (<float64>)	32-bit floating point number, with the floating point number specified in parentheses.
| **float32** (<int32>)	<int32> is binary representation of float.
| **float64** (<float64>)	64-bit floating point number, with the floating point number specified in parentheses.
| **float64** (<int64>)	<int64> is binary representation of double.
| [**unsigned**] **int8** (<int8>)	8-bit integer with the integer specified in parentheses.
| [**unsigned**] **int16** (<int16>)	16-bit integer with the integer specified in parentheses.
| [**unsigned**] **int32** (<int32>)	32-bit integer with the integer specified in parentheses.
| [**unsigned**] **int64** (<int64>)	64-bit integer with the integer specified in parentheses.
| <QSTRING>	String. <QSTRING> is stored as Unicode.
| **nullref**	Null object reference.

ANNOTATION

Implementation-Specific (Microsoft): ilasm does not recognize the optional **unsigned** modifier before the **int8, int16, int32,** or **int64** keywords.

Example (informative):

The following example shows a typical use of this:

```
.field public static literal valuetype ErrorCodes no_error = int8(0)
```

The field named **no_error** is a literal of type **ErrorCodes** (a value type) for which no memory is allocated. Tools and compilers can look up the value and detect that it is intended to be an 8-bit signed integer whose value is 0.

15.3 Embedding Data in a PE File

There are several ways to declare a data field that is stored in a PE file. In all cases, the **.data** directive is used.

Data can be embedded in a PE file by using the **.data** directive at the top level.

<decl> ::=	Section in Partition II
.data <datadecl>	6.6
| ...	

Data may also be declared as part of a type:

<classMember> ::=	Section in Partition II
.data <datadecl>	9.2
| ...	

Yet another alternative is to declare data inside a method:

<methodBodyItem> ::=	Section in Partition II
.data <datadecl>	14.4.1
| ...	

15.3.1 *Data Declaration*

A **.data** directive contains an optional data label and the body which defines the actual data. A data label shall be used if the data is to be accessed by the code.

```
<dataDecl> ::= [<dataLabel> =] <ddBody>
```

The body consists either of one data item or a list of data items in braces. A list of data items is similar to an array.

```
<ddBody> ::=
  <ddItem>
| { <ddItemList> }
```

A list of items consists of any number of items:

```
<ddItemList> ::= <ddItem> [, <ddItemList>]
```

The list may be used to declare multiple data items associated with one label. The items will be laid out in the order declared. The first data item is accessible directly through the label. To access the other items, pointer arithmetic is used, adding the size of each data item to get to the next one in the list. The use of pointer arithmetic will make the application not verifiable. (Each data item shall have a <dataLabel> if it is to be referenced afterward; missing a <dataLabel> is useful in order to insert alignment padding between data items.)

A data item declares the type of the data and provides the data in parentheses. If a list of data items contains items of the same type and initial value, the grammar below can be used as a shortcut for some of the types: the number of times the item shall be replicated is put in brackets after the declaration.

`<ddItem> ::=`	Description
`& ( <id> )`	Address of label
`| bytearray ( <bytes> )`	Array of bytes
`| char * ( <QSTRING> )`	Array of (Unicode) characters
`| float32 [( <float64> )] [[ <int32> ]]`	32-bit floating point number, may be replicated

<ddItem> ::=	Description
| **float64** [(<float64>)] [**[** <int32> **]**]	64-bit floating point number, may be replicated
| **int8** [(<int8>)] [**[** <int32> **]**]	8-bit integer, may be replicated
| **int16** [(<int16>)] [**[** <int32> **]**]	16-bit integer, may be replicated
| **int32** [(<int32>)] [**[** <int32> **]**]	32-bit integer, may be replicated
| **int64** [(<int64>)] [**[** <int32> **]**]	64-bit integer, may be replicated

Example (informative):

The following declares a 32-bit signed integer with value 123:

```
.data theInt = int32(123)
```

The following declares 10 replications of an 8-bit unsigned integer with value 3:

```
.data theBytes = int8 (3) [10]
```

15.3.2 *Accessing Data from the PE File*

The data stored in a PE file using the **.data** directive can be accessed through a **static** variable, either global or a member of a type, declared at a particular position of the data:

```
<fieldDecl> ::= <fieldAttr>* <type> <id> at <dataLabel>
```

The data is then accessed by a program as it would access any other static variable, using instructions such as **ldsfld**, **ldsflda**, and so on (see Partition III).

The ability to access data from within the PE file may be subject to platform-specific rules, typically related to section access permissions within the PE file format itself.

Example (informative):

The following accesses the data declared in the example of Partition II, section 15.3.1. First a static variable needs to be declared for the data -- e.g., a global static variable:

```
.field public static int32 myInt at theInt
```

Then the static variable can be used to load the data:

```
ldsfld int32 myInt
// data on stack
```

[15.3.3 *Unmanaged Thread-Local Storage*]

ANNOTATION

Implementation-Specific (Microsoft): Each PE file has a particular section whose initial contents are copied whenever a new thread is created. This section is called **unmanaged thread-local storage**. The Microsoft implementation of ilasm allows the creation of this unmanaged thread-local storage by extending the data declaration to include an option attribute, **tls**:

```
<dataDecl> ::= [tls] [<dataLabel> =] <ddBody>
```

The CLI provides two mechanisms for dealing with thread-local storage (**tls**): an unmanaged mechanism and a managed mechanism. The unmanaged mechanism has a number of restrictions that are carried forward directly from the underlying platform into the CLI. For example, the amount of thread-local storage is determined when the PE file is loaded and cannot be expanded. The amount is computed based on the static dependencies of the PE file; DLLs that are loaded as a program executes cannot create their own thread-local storage through this mechanism. The managed mechanism, which does not have these restrictions, is part of the Base Class Library.

For unmanaged **tls** there is a particular native code sequence that can be used to locate the start of this section for the current thread. The CLI respects this mechanism. That is, when a reference is made to a static variable with a fixed RVA (Relative Virtual Address) in the PE file and that RVA is in the thread-local section of the PE, the native code generated from the CIL will use the thread-local access sequence.

This has two important consequences:

- A static variable with a specified RVA shall reside entirely in a single section of the PE file. The RVA specifies where the data begins, and the type of the variable specifies how large the data area is.
- When a new thread is created, only the data from the PE file is used to initialize the new copy of the variable. There is no opportunity to run the type initializer. For this reason it is probably wise to restrict the use of unmanaged thread-local storage to the primitive numeric types and value types with explicit layout that have a fixed initial value and no type initializer.

15.4 Initialization of Non-Literal Static Data

This section and its subsections contain only informative text.

Many languages that support static data (i.e., variables that have a lifetime that is the entire program) provide for a means to initialize that data before the program begins running. There are three common mechanisms for doing this, and each is supported in the CLI.

15.4.1 *Data Known at Link Time*

When the correct value to be stored into the static data is known at the time the program is linked (or compiled, for those languages with no linker step), the actual value can be stored directly into the PE file, typically into the data area (see Partition II, section 15.3). References to the variable are made directly to the location where this data has been placed in memory, using the OS-supplied fixup mechanism to adjust any references to this area if the file loads at an address other than the one assumed by the linker.

In the CLI, this technique can be used directly if the static variable has one of the primitive numeric types or is a value type with explicit type layout and no embedded references to managed objects. In this case the data is laid out in the data area as usual, and the static variable is assigned a particular RVA (i.e., offset from the start of the PE file) by using a data label with the field declaration (using the **at** syntax).

ANNOTATION: The RVA (Relative Virtual Address) is the relative offset from the beginning of the file as it is loaded in memory. This is not the same as the byte offset of the file. For more information on RVAs, see Chapter 4 of this book.

This mechanism, however, does not interact well with the CLI notion of an application domain (see Partition I, section 12.5). An application domain is intended to isolate two applications running in the same OS process from one another by guaranteeing that they have no shared data. Since the PE file is shared across the entire process, any data accessed via this mechanism is visible to all application domains in the process, thus violating the application domain isolation boundary.

15.5 Data Known at Load Time

When the correct value is not known until the PE file is loaded (for example, if it contains values computed based on the load addresses of several PE files), it may be possible to supply arbitrary code to run as the PE file is loaded, but this mechanism is platform-specific and may not be available in all conforming implementations of the CLI.

ANNOTATION

Implementation-Specific (Microsoft): This mechanism, while available in Microsoft's CLR, is strongly discouraged. The code runs under the processwide loader lock, and the restrictions imposed by the underlying operating system make this a fragile mechanism. The details are provided in Partition II, section 24.3.3.3.

15.5.1 *Data Known at Runtime*

When the correct value cannot be determined until type layout is computed, the user shall supply code as part of a type initializer to initialize the static data. The guarantees about type initialization are covered in Partition II, section 9.5.3.1. As will be explained below, global statics are modelled in the CLI as though they belonged to a type, so the same guarantees apply to both global and type statics.

Because the layout of managed types need not occur until a type is first referenced, it is not possible to statically initialize managed types by simply laying the data out in the PE file. Instead, there is a type initialization process that proceeds in the following steps:

1. All static variables are zeroed.
2. The user-supplied type initialization procedure, if any, is invoked as described in Partition II, section 9.5.3.

Within a type initialization procedure there are several techniques:

- *Generate explicit code* that stores constants into the appropriate fields of the static variables. For small data structures this can be efficient, but it requires that the initializer be converted to native code, which may prove to be both a code space and an execution time problem.
- *Box value types.* When the static variable is simply a boxed version of a primitive numeric type or a value type with explicit layout, introduce an additional static variable with known RVA that holds the unboxed instance and then simply use the **box** instruction to create the boxed copy.
- *Create a managed array from a static native array of data.* This can be done by marshalling the native array to a managed array. The specific marshaller to be used depends on the native array. For example, it may be a safearray.
- *Default initialize a managed array of a value type.* The Base Class Library provides a method that zeroes the storage for every element of an array of unboxed value types (`System.Runtime.CompilerServices.InitializeArray`).

ANNOTATION

Implementation-Specific (Microsoft): *Use Base Class Library deserialization.* The Microsoft Base Class Library provides serialization and deserialization services. These services can be found in the `System.Runtime.Serialization` namespace. These services were not, however, standardized. An object can be converted to a serialized form, stored in the data section, and accessed using a static variable with known RVA of type unsigned int8[]. The corresponding deserialization mechanism can then be used in the type initializer.

End informative text

16 Defining Properties

A property is declared by the using the **.property** directive. Properties may only be declared inside of types (i.e., global properties are not supported).

`<classMember> ::=`
`.property <propHead> { <propMember>* }`

See Partition II, sections 21.31 and 21.32 for how Property information is stored in metadata.

`<propHead> ::=`
`[specialname] [rtspecialname] <callConv> <type> <id> ( <parameters> )`

The property directive specifies a calling convention (see Partition II, section 14.3), type, name, and parameter in parentheses. **specialname** marks the property as *special* to other tools, while **rtspecialname** marks the property as *special* to the CLI. The signature for the property (i.e., the <propHead> production) shall match the signature of the property's **.get** method (see below).

> **RATIONALE**
> There are currently no property names that are required to be marked with **rtspecialname**. It is provided for extensions, future standardization, and to increase consistency between the declaration of properties and methods (instance and type initializer methods shall be marked with this attribute).

While the CLI places no constraints on the methods that make up a property, the CLS (see Partition I, section 8.11.3) specifies a set of consistency constraints..

A property may contain any number of methods in its body. The following table shows these and provides short descriptions of each item:

<propMember> ::=	Description	Section in Partition II
| **.custom** <customDecl>	Custom attribute.	20
| **.get** <callConv> <type> [<typeSpec> ::] <methodName> (<parameters>)	Specifies the getter for the property.	
| **.other** <callConv> <type> [<typeSpec> ::] <methodName> (<parameters>)	Specifies a method for the property other than the getter or setter.	
| **.set** <callConv> <type> [<typeSpec> ::] <methodName> (<parameters>)	Specifies the setter for the property.	
| <externSourceDecl>	**.line** or #line	5.7

.get specifies the *getter* for this property. The <typeSpec> defaults to the current type. Only one *getter* may be specified for a property. To be CLS-compliant, the definition of *getter* shall be marked **specialname**.

.set specifies the *setter* for this property. The <typeSpec> defaults to the current type. Only one *setter* may be specified for a property. To be CLS-compliant, the definition of *setter* shall be marked **specialname**.

.other is used to specify any other methods that this property comprises.

In addition, custom attributes (see Partition II, section 20) or source line declarations may be specified.

Example (informative):

This example shows the declaration of a property called Count.

```
.class public auto autochar MyCount extends [mscorlib]System.Object {
     .method virtual hidebysig public specialname instance int32 get_Count() {
             // body of getter
     }
     .method virtual hidebysig public specialname instance void set_Count(int32
newCount) {
             // body of setter
     }
     .method virtual hidebysig public instance void reset_Count() {
             // body of refresh method
     }
     // the declaration of the property
     .property int32 Count() {
             .get instance int32 get_Count()
             .set instance void set_Count(int32)
             .other instance void reset_Count()
     }
}
```

ANNOTATION: Properties do not have any special existence in the VES. The methods associated with properties (getter, setter, and any other) carry the information that allow compilers to understand that a property is a property, and to deal with it appropriately. That is why the getter and setter methods must be marked with **specialname** to be CLS-compliant. That designation indicates that they are special to the compiler.

17 Defining Events

Events are declared inside types with the **.event** directive; there are no global events.

<classMember> ::=	Section in Partition II
.event <eventHead> { <eventMember>* }	9
| ...	

See Partition II, section 21.13.

<eventHead> ::=
[specialname] **[rtspecialname]** [<typeSpec>] <id>

In typical usage, the <typeSpec> (if present) identifies a delegate whose signature matches the arguments passed to the event's fire method.

The event head may contain the keywords **specialname** or **rtspecialname**. **specialname** marks the name of the property for other tools, while **rtspecialname** marks the name of the event as special for the runtime.

RATIONALE

There are currently no event names that are required to be marked with **rtspecialname**. It is provided for extensions, future standardization, and to increase consistency between the declaration of events and methods (instance and type initializer methods shall be marked with this attribute).

<eventMember> ::=	Description	Section in Partition II
.addon <callConv> <type> [<typeSpec> ::] <methodName> (<parameters>)	**Add** method for event.	
| **.custom** <customDecl>	Custom attribute.	20
| **.fire** <callConv> <type> [<typeSpec> ::] <methodName> (<parameters>)	Fire method for event.	
| **.other** <callConv> <type> [<typeSpec> ::] <methodName> (<parameters>)	Other method.	
| **.removeon** <callConv> <type> [<typeSpec> ::] <methodName> (<parameters>)	Remove method for event.	
| <externSourceDecl>	**.line** or **#line**	5.7

The **.addon** directive specifies the *add* method, and the <typeSpec> defaults to the same type as the event. The CLS specifies naming conventions and consistency constraints for events, and requires that the definition of the *add* method be marked with **specialname**.

The **.removeon** directive specifies the *remove* method, and the <typeSpec> defaults to the same type as the event. The CLS specifies naming conventions and consistency constraints for events, and requires that the definition of the *remove* method be marked with **specialname**.

The **.fire** directive specifies the *fire* method, and the <typeSpec> defaults to the same type as the event. The CLS specifies naming conventions and consistency constraints for events, and requires that the definition of the *fire* method be marked with **specialname**.

An event may contain any number of other methods specified with the **.other** directive. From the point of view of the CLI, these methods are only associated with each other through the event. If they have special semantics, this needs to be documented by the implementer.

Events may also have custom attributes (see Partition II, section 20) associated with them, and they may declare source line information.

Example (informative):

This shows the declaration of an event, its corresponding delegate, and typical implementations of the add, remove, and fire methods of the event. The event and the methods are declared in a class called Counter.

```
// the delegate
.class private sealed auto autochar TimeUpEventHandler extends
        [mscorlib]System.MulticastDelegate {

    .method public hidebysig specialname rtspecialname instance void
.ctor(object 'object', native int 'method') runtime managed {}

    .method public hidebysig virtual instance void Invoke() runtime managed {}

    .method public hidebysig newslot virtual instance class
        [mscorlib]System.IAsyncResult BeginInvoke(class [mscorlib]System.Asyn
        cCallback callback, object 'object') runtime managed {}

    .method public hidebysig newslot virtual instance void EndInvoke(class
        [mscorlib]System.IAsyncResult result) runtime managed {}

}

// the class that declares the event
.class public auto autochar Counter extends [mscorlib]System.Object {

// field to store the handlers, initialized to null
.field private class TimeUpEventHandler timeUpEventHandler

// the event declaration
.event TimeUpEventHandler startStopEvent {
    .addon instance void add_TimeUp(class TimeUpEventHandler 'handler')
```

```
    .removeon instance void remove_TimeUp(class TimeUpEventHandler 'handler')
    .fire instance void fire_TimeUpEvent()
}
// the add method, combines the handler with existing delegates
.method public hidebysig virtual specialname instance void add_TimeUp(class
      TimeUpEventHandler 'handler') {
    .maxstack 4
    ldarg.0
    dup
    ldfld   class TimeUpEventHandler Counter::TimeUpEventHandler
    ldarg   'handler'
    call    class[mscorlib]System.Delegate [mscorlib]System.Delegate::
      Combine(class [mscorlib]System.Delegate, class [mscorlib]System.Delegate)
    castclass TimeUpEventHandler
    stfld   class TimeUpEventHandler Counter::timeUpEventHandler
    ret
}
// the remove method, removes the handler from the multicast delegate
.method virtual public specialname void remove_TimeUp(class TimeUpEventHandler
      'handler') {
    .maxstack 4
    ldarg.0
    dup
    ldfld   class TimeUpEventHandler Counter::timeUpEventHandler
    ldarg   'handler'
    call    class[mscorlib]System.Delegate [mscorlib]System.Delegate::
      Remove(class [mscorlib]System.Delegate, class [mscorlib]System.Delegate)
    castclass TimeUpEventHandler
    stfld   class TimeUpEventHandler Counter::timeUpEventHandler
    ret
}
// the fire method
.method virtual family specialname void fire_TimeUpEvent() {
    .maxstack 3
    ldarg.0
    ldfld   class TimeUpEventHandler Counter::timeUpEventHandler
```

```
        callvirt instance void TimeUpEventHandler::Invoke()
        ret
    }
}   // end of class Counter
```

ANNOTATION: Like properties, events have no special existence in the VES. The methods associated with properties (*add*, *remove*, *fire*, and any other) carry the information that allow compilers to understand that the entity is an event, and to deal with it appropriately. That is why these methods must be marked with **specialname** to be CLS-compliant. That designation indicates that they are special to the compiler.

---

18 Exception Handling

In the CLI, a method may define a range of CIL instructions that are said to be *protected*. This is called the "try block." It can then associate one or more *handlers* with that try block. If an exception occurs during execution anywhere within the try block, an exception object is created that describes the problem. The CIL then takes over, transferring control from the point at which the exception was thrown, to the block of code that is willing to handle that exception. See Partition I.

ANNOTATION: Pertinent information on exception handling can be found in Partition I, section 12.4.2 and its subsections. Take particular notice of the following sections:

12.4.2.4 Timing of Exceptions

12.4.2.5 Overview of Exception Handling

12.4.2.7 Lexical Nesting of Protected Blocks

12.4.2.8 Control Flow Restrictions on Protected Blocks

<sehBlock> ::=
<tryBlock> <sehClause> [<sehClause>*]

The next few sections expand upon this simple description, by describing the five kinds of code blocks that take part in exception processing: **try**, **catch**, **filter**, **finally**, and **fault**. (Note that there are restrictions upon how many, and what kinds of <sehClause> a given <tryBlock> may have; see Partition I, section 12.4.2 for details.)

The remaining syntax items are described in detail below; they are collected here for reference.

`<tryBlock> ::=`	Description
`.try <label> to <label>`	Protect region from first label to prior to second.
`| .try <scopeBlock>`	<scopeBlock> is protected.

`<sehClause> ::=`	Description
`catch <typeReference> <handlerBlock>`	Catch all objects of the specified type.
`| fault <handlerBlock>`	Handle all exceptions but not normal exit.
`| filter <label> <handlerBlock>`	Enter handler only if filter succeeds.
`| finally <handlerBlock>`	Handle all exceptions and normal exit.

`<handlerBlock> ::=`	Description
`handler <label> to <label>`	Handler range is from first label to prior to second.
`| <scopeBlock>`	<scopeBlock> is the handler block.

ANNOTATION: The stack trace is created at the time the exception is thrown. This is in contrast to Java, where the stack trace is created during the constructioin of the exception object, and not modified when the exception is thrown. When implementing the Java language on top of the CLI, one must therefore take care. This difference is not always apparent, because typically the exception object is created and immediately thrown, so there is no difference in the stack trace. However, when the exception object is created in one method and thrown in another, the difference will be visible to the program that prints the stack trace for that exception.

18.1 Protected Blocks

A *try*, or *protected*, or *guarded*, block is declared with the **.try** directive.

`<tryBlock> ::=`	Description
`.try <label> to <label>`	Protect region from first label to prior to second.
`| .try <scopeBlock>`	<scopeBlock> is protected.

In the first, the protected block is delimited by two labels. The first label is the first instruction to be protected, while the second label is the instruction just beyond the last one to be protected. Both labels shall be defined prior to this point.

The second uses a scope block (see Partition II, section 14.4.4) after the **.try** directive—the instructions within that scope are the ones to be protected.

18.2 Handler Blocks

`<handlerBlock> ::=`	Description
`| handler <label> to <label>`	Handler range is from first label to prior to second.
`| <scopeBlock>`	<scopeBlock> is the handler block.

In the first syntax, the labels enclose the instructions of the handler block, the first label being the first instruction of the handler while the second is the instruction immediately after the handler. Alternatively, the handler block is just a scope block.

ANNOTATION

Implementation-Specific (Microsoft): The Microsoft ilasm requires labels used to specify any exception blocks to be defined *beforehand* in the source. It also supports the following additional syntax for use in round-tripping:

```
<handlerBlock> ::= handler <int32> to <int32>
```

18.3 Catch [Blocks]

A catch block is declared using the **catch** keyword. This specifies the type of exception object the clause is designed to handle, and the handler code itself.

<sehClause> ::=
catch <typeReference> <handlerBlock>

```
Example (informative):
.try {
    ...                              // protected instructions
    leave   exitSEH                  // normal exit
} catch [mscorlib]System.FormatException {
    ...                              // handle the exception
    pop                              // pop the exception object
    leave   exitSEH                  // leave catch handler
}
exitSEH:                             // continue here
```

18.4 Filter [Blocks]

A filter block is declared using the **filter** keyword.

<sehClause> ::= ...
| **filter** <label> <handlerBlock>
| **filter** <scope> <handlerBlock>

The filter code begins at the specified label and ends at the first instruction of the handler block. (Note that the CLI demands that the filter block shall immediately precede, within the CIL stream, its corresponding handler block.)

```
Example (informative):
.method public static void m () {
   .try {
     ...                              // protected instructions
     leave                            exitSEH        // normal exit
   }
   filter {
     ...                              // decide whether to handle
     pop                              // pop exception object
     ldc.i4.1                         // EXCEPTION_EXECUTE_HANDLER
```

```
      endfilter                      // return answer to CLI
    }
    {
      ...                            // handle the exception
      pop                            // pop the exception object
      leave           exitSEH        // leave filter handler
    }
exitSEH:
    ...
}
```

18.5 Finally [Blocks]

A finally block is declared using the **finally** keyword. This specifies the handler code, with this grammar:

<sehClause> ::= ...
| **finally** <handlerBlock>

The last possible CIL instruction that can be executed in a finally handler shall be **endfinally**.

Example (informative):

```
.try {
    ...                        // protected instructions
    leave exitTry              // shall use leave
} finally {
    ...                        // finally handler
    endfinally
}
exitTry:                       // back to normal
```

18.6 Fault Handler [Blocks]

A fault block is declared using the **fault** keyword. This specifies the handler code, with this grammar:

<sehClause> ::= ...
| **fault** <handlerBlock>

The last possible CIL instruction that can be executed in a fault handler shall be **endfault**.

```
Example (informative):
.method public static void m() {
startTry:
             ...                     // protected instructions
             leave   exitSEH         // shall use leave
endTry:

startFault:
             ...                     // fault handler instructions
             endfault
endFault:

      .try startTry to endTry fault handler startFault to endFault

exitSEH:                             // back to normal
}
```

19 Declarative Security

Many languages that target the CLI use attribute syntax to attach declarative security attributes to items in the metadata. This information is actually converted by the compiler into an XML-based representation that is stored in the metadata (see Partition II, section 21.11). By contrast, ilasm requires the conversion information to be represented in its input.

<securityDecl> ::=
.permissionset <secAction> = (<bytes>)
| **.permission** <secAction> <typeReference> (<nameValPairs>)

In **.permission**, <typeReference> specifies the permission class and <nameValPairs> specifies the settings. See Partition II, section 21.11.

In **.permissionset,** the bytes specify the serialized version of the security settings:

<secAction> ::=	Description
assert	Assert permission so that callers do not need it.
| **demand**	Demand permission of all callers.

<secAction> ::=	Description
| **deny**	Deny permission so checks will fail.
| **inheritcheck**	Demand permission of a subclass.
| **linkcheck**	Demand permission of caller.
| **permitonly**	Reduce permissions so check will fail.
| **reqopt**	Request optional additional permissions.
| **reqrefuse**	Refuse to be granted these permissions.
| **request**	Hint that permission may be required.

ANNOTATION

Implementation-Specific (Microsoft): The following security action is Microsoft-specific. A conforming implementation of the CLI may ignore this security action if present in an assembly.

<secAction> ::=	Description
| prejitgrant	**Persisted denied** set at preJIT time.

```
<nameValPairs> ::= <nameValPair> [, <nameValPair>]*
```

```
<nameValPair> ::= <SQSTRING> = <SQSTRING>
```

20 Custom Attributes

Custom attributes add user-defined annotations to the metadata. Custom attributes allow an instance of a type to be stored with any element of the metadata. This mechanism can be used to store application-specific information at compile time and access it either at run-time or when another tool reads the metadata. While any user-defined type can be used as an attribute, CLS compliance requires that attributes will be instances of types whose parent is `System.Attribute`. The CLI predefines some attribute types and uses them to control runtime behavior. Some languages predefine attribute types to represent language features not directly represented in the CTS. Users or other tools are welcome to define and use additional attribute types.

Custom attributes are declared using the directive **.custom**. Followed by this directive is the method declaration for a type constructor, optionally followed by a <bytes> in parentheses:

<customDecl> ::=
<ctor> [= (<bytes>)]

The <ctor> item represents a method declaration (see Partition II, section 14.4), specific for the case where the method's name is **.ctor**.

For example:

```
.custom instance void myAttribute::.ctor(bool, bool) = ( 01 00 00 01 00 00 )
```

Custom attributes can be attached to *any* item in metadata, except a custom attribute itself. Commonly, custom attributes are attached to assemblies, modules, classes, interfaces, value types, methods, fields, properties, and events (the custom attribute is attached to the immediately preceding declaration).

The <bytes> item is not required if the constructor takes no arguments. In these cases, all that matters is the presence of the custom attribute.

If the constructor takes parameters, their values shall be specified in the <bytes> item. The format for this "blob" is defined in Partition II, section 22.3.

Example (informative):

The following example shows a class that is marked with the System. SerializableAttribute and a method that is marked with the System.Runtime. Remoting.OneWayAttribute. The keyword serializable corresponds to the System.SerializableAttribute.

```
.class public MyClass {
      .custom void [mscorlib]System.SerializableAttribute::.ctor ()
      .method public static void main() {
               .custom void [mscorlib]System.Runtime.Remoting.
                   OneWayAttribute::.ctor ()
               ret
      }
}
```

3. Metadata Semantics

20.1 CLS Conventions: Custom Attribute Usage

CLS imposes certain conventions upon the use of Custom Attributes in order to improve cross-language operation. See Partition I, section 9.7 for details.

20.2 Attributes Used by the CLI

There are two kinds of Custom Attributes, called (genuine) Custom Attributes and Pseudo Custom Attributes. Custom Attributes and Pseudo Custom Attributes are treated differently, at the time they are defined, as follows:

- A Custom Attribute is stored directly into the metadata; the "blob" which holds its defining data is stored as is. That "blob" can be retrieved later.
- A Pseudo Custom Attribute is recognized because its name is one of a short list. Rather than store its "blob" directly in metadata, that "blob" is parsed, and the information it contains is used to set bits and/or fields within metadata tables. The "blob" is then discarded; it cannot be retrieved later.

Pseudo Custom Attributes therefore serve to capture user directives, using the same familiar syntax the compiler provides for regular Custom Attributes, but these user directives are then stored into the more space-efficient form of metadata tables. Tables are also faster to check at runtime than (genuine) Custom Attributes.

Many Custom Attributes are invented by higher layers of software. They are stored and returned by the CLI, without its knowing or caring what they "mean." But all Pseudo Custom Attributes, plus a collection of regular Custom Attributes, are of special interest to compilers and to the CLI. An example of such Custom Attributes is `System.Reflection.DefaultMemberAttribute`. This is stored in metadata as a regular Custom Attribute "blob," but reflection uses this Custom Attribute when called to invoke the default member (property) for a type.

The following subsections list all of the Pseudo Custom Attributes and *distinguished* Custom Attributes, where "distinguished" means that the CLI and/or compilers pay direct attention to them, and their behavior is affected in some way.

In order to prevent name collisions into the future, all custom attributes in the `System` namespace are reserved for standardization.

20.2.1 *Pseudo Custom Attributes*

The following table lists the CLI Pseudo Custom Attributes. They are defined in either the `System` or the `System.Reflection` namespaces.

Attribute	Description
`AssemblyAlgorithmIDAttribute`	Records the ID of the hash **algorithm** used (reserved only).
`AssemblyFlagsAttribute`	Records the flags for this assembly (reserved only).
`DllImportAttribute`	Provides information about code implemented within an unmanaged library.
`FieldOffsetAttribute`	Specifies the byte offset of fields within their enclosing class or value type.
`InAttribute`	Indicates that a method parameter is an [in] argument.
`MarshalAsAttribute`	Specifies how a data item should be marshalled between managed and unmanaged code—see Partition II, section 22.4.
`MethodImplAttribute`	Specifies details of how a method is implemented.
`OutAttribute`	Indicates that a method parameter is an [out] argument.
`StructLayoutAttribute`	Allows the caller to control how the fields of a class or value type are laid out in managed memory.

Not all of these Pseudo Custom Attributes are specified in this standard, but all of them are reserved and shall not be used for other purposes. For details on these attributes, see the documentation for the corresponding class in the *.NET Framework Standard Library Annotated Reference*.

The Pseudo Custom Attributes above affect bits and fields in metadata, as follows:

`AssemblyAlgorithmIDAttribute`: Sets the *Assembly.HashAlgId* field.

`AssemblyFlagsAttribute`: Sets the *Assembly.Flags* field.

`DllImportAttribute`: Sets the *Method.Flags.PinvokeImpl* bit for the attributed method; also, adds a new row into the *ImplMap* table (setting *MappingFlags*, *MemberForwarded*, *ImportName*, and *ImportScope* columns).

`FieldOffsetAttribute`: Sets the *FieldLayout.OffSet* value for the attributed field.

`InAttribute`: Sets the *Param.Flags.In* bit for the attributed parameter.

`MarshalAsAttribute`: Sets the *Field.Flags.HasFieldMarshal* bit for the attributed field (or the *Param.Flags.HasFieldMarshal* bit for the attributed parameter); also enters a new row into the FieldMarshal table for both *Parent* and *NativeType* columns.

`MethodImplAttribute`: Sets the *Method.ImplFlags* field of the attributed method.

`OutAttribute`: Sets the *Param.Flags.Out* bit for the attributed parameter.

`StructLayoutAttribute`: Sets the *TypeDef.Flags.LayoutMask* sub-field for the attributed type and, optionally, the *TypeDef.Flags.StringFormatMask* sub-field, the *ClassLayout.PackingSiz*, and *ClassLayout.ClassSize* fields for that type.

ANNOTATION

Implementation-Specific (Microsoft): Use of the following Pseudo Custom Attributes renders the assembly that contains them non-portable; a conforming implementation of the CLI may reject such an assembly when it is loaded, or throw an exception at runtime if any attempt is made to access the metadata items set by those Custom Attributes.

Attribute	Description
`ComImportAttribute`	Provides information about native code reached as a COM component.
`OptionalAttribute`	Marks a method parameter as optional.
`NonSerializedAttribute`	Indicates that a field should not be serialized.
`PreserveSigAttribute`	Specifies HRESULT or retval signature transformation.
`SerializableAttribute`	Indicates that a type can be serialized.

ANNOTATION

Implementation-Specific (Microsoft):

The Pseudo Custom Attributes above affect bits and fields in metadata, as follows:

- `ComImportAttribute`: Sets the *TypeDef.Flags.Import* bit for the attributed type.
- `OptionalAttribute`: Sets the *Param.Flags.Optional* bit for the attributed parameter.
- `NonSerializedAttribute`: Sets the *Field.Flags.NotSerialized* bit for the attributed field.

- `PreserveSigAttribute`: Sets the *Method.ImplFlags.PreserveSig* bit of the attributed method.
- `SerializableAttribute`: Sets the *TypeDef.Flags.Serializable* bit for the attributed type.

20.2.2 *Custom Attributes Defined by the CLS*

The CLS specifies certain Custom Attributes and requires that conformant languages support them. These attributes are located under `System`.

Attribute	Description
`AttributeUsageAttribute`	Used to specify how an attribute is intended to be used.
`ObsoleteAttribute`	Indicates that an element is not to be used.
`CLSCompliantAttribute`	Indicates whether or not an element is declared to be CLS-compliant through an instance field on the attribute object.

[20.2.3 *Custom Attributes for CIL-to-Native-Code Compiler and Debugger]*

ANNOTATION

Implementation-Specific (Microsoft): The following Custom Attributes that control the runtime behavior of a CIL-to-native-code compiler and a runtime debugger are defined in the `System.Diagnostics` namespace. Their use renders the assembly that contains them non-portable; a conforming implementation of the CLI may reject such an assembly when it is loaded, or throw an exception at runtime if any attempt is made to access those Custom Attributes.

Attribute	Description
`DebuggableAttribute`	Controls a CIL-to-native-code compiler to produce code that is easier to debug.
`DebuggerHiddenAttribute`	Specifies that a debugger should step over the attributed method or property.
`DebuggerStepThroughAttribute`	Specifies that a debugger should step through the attributed method or property (it may step into a method called by this one).

[20.2.4 *Custom Attributes for Remoting*]

ANNOTATION

Implementation-Specific (Microsoft): The following Custom Attributes are used to control the behavior of remoting. They are defined in the `System.Runtime.Remoting` namespace of the Microsoft Base Class Library and are not standardized. Their use renders the assembly that contains them non-portable; a conforming implementation of the CLI may reject such an assembly when it is loaded, or throw an exception at runtime if any attempt is made to access those custom attributes.

Attribute	Description
`ContextAttribute`	Root for all context attributes.
`OneWayAttribute`	Marks a method as "fire and forget."
`SynchronizationAttribute`	Specifies the synchronization options for a class.
`ThreadAffinityAttribute`	Refinement of Synchronized Context.

20.2.5 *Custom Attributes for Security*

The following Custom Attributes affect the security checks performed upon method invocations at runtime. They are defined in the `System.Security` namespace.

Attribute	Description
`DynamicSecurityMethodAttribute`	Indicates to the CLI that the method requires space to be allocated for a security object.
`SuppressUnmanagedCodeSecurityAttribute`	Indicates [that] the target method, implemented as unmanaged code, should skip per-call checks.

The following Custom Attributes are defined in the `System.Security.Permissions` namespace. Note that these are all base classes; the actual instances of security attributes found in assemblies will be sub-classes of these.

Attribute	Description
`CodeAccessSecurityAttribute`	Base attribute class for declarative security using custom attributes
`DnsPermissionAttribute`	Custom attribute class for declarative security with DnsPermission
`EnvironmentPermissionAttribute`	Custom attribute class for declarative security with EnvironmentPermission.
`FileIOPermissionAttribute`	Custom attribute class for declarative security with FileIOPermission
`ReflectionPermissionAttribute`	Custom attribute class for declarative security with ReflectionPermission
`SecurityAttribute`	Base attribute class for declarative security from which CodeAccess-SecurityAttribute is derived.
`SecurityPermissionAttribute`	Indicates whether the attributed method can affect security settings
`SiteIdentityPermissionAttribute`	Custom attribute class for declarative security with SiteIdentityPermission
`SocketPermissionAttribute`	Custom attribute class for declarative security with SocketPermission
`StrongNameIdentityPermissionAttribute`	Custom attribute class for declarative security with StrongNameIdentity-Permission
`WebPermissionAttribute`	Custom attribute class for declarative security with WebPermission

Note that any other security-related Custom Attributes (i.e., any Custom Attributes that derive from `System.Security.Permissions.SecurityAttribute`) included in an assembly may cause a conforming implementaion of the CLI to reject such an assembly when it is loaded, or throw an exception at runtime if any attempt is made to access those security-related Custom Attributes. (This statement in fact holds true for any Custom Attributes that cannot be resolved; security-related Custom Attributes are just one particular case.)

ANNOTATION

Implementation-Specific (Microsoft): The following security-related Custom Attributes are defined in the Microsoft Base Class Library `System.Security.Permissions` namespace, and are not standardized. Their use renders the assembly that contains them non-portable; a conforming implementation of the CLI may reject such an assembly when it is loaded, or throw an exception at runtime if any attempt is made to access those Custom Attributes.

Attribute	Description
`RegistryPermissionAttribute`	Indicates whether the attributed method can access the Registry.
`UIPermissionAttribute`	Custom attribute class for declarative security with UIPermission.
`ZoneIdentityPermissionAttribute`	Custom attribute class for declarative security with ZoneIdentityPermission.

20.2.6 *Custom Attributes for TLS*

A Custom Attribute that denotes a TLS (thread-local storage; see Partition II, section 15.3.3) field is defined in the `System` namespace.

Attribute	Description
`ThreadStaticAttribute`	Provides for type member fields that are relative for the thread.

[20.2.7 *Pseudo Custom Attributes for the Assembly Linker]*

ANNOTATION

Implementation-Specific (Microsoft): The following Pseudo Custom Attributes are used by the *al* tool to transfer information between modules and assemblies (they are temporarily attached to a TypeRef to a class called `AssemblyAttributesGoHere`), then merged by *al* and attached to the assembly. These attributes are defined in the `System.Runtime.CompilerServices` namespace. Their use renders the assembly that contains them non-portable; a conforming implementation of the CLI may reject such an assembly when it is loaded, or throw an exception at runtime if any attempt is made to access those Pseudo Custom Attributes.

Attribute	Description
`AssemblyCultureAttribute`	Specifies which culture an assembly supports.
`AssemblyVersionAttribute`	String-holding version of assembly (in the format major.minor.build.revision).

ANNOTATION

Implementation-Specific (Microsoft): The Pseudo Custom Attributes above affect bits and fields in metadata, as follows:

- `AssemblyCulture`: Sets the *Assembly.Culture* field.
- `AssemblyVersion`: Sets the *Assembly.MajorVersion, MinorVersion, BuildNumber*, and *RevisionNumber* fields.

[20.2.8 *Custom Attributes Provided for Interoperation with Unmanaged Code]*

ANNOTATION

Implementation-Specific (Microsoft): The following Custom Attributes are used to control the interoperation with COM 1.x and classical COM. These attributes are located under `System.Runtime.InteropServices`. More information can also be found in the *.NET Framework Standard Library Annotated Reference*. Their use renders the assembly that contains them non-portable; a conforming implementation of the CLI may reject such an assembly when it is loaded, or throw an exception at runtime if any attempt is made to access those Custom Attributes.

Attribute	Description
`ClassInterfaceAttribute`	Specifies how the class is exported to COM (as dispinterface, as a dual interface, or not at all).

Attribute	Description
`ComAliasNameAttribute`	Applied to a parameter or field to indicate the COM alias for the parameter or field type.
`ComConversionLossAttribute`	Indicates that information about a class or interface was lost when it was imported from a type library to an assembly.
`ComEmulateAttribute`	Used on a type to indicate that it is an emulator type for a different type.
`ComRegisterFunctionAttribute`	Used on a method to indicate that the method should be called when the assembly is registered for use from COM.
`ComSourceInterfacesAttribute`	Identifies the list of interfaces that are sources of events for the type.
`ComUnregisterFunctionAttribute`	Used on a method to indicate that the method should be called when the assembly is unregistered for use from COM.
`ComVisibleAttribute`	Can be applied to an individual type or to an entire assembly to control COM visibility.
`DispIdAttribute`	Custom attribute to specify the COM DISPID of a method or field.
`GuidAttribute`	Used to supply the GUID of a type, an interface, or an entire type library.
`HasDefaultInterfaceAttribute`	Used to specify that a class has a COM default interface.
`IDispatchImplAttribute`	Indicates which IDispatch implementation the CLI uses when exposing dual interfaces and dispinterfaces to COM.
`ImportedFromTypeLibAttribute`	Custom attribute to specify that a module is imported from a COM type library.
`InterfaceTypeAttribute`	Indicates whether a managed interface is dual, IDispatch, or IUnknown when exposed to COM.

Attribute	Description
NoComRegistrationAttribute	Used to indicate that an otherwise public, COM-creatable type should not be registered for use from COM applications.
NoIDispatchAttribute	This attribute is used to control how the class responds to queries for an IDispatch interface.
ProgIdAttribute	Custom attribute that allows the user to specify the prog ID of a class.
TypeLibFuncAttribute	Contains the FUNCFLAGS that were originally imported for this function from the COM type library.
TypeLibTypeAttribute	Contains the TYPEFLAGS that were originally imported for this type from the COM type library.
TypeLibVarAttribute	Contains the VARFLAGS that were originally imported for this variable from the COM type library.

20.2.9 *Custom Attributes, Various*

The following Custom Attributes control various aspects of the CLI:

Attribute	Description
ConditionalAttribute	Used to mark methods as callable, based on some compile-time condition. If the condition is false, the method will not be called.
DecimalConstantAttribute	Stores the value of a decimal constant in metadata.
DefaultMemberAttribute	Defines the member of a type that is the default member used by reflection's InvokeMember.
FlagsAttribute	Custom attribute indicating an enumeration should be treated as a bitfield; that is, a set of flags.

Attribute	Description
`IndexerNameAttribute`	Indicates the name by which an indexer will be known in programming languages that do not support indexers directly.
`ParamArrayAttribute`	Indicates that the method will allow a variable number of arguments in its invocation.

4. Overview of File Format

The first half of Partition II of the standard, consisting of sections 1–20 (Chapter 3 in this book), described the semantics of metadata—what it means—using the ilasm assembly language as an illustrative mechanism. Chapter 5 contains the second half of Partition II, sections 21–24, which describes the logical format of metadata and the file format.

This chapter is an overview of the second half of Partition II, describing how to find the information that is pertinent to you. It also provides some information on the PE (Portable Executable) file format for managed files and its relation to the layout of metadata.

The appendix of this book reprints the *Microsoft Portable Executable and Object File Format Specification*.

What Is in Partition IIB (Chapter 5)

The four sections (21 through 24) of Partition II that constitute Chapter 5 in this book present all the details of the file format that are needed for building purely managed, portable applications. Also included are features that permit writing managed code that is not portable, such as code that calls through to the underlying operating system.

The sections in the standard were written in the order of smallest data structure to largest data structure:

- Section 21 defines the metadata tables. Metadata is stored in a file derived from relational databases, and these tables contain most of the information that we refer to as metadata.
- Section 22 defines the values of various bitmasks and flags that are used in the metadata tables described in section 21. It also defines the formats of information referenced from these tables but not stored directly in the tables themselves (stored as

"blobs," in database terminology). It further amplifies the description of metadata tables in section 21 with descriptions of other structures used in those tables:

  - Signatures
  - Custom attributes
  - Marshalling descriptors

- Section 23 describes the metadata layout inside the PE file.
- Section 24 describes the CLI extensions to the PE file format and enough description of a subset of the PE format that a tool or compiler can use the specifications to emit valid CLI images.

This overview will discuss these structures in reverse order, starting with the PE file format, and going down to the layout of the metadata tables in memory.

Overview of the PE File Format for CLI Files

The PE file format is a typical loader format for an operating system. It happens to be the one used for the DOS and Windows operating systems, but it was derived from the DEC VAX/VMS COFF (Common Object File Format) file format. The Microsoft PE file format specification is reprinted in its entirety in the appendix of this book.

Although some operating systems use this as their native file format, from the point of view of the standard the thing that is important is that this is the portable transfer format for programs. As of this writing, implementations that run on platforms with an alternative file format work by requiring a special program to be run that knows how to read this portable file format and execute its contents. An alternative mechanism that would work equally well would be to write a translator from the portable format to the native format. At this time, we know of no implementations that have used that strategy.

PE files already had an extension mechanism built in, in the form of **directory entries**. Managed code is distinguished by having its own directory entry. The directory entries are listed in Partition II, section 24.2.3.3; and the managed code entry, CLI Header, is described in section 24.3.3. If the CLI Header entry is present and is not zero, managed code is considered to be included. The CLI header contains the location of the metadata (among other things). Another important element of a file containing managed code is that it must always reference the file **mscoree.dll**.

Partition II, section 24, specifies in detail the fields that must be filled in, and the values that must be entered. There are a number of fields whose values are specified as 0, to be ignored, etc. They may have meaning to the underlying loader, but they are not relevant to managed code. Therefore, to ensure portability, the suggested value should be written to the file.

In a PE file with unmanaged code, there will be code segments and data segments, and the code segments will consist of native machine instructions. In a PE file for CLI managed code, however, the code sections will contain CIL (Common Intermediate Language) code. Interspersed with this code, for each method, there will be a few bytes of information about the method. This information is referred to as method headers. Method headers typically contain the number of local variables and the exception handlers for the method.

The metadata section stores all of the information needed by compilers and most program analysis tools. It is contained in one contiguous area of memory to make it easy for those tools to find and use it. The information in the method headers is not relevant to such tools but is needed by the runtime. This information is never needed by the class loader, but the information in the metadata is. Typically only interpreters or JIT compilers need the information in the method headers. It makes it easier for these tools that the information they need can be found in the code stream along with what is to be compiled. The information in the method headers is described in Partition III, section 1.

When a PE file is loaded into memory, information in the PE file header describes how it should be modified from its on-disk format to an in-memory format. For each section in the PE file, an entry in the header states where it should be loaded relative to the 0th byte of the file. This is the section's RVA (Relative Virtual Address). The entire file is then loaded into memory starting at some physical address, which becomes the physical address of file address 0. However, nothing in the metadata or managed code ever references physical addresses.

There is an on-disk byte number, and enough information to tell you how it will be relocated when loaded into memory. But all memory locations are expressed with RVAs, which are relative to the start of the file as it would be if loaded into memory.

At the end of this chapter is an annotated dump of a tiny CLI PE file, associating all of the fields and values with their file offsets and RVAs. For anyone attempting to write a valid PE file, it will be very helpful.

Overview of Metadata Physical Layout in PE Files

Section 23 of Partition II describes how the metadata is laid out in PE files. If you look at a dump of a file, the sections relating to the PE file format are described in section 24, and the metadata sections are described in section 23.

Metadata can be stored in either a code or a data segment. From the point of view of the operating system, it is simply a part of that segment. The data is mapped in or not mapped in, depending on whether the segment is to be loaded into memory. At execution time, the metadata is designed to be read-only, and never contains executable code. Presently, Microsoft compilers store the metadata in the code segment, where it is executable but read-only, rather than in its own isolated segment. The standard does not require this, however, and implementations should be prepared to find the metadata anywhere.

The on-disk representation of metadata is stored in streams representing the metadata tables and heaps. It reflects the logical layout described in sections 21 and 22 of Partition II.

The standard deliberately describes only those parts of the format that are intended to be portable—i.e., code that has been completely written and is ready for execution. The standard describes the format needed to transfer such a program. Microsoft compilers typically integrate into a build environment that produces intermediate versions that are not ready for direct execution. These contain additional metadata streams and do not always contain the streams that are described in the standard. In particular, there is a so-called "hard-optimized" metadata format that some compilers use when they produce debugging output or output that is intended to go through a linker. That part of the file format is evolving rapidly, is not portable, and is not intended to be standardized.

As the standard says, metadata is stored in two kinds of structures—tables (arrays of records) and heaps. The tables, the physical representation of the logical metadata tables, are stored as streams in a stream designated "#~". These tables and their schemata are described in detail in section 21 of Partition II.

There are four heaps in any module: String, Blob, Userstring, and Guid.

The **String** heap stores identifiers for the tables. For example, the names of types and their members are stored in the String heap.

The **Blob** heap stores the blobs, chunks of binary data of a known size associated with metadata. Blobs are accessed using the offset of the start of the blob into the Blob heap. The only way to understand the format of a blob is to know where that offset came from. For example, in the metadata table for member definitions, one of the columns is the signature of the member. That will be an offset into the Blob heap; the format for that blob will be the MemberDefSignature.

The **Userstring** heap stores strings specified by a programmer, such as double-quoted strings in source code.

The **Guid** heap is an array of GUIDs, each 16 bytes wide. Its first element is numbered 1, its second 2, and so on.

The first three are byte arrays (so valid indexes into these heaps might be 0, 23, 25, 39, etc.). At present, only a single GUID is used in the CLI. It had been thought that the GUIDs would be used more, but that has not been the case.

Metadata Logical Layout (Sections 21 and 22)

As stated earlier in this chapter, sections 21 and 22 of Partition II describe the logical layout, in detail, of the metadata. Section 22 describes the other structures required in the tables, and section 21 describes, as informative material, the rules for ensuring that metadata emitted into any PE file is valid. These rules are listed as informative rather than normative (part of the standard) because the standardizing body felt that the rules could be deduced from the table schemata, and standards avoid duplicating material. However, deducing those rules would be time-consuming, and their inclusion here greatly simplifies development of a validation mechanism.

The metadata validation rules in the standard are informative rather than normative because they can, in principle, be deduced from other information in the standard. However, the authors of the standard realized that this is both difficult and susceptible to error, so they provide, for your information, their understanding of what those rules are.

Verification ensures type safety according to a strict set of rules, as has been discussed previously. Validation, in contrast, ensures that the bits in a module constitute legal CLI code. If Common Intermediate Language code is not valid, the standard makes no statement on how it will execute—it essentially contains nonsense, and running it will produce unpredictable results. For more information, see Partition II, section 21.1.

The layout of the tables is very complex, so Chris King, of Microsoft, spent the time and energy to create a diagram that provides a map to the layout, which is shown in Figure 4-1.

Annotated Dump of a Tiny PE File

The file **nano.exe** is an attempt to generate the smallest possible CLI executable using Microsoft's tools. This was done by Arch Robison, of Intel Corporation, and a member of the ECMA technical committee working on this standard. Following is the CIL assembly source:

```
.assembly donothing {}
.method static public void main() cil managed
{ .entrypoint
  .maxstack 0
  ret
}
```

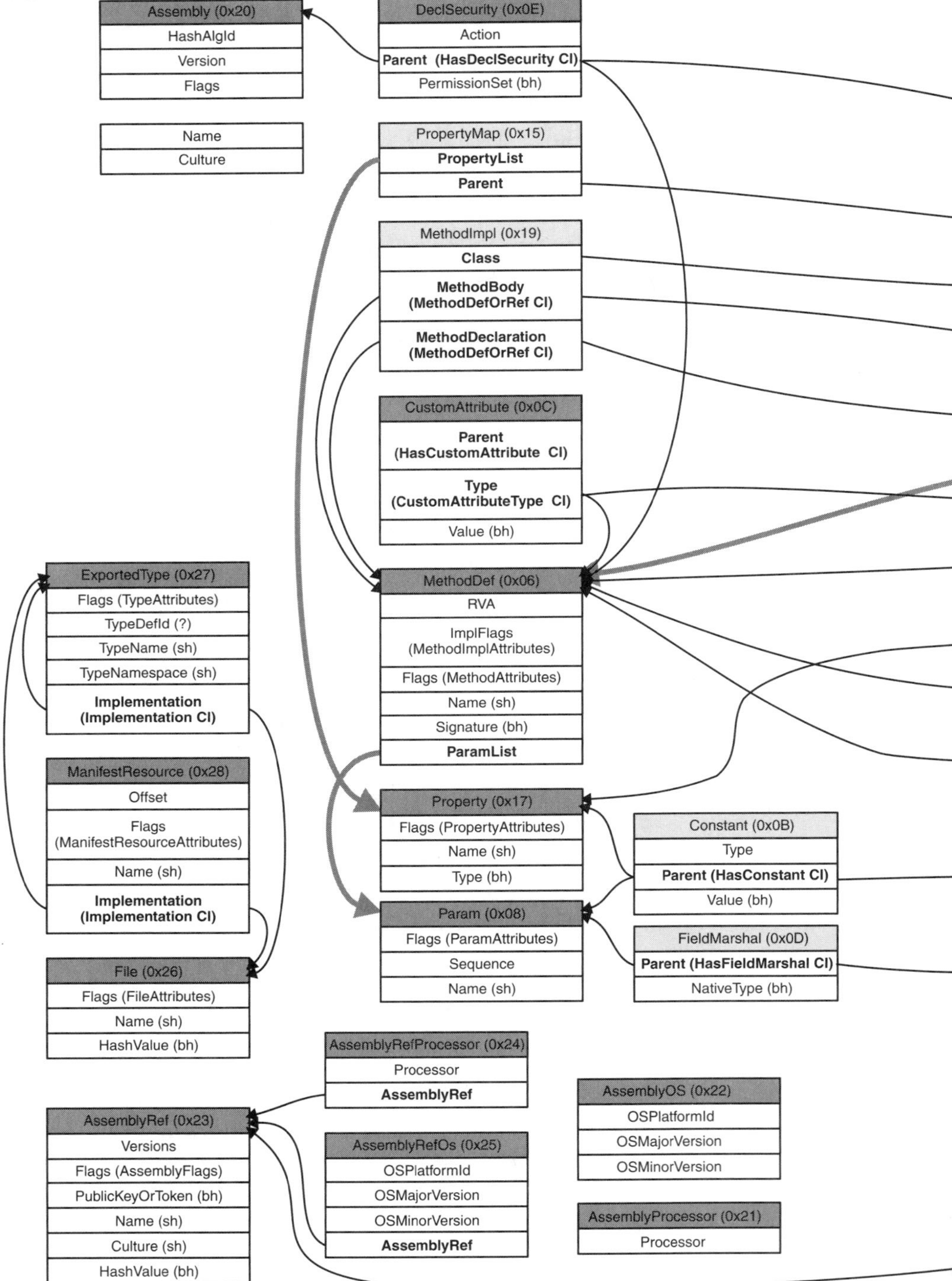

Figure 4.1 Metadata Tables

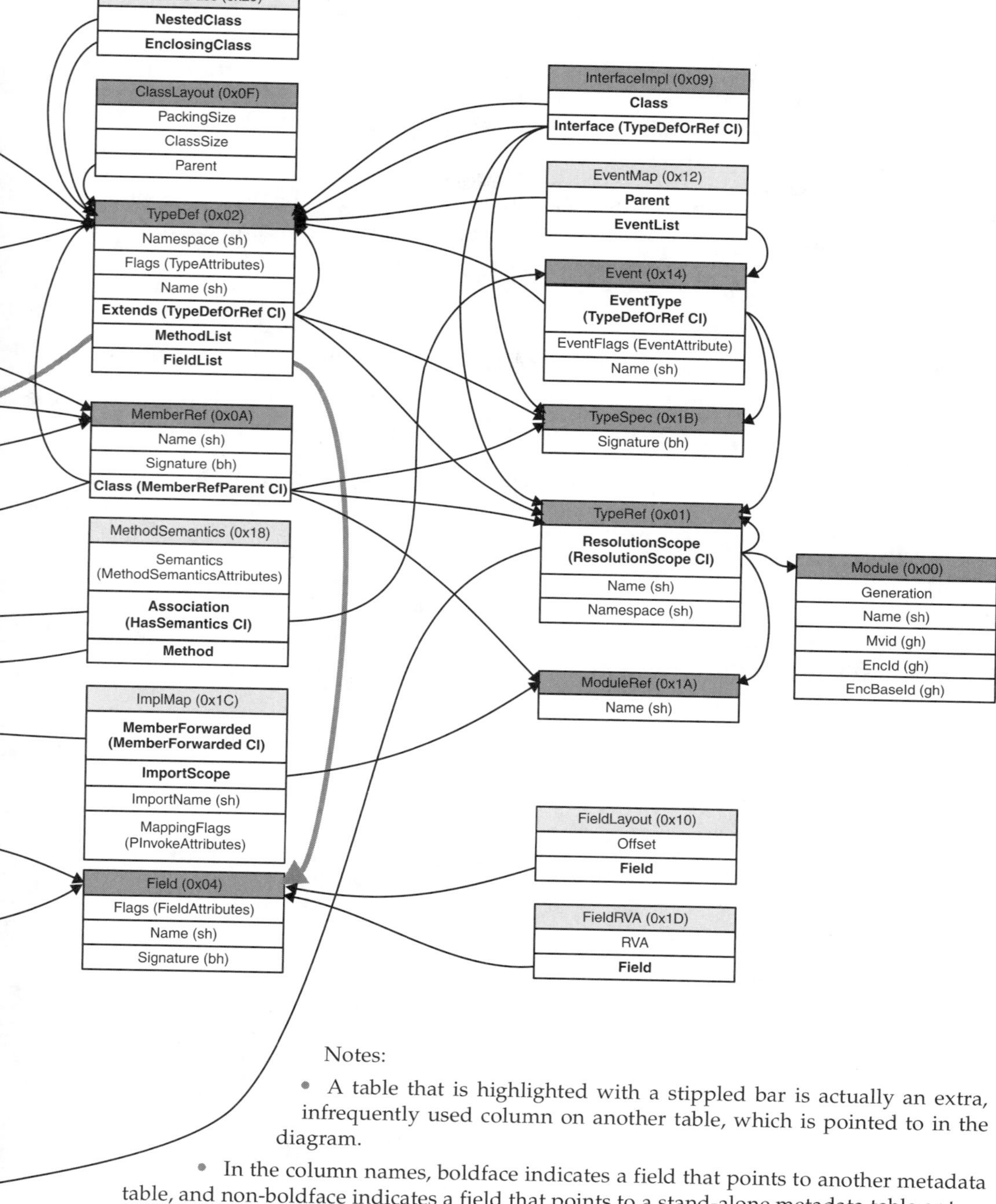

Notes:

- A table that is highlighted with a stippled bar is actually an extra, infrequently used column on another table, which is pointed to in the diagram.
- In the column names, boldface indicates a field that points to another metadata table, and non-boldface indicates a field that points to a stand-alone metadata table or to a Blob, Guid, or String heap as indicated.
- Bold arrows point to a run of rows in the indicated table; non-bold arrows, to a single row.
- In the *Assembly* and *AssemblyRef* tables, the entry "Version" actually represents the four version-related columns *MajorVersion*, *MinorVersion*, *BuildNumber*, and *RevisionNumber*.
- Abbreviations: CI = coded index; bh = Blob heap; gh = Guid heap; sh = String heap.

The resulting nano.exe file was 2,048 bytes long when assembled with the .NET 1.0 ilasm. That's not quite the smallest size allowed by the ECMA specification. Indeed, the .NET 1.1 beta version generates 1,536 bytes.

The descriptions that follow are in order of ascending offset within the file. The intent is to explain the reason for every byte in the file. This exercise uncovered multiple errors in the first edition of the ECMA specification, which were then corrected.

MS-DOS Header

The MS-DOS header matches that in the ECMA specification, with the **lfanew** field set to "0x80 00 00 00".

PE File Header

The PE signature is at offset 0x80, with the ECMA-documented value of "PE\0\0".

The PE file header is at offset 0x84, with the values shown inTable 4-1.

Table 4-1 PR File Header

File Offset	RVA	Field	Contents
0x84	0x84	Machine	0x14C
0x86	0x86	Number of Sections	2
0x88	0x88	Time/Date Stamp	0x3C18B9D8
0x8C	0x8C	Pointer to Symbol Table	0
0x90	0x90	Number of Symbols	0
0x94	0x94	Optional Header Size	0xE0
0x96	0x96	Characteristics	0x10E

The PE header standard fields have the values shown inTable 4-2.

Table 4-2 Standard Fields in the PE Header

File Offset	RVA	Field	Contents
0x98	0x98	Magic	0x10B
0x9A	0x9A	LMajor	6
0x9B	0x9B	LMinor	0
0x9C	0x9C	Code Size	0x400
0xA0	0xA0	Initialized Data Size	0x200
0xA4	0xA4	Uninitialized Data Size	0
0xA8	0xA8	Entry Point RVA	0x21FE
0xAC	0xAC	Base Of Code	0x2000
0xB0	0xB0	Base Of Data	0x4000

The PE header Windows NT–specific fields have the values shown in Table 4-3.

Table 4-3 Windows NT-Specific Fields in the PE Header

File Offset	RVA	Field	Contents
0xB4	0xB4	Image Base	0x400000
0xB8	0xB8	Section Alignment	0x2000
0xBC	0xBC	File Alignment	0x200
0xC0	0xC0	OS Major	4
0xC2	0xC2	OS Minor	0
0xC4	0xC4	User Major	0
0xC6	0xC6	User Minor	0
0xC8	0xC8	SubSys Major	4

Table 4-3 Windows NT-Specific Fields in the PE Header *(continued)*

File Offset	RVA	Field	Contents
0xCA	0xCA	SubSys Minor	0
0xCC	0xCC	Reserved	0
0xD0	0xD0	Image Size	0x6000
0xD4	0xD4	Header Size	0x200
0xD8	0xD8	File Checksum	0
0xDC	0xDC	SubSystem	0x3 (...CE_GUI)
0xDE	0xDE	DLL Flags	0
0xE0	0xE0	Stack Reserve Size	0x100000
0xE4	0xE4	Stack Commit Size	0x1000
0xE8	0xE8	Heap Reserve Size	0x100000
0xEC	0xEC	Heap Commit Size	0x1000
0xF0	0xF0	Loader Flags	0
0xF4	0xF4	Number of Data Directories	0x10

The PE header data directories are shown in Table 4-4.

Table 4-4 PE Header Data Directories

File Offset	RVA	Field	Contents
0xF8	0xF8	Export Table	0
0x100	0x100	Import Table	RVA=0x21A8 Size=0x53
0x108	0x108	Resource Table	0
0x110	0x110	Exception Table	0
0x118	0x118	Certificate Table	0

Table 4-4 PE Header Data Directories *(continued)*

File Offset	RVA	Field	Contents
0x120	0x120	Base Relocation Table	RVA=0x4000 Size=0xC
0x128	0x128	Debug	0
0x130	0x130	Copyright	0
0x138	0x138	Global Ptr	0
0x140	0x140	TLS Table	0
0x148	0x148	Load Config Table	0
0x150	0x150	Bound Import	0
0x158	0x158	IAT	RVA=0x2000 Size=8
0x160	0x160	Delay Import Descriptor	0
0x168	0x168	CLI Header	RVA=0x2008 Size=0x48
0x170	0x170	Reserved	0

PE Section Headers

The section table contains two sections. The first part is shown in Table 4-5; the second, in Table 4-6.

Table 4-5 PE Section Headers: Part 1

File Offset	RVA	Field	Contents
0x178	0x178	Name	".text"
0x180	0x180	VirtualSize	0x204
0x184	0x184	VirtualAddress	0x2000
0x188	0x188	SizeOfRawData	0x400
0x18A	0x18A	PointerToRawData	0x200
0x18E	0x18E	PointerToRelocations	0

Table 4-5 PE Section Headers: Part 1 *(continued)*

File Offset	RVA	Field	Contents
0x192	0x192	PointerToLinenumbers	0
0x196	0x196	NumberOfRelocations	0
0x198	0x198	NumerOfLinenumbers	0
0x19A	0x19A	Characteristics	0x60020 (...CODE, ...EXECUTE, ...READ)

Table 4-6 PE Section Headers: Part 2

File Offset	RVA	Field	Contents
0x1A0	0x1A0	Name	".reloc"
0x1A8	0x1A8	VirtualSize	0xC
0x1AC	0x1AC	VirtualAddress	0x4000
0x1B0	0x1B0	SizeOfRawData	0x200
0x1B4	0x1B4	PointerToRawData	0x600
0x1B8	0x1B8	PointerToRelocations	0
0x1BC	0x1BC	PointerToLinenumbers	0
0x1C0	0x1C0	NumberOfRelocations	0
0x1C2	0x1C2	NumerOfLinenumbers	0
0x1C4	0x1C4	Characteristics	0x42000040 (...INITIALIZED_DATA, ?, ...READ)

The section header tables are followed by zero-fill all the way up to and including offset 0x1FF.

Import Address Table

From file offset 0x200 to 0x400 is the **.text** section. It starts with the Import Address Table (Table 4-7) at 0x200. Note that the beginning RVA for this section is 0x2000, as specified by the VirtualAddress field of the .text section (at file offset 0x184) in the the section table (see Table 4-5).

Table 4-7 Import Address Table

File Offset	RVA	Field	Contents
0x200	0x2000	Hint/Name Table RVA	0x21E0
0x204	0x2004	(Zero-fill for two bytes)	0
0x206	0x2006	2 zeros for sake of alignment	0

CLI Header

The CLI header (Table 4-8) immediately follows at 0x208 (which agrees with the corresponding entry in the data directory):

Table 4-8 CLI Header

File Offset	RVA	Field	Contents
0x208	0x2008	Cb	0x48
0x20C	0x200C	MajorRuntimeVersion	2
0x20E	0x200E	MinorRuntimeVersion	0
0x210	0x2010	MetaData	0x2060
0x214	0x2014	Size of the Metadata	0x148 =(RVA of Import Table) – (RVA of MetaData)
0x218	0x2018	Flags	1
0x218	0x201C	EntryPointToken	0x06000001 (Method #1 in TypeDef table)
0x220	0x2020	Resources	0
0x228	0x2028	StrongNameSignature	0
0x230	0x2030	CodeManagerTable	0
0x238	0x2038	VTableFixups	0
0x240	0x2040	ExportAddressTableJumps	0
0x248	0x2048	ManagedNativeHeader	0

Method Header and CIL

Immediately following the CLI header is a fat method header (Table 4-9) and CIL instructions:

Table 4-9 Method Header

File Offset	RVA	Field	Contents
0x250	0x2050	Flags (lower 12 bits)	0x013 ...Fat, ...InitLocals
+12 bits		Size (upper 4 bits)	0x3
0x252	0x2052	MaxStack	0
0x254	0x2054	CodeSize	0x1
0x258	0x2058	LocalVarSigTok	0
0x25C	0x205C	CIL "ret" instruction	0x2A
0x25D	0x205D	Zero fill for sake of alignment	0

Metadata Root

Next comes the metadata root (Table 4-10).

Table 4-10 Metadata Root

File Offset	RVA	Field	Contents
0x260	0x2060	Signature	0x424A5342
0x264	0x2064	MajorVersion	1
0x266	0x2066	MinorVersion	1
0x268	0x2068	Reserved	0
0x26C	0x206C	Length (of version string)	0xC
0x270	0x2070	Version	"1.0.2914"
0x27C	0x207C	Flags	0
0x27D	0x207D	Streams	4

Metadata Stream Headers

The four stream headers (see Table 4-11) immediately follow.

Table 4-11 Metadata Stream Headers

File Offset	RVA	Field	Contents
0x280	0x2080	Offset	0x60
0x284	0x2084	Size	0x68
0x286	0x2086	Name	"#~\0\0"

File Offset	RVA	Field	Contents
0x28C	0x208C	Offset	0xC8
0x290	0x2090	Size	0x68
0x294	0x2094	Name	"#Strings\0\0\0\0"

File Offset	RVA	Field	Contents
0x2A0	0x20A0	Offset	0x130
0x2A4	0x20A4	Size	0x10
0x2A8	0x20A8	Name	"#GUID\0\0\0"

File Offset	RVA	Field	Contents
0x2B0	0x20B0	Offset	0x140
0x2B4	0x20B4	Size	0x8
0x2B8	0x20B8	Name	"#Blob"

The #~ Stream

The data for the #~ stream (Table 4-12) immediately follows.

Table 4-12 The #~ Stream

File Offset	RVA	Field	Contents
0x2C0	20C0	Reserved	0
0x2C4	20C4	MajorVersion	1
0x2C5	20C5	MinorVersion	0
0x2C6	20C6	HeapSizes	0 (all heap indices are 16 bits wide)
0x2C7	20C7	Reserved	1
0x2C8	20C8	Valid	0x100000045 (Assembly, Method, TypeDef, Module)
0x2D0	20D0	Sorted	0x2003301FA00
0x2D8	20D8	Rows [Module]	1
0x2DC	20DC	Rows [TypeDef]	1
0x2E0	20E0	Rows [Method]	1
0x2E4	20E4	Rows [Assembly]	1

The Module table (Table 4-13) immediately follows.

Table 4-13 Module Table

File Offset	RVA	Field	Contents
0x2E8	20E8	Generation	0
0x2EA	20EA	Name	0x4D
0x2EC	20EC	Mvid	1
0x2EE	20EE	EncId	0
0x2F0	20F0	EncBaseId	0

The TypeDef table (Table 4-14) immediately follows.

Table 4-14 TypeDef Table

File Offset	RVA	Field	Contents
0x2F2	0x20F2	Flags	0
0x2F4	0x20F4	Name	0x44
0x2F6	0x20F6	Namespace	0
0x2F8	0x20F8	Extends	0
0x2FA	0x20FA	FieldList	1
0x2FC	0x20FC	MethodList	1

The Method table (Table 4-15) immediately follows.

Table 4-15 Method Table

File Offset	RVA	Field	Contents
0x300	0x2100	RVA	0x2050
0x304	0x2104	ImpFlags	0x44
0x306	0x2106	Flags	0x0016
0x308	0x2108	Name	0x60
0x30A	0x210A	Signature	1
+12	0210C	ParamList	1

The Assembly table (Table 4-16) immediately follows.

Table 4-16 Assembly Table

File Offset	RVA	Field	Contents
0x30E	0x210E	HashAlgId	0
0x312	0x2112	MajorVersion	0
0x314	0x2114	MinorVersion	0
0x316	0x2116	BuildNumber	0
0x318	0x2118	RevisionNumber	0
0x31A	0x211A	Flags	0
0x31E	0x211E	PublicKey	0
0x320	0x2120	Name	0x56 (index of string "donothing")
0x322	0x2122	Culture	0

String Heap

The String heap (Table 4-17) follows.

Table 4-17 String Heap

File Offset	RVA	String
0x328	0x2128	"\0"
0x329	0x2129	"Version of runtime against which the binary is built : 1.0.2914.16\0"
0x36C	0x216C	"<Module>"
0x375	0x2175	"nano.exe"
0x37E	0x217E	"donothing"
0x388	0x2188	"main"
0x38D	0x218D	0 fill for 3 bytes

Guid Heap

Next comes the Guid heap (Table 4-18).

Table 4-18 Guid Heap

File Offset	RVA	GUID
0x390	0x2190	0xE22D90FB 0x446C1C25 0x5D9D0B95 0x4D6C243E

Blob Heap

Immediately afterward is the Blob heap (Table 4-19).

Table 4-19 Blob Heap

File Offset	RVA	Blob
0x3A0	0x21A0	{}
0x3A1	0x21A1	{0,0,1}
0x3A5	0x21A5	0 fill for 3 bytes

At this point we are at the end of the metadata.

Import Table

We have reached the Import Table (Partition II, section 24.3.1) pointed to by the data directory. The Import Table's contents are as shown inTable 4-20.

Table 4-20 Import Table

File Offset	RVA	Field	Contents
0x3A8	0x21A8	ImportLookupTable	0x21D0
0x3A8	0x21AC	DateTimeStamp	0
0x3B0	0x21B0	ForwarderChain	0
0x3B4	0x21B4	Name	0x21EE
0x3B8	0x21B8	ImportAddressTable	0x2000
0x3BC	0x21BC	Filled with twenty zeros	

Immedately following is the Import Lookup Table (Table 4-21).

Table 4-21 Import Lookup Table

File Offset	RVA	Field	Contents
0x3D0	0x21D0	Hint/Name Table RVA	0x21E0
0x3D4	0x21D4	Filled with two zeros	0
0x3DA	0x21DA	Undocumented	Ten zeros not documented in II.24.3.1

Following the Import Lookup Table is the Hint/Name table (Table 4-22) and some miscellanea.

Table 4-22 Hint/Name Table

File Offset	RVA	Field	Contents
0x3E0	0x21E0	Hint	0x21E0
0x3E2	0x21E2	Name	"_CorExeMain\0"
0x3EE	0x21EE		"mscoree.dll\0"
0x3FA	0x21FA	*4 undocumented zero bytes*	
0x3FE	0x21FE	Entry point per II.24.2.3.1	0xFF 0x25
0x400	0x2200	RVA that must follow	0x402000

Relocation Section

The rest of the file is zeros until we reach offset 0x600, which is the raw data for the relocation section (**.reloc**) (see Table 4-23).

Table 4-23 Raw Data for Relocation

File Offset	RVA	Field	Contents
0x600	0x4000	RVA for page	0x2000
0x604	0x4004	Size of this structure	0xC
0x608	0x4008	Relocation	0x3200 IMAGE_REL_BASED_HIGHLOW at 0x200
0x60A	0x400A	Placeholder	0

This is a request for the loader to add a fix-up delta to the RVA following the "0xFF 0x25" stub.

The rest of the file is zeros, up to the last offset of 0x7FF.

COMMON LANGUAGE INFRASTRUCTURE (CLI)

5. Partition IIB: Metadata File Format

21 Metadata Logical Format: Tables

This section defines the structures that describe metadata, and how they are cross-indexed. This corresponds to how metadata is laid out, after being read into memory from a PE file. (For a description of metadata layout inside the PE file itself, see Partition II, section 23.)

Metadata is stored in two kinds of structures—tables (arrays of records) and heaps. There are four heaps in any module: String, Blob, Userstring, and Guid. The first three are byte arrays (so valid indices into these heaps might be 0, 23, 25, 39, etc.). The Guid heap is an array of GUIDs, each 16 bytes wide. Its first element is numbered 1, its second 2, and so on.

Each entry in each column of each table is either a constant or an index.

Constants are either literal values (e.g., ALG_SID_SHA1 = 4, stored in the *HashAlgId* column of the *Assembly* table), or, more commonly, bitmasks. Most bitmasks (they are almost all called "*Flags*") are 2 bytes wide (e.g., the *Flags* column in the *Field* table), but there are a few that are 4 bytes (e.g., the *Flags* column in the *TypeDef* table).

Each index is either 2 bytes wide or 4 bytes wide. The index points into another (or the same) table, or into one of the four heaps. The size of each index column in a table is only made 4 bytes if it needs to be, for that particular module. So, if a particular column indexes a table, or tables, whose highest row number fits in a 2-byte value, the indexer column need only be 2 bytes wide. Conversely, for huge tables, containing 64K rows or more, an indexer of that table will be 4 bytes wide.

Note that indices begin at 1, meaning the first row in any given metadata table. An index value of zero denotes that it does not index a row at all (it behaves like a null reference).

The columns that index a metadata table are of two sorts:

- Simple – that column indexes one, and only one, table. For example, the *FieldList* column in the *TypeDef* table always indexes the *Field* table. So all values in that column are simple integers, giving the row number in the target table.
- Coded – that column indexes any of several tables. For example, the *Extends* column in the *TypeDef* table can index into the *TypeDef* table or into the *TypeRef* table. A few bits of that index value are reserved to define which table it targets. For the most part, this specification talks of index values after being decoded into row numbers within the target table. However, the specification includes a description of these coded indices in the section that describes the physical layout of metadata (Partition II, section 23).

Metadata preserves name strings, as created by a compiler or code generator, unchanged. Essentially it treats each string as an opaque "blob." In particular, it preserves case. The CLI imposes no limit on the size of names stored in metadata and subsequently processed by the CLI.

ANNOTATION

Implementation-Specific (Microsoft): For first release, strings are limited in length. Depending on its purpose, a string can be no larger than `MAX_CLASS_NAME` (defined as 1024) or `MAX_PATH_NAME` (defined as 260). These values refer to the maximum number of bytes that the string, after being converted into UTF8 format, may occupy; that includes a terminating null character. It is intended that this limitation be removed in a future release. Within this document, the above restrictions are abbreviated to the phrase "is limited to `MAX_CLASS_NAME`" or "is limited to `MAX_PATH_NAME`".

Matching *AssemblyRefs* and *ModuleRefs* to their corresponding Assembly and Module shall be performed case-blind. However, all other name matches (type, field, method, property, event) are exact—so that this level of resolution is the same across all platforms, whether their OS is case-sensitive or not.

Tables are given both a name (e.g., "Assembly") and a number (e.g., 0x20). The number for each table is listed immediately with its title in the following sections.

A few of the tables represent extensions to regular CLI files. Specifically, ENCLog and ENCMap, which occur in temporary images, generated during "Edit and Continue" or "incremental compilation" scenarios, while debugging. Both table types are reserved for future use.

References to the methods or fields of a Type are stored together in a metadata table called the *MemberRef* table. However, sometimes, for clearer explanation, this specification distinguishes between these two kinds of references, calling them "MethodRef" and "FieldRef."

Certain tables are required to be sorted by a primary key, as follows:

Table	Primary Key Column
Constant	Parent
FieldMarshal	Parent
MethodSemantics	Association
ClassLayout	Parent
FieldLayout	Field
ImplMap	MemberForwarded
FieldRVA	Field
NestedClass	NestedClass
MethodImpl	Class
CustomAttribute	Parent
DeclSecurity	Parent

Furthermore, the *InterfaceImpl* table is subsorted using the *Interface* column as a secondary key.

Finally, the *TypeDef* table has a special ordering constraint: the definition of an enclosing class must precede the definition of all classes it encloses.

21.1 Metadata Validation Rules

This contains informative text only.

The sections that follow describe the schema for each kind of metadata table and explain the detailed rules that guarantee [that] metadata emitted into any PE file is valid. Checking that metadata is valid ensures that later processing—checking the CIL instruction stream for type safety, building method tables, CIL-to-native-code compilation, data marshalling, etc.— will not cause the CLI to crash or behave in an insecure fashion.

In addition, some of the rules are used to check compliance with the CLS requirements (see Partition I, section 11) even though these are not related to valid metadata. These are marked with a trailing **[CLS]** tag.

The rules for valid metadata refer to an individual module. A module is any collection of metadata that *could* typically be saved to a disk file. This includes the output of compilers and linkers, or the output of script compilers (where often the metadata is held only in memory, but never actually saved to a file on disk).

The rules address intra-module validation only. So, validator software, for example, that checks conformance with this spec, need not resolve references or walk type hierarchies defined in other modules. However, it should be clear that even if two modules, A and B, analyzed separately, contain only valid metadata, they may still be in error when viewed together (e.g., a call from module A, to a method defined in module B, might specify a call-site signature that does not match the signatures defined for that method in B).

All checks are categorized as ERROR, WARNING, or CLS.

- An ERROR reports something that might cause a CLI to crash or hang, might run but produce wrong answers, or might be entirely benign. There may exist conforming implementations of the CLI that will not accept metadata that violates an ERROR rule, and therefore such metadata is invalid and is not portable.
- A WARNING reports something, not actually wrong, but possibly a slip on the part of the compiler. Normally, it indicates a case where a compiler could have encoded the same information in a more compact fashion or where the metadata represents a construct that can have no actual use at runtime. All conforming implementations will support metadata that violates only WARNING rules; hence such metadata is both valid and portable.
- A CLS reports lack of compliance with the Common Language Specification (see Partition I [section 7]). Such metadata is both valid and portable, but there may exist programming languages that cannot process it, even though all conforming implementations of the CLI support the constructs.

Validation rules fall into a few broad categories, as follows:

- **Number of Rows:** A few tables are allowed only one row (e.g., the *Module* table). Most have no such restriction.
- **Unique Rows:** No table may contain duplicate rows, where "duplicate" is defined in terms of its *key* column, or combination of columns.
- **Valid Indices:** Columns which are indices shall point somewhere sensible, as follows:

  - Every index into the String, Blob, or Userstring heaps shall point *into* that heap, neither before its start (offset 0), nor after its end.
  - Every index into the Guid heap shall lie between 1 and the maximum element number in this module, inclusive.
  - Every index (row number) into another metadata table shall lie between 0 and that table's row count + 1 (for some tables, the index may point just past the end of any target table, meaning it indexes nothing).
- **Valid Bitmasks:** Columns which are bitmasks shall only have valid permutations of bits set.
- **Valid RVAs:** There are restrictions upon fields and methods that are assigned RVAs (Relative Virtual Addresses; these are byte offsets, expressed from the address at which the corresponding PE file is loaded into memory).

Note that some of the rules listed below say "nothing"—for example, some rules state that a particular table is allowed zero or more rows—so there is no way that the check can fail. This is done simply for completeness, to record that such details have indeed been addressed, rather than overlooked.

End informative text

The CLI imposes no limit on the size of names stored in metadata and subsequently processed by a CLI implementation.

21.2 Assembly: 0x20

The *Assembly* table has the following columns:

- *HashAlgId* (a 4-byte constant of type *AssemblyHashAlgorithm*; see Partition II, section 22.1.1)
- *MajorVersion, MinorVersion, BuildNumber, RevisionNumber* (2-byte constants)
- *Flags* (a 4-byte bitmask of type *AssemblyFlags*; see Partition II, section 22.1.2)
- *PublicKey* (index into Blob heap)
- *Name* (index into String heap)
- *Culture* (index into String heap)

The *Assembly* table is defined using the **.assembly** directive (see Partition II, section 6.2); its columns are obtained from the respective **.hash algorithm**, **.ver**, **.publickey**, and **.culture** [directives] (see Partition II, section 6.2.1). For an example, see Partition II, section 6.2.

This contains informative text only.

1. The *Assembly* table may contain zero or one row. [ERROR]
2. *HashAlgId* should be one of the specified values. [ERROR]

ANNOTATION

Implementation-Specific (Microsoft): The Microsoft implementation treats this as a WARNING rather than an error, using numbers based on the Crypto APIs. This means that the Microsoft implementation can handle additional algorithms based on the constants of type `ALG_CLASS_HASH` in WinCrypt.h, as well as those dynamically discovered at runtime.

3. *Flags* may have only those values set that are specified. [ERROR]
4. *PublicKey* may be null or non-null.
5. *Name* shall index a non-null string in the String heap. [ERROR]
6. The string indexed by *Name* can be of unlimited length.
7. *Culture* may be null or non-null.
8. If *Culture* is non-null, it shall index a single string from the list specified (see Partition II, section 22.1.3). [ERROR]

NOTE

Name is a simple name (e.g., "Foo"—no drive letter, no path, no file extension); on POSIX-compliant systems, *Name* contains no colon, no forward-slash, no backslash, no period.

End informative text

21.3 AssemblyOS: 0x22

The *AssemblyOS* table has the following columns:

- *OSPlatformID* (a 4-byte constant)

- *OSMajorVersion* (a 4-byte constant)
- *OSMinorVersion* (a 4-byte constant)

This record should not be emitted into any PE file. If present in a PE file, it should be treated as if all its fields were zero. It should be ignored by the CLI.

21.4 AssemblyProcessor: 0x21

The *AssemblyProcessor* table has the following column:

- *Processor* (a 4-byte constant)

This record should not be emitted into any PE file. If present in a PE file, it should be treated as if its field were zero. It should be ignored by the CLI.

21.5 AssemblyRef: 0x23

The *AssemblyRef* table has the following columns:

- *MajorVersion, MinorVersion, BuildNumber, RevisionNumber* (2-byte constants)
- *Flags* (a 4-byte bitmask of type *AssemblyFlags*; see Partition II, section 22.1.2)
- *PublicKeyOrToken* (index into Blob heap—the public key or token that identifies the author of this assembly)
- *Name* (index into String heap)
- *Culture* (index into String heap)
- *HashValue* (index into Blob heap)

The table is defined by the **.assembly extern** directive (see Partition II, section 6.3). Its columns are filled using directives similar to those of the *Assembly* table, except for the *PublicKeyOrToken* column, which is defined using the **.publickeytoken** directive. For an example, see Partition II, section 6.3.

This contains informative text only.

---

1. *MajorVersion, MinorVersion, BuildNumber, RevisionNumber* can each have any value.
2. *Flags* may have only one possible bit set—the **PublicKey** bit (see Partition II, section 22.1.2). All other bits shall be zero. [ERROR]
3. *PublicKeyOrToken* may be null or non-null (note that the **Flags.PublicKey** bit specifies whether the "blob" is a full public key or the short hashed token).
4. If non-null, then *PublicKeyOrToken* shall index a valid offset in the Blob heap. [ERROR]

5. *Name* shall index a non-null string, in the String heap (there is no limit to its length). [ERROR]
6. *Culture* may be null or non-null. If non-null, it shall index a single string from the list specified (see Partition II, section 22.1.3). [ERROR]
7. *HashValue* may be null or non-null.
8. If non-null, then *HashValue* shall index a non-empty "blob" in the Blob heap. [ERROR]
9. The *AssemblyRef* table shall contain no duplicates, where duplicate rows have the same *MajorVersion*, *MinorVersion*, *BuildNumber*, *RevisionNumber*, *PublicKeyOrToken*, *Name*, and *Culture* [values]. [WARNING]

> **NOTE**
> *Name* is a simple name (e.g., "Foo"—no drive letter, no path, no file extension); on POSIX-compliant systems, *Name* contains no colon, no forward-slash, no backslash, no period.

End informative text

21.6 AssemblyRefOS: 0x25

The *AssemblyRefOS* table has the following columns:

- *OSPlatformId* (4-byte constant)
- *OSMajorVersion* (4-byte constant)
- *OSMinorVersion* (4-byte constant)
- *AssemblyRef* (index into the *AssemblyRef* table)

These records should not be emitted into any PE file. If present in a PE file, they should be treated as if their fields were zero. They should be ignored by the CLI.

21.7 AssemblyRefProcessor: 0x24

The *AssemblyRefProcessor* table has the following columns:

- *Processor* (4-byte constant)
- *AssemblyRef* (index into the *AssemblyRef* table)

These records should not be emitted into any PE file. If present in a PE file, they should be treated as if their fields were zero. They should be ignored by the CLI.

21.8 ClassLayout: 0x0F

The *ClassLayout* table is used to define how the fields of a class or value type shall be laid out by the CLI (normally, the CLI is free to reorder and/or insert gaps between the fields defined for a class or value type).

> **RATIONALE**
>
> This feature is used to make a managed value type be laid out in exactly the same way as an unmanaged C struct—with this condition true, the managed value type can be handed to unmanaged code, which accesses the fields exactly as if that block of memory had been laid out by unmanaged code.

The information held in the *ClassLayout* table depends upon the *Flags* value for {*AutoLayout*, *SequentialLayout*, *ExplicitLayout*} in the owner class or value type.

A type *has layout* if it is marked *SequentialLayout* or *ExplicitLayout*. If any type within an inheritance chain has layout, then so shall all its parents, up to the one that descends immediately from `System.Object, or from System.ValueType.`

This contains informative text only.

Layout cannot begin partway down the chain. But it *is* legal to *stop* "having layout" at any point down the chain.

For example, in the diagrams below, class A derives from `System.Object`; class B derives from A; class C derives from B. `System.Object` has no layout. But A, B, and C are all defined with layout, and that is legal.

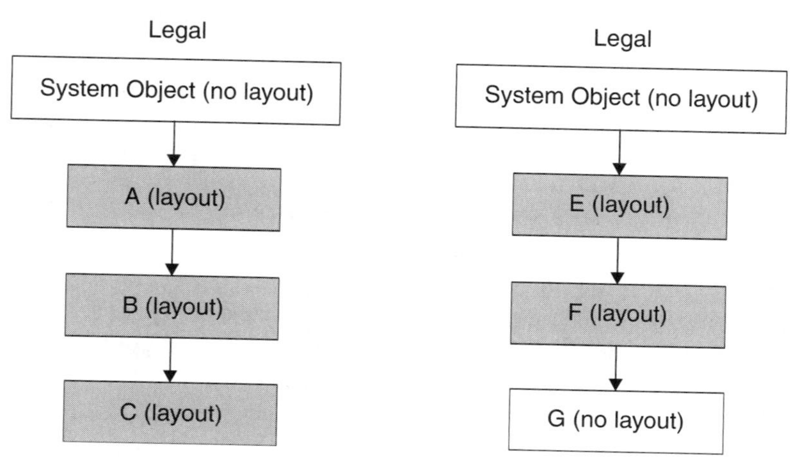

Similarly with classes E, F, and G, G has no layout. This, too, is legal. The following picture shows two *illegal* setups:

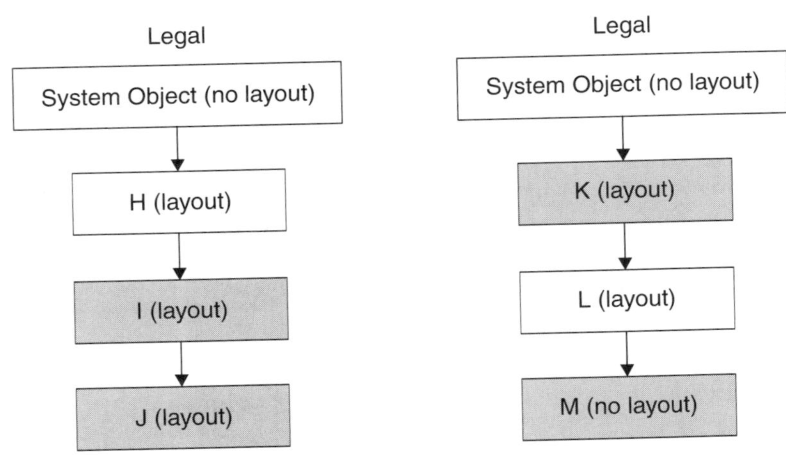

On the left, the "chain with layout" does not start at the "highest" class. And on the right, there is a "hole" in the "chain with layout."

Layout information for a class or value type is held in two tables—the *ClassLayout* and *FieldLayout* tables, as shown in this diagram:

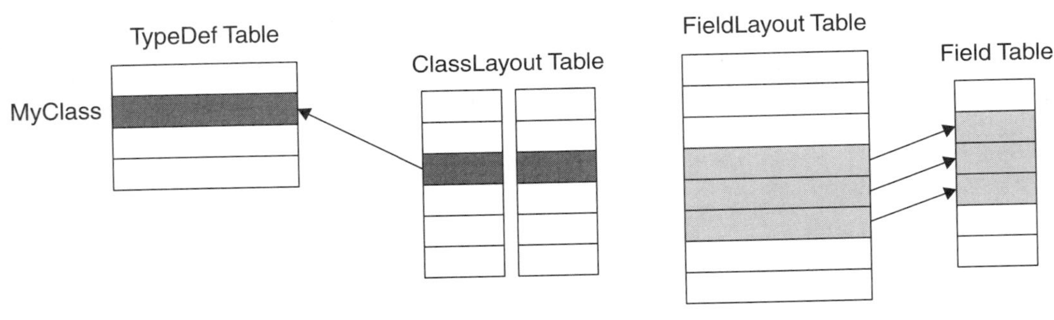

This example shows how row 3 of the *ClassLayout* table points to row 2 in the *TypeDef* table (the definition for a Class, called "MyClass"). Rows 4 through 6 of the *FieldLayout* table point to corresponding rows in the *Field* table. This illustrates how the CLI stores the explicit offsets for the three fields that are defined in "MyClass" (there is always one row in the *FieldLayout* table for each field in the owning class or value type). So, the *ClassLayout*

table acts as an extension to those rows of the *TypeDef* table that have layout info; since many classes do not have layout info, this design overall saves space.

End informative text

The *ClassLayout* table has the following columns:

- *PackingSize* (a 2-byte constant)
- *ClassSize* (a 4-byte constant)
- *Parent* (index into *TypeDef* table)

The rows of the *ClassLayout* table are defined by placing **.pack** and **.size** directives on the body of a parent type declaration (see Partition II, section 9.2). For an example, see Partition II, section 9.7.

This contains informative text only.

---

1. A *ClassLayout* table may contain zero or more or rows.
2. *Parent* shall index a valid row in the *TypeDef* table, corresponding to a Class or ValueType (not to an Interface). [ERROR]
3. The Class or ValueType indexed by *Parent* shall *not* be *AutoLayout*—i.e., it shall be one of *SequentialLayout* or *ExplicitLayout*. (See Partition II, section 22.1.14.) Put another way, *AutoLayout* types shall not own any rows in the *ClassLayout* table. [ERROR]
4. If *Parent* indexes a *SequentialLayout* type, then: [ERROR]
   - *PackingSize* shall be one of {0, 1, 2, 4, 8, 16, 32, 64, 128} (0 means use the default pack size for the platform that the application is running on).
   - If *ClassSize* is non-zero, then it shall be greater than or equal to the calculated size of the class, based upon its field sizes and *PackingSize* (compilers request padding at the end of a class by providing a value for *ClassSize* that is larger than its calculated size). [ERROR]
   - A *ClassSize* of zero does not mean the class has zero size. It means that no size was specified at definition time. Instead, the actual size is calculated from the field types, taking account of packing size (default or specified) and natural alignment on the target, runtime platform.
   - If *Parent* indexes a ValueType, then *ClassSize* shall be less than 1 MByte (0x100000 bytes).

5. Metadata File Format

ANNOTATION

Implementation-Specific (Microsoft): Current implementation of desktop CLI allows 0x3F0000 bytes, but this size may be reduced in future.

---

5. Note that *ExplicitLayout* types *might* result in verifiable types, so long as that layout does not create *union* types.
6. If *Parent* indexes an *ExplicitLayout* type, then: [ERROR]
   - If *ClassSize* is non-zero, then it shall be greater than or equal to the calculated size of the class, based upon the rows it owns in the *FieldLayout* table (compilers create padding at the end of a class by providing a value for *ClassSize* that is larger than its calculated size).
   - A *ClassSize* of zero does not mean the class has zero size. It means that no size was specified at definition time. Instead, the actual size is calculated from the field types, their specified offsets, and any beyond-end **alignment** packing performed by the target platform.
   - If *Parent* indexes a ValueType, then *ClassSize* shall be less than 1 MByte (0x100000 bytes).

ANNOTATION

Implementation-Specific (Microsoft): Current implementation allows 0x3F0000 bytes, but this size may be reduced in future.

   - *PackingSize* shall be 0 (because it makes no sense to provide explicit offsets for each field, as well as a packing size).
7. Layout along the length of an inheritance chain shall follow the rules specified above (starts at "highest" Type, with no "holes", etc.). [ERROR]

End informative text

21.9 Constant: 0x0B

The *Constant* table is used to store compile-time, constant values for fields, parameters, and properties.

The *Constant* table has the following columns:

- *Type* (a 1-byte constant, followed by a 1-byte padding zero); see Partition II, section 22.1.15. The encoding of *Type* for the **nullref** value for <fieldInit> in ilasm (see Partition II, section 15.2) is `ELEMENT_TYPE_CLASS` with a *Value* of a 4-byte zero. Unlike uses of `ELEMENT_TYPE_CLASS` in signatures, this one is *not* followed by a type token.
- *Parent* (index into the *Param* or *Field* or *Property* table; more precisely, a *HasConstant* coded index).
- *Value* (index into Blob heap).

Note that *Constant* information does not directly influence runtime behavior, although it is visible via reflection (and hence may be used to implement functionality such as that provided by `System.Enum.ToString`). Compilers inspect this information, at compile time, when importing metadata; but the value of the constant itself, if used, becomes embedded into the CIL stream the compiler emits. There are no CIL instructions to access the *Constant* table at runtime.

A row in the *Constant* table for a parent is created whenever a compile-time value is specified for that parent. For an example, see Partition II, section 15.2.

This contains informative text only.

---

1. *Type* shall be exactly one of: `ELEMENT_TYPE_BOOLEAN`, `ELEMENT_TYPE_CHAR`, `ELEMENT_TYPE_I1`, `ELEMENT_TYPE_U1`, `ELEMENT_TYPE_I2`, `ELEMENT_TYPE_U2`, `ELEMENT_TYPE_I4`, `ELEMENT_TYPE_U4`, `ELEMENT_TYPE_I8`, `ELEMENT_TYPE_U8`, `ELEMENT_TYPE_R4`, `ELEMENT_TYPE_R8`, `ELEMENT_TYPE_STRING`; or `ELEMENT_TYPE_CLASS` with a *Value* of zero (see Partition II, section 22.1.15). [ERROR]
2. *Type* shall not be any of: `ELEMENT_TYPE_I1, ELEMENT_TYPE_U2, ELEMENT_TYPE_U4, ELEMENT_TYPE_U8 (see Partition II, section 22.1.15). [CLS]`
3. *Parent* shall index a valid row in the *Field* or *Property* or *Param* table. [ERROR]
4. There shall be no duplicate rows, based upon *Parent*. [ERROR]
5. *Constant.Type* must match exactly the declared type of the *Param*, *Field*, or *Property* identified by *Parent* (in the case where the parent is an enum, it must match exactly the underlying type of that enum). [CLS]

End informative text

21.10 CustomAttribute: 0x0C

The *CustomAttribute* table has the following columns:

- *Parent* (index into *any* metadata table, except the *CustomAttribute* table itself; more precisely, a *HasCustomAttribute* coded index)
- *Type* (index into the *MethodDef* or *MethodRef* table; more precisely, a *CustomAttributeType* coded index)
- *Value* (index into Blob heap)

The *CustomAttribute* table stores data that can be used to instantiate a Custom Attribute (more precisely, an object of the specified Custom Attribute class) at runtime. The column called *Type* is slightly misleading—it actually indexes a constructor method—the owner of that constructor method is the Type of the Custom Attribute.

A row in the *CustomAttribute* table for a parent is created by the **.custom** attribute, which gives the value of the *Type* column and optionally that of the *Value* column (see Partition II, section 20).

This contains informative text only.

All binary values are stored in little-endian format (except *PackedLen* items—used only as counts for the number of bytes to follow in a UTF8 string).

1. It is legal for there to be no *CustomAttribute* present at all—that is, for the *CustomAttribute.Value* field to be null.
2. *Parent* can be an index into *any* metadata table, *except* the *CustomAttribute* table itself. [ERROR]
3. *Type* shall index a valid row in the *Method* or *MethodRef* table. That row shall be a constructor method (for the class of which this information forms an instance). [ERROR]
4. *Value* may be null or non-null.
5. If *Value* is non-null, it shall index a "blob" in the Blob heap. [ERROR]
6. The following rules apply to the overall structure of the *Value* "blob" (see Partition II, section 22.3):
   - *Prolog* shall be 0x0001. [ERROR]
   - There shall be as many occurrences of *FixedArg* as are declared in the constructor method. [ERROR]
   - *NumNamed* may be zero or more.

- There shall be exactly *NumNamed* occurrences of *NamedArg*. [ERROR]
- Each *NamedArg* shall be accessible by the caller. [ERROR]
- If *NumNamed* = 0, then there shall be no further items in the *CustomAttrib*. [ERROR]

7. The following rules apply to the structure of *FixedArg* (see Partition II, section 22.3):
   - If this item is not for a vector (a single-dimension array with lower bound of 0), then there shall be exactly one *Elem*. [ERROR]
   - If this item is for a vector, then:
     - *NumElem* shall be 1 or more. [ERROR]
     - This shall be followed by *NumElem* occurrences of *Elem*. [ERROR]
8. The following rules apply to the structure of *Elem* (see Partition II, section 22.3):
   - If this is a simple type or an enum (see Partition II, section 22.3 for how this is defined), then *Elem* consists simply of its value. [ERROR]
   - If this is a string, or a Type, then *Elem* consists of a *SerString*—a *PackedLen* count of bytes, followed by the UTF8 characters. [ERROR]
   - If this is a boxed simple value type (bool, char, float32, float64, int8, int16, int32, int64, unsigned int8, unsigned int16, unsigned int32 or unsigned int64), then *Elem* consists of the corresponding type denoter (`ELEMENT_TYPE_BOOLEAN`, `ELEMENT_TYPE_CHAR`, `ELEMENT_TYPE_I1`, `ELEMENT_TYPE_U1`, `ELEMENT_TYPE_I2`, `ELEMENT_TYPE_U2`, `ELEMENT_TYPE_I4`, `ELEMENT_TYPE_U4`, `ELEMENT_TYPE_I8`, `ELEMENT_TYPE_U8`, `ELEMENT_TYPE_R4`, `ELEMENT_TYPE_R8`), followed by its value. [ERROR]
9. The following rules apply to the structure of *NamedArg* (see Partition II, section 22.3):
   - The single-byte `FIELD (0x53) or PROPERTY (0x54) [ERROR]`
   - The type of the field or property—one of `ELEMENT_TYPE_BOOLEAN`, `ELEMENT_TYPE_CHAR`, `ELEMENT_TYPE_I1`, `ELEMENT_TYPE_U1`, `ELEMENT_TYPE_I2`, `ELEMENT_TYPE_U2`, `ELEMENT_TYPE_I4`, `ELEMENT_TYPE_U4`, `ELEMENT_TYPE_I8`, `ELEMENT_TYPE_U8`, `ELEMENT_TYPE_R4`, `ELEMENT_TYPE_R8`, `ELEMENT_TYPE_STRING`, or the constant 0x50 (for an argument of type `System.Type`)
   - The name of the field or property, respectively, with the previous item, as a *SerString*—a *PackedLen* count of bytes, followed by the UTF8 characters of the name [ERROR]
   - A *FixedArg* (see above) [ERROR]

End informative text

21.11 DeclSecurity: 0x0E

Security attributes, which derive from `System.Security.Permissions.SecurityAttribute` (see the *.NET Framework Standard Library Annotated Reference*), can be attached to a *TypeDef*, a *Method*, or an *Assembly*. All constructors of this class shall take a `System.Security.Permissions.SecurityAction` value as their first parameter, describing what should be done with the permission on the type, method, or assembly to which it is attached. Code access security attributes, which derive from `System.Security.Permissions.CodeAccessSecurityAttribute`, may have any of the security actions.

These different security actions are encoded in the *DeclSecurity* table as a 2-byte enum (see below). All security custom attributes for a given security action on a method, type, or assembly shall be gathered together and one `System.Security.PermissionSet` instance shall be created, stored in the Blob heap, and referenced from the *DeclSecurity* table.

> **NOTE**
>
> The general flow from a compiler's point of view is as follows. The user specifies a custom attribute through some language-specific syntax that encodes a call to the attribute's constructor. If the attribute's type is derived (directly or indirectly) from `System.Security.Permissions.SecurityAttribute`, then it is a security custom attribute and requires special treatment, as follows (other custom attributes are handled by simply recording the constructor in the metadata as described in Partition II, section 21.10). The attribute object is constructed, and provides a method (`CreatePermission`) to convert it into a security permission object (an object derived from `System.Security.Permission`). All the permission objects attached to a given metadata item with the same security action are combined together into a `System.Security.PermissionSet`. This permission set is converted into a form that is ready to be stored in XML using its ToXML method to create a `System.Security.SecurityElement`. Finally, the XML that is required for the metadata is created using the `ToString` method on the security element.

The *DeclSecurity* table has the following columns:

- *Action* (2-byte value)
- *Parent* (index into the *TypeDef*, *MethodDef*, or *Assembly* table; more precisely, a *HasDeclSecurity* coded index)
- *PermissionSet* (index into Blob heap)

Action is a 2-byte representation of security actions, see `System.Security.SecurityAction` in the *.NET Framework Standard Library Annotated Reference.* The values 0 through 0xFF are reserved for future standards use. Values 0x20 through 0x7F, and 0x100 through 0x07FF, are for uses where the action may be ignored if it is not understood or supported. Values 0x80 through 0xFF, and 0x0800 through 0xFFFF, are for uses where the action shall be implemented for secure operation; in implementations where the action is not available, no access to the assembly, type, or method shall be permitted.

Security Action	Note	Explanation of Behavior	Legal Scope
Assert	1	Without further checks, satisfy Demand for specified permission.	Method, Type
Demand	1	Check [that] all callers in the call chain have been granted specified permission, throw `SecurityException` (see the *.NET Framework Standard Library Annotated Reference*) on failure.	Method, Type
Deny	1	Without further checks, refuse Demand for specified permission.	Method, Type
InheritanceDemand	1	Specified permission shall be granted in order to inherit from class or override virtual method.	Method, Type
LinkDemand	1	Check [that] immediate caller has been granted specified permission, throw `SecurityException` (see the *.NET Framework Standard Library Annotated Reference*) on failure.	Method, Type
PermitOnly	1	Without further checks, refuse Demand for all permissions other than those specified.	Method, Type
RequestMinimum		Specify minimum permissions required to run.	Assembly
RequestOptional		Specify optional permissions to grant.	Assembly
RequestRefuse		Specify permissions not to be granted.	Assembly
NonCasDemand	2	Check that current assembly has been granted specified permission, throw `SecurityException` (see the *.NET Framework Standard Library Annotated Reference* otherwise).	Method, Type

Security Action	Note	Explanation of Behavior	Legal Scope
NonCasLinkDemand	2	Check that immediate caller has been granted specified permission, throw `Security-Exception` (see the *.NET Framework Standard Library Annotated Reference*) otherwise.	Method, Type
PrejitGrant		Reserved for implementation-specific use.	Assembly

Note 1: Specified attribute shall derive from `System.Security.Permissions.Code-Access-SecurityAttribute`.

Note 2: Attribute shall derive from `System.Security.Permissions.Security-Attribute`, but shall not derive from `System.Security.Permissions.CodeAccessSecurityAttribute`.

Parent is a metadata token that identifies the *Method, Type,* or *Assembly* on which security custom attributes serialized in *PermissionSet* were defined.

PermissionSet is a "blob" that contains the XML serialization of a permission set. The permission set contains the permissions that were requested with an *Action* on a specific *Method, Type,* or *Assembly* (see *Parent*).

The rows of the *DeclSecurity* table are filled by attaching a **.permission** or **.permissionset** directive that specifies the *Action* and *PermissionSet* on a parent assembly (see Partition II, section 6.6) or parent type or method (see Partition II, section 9.2).

This contains informative text only.

---

1. *Action* may have only those values set that are specified. [ERROR]
2. *Parent* shall be one of *TypeDef, MethodDef,* or *Assembly.* That is, it shall index a valid row in the *TypeDef* table, the *MethodDef* table, or the *Assembly* table. [ERROR]
3. If *Parent* indexes a row in the *TypeDef* table, that row should not define an Interface. The security system ignores any such parent; compilers should not emit such permissions sets. [WARNING]
4. If *Parent* indexes a *TypeDef*, then its *TypeDef.Flags.HasSecurity* bit should be set. [ERROR]
5. If *Parent* indexes a *MethodDef*, then its *MethodDef.Flags.HasSecurity* bit should be set, [ERROR]
6. *PermissionSet* should index a "blob" in the Blob heap. [ERROR]

7. The format of the "blob" indexed by *PermissionSet* should represent a valid, serialized CLI object graph. The serialized form of all standardized permissions is specified in the *.NET Framework Standard Library Annotated Reference*. [ERROR]

End informative text

21.12 EventMap: 0x12

The *EventMap* table has the following columns:

- *Parent* (index into the *TypeDef* table)
- *EventList* (index into *Event* table). It marks the first of a contiguous run of Events owned by this Type. The run continues to the smaller of:
  - The last row of the *Event* table
  - The next run of Events, found by inspecting the *EventList* of the next row in the *EventMap* table

Note that *EventMap* info does not directly influence runtime behavior; what counts is the info stored for each method that the event comprises.

This contains informative text only.

---

1. The *EventMap* table may contain zero or more rows.
2. There shall be no duplicate rows, based upon *Parent* (a given class has only one "pointer" to the start of its event list). [ERROR]
3. There shall be no duplicate rows, based upon *EventList* (different classes cannot share rows in the *Event* table). [ERROR]

End informative text

21.13 Event: 0x14

Events are treated within metadata much like Properties—a way to associate a collection of methods defined on given class. There are two required methods—*add_* and *remove_*—plus optional *raise_* and *others*. All of the methods gathered together as an Event shall be defined on the class.

The association between a row in the *TypeDef* table and the collection of methods that make up a given Event is held in three separate tables (exactly analogous to that used for Properties)—see the [diagram] below:

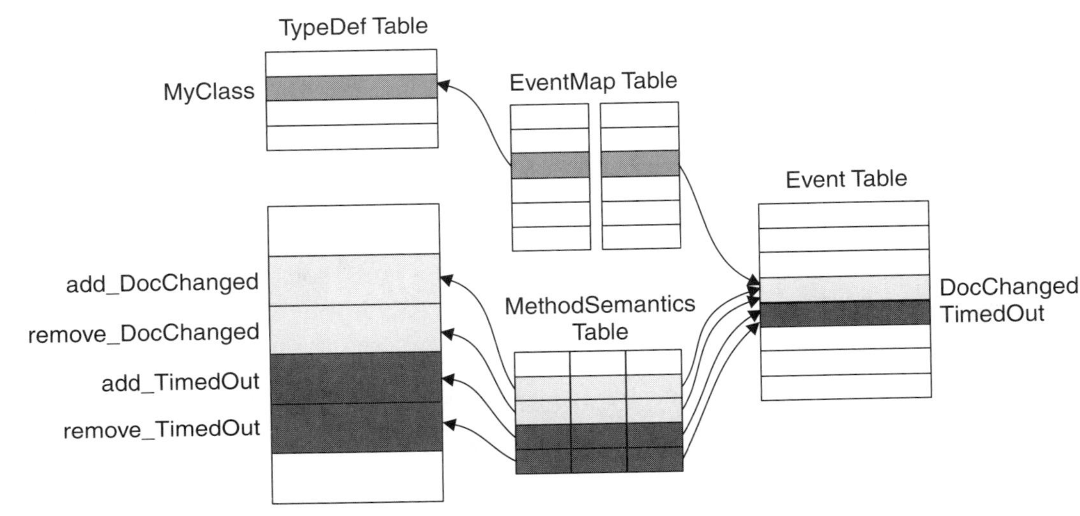

Row 3 of the *EventMap* table indexes row 2 of the *TypeDef* table on the left (*MyClass*), while indexing row 4 of the *Event* table on the right—the row for an Event called *DocChanged*. This setup establishes that *MyClass* has an Event called *DocChanged*. But what methods in the *MethodDef* table are gathered together as "belonging" to event *DocChanged*? That association is contained in the *MethodSemantics* table—its row 2 indexes event *DocChanged* to the right, and row 2 in the *MethodDef* table to the left (a method called *add_DocChanged*). Also, row 3 of the *MethodSemantics* table indexes *DocChanged* to the right, and row 3 in the *MethodDef* table to the left (a method called *remove_DocChanged*). As the shading suggests, *MyClass* has another event, called *TimedOut*, with two methods, *add_TimedOut* and *remove_TimedOut*.

Event tables do a little more than group together existing rows from other tables. The *Event* table has columns for *EventFlags*, *Name* (e.g., *DocChanged* and *TimedOut* in the example here) and *EventType*. In addition, the *MethodSemantics* table has a column to record whether the method it points at is an *add_*, a *remove_*, a *raise_*, or *other*.

The *Event* table has the following columns:

- *EventFlags* (a 2-byte bitmask of type *EventAttribute*; see Partition II, section 22.1.4)
- *Name* (index into String heap)
- *EventType* (index into *TypeDef*, *TypeRef*, or *TypeSpec* tables; more precisely, a *TypeDefOrRef* coded index) (this corresponds to the Type of the Event; it is *not* the Type that owns this event)

Note that *Event* information does not directly influence runtime behavior; what counts is the information stored for each method that the event comprises.

The *EventMap* and *Event* tables result from putting the **.event** directive on a class (see Partition II, section 17).

This contains informative text only.

---

1. The *Event* table may contain zero or more rows.
2. Each row shall have one, and only one, owner row in the *EventMap* table. [ERROR]
3. *EventFlags* may have only those values set that are specified (all combinations valid). [ERROR]
4. *Name* shall index a non-null string in the String heap. [ERROR]

ANNOTATION

Implementation-Specific (Microsoft): This string is limited to `MAX_CLASS_NAME`.

---

5. The *Name* string shall be a valid CLS identifier. [CLS]
6. *EventType* may be null or non-null.
7. If *EventType* is non-null, then it shall index a valid row in the *TypeDef* or *TypeRef* table. [ERROR]
8. If *EventType* is non-null, then the row in *TypeDef*, *TypeRef*, or *TypeSpec* table that it indexes shall be a Class (not an Interface; not a ValueType). [ERROR]
9. For each row, there shall be one *add_* and one *remove_* row in the *MethodSemantics* table. [ERROR]
10. For each row, there can be zero or one *raise_* row, as well as zero or more *other* rows in the *MethodSemantics* table. [ERROR]
11. Within the rows owned by a given row in the *TypeDef* table, there shall be no duplicates based upon *Name*. [ERROR]
12. There shall be no duplicate rows based upon *Name*, where *Name* fields are compared using CLS conflicting-identifier-rules. [CLS]

End informative text

---

5. Metadata File Format

21.14 ExportedType: 0x27

The *ExportedType* table holds a row for each type, defined within *other* modules of this Assembly, that is exported out of this Assembly. In essence, it stores *TypeDef* row numbers of all types that are marked public in *other* modules that this Assembly comprises.

The actual target row in a *TypeDef* table is given by the combination of *TypeDefId* (in effect, row number) and *Implementation* (in effect, the module that holds the target *TypeDef* table). Note that this is the only occurrence in metadata of *foreign* tokens—that is, token values that have a meaning in *another* module. (Regular token values are indices into the table in the *current* module.)

The full name of the type need not be stored directly. Instead, it may be split into two parts at any included "." (although typically this is done at the last "." in the full name). The part preceding the "." is stored as the *TypeNamespace*, and that following the "." is stored as the *TypeName*. If there is no "." in the full name, then the *TypeNamespace* shall be the index of the empty string.

The *ExportedType* table has the following columns:

- *Flags* (a 4-byte bitmask of type *TypeAttributes*; see Partition II, section 22.1.14).
- *TypeDefId* (4-byte index into a *TypeDef* table of another module in this Assembly). This field is used as a hint only. If the entry in the target *TypeDef* table matches the *TypeName* and *TypeNamespace* entries in this table, resolution has succeeded. But if there is a mismatch, the CLI shall fall back to a search of the target *TypeDef* table.
- *TypeName* (index into the String heap).
- *TypeNamespace* (index into the String heap).
- *Implementation*. This can be an index (more precisely, an *Implementation* coded index) into one of two tables, as follows:
  - *File* table, where that entry says which module in the current assembly holds the *TypeDef*
  - *ExportedType* table, where that entry is the enclosing Type of the current nested Type

The rows in the *ExportedType* table are the result of the **.class extern** directive (see Partition II, section 6.7).

This contains informative text only.

The term "FullName" refers to the string created as follows: if the *TypeNamespace* is null, then use the *TypeName*; otherwise use the concatenation of *Typenamespace*, ".", and *TypeName*.

1. The *ExportedType* table may contain zero or more rows.
2. There shall be no entries in the *ExportedType* table for Types that are defined in the current module—just for Types defined in other modules within the Assembly. [ERROR]
3. *Flags* may have only those values set that are specified. [ERROR]
4. If *Implementation* indexes the *File* table, then *Flags.VisibilityMask* shall be `Public` (see Partition II, section 22.1.14). [ERROR]
5. If *Implementation* indexes the *ExportedType* table, then *Flags.VisibilityMask* shall be `NestedPublic` (see Partition II, section 22.1.14). [ERROR]
6. If non-null, *TypeDefId* should index a valid row in a *TypeDef* table in a module somewhere within this Assembly (but not *this* module), and the row so indexed should have its *Flags.Public* = 1 (see Partition II, section 22.1.14). [WARNING]
7. *TypeName* shall index a non-null string in the String heap. [ERROR]

ANNOTATION

Implementation-Specific (Microsoft): This string is limited to `MAX_CLASS_NAME`.

---

8. *TypeNamespace* may be null or non-null.
9. If *TypeNamespace* is non-null, then it shall index a non-null string in the String heap. [ERROR]

ANNOTATION

Implementation-Specific (Microsoft): This string is limited to MAX_CLASS_NAME. Also, the FullName (concatenated TypeNamespace+"."+TypeName) shall be less than `MAX_CLASS_NAME`.

---

10. *FullName* shall be a valid CLS identifier. [CLS]
11. If this is a nested Type, then *TypeNamespace* should be null, and *TypeName* should represent the unmangled, simple name of the nested Type. [ERROR]
12. *Implementation* shall be a valid index into either: [ERROR]
    - The *File* table; that file shall hold a definition of the target Type in its *TypeDef* table.
    - A *different* row in the current *ExportedType* table—this identifies the enclosing Type of the current, nested Type.
13. *FullName* shall match exactly the corresponding *FullName* for the row in the *TypeDef* table indexed by *TypeDefId*. [ERROR]

14. Ignoring nested Types, there shall be no duplicate rows, based upon *FullName*. [ERROR]
15. For nested Types, there shall be no duplicate rows, based upon *TypeName* and enclosing Type. [ERROR]
16. The complete list of Types exported from the current Assembly is given as the catenation of the *ExportedType* table with all public Types in the current *TypeDef* table, where "public" means a *Flags.tdVisibilityMask* of either `Public` or `NestedPublic`. There shall be no duplicate rows, in this concatenated table, based upon *FullName* (add Enclosing Type into the duplicates check if this is a nested Type). [ERROR]

End informative text

21.15 Field: 0x04

The *Field* table has the following columns:

- *Flags* (a 2-byte bitmask of type *FieldAttributes*; see Partition II, section 22.1.5)
- *Name* (index into String heap)
- *Signature* (index into Blob heap)

Conceptually, each row in the *Field* table is owned by one, and only one, row in the *TypeDef* table. However, the owner of any row in the *Field* table is not stored anywhere in the *Field* table itself. There is merely a "forward-pointer" from each row in the *TypeDef* table (the *FieldList* column), as shown in the following illustration:

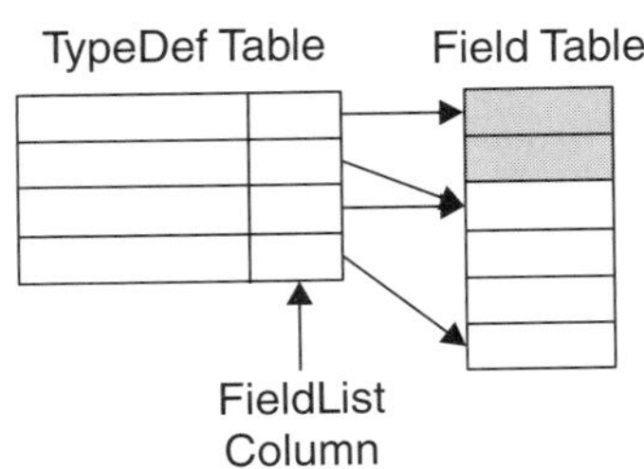

The *TypeDef* table has rows 1 through 4. The first row in the *TypeDef* table corresponds to a pseudo type, inserted automatically by the CLI. It is used to denote those rows in the *Field* table corresponding to global variables. The *Field* table has rows 1 through 6. Type 1 (pseudo type for "module") owns rows 1 and 2 in the *Field* table. Type 2 owns no rows in the *Field* table, even though its *FieldList* indexes row 3 in the *Field* table. Type 3 owns rows 3 through 5 in the *Field* table. Type 4 owns row 6 in the *Field* table. (The *next* pointers in the diagram show the next free row in each table) So, in the *Field* table, rows 1 and 2 belong to Type 1 (global variables); rows 3 through 5 belong to Type 3; row 6 belongs to Type 4.

Each row in the *Field* table results from a toplevel **.field** directive (see Partition II, section 5.10), or a **.field** directive inside a Type (see Partition II, section 9.2). For an example, see Partition II, section 13.5.

This contains informative text only.

---

1. The *Field* table may contain zero or more rows.
2. Each row shall have one, and only one, owner row in the *TypeDef* table. [ERROR]
3. The owner row in the *TypeDef* table shall not be an Interface. [CLS]
4. *Flags* may have only those set that are specified. [ERROR]
5. The *FieldAccessMask* subfield of *Flags* shall contain precisely one of `CompilerControlled`, `Private`, `FamANDAssem`, `Assembly`, `Family`, `FamORAssem`, or `Public` (see Partition II, section 22.1.5). [ERROR]
6. *Flags* may set 0 or 1 of `Literal` or `InitOnly` (not both) (see Partition II, section 22.1.5). [ERROR]
7. If *Flags.Literal* = 1, then *Flags.Static* shall be 1 too (see Partition II, section 22.1.5). [ERROR]
8. If *Flags.RTSpecialName* = 1, then *Flags.SpecialName* shall also be 1 (see Partition II, section 22.1.5). [ERROR]
9. If *Flags.HasFieldMarshal* = 1, then this row shall "own" exactly one row in the *FieldMarshal* table (see Partition II, section 22.1.5). [ERROR]
10. If *Flags.HasDefault* = 1, then this row shall "own" exactly one row in the *Constant* table (see Partition II, section 22.1.5). [ERROR]
11. If *Flags.HasFieldRVA* = 1, then this row shall "own" exactly one row in the *Field*'s *RVA* table (see Partition II, section 22.1.5). [ERROR]
12. *Name* shall index a non-null string in the String heap. [ERROR]

ANNOTATION

Implementation-Specific (Microsoft): This string is limited to `MAX_CLASS_NAME`.

---

13. The *Name* string shall be a valid CLS identifier. [CLS]

14. *Signature* shall index a valid field signature in the Blob heap, [ERROR]
15. If *Flags.CompilerControlled* = 1 (see Partition II, section 22.1.5), then this row is ignored completely in duplicate checking.
16. If the owner of this field is the internally generated type called <Module>, it denotes that this field is defined at module scope (commonly called a global variable). In this case:
    - *Flags.Static* shall be 1. [ERROR]
    - The *Flags.MemberAccessMask* subfield shall be one of `Public`, `CompilerControlled`, or `Private` (see Partition II, section 22.1.5). [ERROR]
    - Module-scope fields are not allowed. [CLS]
17. There shall be no duplicate rows in the *Field* table, based upon owner+*Name*+*Signature* (where owner is the owning row in the *TypeDef* table, as described above). (Note, however, that if *Flags.CompilerControlled* = 1, then this row is completely excluded from duplicate checking.) [ERROR]
18. There shall be no duplicate rows in the *Field* table, based upon owner+*Name*, where *Name* fields are compared using CLS conflicting-identifier-rules. So, for example, `"int i"` and `"float i"` would be considered CLS duplicates. (Note, however, that if *Flags.CompilerControlled* = 1, then this row is completely excluded from duplicate checking, as noted above.) [CLS]
19. If this is a field of an Enum, and *Name* string = "value__", then:
    a. `RTSpecialName` shall be 1. [ERROR]
    b. The owner row in the *TypeDef* table shall derive directly from `System.Enum`. [ERROR]
    c. The owner row in the *TypeDef* table shall have no other instance fields. [CLS]
    d. Its *Signature* shall be one of (see Partition II, section 22.1.15): [CLS]
        - `ELEMENT_TYPE_U1`
        - `ELEMENT_TYPE_I2`
        - `ELEMENT_TYPE_I4`
        - `ELEMENT_TYPE_I8`
20. Its *Signature* shall be an integral type.

End informative text

21.16 FieldLayout: 0x10

The *FieldLayout* table has the following columns:

- *Offset* (a 4-byte constant)
- *Field* (index into the *Field* table)

Note that each Field in any Type is defined by its Signature. When a Type instance (ie, an object) is laid out by the CLI, each Field is one of four kinds:

- Scalar – for any member of built-in, such as int32. The size of the field is given by the size of that intrinsic, which varies between 1 and 8 bytes.
- ObjectRef – for `CLASS`, `STRING`, `OBJECT`, `ARRAY`, `SZARRAY`.
- Pointer – for `PTR`, `FNPTR`.
- ValueType – for `VALUETYPE`. The instance of that ValueType is actually laid out in this object, so the size of the field is the size of that ValueType.

(The list above uses an abbreviation—each all-caps name should be prefixed by `ELEMENT_TYPE_`; so, for example, `STRING` is actually `ELEMENT_TYPE_STRING`. See Partition II, section 22.1.15.)

Note that metadata specifying explicit structure layout may be valid for use on one platform but not another, since some of the rules specified here are dependent on platform-specific alignment rules.

A row in the *FieldLayout* table is created if the **.field** directive for the parent field has specified a field offset (see Partition II, section 9.7).

This contains informative text only.

---

1. A *FieldLayout* table may contain zero or more or rows.
2. The Type whose Fields are described by each row of the *FieldLayout* table shall have *Flags.ExplicitLayout* (see Partition II, section 22.1.14) set. [ERROR]
3. *Offset* shall be zero or more (cannot be negative). [ERROR]
4. *Field* shall index a valid row in the *Field* table. [ERROR]
5. The row in the *Field* table indexed by *Field* shall be non-static (i.e., its *Flags.Static* shall be 0). [ERROR]
6. Among the rows owned by a given Type, there shall be no duplicates, based upon *Field*. That is, a given Field of a Type cannot be given two offsets. [ERROR]

7. Each Field of kind *ObjectRef* shall be naturally aligned within the Type. [ERROR]
8. No Field of kind *ObjectRef* may overlap any other Field no matter what its kind, wholly or partially. [ERROR]
9. Among the rows owned by a given Type, it is perfectly legal for several rows to have the same value of *Offset*, so long as they are *not* of type *ObjectRef* (used to define C *unions*, for example). [ERROR]
10. If *ClassSize* in the owner *ClassLayout* row is non-zero, then no Field may extend beyond that *ClassSize* (i.e., the Field *Offset* value plus the Field's calculated size shall not exceed *ClassSize*) (note that it is legal, and common, for *ClassSize* to be supplied as *larger* than the calculated object size—the CLI pads the object with trailing bytes up to the *ClassSize* value.) [ERROR]
11. Every Field of an *ExplicitLayout* Type shall be given an offset—that is, it shall have a row in the *FieldLayout* table. [ERROR]

ANNOTATION

Implementation-Specific (Microsoft): Note that the rules above specify what is legal, or non-legal, metadata. However, there is a finer distinction that can be drawn—what layouts permit typesafe access by code? For example, a class that overlaps two ValueTypes constitutes legal metadata, but accesses to that class may result in code that is not provably typesafe. At runtime, it is the Class loader that will perform these type-safety checks. Version 1 takes a simple approach—if the type has any explicit layout, it is not typesafe. (This may be refined in future versions.)

End informative text

21.17 FieldMarshal: 0x0D

The *FieldMarshal* table has two columns. It "links" an existing row in the *Field* or *Param* table to information in the Blob heap that defines how that field or parameter (which, as usual, covers the method return, as parameter number 0) should be marshalled when calling to or from unmanaged code via PInvoke dispatch.

Note that *FieldMarshal* information is used only by code paths that arbitrate operation with unmanaged code. In order to execute such paths, the caller, on most platforms, would be installed with elevated security permission. Once it invokes unmanaged code, it lies outside the regime that the CLI can check—it is simply trusted not to violate the type system.

The *FieldMarshal* table has the following columns:

- *Parent* (index into *Field* or *Param* table; more precisely, a *HasFieldMarshal* coded index)
- *NativeType* (index into the Blob heap)

For the detailed format of the "blob," see Partition II, section 22.4.

A row in the *FieldMarshal* table is created if the **.field** directive for the parent field has specified a **.marshal** attribute (see Partition II, section 15.1).

This contains informative text only.

---

1. A *FieldMarshal* table may contain zero or more rows.
2. *Parent* shall index a valid row in the *Field* or *Param* table (*Parent* values are encoded to say which of these two tables each refers to). [ERROR]
3. *NativeType* shall index a non-null "blob" in the Blob heap. [ERROR]
4. No two rows can point to the same parent. In other words, after the *Parent* values have been decoded to determine whether they refer to the *Field* or the *Param* table, no two rows can point to the same row in the *Field* table or in the *Param* table. [ERROR]
5. The following checks apply to the *MarshalSpec* "blob" (see Partition II, section 22.4):
   a. *NativeIntrinsic* shall be exactly one of the constant values in its production. [ERROR]
   b. If *NativeIntrinsic* has the value `BYVALSTR`, then *Parent* shall point to a row in the *Field* table, not the *Param* table. [ERROR]
   c. If `FIXEDARRAY`, then *Parent* shall point to a row in the *Field* table, not the *Param* table. [ERROR]
   d. If `FIXEDARRAY`, then *NumElem* shall be 1 or more. [ERROR]
   e. If `FIXEDARRAY`, then *ArrayElemType* shall be exactly one of the constant values in its production. [ERROR]
   f. If `ARRAY`, then *ArrayElemType* shall be exactly one of the constant values in its production. [ERROR]
   g. If `ARRAY`, then *ParamNum* may be zero.
   h. If `ARRAY`, then *ParamNum* cannot be < 0. [ERROR]
   i. If `ARRAY` and *ParamNum* > 0, then *Parent* shall point to a row in the *Param* table, not in the *Field* table. [ERROR]

j. If `ARRAY` and *ParamNum* > 0, then *ParamNum* cannot exceed the number of parameters supplied to the *MethodDef* (or *MethodRef* if a `VARARG` call) of which the parent *Param* is a member. [ERROR]

k. If `ARRAY`, then *ElemMult* shall be >= 1. [ERROR]

l. If `ARRAY` and *ElemMult* <> 1 issue a warning, because it is probably a mistake [WARNING]

m. If `ARRAY` and *ParamNum* == 0, then *NumElem* shall be >= 1. [ERROR]

n. If `ARRAY` and *ParamNum* != 0 and *NumElem* != 0, then issue a warning because it is probably a mistake. [WARNING]

ANNOTATION

Implementation-Specific (Microsoft): The following rules apply to Microsoft-specific features:

a. If `CUSTOMMARSHALLER`, then Guid shall be an in-place, counted-UTF8 string that represents a string-format GUID. Its length, when expanded from UTF8, shall be exactly 38 characters, to include leading (and trailing). [ERROR]

b. If `CUSTOMMARSHALLER`, then *UnmanagedType* shall be a non-empty, counted-UTF8 string. [ERROR]

c. If `CUSTOMMARSHALLER`, then *ManagedType* shall be a non-empty, counted-UTF8 string that represents the fully qualified *Namespace*+"."+*Name* of a Class or Value-Type defined somewhere within the current Assembly. [ERROR]

d. If `CUSTOMMARSHALLER`, then *Cookie* shall be a counted-UTF8 string—its size may legally be zero. [ERROR]

e. If `SAFEARRAY`, then *SafeArrayElemType* shall be exactly one of the constant values in its production. [ERROR]

End informative text

21.18 FieldRVA: 0x1D

The *FieldRVA* table has the following columns:

- *RVA* (a 4-byte constant)
- *Field* (index into *Field* table)

Conceptually, each row in the *FieldRVA* table is an extension to exactly one row in the *Field* table, and records the RVA (Relative Virtual Address) within the image file at which this field's initial value is stored.

A row in the *FieldRVA* table is created for each static parent field that has specified the optional **data** label (see Partition II, section 15). The RVA column is the Relative Virtual Address of the data in the PE file (see Partition II, section 15.3).

This contains informative text only.

---

1. *RVA* shall be non-zero. [ERROR]
2. *RVA* shall point into the current module's data area (not its metadata area). [ERROR]
3. *Field* shall index a valid table in the *Field* table. [ERROR]
4. Any field with an RVA shall be a ValueType (not a Class, and not an Interface). Moreover, it shall not have any private fields (and likewise for any of its fields that are themselves ValueTypes). (If any of these conditions were breached, code could overlay that global static and access its private fields.) Moreover, no fields of that ValueType can be Object References (into the GC heap). [ERROR]
5. So long as two RVA-based fields comply with the previous conditions, the ranges of memory spanned by the two ValueTypes may overlap, with no further constraints. This is not actually an additional rule; it simply clarifies the position with regard to overlapped RVA-based fields.

End informative text

21.19 File: 0x26

The *File* table has the following columns:

- *Flags* (a 4-byte bitmask of type *FileAttributes*; see Partition II, section 22.1.6)
- *Name* (index into String heap)
- *HashValue* (index into Blob heap)

The rows of the *File* table result from **.file** directives in an Assembly (see Partition II, section 6.2.3).

This contains informative text only.

1. Flags may have only those values set that are specified (all combinations valid). [ERROR]
2. *Name* shall index a non-null string in the String heap. It shall be in the format <file-name>.<extension> (e.g., "foo.dll", but *not* "c:\utils\foo.dll"). [ERROR]

ANNOTATION

Implementation-Specific (Microsoft): This string is limited to `MAX_PATH_NAME`.

Also, the following values for *Name* are illegal (these represent device, rather than file, names):

S [N] [[C]*]

where
S ::= con | aux | lpt | prn | null | com (case-blind)
N ::= a number 0 .. 9
C ::= $ | :
"[]" denotes optional, "*" denotes Kleene closure, " | " denotes alternatives. [ERROR]

The CLI also checks dynamically against opening a device, which can be assigned an arbitrary name by the user.

3. *HashValue* shall index a non-empty "blob" in the Blob heap. [ERROR]
4. There shall be no duplicate rows—rows with the same *Name* value. [ERROR]
5. If this module contains a row in the *Assembly* table (that is, if this module "holds the manifest"), then there shall not be any row in the *File* table for this module—i.e., no self-reference. [ERROR]
6. If the *File* table is empty, then this, by definition, is a single-file assembly. In this case, the *ExportedType* table should be empty. [WARNING]

End informative text

21.20 ImplMap: 0x1C

The *ImplMap* table holds information about unmanaged methods that can be reached from managed code, using PInvoke dispatch.

Each row of the *ImplMap* table associates a row in the *MethodDef* table (*MemberForwarded*) with the name of a routine (*ImportName*) in some unmanaged DLL (*ImportScope*).

> **NOTE**
>
> A typical example would be: associate the managed Method stored in row N of the *Method* table (so *MemberForwarded* would have the value N) with the routine called "GetEnvironmentVariable" (the string indexed by *ImportName*) in the DLL called "kernel32" (the string in the *ModuleRef* table indexed by *ImportScope*). The CLI intercepts calls to managed Method number N, and instead forwards them as calls to the unmanaged routine called "GetEnvironmentVariable" in "kernel32.dll" (including marshalling any arguments, as required).
>
> The CLI does not support this mechanism to access *fields* that are exported from a DLL—only methods.

The *ImplMap* table has the following columns:

- *MappingFlags* (a 2-byte bitmask of type *PInvokeAttributes*; see Partition II, section 22.1.7)
- *MemberForwarded* (index into the *Field* or *MethodDef* table; more precisely, a *MemberForwarded* coded index. However, it only ever indexes the *MethodDef* table, since *Field* export is not supported.
- *ImportName* (index into the String heap)
- *ImportScope* (index into the *ModuleRef* table)

A row is entered in the *ImplMap* table for each parent Method (see Partition II, section 14.5) that is defined with a **.pinvokeimpl** interoperation attribute specifying the *MappingFlags*, *ImportName*, and *ImportScope*. For an example see Partition II, section 14.5.

This contains informative text only.

---

1. *ImplMap* may contain zero or more rows.
2. *MappingFlags* may have only those values set that are specified. [ERROR]
3. *MemberForwarded* shall index a valid row in the *MethodDef* table. [ERROR]

4. The *MappingFlags.CharSetMask* (see Partition II, section 22.1.7) in the row of the *MethodDef* table indexed by *MemberForwarded* shall have at most one of the following bits set: `CharSetAnsi`, `CharSetUnicode`, or `CharSetAuto` (if none set, the default is `CharSetNotSpec`). [ERROR]

ANNOTATION

Implementation-Specific (Microsoft): The *MappingFlags.CallConvMask* in the row of the Method table indexed by *MemberForwarded* may have at most one of the following values: `CallConvWinapi`, `CallConvCdecl`, `CallConvStdcall`. It cannot have the value `CallConvFastcall` or `CallConvThiscall`. [ERROR]

---

5. *ImportName* shall index a non-null string in the String heap. [ERROR]

ANNOTATION

Implementation-Specific (Microsoft): This string is limited to `MAX_CLASS_NAME`.

---

6. *ImportScope* shall index a valid row in the *ModuleRef* table. [ERROR]
7. The row indexed in the *MethodDef* table by *MemberForwarded* shall have its *Flags.PinvokeImpl* = 1, and *Flags.Static* = 1. [ERROR]

End informative text

21.21 InterfaceImpl: 0x09

The *InterfaceImpl* table has the following columns:

- *Class* (index into the *TypeDef* table)
- *Interface* (index into the *TypeDef*, *TypeRef*, or *TypeSpec* table; more precisely, a *TypeDefOrRef* coded index)

The *InterfaceImpl* table records which interfaces a Type implements. Conceptually, each row in the *InterfaceImpl* table says that *Class* implements *Interface*.

This contains informative text only.

---

1. The *InterfaceImpl* table may contain zero or more rows.
2. *Class* shall be non-null. [ERROR]

ANNOTATION

Implementation-Specific (Microsoft): If *Class* = null, this row should be treated as if it did not exist. Used to mark a class deleted, in incremental compilation scenarios, without physically deleting its metadata.

---

3. If *Class* is non-null, then:
   - *Class* shall index a valid row in the *TypeDef* table. [ERROR]
   - *Interface* shall index a valid row in the *TypeDef* or *TypeRef* table. [ERROR]
   - The row in the *TypeDef, TypeRef,* or *TypeSpec* table indexed by *Interface* shall be an Interface (*Flags.Interface* = 1), not a Class or ValueType. [ERROR]
4. There should be no duplicates in the *InterfaceImpl* table, based upon non-null *Class* and *Interface* values. [WARNING]
5. There can be many rows with the same value for *Class* (a class can implement many interfaces).
6. There can be many rows with the same value for *Interface* (many classes can implement the same interface).

End informative text

21.22 ManifestResource: 0x28

The *ManifestResource* table has the following columns:

- *Offset* (a 4-byte constant)
- *Flags* (a 4-byte bitmask of type *ManifestResourceAttributes*; see Partition II, section 22.1.8)
- *Name* (index into the String heap)
- *Implementation* (index into *File* table, or *AssemblyRef* table, or null; more precisely, an *Implementation* coded index)

The *Offset* specifies the byte offset within the referenced file at which this resource record begins. The *Implementation* specifies which file holds this resource. The rows in the table result from **.mresource** directives on the Assembly (see Partition II, section 6.2.2).

5. Metadata File Format

This contains informative text only.

1. The *ManifestResource* table may contain zero or more rows.
2. *Offset* shall be a valid offset into the target file, starting from the Resource entry in the COR header. [ERROR]
3. *Flags* may have only those values set that are specified. [ERROR]
4. The *VisibilityMask* (see Partition II, section 22.1.8) subfield of *Flags* shall be one of `Public` or `Private`. [ERROR]
5. *Name* shall index a non-null string in the String heap. [ERROR]

ANNOTATION

Implementation-Specific (Microsoft): This string is limited to `MAX_CLASS_NAME`.

6. *Implementation* may be null or non-null (if null, it means the resource is stored in the current file).
7. If *Implementation* is null, then *Offset* shall be a valid offset in the current file, starting from the Resource entry in the CLI header. [ERROR]
8. If *Implementation* is non-null, then it shall index a valid row in the *File* or *AssemblyRef* table. [ERROR]
9. There shall be no duplicate rows, based upon *Name*. [ERROR]
10. If the resource is an index into the *File* table, *Offset* shall be zero. [ERROR]

End informative text

21.23 MemberRef: 0x0A

The *MemberRef* table combines two sorts of references—to Fields and to Methods of a class, known as "MethodRef" and "FieldRef", respectively. The *MemberRef* table has the following columns:

- *Class* (index into the *TypeRef*, *ModuleRef*, *MethodDef*, *TypeSpec*, or *TypeDef* tables; more precisely, a *MemberRefParent* coded index)
- *Name* (index into String heap)
- *Signature* (index into Blob heap)

An entry is made into the *MemberRef* table whenever a reference is made, in the CIL code, to a method or field which is defined in another module or assembly. (Also, an entry is made for a call to a method with a `VARARG` signature, even when it is defined in the same module as the call site.)

This contains informative text only.

1. *Class* shall be one of: [ERROR]
   a. A *TypeRef* token, if the class that defines the member is defined in another module. (**Note:** It is unusual, but legal, to use a *TypeRef* token when the member is defined in this same module—its *TypeDef* token can be used instead.)
   b. A *ModuleRef* token, if the member is defined, in another module of the same assembly, as a global function or variable.
   c. A *MethodDef* token, when used to supply a call-site signature for a varargs method that is defined in this module. The *Name* shall match the *Name* in the corresponding *MethodDef* row. The *Signature* shall match the *Signature* in the target method definition. [ERROR]
   d. A *TypeSpec* token, if the member is a member of a constructed type.
2. *Class* shall not be null (this would indicate an unresolved reference to a global function or variable). [ERROR]
3. *Name* shall index a non-null string in the String heap. [ERROR]

ANNOTATION

Implementation-Specific (Microsoft): This string is limited to `MAX_CLASS_NAME`.

4. The *Name* string shall be a valid CLS identifier. [CLS]
5. *Signature* shall index a valid field or method signature in the Blob heap. In particular, it shall embed exactly one of the following "calling conventions": [ERROR]
   a. `DEFAULT` (0x0)
   b. `VARARG` (0x5)
   c. `FIELD` (0x6)

5. Metadata File Format

ANNOTATION

Implementation-Specific (Microsoft): The above names are defined in the file **inc\CorHdr.h** as part of the Microsoft .NET SDK, using the prefix `IMAGE_CEE_CS_CALLCONV_`.

6. The *MemberRef* table shall contain no duplicates, where duplicate rows have the same *Class*, *Name*, and *Signature*. [WARNING]
7. *Signature* shall not have the `VARARG` (0x5) calling convention. [CLS]
8. There shall be no duplicate rows, where *Name* fields are compared using CLS conflicting-identifier-rules. [CLS]
9. There shall be no duplicate rows, where *Name* fields are compared using CLS conflicting-identifier-rules. (Note, in particular, that the return type, and whether parameters are marked `ELEMENT_TYPE_BYREF` (see Partition II, section 22.1.15) are ignored in the CLS. For example, `int foo()` and `double foo()` result in duplicate rows by CLS rules. Similarly, `void bar(int i)` and `void bar(int& i)` also result in duplicate rows by CLS rules.) [CLS]

ANNOTATION

Implementation-Specific (Microsoft): *Name* shall not be of the form _VtblGapSequenceNumber<_CountOfSlots>—such methods are dummies, used to pad entries in the vtable that CLI generates for COM interop. Such methods cannot be called from managed or unmanaged code. [ERROR]

10. If *Class* and *Name* resolve to a field, then that field shall not have a value of `CompilerControlled` (see Partition II, section 22.1.5) in its *Flags.FieldAccessMask* subfield. [ERROR]
11. If *Class* and *Name* resolve to a method, then that method shall not have a value of `CompilerControlled` in its *Flags.MemberAccessMask* (see Partition II, section 22.1.9) subfield. [ERROR]

End informative text

21.24 MethodDef: 0x06

The *MethodDef* table has the following columns:

- *RVA* (a 4-byte constant).
- *ImplFlags* (a 2-byte bitmask of type *MethodImplAttributes*; see Partition II, section 22.1.10).
- *Flags* (a 2-byte bitmask of type *MethodAttributes*; see Partition II, section 22.1.9).
- *Name* (index into String heap).
- *Signature* (index into Blob heap).
- *ParamList* (index into *Param* table). It marks the first of a contiguous run of Parameters owned by this method. The run continues to the smaller of:
  - The last row of the *Param* table
  - The next run of Parameters, found by inspecting the *ParamList* of the next row in the *MethodDef* table

Conceptually, every row in the *MethodDef* table is owned by one, and only one, row in the *TypeDef* table.

The rows in the *MethodDef* table result from **.method** directives (see Partition II, section 14). The RVA column is computed when the image for the PE file is emitted and points to the `Cor_ILMethod` structure for the body of the method (see Partition II, section 24.4).

This contains informative text only.

---

1. The *MethodDef* table may contain zero or more rows.
2. Each row shall have one, and only one, owner row in the *TypeDef* table. [ERROR]
3. *ImplFlags* may have only those values set that are specified. [ERROR]
4. *Flags* may have only those values set that are specified. [ERROR]
5. The *MemberAccessMask* (see Partition II, section 22.1.9) subfield of *Flags* shall contain precisely one of `CompilerControlled`, `Private`, `FamANDAssem`, `Assem`, `Family`, `FamORAssem`, or `Public`. [ERROR]
6. The following combined bit settings in *Flags* are illegal: [ERROR]
   a. `Static | Final`
   b. `Static | Virtual`
   c. `Static | NewSlot`
   d. `Final | Abstract`

5. Metadata File Format

e. `Abstract | PinvokeImpl`

f. `CompilerControlled | Virtual`

g. `CompilerControlled | Final`

h. `CompilerControlled | SpecialName`

i. `CompilerControlled | RTSpecialName`

7. An abstract method shall be virtual. So: if *Flags.Abstract* = 1, then *Flags.Virtual* shall also be 1. [ERROR]
8. If *Flags.RTSpecialName* = 1, then *Flags.SpecialName* shall also be 1. [ERROR]

ANNOTATION

Implementation-Specific (Microsoft): An abstract method cannot have `ForwardRef` (see Partition II, section 22.1.10) set, and vice versa. So:

- If *Flags.Abstract* = 1, then *ImplFlags.ForwardRef* shall be 0. [ERROR]
- If *ImplFlags.ForwardRef* = 1, then *Flags.Abstract* shall be 0. [ERROR]

The `ForwardRef` bit may be set only in an OBJ file (used by managed extensions for C++). By the time a method executes, its `ForwardRef` shall be 0. [ERROR]

---

9. If *Flags.HasSecurity* = 1, then at least one of the following conditions shall be true: [ERROR]
   - This Method owns at least [one] row in the *DeclSecurity* table.
   - This Method has a custom attribute called *SuppressUnmanagedCodeSecurityAttribute*.
10. If this Method owns one (or more) rows in the *DeclSecurity* table, then *Flags.HasSecurity* shall be 1. [ERROR]
11. If this Method has a custom attribute called *SuppressUnmanagedCodeSecurityAttribute*, then *Flags.HasSecurity* shall be 1. [ERROR]
12. A Method may have a custom attribute called *DynamicSecurityMethodAttribute*—but this has no effect whatsoever upon the value of its *Flags.HasSecurity*.
13. *Name* shall index a non-null string in the String heap. [ERROR]

ANNOTATION

Implementation-Specific (Microsoft): This string is limited to `MAX_CLASS_NAME`.

---

14. Interfaces cannot have instance constructors. So, if this Method is owned by an Interface, then its *Name* cannot be **.ctor**. [ERROR]
15. Interfaces can only own virtual methods (not static or instance methods). So, if this Method is owned by an Interface, *Flags.Static* shall be clear. [ERROR]
16. The *Name* string shall be a valid CLS identifier (unless *Flags.RTSpecialName* is set—for example, **.cctor** is legal). [CLS]
17. *Signature* shall index a valid method signature in the Blob heap. [ERROR]
18. If *Flags.CompilerControlled* = 1, then this row is ignored completely in duplicate checking.
19. If the owner of this method is the internally generated type called <Module>, it denotes that this method is defined at module scope. (In C++, the method is called "global" and can be referenced only within its compiland, from its point of declaration forward.) In this case:
    a. *Flags.Static* shall be 1. [ERROR]
    b. *Flags.Abstract* shall be 0. [ERROR]
    c. *Flags.Virtual* shall be 0. [ERROR]
    d. The *Flags.MemberAccessMask* subfield shall be one of `CompilerControlled`, `Public`, or `Private`. [ERROR]
    e. Module-scope methods are not allowed. [CLS]
20. It makes no sense for ValueTypes, which have no *identity*, to have synchronized methods (unless they are boxed). So, if the owner of this method is a ValueType, then the method cannot be synchronized; i.e., *ImplFlags.Synchronized* shall be 0. [ERROR]
21. There shall be no duplicate rows in the *MethodDef* table, based upon owner+*Name*+*Signature* (where owner is the owning row in the *TypeDef* table). (Note, however, that if *Flags.CompilerControlled* = 1, then this row is completely excluded from duplicate checking.) [ERROR]
22. There shall be no duplicate rows in the *MethodDef* table, based upon owner+*Name*+*Signature*, where *Name* fields are compared using CLS conflicting-identifier-rules; also, the Type defined in the signatures shall be different. So, for example, `"int i"` and `"float i"` would be considered CLS duplicates; also, the return type of the method is ignored. (Note, however, that if *Flags.CompilerControlled* = 1, then this row is completely excluded from duplicate checking, as explained above.) [CLS]
23. If `Final` or `NewSlot` is set in *Flags*, then *Flags.Virtual* shall also be set. [ERROR]
24. If *Flags.PInvokeImpl* is set, then *Flags.Virtual* shall be 0. [ERROR]
25. If *Flags.Abstract* != 1, then exactly one of the following shall also be true: [ERROR]
    - *RVA* != 0

5. Metadata File Format

- *Flags.PInvokeImpl* = 1
- *ImplFlags.Runtime* = 1

ANNOTATION

Implementation-Specific (Microsoft): There is an additional mutually exclusive possibility related to COM interop: the owner of this method is marked `Import` = 1.

---

26. If the method is `CompilerControlled`, then the RVA shall be non-zero or marked with `PinvokeImpl` = 1. [ERROR]
27. *Signature* shall have exactly one of the following managed calling conventions: [ERROR]
    a. `DEFAULT` (0x0)
    b. `VARARG` (x5)

ANNOTATION

Implementation-Specific (Microsoft): The above names are defined in the file **inc\CorHdr.h** as part of the Microsoft .NET SDK, using a prefix of `IMAGE_CEE_CS_CALLCONV_`.

---

28. *Signature* shall have the calling-convention `DEFAULT` (0x0). [CLS]
29. *Signature*: If and only if the method is not `Static`, then the calling convention byte in Signature has its `HASTHIS` (0x20) bit set. [ERROR]
30. *Signature*: If the method is `Static`, then the `HASTHIS` (0x20) bit in the calling convention byte shall be 0. [ERROR]
31. If `EXPLICITTHIS` (0x40) in the signature is set, then `HASTHIS` (0x20) shall also be set (note in passing: if `EXPLICITTHIS` is set, then the code is not verifiable). [ERROR]
32. The `EXPLICITTHIS` (0x40) bit can be set only in signatures for function pointers: signatures whose *MethodDefSig* is preceded by `FNPTR` (0x1B). [ERROR]
33. If *RVA* = 0, then either: [ERROR]
    - *Flags.Abstract* = 1, or
    - *ImplFlags.Runtime* = 1, or
    - *Flags.PinvokeImpl* = 1

ANNOTATION

Implementation-Specific (Microsoft): There are two additional mutually exclusive possibilities:

- *ImplFlags.InternalCall* = 1, or
- The owner row in the *TypeDef* table has *Flags.Import* = 1

34. If *RVA* != 0, then: [ERROR]
    a. *Flags.Abstract* shall be 0, and
    b. *ImplFlags.CodeTypeMask* shall be exactly one of the following values: `Native`, `CIL`, or `Runtime`, and
    c. *RVA* shall point into the CIL code stream in this file.

ANNOTATION

Implementation-Specific (Microsoft): There are two additional requirements:

- *ImplFlags.InternalCall* = 0, and
- The owner row in the *TypeDef* table has *Flags.tdImport* = 0

35. If *Flags.PinvokeImpl* = 1, then: [ERROR]
    - *RVA* = 0 *and* the method owns a row in the *ImplMap* table, **OR**

ANNOTATION

Implementation-Specific (Microsoft): For IJW ("It Just Works") thunks there is an additional possibility, where the method is actually a managed method in the current module:

RVA != 0 *and* the method does not own a row in the *ImplMap* table *and* the method signature includes a custom modifier that specifies the native calling convention.

36. If *Flags.RTSpecialName* = 1, then *Name* shall be one of: [ERROR]
    a. **.ctor** (object constructor method)
    b. **.cctor** (class constructor method)

ANNOTATION

Implementation-Specific (Microsoft): For COM interop, an additional class of method names is permitted:

VtblGap<SequenceNumber><CountOfSlots>

where <SequenceNumber> and <CountOfSlots> are decimal numbers.

37. Conversely, if *Name* is any of the above special names, then *Flags.RTSpecialName* shall be set. [ERROR]
38. If *Name* = **.ctor** (object constructor method), then:
    a. The return type in *Signature* shall be `ELEMENT_TYPE_VOID` (see Partition II, section 22.1.15). [ERROR]
    b. *Flags.Static* shall be 0. [ERROR]
    c. *Flags.Abstract* shall be 0. [ERROR]
    d. *Flags.Virtual* shall be 0. [ERROR]
    e. The "owner" type shall be a valid Class or ValueType (not <Module> and not an Interface) in the *TypeDef* table. [ERROR]
    f. There can be 0 or more **.ctors** for any given "owner."
39. If *Name* = **.cctor** (class constructor method), then:
    a. The return type in *Signature* shall be `ELEMENT_TYPE_VOID` (see Partition II, section 22.1.15). [ERROR]
    b. *Signature* shall have `DEFAULT` (0x0) for its calling convention. [ERROR]
    c. There shall be no parameters supplied in *Signature*. [ERROR]
    d. *Flags.Static* shall be set. [ERROR]
    e. *Flags.Virtual* shall be clear. [ERROR]
    f. *Flags.Abstract* shall be clear. [ERROR]
40. Among the set of methods owned by any given row in the *TypeDef* table, there can be zero or one method named **.cctor** (never two or more). [ERROR]

End informative text

21.25 MethodImpl: 0x19

MethodImpls let a compiler override the default inheritance rules provided by the CLI. Their original use was to allow a class "C" that inherited method "Foo" from interfaces I *and* J, to provide implementations for *both* methods (rather than have only *one* slot for "Foo" in its vtable). But *MethodImpls* can be used for other reasons too, limited only by the compiler writer's ingenuity within the constraints defined in the validation rules below.

In the example above, *Class* specifies "C", *MethodDeclaration* specifies I::Foo, and *MethodBody* specifies the method which provides the implementation for I::Foo (either a method body within "C", or a method body implemented by a superclass of "C").

The *MethodImpl* table has the following columns:

- *Class* (index into *TypeDef* table)
- *MethodBody* (index into *MethodDef* or *MemberRef* table; more precisely, a *MethodDefOrRef* coded index)
- *MethodDeclaration* (index into *MethodDef* or *MemberRef* table; more precisely, a *MethodDefOrRef* coded index)

ilasm uses the **.override** directive to specify the rows of the *MethodImpl* table (see Partition II, section 9.3.2).

This contains informative text only.

---

1. The *MethodImpl* table may contain zero or more rows.
2. *Class* shall index a valid row in the *TypeDef* table. [ERROR]
3. *MethodBody* shall index a valid row in the *Method* or *MethodRef* table. [ERROR]
4. The method indexed by *MethodDeclaration* shall have *Flags.Virtual* set. [ERROR]
5. The owner Type of the method indexed by *MethodDeclaration* shall not have *Flags.Sealed* = 0. [ERROR]
6. The method indexed by *MethodBody* shall be a member of *Class* or some superclass of *Class* (*MethodImpls* do not allow compilers to "hook" arbitrary method bodies). [ERROR]
7. The method indexed by *MethodBody* shall be virtual. [ERROR]
8. The method indexed by *MethodBody* shall have its *Method.RVA* != 0 (cannot be an unmanaged method reached via PInvoke, for example). [ERROR]

9. *MethodDeclaration* shall index a method in the ancestor chain of *Class* (reached via its *Extends* chain) or in the interface tree of *Class* (reached via its *InterfaceImpl* entries). [ERROR]
10. The method indexed by *MethodDeclaration* shall not be final (its *Flags.Final* shall be 0). [ERROR]
11. The method indexed by *MethodDeclaration* shall be accessible to *Class*. [ERROR]
12. The method signature defined by *MethodBody* shall match those defined by *MethodDeclaration*. [ERROR]
13. There shall be no duplicate rows, based upon *Class+MethodDeclaration*. [ERROR]

End informative text

21.26 MethodSemantics: 0x18

The *MethodSemantics* table has the following columns:

- *Semantics* (a 2-byte bitmask of type *MethodSemanticsAttributes*; see Partition II, section 22.1.11)
- *Method* (index into the *MethodDef* table)
- *Association* (index into the *Event* or *Property* table; more precisely, a *HasSemantics* coded index)

The rows of the *MethodSemantics* table are filled by **.property** (see Partition II, section 16) and **.event** (see Partition II, section 17) directives. See Partition II, section 21.13 for more information.

This contains informative text only.

---

1. The *MethodSemantics* table may contain zero or more rows.
2. *Semantics* may have only those values set that are specified. [ERROR]
3. *Method* shall index a valid row in the *MethodDef* table, and that row shall be for a method defined on the same class as the Property or Event this row describes. [ERROR]
4. All methods for a given Property or Event shall have the same accessibility (i.e., the *MemberAccessMask* subfield of their *Flags* row) and cannot be `CompilerControlled`. [CLS]

5. *Semantics*: constrained as follows:
   - If this row is for a Property, then exactly one of `Setter`, `Getter`, or `Other` shall be set. [ERROR]
   - If this row is for an Event, then exactly one of `AddOn`, `RemoveOn`, `Fire`, or `Other` shall be set. [ERROR]
6. If this row is for an Event, and its *Semantics* is `Addon` or `RemoveOn`, then the row in the *MethodDef* table indexed by *Method* shall take a Delegate as a parameter, and return void. [ERROR]
7. If this row is for an Event, and its *Semantics* is `Fire`, then the row indexed in the *MethodDef* table by *Method* may return any type.

ANNOTATION

Implementation-Specific (Microsoft): The Microsoft implementation limits the return type of the `Fire method to void.`

---

8. For each property, there shall be a setter, or a getter, or both. [CLS]
9. Any getter method for a property whose *Name* is **xxx** shall be called **get_xxx**. [CLS]
10. Any setter method for a property whose *Name* is **xxx** shall be called **set_xxx**. [CLS]
11. If a property provides both getter and setter methods, then these methods shall have the same value in the *Flags.MemberAccessMask* subfield. [CLS]
12. If a property provides both getter and setter methods, then these methods shall have the same value for their *Method.Flags.Virtual*. [CLS]
13. Any getter and setter methods shall have *Method.Flags.SpecialName* = 1. [CLS]
14. Any getter method shall have a return type which matches the signature indexed by the *Property.Type* field. [CLS]
15. The last parameter for any setter method shall have a type which matches the signature indexed by the *Property.Type* field. [CLS]
16. Any setter method shall have return type `ELEMENT_TYPE_VOID` (see Partition II, section 22.1.15) in *Method.Signature*. [CLS]
17. If the property is indexed, the indices for getter and setter shall agree in number and type. [CLS]
18. Any *AddOn* method for an event whose *Name* is **xxx** shall have the signature: **void add_xxx (**<DelegateType> **handler)** [CLS]

19. Any *RemoveOn* method for an event whose *Name* is **xxx** shall have the signature: **void remove_xxx(<DelegateType> handler)**. [CLS]
20. Any *Fire* method for an event whose *Name* is **xxx** shall have the signature: **void raise_xxx(Event e)**. [CLS]

End informative text

21.27 Module: 0x00

The *Module* table has the following columns:

- *Generation* (2-byte value, reserved, shall be zero)
- *Name* (index into String heap)
- *Mvid* (index into Guid heap; simply a GUID used to distinguish between two versions of the same module)
- *EncId* (index into Guid heap, reserved, shall be zero)
- *EncBaseId* (index into Guid heap, reserved, shall be zero)

The *Mvid* column shall index a unique GUID in the Guid heap (see Partition II, section 23.2.5) that identifies this instance of the module. The *Mvid* may be ignored on read by conforming implementations of the CLI. The *Mvid* should be newly generated for every module, using the algorithm specified in ISO/IEC 11578:1996 (Annex A) or another compatible algorithm.

NOTE

The term "GUID" stands for "Globally Unique IDentifier," a 16-byte-long number typically displayed using its hexadecimal encoding. A GUID may be generated by several well-known algorithms, including those used for UUIDs (Universally Unique IDentifiers) in RPC and CORBA, as well as CLSIDs, GUIDs, and IIDs in COM.

RATIONALE

While the VES itself makes no use of the Mvid, other tools (such as debuggers, which are outside the scope of this standard) rely on the fact that the Mvid almost always differs from one module to another.

The *Generation*, *EncId*, and *EncBaseId* columns can be written as zero, and can be ignored by conforming implementations of the CLI. The rows in the *Module* table result from **.module** directives in the Assembly (see Partition II, section 6.4).

This contains informative text only.

1. The *Module* table shall contain one, and only one, row. [ERROR]
2. *Name* shall index a non-null string. This string should match exactly any corresponding *ModuleRef.Name* string that resolves to this module. [ERROR]

ANNOTATION

Implementation-Specific (Microsoft): *Name* is limited to `MAX_PATH_NAME`. The format of *Name* is <file name>.<file extension> with no path or drive letter; on POSIX-compliant systems *Name* contains no colon, no forward-slash, no backslash.

3. *Mvid* shall index a non-null GUID in the Guid heap. [ERROR]

End informative text

21.28 ModuleRef: 0x1A

The *ModuleRef* table has the following column:

- *Name* (index into String heap)

The rows in the *ModuleRef* table result from **.module extern** directives in the Assembly (see Partition II, section 6.5).

This contains informative text only.

1. *Name* shall index a non-null string in the String heap. This string shall enable the CLI to locate the target module (typically, it might name the file used to hold the module). [ERROR]

ANNOTATION

Implementation-Specific (Microsoft): *Name* is limited to `MAX_PATH_NAME`. The format of *Name* is <filename>.<extension> (e.g., "Foo.DLL"—no drive letter, no path); on POSIX-compliant systems *Name* contains no colon, no forward-slash, and no backslash.

---

2. There should be no duplicate rows. [WARNING]
3. *Name* should match an entry in the *Name* column of the *File* table. Moreover, that entry shall enable the CLI to locate the target module (typically it might name the file used to hold the module). [ERROR]

End informative text

21.29 NestedClass: 0x29

The *NestedClass* table has the following columns:

- *NestedClass* (index into the *TypeDef* table)
- *EnclosingClass* (index into the *TypeDef* table)

The *NestedClass* table records which Type definitions are nested within which other Type definitions. In a typical high-level language, including ilasm, the nested class is defined as lexically "inside" the text of its enclosing Type.

This contains informative text only.

The *NestedClass* table records which Type definitions are nested within which other Type definitions. In a typical high-level language, the nested class is defined as lexically "inside" the text of its enclosing Type.

1. The *NestedClass* table may contain zero or more rows.
2. *NestedClass* shall index a valid row in the *TypeDef* table. [ERROR]
3. *EnclosingClass* shall index a valid row in the *TypeDef* table (note, particularly, that it is not allowed to index the *TypeRef* table). [ERROR]
4. There should be no duplicate rows (i.e., same values for *NestedClass* and *EnclosingClass*). [WARNING]

5. A given Type can only be nested by *one* encloser. So, there cannot be two rows with the same value for *NestedClass*, but a different value for *EnclosingClass*. [ERROR]
6. A given Type can "own" several different nested Types, so it is perfectly legal to have two or more rows with the same value for *EnclosingClass*, but different values for *NestedClass*.

End informative text

21.30 Param: 0x08

The *Param* table has the following columns:

- *Flags* (a 2-byte bitmask of type *ParamAttributes*; see Partition II, section 22.1.12)
- *Sequence* (a 2-byte constant)
- *Name* (index into String heap)

Conceptually, every row in the *Param* table is owned by one, and only one, row in the *MethodDef* table.

The rows in the *Param* table result from the parameters in a method declaration (see Partition II, section 14.4), or from a **.param** attribute attached to a method (see Partition II, section 14.4.1).

This contains informative text only.

---

1. The *Param* table may contain zero or more rows.
2. Each row shall have one, and only one, owner row in the *MethodDef* table. [ERROR]
3. *Flags* may have only those values set that are specified (all combinations valid). [ERROR]
4. *Sequence* shall have a value >= 0 and <= number of parameters in owner method. A *Sequence* value of 0 refers to the owner method's return type; its parameters are then numbered from 1 onward. [ERROR]
5. Successive rows of the *Param* table that are owned by the same method shall be ordered by increasing *Sequence* value—although gaps in the sequence are allowed. [WARNING]
6. If *Flags.HasDefault* = 1, then this row shall own exactly one row in the *Constant* table. [ERROR]

7. If *Flags.HasDefault* = 0, then there shall be no rows in the *Constant* table owned by this row. [ERROR]
8. Parameters cannot be given default values, so *Flags.HasDefault* shall be 0. [CLS]
9. If *Flags.FieldMarshal* = 1, then this row shall own exactly one row in the *FieldMarshal* table. [ERROR]
10. *Name* may be null or non-null.
11. If *Name* is non-null, then it shall index a non-null string in the String heap. [WARNING]

ANNOTATION

Implementation-Specific (Microsoft): This string is limited to `MAX_CLASS_NAME`.

End informative text

21.31 Property: 0x17

Properties within metadata are best viewed as a means to gather together collections of methods defined on a class, give them a name, and not much else. The methods are typically *get_* and *set_* methods, already defined on the class, and inserted like any other methods into the *MethodDef* table. The association is held together by three separate tables:

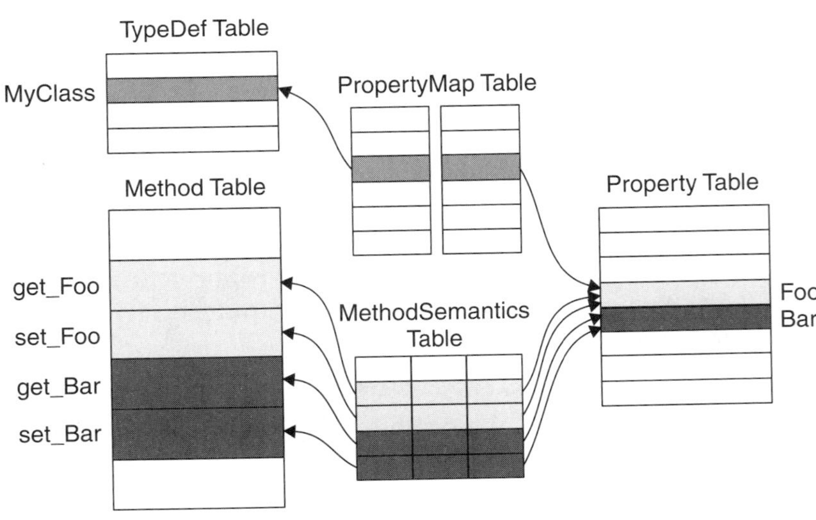

Row 3 of the *PropertyMap* table indexes row 2 of the *TypeDef* table on the left (*MyClass*), while indexing row 4 of the *Property* table on the right—the row for a property called *Foo*. This setup establishes that *MyClass* has a property called *Foo*. But what methods in the *MethodDef* table are gathered together as "belonging" to property *Foo*? That association is contained in the *MethodSemantics* table—its row 2 indexes property *Foo* to the right, and row 2 in the *MethodDef* table to the left (a method called *get_Foo*). Also, row 3 of the *MethodSemantics* table indexes *Foo* to the right, and row 3 in the *Method* table to the left (a method called *set_Foo*). As the shading suggests, *MyClass* has another property, called *Bar*, with two methods, *get_Bar* and *set_Bar*.

Property tables do a little more than group together existing rows from other tables. The *Property* table has columns for *Flags*, *Name* (e.g., *Foo* and *Bar* in the example here) and *Type*. In addition, the *MethodSemantics* table has a column to record whether the method it points at is a *set_*, a *get_*, or *other*.

NOTE

The CLS (see Partition I [section 7]) refers to instance, virtual, and static properties. The signature of a property (from the *Type* column) can be used to distinguish a static property, since instance and virtual properties will have the `HASTHIS` bit set in the signature (see Partition II, section 22.2.1), while a static property will not. The distinction between an instance and a virtual property depends on the signature of the getter and setter methods, which the CLS requires to be either both virtual or both instance.

The *Property* (0x17) table has the following columns:

- *Flags* (a 2-byte bitmask of type *PropertyAttributes*; see Partition II, section 22.1.13)
- *Name* (index into String heap)
- *Type* (index into Blob heap) (The name of this column is misleading. It does not index a *TypeDef* or *TypeRef* table—instead it indexes the signature in the Blob heap of the Property.)

This contains informative text only.

1. The *Property* table may contain zero or more rows.
2. Each row shall have one, and only one, owner row in the *PropertyMap* table (as described above). [ERROR]

3. *PropFlags* may have only those values set that are specified (all combinations valid). [ERROR]
4. *Name* shall index a non-null string in the String heap. [ERROR]

ANNOTATION

Implementation-Specific (Microsoft): This string is limited to `MAX_CLASS_NAME`.

---

5. The *Name* string shall be a valid CLS identifier. [CLS]
6. *Type* shall index a non-null signature in the Blob heap. [ERROR]
7. The signature indexed by *Type* shall be a valid signature for a property (i.e., low nibble of leading byte is 0x8). Apart from this leading byte, the signature is the same as the property's *get_* method. [ERROR]
8. Within the rows owned by a given row in the *TypeDef* table, there shall be no duplicates based upon *Name+Type*. [ERROR]
9. There shall be no duplicate rows based upon *Name*, where *Name* fields are compared using CLS conflicting-identifier-rules (in particular, properties cannot be overloaded by their *Type*—a class cannot have two properties, `"int Foo"` and `"String Foo"`, for example). [CLS]

End informative text

21.32 PropertyMap: 0x15

The *PropertyMap* table has the following columns:

- *Parent* (index into the *TypeDef* table)
- *PropertyList* (index into the *Property* table). It marks the first of a contiguous run of Properties owned by *Parent*. The run continues to the smaller of:
    - The last row of the *Property* table
    - The next run of Properties, found by inspecting the *PropertyList* of the next row in this *PropertyMap* table

The *PropertyMap* and *Property* tables result from putting the **.property** directive on a class (see Partition II, section 16).

This contains informative text only.

1. The *PropertyMap* table may contain zero or more rows.
2. There shall be no duplicate rows, based upon *Parent* (a given class has only one "pointer" to the start of its property list). [ERROR]
3. There shall be no duplicate rows, based upon *PropertyList* (different classes cannot share rows in the *Property* table). [ERROR]

End informative text

21.33 StandAloneSig: 0x11

Signatures are stored in the metadata Blob heap. In most cases, they are indexed by a column in some table—*Field.Signature*, *Method.Signature*, *MemberRef.Signature*, etc. However, there are two cases that require a metadata token for a signature that is not indexed by any metadata table. The *StandAloneSig* table fulfills this need. It has just one column, that points to a Signature in the Blob heap.

The signature shall describe either:

- A method – code generators create a row in the *StandAloneSig* table for each occurrence of a **calli** CIL instruction. That row indexes the call-site signature for the function pointer operand of the **calli** instruction.
- Local variables – code generators create one row in the *StandAloneSig* table for each method, to describe all of its local variables. The **.locals** directive in ilasm generates a row in the *StandAloneSig* table.

The *StandAloneSig* table has the following column:

- *Signature* (index into the Blob heap)

  Example (informative):

```
// On encountering the calli instruction, ilasm generates a signature
// in the blob heap (DEFAULT, ParamCount = 1, RetType = int32, Param1 = int32),
// indexed by the StandAloneSig table:

.assembly Test {}
```

```
.method static int32 AddTen(int32)
{ ldarg.0
  ldc.i4  10
  add
  ret
}

.class Test
{ .method static void main()
  { .entrypoint
    ldc.i4.1
    ldftn int32 AddTen(int32)
    calli int32(int32)
    pop
    ret
  }
}
```


This contains informative text only.

1. The *StandAloneSig* table may contain zero or more rows.
2. *Signature* shall index a valid signature in the Blob heap. [ERROR]
3. The signature "blob" indexed by *Signature* shall be a valid `METHOD` or `LOCALS` signature. [ERROR]
4. Duplicate rows are allowed.

End informative text

21.34 TypeDef: 0x02

The *TypeDef* table has the following columns:

- *Flags* (a 4-byte bitmask of type *TypeAttributes*; see Partition II, section 22.1.14)

- *Name* (index into String heap)
- *Namespace* (index into String heap)
- *Extends* (index into *TypeDef*, *TypeRef*, or *TypeSpec* table; more precisely, a *TypeDefOrRef* coded index)
- *FieldList* (index into *Field* table; it marks the first of a continguous run of Fields owned by this Type). The run continues to the smaller of:
  - The last row of the *Field* table
  - The next run of Fields, found by inspecting the *FieldList* of the next row in this *TypeDef* table
- *MethodList* (index into the *MethodDef* table; it marks the first of a continguous run of Methods owned by this Type). The run continues to the smaller of:
  - The last row of the *MethodDef* table
  - The next run of Methods, found by inspecting the *MethodList* of the next row in this *TypeDef* table

Note that any *type* shall be one, and only one, of

- Class (*Flags.Interface* = 0, and derives ultimately from `System.Object`)
- Interface (*Flags.Interface* = 1)
- Value type, derived ultimately from `System.ValueType`

For any given type, there are two separate, and quite distinct "inheritance" chains of pointers to other types (the pointers are actually implemented as indices into metadata tables). The two chains are:

- Extension chain – defined via the *Extends* column of the *TypeDef* table. Typically, a *derived* Class *extends* a *base* Class (always one, and only one, base Class).
- Interface chains – defined via the *InterfaceImpl* table. Typically, a Class implements zero, one, or more Interfaces.

These two chains (extension and interface) are always kept separate in metadata. The *Extends* chain represents one-to-one relations—that is, one Class *extends* (or "derives from") exactly one other Class (called its immediate base Class). The *Interface* chains may represent one-to-many relations—that is, one Class might well implement two or more Interfaces.

Example (informative, written in C#):

```
interface IA {void m1(int i);        }

interface IB {void m2(int i, int j); }

class C : IA, IB {
```

```
  int f1, f2;
  public void m1(int i)         {f1 = i;         }
  public void m2(int i, int j) {f1 = i; f2 = j;}
}
// In metadata, Interface IA extends nothing; Interface IB
// extends nothing; class C extends System.Object and implements
// Interfaces IA and IB.
```

An Interface can also "inherit" from one or more other Interfaces—metadata stores those links via the *InterfaceImpl* table (the nomenclature is a little inappropriate here—there is no "implementation" involved—perhaps a clearer name might have been *Interface* table, or *InterfaceInherit* table).

Example (informative, written in C#):

```
interface IA           {void m1(int i);         }
interface IB           {void m2(int i, int j); }
interface IC : IA, IB {void m3(int i, int j, int k);}
class C : IC {
  int f1, f2, f3;
  public void m1(int i)                {f1 = i;                 }
  public void m2(int i, int j)         {f1 = i; f2 = j;         }
  public void m3(int i, int j, int k) {f1 = i; f2 = j; f3 = k;}
}
// In metadata, Interface IA extends nothing; Interface IB extends
// nothing; Interface IC "inherits" Interfaces IA and IB (defined via
// the InterfaceImpl table); Class C extends System.Object and
// implements Interface IC (see InterfaceImpl table)
```

There are also a few specialized types. One is the user-defined Enum—which shall derive directly from `System.Enum` (via the *Extends* field).

Another slightly specialized type is a *nested* type which is declared in ilasm as lexically nested within an enclosing type declaration. Whether a type is nested can be determined by the value of its *Flags.Visibility* sub-field—it shall be one of the set {*NestedPublic, NestedPrivate, NestedFamily, NestedAssembly, NestedFamANDAssem, NestedFamORAssem*}.

The roots of the inheritance hierarchies look like this:

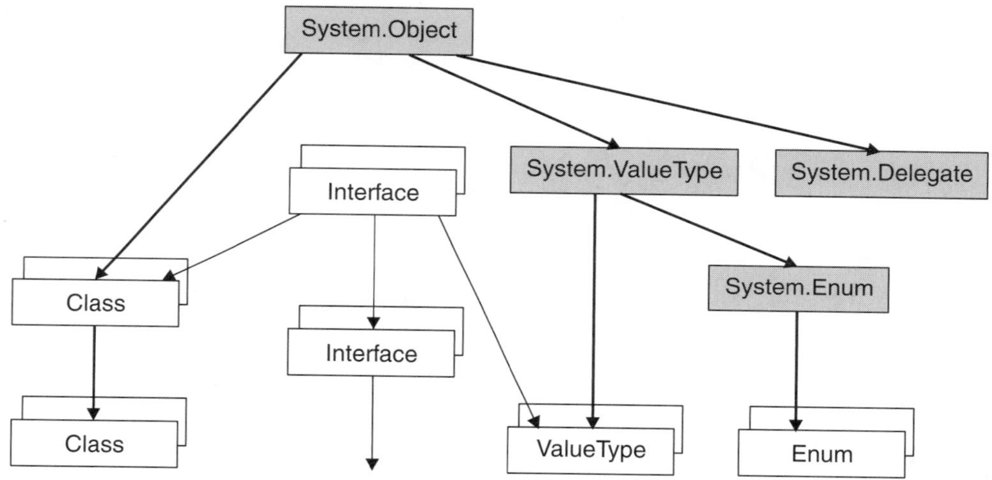

There is one system-defined root—`System.Object`. All Classes and ValueTypes shall derive, ultimately, from `System.Object`; Classes can derive from other Classes (through a single, non-looping chain) to any depth required. This *Extends* inheritance chain is shown with heavy arrows.

(See below for details of the `System.Delegate` Class).

Interfaces do not inherit from one another; however, they specify zero or more other interfaces which shall be implemented. The *Interface* requirement chain is shown as light, dashed arrows. This includes links between Interfaces and Classes/ValueTypes—where the latter are said to *implement* that interface or interfaces.

Regular ValueTypes (i.e., excluding Enums—see later) are defined as deriving directly from `System.ValueType`. Regular ValueTypes cannot be derived to a depth of more than one. (Another way to state this is that user-defined ValueTypes shall be *sealed*.) User-defined Enums shall derive directly from `System.Enum`. Enums cannot be derived to a depth of more than one below `System.Enum`. (Another way to state this is that user-defined Enums shall be *sealed*.) `System.Enum` derives directly from `System.ValueType`.

The hierarchy below `System.Delegate` is as follows:

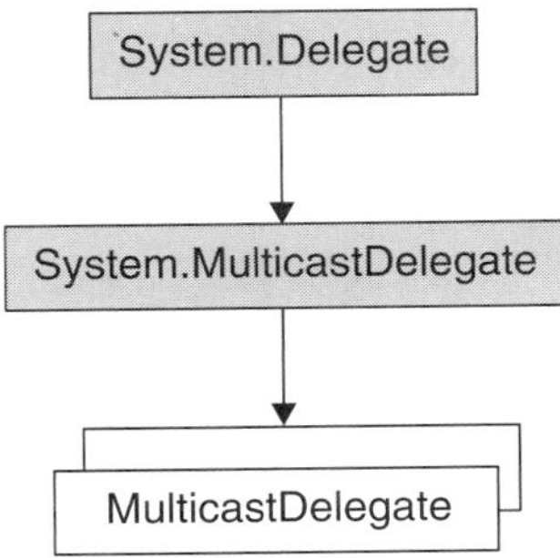

User-defined delegates derive directly from `System.MulticastDelegate`. Delegates cannot be derived to a depth of more than one.

For the directives to declare types, see Partition II, section 9.

This contains informative text only.

---

1. The *TypeDef* table may contain one or more rows. There is always one row (row zero) that represents the pseudo class that acts as parent for functions and variables defined at module scope.
2. *Flags*:
   a. May have only those values set that are specified. [ERROR]
   b. Can set 0 or 1 of `SequentialLayout` and `ExplicitLayout` (if none set, then defaults to `AutoLayout`) [ERROR]
   c. Can set 0 or 1 of `UnicodeClass` and `AutoClass` (if none set, then defaults to `AnsiClass`) [ERROR]

ANNOTATION

Implementation-Specific (Microsoft): If `RTSpecialName` is set, then this Type is regarded as deleted (used in Edit&Continue and incremental compilation scenarios). Perform no checks on this Type or any of its members (the information is not physically deleted; it is just "flagged" as logically deleted). Note: this situation can only be seen on in-memory metadata—it is not persisted to disk, and therefore it is irrelevant to checks done by an offline tool.

If `Import` is set (denotes a Type defined via the tlbimp tool), then all the methods owned by this Type shall have their *Method.RVA* = 0. [ERROR]

---

d. If *Flags.HasSecurity* = 1, then at least one of the following conditions shall be true: [ERROR]

- This Type owns at least one row in the *DeclSecurity* table.
- This Type has a custom attribute called `SuppressUnmanagedCodeSecurity-Attribute`.

e. If this Type owns one (or more) rows in the *DeclSecurity* table, then *Flags.HasSecurity* shall be 1. [ERROR]

f. If this Type has a custom attribute called `SuppressUnmanagedCodeSecu-rityAttribute`, then *Flags.HasSecurity* shall be 1. [ERROR]

g. Note that it is legal for an Interface to have `HasSecurity` set. However, the security system ignores any permission requests attached to that Interface.

3. *Name* shall index a non-null string in the String heap. [ERROR]

ANNOTATION

Implementation-Specific (Microsoft): This string is limited to `MAX_CLASS_NAME`.

---

4. The *Name* string shall be a valid CLS identifier. [CLS]
5. *Namespace* may be null or non-null.
6. If non-null, then *Namespace* shall index a non-null string in the String heap. [ERROR]

ANNOTATION

Implementation-Specific (Microsoft): This string is limited to `MAX_CLASS_NAME`. Also, the concatenated *TypeNamespace*+"."+*TypeName* shall be less than `MAX_CLASS_NAME`.

---

7. If non-null, *Namespace*'s string shall be a valid CLS identifier. [CLS]
8. Every Class (with the sole exception of `System.Object`) shall extend one, and only one, other Class—so *Extends* for a Class shall be non-null. [ERROR]
9. `System.Object` shall have an *Extends* value of null. [ERROR]

10. `System.ValueType` shall have an *Extends* value of `System.Object`. [ERROR]
11. With the sole exception of `System.Object`, for any Class, *Extends* shall index a valid row in the *TypeDef* or *TypeRef* table, where valid means 1 <= row <= rowcount. In addition, that row itself shall be a Class (not an Interface or ValueType). In addition, that base Class shall not be sealed (its *Flags.Sealed* shall be 0). [ERROR]

ANNOTATION

Implementation-Specific (Microsoft): *Extends* may index a row in the *TypeSpec* table—this is an extension for prototyping parametric-polymorphism. [WARNING]

12. A Class cannot extend itself, or any of its children (i.e., its derived Classes), since this would introduce loops in the hierarchy tree. [ERROR]
13. An Interface never *extends* another Type—so *Extends* shall be null (Interfaces *do* implement other Interfaces, but recall that this relationship is captured via the *InterfaceImpl* table, rather than the *Extends* column). [ERROR]
14. *FieldList* can be null or non-null.
15. A Class or Interface may "own" zero or more fields.
16. A ValueType shall have a non-zero size—either by defining at least one field, or by providing a non-zero *ClassSize*. [ERROR]
17. If *FieldList* is non-null, it shall index a valid row in the *Field* table, where valid means 1 <= row <= rowcount+1. [ERROR]
18. *MethodList* can be null or non-null.
19. A Type may "own" zero or more methods.
20. The runtime size of a ValueType shall not exceed 1 MByte (0x100000 bytes). [ERROR]

ANNOTATION

Implementation-Specific (Microsoft): The current implementation actually allows 0x3F0000 bytes, but this size may be reduced in future.

21. If *MethodList* is non-null, it shall index a valid row in the *MethodDef* table, where valid means 1 <= row <= rowcount+1. [ERROR]
22. A Class which has one or more abstract methods cannot be instantiated, and shall have *Flags.Abstract* = 1. Note that the methods *owned* by the class include all of those inherited from its base class and interfaces it implements, plus those defined via its *Method-*

List. (The CLI shall analyze class definitions at runtime; if it finds a class to have one or more abstract methods, but has *Flags.Abstract* = 0, it will throw an exception.) [ERROR]

23. An Interface shall have *Flags.Abstract* = 1. [ERROR]
24. It is legal for an abstract Type to have a constructor method (i.e., a method named **.ctor**).
25. Any non-abstract Type (i.e., *Flags.Abstract* = 0) shall provide an implementation (body) for every method its contract requires. Its methods may be inherited from its base class, from the interfaces it implements, or defined by itself. The implementations may be inherited from its base class or defined by itself. [ERROR]
26. An Interface (*Flags.Interface* == 1) can own static fields (*Field.Static* == 1) but cannot own instance fields (*Field.Static* == 0). [ERROR]
27. An Interface cannot be sealed (if *Flags.Interface* == 1, then *Flags.Sealed* shall be 0). [ERROR]
28. All of the methods owned by an Interface (*Flags.Interface* == 1) shall be abstract (*Flags.Abstract* == 1). [ERROR]
29. There shall be no duplicate rows in the *TypeDef* table, based on *Namespace+Name* (unless this is a nested type—see below). [ERROR]
30. If this is a nested type, there shall be no duplicate row in the *TypeDef* table, based upon *Namespace+Name+OwnerRowInNestedClassTable*. [ERROR]
31. There shall be no duplicate rows, where *Namespace+Name* fields are compared using CLS conflicting-identifier-rules (unless this is a nested type—see below). [CLS]
32. If this is a nested type, there shall be no duplicate rows, based upon *Namespace+Name+OwnerRowInNestedClassTable* and where *Namespace+Name* fields are compared using CLS conflicting-identifier-rules. [CLS]
33. If *Extends* = System.Enum (i.e., type is a user-defined Enum), then:
    a. [It] shall be sealed (`Sealed` = 1). [ERROR]
    b. [It] shall not have any methods of its own (*MethodList* chain shall be zero length). [ERROR]
    c. [It] shall not implement any interfaces (no entries in *InterfaceImpl* table for this type). [ERROR]
    d. [It] shall not have any properties. [ERROR]
    e. [It] shall not have any events. [ERROR]
    f. Any static fields shall be literal (have *Flags.Literal* = 1). [ERROR]
    g. [It] shall have at least one static, literal field. If more than one, they shall all be of the same type. Any such static literal fields shall be of the type of the Enum. [CLS]
    h. [There] shall be at least one instance field, of integral type. [ERROR]
    i. [There] shall be exactly one instance field. [CLS]

j. The *Name* string of the instance field shall be "value__"; it shall be marked `RTSpecialName`; its type shall be one of (see Partition II, section 22.1.15): [CLS]

- `ELEMENT_TYPE_U1`
- `ELEMENT_TYPE_I2`
- `ELEMENT_TYPE_I4`
- `ELEMENT_TYPE_I8`

k. [There] shall be no other members (i.e., apart from any static literals, and the one instance field called "value__"). [CLS]

34. A Nested type (defined above) shall own exactly one row in the *NestedClass* table—where "owns" means a row in that *NestedClass* table whose *NestedClass* column holds the *TypeDef* token for this type definition. [ERROR]

35. A ValueType shall be sealed. [ERROR]

End informative text

21.35 TypeRef: 0x01

The *TypeRef* table has the following columns:

- *ResolutionScope* (index into *Module*, *ModuleRef*, *AssemblyRef*, or *TypeRef* tables, or null; more precisely, a *ResolutionScope* coded index)
- *Name* (index into String heap)
- *Namespace* (index into String heap)

This contains informative text only.

---

1. *ResolutionScope* shall be exactly one of:

   a. null – in this case, there shall be a row in the *ExportedType* table for this Type—its *Implementation* field shall contain a *File* token or an *AssemblyRef* token that says where the type is defined. [ERROR]

   b. A *TypeRef* token, if this is a nested type (which can be determined by, for example, inspecting the *Flags* column in its *TypeDef* table—the accessibility subfield is one of the `tdNestedXXX` set). [ERROR]

   c. A *ModuleRef* token, if the target type is defined in another module within the same Assembly as this one. [ERROR]

   d. A *Module* token, if the target type is defined in the current module—this should not occur in a CLI ("compressed metadata") module. [WARNING]

   e. An *AssemblyRef* token, if the target type is defined in a different Assembly from the current module. [ERROR]

2. *Name* shall index a non-null string in the String heap. [ERROR]

ANNOTATION

Implementation-Specific (Microsoft): This string is limited to `MAX_CLASS_NAME`.

---

3. *Namespace* may be null or non-null.
4. If non-null, *Namespace* shall index a non-null string in the String heap. [ERROR]

ANNOTATION

Implementation-Specific (Microsoft): This string is limited to `MAX_CLASS_NAME`. Also, the concatenated *TypeNamespace*+"."+*TypeName* shall be less than `MAX_CLASS_NAME`.

---

5. The *Name* string shall be a valid CLS identifier. [CLS]
6. There shall be no duplicate rows, where a duplicate has the same *ResolutionScope*, *Name*, and *Namespace*. [ERROR]
7. There shall be no duplicate rows, where *Name* and *Namespace* fields are compared using CLS conflicting-identifier-rules. [CLS]

End informative text

21.36 TypeSpec: 0x1B

The *TypeSpec* table has just one column, which indexes the specification of a Type, stored in the Blob heap. This provides a metadata token for that Type (rather than simply an index into the Blob heap)—this is required, typically, for array operations—creating, or calling methods on the array class.

The *TypeSpec* table has the following column:

- *Signature* (index into the Blob heap, where the blob is formatted as specified in Partition II, section 22.2.14)

Note that *TypeSpec* tokens can be used with any of the CIL instructions that take a *TypeDef* or *TypeRef* token—specifically:

castclass, cpobj, initobj, isinst, ldelema, ldobj, mkrefany, newarr, refanyval, sizeof, stobj, box, unbox

This contains informative text only.

1. The *TypeSpec* table may contain zero or more rows.
2. *Signature* shall index a validType specification in the Blob heap. [ERROR]
3. There shall be no duplicate rows, based upon *Signature*. [ERROR]

End informative text

22 Metadata Logical Format: Other Structures

22.1 Bitmasks and Flags

This section explains the various flags and bitmasks used in the various metadata tables.

22.1.1 *Values for AssemblyHashAlgorithm*

Algorithm	Value
`None`	0x0000
`Reserved (MD5)`	0x8003
`SHA1`	0x8004

ANNOTATION: For more information on the SHA1 hash algorithm, see Partition II, section 6.2.1.1.

22.1.2 *Values for AssemblyFlags*

Flag	Value	Description
`PublicKey`	`0x0001`	The assembly reference holds the full (unhashed) public key.
`SideBySideCompatible`	`0x0000`	The assembly is side by side compatible.
`<reserved>`	`0x0030`	Reserved: both bits shall be zero.
`Retargetable`	`0x0100`	The implementation of this assembly used at runtime is not expected to match the version seen at compile time. (See the text following this table.)
`EnableJITcompileTracking`	`0x8000`	Reserved (a conforming implementation of the CLI may ignore this setting on read; some implementations might use this bit to indicate that a CIL-to-native-code compiler should generate CIL-to-native-code map).
`DisableJITcompileOptimizer`	`0x4000`	Reserved (a conforming implementation of the CLI may ignore this setting on read; some implementations might use this bit to indicate that a CIL-to-native-code compiler should not generate optimized code).

In portable programs, the `Retargetable` (0x100) bit shall be set on all references to assemblies specified in this standard.

ANNOTATION: For more information on the originator's public key, see Partition II, section 6.2.1.3.

22.1.3 *Values for Culture*

`ar-SA`	`ar-IQ`	`ar-EG`	`ar-LY`
`ar-DZ`	`ar-MA`	`ar-TN`	`ar-OM`
`ar-YE`	`ar-SY`	`ar-JO`	`ar-LB`

ar-KW	ar-AE	ar-BH	ar-QA
bg-BG	ca-ES	zh-TW	zh-CN
zh-HK	zh-SG	zh-MO	cs-CZ
da-DK	de-DE	de-CH	de-AT
de-LU	de-LI	el-GR	en-US
en-GB	en-AU	en-CA	en-NZ
en-IE	en-ZA	en-JM	en-CB
en-BZ	en-TT	en-ZW	en-PH
es-ES-Ts	es-MX	es-ES-Is	es-GT
es-CR	es-PA	es-DO	es-VE
es-CO	es-PE	es-AR	es-EC
es-CL	es-UY	es-PY	es-BO
es-SV	es-HN	es-NI	es-PR
Fi-FI	fr-FR	fr-BE	fr-CA
Fr-CH	fr-LU	fr-MC	he-IL
hu-HU	is-IS	it-IT	it-CH
Ja-JP	ko-KR	nl-NL	nl-BE
nb-NO	nn-NO	pl-PL	pt-BR
pt-PT	ro-RO	ru-RU	hr-HR
Lt-sr-SP	Cy-sr-SP	sk-SK	sq-AL
sv-SE	sv-FI	th-TH	tr-TR
ur-PK	id-ID	uk-UA	be-BY
sl-SI	et-EE	lv-LV	lt-LT
fa-IR	vi-VN	hy-AM	Lt-az-AZ

Cy-az-AZ	eu-ES	mk-MK	af-ZA
ka-GE	fo-FO	hi-IN	ms-MY
ms-BN	kk-KZ	ky-KZ	sw-KE
Lt-uz-UZ	Cy-uz-UZ	tt-TA	pa-IN
gu-IN	ta-IN	te-IN	kn-IN
mr-IN	sa-IN	mn-MN	gl-ES
kok-IN	syr-SY	div-MV	

Note on RFC 1766 Locale names: a typical string would be "en-US". The first part ("en" in the example) uses ISO 639 characters ("Latin-alphabet characters in lowercase. No diacritical marks of modified characters are used"). The second part ("US" in the example) uses ISO 3166 characters (similar to ISO 639, but uppercase). In other words, the familiar ASCII characters—a–z and A–Z, respectively. However, while RFC 1766 recommends the first part is lowercase, the second part uppercase, it allows mixed case. Therefore, the validation rule checks only that *Culture* is one of the strings in the list above—but the check is totally case-blind—where case-blind is the familiar fold on values less than U+0080.

ANNOTATION: For more information on the culture, see Partition II, section 6.2.1.2.

22.1.4 *Flags for Events (EventAttributes)*

Flag	Value	Description
`SpecialName`	`0x0200`	Event is special.
`RTSpecialName`	`0x0400`	CLI provides "special" behavior, depending upon the name of the event.

ANNOTATION: The *SpecialName* attribute is also used for properties, and compilers can designate any name they choose as *SpecialName*. *RTSpecialName* is used for certain other names that require special treatment by the VES. For more information on designating names as special, to either the compiler or the runtime, see Partition II, section 9.1.6, and Partition I, sections 8.11.3 and 8.11.4.

22.1.5 *Flags for Fields (FieldAttributes)*

Flag	Value	Description
`FieldAccessMask`	`0x0007`	
`CompilerControlled`	`0x0000`	Member not referenceable.
`Private`	`0x0001`	Accessible only by the parent type.
`FamANDAssem`	`0x0002`	Accessible by subtypes only in this Assembly.
`Assembly`	`0x0003`	Accessibly by anyone in the Assembly.
`Family`	`0x0004`	Accessible only by type and subtypes.
`FamORAssem`	`0x0005`	Accessibly by subtypes anywhere, plus anyone in assembly.
`Public`	`0x0006`	Accessibly by anyone who has visibility to this scope field contract attributes.
`Static`	`0x0010`	Defined on type, else per instance.
`InitOnly`	`0x0020`	Field may only be initialized, not written to after init.
`Literal`	`0x0040`	Value is compile-time constant.
`NotSerialized`	`0x0080`	Field does not have to be serialized when type is remoted.
`SpecialName`	`0x0200`	Field is special.
Interop Attributes		
`PInvokeImpl`	`0x2000`	Implementation is forwarded through PInvoke.
Additional Flags		
`RTSpecialName`	`0x0400`	CLI provides "special" behavior, depending upon the name of the field.
`HasFieldMarshal`	`0x1000`	Field has marshalling information.

Flag	Value	Description
`HasDefault`	`0x8000`	Field has default.
`HasFieldRVA`	`0x0100`	Field has RVA.

ANNOTATION: For more information on *NotSerialized*, see Partition II, sections 9.1.6 and 15.1.2.

For more information on the accessibility options, see Partition II, section 8 and its subsections.

22.1.6 *Flags for Files (FileAttributes)*

Flag	Value	Description
`ContainsMetaData`	`0x0000`	This is not a resource file.
`ContainsNoMetaData`	`0x0001`	This is a resource file or other non-metadata-containing file.

22.1.7 *Flags for ImplMap (PInvokeAttributes)*

Flag	Value	Description
`NoMangle`	`0x0001`	PInvoke is to use the member name as specified.
Character Set		
`CharSetMask`	`0x0006`	This is a resource file or other non-metadata-containing file.
`CharSetNotSpec`	`0x0000`	
`CharSetAnsi`	`0x0002`	
`CharSetUnicode`	`0x0004`	
`CharSetAuto`	`0x0006`	

Flag	Value	Description
SupportsLastError	0x0040	Information about target function. Not relevant for fields.
Calling Convention		
CallConvMask	0x0700	
CallConvWinapi	0x0100	
CallConvCdecl	0x0200	
CallConvStdcall	0x0300	
CallConvThiscall	0x0400	
CallConvFastcall	0x0500	

ANNOTATION: For more information on character sets, see Partition II, section 9.1.5. For more information on calling conventions, see Partition II, section 14.3.

22.1.8 *Flags for ManifestResource (ManifestResourceAttributes)*

Flag	Value	Description
VisibilityMask	0x0007	
Public	0x0001	The Resource is exported from the Assembly.
Private	0x0002	The Resource is private to the Assembly.

ANNOTATION: For more information on visibility, see Partition II, section 8 and its subsections.

22.1.9 *Flags for Methods (MethodAttributes)*

Flag	Value	Description
`MemberAccessMask`	`0x0007`	
`CompilerControlled`	`0x0000`	Member not referenceable.
`Private`	`0x0001`	Accessible only by the parent type.
`FamANDAssem`	`0x0002`	Accessible by subtypes only in this Assembly.
`Assem`	`0x0003`	Accessibly by anyone in the Assembly.
`Family`	`0x0004`	Accessible only by type and subtypes.
`FamORAssem`	`0x0005`	Accessibly by subtypes anywhere, plus anyone in assembly.
`Public`	`0x0006`	Accessibly by anyone who has visibility to this scope.
`Static`	`0x0010`	Defined on type, else per instance.
`Final`	`0x0020`	Method may not be overridden.
`Virtual`	`0x0040`	Method is virtual.
`HideBySig`	`0x0080`	Method hides by name+sig, else just by name.
`VtableLayoutMask`	`0x0100`	Use this mask to retrieve vtable attributes.
`ReuseSlot`	`0x0000`	Method reuses existing slot in vtable.
`NewSlot`	`0x0100`	Method always gets a new slot in the vtable.
`Abstract`	`0x0400`	Method does not provide an implementation.
`SpecialName`	`0x0800`	Method is special.
Interop Attributes		
`PInvokeImpl`	`0x2000`	Implementation is forwarded through PInvoke.
`UnmanagedExport`	`0x0008`	Reserved: shall be zero for conforming implementations.

5. Metadata File Format

Flag	Value	Description
Additional Flags		
`RTSpecialName`	`0x1000`	CLI provides "special" behavior, depending upon the name of the method.
`HasSecurity`	`0x4000`	Method has security associate with it.
`RequireSecObject`	`0x8000`	Method calls another method containing security code.

ANNOTATION: For more information on the accessibility options and hiding, see Partition II, section 8 and its subsections. For information on overriding (the *NewSlot* flag), see Partition II, section 9.3.1.

ANNOTATION

Implementation-Specific (Microsoft): *UnmanagedExport* indicates a managed method exported via thunk to unmanaged code.

22.1.10 *Flags for Methods (MethodImplAttributes)*

Flag	Value	Description
`CodeTypeMask`	`0x0003`	
`IL`	`0x0000`	Method impl is CIL.
`Native`	`0x0001`	Method impl is native.
`OPTIL`	`0x0002`	Reserved: shall be zero in conforming implementations.
`Runtime`	`0x0003`	Method impl is provided by the runtime.
`ManagedMask`	`0x0004`	Flags specifying whether the code is managed or unmanaged.
`Unmanaged`	`0x0004`	Method impl is unmanaged, otherwise managed.
`Managed`	`0x0000`	Method impl is managed.

Flag	Value	Description
Implementation Info and Interop		
`ForwardRef`	`0x0010`	Indicates method is defined; used primarily in merge scenarios.
`PreserveSig`	`0x0080`	Reserved: conforming implementations may ignore.
`InternalCall`	`0x1000`	Reserved: shall be zero in conforming implementations.
`Synchronized`	`0x0020`	Method is single-threaded through the body.
`NoInlining`	`0x0008`	Method may not be inlined.
`MaxMethodImplVal`	`0xffff`	Range check value.

ANNOTATION

Implementation-Specific (Microsoft): The *PreserveSig* method signature is not to be mangled to do HRESULT conversion.

22.1.11 *Flags for MethodSemantics (MethodSemanticsAttributes)*

Flag	Value	Description
`Setter`	`0x0001`	Setter for property
`Getter`	`0x0002`	Getter for property
`Other`	`0x0004`	Other method for property or event
`AddOn`	`0x0008`	AddOn method for event
`RemoveOn`	`0x0010`	RemoveOn method for event
`Fire`	`0x0020`	Fire method for event

ANNOTATION: For more information on properties and events, see Partition II, sections 16 and 17.

22.1.12 *Flags for Params (ParamAttributes)*

Flag	Value	Description
`In`	`0x0001`	Param is [In].
`Out`	`0x0002`	Param is [Out].
`Optional`	`0x0010`	Param is optional.
`HasDefault`	`0x1000`	Param has default value.
`HasFieldMarshal`	`0x2000`	Param has FieldMarshal.
`Unused`	`0xcfe0`	Reserved: shall be zero in a conforming implementation.

22.1.13 *Flags for Properties (PropertyAttributes)*

Flag	Value	Description
`SpecialName`	`0x0200`	Property is special.
`RTSpecialName`	`0x0400`	Runtime (metadata internal APIs) should check name encoding.
`HasDefault`	`0x1000`	Property has default.
`Unused`	`0xe9ff`	Reserved: shall be zero in a conforming implementation.

22.1.14 *Flags for Types (TypeAttributes)*

Flag	Value	Description
Visibility Attributes		
`VisibilityMask`	`0x00000007`	Use this mask to retrieve visibility information.
`NotPublic`	`0x00000000`	Class has no public scope.
`Public`	`0x00000001`	Class has public scope.
`NestedPublic`	`0x00000002`	Class is nested with public visibility.

Flag	Value	Description
NestedPrivate	0x00000003	Class is nested with private visibility.
NestedFamily	0x00000004	Class is nested with family visibility.
NestedAssembly	0x00000005	Class is nested with assembly visibility.
NestedFamANDAssem	0x00000006	Class is nested with family and assembly visibility.
NestedFamORAssem	0x00000007	Class is nested with family or assembly visibility.
Class Layout Attributes		
LayoutMask	0x00000018	Use this mask to retrieve class layout information.
AutoLayout	0x00000000	Class fields are auto-laid out.
SequentialLayout	0x00000008	Class fields are laid out sequentially.
ExplicitLayout	0x00000010	Layout is supplied explicitly.
Class Semantics Attributes		
ClassSemanticsMask	0x00000020	Use this mask to retrieve class semantics information.
Class	0x00000000	Type is a class.
Interface	0x00000020	Type is an interface.
Special Semantics in Addition to Class Semantics		
Abstract	0x00000080	Class is abstract.
Sealed	0x00000100	Class cannot be extended.
SpecialName	0x00000400	Class name is special.
Implementation Attributes		
Import	0x00001000	Class/Interface is imported.
Serializable	0x00002000	Class is serializable.
String Formatting Attributes		
StringFormatMask	0x00030000	Use this mask to retrieve string information for native interop.

Flag	Value	Description
AnsiClass	0x00000000	LPSTR is interpreted as ANSI.
UnicodeClass	0x00010000	LPSTR is interpreted as Unicode.
AutoClass	0x00020000	LPSTR is interpreted automatically.
Class Initialization Attributes		
BeforeFieldInit	0x00100000	Initialize the class before first static field access.
Additional Flags		
RTSpecialName	0x00000800	CLI provides "special" behavior, depending upon the name of the Type.
HasSecurity	0x00040000	Type has security associated with it.

22.1.15 *Element Types Used in Signatures*

The following table lists the values for ELEMENT_TYPE constants. These are used extensively in metadata signature *blobs*—see Partition II, section 22.2.

ANNOTATION: For more information on element types, see Partition II, sections 21.9 and 21.10.

ANNOTATION

Implementation-Specific (Microsoft): These values are defined in the file **inc\CorHdr.h** in the Microsoft .NET SDK.

Name	Value	Remarks
ELEMENT_TYPE_END	0x00	Marks end of a list.
ELEMENT_TYPE_VOID	0x01	
ELEMENT_TYPE_BOOLEAN	0x02	

Name	Value	Remarks
ELEMENT_TYPE_CHAR	0x03	
ELEMENT_TYPE_I1	0x04	
ELEMENT_TYPE_U1	0x05	
ELEMENT_TYPE_I2	0x06	
ELEMENT_TYPE_U2	0x07	
ELEMENT_TYPE_I4	0x08	
ELEMENT_TYPE_U4	0x09	
ELEMENT_TYPE_I8	0x0a	
ELEMENT_TYPE_U8	0x0b	
ELEMENT_TYPE_R4	0x0c	
ELEMENT_TYPE_R8	0x0d	
ELEMENT_TYPE_STRING	0x0e	
ELEMENT_TYPE_PTR	0x0f	Followed by <type> token.
ELEMENT_TYPE_BYREF	0x10	Followed by <type> token.
ELEMENT_TYPE_VALUETYPE	0x11	Followed by TypeDef or TypeRef token.
ELEMENT_TYPE_CLASS	0x12	Followed by TypeDef or TypeRef token.
ELEMENT_TYPE_ARRAY	0x14	<type> <rank> <boundsCount> <bound1> ... <loCount> <lo1> ...
ELEMENT_TYPE_TYPEDBYREF	0x16	
ELEMENT_TYPE_I	0x18	System.IntPtr.
ELEMENT_TYPE_U	0x19	System.UIntPtr.
ELEMENT_TYPE_FNPTR	0x1b	Followed by full method signature.
ELEMENT_TYPE_OBJECT	0x1c	System.Object.

Name	Value	Remarks
ELEMENT_TYPE_SZARRAY	0x1d	Single-dim array with 0 lower bound.
ELEMENT_TYPE_CMOD_REQD	0x1f	Required modifier: followed by a TypeDef or TypeRef token.
ELEMENT_TYPE_CMOD_OPT	0x20	Optional modifier: followed by a TypeDef or TypeRef token.
ELEMENT_TYPE_INTERNAL	0x21	Implemented within the CLI.
ELEMENT_TYPE_MODIFIER	0x40	OR'd with following element types.
ELEMENT_TYPE_SENTINEL	0x41	Sentinel for varargs method signature.
ELEMENT_TYPE_PINNED	0x45	Denotes a local variable that points at a pinned object.

22.2 Blobs and Signatures

The word "signature" is conventionally used to describe the type info for a function or method—that is, the type of each of its parameters, and the type of its return value. Within metadata, the word "signature" is also used to describe the type info for fields, properties, and local variables. Each Signature is stored as a (counted) byte array in the Blob heap. There are six kinds of Signatures, as follows:

- MethodRefSig – differs from a MethodDefSig only for VARARG calls
- MethodDefSig
- FieldSig
- PropertySig
- LocalVarSig
- TypeSpec

The value of the leading byte of a Signature "blob" indicates what kind of Signature it is. This section defines the binary "blob" format for each kind of Signature.

Note that Signatures are compressed before being stored into the Blob heap (described below) by compressing the integers embedded in the signature. The maximum encodable integer is 29 bits long, 0x1FFFFFFF. The compression algorithm used is as follows (bit 0 is the least significant bit):

- If the value lies between 0 (0x00) and 127 (0x7F), inclusive, encode as a 1-byte integer (bit #7 is clear, value held in bits #6 through #0).

- If the value lies between 2^8 (0x80) and $2^{14} - 1$ (0x3FFF), inclusive, encode as a 2-byte integer with bit #15 set, bit #14 clear (value held in bits #13 through #0).
- Otherwise, encode as a 4-byte integer, with bit #31 set, bit #30 set, bit #29 clear (value held in bits #28 through #0).
- A null string should be represented with the reserved single-byte 0xFF, and no following data.

NOTE

The table below shows several examples. The first column gives a value, expressed in familiar (C-like) hex notation. The second column shows the corresponding, compressed result, as it would appear in a PE file, with successive bytes of the result lying at successively higher byte offsets within the file. (This is the opposite order from how regular binary integers are laid out in a PE file.)

Original Value	Compressed Representation
0x03	03
0x7F	7F (7 bits set)
0x80	8080
0x2E57	AE57
0x3FFF	BFFF
0x4000	C000 4000
0x1FFF FFFF	DFFF FFFF

Thus, the most significant bits (the first ones encountered in a PE file) of a "compressed" field, can reveal whether it occupies 1, 2, or 4 bytes, as well as its value. For this to work, the "compressed" value, as explained above, is stored in big-endian order—with the most significant byte at the smallest offset within the file.

ANNOTATION: As you will note, the "compressions" above do not always reduce the size of the values. This type of compression allows smaller values to be stored in fewer than 4 bytes, because statistically, more small positive or negative numbers are used than larger values. Integers near zero use only 1 byte instead of 4, and slightly larger values use 2 bytes instead of 4.

Signatures make extensive use of constant values called `ELEMENT_TYPE_xxx`—see Partition II, section 22.1.15. In particular, signatures include two modifiers called:

`ELEMENT_TYPE_BYREF` – this element is a managed pointer [see the annotation to Partition I, section 8.9.2]. This modifier can only occur in the definition of *Param* (Partition II, section 22.2.10) or *RetType* (Partition II, section 22.2.11). It shall *not* occur within the definition of a *Field* (Partition II, section 22.2.4).

`ELEMENT_TYPE_PTR` – this element is an unmanaged pointer (see Partition I [section 8.9.2]). This modifier can occur in the definition of *Param* (Partition II, section 22.2.10) or *RetType* (Partition II, section 22.2.11) or *Field* (Partition II, section 22.2.4).

ANNOTATION: For a field, the signature would be the type of the field. For a method, it would be the return type, the number of parameters, all of the parameter types, etc.

22.2.1 *MethodDefSig*

A MethodDefSig is indexed by the *Method.Signature* column. It captures the *signature* of a method or global function. The syntax chart for a MethodDefSig is:

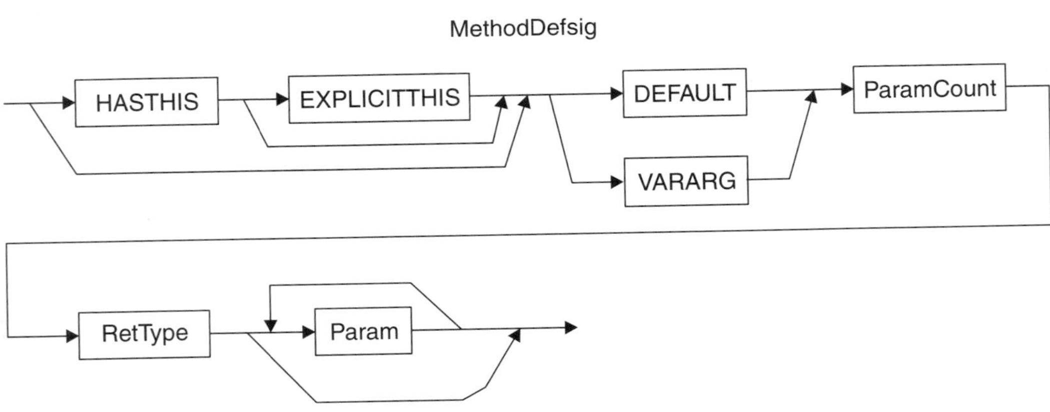

This chart uses the following abbreviations (see Partition II, section 14.3):

`HASTHIS = 0x20`, used to encode the keyword **instance** in the calling convention

`EXPLICITTHIS = 0x40`, used to encode the keyword **explicit** in the calling convention

`DEFAULT = 0x0`, used to encode the keyword **default** in the calling convention

`VARARG = 0x5`, used to encode the keyword **vararg** in the calling convention

---

ANNOTATION

Implementation-Specific (Microsoft): The above names are defined in the file **inc\CorHdr.h** as part of the Microsoft .NET SDK, using a prefix of `IMAGE_CEE_CS_CALLCONV_`.

The first byte of the Signature holds bits for `HASTHIS`, `EXPLICITTHIS`, and calling convention—`DEFAULT` or `VARARG`. These are OR'd together.

ParamCount is an integer that holds the number of parameters (0 or more). It can be any number between 0 and 0x1FFFFFFF. The compiler compresses it too (see Partition II, Metadata Validation [section 3])—before storing into the "blob" (*ParamCount* counts just the method parameters—it does not include the method's return type).

The *RetType* item describes the type of the method's return value (see Partition II, section 22.2.11).

The *Param* item describes the type of each of the method's parameters. There shall be *ParamCount* instances of the *Param* item (see Partition II, section 22.2.10).

22.2.2 *MethodRefSig*

A MethodRefSig is indexed by the *MemberRef.Signature* column. This provides the *call-site* Signature for a method. Normally, this call-site Signature shall match exactly the Signature specified in the definition of the target method. For example, if a method Foo is defined that takes two uint32's and returns void; then any call site shall index a signature that takes exactly two uint32's and returns void. In this case, the syntax chart for a MethodRefSig is identical with that for a MethodDefSig—see Partition II, section 22.2.1.

The Signature at a call site differs from that at its definition, only for a method with the VARARG calling convention. In this case, the call-site Signature is extended to include info about the extraVARARG arguments (for example, corresponding to the "..." in C syntax). The syntax chart for this case is:

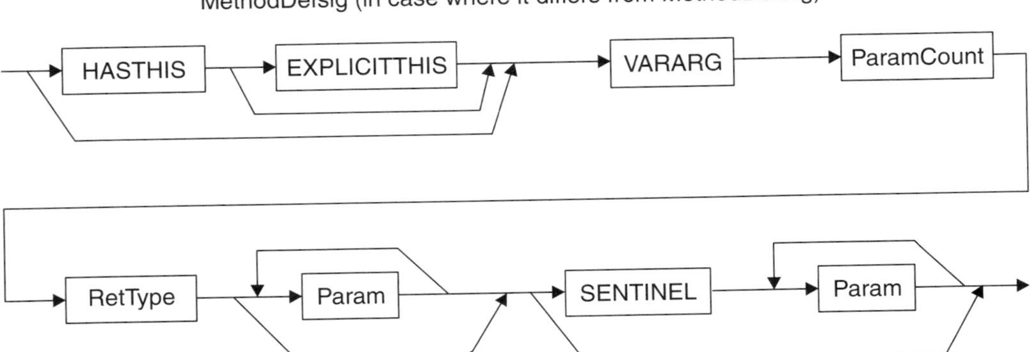

This chart uses the following abbreviations (see Partition II, section 14.3):

`HASTHIS = 0x20`, used to encode the keyword **instance** in the calling convention

`EXPLICITTHIS = 0x40`, used to encode the keyword **explicit** in the calling convention

`DEFAULT = 0x0`, used to encode the keyword **default** in the calling convention

`VARARG = 0x5`, used to encode the keyword **vararg** in the calling convention

`SENTINEL = 0x41` (see Partition II, section 22.1.15), used to encode "**...**" in the parameter list

ANNOTATION

Implementation-Specific (Microsoft): The above names are defined in the file **inc\CorHdr.h** as part of the SDK, using a prefix of `IMAGE_CEE_CS_CALLCONV_`.

- The first byte of the Signature holds bits for `HASTHIS`, `EXPLICITTHIS`, and calling convention—`DEFAULT`, `VARARG`, `C`, `STDCALL`, `THISCALL`, or `FASTCALL`. These are OR'd together.
- *ParamCount* is an integer that holds the number of parameters (0 or more). It can be any number between 0 and 0x1FFFFFFF. The compiler compresses it too (see Partition II, Metadata Validation [section 3])—before storing into the "blob" (*ParamCount* counts just the method parameters—it does not include the method's return type).
- The *RetType* item describes the type of the method's return value (see Partition II, section 22.2.11).

- The *Param* item describes the type of each of the method's parameters. There shall be *ParamCount* instances of the *Param* item (see Partition II, section 22.2.10).

The *Param* item describes the type of each of the method's parameters. There shall be *ParamCount* instances of the *Param* item. This starts just like the MethodDefSig for a `VARARG` method (see Partition II, section 22.2.1). But then a `SENTINEL` token is appended, followed by extra *Param* items to describe the extra `VARARG` arguments. Note that the *ParamCount* item shall indicate the total number of *Param* items in the Signature—before and after the `SENTINEL` byte (0x41).

In the unusual case that a call site supplies no extra arguments, the signature shall *not* include a `SENTINEL` (this is the route shown by the lower arrow that bypasses `SENTINEL` and goes to the end of the MethodRefSig definition).

22.2.3 *StandAloneMethodSig*

A StandAloneMethodSig is indexed by the *StandAloneSig.Signature* column. It is typically created as preparation for executing a **calli** instruction. It is similar to a MethodRefSig, in that it represents a call-site signature, but its calling convention may specify an unmanaged target (the **calli** instruction invokes either managed or unmanaged code). Its syntax chart is:

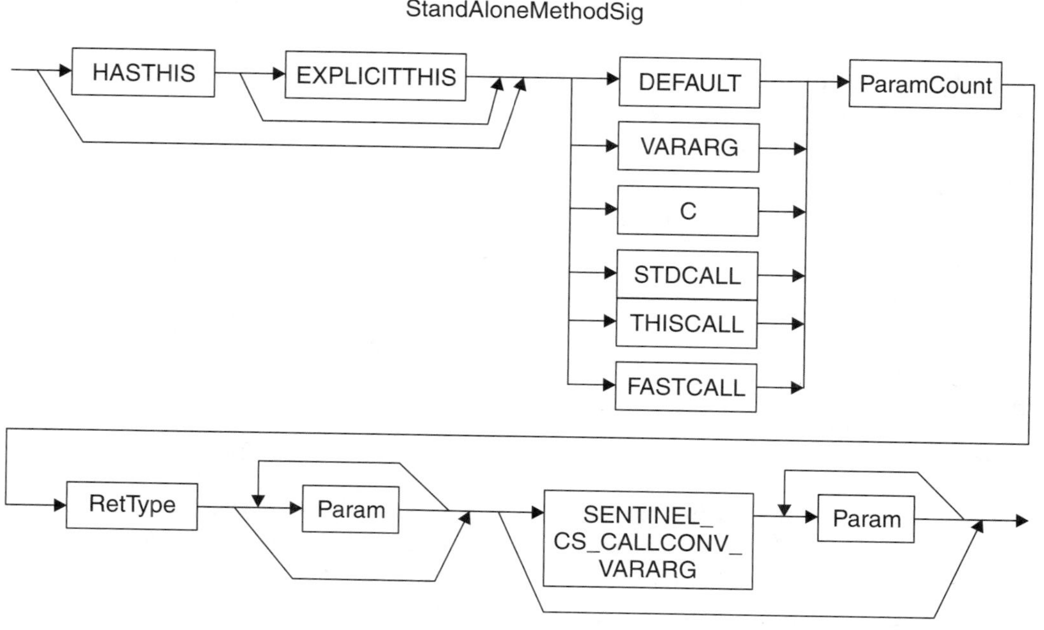

This chart uses the following abbreviations (see Partition II, section 14.3):

`HASTHIS` for `0x20`

`EXPLICITTHIS` for `0x40`

`DEFAULT` for `0x0`

`VARARG` for `0x5`

`C` for `0x1`

`STDCALL` for `0x2`

`THISCALL` for `0x3`

`FASTCALL` for `0x4`

`SENTINEL` for `0x41` (see Partition II, section 22.1.15 and Partition II, section 14.3)

ANNOTATION

Implementation-Specific (Microsoft): The above names are defined in the file **inc\CorHdr.h** as part of the Microsoft .NET SDK, using a prefix of `IMAGE_CEE_CS_CALLCONV_`.

- The first byte of the Signature holds bits for `HASTHIS`, `EXPLICITTHIS`, and calling convention—`DEFAULT`, `VARARG`, `C`, `STDCALL`, `THISCALL`, or `FASTCALL`. These are OR'd together.
- *ParamCount* is an integer that holds the number of parameters (0 or more). It can be any number between 0 and 0x1FFFFFFF. The compiler compresses it too (see Partition II, Metadata Validation [section 3])—before storing into the "blob" (*ParamCount* counts just the method parameters—it does not include the method's return type).
- The *RetType* item describes the type of the method's return value (see Partition II, section 22.2.11).
- The *Param* item describes the type of each of the method's parameters. There shall be *ParamCount* instances of the *Param* item (see Partition II, section 22.2.10).

This is the most complex of the various method signatures. Two separate charts have been combined into one in this diagram, using shading to distinguish between them. Thus, for the following calling conventions: `DEFAULT` (managed), `STDCALL`, `THISCALL`, and `FASTCALL` (unmanaged), the signature ends just before the `SENTINEL` item (these are all nonvararg signatures). However, for the managed and unmanaged vararg calling conventions: `VARARG` (managed) and `C` (unmanaged), the signature can include the `SENTINEL` and final Param items (they are not required, however). These options are indicated by the shading of boxes in the syntax chart.

22.2.4 *FieldSig*

A FieldSig is indexed by the *Field.Signature* column or by the *MemberRef.Signature* column (in the case where it specifies a reference to a field, not a method, of course). The Signature captures the field's definition. The field may be a static or instance field in a class, or it may be a global variable. The syntax chart for a FieldSig looks like this:

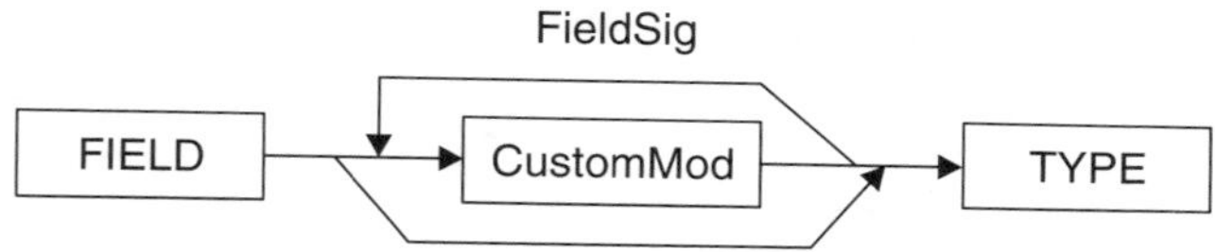

This chart uses the following abbreviations:

`FIELD` for `0x6`

ANNOTATION

Implementation-Specific (Microsoft): The above name is defined in the file **inc\CorHdr.h** as part of the Microsoft .NET SDK, using a prefix of `IMAGE_CEE_CS_CALLCONV_FIELD`.

CustomMod is defined in Partition II, section 22.2.7. *Type* is defined in Partition II, section 22.2.12.

22.2.5 *PropertySig*

A PropertySig is indexed by the *Property.Type* column. It captures the type information for a Property—essentially, the signature of its *getter* method:

How many parameters are supplied to its *getter* method

The base type of the Property—the type returned by its *getter* method

Type information for each parameter in the *getter* method—that is, the index parameters

Note that the signatures of the getter and setter are related precisely as follows:

- The types of a *getter's paramCount* parameters are exactly the same as the first *paramCount* parameters of the *setter*.
- The return type of a *getter* is exactly the same as the type of the last parameter supplied to the *setter*.

The syntax chart for a PropertySig looks like this:

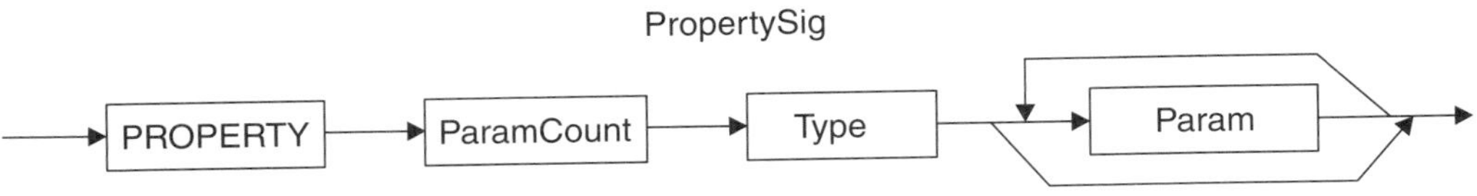

This chart uses the following abbreviations:

`PROPERTY` for `0x8`

ANNOTATION

Implementation-Specific (Microsoft): The above name is defined in the file **inc\CorHdr.h** as part of the Microsoft .NET SDK, using a prefix of `IMAGE_CEE_CS_CALLCONV_PROPERTY`.

Type specifies the type returned by the *getter* method for this property. *Type* is defined in Partition II, section 22.2.12. *Param* is defined in Partition II, section 22.2.10.

ParamCount is an integer that holds the number of index parameters in the *getter* methods (0 or more) (see Partition II, section 22.2.1). (*ParamCount* counts just the method parameters—it does not include the method's base type of the Property.)

22.2.6 *LocalVarSig*

A LocalVarSig is indexed by the *StandAloneSig.Signature* column. It captures the type of all the local variables in a method. Its syntax chart is:

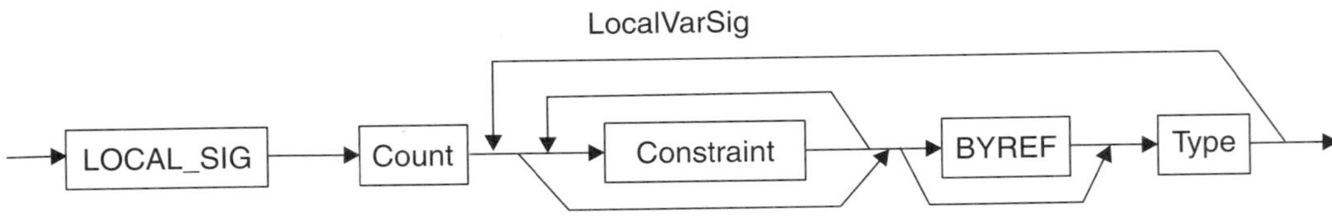

This chart uses the following abbreviations:

LOCAL_SIG for 0x7, used for the **.locals** directive (see Partition II, section 14.4.1.3)

ANNOTATION

Implementation-Specific (Microsoft): The above name is defined in the file **inc\CorHdr.h** as part of the Microsoft .NET SDK, using a prefix of IMAGE_CEE_CS_CALLCONV_LOCAL_SIG.

BYREF for ELEMENT_TYPE_BYREF (see Partition II, section 22.1.15)

Constraint is defined in Partition II, section 22.2.9.

Type is defined in Partition II, section 22.2.12.

Count is an unsigned integer that holds the number of local variables. It can be any number between 1 and 0xFFFE.

There shall be *Count* instances of the *Type* in the LocalVarSig.

22.2.7 *CustomMod*

The *CustomMod* (custom modifier) item in Signatures has a syntax chart like this:

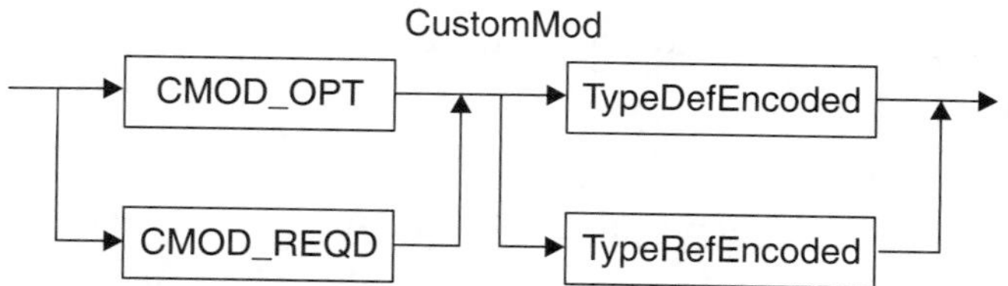

This chart uses the following abbreviations:

CMOD_OPT for ELEMENT_TYPE_CMOD_OPT (see Partition II, section 22.1.15)

CMOD_REQD for ELEMENT_TYPE_CMOD_REQD (see Partition II, section 22.1.15)

The CMOD_OPT or CMOD_REQD value is compressed (see Partition II, section 22.2).

The CMOD_OPT or CMOD_REQD is followed by a metadata token that indexes a row in the *TypeDef* table or the *TypeRef* table. However, these tokens are encoded and compressed—see Partition II, section 22.2.8 for details.

If the custom modifier is tagged `CMOD_OPT`, then any importing compiler can freely ignore it entirely. Conversely, if the custom modifier is tagged `CMOD_REQD`, any importing compiler shall "understand | " the semantic implied by this custom modifier in order to reference the surrounding Signature.

ANNOTATION

Implementation-Specific (Microsoft): A typical use for a custom modifier is for Visual C++ .NET to denote a method parameter as **const**. It does this using a `CMOD_OPT`, followed by a *TypeRef* to `Microsoft.VisualC.IsConstModifier` (defined in Microsoft.VisualC.DLL).

Visual C++ .NET also uses a custom modifier (embedded within a *RetType*—see Partition II, section 22.2.11) to mark the native calling convention of a function. Of course, if that routine is implemented as managed code, this info is not used. But if it turns out to be implemented as unmanaged code, it becomes crucial that automatically generated thunks marshal the arguments correctly. This technique is used in IJW ("It Just Works") scenarios. Strictly speaking, such a custom modifier does not apply only to the *RetType*; it really applies to the whole function. In these cases, the *TypeRef* following the `CMOD_OPT` is to one of `CallConvCdecl`, `CallConvStdcall`, `CallConvThiscall`, or `CallConvFastcall`.

22.2.8 *TypeDef or Ref Encoded*

These items are compact ways to store a *TypeDef* or *TypeRef* token in a Signature (see Partition II, section 22.2.12).

Consider a regular *TypeRef* token, such as 0x01000012. The top byte of 0x01 indicates that this is a *TypeRef* token (see Partition V for a list of the supported metadata token types). The lower 3 bytes (0x000012) index row number 0x12 in the *TypeRef* table.

The encoded version of this *TypeRef* token is made up as follows:

1. Encode the table that this token indexes as the least significant 2 bits. The bit values to use are 0, 1, and 2, specifying the target table is the *TypeDef*, *TypeRef*, or *TypeSpec* table, respectively.
2. Shift the 3-byte row index (0x000012 in this example) left by 2 bits, and OR into the 2-bit encoding from step 1.
3. Compress the resulting value (see Partition II, section 22.2). This example yields the following encoded value:

```
a)  encoded = value for TypeRef table = 0x01 (from 1. above)
```

```
b)   encoded = ( 0x000012 << 2 ) |  0x01
             = 0x48 | 0x01
             = 0x49
c)   encoded = Compress (0x49)
             = 0x49
```

So, instead of the original, regular *TypeRef* token value of 0x01000012, requiring 4 bytes of space in the Signature "blob," this *TypeRef* token is encoded as a single byte.

22.2.9 *Constraint*

The *Constraint* item in Signatures currently has only one possible value—`ELEMENT_TYPE_PINNED` (see Partition II, section 22.1.15), which specifies that the target type is pinned in the runtime heap, and will not be moved by the actions of garbage collection.

A *Constraint* can only be applied within a LocalVarSig (not a FieldSig). The Type of the local variable shall either be a reference type (in other words, it *points* to the actual variable—for example, an Object or a String); or it shall include the `BYREF` item. The reason is that local variables are allocated on the runtime stack—they are never allocated from the runtime heap; so unless the local variable *points* at an object allocated in the GC heap, pinning makes no sense.

22.2.10 *Param*

The *Param* (parameter) item in Signatures has this syntax chart:

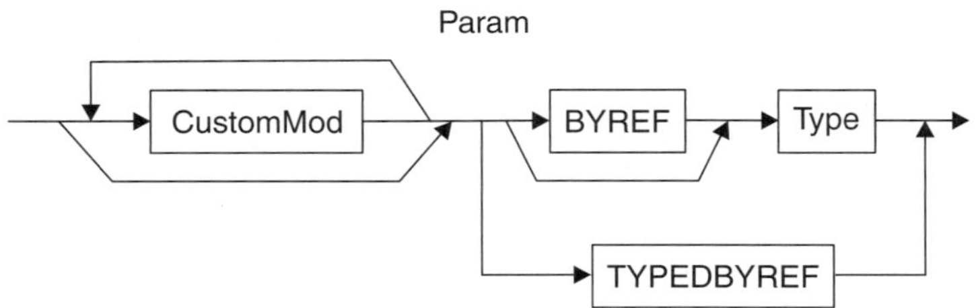

This chart uses the following abbreviations:

`BYREF`	for	`0x10` (see Partition II, section 22.1.15)
`TYPEDBYREF`	for	`0x16` (see Partition II, section 22.1.15)

CustomMod is defined in Partition II, section 22.2.7. *Type* is defined in Partition II, section 22.2.12.

22.2.11 *RetType*

The *RetType* (return type) item in Signatures has this syntax chart:

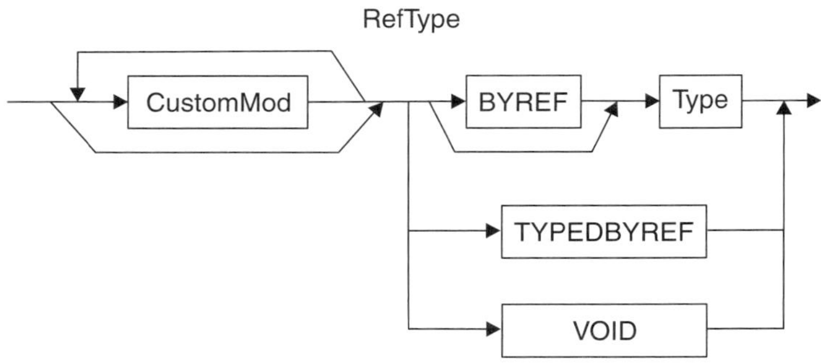

RetType is identical to *Param* except for one extra possibility, that it can include the type VOID. This chart uses the following abbreviations:

`BYREF`	for	`ELEMENT_TYPE_BYREF` (see Partition II, section 22.1.15)
`TYPEDBYREF`	for	`ELEMENT_TYPE_TYPEDBYREF` (see Partition II, section 22.1.15)
`VOID`	for	`ELEMENT_TYPE_VOID` (see Partition II, section 22.1.15)

22.2.12 *Type*

Type is encoded in signatures as follows (`I1` is an abbreviation for `ELEMENT_TYPE_I1`, etc.; see Partition II, section 22.1.15):

```
Type ::=
BOOLEAN | CHAR | I1 | U1 | I2 | U2 | I4 | U4 | I8 | U8 | R4 | R8 | I  | U |
| VALUETYPE TypeDefOrRefEncoded
| CLASS TypeDefOrRefEncoded
| STRING
| OBJECT
| PTR CustomMod* VOID
| PTR CustomMod* Type
| FNPTR MethodDefSig
| FNPTR MethodRefSig
| ARRAY Type ArrayShape  (general array, see Partition II, section 22.2.13)
| SZARRAY CustomMod* Type (single-dimensional, zero-based array--i.e., vector)
```

22.2.13 *ArrayShape*

An ArrayShape has the following syntax chart:

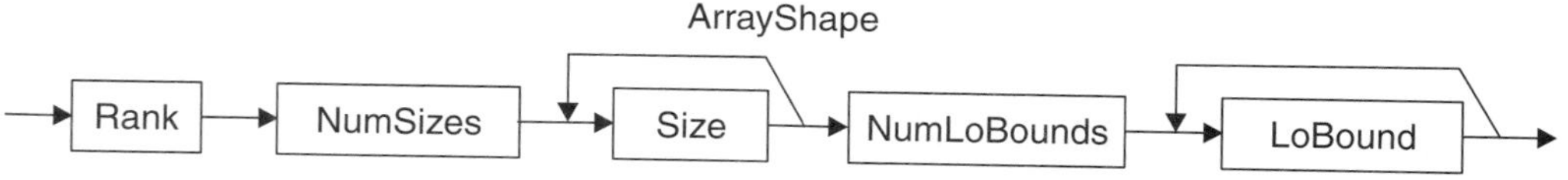

Rank is an integer (stored in compressed form; see Partition II, section 22.2) that specifies the number of dimensions in the array (shall be 1 or more). *NumSizes* is a compressed integer that says how many dimensions have specified sizes (it shall be 0 or more). *Size* is a compressed integer specifying the size of that dimension—the sequence starts at the first dimension, and goes on for a total of *NumSizes* items. Similarly, *NumLoBounds* is a compressed integer that says how many dimensions have specified lower bounds (it shall be 0 or more). And *LoBound* is a compressed integer specifying the lower bound of that dimension—the sequence starts at the first dimension and goes on for a total of *NumLoBounds* items. None of the dimensions in these two sequences can be skipped, but the number of specified dimensions can be less than *Rank*.

Here are a few examples, all for element type `int32`:

	Type	Rank	NumSizes	Size	NumLoBounds	LoBound
`[0...2]`	`I4`	`1`	`1`	`3`	`0`	
`[,,,,,,]`	`I4`	`7`	`0`		`0`	
`[0...3, 0...2,,,,]`	`I4`	`6`	`2`	`4 3`	`2`	`0 0`
`[1...2, 6...8]`	`I4`	`2`	`2`	`2 3`	`2`	`1 6`
`[5, 3...5, , ]`	`I4`	`4`	`2`	`5 3`	`2`	`0 3`

> **NOTE**
> Definitions can nest, since the Type may itself be an array.

5. Metadata File Format

22.2.14 *TypeSpec*

The signature in the Blob heap indexed by a *TypeSpec* token has the following format:

```
TypeSpecBlob ::=
    PTR       CustomMod*  VOID
  | PTR       CustomMod*  Type
  | FNPTR     MethodDefSig
  | FNPTR     MethodRefSig
  | ARRAY     Type  ArrayShape
  | SZARRAY   CustomMod*  Type
```

For compactness, the ELEMENT_TYPE_ prefixes have been omitted from this list. So, for example, PTR is shorthand for ELEMENT_TYPE_PTR (see Partition II, section 22.1.15). Note that a *TypeSpecBlob* does *not* begin with a calling-convention byte, so it differs from the various other signatures that are stored into metadata.

22.2.15 *Short-Form Signatures*

The general specification for signatures leaves some leeway in how to encode certain items. For example, it appears legal to encode a String as either

Long-form: ELEMENT_TYPE_CLASS, TypeRef-to-System.String

Short-form: ELEMENT_TYPE_STRING

Only the short form is valid. The following table shows which short forms should be used in place of each long-form item. (As usual, for compactness, the ELEMENT_TYPE_ prefixes have been omitted here—so VALUETYPE is short for ELEMENT_TYPE_VALUETYPE.)

Long Form		**Short Form**
Prefix	**TypeRef to:**	
CLASS	System.String	STRING
CLASS	System.Object	OBJECT
VALUETYPE	System.Void	VOID
VALUETYPE	System.Boolean	BOOLEAN
VALUETYPE	System.Char	CHAR
VALUETYPE	System.Byte	U1
VALUETYPE	System.Sbyte	I1

Long Form		Short Form
Prefix	TypeRef to:	
VALUETYPE	System.Int16	I2
VALUETYPE	System.UInt16	U2
VALUETYPE	System.Int32	I4
VALUETYPE	System.UInt32	U4
VALUETYPE	System.Int64	I8
VALUETYPE	System.UInt64	U8
VALUETYPE	System.IntPtr	I
VALUETYPE	System.UIntPtr	U
VALUETYPE	System.TypedReference	TYPEDBYREF

NOTE

Arrays shall be encoded in signatures using one of `ELEMENT_TYPE_ARRAY` or `ELEMENT_TYPE_SZARRAY`. There is no long form involving a TypeRef to `System.Array`.

22.3 Custom Attributes

A Custom Attribute has the following syntax chart:

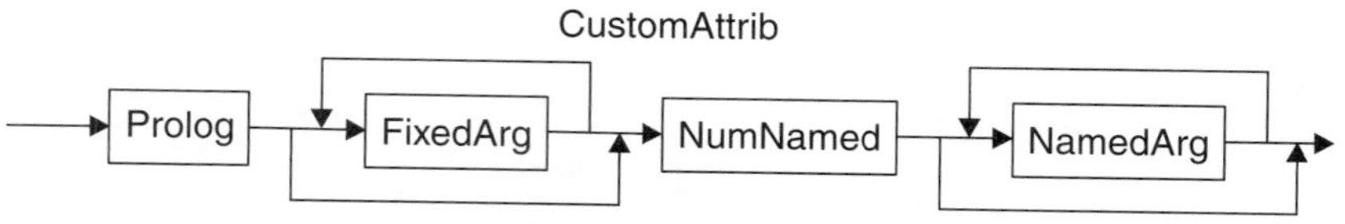

All binary values are stored in little-endian format (except *PackedLen* items—used only as counts for the number of bytes to follow in a UTF8 string). If there are no fields, parameters, or properties specified, the entire attribute may be represented as an empty blob.

CustomAttrib starts with a *Prolog*—an unsigned int16, with value 0x0001.

Next comes a description of the fixed arguments for the constructor method. Their number and type is found by examining that constructor's *MethodDef*; this info is *not* repeated in the *CustomAttrib* itself. As the syntax chart shows, there can be zero or more *FixedArgs*. (Note that `VARARG` constructor methods are not allowed in the definition of Custom Attributes.)

Next is a description of the optional "named" fields and properties. This starts with *NumNamed*—an unsigned int16 giving the number of "named" properties or fields that follow. Note that *NumNamed* shall always be present. If its value is zero, there are no "named" properties or fields to follow (and of course, in this case, the *CustomAttrib* shall end immediately after *NumNamed*). In the case where *NumNamed* is non-zero, it is followed by *NumNamed* repeats of *NamedArgs*.

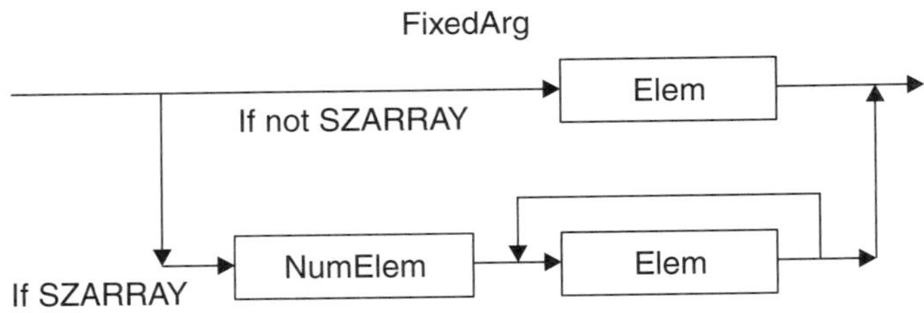

The format for each *FixedArg* depends upon whether that argument is single, or an `SZARRAY`—this is shown in the upper and lower paths, respectively, of the syntax chart [above]. So each *FixedArg* is either a single *Elem*, or *NumElem* repeats of *Elem*.

(`SZARRAY` is the single byte 0x1d and denotes a vector—a single-dimension array with a lower bound of zero.)

NumElem is an unsigned int32 specifying the number of elements in the `SZARRAY`, or 0xFFFFFFFF to indicate that the value is null.

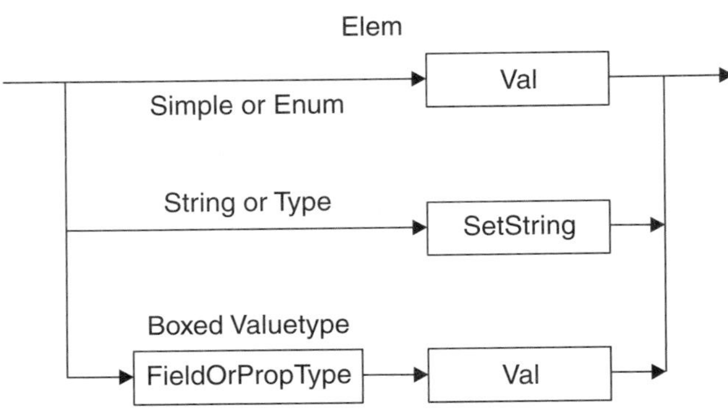

An *Elem* takes one of three forms:

- If the parameter kind is simple (**bool**, **char**, **float32**, **float64**, **int8**, **int16**, **int32**, **int64**, **unsigned int8**, **unsigned int16**, **unsigned int32**, or **unsigned int64**) then the "blob" contains its binary value (*Val*). This pattern is also used if the parameter kind is an *enum*—simply store the value of the enum's underlying integer type.
- If the parameter kind is string or type, then the blob contains a *SerString*—a *PackedLen* count of bytes, followed by the UTF8 characters. A type is stored as a string giving the full name of that type. Where the actual argument value is **null**, it shall be encoded as the single byte 0xFF.
- For parameters, fields, or properties whose formal (static) type is **System.Object**, the blob contains the actual type's **FieldOrPropType** (see below), followed by the representation of the actual parameter. (Note: it is not possible to pass a value of **null** in this case.)

Val is the binary value for a simple type. A bool is a single byte with value 0 (false) or 1 (true); char is a two-byte unicode character; and the others have their obvious meaning.

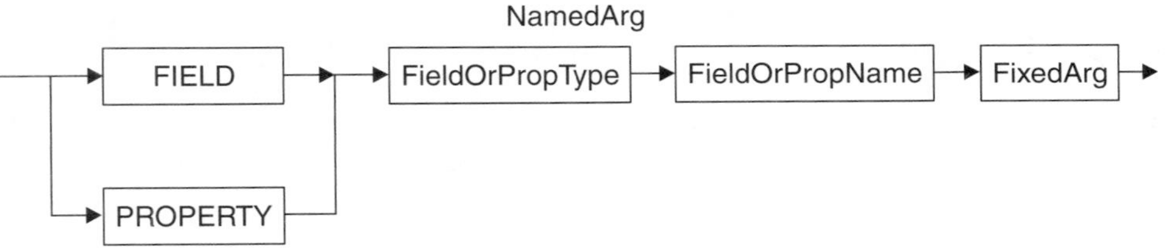

A *NamedArg* is simply a *FixedArg* (discussed above) preceded by information to identify which field or property it represents.

`FIELD` is the single byte 0x53.

`PROPERTY` is the single byte 0x54.

If the parameter kind is a boxed simple value type (**bool**, **char**, **float32**, **float64**, **int8**, **int16**, **int32**, **int64**, **unsigned int8**, **unsigned int16**, **unsigned int32**, or **unsigned int64**), then **FieldOrPropType** is immediately preceded by a byte containing the value **0x51**.

The *FieldOrPropType* shall be exactly one of: `ELEMENT_TYPE_BOOLEAN`, `ELEMENT_TYPE_CHAR`, `ELEMENT_TYPE_I1`, `ELEMENT_TYPE_U1`, `ELEMENT_TYPE_I2`, `ELEMENT_TYPE_U2`, `ELEMENT_TYPE_I4`, `ELEMENT_TYPE_U4`, `ELEMENT_TYPE_I8`, `ELEMENT_TYPE_U8`, `ELEMENT_TYPE_R4`, `ELEMENT_TYPE_R8`, `ELEMENT_TYPE_STRING`, or the constant 0x50 (for an argument of type Type). A single-dimensional, zero-based array is specified as a single byte 0x1D followed by the **FieldOrPropType** of the element type. (See Partition II, section 22.1.15.)

The *FieldOrPropName* is the name of the field or property, stored as a *SerString* (defined above).

The *SerString* used to encode an argument of type `Type` includes the full type name, followed optionally by the assembly where it is defined, its version, culture, and public key token. If the assembly name is omitted, the CLI looks first in this assembly, and then the assembly named **mscorlib**.

For example, consider the Type string "Ozzy.OutBack.Kangaroo+Wallaby, MyAssembly" for a class "Wallaby" nested within class "Ozzy.OutBack.Kangaroo", defined in the assembly "MyAssembly".

22.4 Marshalling Descriptors

A marshalling descriptor is like a signature—it's a "blob" of binary data. It describes how a field or parameter (which, as usual, covers the method return, as parameter number 0) should be marshalled when calling to or from unmanaged code via PInvoke dispatch. The ilasm syntax **marshal** can be used to create a marshalling descriptor, as can the pseudo custom attribute *MarshalAsAttribute*—see Partition II, section 20.2.1.)

Note that a conforming implementation of the CLI need only support marshalling of the types specified earlier—see Partition II, section 14.5.5.

Marshalling descriptors make use of constants named `NATIVE_TYPE_xxx`. Their names and values are listed in the following table:

Name	Value
`NATIVE_TYPE_BOOLEAN`	`0x02`
`NATIVE_TYPE_I1`	`0x03`
`NATIVE_TYPE_U1`	`0x04`
`NATIVE_TYPE_I2`	`0x05`
`NATIVE_TYPE_U2`	`0x06`
`NATIVE_TYPE_I4`	`0x07`
`NATIVE_TYPE_U4`	`0x08`
`NATIVE_TYPE_I8`	`0x09`
`NATIVE_TYPE_U8`	`0x0a`

Name	Value
NATIVE_TYPE_R4	0x0b
NATIVE_TYPE_R8	0x0c
NATIVE_TYPE_LPSTR	0x14
NATIVE_TYPE_INT	0x1f
NATIVE_TYPE_UINT	0x20
NATIVE_TYPE_FUNC	0x26
NATIVE_TYPE_ARRAY	0x2a

ANNOTATION

Implementation-Specific (Microsoft): The Microsoft implementation supports a richer set of types to describe marshalling between Windows native types and COM. These additional options are listed in the following table:

Name	Value	Remarks
NATIVE_TYPE_CURRENCY	0x0f	
NATIVE_TYPE_BSTR	0x13	
NATIVE_TYPE_LPWSTR	0x15	
NATIVE_TYPE_LPTSTR	0x16	
NATIVE_TYPE_FIXEDSYSSTRING	0x17	
NATIVE_TYPE_IUNKNOWN	0x19	
NATIVE_TYPE_IDISPATCH	0x1a	
NATIVE_TYPE_STRUCT	0x1b	
NATIVE_TYPE_INTF	0x1c	
NATIVE_TYPE_SAFEARRAY	0x1d	

Name	Value	Remarks
NATIVE_TYPE_FIXEDARRAY	0x1e	
NATIVE_TYPE_BYVALSTR	0x22	
NATIVE_TYPE_ANSIBSTR	0x23	
NATIVE_TYPE_TBSTR	0x24	Selects BSTR or ANSIBSTR depending on platform.
NATIVE_TYPE_VARIANTBOOL	0x25	2-byte Boolean value: false = 0; true = –1.
NATIVE_TYPE_ASANY	0x28	
NATIVE_TYPE_LPSTRUCT	0x2b	
NATIVE_TYPE_CUSTOMMARSHALER	0x2c	Custom marshaller native type. Shall be followed by a string in the format: "Native type name/0Custom marshaler type name/0Optional cookie/0" OR "{Native type GUID}/0Custom marshaler type name/0Optional cookie/0"
NATIVE_TYPE_ERROR	0x2d	This native type coupled with ELEMENT_TYPE_I4 will map to VT_HRESULT.
NATIVE_TYPE_MAX	0X50	Used to indicate "no info."

The "blob" has the following format:

```
MarshalSpec ::=
  NativeInstrinsic
| ARRAY ArrayElemType ParamNum ElemMult NumElem
```

ANNOTATION

Implementation-Specific (Microsoft): The Microsoft implementation supports a wider range of options:

MarshalSpec ::=

NativeIntrinsic

```
| ARRAY ArrayElemType ParamNum ElemMult NumElem
| CUSTOMMARSHALLER Guid UnmanagedType ManagedType Cookie
| FIXEDARRAY NumElem ArrayElemType
| SAFEARRAY SafeArrayElemType
```

```
NativeInstrinsic ::=
  BOOLEAN | I1 | U1 | I2 | U2 | I4 | U4 | I8 | U8 | R4 | R8
| CURRENCY | BSTR | LPSTR | LPWSTR | LPTSTR
| INT | UINT | FUNC | LPVOID
```

For compactness, the `NATIVE_TYPE_` prefixes have been omitted in the above lists. So, for example, `ARRAY` is shorthand for `NATIVE_TYPE_ARRAY`.

ANNOTATION

Implementation-Specific (Microsoft): `NativeIntrinsic ::= ...`

```
| FIXEDSYSSTRING | STRUCT | INTF | FIXEDARRAY | BYVALSTR |
ANSIBSTR |
| TBSTR | VARIANTBOOL | ASANY | LPSTRUCT | ERROR
```

Guid is a counted-UTF8 string—e.g., "{90883F05-3D28-11D2-8F17-00A0C9A6186D}"—it shall include leading "{" and trailing "}" and be exactly 38 characters long.

UnmanagedType is a counted-UTF8 string—e.g., "Point".

ManagedType is a counted-UTF8 string—e.g., "System.Util.MyGeometry"—it shall be the fully qualified name (namespace and name) of a managed Type defined within the current Assembly (that Type shall implement ICustomMarshaller, and provides a "to" and "from" marshalling method).

Cookie is a counted-UTF8 string—e.g., "123"—an empty string is allowed.

NumElem is an integer (compressed as described in Partition II, section 22.2) that specifies how many elements are in the array.

```
ArrayElemType :==
   NativeInstrinsic | BOOLEAN | I1 | U1 | I2 | U2
|  I4 | U4 | I8 | U8 | R4 | R8 | LPSTR | INT | UINT | FUNC | LPVOID
```

ANNOTATION

Implementation-Specific (Microsoft): ArrayElemType ::= …

| BSTR | LPWSTR | LPTSTR | FIXEDSYSSTRING | STRUCT | INTF | BYVALSTR

| ANSIBSTR | TBSTR | VARIANTBOOL | ASANY | LPSTRUCT | ERROR | MAX

The value MAX is used to indicate "no info."

The following information and table are specific to the Microsoft implementation of the CLI:

```
SafeArrayElemType ::=
  I2 | I4 | R4 | R8 | CY | DATE | BSTR | DISPATCH |
  | ERROR | BOOL | VARIANT | UNKNOWN | DECIMAL | I1 | UI1 | UI2
  | UI4 | INT | UINT
```

where each is prefixed by VT_. The values for the VT_xxx constants are given in the following table:

Constant	Value
VT_I2	= 2,
VT_I4	= 3,
VT_R4	= 4,
VT_R8	= 5,
VT_CY	= 6,
VT_DATE	= 7,
VT_BSTR	= 8,
VT_DISPATCH	= 9,
VT_ERROR	= 10,
VT_BOOL	= 11,

Constant	Value
`VT_VARIANT`	= 12,
`VT_UNKNOWN`	= 13,
`VT_DECIMAL`	= 14,
`VT_I1`	= 16,
`VT_UI1`	= 17,
`VT_UI2`	= 18,
`VT_UI4`	= 19,
`VT_INT`	= 22,
`VT_UINT`	= 23,

ParamNum is an integer (compressed as described in Partition II, section 22.2) specifying the parameter in the method call that provides the number of elements in the array—see below.

ElemMult is an integer compressed as described in Partition II, section 22.2 (says by what-factor to multiply—see below).

> **NOTE**
> For example, in the method declaration:
>
> ```
> Foo (int ar1[], int size1, byte ar2[], int size2)
> ```
>
> The *ar1* parameter might own a row in the *FieldMarshal* table, which indexes a *MarshalSpec* in the Blob heap with the format:
>
> ```
> ARRAY  MAX 2 1 0
> ```
>
> This says the parameter is marshalled to a `NATIVE_TYPE_ARRAY`. There is no additional info about the type of each element (signified by that `NATIVE_TYPE_MAX`). The value of *ParamNum* is 2, which indicates that parameter number 2 in the method (the one called "size1") will specify the number of elements in the actual array—let's suppose its value on a particular call is 42. The value of *ElemMult* is 1. The value of NumElem is 0. The calculated total size, in bytes, of the array is given by the formula:

```
if ParamNum == 0
SizeInBytes = NumElem * sizeof (elem)
else
SizeInBytes = ( @ParamNum * ElemMult + NumElem ) * sizeof (elem)
endif
```

The syntax "*@ParamNum*" is used here to denote the value passed in for parameter number *ParamNum*—it would be 42 in this example. The size of each element is calculated from the metadata for the *ar1* parameter in *Foo*'s signature—an `ELEMENT_TYPE_I4` (see Partition II, section 22.1.15) of size 4 bytes.

23 Metadata Physical Layout

The physical on-disk representation of metadata is a direct reflection of the logical representation described in Partition II, sections 21 and 22. That is, data is stored in streams representating the metadata tables and heaps. The main complication is that, where the logical representation is abstracted from the number of bytes needed for indexing into tables and columns, the physical representation has to take care of that explicitly by defining how to map logical metadata heaps and tables into their physical representations.

Unless stated otherwise, all binary values are stored in little-endian format.

23.1 Fixed Fields

Complete CLI components (metadata and CIL instructions) are stored in a subset of the current Portable Executable (PE) file format (see Partition II, section 24). Because of this heritage, some of the fields in the physical representation of metadata have fixed values. When writing these fields, they shall be set to the value indicated; on reading they may be ignored.

23.2 File Headers

23.2.1 *Metadata Root*

The root of the physical metadata starts with a magic signature, several bytes of version and other miscellaneous information, followed by a count and an array of stream headers, one for each stream that is present. The actual encoded tables and heaps are stored in the streams, which immediately follow this array of headers.

Offset	Size	Field	Description
0	4	Signature	Magic signature for physical metadata: 0x424A5342
4	2	MajorVersion	Major version, 1 (ignore on read)
6	2	MinorVersion	Minor version, 1 (ignore on read)
8	4	Reserved	Reserved, always 0 (see Partition II, section 21)
12	4	Length	Length of version string in bytes—say, *m* (<= 255)—rounded up to a multiple of four
16	m	Version	UTF8-encoded version string of length *m* (see below)
16+m			Padding to next 4-byte boundary—say, *x*
x	2	Flags	Reserved, always 0
x+2	2	Streams	Number of streams—say, *n*
x+4		StreamHeaders	Array of *n* StreamHdr structures

The Version string shall be "Standard CLI 2002" for any file that is intended to be executed on any conforming implementation of the CLI, and all conforming implementations of the CLI shall accept files that use this version string. Other strings shall be used when the file is restricted to a vendor-specific implementation of the CLI. Future versions of this standard shall specify different strings, but they shall begin "Standard CLI". Other standards that specify additional functionality shall specify their own specific version strings beginning with "Standard". Vendors that provide implementation-specific extensions shall provide a version string that does *not* begin with "Standard".

23.2.2 Stream Header

A stream header gives the names, and the position and length of a particular table or heap. Note that the length of a stream header structure is not fixed, but depends on the length of its name field (a variable-length, null-terminated string).

Offset	Size	Field	Description
0	4	Offset	Memory offset to start of this stream from start of the metadata root (see Partition II, section 23.2.1)
4	4	Size	Size of this stream in bytes; shall be a multiple of 4
8		Name	Name of the stream as null-terminated, variable-length array of ASCII characters, padded to the next 4-byte boundary with \0 characters

Both logical tables and heaps are stored in streams. There are five possible kinds of streams: a stream header with name "#Strings" that points to the physical representation of the String heap where identifier strings are stored; a stream header with name "#US" that points to the physical representation of the Userstring heap; a stream header with name "#Blob" that points to the physical representation of the Blob heap; a stream header with name "#GUID" that points to the physical representation of the Guid heap; and a stream header with name "#~" that points to the physical representation of a set of tables (see Partition II, section 22).

ANNOTATION

Implementation-Specific (Microsoft): Some compilers store metadata in a "#~" stream, which holds an uncompressed, or non-optimized, representation of metadata tables; this includes extra metadata "pointer" tables. Such PE files do not form part of this International Standard.

Each kind of stream may occur at most once; that is, a metadata file may not contain two "#US" streams, or five "#Blob" streams. Streams need not be there if they are empty.

The next sections will describe the structure of each kind of stream in more detail.

23.2.3 *#Strings Heap*

The stream of bytes pointed to by a "#Strings" header is the physical representation of the logical string heap. The physical heap may contain garbage; that is, it may contain parts that are unreachable from any of the tables, but parts that are reachable from a table shall contain a valid null-terminated UTF8 string. When the #String heap is present, the first entry is always the empty string (i.e., \0).

23.2.4 *#US and #Blob Heaps*

The stream of bytes pointed to by a "#US" or "#Blob" header are the physical representation of logical Userstring and Blob heaps, respectively. Both these heaps may contain garbage, as long as any part that is reachable from any of the tables contains a valid "blob." Individual blobs are stored with their length encoded in the first few bytes:

- If the first 1 byte of the "blob" is 0*bs*, then the rest of the "blob" contains the (*bs*) bytes of actual data.
- If the first 2 bytes of the "blob" are 10*bs* and *x*, then the rest of the "blob" contains the (*bs* << 8 + *x*) bytes of actual data.
- If the first 4 bytes of the "blob" are 110*bs*, *x*, *y*, and *z*, then the rest of the "blob" contains the (*bs* << 24 + *x* << 16 + *y* << 8 + *z*) bytes of actual data.

The first entry in both these heaps is the empty "blob" that consists of the single byte 0x00.

Strings in the #US (Userstring) heap are encoded using 16-bit Unicode encodings. The count on each string is the number of bytes (not characters) in the string. Furthermore, there is an additional terminal byte (so all byte counts are odd, not even). This final byte holds the value 1 if and only if any UTF16 character within the string has any bit set in its top byte, or its low byte is any of the following: 0x01–0x08, 0x0E–0x1F, 0x27, 0x2D, 0x7F. Otherwise, it holds 0. The 1 signifies Unicode characters that require handling beyond that normally provided for 8-bit encoding sets.

23.2.5 *#GUID Heap*

The "#GUID" header points to a sequence of 128-bit GUIDs. There might be unreachable GUIDs stored in the stream.

23.2.6 *#~ Stream*

The "#~" streams contain the actual physical representations of the logical metadata tables (see Partition II, section 21). A "#~" stream has the following top-level structure:

Offset	Size	Field	Description
0	4	Reserved	Reserved, always 0
4	1	MajorVersion	Major version of table schemata, always 1
5	1	MinorVersion	Minor version of table schemata, always 0
6	1	HeapSizes	Bit vector for heap sizes

5. Metadata File Format

Offset	Size	Field	Description
7	1	Reserved	Reserved, always 1
8	8	Valid	Bit vector of present tables, let *n* be the number of bits that are 1
16	8	Sorted	Bit vector of sorted tables
24	4*n	Rows	Array of *n* 4-byte unsigned integers indicating the number of rows for each present table
24+4*n		Tables	The sequence of physical tables

The HeapSizes field is a bit vector that encodes how wide indices into the various heaps are. If bit 0 is set, indices into the "#String" heap are 4 bytes wide; if bit 1 is set, indices into the "#GUID" heap are 4 bytes wide; bit 2 is not used; if bit 3 is set, indices into the "#Blob" heap are 4 bytes wide. Conversely, if the HeapSize bit for a particular heap is not set, indices into that heap are 2 bytes wide.

Bit Position	Description
0x01	Size of "#String" stream >= 2^{16}.
0x02	Size of "#GUID" stream >= 2^{16}.
0x04	Size of "#Blob" stream >= 2^{16}.

The Valid field is a 64-bit-wide bit vector that has a specific bit set for each table that is stored in the stream; the mapping of tables to indices is given at the start of Partition II, section 21. For example when the *DeclSecurity* table is present in the logical metadata, bit 0x0e should be set in the Valid vector. It is illegal to include non-existent tables in Valid, so all bits above 0x2b shall be zero.

The Rows array contains the number of rows for each of the tables that are present. When decoding physical metadata to logical metadata, the number of 1's in Valid indicates the number of elements in the Rows array.

A crucial aspect in the encoding of a logical table is its *schema*. The schema for each table is given in Partition II, section 21. For example, the table with assigned index 0x02 is a *TypeDef* table, which, according to its specification in Partition II, section 21.34, has the following columns: 4-byte-wide flags, index into the String heap, another index into the String heap, index into the *TypeDef* or *TypeRef* table, index into the *Field* table, index into the *MethodDef* table.

The physical representation of a table with schema (C_0,…,C_{n-1}) with n rows consists of the concatenation of the physical representation of each of its rows. The physical representation of a row with schema (C_0,…,C_{n-1}) is the concatenation of the physical representation of each of its elements. The physical representation of a row cell e at a column with type C is defined as follows:

- If e is a constant, it is stored using the number of bytes as specified for its column type C (i.e., a 2-byte bitmask of type *PropertyAttributes*).
- If e is an index into the Guid heap, Blob [heap], or String heap, it is stored using the number of bytes as defined in the HeapSizes field.
- If e is a simple index into a table with index i, it is stored using 2 bytes if table i has less than 2^{16} rows, otherwise it is stored using 4 bytes.
- If e is a *coded index* (see Partition II, section 21) that points into table t_i out of n possible tables t_0, …t_{n-1}, then it is stored as e << (log n) | tag{ t_0, …t_{n-1}}[t_i] using 2 bytes if the maximum number of rows of tables, t_0, …t_{n-1}, is less than $2^{16-(\log n)}$, and using 4 bytes otherwise. The family of finite maps tag{ t_0, …t_{n-1}} is defined below. Note that decoding a physical row requires the inverse of this mapping. (For example, the *Parent* column of the *Constant* table indexes a row in the *Field*, *Param*, or *Property* tables. The actual table is encoded into the low 2 bits of the number, using the values: 0 => *Field*, 1 => *Param*, 2 => *Property*. The remaining bits hold the actual row number being indexed. For example, a value of 0x321 indexes row number 0xC8 in the *Param* table.)

TypeDefOrRef: 2 bits to encode tag	Tag
`TypeDef`	0
`TypeRef`	1
`TypeSpec`	2

HasConstant: 2 bits to encode tag	Tag
`FieldDef`	0
`ParamDef`	1
`Property`	2

HasCustomAttribute: 5 bits to encode tag	Tag
MethodDef	0
FieldDef	1
TypeRef	2
TypeDef	3
ParamDef	4
InterfaceImpl	5
MemberRef	6
Module	7
Permission	8
Property	9
Event	10
StandAloneSig	11
ModuleRef	12
TypeSpec	13
Assembly	14
AssemblyRef	15
File	16
ExportedType	17
ManifestResource	18

HasFieldMarshall: 1 bit to encode tag	Tag
FieldDef	0
ParamDef	1

HasDeclSecurity: 2 bits to encode tag	Tag
TypeDef	0
MethodDef	1
Assembly	2

MemberRefParent: 3 bits to encode tag	Tag
Not used	0
TypeRef	1
ModuleRef	2
MethodDef	3
TypeSpec	4

HasSemantics: 1 bit to encode tag	Tag
Event	0
Property	1

MethodDefOrRef: 1 bit to encode tag	Tag
MethodDef	0
MemberRef	1

MemberForwarded: 1 bit to encode tag	Tag
FieldDef	0
MethodDef	1

Implementation: 2 bits to encode tag	Tag
`File`	0
`AssemblyRef`	1
`ExportedType`	

CustomAttributeType: 3 bits to encode tag	Tag
Not used	0
Not used	1
`MethodDef`	2
`MemberRef`	3
Not used	4

ResolutionScope: 2 bits to encode tag	Tag
`Module`	0
`ModuleRef`	1
`AssemblyRef`	2
`TypeRef`	3

24 File Format Extensions to PE

This contains informative text only.

The file format for CLI components is a strict extension of the current Portable Executable (PE) file format. This extended PE format enables the operating system to recognize runtime images, accommodates code emitted as CIL or native code, and accommodates runtime metadata as an integral part of the emitted code. There are also specifications for a subset of the full Windows PE/COFF file format, in sufficient detail that a tool or compiler can use the specifications to emit valid CLI images.

The PE format frequently uses the term RVA (Relative Virtual Address). An RVA is the address of an item *once loaded into memory*, with the base address of the image file subtracted from it (i.e., the offset from the base address where the file is loaded). The RVA of an item will almost always differ from its position within the file on disk. To compute the file position of an item with RVA r, search all the sections in the PE file to find the section with RVA s, length l, and file position p in which the RVA lies—i.e., $s \leq r < s+l$. The file position of the item is then given by $p+(r-s)$.

Unless stated otherwise, all binary values are stored in little-endian format.

End informative text

24.1 Structure of the Runtime File Format

The figure below provides a high-level view of the CLI file format. All runtime images contain the following:

- PE headers, with specific guidelines on how field values should be set in a runtime file.
- A CLI header that contains all of the runtime-specific data entries. The runtime header is read-only and shall be placed in any read-only section.
- The sections that contain the actual data as described by the headers, including imports/exports, data, and code.

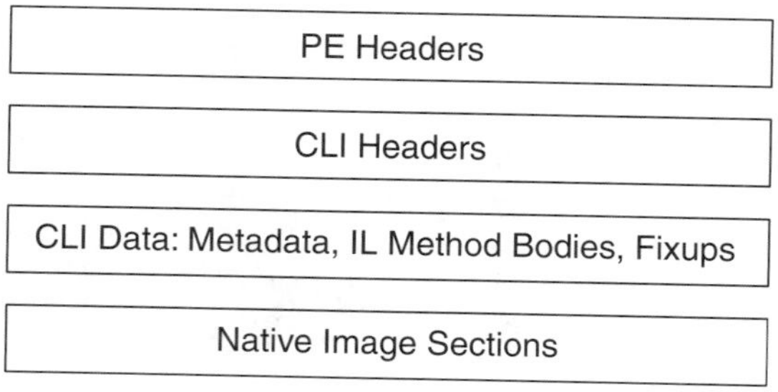

PE Headers
CLI Headers
CLI Data: Metadata, IL Method Bodies, Fixups
Native Image Sections

The CLI header (see Partition II, section 24.3.3) is found using the "CLI Header" directory entry in the PE header. The CLI header in turn contains the address and sizes of the runtime data (metadata, see Partition II, section 23; and CIL, see Partition II, section 24.4) in the rest of the image. Note that the runtime data can be merged into other areas of the PE format with the other data based on the attributes of the sections (such as read-only versus execute, etc.).

24.2 PE Headers

A PE image starts with an MS-DOS header followed by a PE signature, followed by the PE file header, and then the PE optional header followed by PE section headers.

ANNOTATION: Many of the entries in the tables in this whole section 24 are prescribed, and certain values are required. In some cases, the value is 0, or marked "to be ignored," in which case it is not relevant to managed code. If you write the values specified, a PE file so created will run. Great care has been taken to ensure the accuracy of these values. Some errors have been found and corrected, but so far, all errors are in the direction of a differing value not causing a problem. In general, if you write what we tell you, it will run.

24.2.1 *MS-DOS Header*

The PE format starts with an MS-DOS stub of exactly the following 128 bytes to be placed at the front of the module. At offset 0x3c in the DOS header is a 4-byte unsigned integer, offset **lfa***new* to the PE signature (shall be "PE\0\0"), immediately followed by the PE file header.

0x4d	0x5a	0x90	0x00	0x03	0x00	0x00	0x00
0x04	0x00	0x00	0x00	0xFF	0xFF	0x00	0x00
0xb8	0x00	0x00	0x00	0x00	0x00	0x00	0x00
0x40	0x00	0x00	0x00	0x00	0x00	0x00	0x00
0x00	0x00	0x00	0x00	0x00	0x00	0x00	0x00
0x00	0x00	0x00	0x00	0x00	0x00	0x00	0x00
0x00	0x00	0x00	0x00	0x00	0x00	0x00	0x00
0x00	0x00	0x00	0x00	*lfanew*			
0x0e	0x1f	0xba	0x0e	0x00	0xb4	0x09	0xcd
0x21	0xb8	0x01	0x4c	0xcd	0x21	0x54	0x68
0x69	0x73	0x20	0x70	0x72	0x6f	0x67	0x72
0x61	0x6d	0x20	0x63	0x61	0x6e	0x6e	0x6f
0x74	0x20	0x62	0x65	0x20	0x72	0x75	0x6e

0x20	0x69	0x6e	0x20	0x44	0x4f	0x53	0x20
0x6d	0x6f	0x64	0x65	0x2e	0x0d	0x0d	0x0a
0x24	0x00	0x00	0x00	0x00	0x00	0x00	0x00

24.2.2 *PE File Header*

Immediately after the PE signature is the PE file header consisting of the following:

Offset	Size	Field	Description
0	2	Machine	Always 0x14c
2	2	Number of Sections	Number of sections; indicates size of the section table, which immediately follows the headers.
4	4	Time/Date Stamp	Time and date the file was created in seconds since January 1st 1970 00:00:00 or 0.
8	4	Pointer to Symbol Table	Always 0
12	4	Number of Symbols	Always 0
16	2	Optional Header Size	Size of the optional header; the format is described below.
18	2	Characteristics	Flags indicating attributes of the file, see section 24.2.2.1.

ANNOTATION: Notice that *Pointer to Symbol Table* and *Number of Symbols* are always 0. These symbol tables are for unmanaged code and data.

24.2.2.1 Characteristics

A CIL-only DLL sets flag 0x2000 to 1, while a CIL-only .exe has flag 0x2000 set to zero:

Flag	Value	Description
IMAGE_FILE_DLL	0x2000	The image file is a dynamic-link library (DLL).

5. Metadata File Format

Except for the `IMAGE_FILE_DLL` flag (0x2000), flags 0x0002, 0x0004, 0x008, and 0x0100 shall all be set, while all others shall always be zero.

ANNOTATION: The value of the characteristics field shall be either 0x210D or 0x10D.

24.2.3 *PE Optional Header*

Immediately after the PE header is the PE optional header. This header contains the following information:

Offset	Size	Header Part	Description
0	28	Standard fields	These define general properties of the PE file, see Partition II, section 24.2.3.1.
28	68	NT-specific fields	These include additional fields to support specific features of Windows, see Partition II, section 24.2.3.2.
96	128	Data directories	These fields are address/size pairs for special tables, found in the image file (for example, Import Table and Export Table).

24.2.3.1 PE Header Standard Fields

These fields are required for all PE files and contain the following information:

Offset	Size	Field	Description
0	2	Magic	Always 0x10B
2	1	LMajor	Always 6
3	1	LMinor	Always 0
4	4	Code Size	Size of the code (text) section, or the sum of all code sections if there are multiple sections.
8	4	Initialized Data Size	Size of the initialized data section, or the sum of all such sections if there are multiple data sections.

Offset	Size	Field	Description
12	4	Uninitialized Data Size	Size of the uninitialized data section, or the sum of all such sections if there are multiple uninitialized data sections.
16	4	Entry Point RVA	RVA of entry point; needs to point to bytes 0xFF25 followed by the RVA in a section marked execute/read for EXEs or 0 for DLLs.
20	4	Base Of Code	RVA of the code section, always 0x00400000 for EXEs and 0x10000000 for DLLs.
24	4	Base Of Data	RVA of the data section.

ANNOTATION: The first three values in this table must be as specified here, or the file is invalid.

Managed code always starts at a given entry point within the file **mscoree.dll**. See Chapter 4 of this book for an example.

This contains informative text only.

The entry point RVA shall always be either the x86 entry point stub or 0. On non-CLI-aware platforms, this stub will call the entry point API of mscoree (_CorExeMain or _CorDllMain). The mscoree entry point will use the module handle to load the metadata from the image, and invoke the entry point specified in the CLI header.

End informative text

24.2.3.2 PE Header Windows NT–Specific Fields

These fields are Windows NT–specific:

Offset	Size	Field	Description
28	4	Image Base	Always 0x400000.

Offset	Size	Field	Description
32	4	Section Alignment	Always 0x2000.
36	4	File Alignment	Either 0x200 or 0x1000.
40	2	OS Major	Always 4.
42	2	OS Minor	Always 0.
44	2	User Major	Always 0.
46	2	User Minor	Always 0.
48	2	SubSys Major	Always 4.
50	2	SubSys Minor	Always 0.
52	4	Reserved	Always 0.
56	4	Image Size	Size, in bytes, of image, including all headers and padding; shall be a multiple of Section Alignment.
60	4	Header Size	Combined size of MS-DOS header, PE header, PE optional header and padding; shall be a multiple of the file alignment.
64	4	File Checksum	Always 0.
68	2	SubSystem	Subsystem required to run this image. Shall be either IMAGE_SUBSYSTEM_WINDOWS_CE_GUI (0x3) or IMAGE_SUBSYSTEM_WINDOWS_GUI (0x2).
70	2	DLL Flags	Always 0.
72	4	Stack Reserve Size	Always 0x100000 (1Mb).
76	4	Stack Commit Size	Always 0x1000 (4Kb).
80	4	Heap Reserve Size	Always 0x100000 (1Mb).
84	4	Heap Commit Size	Always 0x1000 (4Kb).
88	4	Loader Flags	Always 0.
92	4	Number of Data Directories	Always 0x10.

ANNOTATION: The specified values are standard values that work, and should continue to work in the future. Setting other values removes the guarantee that they will work, although alternative values may also work on some operating systems.

The number of data directories is set at 0x10, and the last of these is the data directory that contains the IL metadata pointer.

24.2.3.3 PE Header Data Directories

The optional header data directories give the address and size of several tables that appear in the sections of the PE file. Each data directory entry contains the RVA and Size of the structure it describes.

Offset	Size	Field	Description
96	8	Export Table	Always 0.
104	8	Import Table	RVA of Import Table (see Partition II, section 24.3.1).
112	8	Resource Table	Always 0.
120	8	Exception Table	Always 0.
128	8	Certificate Table	Always 0.
136	8	Base Relocation Table	Relocation Table; set to 0 if unused (see Partition II, section 24.3.2).
144	8	Debug	Always 0.
152	8	Copyright	Always 0.
160	8	Global Ptr	Always 0.
168	8	TLS Table	Always 0.
176	8	Load Config Table	Always 0.
184	8	Bound Import	Always 0.
192	8	IAT	RVA of Import Address Table (see Partition II, section 24.3.1).

Offset	Size	Field	Description
200	8	Delay Import Descriptor	Always 0.
208	8	CLI Header	CLI header with directories for runtime data, (see Partition II, section 24.3.3).
216	8	Reserved	Always 0.

The tables pointed to by the directory entries are stored in one of the PE file's sections; these sections themselves are described by section headers.

ANNOTATION: The CLI header, if present and non-zero, always indicates that the file contains managed code. It specifies where the metadata information is.

24.3 Section Headers

Immediately following the optional header is the section table, which contains a number of section headers. This positioning is required because the file header does not contain a direct pointer to the section table; the location of the section table is determined by calculating the location of the first byte after the headers.

Each section header has the following format, for a total of 40 bytes per entry:

Offset	Size	Field	Description
0	8	Name	An 8-byte, null-padded ASCII string. There is no terminating null if the string is exactly eight characters long.
8	4	VirtualSize	Total size of the section when loaded into memory in bytes rounded to Section Alignment. If this value is greater than SizeofRawData, the section is zero-padded.
12	4	VirtualAddress	For executable images this is the address of the first byte of the section, when loaded into memory, relative to the image base.

Offset	Size	Field	Description
16	4	SizeOfRawData	Size of the initialized data on disk in bytes; shall be a multiple of File Alignment from the PE header. If this is less than VirtualSize, the remainder of the section is zero-filled. Because this field is rounded while the VirtualSize field is not, it is possible for this to be greater than VirtualSize as well. When a section contains only uninitialized data, this field should be 0.
20	4	PointerToRawData	Offset of section's first page within the PE file. This shall be a multiple of File Alignment from the optional header. When a section contains only uninitialized data, this field should be 0.
24	4	PointerToRelocations	RVA of Relocation section [see Partition II, section 24.3.2].
28	4	PointerToLinenumbers	Always 0.
32	2	NumberOfRelocations	Number of relocations, set to 0 if unused.
34	2	NumberOfLinenumbers	Always 0.
36	4	Characteristics	Flags describing section's characteristics; see below.

The following table defines the possible characteristics of the section.

Flag	Value	Description
IMAGE_SCN_CNT_CODE	0x00000020	Section contains executable code.
IMAGE_SCN_CNT_INITIALIZED_DATA	0x00000040	Section contains initialized data.
IMAGE_SCN_CNT_UNINITIALIZED_DATA	0x00000080	Section contains uninitialized data.
IMAGE_SCN_MEM_EXECUTE	0x20000000	Section can be executed as code.
IMAGE_SCN_MEM_READ	0x40000000	Section can be read.
IMAGE_SCN_MEM_WRITE	0x80000000	Section can be written to.

24.3.1 *Import Table and Import Address Table (IAT)*

The Import Table and the Import Address Table (IAT) are used to import the `_CorExeMain` (for a .exe) or `_CorDllMain` (for a .dll) entries of the runtime engine (mscoree.dll). The Import Table directory entry points to a one-element, zero-terminated array of Import Directory entries (in a general PE file there is one entry for each imported DLL):

Offset	Size	Field	Description
0	4	ImportLookupTable	RVA of the Import Lookup Table.
4	4	DateTimeStamp	Always 0.
8	4	ForwarderChain	Always 0.
12	4	Name	RVA of null-terminated ASCII string "mscoree.dll".
16	4	ImportAddressTable	RVA of Import Address Table (this is the same as the RVA of the IAT descriptor in the optional header).
20	20		End of Import Table; shall be filled with zeros.

The Import Lookup Table and the Import Address Table (IAT) are both one-element, zero-terminated arrays of RVAs into the Hint/Name table. Bit 31 of the RVA shall be set to 0. In a general PE file there is one entry in this table for every imported symbol.

Offset	Size	Field	Description
0	4	Hint/Name Table RVA	A 31-bit RVA into the Hint/Name table. Bit 31 shall be set to 0, indicating import by name.
4	4		End of table; shall be filled with zeros.

The IAT should be in an executable and writable section, as the loader will replace the pointers into the Hint/Name table by the actual entry points of the imported symbols.

The Hint/Name table contains the name of the dll entry that is imported.

Offset	Size	Field	Description
0	2	Hint	Shall be 0.
2	variable	Name	Case-sensitive, null-terminated ASCII string containing name to import. Shall be "_CorExeMain" for a .exe file and "_CorDllMain" for a .dll file.

ANNOTATION: In short, the previous section is saying that for managed code, the Import Table (the first table in this section) imports only the single file **mscoree.dll**, which executes the VES software. The Import Address Table (IAT) then says which routine to run. If your PE file is a .exe file, it must be **_CorExeMain**; if it is a .dll, it must be **_CorDllMain**.

From the point of view of the operating system, it loads **mscoree.dll**, calls one of the two routines, and stops. From the point of view of the VES, the call to one of those two routines is where the managed code starts running. When the managed code finishes executing the program and returns, it hands off to the operating system.

24.3.2 *Relocations*

In a pure CIL image, a single fixup of type IMAGE_REL_BASED_HIGHLOW (0x3) is required for the x86 startup stub which accesses the IAT to load the runtime engine on down-level loaders. When building a mixed CIL/native image or when the image contains embedded RVAs in user data, the relocation section contains relocations for these as well.

The relocations shall be in their own section, named ".reloc", which shall be the final section in the PE file. The relocation section contains a fixup table. The fixup table is broken into blocks of fixups. Each block represents the fixups for a 4K page, and each block shall start on a 32-bit boundary.

Each fixup block starts with the following structure:

Offset	Size	Field	Description
0	4	PageRVA	The RVA of the block in which the fixup needs to be applied. The low 12 bits shall be zero.
4	4	Block Size	Total number of bytes in the fixup block, including the PageRVA and Block Size fields, as well as the Type/Offset fields that follow, rounded up to the next multiple of 4.

5. Metadata File Format

The Block Size field is then followed by (BlockSize – 8)/2 Type/Offset. Each entry is a word (2 bytes) and has the following structure (if necessary, insert 2 bytes of 0 to pad to a multiple of 4 bytes in length):

Offset	Size	Field	Description
0	4 bits	Type	Stored in high 4 bits of word. Value indicating which type of fixup is to be applied (described below).
0	12 bits	Offset	Stored in remaining 12 bits of word. Offset from starting address specified in the PageRVA field for the block. This offset specifies where the fixup is to be applied.

24.3.3 *CLI Header*

The CLI header contains all of the runtime-specific data entries and other information. The header should be placed in a read-only, sharable section of the image. This header is defined as follows:

Offset	Size	Field	Description
0	4	Cb	Size of the header in bytes.
4	2	MajorRuntimeVersion	The minimum version of the runtime required to run this program, currently 2.
6	2	MinorRuntimeVersion	The minor portion of the version, currently 0.
8	8	MetaData	RVA and size of the physical metadata (see Partition II, section 23).
16	4	Flags	Flags describing this runtime image. (see Partition II, section 24.3.3.1).
20	4	EntryPointToken	Token for the MethodDef or File of the entry point for the image.
24	8	Resources	Location of CLI resources (see Partition V).
32	8	StrongNameSignature	RVA of the hash data for this PE file used by the CLI loader for binding and versioning,
40	8	CodeManagerTable	Always 0.

Offset	Size	Field	Description
48	8	VTableFixups	RVA of an array of locations in the file that contain an array of function pointers (e.g., vtable slots); see below.
56	8	ExportAddressTableJumps	Always 0.
64	8	ManagedNativeHeader	Always 0.

ANNOTATION: The CLI header is what distinguishes a managed executable file. It is through this header that the metadata of the image is located.

24.3.3.1 Runtime Flags

The following flags describe this runtime image and are used by the loader.

Flag	Value	Description
COMIMAGE_FLAGS_ILONLY	0x00000001	Always 1.
COMIMAGE_FLAGS_32BITREQUIRED	0x00000002	Image may only be loaded into a 32-bit process—for instance, if there are 32-bit vtable fixups, or casts from native integers to int32. CLI implementations that have 64-bit native integers shall refuse loading binaries with this flag set.
COMIMAGE_FLAGS_STRONGNAMESIGNED	0x00000008	Image has a strong name signature.
COMIMAGE_FLAGS_TRACKDEBUGDATA	0x00010000	Always 0.

24.3.3.2 Entry Point Metadata Token

- The entry point token (see Partition II, section 14.4.1.2) is always a *MethodDef* token (see Partition II, section 21.24) or *File* token (see Partition II, section 21.19) when the entry point for a multi-module assembly is not in the manifest assembly. The signature and implementation flags in metadata for the method indicate how the entry is run.

ANNOTATION: If you have a managed entry point, the entry point token is either the method that is the entry point, or if the entry point method is in another file in the assembly, a file token for that file. That file must have the entry point. For more information, see Partition II, section 14.4.1.2, on the ilasm **.entrypoint** directive. Do not confuse the **EntryPointToken** with the Entry Point RVA in the CLI header portion of the PE file, which tells the operating system to load the **mscoree.dll** file, which loads the VES.

24.3.3.3 Vtable Fixup

Certain languages, which choose not to follow the common type system runtime model, may have virtual functions which need to be represented in a vtable. These vtables are laid out by the compiler, not by the runtime. Finding the correct vtable slot and calling indirectly through the value held in that slot is also done by the compiler. The **VtableFixups** field in the runtime header contains the location and size of an array of vtable fixups (see Partition II, section 14.5.1). Vtables shall be emitted into a *read-write* section of the PE file.

Each entry in this array describes a contiguous array of vtable slots of the specified size. Each slot starts out initialized to the metadata token value for the method they need to call. At image load time, the runtime loader will turn each entry into a pointer to machine code for the CPU and can be called directly.

Offset	Size	Field	Description
0	4	VirtualAddress	RVA of Vtable
4	2	Size	Number of entries in Vtable
6	2	Type	Type of the entries, as defined in table below

Constant	Value	Description
COR_VTABLE_32BIT	0x01	Vtable slots are 32 bits.
COR_VTABLE_64BIT	0x02	Vtable slots are 64 bits.
COR_VTABLE_FROM_UNMANAGED	0x04	Transition from unmanaged to managed code.
COR_VTABLE_CALL_MOST_DERIVED	0x10	Call most derived method described by the token (only valid for virtual methods).

24.3.3.4 Strong Name Signature

This header entry points to the strong name hash for an image that can be used to deterministically identify a module from a referencing point (see Partition II, section 6.2.1.3).

24.4 Common Intermediate Language Physical Layout

This section contains the layout of the data structures used to describe a CIL method and its exceptions. Method bodies can be stored in any read-only section of a PE file. The*MethodDef* (see Partition II, section 21.24) records in metadata carry each method's RVA.

A method consists of a method header immediately followed by the method body, possible followed by extra method data sections (see Partition II, section 24.4.5), typically exception handling data. If exception handling data is present, then the CorILMethod_MoreSects flag (see Partition II, section 24.4.4) shall be specified in the method header and for each chained item after that.

There are two flavors of method headers—tiny (see Partition II, section 24.4.2) and fat (see Partition II, section 24.4.3). The three least significant bits in a method header indicate which type is present (see Partition II, section 24.4.1). The tiny header is 1 byte long and represents only the method's code size. A method is given a tiny header if it has no local variables, maxstack is 8 or less, the method has no exceptions, the method size is less than 64 bytes, and the method has no flags above 0x7. Fat headers carry full information—local vars signature token, maxstack, code size, flag. Method headers shall be 4-byte aligned.

24.4.1 *Method Header Type Values*

The three least significant bits of the first byte of the method header indicate what type of header is present. These 3 bits will be one, and only one, of the following:

Value	Value	Description
`CorILMethod_TinyFormat`	`0x2`	The method header is tiny (see Partition II, section 24.4.2).
`CorILMethod_FatFormat`	`0x3`	The method header is fat (see Partition II, section 24.4.3).

24.4.2 *Tiny Format*

Tiny headers use a 5-bit length encoding. The following is true for all tiny headers:

- No local variables are allowed.
- No exceptions.
- No extra data sections.
- The operand stack need be no bigger than eight entries.

The first encoding has the following format:

Start Bit	Count of Bits	Description
0	2	Flags (CorILMethod_TinyFormat shall be set; see Partition II, section 24.4.4).
2	6	Size of the method body immediately following this header. Used only when the size of the method is less than 2^6 bytes.

24.4.3 *Fat Format*

The fat format is used whenever the tiny format is not sufficient. This may be true for one or more of the following reasons:

- The method is too large to encode the size.
- There are exceptions.
- There are extra data sections.
- There are local variables.
- The operand stack needs more than eight entries.

A fat header has the following structure:

Offset	Size	Field	Description
0	12 (bits)	Flags	Flags (CorILMethod_FatFormat shall be set; see Partition II, section 24.4.4).
12 (bits)	4 (bits)	Size	Size of this header expressed as the count of 4-byte integers occupied.
2	2	MaxStack	Maximum number of items on the operand stack.
4	4	CodeSize	Size in bytes of the actual method body.
8	4	LocalVarSigTok	Metadata token for a signature describing the layout of the local variables for the method. 0 means there are no local variables present.

24.4.4 *Flags for Method Headers*

The first byte of a method header may also contain the following flags, valid only for the fat format, that indicate how the method is to be executed:

Flag	Value	Description
CorILMethod_FatFormat	0x3	Method header is fat.
CorILMethod_TinyFormat	0x2	Method header is tiny.
CorILMethod_MoreSects	0x8	More sections follow after this header (see Partition II, section 24.4.5).
CorILMethod_InitLocals	0x10	Call default constructor on all local variables.

24.4.5 *Method Data Section*

At the next 4-byte boundary following the method body can be extra method data sections. These method data sections start with a 2-byte header (1 byte for flags, 1 byte for the length of the actual data) or a 4-byte header (1 byte for flags, and 3 bytes for length of the actual data). The first byte determines the kind of the header, and what data is in the actual section:

Flag	Value	Description
CorILMethod_Sect_EHTable	0x1	Exception handling data.
CorILMethod_Sect_OptILTable	0x2	Reserved, shall be 0.
CorILMethod_Sect_FatFormat	0x40	Data format is of the fat variety, meaning there is a 3-byte length. If not set, the header is small, with a 1-byte length.
CorILMethod_Sect_MoreSects	0x80	Another data section occurs after this current section.

Currently, the method data sections are only used for exception tables (see Partition II, section 18). The layout of a small exception header structure as is a follows:

Offset	Size	Field	Description
0	1	Kind	Flags as described above.
1	1	DataSize	Size of the data for the block, including the header—say, *n**12+4.
2	2	Reserved	Padding, always 0.
4	n	Clauses	*n* small exception clauses (see Partition II, section 24.4.6).

The layout of a fat exception header structure is as follows:

Offset	Size	Field	Description
0	1	Kind	Which type of exception block is being used
1	3	DataSize	Size of the data for the block, including the header—say, *n**24+4.
4	n	Clauses	*n* fat exception clauses (see Partition II, section 24.4.6).

24.4.6 *Exception Handling Clauses*

Exception handling clauses also come in small and fat versions.

The small form of the exception clause should be used whenever the code size for the try block and handler code is smaller than or equal to 256 bytes. The format for a small exception clause is as follows:

Offset	Size	Field	Description
0	2	Flags	Flags; see below
2	2	TryOffset	Offset in bytes of try block from start of the header
4	1	TryLength	Length in bytes of the try block
5	2	HandlerOffset	Location of the handler for this try block
7	1	HandlerLength	Size of the handler code in bytes
8	4	ClassToken	Metadata token for a type-based exception handler
8	4	FilterOffset	Offset in method body for filter-based exception handler

The layout of fat form of exception handling clauses is as follows:

Offset	Size	Field	Description
0	4	Flags	Flags; see below
4	4	TryOffset	Offset in bytes of try block from start of the header
8	4	TryLength	Length in bytes of the try block
12	4	HandlerOffset	Location of the handler for this try block
16	4	HandlerLength	Size of the handler code in bytes
20	4	ClassToken	Metadata token for a type-based exception handler
20	4	FilterOffset	Offset in method body for filter-based exception handler

The following flag values are used for each exception handling clause:

Flag	Value	Description
COR_ILEXCEPTION_CLAUSE_EXCEPTION	0x0000	A typed exception clause
COR_ILEXCEPTION_CLAUSE_FILTER	0x0001	An exception filter and handler clause
COR_ILEXCEPTION_CLAUSE_FINALLY	0x0002	A finally clause
COR_ILEXCEPTION_CLAUSE_FAULT	0x0004	Fault clause (finally [clause] that is called on exception only)

6. Partition III: CIL Instruction Set

1 Scope

This specification is a detailed description of the Common Intermediate Language (CIL) instruction set, part of the specification of the Common Language Infrastructure. Partition I describes the architecture of the CLI and provides an overview of a large number of issues relating to the CIL instruction set. That overview is essential to an understanding of the instruction set as described here.

ANNOTATION: The importance of section 1 in Partition III cannot be overemphasized, particularly if you are writing a compiler or want to understand the output of a compiler. It will also help you if you care about the numeric characteristics of your computation, and it should help you pick a language that provides the numeric characteristics you want.

Each instruction description describes a set of related CLI machine instructions. Each instruction definition consists of five parts:

- A table describing the binary format, assembly language notation, and description of each variant of the instruction. See Partition III, section 1.2.
- A stack transition diagram that describes the state of the evaluation stack before and after the instruction is executed. See Partition III, section 1.3.
- An English description of the instruction. See Partition III, section 1.4.
- A list of exceptions that might be thrown by the instruction. See Partition I, section 12.4.2 for details. There are three exceptions which may be thrown by any instruction and are not listed with the instruction:

`ExecutionEngineException` indicates that the internal state of the Execution Engine is corrupted and execution cannot continue. (**Note:** In a system that executes only verifiable code this exception is not thrown.)

`StackOverflowException` indicates that the hardware stack size has been exceeded. The precise timing of this exception and the conditions under which it occurs are implementation-specific. (**Note:** This exception is unrelated to the maximum stack size described in Partition III, section 1.7.4. That size relates to the depth of the evaluation stack that is part of the method state described in Partition I [section 12.3.2], while this exception has to do with the implementation of that method state on physical hardware.)

`OutOfMemoryException` indicates that the available memory space has been exhausted, either because the instruction inherently allocates memory (`newobj`, `newarr`) or for an implementation-specific reason (for example, an implementation based on just-in-time compilation to native code may run out of space to store the translated method while executing the first `call` or `callvirt` to a given method).

- A section describing the verifiability conditions associated with the instruction. See Partition III, section 1.8.

In addition, operations that have a numeric operand also specify an operand type table that describes how they operate based on the type of the operand. See Partition III, section 1.5.

Note that not all instructions are included in all CLI profiles. See Partition IV for details.

1.1 Data Types

While the Common Type System (CTS) defines a rich type system and the Common Language Specification (CLS) specifies a subset that can be used for language interoperability, the CLI itself deals with a much simpler set of types. These types include user-defined value types and a subset of the built-in types. The subset is collectively known as the "basic CLI types":

- A subset of the full numeric types (`int32`, `int64`, `native int`, and `F`)
- Object references (`O`) without distinction between the type of object referenced
- Pointer types (`native unsigned int` and `&`) without distinction as to the type pointed to

Note that object references and pointer types may be assigned the value `null`. This is defined throughout the CLI to be zero (a bit pattern of all bits zero).

ANNOTATION: Understanding the descriptions in this section of data types, particularly information on the numeric types, is an important part of understanding the VES. Although the CTS specifies a full set of data types, the instruction set clearly supports a much smaller set. The first section of Partition III describes how the VES, without having the full type set built in, handles all of the CTS data types.

One way to view the CLI is that there are actually three type systems, compatible but different. First is the Common Type System (CTS), supported by the metadata, and described in Partition I and the first half of Partition II. This is the richest type system, describing types for all languages, and having many features that affect only a subset of languages. This is the type system that *programmers* see, through the filter of the languages they use.

The next type system, smaller than the CTS, is the type system that *verifiers* use. A verifier checks for subtype relationships between reference types, and the distinctions among all the value types, etc., but sees no distinction, for example, between a signed and an unsigned integer.

Finally, there is the smallest type system—the type system of which the *VES* is aware. This type system contains a subset of the full numeric type system (32- and 64-bit integers, native-size integers, and floating point), both managed and unmanaged pointers, and distinguishes between value types. Although the VES needs to know about the size and shape of value types, it sees objects only as a reference. From the point of view of the VES, all reference types are treated as one type—`O`. This reflects the fact that from an implementation point of view, objects are all represented the same way (typically, as a pointer to data with a standard header on the heap). There are a few object model instructions, but beyond that, the VES has a very simple view of objects, leaving type checking to languages and verifiers.

From that small data type set, then, the class library uses the CIL instruction set to produce all of the CTS data types. For example, although the VES knows only about signed integers, there are both signed and unsigned instructions like `add`. Similarly, some instructions check for overflow, while others do not.

It is the job of the compiler to use the appropriate instruction to get the desired result. For example, as far as the VES operations on the evaluation stack are concerned, it is legitimate to have only one floating point type, and it does not care about its size, which can be anything greater than or equal to 64 bits. It is also legitimate to have more than one floating point type, typically a 32-bit representation and a 64-bit representation. The VES makes the distinction about the size of numeric values only when storing these values to or reading from the heap, statics, local variables, or method arguments. Microsoft's Common Language Runtime, an implementation of the VES, has set that VES floating point size at 64 bits. The compiler must use CIL instructions that force that value back to 32 bits, when appropriate.

If you are writing a compiler, want to understand the output of your compiler, or want to understand the VES, it is essential to understand this section.

1.1.1 *Numeric Data Types*

- The CLI only operates on the numeric types `int32` (4-byte signed integers), `int64` (8-byte signed integers), `native int` (native-size integers), and `F` (native-size floating point numbers). The CIL instruction set, however, allows additional data types to be implemented:
- **Short integers**. The evaluation stack only holds 4- or 8-byte integers, but other locations (arguments, local variables, statics, array elements, fields) may hold 1- or 2-byte integers. Loading from these locations onto the stack either zero-extends (`ldind.u*`, `ldelem.u*`, etc.) or sign-extends (`ldind.i*`, `ldelem.i*`, etc.) to a 4-byte value. Storing to integers (`stind.u1`, `stelem.i2`, etc.) truncates. Use the `conv.ovf.*` instructions to detect when this truncation results in a value that doesn't correctly represent the original value.

> **NOTE**
> Short integers are loaded as 4-byte numbers on all architectures, and these 4-byte numbers must always be tracked as distinct from 8-byte numbers. This helps portability of code by ensuring that the default arithmetic behavior (i.e., when no `conv` or `conv.ovf` instructions are executed) will have identical results on all implementations.

Convert instructions that yield short integer values actually leave an `int32` (32-bit) value on the stack, but it is guaranteed that only the low bits have meaning (i.e., the more significant bits are all zero for the unsigned conversions or a sign extension for the signed conversions). To correctly simulate the full set of short integer operations, a conversion to the short form is required before the `div`, `rem`, `shr`, comparison, and conditional branch instructions.

In addition to the explicit conversion instructions, there are four cases where the CLI handles short integers in a special way:

- Assignment to a local (`stloc`) or argument (`starg`) whose type is declared to be a short integer type automatically truncates to the size specified for the local or argument.

- Loading from a local (`ldloc`) or argument (`ldarg`) whose type is declared to be a short signed integer type automatically sign-extends.
- Calling a procedure with an argument that is a short integer type is equivalent to assignment to the argument value, so it truncates.
- Returning a value from a method whose return type is a short integer is modeled as storing into a short integer within the called procedure (i.e., the CLI automatically truncates) and then loading from a short integer within the calling procedure (i.e., the CLI automatically zero- or sign-extends).

In the last two cases it is up to the native calling convention to determine whether values are actually truncated or extended, as well as whether this is done in the called procedure or the calling procedure. The CIL instruction sequence is unaffected, and it is as though the CIL sequence included an appropriate `conv` instruction.

- **4-byte integers**. The shortest value actually stored on the stack is a 4-byte integer. These can be converted to 8-byte integers or native-size integers using `conv.*` instructions. Native-size integers can be converted to 4-byte integers, but doing so is not portable across architectures. The `conv.i4` and `conv.u4` can be used for this conversion if the excess significant bits should be ignored; the `conv.ovf.i4` and `conv.ovf.u4` instructions can be used to detect the loss of information. Arithmetic operations allow 4-byte integers to be combined with native-size integers, resulting in native-size integers. Four-byte integers may not be directly combined with 8-byte integers (they must be converted to 8-byte integers first).
- **Native-size integers**. Native-size integers can be combined with 4-byte integers using any of the normal arithmetic instructions, and the result will be a native-size integer. Native-size integers must be explicitly converted to 8-byte integers before they can be combined with 8-byte integers.
- **8-byte integers**. Supporting 8-byte integers on 32-bit hardware may be expensive, whereas 32-bit arithmetic is available and efficient on current 64-bit hardware. For this reason, numeric instructions allow `int32` and `native int` data types to be intermixed (yielding the largest type used as input), but these types *cannot* be combined with `int64`s. Instead, a `native int` or `int32` must be explicitly converted to `int64` before it can be combined with an `int64`.
- **Unsigned integers**. Special instructions are used to interpret integers on the stack as though they were unsigned, rather than tagging the stack locations as being unsigned.
- **Floating point numbers**. See also Partition I, section 12.1.3. Storage locations for floating point numbers (statics, array elements, and fields of classes) are of fixed size. The supported storage sizes are `float32` and `float64`. Everywhere else (on the evaluation stack, as arguments, as return types, and as local variables), floating point numbers are represented using an internal floating point type. In each such instance, the

nominal type of the variable or expression is either `float32` or `float64`, but its value may be represented internally with additional range and/or precision. The size of the internal floating point representation is implementation-dependent, may vary, and shall have precision at least as great as that of the variable or expression being represented. An implicit widening conversion to the internal representation from `float32` or `float64` is performed when those types are loaded from storage. The internal representation is typically the natural size for the hardware, or as required for efficient implementation of an operation. The internal representation shall have the following characteristics:

- The internal representation shall have precision and range greater than or equal to the nominal type.
- Conversions to and from the internal representation shall preserve value. (**Note:** This implies that an implicit widening conversion from `float32` (or `float64`) to the internal representation, followed by an explicit conversion from the internal representation to `float32` (or `float64`), will result in a value that is identical to the original `float32` (or `float64`) value.)

NOTE

The above specification allows a compliant implementation to avoid rounding to the precision of the target type on intermediate computations, and thus permits the use of wider precision hardware registers, as well as the application of optimizing transformations which result in the same or greater precision, such as contractions. Where exactly reproducible behavior is required by a language or application, explicit conversions may be used.

When a floating point value whose internal representation has greater range and/or precision than its nominal type is put in a storage location, it is automatically coerced to the type of the storage location. This may involve a loss of precision or the creation of an out-of-range value (NaN, +infinity, or –infinity). However, the value may be retained in the internal representation for future use, if it is reloaded from the storage location without having been modified. It is the responsibility of the compiler to ensure that the memory location is still valid at the time of a subsequent load, taking into account the effects of aliasing and other execution threads (see Partition I, section 12.6). This freedom to carry extra precision is not permitted, however, following the execution of an explicit conversion (`conv.r4` or `conv.r8`), at which time the internal representation must be exactly representable in the associated type.

> **NOTE**
> To detect values that cannot be converted to a particular storage type, use a conversion instruction (`conv.r4`, or `conv.r8`) and then check for an out-of-range value using `ckfinite`. To detect underflow when converting to a particular storage type, a comparison to zero is required before and after the conversion.

> **NOTE**
> This standard does not specify the behavior of arithmetic operations on denormalized floating point numbers, nor does it specify when or whether such representations should be created. This is in keeping with IEC 60559:1989. In addition, this standard does not specify how to access the exact bit pattern of NaNs that are created, nor the behavior when converting a NaN between 32-bit and 64-bit representation. All of this behavior is deliberately left implementation-specific.

1.1.2 *Boolean Data Type*

A CLI Boolean type occupies 1 byte in memory. A bit pattern of all zeros denotes a value of false. A bit pattern with any bit set (analogous to a non-zero integer) denotes a value of true.

1.1.3 *Object References*

Object references (type `O`) are completely opaque. There are no arithmetic instructions that allow object references as operands, and the only comparison operations permitted are equality (and inequality) between two object references. There are no conversion operations defined on object references. Object references are created by certain CIL object instructions (notably `newobj` and `newarr`). Object references can be passed as arguments, stored as local variables, returned as values, and stored in arrays and as fields of objects.

1.1.4 *Runtime Pointer Types*

There are two kinds of pointers: unmanaged pointers and managed pointers. For pointers into the same array or object, the following arithmetic operations are defined:

- Adding an integer to a pointer, where the integer is interpreted as a number of bytes, results in a pointer of the same kind.
- Subtracting an integer (number of bytes) from a pointer results in a pointer of the same kind. Note that subtracting a pointer from an integer is not permitted.
- Two pointers, regardless of kind, can be subtracted from one another, producing an integer that specifies the number of bytes between the addresses they reference.

None of these operations is allowed in verifiable code.

It is important to understand the impact on the garbage collector of using arithmetic on the different kinds of pointers. Since unmanaged pointers must never reference memory that is controlled by the garbage collector, performing arithmetic on them can endanger the memory safety of the system (hence it is not verifiable), but since they are not reported to the garbage collector there is no impact on its operation.

Managed pointers, however, are reported to the garbage collector. As part of garbage collection both the contents of the location to which they point *and* the pointer itself can be modified. The garbage collector will ignore managed pointers if they point into memory that is not under its control (the evaluation stack, the call stack, static memory, or memory under the control of another allocator). If, however, a managed pointer refers to memory controlled by the garbage collector it *must* point to either a field of an object, an element of an array, or the address of the element just past the end of an array. If address arithmetic is used to create a managed pointer that refers to any other location (an object header or a gap in the allocated memory), the garbage collector's operation is unspecified.

1.1.4.1 Unmanaged Pointers

Unmanaged pointers are the traditional pointers used in languages like C and C++. There are no restrictions on their use, although for the most part they result in code that cannot be verified. While it is perfectly legal to mark locations that contain unmanaged pointers as though they were unsigned integers (and this is, in fact, how they are treated by the CLI), it is often better to mark them as unmanaged pointers to a specific type of data. This is done by using `ELEMENT_TYPE_PTR` in a signature for a return value, a local variable, or an argument or by using a pointer type for a field or array element.

Unmanaged pointers are not reported to the garbage collector and can be used in any way that an integer can be used.

- Unmanaged pointers should be treated as unsigned (i.e., use `conv.ovf.u` rather than `conv.ovf.i`, etc.).
- Verifiable code cannot use unmanaged pointers to reference memory.
- Unverified code can pass an unmanaged pointer to a method that expects a managed pointer. This is safe only if one of the following is true:
  - The unmanaged pointer refers to memory that is not in memory managed by the garbage collector.
  - The unmanaged pointer refers to a field within an object.
  - The unmanaged pointer refers to an element within an array.
  - The unmanaged pointer refers to the location where the element following the last element in an array would be located.

1.1.4.2 Managed Pointers (type &)

Managed pointers (&) may point to a local variable, a method argument, a field of an object [(this includes an instance or static field of an object)], a field of a value type, an element of an array, or the address where an element just past the end of an array would be stored (for pointer indexes into managed arrays). Managed pointers cannot be `null`. (They must be reported to the garbage collector, even if they do not point to managed memory.)

ANNOTATION: Managed pointers are an innovation of the CLI. Although the designers of the C# language initially did not want to include them, ultimately they have found them useful. By including managed pointers in C#, it becomes possible to implement **out** parameters, so that, in contrast to Java, it is not necessary to create a data structure to return multiple **out** parameters.

Managed pointers are specified by using `ELEMENT_TYPE_BYREF` in a signature for a return value, a local variable, or an argument or by using a by-ref type for a field or array element.

- Managed pointers can be passed as arguments and stored in local variables.
- If you pass a parameter by reference, the corresponding argument is a managed pointer.
- Managed pointers cannot be stored in static variables, array elements, or fields of objects or value types.
- Managed pointers are *not* interchangeable with object references.
- A managed pointer cannot point to another managed pointer, but it can point to an object reference or a value type.
- Managed pointers that do not point to managed memory can be converted (using `conv.u` or `conv.ovf.u`) into unmanaged pointers, but this is not verifiable.
- Unverified code that erroneously converts a managed pointer into an unmanaged pointer can seriously compromise the integrity of the CLI. This conversion is safe if any of the following is known to be true:
    a. The managed pointer does not point into the garbage collector's memory area.
    b. The memory referred to has been pinned for the entire time that the unmanaged pointer is in use.
    c. A garbage collection cannot occur while the unmanaged pointer is in use.
    d. The garbage collector for the given implementation of the CLI is known to not move the referenced memory.

ANNOTATION: It is important to understand these rules concerning when you can safely convert managed pointers to unmanaged pointers, and when you cannot. The detailed rules above are complicated, but the model is simple. Managed pointers that represent value types on the stack can be converted to unmanaged pointers, as long as the data referenced cannot move. Otherwise, managed pointers cannot be converted.

Two points are captured in these rules. First, it is verifiable to convert a managed pointer to an unmanaged pointer only if you can prove that the data it references cannot move. Second, uses of managed pointers that are verifiable guarantee that the managed pointer always points to something that exists. For example, you cannot point a managed pointer to something on the stack and return it as a value, because the stack frame may have gone away. This is also why you cannot store a managed pointer in a static variable: the managed pointer might point to something on the stack when the stack frame has gone away.

1.2 Instruction Variant Table

In Partition III, section 3, an instruction variant table is presented for each instruction. It describes each variant of the instructions. The *Format* column of the table lists the opcode for the instruction variant, along with any arguments that follow the instruction in the instruction stream. For example:

Format	Assembly Format	Description
FE 0A **<unsigned int16>**	Ldarga *argNum*	Fetch the address of argument *argNum*.
0F **<unsigned int8>**	Ldarga.s *argNum*	Fetch the address of argument *argNum*, short form.

The first one or two hex numbers in the *Format* column show how this instruction is encoded (its "opcode"). So, the `ldarga` instruction is encoded as a byte holding FE, followed by another holding 0A. Italicized type names represent numbers that should follow in the instruction stream. In this example a 2-byte quantity that is to be treated as an unsigned integer directly follows the FE 0A opcode.

Any of the fixed-size built-in types (`int8`, `unsigned int8`, `int16`, `unsigned int16`, `int32`, `unsigned int32`, `int64`, `unsigned in64`, `float32`, and `float64`) can appear in format descriptions. These types define the number of bytes for the argument and how it should be interpreted (signed, unsigned, or floating point). In addition, a metadata token can appear, indicated as *<T>*. Tokens are encoded as 4-byte integers. All argument numbers are encoded least-significant-byte-at-smallest-address (a pattern commonly termed "little-endian"). Bytes for instruction opcodes and arguments are packed as tightly as possible (no alignment padding is done).

The *Assembly Format* column defines an assembly code mnemonic for each instruction variant. For those instructions that have instruction stream arguments, this column also assigns names to each of the arguments to the instruction. For each instruction argument, there is a name in the assembly format. These names are used later in the instruction description.

1.2.1 *Opcode Encodings*

CIL opcodes are 1 or more bytes long; they may be followed by zero or more operand bytes. All opcodes whose first byte lies in the range 0x00 through 0xEF, or 0xFC through 0xFF, are reserved for standardization. Opcodes whose first byte lies in the range 0xF0 through 0xFB, inclusive, are available for experimental purposes. The use of experimental opcodes in any method renders the method invalid and hence unverifiable.

ANNOTATION: The opcode encodings in this section are important if you are implementing a VES or writing a compiler. Some analysis tools may also require this information.

The currently defined encodings are specified in Table 6-1, Opcode Encodings.

Table 6-1 Opcode Encodings

0x00	nop
0x01	break
0x02	ldarg.0
0x03	ldarg.1
0x04	ldarg.2
0x05	ldarg.3
0x06	ldloc.0
0x07	ldloc.1
0x08	ldloc.2
0x09	ldloc.3
0x0a	stloc.0
0x0b	stloc.1
0x0c	stloc.2
0x0d	stloc.3
0x0e	ldarg.s
0x0f	ldarga.s

continues

Table 6-1 Opcode Encodings *(continued)*

0x10	starg.s
0x11	ldloc.s
0x12	ldloca.s
0x13	stloc.s
0x14	ldnull
0x15	ldc.i4.m1
0x16	ldc.i4.0
0x17	ldc.i4.1
0x18	ldc.i4.2
0x19	ldc.i4.3
0x1a	ldc.i4.4
0x1b	ldc.i4.5
0x1c	ldc.i4.6
0x1d	ldc.i4.7
0x1e	ldc.i4.8
0x1f	ldc.i4.s
0x20	ldc.i4
0x21	ldc.i8
0x22	ldc.r4
0x23	ldc.r8
0x25	dup
0x26	pop
0x27	jmp
0x28	call
0x29	calli
0x2a	ret
0x2b	br.s
0x2c	brfalse.s
0x2d	brtrue.s
0x2e	beq.s
0x2f	bge.s
0x30	bgt.s
0x31	ble.s
0x32	blt.s
0x33	bne.un.s
0x34	bge.un.s
0x35	bgt.un.s
0x36	ble.un.s
0x37	blt.un.s
0x38	br
0x39	brfalse
0x3a	brtrue
0x3b	beq
0x3c	bge
0x3d	bgt
0x3e	ble

Table 6-1 Opcode Encodings *(continued)*

0x3f	blt
0x40	bne.un
0x41	bge.un
0x42	bgt.un
0x43	ble.un
0x44	blt.un
0x45	switch
0x46	ldind.i1
0x47	ldind.u1
0x48	ldind.i2
0x49	ldind.u2
0x4a	ldind.i4
0x4b	ldind.u4
0x4c	ldind.i8
0x4d	ldind.i
0x4e	ldind.r4
0x4f	ldind.r8
0x50	ldind.ref
0x51	stind.ref
0x52	stind.i1
0x53	stind.i2
0x54	stind.i4
0x55	stind.i8
0x56	stind.r4
0x57	stind.r8
0x58	add
0x59	sub
0x5a	mul
0x5b	div
0x5c	div.un
0x5d	rem
0x5e	rem.un
0x5f	and
0x60	or
0x61	xor
0x62	shl
0x63	shr
0x64	shr.un
0x65	neg
0x66	not
0x67	conv.i1
0x68	conv.i2
0x69	conv.i4
0x6a	conv.i8
0x6b	conv.r4
0x6c	conv.r8

continues

Table 6-1 Opcode Encodings *(continued)*

0x6d	conv.u4
0x6e	conv.u8
0x6f	callvirt
0x70	cpobj
0x71	ldobj
0x72	ldstr
0x73	newobj
0x74	castclass
0x75	isinst
0x76	conv.r.un
0x79	unbox
0x7a	throw
0x7b	ldfld
0x7c	ldflda
0x7d	stfld
0x7e	ldsfld
0x7f	ldsflda
0x80	stsfld
0x81	stobj
0x82	conv.ovf.i1.un
0x83	conv.ovf.i2.un
0x84	conv.ovf.i4.un
0x85	conv.ovf.i8.un
0x86	conv.ovf.u1.un
0x87	conv.ovf.u2.un
0x88	conv.ovf.u4.un
0x89	conv.ovf.u8.un
0x8a	conv.ovf.i.un
0x8b	conv.ovf.u.un
0x8c	box
0x8d	newarr
0x8e	ldlen
0x8f	ldelema
0x90	ldelem.i1
0x91	ldelem.u1
0x92	ldelem.i2
0x93	ldelem.u2
0x94	ldelem.i4
0x95	ldelem.u4
0x96	ldelem.i8
0x97	ldelem.i
0x98	ldelem.r4
0x99	ldelem.r8
0x9a	ldelem.ref

Table 6-1 Opcode Encodings *(continued)*

0x9b	stelem.i
0x9c	stelem.i1
0x9d	stelem.i2
0x9e	stelem.i4
0x9f	stelem.i8
0xa0	stelem.r4
0xa1	stelem.r8
0xa2	stelem.ref
0xb3	conv.ovf.i1
0xb4	conv.ovf.u1
0xb5	conv.ovf.i2
0xb6	conv.ovf.u2
0xb7	conv.ovf.i4
0xb8	conv.ovf.u4
0xb9	conv.ovf.i8
0xba	conv.ovf.u8
0xc2	refanyval
0xc3	ckfinite
0xc6	mkrefany
0xd0	ldtoken
0xd1	conv.u2
0xd2	conv.u1
0xd3	conv.i
0xd4	conv.ovf.i
0xd5	conv.ovf.u
0xd6	add.ovf
0xd7	add.ovf.un
0xd8	mul.ovf
0xd9	mul.ovf.un
0xda	sub.ovf
0xdb	sub.ovf.un
0xdc	endfinally
0xdd	leave
0xde	leave.s
0xdf	stind.i
0xe0	conv.u
0xfe 0x00	arglist
0xfe 0x01	ceq
0xfe 0x02	cgt
0xfe 0x03	cgt.un
0xfe 0x04	clt
0xfe 0x05	clt.un
0xfe 0x06	ldftn
0xfe 0x07	ldvirtftn
0xfe 0x09	ldarg
0xfe 0x0a	ldarga

continues

Table 6-1 Opcode Encodings *(continued)*

0xfe 0x0b	starg
0xfe 0x0c	ldloc
0xfe 0x0d	ldloca
0xfe 0x0e	stloc
0xfe 0x0f	localloc
0xfe 0x11	endfilter
0xfe 0x12	unaligned.
0xfe 0x13	volatile.
0xfe 0x14	tail.
0xfe 0x15	initobj
0xfe 0x17	cpblk
0xfe 0x18	initblk
0xfe 0x1a	rethrow
0xfe 0x1c	sizeof
0xfe 0x1d	refanytype

1.3 Stack Transition Diagram

The stack transition diagram displays the state of the evaluation stack before and after the instruction is executed. Below is a typical stack transition diagram.

…, value1, value2 → …, result

This diagram indicates that the stack must have at least two elements on it, and in the definition the topmost value ("top of stack" or "most recently pushed") will be called *value2* and the value underneath (pushed prior to *value2*) will be called *value1*. (In diagrams like this, the stack grows to the right, along the page.) The instruction removes these values from the stack and replaces them by another value, called *result* in the description.

1.4 English Description

The English description describes any details about the instructions that are not immediately apparent once the format and stack transition have been described.

1.5 Operand Type Table

Many CIL operations take numeric operands on the stack. These operations fall into several categories, depending on how they deal with the types of the operands. The following tables summarize the valid kinds of operand types and the type of the result. Notice that the types referred to here are the types as tracked by the CLI rather than the more detailed types used by tools such as CIL verification. The types tracked by the CLI are: `int32`, `int64`, `native int`, F, O, and &.

ANNOTATION: There is a great deal of data in these tables that may be easy to overlook, and in some cases to misunderstand. Each table is important and describes the effect on the numeric types of a set of CIL instructions. The CIL instruction descriptions throughout Partition III refer back to these tables.

Compiler writers need to look at these tables in light of what their language requires. For example, if a language allows adding a 32- and a 64-bit value, then the compiler must decide whether the 32-bit value must be sign-extended. Depending on the decision, the compiler must emit either the sign-extension or non-sign-extension instruction. It is the compiler's job to match its type system to the VES's type system.

Portable CIL programs cannot depend on invalid operations. Any compiler that emits invalid operations is relying on implementation details of a particular VES, which is inadvisable. The standard does not specify what happens when such operations are executed. Among the possibilities are that the VES may terminate operation of the program, proceed with an incorrect result, or generate a runtime exception.

[1.5.1 *Binary Numeric Operations]*

A op B (used for `add`, `div`, `mul`, `rem`, and `sub`). Table 6-2, Binary Numeric Operations, shows the result type, for each possible combination of operand types. Boxes holding simply a result type apply to all five instructions. Boxes marked ✘ indicate an invalid CIL instruction. Shaded boxes indicate a CIL instruction that is not verifiable. Boxes with a list of instructions are valid only for those instructions.

Table 6-2 Binary Numeric Operations

		B's Type					
		int32	**int64**	**native int**	**F**	**&**	**O**
A's Type	**int32**	int32	✘	native int	✘	& (add)	✘
	int64	✘	int64	✘	✘	✘	✘
	native int	native int	✘	native int	✘	& (add)	✘
	F	✘	✘	✘	F	✘	✘
	&	& (add, sub)	✘	& (add, sub)	✘	native int (sub)	✘
	O	✘	✘	✘	✘	✘	✘

ANNOTATION: For all VES types except objects, you are allowed arithmetic operations on two of the same numeric type. In most cases, the result is the same type. But for pointers, subtracting two pointers results in an integer, which is the distance between them. Pointer arithmetic is allowed, and involves adding an integer to, or subtracting an integer from a pointer. For example, if you have a pointer to a field in an array, you can add a known integer to get to the next array, or subtract to get to the previous array. If you know the distance between two fields within an object, it is possible to add or subtract a value to get there, but these operations are always unverifiable.

[1.5.2 *Unary Numeric Operations]*

Used for the `neg` instruction. Boxes marked ✘ [in Table 6-3, Unary Numeric Operations,] indicate an invalid CIL instruction. All valid uses of this instruction are verifiable.

Table 6-3 Unary Numeric Operations

Operand Type	`int32`	`int64`	`native int`	`F`	`&`	`O`
Result Type	`int32`	`int64`	`native int`	`F`	✘	✘

[1.5.3 *Binary Comparison or Branch Operations]*

These return a Boolean value or branch based on the top two values on the stack. Used for `beq`, `beq.s`, `bge`, `bge.s`, `bge.un`, `bge.un.s`, `bgt`, `bgt.s`, `bgt.un`, `bgt.un.s`, `ble`, `ble.s`, `ble.un`, `ble.un.s`, `blt`, `blt.s`, `blt.un`, `blt.un.s`, `bne.un`, `bne.un.s`, `ceq`, `cgt`, `cgt.un`, `clt`, `clt.un`. Boxes marked ✓ [in Table 6-4, Binary Comparison or Branch Operations,] indicate that all instructions are valid for that combination of operand types. Boxes marked ✘ indicate invalid CIL sequences. Shaded boxes indicate a CIL instruction that is not verifiable. Boxes with a list of instructions are valid only for those instructions.

ANNOTATION: It is always possible to compare two values of the same type. The only possible comparison for objects is to branch on whether they are the same or not the same, and compare for equality. In comparisons where the types are not the same, in most cases the standard does not specify a result. Although you can compare 32-bit integers and native integers, because native integers are assumed to be at least 32 bits, if the compiler knows that native integers are 64 bits, it can also ensure that 64-bit/native integer comparisons are valid. If you know that native integers are 64 bits, it is

Table 6-4 Binary Comparison or Branch Operations

	int32	int64	native int	F	&	O
int32	✓	✗	✓	✗	✗	✗
int64	✗	✓	✗	✗	✗	✗
native int	✓	✗	✓	✗	`beq[.s]`, `bne.un[.s]`, `ceq`	✗
F	✗	✗	✗	✓	✗	✗
&	✗	✗	`beq[.s]`, `bne.un[.s]`, `ceq`	✗	✓[1]	✗
O	✗	✗	✗	✗	✗	`beq[.s]`, `bne.un[.s]`, `ceq`[2]

1. Except for `beq`, `bne.un` (or short versions), or `ceq`, these combinations make sense if both operands are known to be pointers to elements of the same array. However, there is no security issue for a CLI that does not check this constraint.

Note: If the two operands are *not* pointers into the same array, then the result is simply the distance apart in the garbage-collected heap of two unrelated data items. This distance apart will almost certainly change at the next garbage collection. Essentially, the result cannot be used to compute anything useful.

2. `cgt.un` is allowed and verifiable on ObjectRefs (O). This is commonly used when comparing an ObjectRef with null (there is no "compare-not-equal" instruction, which would otherwise be a more obvious solution).

up to the compiler to make the comparison valid. In comparing a pointer to a native integer, the only valid operations are the same as when comparing two objects (branch on equal or not equal, compare for equality).

[1.5.4 *Integer Operations]*

These operate only on integer types. Used for and, `div.un`, `not`, `or`, `rem.un`, `xor`. The `div.un` and `rem.un` instructions treat their arguments as unsigned integers and produce the bit pattern corresponding to the unsigned result. As described in the CLI specification, however, the CLI makes no distinction between signed and unsigned integers on the stack. The `not` instruction is unary and returns the same type as the input. The `shl` and `shr`

Table 6-5 Integer Operations

	int32	**int64**	**native int**	**F**	**&**	**O**
int32	int32	✘	native int	✘	✘	✘
int64	✘	int64	✘	✘	✘	✘
native int	native int	✘	native int	✘	✘	✘
F	✘	✘	✘	✘	✘	✘
&	✘	✘	✘	✘	✘	✘
O	✘	✘	✘	✘	✘	✘

instructions return the same type as their first operand, and their second operand must be of type `native unsigned int`. Boxes marked ✘ [in Table 6-5, Integer Operations,] indicate invalid CIL sequences. All other boxes denote verifiable combinations of operands.

[1.5.5 *Shift Operations]*

Table 6-6, Shift Operations, lists the legal combinations of operands and results for the shift instructions: `shl`, `shr`, `shr_un`. Boxes marked ✘ indicate invalid CIL sequences. All other boxes denote verifiable combinations of operand. If the "Shift-By" operand is larger than the width of the "To-Be-Shifted" operand, then the results are implementation-defined (e.g., shift an int32 integer left by 37 bits).

Table 6-6 Shift Operations

		Shift-By					
		int32	**int64**	**native int**	**F**	**&**	**O**
To Be Shifted	**int32**	int32	✘	int32	✘	✘	✘
	int64	int64	✘	int64	✘	✘	✘
	native int	native int	✘	native int	✘	✘	✘
	F	✘	✘	✘	✘	✘	✘
	&	✘	✘	✘	✘	✘	✘
	O	✘	✘	✘	✘	✘	✘

[1.5.6 *Overflow Arithmetic Operations]*

These operations generate an exception if the result cannot be represented in the target data type. Used for `add.ovf`, `add.ovf.un`, `mul.ovf`, `mul.ovf.un`, `sub.ovf`, `sub.ovf.un`. The shaded uses [in Table 6-7, Overflow Arithmetic Operations,] are not verifiable, while boxes marked ✘ indicate invalid CIL sequences.

Table 6-7 Overflow Arithmetic Operations

	int32	int64	native int	F	&	O
int32	int32	✘	native int	✘	& `add.ovf.un`	✘
int64	✘	int64	✘	✘	✘	✘
native int	native int	✘	native int	✘	& `add.ovf.un`	✘
F	✘	✘	✘	✘	✘	✘
&	& `add.ovf.un`, `sub.ovf.un`	✘	& `add.ovf.un`, `sub.ovf.un`	✘	native int `sub.ovf.un`	✘
O	✘	✘	✘	✘	✘	✘

ANNOTATION: Some languages require that an overflow in an operation throws an exception, and some languages ignore it. The CLI standard supports both approaches, but the rules, as stated in this section, are different from the other operations.

[1.5.7 *Conversion Operations]*

These operations convert the top item on the evaluation stack from one numeric type to another. The result type is guaranteed to be representable as the data type specified as part of the operation (i.e., the `conv.u2` instruction returns a value that can be stored in an `unsigned int16`). The stack, however, can only store values that are a minimum of 4 bytes wide. Used for the `conv.`<to type>, `conv.ovf.`<to type>, and `conv.ovf.`<to type>`.un` instructions. The shaded uses [in Table 6-8, Conversion Operations,] are not verifiable, while boxes marked ✘ indicate invalid CIL sequences.

Table 6-8 Conversion Operations

		Input (from Evaluation Stack)					
		int32	**int64**	**native int**	**F**	**&**	**O**
Convert To	**int8** **unsigned int8** **int16** **unsigned int16**	Truncate[1]	Truncate[1]	Truncate[1]	Truncate to zero[2]	✘	✘
	int32 **unsigned int32**	Nop	Truncate[1]	Truncate[1]	Truncate to zero[2]	✘	✘
	int64	Sign-extend	Nop	Sign-extend	Truncate to zero[2]	Stop GC tracking[4]	Stop GC tracking[4]
	unsigned int64	Zero-extend	Nop	Zero-extend	Truncate to zero[2]	Stop GC tracking[4]	Stop GC tracking[4]
	native int	Sign-extend	Truncate[1]	Nop	Truncate to zero[2]	Stop GC tracking[4]	Stop GC tracking[4]
	native unsigned int	Zero-extend	Truncate[1]	Nop	Truncate to zero[2]	Stop GC tracking[4]	Stop GC tracking[4]
	All Float Types	To Float	To Float	To Float	Change precision[3]	✘	✘

1. "Truncate" means that the number is truncated to the desired size; i.e., the most significant bytes of the input value are simply ignored. If the result is narrower than the minimum stack width of 4 bytes, then this result is zero-extended (if the target type is unsigned) or sign-extended (if the target type is signed). Thus, converting the value 0x1234 ABCD from the evaluation stack to an 8-bit datum yields the result 0xCD; if the target type were int8, this would be sign-extended to give 0xFFFF FFCD; if, instead, the target type were unsigned int8, this would be zero-extended to give 0x0000 00CD.
2. "Truncate to zero" means that the floating point number will be converted to an integer by truncation toward zero. Thus, 1.1 is converted to 1, and –1.1 is converted to –1.
3. Converts from the current precision available on the evaluation stack to the precision specified by the instruction. If the stack has more precision than the output size, the conversion is performed using the IEC 60559:1989 "round to nearest" mode to compute the low-order bit of the result.
4. "Stop GC tracking" means that, following the conversion, the item's value will *not* be reported to subsequent garbage-collection operations (and therefore will not be updated by such operations).

ANNOTATION: Table 6-8 is very important because it shows the implicit conversions that the VES does—and does not—do. This table encapsulates information that is most often misunderstood. In conversion operations, it is what you are converting *to* that determines how you treat the input parameter. For example, suppose there is a 32-bit quantity that you want to convert to a 32-bit signed quantity. What happens if it already has a sign? If it was negative on the stack, the conversion should fail if you are checking for overflow because a negative number will not go into the unsigned representation. Some conversions cause the VES to truncate the value; others cause the VES to extend.

1.6 Implicit Argument Coercion

While the CLI operates only on six types (`int32`, `native int`, `int64`, `F`, `O`, and `&`), the metadata supplies a much richer model for parameters of methods. When about to call a method, the VES performs implicit type conversions, detailed in Table 6-9, Signature Matching. (Conceptually, it inserts the appropriate `conv.*` instruction into the CIL stream, which may result in an information loss through truncation or rounding.) This implicit conversion occurs for boxes marked ✓. Shaded boxes are not verifiable. Boxes marked ✘ indicate invalid CIL sequences. (A compiler is of course free to emit explicit `conv.*` or `conv.*.ovf` instructions to achieve any desired effect.)

Further notes concerning this table:

- On a 32-bit machine, passing a `native int` argument to an `unsigned int32` parameter involves no conversion. On a 64-bit machine, it is implicitly converted.
- "Start GC tracking" means that, following the implicit conversion, the item's value will be reported to any subsequent garbage-collection operations, and perhaps changed as a result of the item pointed-to being relocated in the heap.

ANNOTATION: Table 6-9 is another very important table. It details the implicit type conversions that the VES will do when a method is to be called, referred to as **signature matching**. Compilers need to know which conversions happen automatically. Where a CIL sequence is invalid, the compiler must issue the `conv.*` or `conv.*.ovf` instruction to turn it into a valid sequence.

For example, the compiler is responsible for what happens if a floating point value is passed to someone expecting an 8-bit integer. On the other hand, passing a full-sized integer to someone expecting an 8-bit integer triggers an implicit conversion by the VES. In the VES, it is the full 32-bit integer that is passed. If the compiler wanted to

Table 6-9 Signature Matching

		Stack Parameter					
		int32	**native int**	**int64**	**F**	**&**	**O**
Type in Signature	**int8**	✓	✓	✗	✗	✗	✗
	unsigned int8, bool	✓	✓	✗	✗	✗	✗
	int16	✓	✓	✗	✗	✗	✗
	unsigned int16, char	✓	✓	✗	✗	✗	✗
	int32	✓	✓	✗	✗	✗	✗
	unsigned int32	✓	✓	✗	✗	✗	✗
	int64	✗	✗	✓	✗	✗	✗
	unsigned int64	✗	✗	✓	✗	✗	✗
	native int	✓ Sign-0extend	✓	✗	✗	✗	✗
	native unsigned int	✓ Zero-extend	✓ Zero-extend	✗	✗	✗	✗
	float32	✗	✗	✗	Note[4]	✗	✗
	float64	✗	✗	✗	Note[4]	✗	✗
	Class	✗	✗	✗	✗	✗	✓
	Value Type (Note[2])	Note[1]	Note[1]	Note[1]	Note[1]	✗	✗
	By-Ref (&)	✗	✓ Start GC tracking	✗	✗	✓	✗
	Ref Any (Note[3])	✗	✗	✗	✗	✗	✗

1. Passing a built-in type to a parameter that is required to be a value type is not allowed.
2. The CLI's stack can contain a value type. These may only be passed if the particular value type on the stack exactly matches the class required by the corresponding parameter.
3. There are special instructions to construct and pass a `Ref Any`.
4. The CLI is permitted to pass floating point arguments using its internal `F` type (see Partition III, section 1.1.1). CIL generators may, of course, include an explicit `conv.r4`, `conv.r4.ovf`, or similar instruction.

make a check, it could truncate the value to 8 bits to make sure it would fit into 8 bits, but that particular operation is not built into the VES.

The VES does type conversions with the equivalent of the convert instruction, but not the convert with overflow. If a compiler needs overflow checking, it must explicitly insert a `conv.*.ovf` instruction. The implicit conversions by the VES detailed in this table were standardized to save the compiler from inserting numerous convert operations that are mostly harmless and often used in any case.

As it says in this section, a value type may be on the stack, and as it says in note 2 of Table 6-9, it may be passed only if the value type on the stack exactly matches the class required by the corresponding parameter. There is no conversion of value types.

There is one source of confusion: the class library has value types that correspond to certain built-in numeric types. For example, a value type called `System.Int32` corresponds to the built-in type `int32`. Although a programmer may specify the class library's value class, the compiler is responsible for ensuring that it is the built-in int32 that goes into the actual signature in the metadata.

1.7 Restrictions on CIL Code Sequences

As well as detailed restrictions on CIL code sequences to ensure:

- Valid CIL
- Verifiable CIL

there are a few further restrictions, imposed to make it easier to construct a simple CIL-to-native-code compiler. This section specifies the general restrictions that apply in addition to those listed for individual instructions.

ANNOTATION: This section and its subsections are important to those interested in implementing or understanding a VES, compiler designers, and those implementing a JIT compiler. From the point of view of the VES, of interest is mainly what it does *not* have to do—there are some sequences of code the VES never has to handle. Some of the restrictions in this section were included to make it easier to write a VES. The restrictions that were included to make it easier to write a VES, in turn, place restrictions on source language compilers because there are some things they might like to generate but cannot because the VES is not required to handle them.

1.7.1 *The Instruction Stream*

The implementation of a method is provided by a contiguous block of CIL instructions, encoded as specified below. The address of the instruction block for a method, as well as its length, is specified in the file format (see Partition II, section 24.4, Common Intermediate Language Physical Layout). The first instruction is at the first byte (lowest address) of the instruction block.

Instructions are variable in size. The size of each instruction can be determined (decoded) from the content of the instruction bytes themselves. The size of and ordering of the bytes within an instruction are specified by each instruction definition. Instructions follow each other without padding in a stream of bytes that is both alignment- and byte-order-insensitive.

Each instruction occupies an exact number of bytes, and until the end of the instruction block, the next instruction begins immediately at the next byte. It is invalid for the instruction block (as specified by the block's length) to end without forming a complete last instruction.

Instruction prefixes extend the length of an instruction without introducing a new instruction; an instruction having one or more prefixes introduces only one instruction that begins at the first byte of the first instruction prefix.

NOTE

Until the end of the instruction block, the instruction following any control transfer instruction is decoded as an instruction and thus participates in locating subsequent instructions even if it is not the target of a branch. Only instructions may appear in the instruction stream, even if unreachable. There are no address-relative data addressing modes, and raw data cannot be directly embedded within the instruction stream. Certain instructions allow embedding of immediate data as part of the instruction; however, that differs from allowing raw data embedded directly in the instruction stream. Unreachable code may appear as the result of machine-generated code and is allowed, but it must always be in the form of properly formed instruction sequences.

The instruction stream can be translated and the associated instruction block discarded prior to execution of the translation. Thus, even instructions that capture and manipulate code addresses, such as `call`, `ret`, etc. can be virtualized to operate on translated addresses instead of addresses in the CIL instruction stream.

1.7.2 *Valid Branch Targets*

The set of addresses composed of the first byte of each instruction identified in the instruction stream defines the only valid instruction targets. Instruction targets include branch targets as specified in branch instructions, targets specified in exception tables such as protected ranges (see Partition I, section 12.4.2 and Partition II, section 18), filters, and handler targets.

Branch instructions specify branch targets as either a 1-byte or a 4-byte signed relative offset; the size of the offset is differentiated by the opcode of the instruction. The offset is defined as being relative to the byte following the branch instruction. (**Note**: Thus, an offset value of zero targets the immediately following instruction.)

The value of a 1-byte offset is computed by interpreting that byte as a signed 8-bit integer. The value of a 4-byte offset can be computed by concatenating the bytes into a signed integer in the following manner: the byte of lowest address forms the least significant byte, and the byte with the highest address forms the most significant byte of the integer. (**Note**: This representation is often called "a signed integer in little-endian byte-order.")

ANNOTATION: The major point of this section is that it is invalid to jump into the middle of an instruction. This would be of concern in instructions that take more than 1 byte.

1.7.3 *Exception Ranges*

Exception tables describe ranges of instructions that are protected by catch, fault, or finally handlers (see Partition I, section 12.4.2 and Partition II, section 18). The starting address of a protected block, `filter` clause, or handler shall be a valid branch target as specified in Partition III, section 1.7.2. It is invalid for a protected block, `filter` clause, or handler to end without forming a complete last instruction.

ANNOTATION: The focus of this section is that multi-byte instructions cannot be split across exception boundaries.

1.7.4 *Must Provide Maxstack*

Every method specifies a maximum number of items that can be pushed onto the CIL evaluation [stack]. The value is stored in the `IMAGE_COR_ILMETHOD` structure that precedes the CIL body of each method. A method that specifies a maximum number of items less than the amount required by a static analysis of the method (using a traditional control flow graph without analysis of the data) is invalid (hence also unverifiable) and need not be supported by a conforming implementation of the CLI.

NOTE

Maxstack is related to analysis of the program, not to the size of the stack at runtime. It does not specify the maximum size in bytes of a stack frame, but rather the number of items that must be tracked by an analysis tool.

RATIONALE

By analyzing the CIL stream for any method, it is easy to determine how many items will be pushed onto the CIL evaluation stack. However, specifying that maximum number ahead of time helps a CIL-to-native-code compiler (especially a simple one that does only a single pass through the CIL stream) in allocating internal data structures that model the stack and/or verification algorithm.

ANNOTATION: **Maxstack** is the maximum number of values pushed onto the evaluation stack within the method. It should not be confused with the space allocated at runtime. Maxstack is provided for JIT compilers and verifiers because they need to allocate space to simulate the method evaluation stack. Language compilers are required to compute this required space so that interpreters and JIT compilers can be written without having to scan the method before simulating or executing it.

1.7.5 *Backward Branch Constraints*

It must be possible, with a single forward-pass through the CIL instruction stream for any method, to infer the exact state of the evaluation stack at every instruction (where by "state" we mean the number and type of each item on the evaluation stack).

In particular, if that single-pass analysis arrives at an instruction, call it location X, that immediately follows an unconditional branch, and where X is not the target of an earlier branch instruction, then the state of the evaluation stack at X, clearly, cannot be derived from existing information. In this case, the CLI demands that the evaluation stack at X be empty.

Following on from this rule, it would clearly be invalid CIL if a later branch instruction to X were to have a non-empty evaluation stack

RATIONALE

This constraint ensures that CIL code can be processed by a simple CIL-to-native-code compiler. It ensures that the state of the evaluation stack at the beginning of each CIL can be inferred from a single, forward-pass analysis of the instruction stream.

Note: The stack state at location X in the above can be inferred by various means: from a previous forward branch to X, because X marks the start of an exception handler, etc.

See the following sections for further information:

- Exceptions: Partition I, section 12.4.2
- Verification conditions for branch instructions: Partition III, section 3
- The `tail.` prefix: Partition III, section 2.1

ANNOTATION: The backward branch constraint improves the efficiency of the JIT compiler and makes it easier to implement. For the verifier, it is necessary to figure out the data types that have to be on the stack, in a single pass of the code from front to back. This restriction prevents loop rotations that make the early code appear to have something on the stack. Loop rotations are done in native code, and they make sense in some circumstances, but much less in CIL. If that optimization is needed, the JIT could implement it in native code—source coming in must not.

1.7.6 *Branch Verification Constraints*

The *target* of all branch instructions must be a valid branch target (see Partition III, section 1.7.2) within the method holding that branch instruction.

1.8 Verifiability

Memory safety is a property that ensures programs running in the same address space are correctly isolated from one another (see Partition I, section 8.8). Thus, it is desirable to test whether programs are memory-safe prior to running them. Unfortunately, it is provably impossible to do this with 100% accuracy. Instead, the CLI can test a stronger restriction, called **verifiability**. Every program that is verified is memory-safe, but some programs that are not verifiable are still memory-safe.

It is perfectly acceptable to generate CIL code that is not verifiable, but that is known to be memory-safe by the compiler writer. Thus, conforming CIL may not be verifiable, even though the producing compiler may *know* that it is memory-safe. Several important uses of CIL instructions are not verifiable, such as the pointer arithmetic versions of `add` that are required for the faithful and efficient compilation of C programs. For non-verifiable code, memory safety is the responsibility of the application programmer.

CIL contains a **verifiable subset**. The verifiability description [for each instruction] gives details of the conditions under which use of an instruction falls within the verifiable subset of CIL. Verification tracks the types of values in much finer detail than is required for the basic functioning of the CLI, because it is checking that a CIL code sequence respects not only the basic rules of the CLI with respect to the safety of garbage collection, but also the typing rules of the CTS. This helps to guarantee the sound operation of the entire CLI.

The verifiability section of each operation description specifies requirements both for correct CIL generation and for verification. Correct CIL generation always requires guaranteeing that the top items on the stack correspond to the types shown in the stack transition diagram. The verifiability section specifies only requirements for correct CIL generation that are not captured in that diagram. Verification tests both the requirements for correct CIL generation and the specific verification conditions that are described with the instruction. The operation of CIL sequences that do not meet the CIL correctness requirements is unspecified. The operation of CIL sequences that meet the correctness requirements but are not verifiable may violate type safety and hence may violate security or memory access constraints.

1.8.1 *Flow Control Restrictions for Verifiable CIL*

This section specifies a verification algorithm that, combined with information on individual CIL instructions (see Partition III, section 3) and metadata validation (see Partition II), guarantees memory integrity.

The algorithm specified here creates a minimum level for all compliant implementations of the CLI in the sense that any program that is considered verifiable by this algorithm shall be considered verifiable and run correctly on all compliant implementations of the CLI.

The CLI provides a security permission that controls whether or not the CLI shall run programs that may violate memory safety. Any program that is verifiable according to this specification does not violate memory safety, and a conforming implementation of the CLI shall run such programs. The implementation may also run other programs, provided it is able to show they do not violate memory safety (typically because they use a verification algorithm that makes use of specific knowledge about the implementation).

> **NOTE**
>
> While a compliant implementation is required to accept and run any program this verification algorithm states is verifiable, there may be programs that are accepted as verifiable by a given implementation but that this verification algorithm will fail to consider verifiable. Such programs will run in the given implementation but need not be considered verifiable by other implementations.
>
> For example, an implementation of the CLI may choose to correctly track full signatures on method pointers and permit programs to execute the `calli` instruction even though this is not permitted by the verification algorithm specified here.
>
> Implementers of the CLI are urged to provide a means for testing whether programs generated on their implementation meet this portable verifiability standard. They are also urged to specify where their verification algorithms are more permissive than this standard.

ANNOTATION

Implementation-Specific (Microsoft): The various implementations of the CLI produced by Microsoft use slightly different verification algorithms. In all cases, however, the PEVerify program (part of the .NET SDK) implements the portable verification algorithm as specified in this standard. Programmers are urged to run PEVerify over all code before shipping it for possible use on other implementations of the CLI.

Only valid programs shall be verifiable. For ease of explanation, the verification algorithm described here assumes that the program is valid and does not explicitly call for tests of all validity conditions. Validity conditions are specified on a per-CIL instruction basis (see Partition III, section 3), and on the overall file format in Partition II, section 21.

1.8.1.1 Verification Algorithm

The verification algorithm shall attempt to associate a valid `stack state` with every CIL instruction. The stack state specifies the number of slots on the CIL stack at that point in the code and, for each slot, a required type that must be present in that slot. The initial stack state is empty (there are no items on the stack).

Verification assumes that the CLI zeros all memory other than the evaluation stack before it is made visible to programs. A conforming implementation of the CLI shall provide this observable behavior. Furthermore, verifiable methods shall have the "zero initialize" bit set, see Partition II, section 24.4.4. If this bit is not set, then a CLI may throw a *Verification* exception at any point where a local variable is accessed, and where the assembly containing that method has not been granted *SecurityPermission.SkipVerification*.

ANNOTATION: The "zero init flag" syntax in the assembler syntax is the **.local init** directive; and in the file format, it is the flag **CorILMethod_InitLocals** (see Partition II, section 24.4.4).

RATIONALE

This requirement strongly enhances program portability, and a well-known technique (definite-assignment analysis) allows a compiler from CIL to native code to minimize its performance impact. Note that a CLI may optionally choose to perform definite-assignment analysis—in such a case, it may confirm that a method, even without the "zero initialize" bit set, may in fact be verifiable (and therefore not throw a *Verification* exception).

NOTE

Definite-assignment analysis can be used by the CLI to determine which locations are written before they are read. Such locations needn't be zeroed, since it isn't possible to observe the contents of the memory as it was provided by the EE.

Performance measurements on C++ implementations (which do not require definite-assignment analysis) indicate that adding this requirement has almost no impact, even in highly optimized code. Furthermore, customers incorrectly attribute bugs to the compiler when this zeroing is not performed, since such code often fails when small, unrelated changes are made to the program.

The verification algorithm shall simulate all possible control flow paths through the code and ensures that a legal stack state exists for every reachable CIL instruction. The verification algorithm does not take advantage of any data values during its simulation (e.g., it does not perform constant propagation), but uses only type assignments. Details of the type system used for verification and the algorithm used to merge stack states are provided in Partition III, section 1.8.1.3. The verification algorithm terminates as follows:

1. Successfully when all control paths have been simulated
2. Unsuccessfully when it is not possible to compute a valid stack state for a particular CIL instruction
3. Unsuccessfully when additional tests specified in this clause fail

There is a control flow path from every instruction to the subsequent instruction, with the exception of the unconditional branch instructions, `throw`, `rethrow`, and `ret`. Finally, there is a control flow path from each branch instruction (conditional or unconditional) to the branch target (targets, plural, for the `switch` instruction).

Verification simulates the operation of each CIL instruction to compute the new stack state, and any type mismatch between the specified conditions on the stack state (see Partition III, section 3) and the simulated stack state shall cause the verification algorithm to fail. (Note that verification simulates only the effect on the stack state; it does not perform the actual computation.) The algorithm shall also fail if there is an existing stack state at the next instruction address (for conditional branches or instructions within a `try` block there may be more than one such address) that cannot be merged with the stack state just computed. For rules of this merge operation, see Partition III, section 1.8.1.3.

ANNOTATION: In Partition III, section 1.8 and its subsections provide a detailed and accurate description of the verification standard. Verifying code according to the rules described here guarantees that all conforming implementations of the CLI will consider it to be verifiable, and the code to be memory-safe. Code that is intended to be portable, such as frameworks, should be verified with a verifier built according to this standard.

Many verifiers permit as verifiable some things that are not allowed according to this description. This does not mean the code is not safe—these things are permitted usually to take advantage of features of the platform on which the code is expected to be run. There is no reason that one implementation cannot run as verifiable some things that are not considered verifiable in another implementation. It does mean, however, that if you are a compiler writer, you should be testing your code not by running it through your implementation's verifier, but through this standard verification test, using a tool such as Microsoft's PEVerify, which was designed according to these rules.

1.8.1.2 Verification Type System

The verification algorithm compresses types that are logically equivalent, since they cannot lead to memory safety violations. The types used by the verification algorithm are specified in Partition III, section 1.8.1.2.1; the type compatibility rules are specified in Partition III, section 1.8.1.2.2; and the rules for merging stack states are in Partition III, section 1.8.1.3.

1.8.1.2.1 ***Verification Types***

The following table specifies the mapping of types used in the CLI and those used in verification. Notice that verification compresses the CLI types to a smaller set that maintains information about the size of those types in memory, but then compresses these again to represent the fact that the CLI stack expands 1-, 2-, and 4-byte built-in types into 4-byte types on the stack. Similarly, verification treats floating point numbers on the stack as 64-bit quantities regardless of the actual representation.

Arrays are objects, but with special compatibility rules.

There is a special encoding for `null` that represents an object known to be the null value, hence with indeterminate actual type.

In the following table, *CLI Type* is the type as it is described in metadata. The *Verification Type* is a corresponding type used for type compatibility rules in verification (see Partition III, section 1.8.1.2.2) when considering the types of local variables, incoming arguments, and formal parameters on methods being called. The column *Verification Type (in Stack State)* is used to simulate instructions that load data onto the stack, and shows the types that are actually maintained in the stack state information of the verification algorithm. The column *Managed Pointer to Type* shows the type tracked for managed pointers.

CLI Type	Verification Type	Verification Type (in Stack State)	Managed Pointer to Type
`int8, unsigned int8, bool`	`int8`	`int32`	`& int8`
`int16, unsigned int16, char`	`int16`	`int32`	`& int16`
`int32, unsigned int32`	`int32`	`int32`	`& int32`
`int64, unsigned int64`	`int64`	`int64`	`& int64`
`native int, native unsigned int`	`native int`	`native int`	`& native int`
`float32`	`float32`	`float64`	`& float32`
`float64`	`float64`	`float64`	`& float64`
`Any value type`	`Same type`	`Same type`	`& Same type`
`Any object type`	`Same type`	`Same type`	`& Same type`
`Method pointer`	`Same type`	`Same type`	`Not valid`

A method can be defined as returning a managed pointer, but calls upon such methods are not verifiable.

> **RATIONALE**
> Some uses of returning a managed pointer are perfectly verifiable (e.g., returning a reference to a field in an object); but some are not (e.g., returning a pointer to a local variable of the called method). Tracking this in the general case is a burden, and therefore not included in this standard.

1.8.1.2.2 ***Verification Type Compatibility***

The following rules define type compatibility. We use `S` and `T` to denote verification types, and the notation "`S := T`" to indicate that the verification type T can be used wherever the verification type S can be used, while "`S !:= T`" indicates that `T` cannot be used where `S` is expected. These are the verification type compatibility rules. We use `T[]` to denote an array (of any rank) whose elements are of type `T`, and `T&` to denote a managed pointer to type `T`.

1. [:= is reflexive] for all verification types `S`, `S := S`
2. [:= is transitive] for all verification types `S`, `T`, and `U`; if `S := T` and `T := U`, then `S := U`.
3. `S := T` if `S` is the base class of `T` or an interface implemented by `T`, and `T` is not a value type.
4. `S := T` if `S` and `T` are both interfaces, and the implementation of `T` requires the implementation of `S`.
5. `S := null` if `S` is an object type or an interface.
6. `S[] := T[]` if `S := T` and the arrays are either both vectors (zero-based, rank one), or neither is a vector and both have the same rank.
7. If `S` and `T` are method pointers, then `S := T` if the signatures (return types, parameter types, calling convention, and any custom attributes or custom modifiers) are the same.
8. Otherwise `S !:= T`.

1.8.1.3 **Merging Stack States**

As the verification algorithm simulates all control flow paths, it shall merge the simulated stack state with any existing stack state at the next CIL instruction in the flow. If there is no existing stack state, the simulated stack state is stored for future use. Otherwise the merge shall be computed as follows and stored to replace the existing stack state for the CIL instruction. If the merge fails, the verification algorithm shall fail.

The merge shall be computed by comparing the number of slots in each stack state. If they differ, the merge shall fail. If they match, then the overall merge shall be computed by merging the states slot-by-slot as follows. Let `T` be the type from the slot on the newly computed state and S be the type from the corresponding slot on the previously stored state. The merged type, `U`, shall be computed as follows (recall that `S := T` is the compatibility function defined in Partition III, section 1.8.1.2.2):

1. If `S := T`, then `U=S`.
2. Otherwise if `T := S`, then `U=T`.
3. Otherwise, if `S` and `T` are both object types, then let `V` be the closest common supertype of `S` and `T`; then `U=V`.
4. Otherwise, the merge shall fail.

ANNOTATION:

Implementation-Specific (Microsoft): The V1.0 release of the Microsoft CLI will merge interfaces by arbitrarily choosing the first common interface between the two verification types being merged.

ANNOTATION: For those already familiar with verification, this section may be the single most surprising piece of this algorithm, so it is important to read and understand it completely. This definition makes sense for a standard, but it prohibits a large class of perfectly good programs. Adjusting this rule produces rules that depend on the order in which the verifier does its analysis and requires some control flow analysis that not all verifiers can do. It would be inappropriate to standardize an analysis order for verifiers, so this rule, while limiting, ensures portable files. Some implementations of verifiers that have a specific order to their analysis weaken this rule to allow many more programs to be verifiable.

The issue here is the merging of the stack model at points where multiple flows of control converge. Consider the following C program:

```
interface I { int M(); }
class A implements I { .... };
class B implements I { .... };
```

```
static int Main()
{ A myA = new A();
   B myB = new B();
   boolean IsSunday = (System.DateTime.Today.DayOfWeek==System.DateTime.DayOf-
      Week.Sunday);
   return 3+((IsSunday ? myA : myB).M());
}
```

The verifier would see a flow join where the stack has A on one branch and B on the other and might not be able to pick the correct common parent type. So the trade-off is performance versus assured verifiability.

The following is an approximation of the CIL code for `Main()`:

```
.class Test
{ .method static void Main()
  { .entrypoint
    .locals (class A myA, class B myB, bool IsSunday)
    call int32 [System]DateTime::get_DayOfWeek()
    ldc.i4.0              // Assuming Sunday is 0
    stloc.2            // IsSunday
    ldc.i4.3
    ldloc.2
    brfalse NotSunday
    ldloc.0            // myA
    brfalse Join
NotSunday:
    ldloc.1            // myB
Join:  // Stack has A or B on it
    callvirt int32 I::M() // Not verifiable
    ret
  }
}
```

1.8.1.4 Class and Object Initialization Rules

The VES ensures that all statics are initially zeroed (i.e., built-in types are 0 or false, object references are null), hence the verification algorithm does not test for definite assignment to statics.

An object constructor shall not return unless a constructor for the base class or a different construct for the object's class has been called on the newly constructed object. The verification algorithm shall treat the `this` pointer as uninitialized unless the base class constructor has been called. No operations can be performed on an uninitialized `this` except for storing into and loading from the object's fields.

> **NOTE**
> If the constructor generates an exception, the `this` pointer in the corresponding `catch` block is still uninitialized.

1.8.1.5 Delegate Constructors

The verification algorithm shall require that one of the following code sequences is used for constructing delegates; no other code sequence in verifiable code shall contain a `newobj` instruction for a delegate type. There shall be only one instance constructor method for a delegate (overloading is not allowed).

The verification algorithm shall fail if a branch target is within these instruction sequences (other than at the start of the sequence).

> **NOTE**
> See Partition II [section 7] for the signature of delegates and a validity requirement regarding the signature of the method used in the constructor and the signature of `Invoke` and other methods on the delegate class.

1.8.1.5.1 Delegating via Virtual Dispatch

The following CIL instruction sequence shall be used or the verification algorithm shall fail. The sequence begins with an object on the stack.

```
dup
ldvirtftn mthd; Method shall be on the class of the object,
          ; or one of its parent classes, or an interface
          ; implemented by the object
newobj delegateclass::.ctor(object, native int)
```

> **RATIONALE**
> The dup is required to ensure that it is precisely the same object stored in the delegate as was used to compute the virtual method. If another object of a subtype were used, the object and the method wouldn't match and could lead to memory violations.

1.8.1.5.2 *Delegating via Instance Dispatch*

The following CIL instruction sequence shall be used or the verification algorithm shall fail. The sequence begins with either `null` or an object on the stack.

```
ldftn mthd; Method shall either be a static method or
          ; a method on the class of the object on the stack or
          ; one of the object's parent classes
newobj delegateclass::.ctor(object, native int)
```

1.9 Metadata Tokens

Many CIL instructions are followed by a "metadata token." This is a 4-byte value that specifies a row in a metadata table, or a starting byte offset in the Userstring heap. The most-significant byte of the token specifies the table or heap. For example, a value of 0x02 specifies the *TypeDef* table; a value of 0x70 specifies the Userstring heap. The value corresponds to the number assigned to that metadata table (see Partition II [section 21] for the full list of tables) or to 0x70 for the Userstring heap. The least-significant 3 bytes specify the target row within that metadata table, or starting byte offset within the Userstring heap. The rows within metadata tables are numbered one upward, while offsets in the heap are numbered zero upward. (So, for example, the metadata token with value 0x02000007 specifies row number 7 in the *TypeDef* table.)

1.10 Exceptions Thrown

A CIL instruction can throw a range of exceptions. The CLI can also throw the general-purpose exception called `ExecutionEngineException`. See Partition I, section 12.4.2.

2 Prefixes to Instructions

These special values are reserved to precede specific instructions. They do not constitute full instructions in their own right. It is not valid CIL to branch to the instruction following the prefix, but the prefix itself is a valid branch target. It is not valid CIL to have a prefix without immediately following it by one of the instructions it is permitted to precede.

2.1 tail. (Prefix) – Call Terminates Current Method

Format	Assembly Format	Description
FE 14	tail.	Subsequent call terminates current method.

Description:

The `tail.` instruction must immediately precede a `call`, `calli`, or `callvirt` instruction. It indicates that the current method's stack frame is no longer required and thus can be removed before the call instruction is executed. Because the value returned by the call will be the value returned by this method, the call can be converted into a cross-method jump.

The evaluation stack must be empty except for the arguments being transferred by the following call. The instruction following the call instruction must be a `ret`. Thus the only legal code sequence is

`tail. call` (or `calli` or `callvirt`) *somewhere*
`ret`

Correct CIL must not branch to the `call` instruction, but it is permitted to branch to the `ret`. The only values on the stack must be the arguments for the method being called.

The `tail.call` (or `calli` or `callvirt`) instruction cannot be used to transfer control out of a `try`, `filter`, `catch`, or `finally` block. See Partition I, section 12.4.2.6.

The current frame cannot be discarded when control is transferred from untrusted code to trusted code, since this would jeopardize code identity security. Security checks may therefore cause the `tail.` to be ignored, leaving a standard call instruction.

Similarly, in order to allow the exit of a synchronized region to occur after the call returns, the `tail.` prefix is ignored when used to exit a method that is marked synchronized.

There may also be implementation-specific restrictions that prevent the `tail.` prefix from being obeyed in certain cases. While an implementation is free to ignore the `tail.` prefix under these circumstances, they should be clearly documented as they can affect the behavior of programs.

CLI implementations are required to honor `tail. call` requests where caller and callee methods can be statically determined to lie in the same assembly; and where the caller is not in a synchronized region; and where caller and callee satisfy all conditions listed in the "Verifiability" rules below. (To "honor" the `tail.` prefix means to remove the caller's frame, rather than revert to a regular call sequence.) Consequently, a CLI implementation need not honor `tail. calli` or `tail. callvirt` sequences.

RATIONALE

`tail.` calls allow some linear space algorithms to be converted to constant space algorithms and are required by some languages. In the presence of `ldloca` and `ldarga` instructions it isn't always possible for a compiler from CIL to native code to optimally determine when a `tail.` can be automatically inserted.

Exceptions:
None.

Verifiability:
Correct CIL obeys the control transfer constraints listed above. In addition, no managed pointers can be passed to the method being called if they point into the stack frame that is about to be removed. The return type of the method being called must be compatible with the return type of the current method. Verification requires that no managed pointers are passed to the method being called, since it does not track pointers into the current frame.

2.2 unaligned. (Prefix) – Pointer Instruction May Be Unaligned

Format	Assembly Format	Description
FE 12 <**unsigned int8**>	unaligned. *alignment*	Subsequent pointer instruction may be unaligned.

Stack Transition:
…, addr → …, addr

Description:
`unaligned.` specifies that *address* (an unmanaged pointer (`&`), or `native int`) on the stack may not be aligned to the natural size of the immediately following `ldind`, `stind`, `ldfld`, `stfld`, `ldobj`, `stobj`, `initblk`, or `cpblk` instruction. That is, for a `ldind.i4` instruction the alignment of *addr* may not be to a 4-byte boundary. For `initblk` and `cpblk` the default alignment is architecture-dependent (4-byte on 32-bit CPUs, 8-byte on 64-bit CPUs). Code generators that do not restrict their output to a 32-bit word size (see Partitions I and II) must use `unaligned.` if the alignment is not known at compile time to be 8-byte.

The value of *alignment* shall be 1, 2, or 4 and means that the generated code should assume that *addr* is byte, double byte, or quad byte aligned, respectively.

> **RATIONALE**
> While the alignment for a `cpblk` instruction would logically require two numbers (one for the source and one for the destination), there is no noticeable impact on performance if only the lower number is specified.

The `unaligned.` and `volatile.` prefixes may be combined in either order. They must immediately precede a `ldind`, `stind`, `ldfld`, `stfld`, `ldobj`, `stobj`, `initblk`, or `cpblk` instruction. Only the `volatile.` prefix is allowed for the `ldsfld` and `stsfld` instructions.

> **NOTE**
> See Partition I, section 12.6 and its subsections for information about atomicity and data alignment.

Exceptions:
None.

Verifiability:
An `unaligned.` prefix shall be immediately followed by one of the instructions listed above.

2.3 volatile. (Prefix) – Pointer Reference Is Volatile

Format	Assembly Format	Description
FE 13	volatile.	Subsequent pointer reference is volatile.

Stack Transition:
…, addr → …, addr

Description:
`volatile.` specifies that *addr* is a volatile address (i.e., it may be referenced externally to the current thread of execution) and the results of reading that location cannot be cached, or that multiple stores to that location cannot be suppressed. Marking an access as `volatile.` affects only that single access; other accesses to the same location must be marked separately. Access to volatile locations need not be performed atomically. (See Partition I [section 12.6, Memory Model and Optimizations].)

The `unaligned.` and `volatile.` prefixes may be combined in either order. They must immediately precede a `ldind`, `stind`, `ldfld`, `stfld`, `ldobj`, `stobj`, `initblk`, or `cpblk` instruction. Only the `volatile.` prefix is allowed for the `ldsfld` and `stsfld` instructions.

Exceptions:
None.

Verifiability:
A `volatile.` prefix should be immediately followed by one of the instructions listed above.

3 Base Instructions

These instructions form a "Turing complete" set of basic operations. They are independent of the object model that may be employed. Operations that are specifically related to the CTS's object model are contained in the Object Model Instructions section [Partition III, section 4].

3.1 add – Add Numeric Values

Format	Assembly Format	Description
58	add	Add two values, returning a new value.

Stack Transition:
…, value1, value2 → …, result

Description:
The `add` instruction adds *value2* to *value1* and pushes the result onto the stack. Overflow is not detected for integral operations (but see `add.ovf`); floating point overflow returns `+inf` or `-inf`.

The acceptable operand types and their corresponding result data type are encapsulated in Table 6-2, Binary Numeric Operations.

Exceptions:
None.

Verifiability:
See Table 6-2, Binary Numeric Operations.

3.2 add.ovf.<signed> – Add Integer Values with Overflow Check

Format	Assembly Format	Description
D6	add.ovf	Add signed integer values with overflow check.
D7	add.ovf.un	Add unsigned integer values with overflow check.

Stack Transition:
..., value1, value2 → ..., result

Description:
The `add.ovf` instruction adds *value1* and *value2* and pushes the result onto the stack. The acceptable operand types and their corresponding result data type are encapsulated in Table 6-7, Overflow Arithmetic Operations.

Exceptions:
`OverflowException` is thrown if the result cannot be represented in the result type.

Verifiability:
See Table 6-7, Overflow Arithmetic Operations.

3.3 and – Bitwise AND

Format	Instruction	Description
5F	and	Bitwise AND of two integral values; returns an integral value.

Stack Transition:
..., value1, value2 → ..., result

Description:
The `and` instruction computes the bitwise AND of *value1* and *value2* and pushes the result onto the stack. The acceptable operand types and their corresponding result data type are encapsulated in Table 6-5, Integer Operations.

Exceptions:
None.

Verifiability:
See Table 6-5, Integer Operations.

3.4 arglist – Get Argument List

Format	Assembly Format	Description
FE 00	arglist	Return argument list handle for the current method.

Stack Transition:
... → ..., argListHandle

Description:

The `arglist` instruction returns an opaque handle (an unmanaged pointer, type `native int`) representing the argument list of the current method. This handle is valid only during the lifetime of the current method. The handle can, however, be passed to other methods as long as the current method is on the thread of control. The `arglist` instruction may only be executed within a method that takes a variable number of arguments.

> **RATIONALE**
> This instruction is needed to implement the C "va_*" macros used to implement procedures like "printf". It is intended for use with the class library implementation of `System.ArgIterator`.

Exceptions:

None.

Verifiability:

It is incorrect CIL generation to emit this instruction except in the body of a method whose signature indicates that it accepts a variable number of arguments. Within such a method its use is verifiable, but verification requires that the result is an instance of the `System.RuntimeArgumentHandle` class.

3.5 beq.<length> – Branch on Equal

Format	Assembly Format	Description
3B <int32>	beq *target*	Branch to *target* if equal.
2E <int8>	beq.s *target*	Branch to *target* if equal, short form.

Stack Transition:

…, value1, value2 → …

Description:

The `beq` instruction transfers control to *target* if *value1* is equal to *value2*. The effect is identical to performing a `ceq` instruction followed by a `brtrue` *target*. *target* is represented as a signed offset (4 bytes for `beq`, 1 byte for `beq.s`) from the beginning of the instruction following the current instruction.

The acceptable operand types are encapsulated in Table 6-4, Binary Comparison or Branch Operations.

If the target instruction has one or more prefix codes, control can only be transferred to the first of these prefixes.

Control transfers into and out of `try`, `catch`, `filter`, and `finally` blocks cannot be performed by this instruction. (Such transfers are severely restricted and must use the `leave` instruction instead; see Partition I [sections 12.4.2.5 through 12.4.2.8] for details).

Exceptions:
None.

Verifiability:
Correct CIL must observe all of the control transfer rules specified above and must guarantee that the top two items on the stack correspond to the types shown in Table 6-4, Binary Comparison or Branch Operations.

In addition, verifiable code requires the type-consistency of the stack, locals, and arguments for every possible path to the destination instruction. See Partition III, section 1.5 for more details.

3.6 bge.<length> – Branch on Greater Than or Equal To

Format	Assembly Format	Description
3C <int32>	bge *target*	Branch to *target* if greater than or equal to.
2F <int8>	bge.s *target*	Branch to *target* if greater than or equal to, short form.

Stack Transition:
…, value1, value2 → …

Description:
The `bge` instruction transfers control to *target* if *value1* is greater than or equal to *value2*. The effect is identical to performing a `clt.un` instruction followed by a `brfalse` *target*. *target* is represented as a signed offset (4 bytes for `bge`, 1 byte for `bge.s`) from the beginning of the instruction following the current instruction.

The effect of a "`bge` *target*" instruction is identical to:

- If stack operands are integers, then: `clt` followed by a `brfalse` *target*.
- If stack operands are floating point, then : `clt.un` followed by a `brfalse` *target*.

The acceptable operand types are encapsulated in Table 6-4, Binary Comparison or Branch Operations.

If the target instruction has one or more prefix codes, control can only be transferred to the first of these prefixes.

Control transfers into and out of `try`, `catch`, `filter`, and `finally` blocks cannot be performed by this instruction. (Such transfers are severely restricted and must use the `leave` instruction instead; see Partition I [sections 12.4.2.5 through 12.4.2.8] for details).

Exceptions:
None.

Verifiability:
Correct CIL must observe all of the control transfer rules specified above and must guarantee that the top two items on the stack correspond to the types shown in Table 6-4, Binary Comparison or Branch Operations.

In addition, verifiable code requires the type-consistency of the stack, locals, and arguments for every possible path to the destination instruction. See Partition III, section 1.5 for more details.

3.7 bge.un.<length> – Branch on Greater Than or Equal To, Unsigned or Unordered

Format	Assembly Format	Description
41 <int32>	bge.un *target*	Branch to *target* if greater than or equal to (unsigned or unordered).
34 <int8>	bge.un.s *target*	Branch to *target* if greater than or equal to (unsigned or unordered), short form.

Stack Transition:
…, value1, value2 → …

Description:
The `bge.un` instruction transfers control to *target* if *value1* is greater than or equal to *value2*, when compared unsigned (for integer values) or unordered (for floating point values). The effect is identical to performing a `clt` instruction followed by a `brfalse` *target*. *target* is represented as a signed offset (4 bytes for `bge.un`, 1 byte for `bge.un.s`) from the beginning of the instruction following the current instruction.

The acceptable operand types are encapsulated in Table 6-4, Binary Comparison or Branch Operations.

If the target instruction has one or more prefix codes, control can only be transferred to the first of these prefixes.

Control transfers into and out of `try`, `catch`, `filter`, and `finally` blocks cannot be performed by this instruction. (Such transfers are severely restricted and must use the `leave` instruction instead; see Partition I [sections 12.4.2.5 through 12.4.2.8] for details).

Exceptions:
None.

Verifiability:
Correct CIL must observe all of the control transfer rules specified above and must guarantee that the top two items on the stack correspond to the types shown in Table 6-4, Binary Comparison or Branch Operations.

In addition, verifiable code requires the type-consistency of the stack, locals, and arguments for every possible path to the destination instruction. See Partition III, section 1.5 for more details.

3.8 bgt.<length> – Branch on Greater Than

Format	Assembly Format	Description
3D <int32>	bgt *target*	Branch to *target* if greater than.
30 <int8>	bgt.s *target*	Branch to *target* if greater than, short form.

Stack Transition:
…, value1, value2 → …

Description:
The `bgt` instruction transfers control to *target* if *value1* is greater than *value2*. The effect is identical to performing a `cgt` instruction followed by a `brtrue` *target*. *target* is represented as a signed offset (4 bytes for `bgt`, 1 byte for `bgt.s`) from the beginning of the instruction following the current instruction.

The acceptable operand types are encapsulated in Table 6-4, Binary Comparison or Branch Operations.

If the target instruction has one or more prefix codes, control can only be transferred to the first of these prefixes.

Control transfers into and out of `try`, `catch`, `filter`, and `finally` blocks cannot be performed by this instruction. (Such transfers are severely restricted and must use the `leave` instruction instead; see Partition I [sections 12.4.2.5 through 12.4.2.8] for details.)

Exceptions:
None.

Verifiability:
Correct CIL must observe all of the control transfer rules specified above and must guarantee that the top two items on the stack correspond to the types shown in Table 6-4, Binary Comparison or Branch Operations.

In addition, verifiable code requires the type-consistency of the stack, locals, and arguments for every possible path to the destination instruction. See Partition III, section 1.5 for more details.

3.9 bgt.un.<length> – Branch on Greater Than, Unsigned or Unordered

Format	Assembly Format	Description
42 <int32>	bgt.un *target*	Branch to *target* if greater than (unsigned or unordered).
35 <int8>	bgt.un.s *target*	Branch to *target* if greater than (unsigned or unordered), short form.

Stack Transition:
…, value1, value2 → …

Description:
The `bgt.un` instruction transfers control to *target* if *value1* is greater than *value2*, when compared unsigned (for integer values) or unordered (for floating point values). The effect is identical to performing a `cgt.un` instruction followed by a `brtrue` *target*. *target* is represented as a signed offset (4 bytes for `bgt.un`, 1 byte for `bgt.un.s`) from the beginning of the instruction following the current instruction.

The acceptable operand types are encapsulated in Table 6-4, Binary Comparison or Branch Operations.

If the target instruction has one or more prefix codes, control can only be transferred to the first of these prefixes.

Control transfers into and out of `try`, `catch`, `filter`, and `finally` blocks cannot be performed by this instruction. (Such transfers are severely restricted and must use the `leave` instruction instead; see Partition I [sections 12.4.2.5 through 12.4.2.8] for details.)

Exceptions:
None.

Verifiability:

Correct CIL must observe all of the control transfer rules specified above and must guarantee that the top two items on the stack correspond to the types shown in Table 6-4, Binary Comparison or Branch Operations.

In addition, verifiable code requires the type-consistency of the stack, locals, and arguments for every possible path to the destination instruction. See Partition III, section 1.5 for more details.

3.10 ble.<length> – Branch on Less Than or Equal To

Format	Assembly Format	Description
3E <int32>	ble *target*	Branch to *target* if less than or equal to.
31 <int8>	ble.s *target*	Branch to *target* if less than or equal to, short form.

Stack Transition:

…, value1, value2 → …

Description:

The `ble` instruction transfers control to *target* if *value1* is less than or equal to *value2*. *target* is represented as a signed offset (4 bytes for `ble`, 1 byte for `ble.s`) from the beginning of the instruction following the current instruction.

The effect of a "`ble` *target*" instruction is identical to:

- If stack operands are integers, then: `cgt` followed by a `brfalse` *target*.
- If stack operands are floating point, then: `cgt.un` followed by a `brfalse` *target*.

The acceptable operand types are encapsulated in Table 6-4, Binary Comparison or Branch Operations.

If the target instruction has one or more prefix codes, control can only be transferred to the first of these prefixes.

Control transfers into and out of `try`, `catch`, `filter`, and `finally` blocks cannot be performed by this instruction. (Such transfers are severely restricted and must use the `leave` instruction instead; see Partition I [sections 12.4.2.5 through 12.4.2.8] for details.)

Exceptions:

None.

Verifiability:

Correct CIL must observe all of the control transfer rules specified above and must guarantee that the top two items on the stack correspond to the types shown in Table 6-4, Binary Comparison or Branch Operations.

In addition, verifiable code requires the type-consistency of the stack, locals, and arguments for every possible path to the destination instruction. See Partition III, section 1.5 for more details.

3.11 ble.un.<length> – Branch on Less Than or Equal To, Unsigned or Unordered

Format	Assembly Format	Description
43 <int32>	ble.un *target*	Branch to *target* if less than or equal to (unsigned or unordered).
36 <int8>	ble.un.s *target*	Branch to *target* if less than or equal to (unsigned or unordered), short form.

Stack Transition:

…, value1, value2 → …

Description:

The `ble.un` instruction transfers control to *target* if *value1* is less than or equal to *value2*, when compared unsigned (for integer values) or unordered (for floating point values). *target* is represented as a signed offset (4 bytes for `ble.un`, 1 byte for `ble.un.s`) from the beginning of the instruction following the current instruction.

The effect of a "`ble.un` *target*" instruction is identical to:

- If stack operands are integers, then: `cgt.un` followed by a `brfalse` *target*.
- If stack operands are floating point, then: `cgt` followed by a `brfalse` *target*.

The acceptable operand types are encapsulated in Table 6-4, Binary Comparison or Branch Operations.

If the target instruction has one or more prefix codes, control can only be transferred to the first of these prefixes.

Control transfers into and out of `try`, `catch`, `filter`, and `finally` blocks cannot be performed by this instruction. (Such transfers are severely restricted and must use the `leave` instruction instead; see Partition I [sections 12.4.2.5 through 12.4.2.8] for details.)

Exceptions:
None.

Verifiability:
Correct CIL must observe all of the control transfer rules specified above and must guarantee that the top two items on the stack correspond to the types shown inTable 6-4, Binary Comparison or Branch Operations.

In addition, verifiable code requires the type-consistency of the stack, locals, and arguments for every possible path to the destination instruction. See Partition III, section 1.5 for more details.

3.12 blt.<length> – Branch on Less Than

Format	Assembly Format	Description
3F <int32>	blt *target*	Branch to *target* if less than.
32 <int8>	blt.s *target*	Branch to *target* if less than, short form.

Stack Transition:
…, value1, value2 → …

Description:
The `blt` instruction transfers control to *target* if *value1* is less than *value2*. The effect is identical to performing a `clt` instruction followed by a `brtrue` *target*. *target* is represented as a signed offset (4 bytes for `blt`, 1 byte for `blt.s`) from the beginning of the instruction following the current instruction.

The acceptable operand types are encapsulated inTable 6-4, Binary Comparison or Branch Operations.

If the target instruction has one or more prefix codes, control can only be transferred to the first of these prefixes.

Control transfers into and out of `try`, `catch`, `filter`, and `finally` blocks cannot be performed by this instruction. (Such transfers are severely restricted and must use the `leave` instruction instead; see Partition I [sections 12.4.2.5 through 12.4.2.8] for details.)

Exceptions:
None.

Verifiability:
Correct CIL must observe all of the control transfer rules specified above and must guarantee that the top two items on the stack correspond to the types shown in Table 6-4, Binary Comparison or Branch Operations.

In addition, verifiable code requires the type-consistency of the stack, locals, and arguments for every possible path to the destination instruction. See Partition III, section 1.5 for more details.

3.13 blt.un.<length> – Branch on Less Than, Unsigned or Unordered

Format	Assembly Format	Description
44 <int32>	blt.un *target*	Branch to *target* if less than (unsigned or unordered) .
37 <int8>	blt.un.s *target*	Branch to *target* if less than (unsigned or unordered), short form.

Stack Transition:
…, value1, value2 → …

Description:
The `blt.un` instruction transfers control to *target* if *value1* is less than *value2*, when compared unsigned (for integer values) or unordered (for floating point values). The effect is identical to performing a `clt.un` instruction followed by a `brtrue` *target*. *target* is represented as a signed offset (4 bytes for `blt.un`, 1 byte for `blt.un.s`) from the beginning of the instruction following the current instruction.

The acceptable operand types are encapsulated in Table 6-4, Binary Comparison or Branch Operations.

If the target instruction has one or more prefix codes, control can only be transferred to the first of these prefixes.

Control transfers into and out of `try`, `catch`, `filter`, and `finally` blocks cannot be performed by this instruction. (Such transfers are severely restricted and must use the `leave` instruction instead; see Partition I [sections 12.4.2.5 through 12.4.2.8] for details.)

Exceptions:
None.

Verifiability:
Correct CIL must observe all of the control transfer rules specified above and must guarantee that the top two items on the stack correspond to the types shown in Table 6-4, Binary Comparison or Branch Operations.

In addition, verifiable code requires the type-consistency of the stack, locals, and arguments for every possible path to the destination instruction. See Partition III, section 1.5 for more details.

3.14 bne.un<length> – Branch on Not Equal or Unordered

Format	Assembly Format	Description
40 <int32>	bne.un *target*	Branch to *target* if unequal or unordered.
33 <int8>	bne.un.s *target*	Branch to *target* if unequal or unordered, short form.

Stack Transition:
…, value1, value2 → …

Description:
The `bne.un` instruction transfers control to *target* if *value1* is not equal to *value2*, when compared unsigned (for integer values) or unordered (for floating point values). The effect is identical to performing a `ceq` instruction followed by a `brfalse` *target*. *target* is represented as a signed offset (4 bytes for `bne.un`, 1 byte for `bne.un.s`) from the beginning of the instruction following the current instruction.

The acceptable operand types are encapsulated in Table 6-4, Binary Comparison or Branch Operations.

If the target instruction has one or more prefix codes, control can only be transferred to the first of these prefixes.

Control transfers into and out of `try`, `catch`, `filter`, and `finally` blocks cannot be performed by this instruction. (Such transfers are severely restricted and must use the `leave` instruction instead; see Partition I [sections 12.4.2.5 through 12.4.2.8] for details.)

Exceptions:
None.

Verifiability:
Correct CIL must observe all of the control transfer rules specified above and must guarantee that the top two items on the stack correspond to the types shown in Table 6-4, Binary Comparison or Branch Operations.

In addition, verifiable code requires the type-consistency of the stack, locals, and arguments for every possible path to the destination instruction. See Partition III, section 1.5 for more details.

3.15 br.<length> – Unconditional Branch

Format	Assembly Format	Description
38 <int32>	br *target*	Branch to *target*
2B <int8>	br.s *target*	Branch to *target*, short form.

Stack Transition:

…, → …

Description:

The `br` instruction unconditionally transfers control to *target*. *target* is represented as a signed offset (4 bytes for `br`, 1 byte for `br.s`) from the beginning of the instruction following the current instruction.

If the target instruction has one or more prefix codes, control can only be transferred to the first of these prefixes.

Control transfers into and out of `try`, `catch`, `filter`, and `finally` blocks cannot be performed by this instruction. (Such transfers are severely restricted and must use the `leave` instruction instead; see Partition I [sections 12.4.2.5 through 12.4.2.8] for details.)

> **RATIONALE**
>
> While a `leave` instruction can be used instead of a `br` instruction when the evaluation stack is empty, doing so may increase the resources required to compile from CIL to native code and/or lead to inferior native code. Therefore CIL generators should use a `br` instruction in preference to a `leave` instruction when both are legal.

Exceptions:

None.

Verifiability:

Correct CIL must observe all of the control transfer rules specified above.

In addition, verifiable code requires the type-consistency of the stack, locals, and arguments for every possible path to the destination instruction. See Partition III, section 1.5 for more details.

3.16 break – Breakpoint Instruction

Format	Assembly Format	Description
01	break	Inform a debugger that a breakpoint has been reached.

Stack Transition:

…, → …

Description:

The `break` instruction is for debugging support. It signals the CLI to inform the debugger that a breakpoint has been tripped. It has no other effect on the interpreter state.

The `break` instruction has the smallest possible instruction size so that code can be patched with a breakpoint with minimal disturbance to the surrounding code.

The `break` instruction may trap to a debugger, do nothing, or raise a security exception: the exact behavior is implementation-defined.

ANNOTATION: Typically, in an externally written PE file, the `break` instruction would not be present in the CIL instructions. It is intended for use by debuggers in the in-memory representation of CLI methods.

Exceptions:

None.

Verifiability:

The `break` instruction is always verifiable.

3.17 brfalse.<length> – Branch on False, Null, or Zero

Format	Assembly Format	Description
39 <int32>	brfalse *target*	Branch to *target* if *value* is zero (false).
2C <int8>	brfalse.s *target*	Branch to *target* if *value* is zero (false), short form.

Format	Assembly Format	Description
39 <int32>	brnull *target*	Branch to *target* if *value* is null (*alias for* `brfalse`).
2C <int8>	brnull.s *target*	Branch to *target* if *value* is null (*alias for* `brfalse.s`), short form.
39 <int32>	brzero *target*	Branch to *target* if *value* is zero (*alias for* `brfalse`).
2C <int8>	brzero.s *target*	Branch to *target* if *value* is zero (*alias for* `brfalse.s`), short form.

Stack Transition:

…, value → …

Description:

The `brfalse` instruction transfers control to *target* if *value* (of type `int32`, `int64`, `object reference`, `managed pointer`, `unmanaged pointer`, or `native int`) is zero (false). If *value* is non-zero (true), execution continues at the next instruction.

target is represented as a signed offset (4 bytes for `brfalse`, 1 byte for `brfalse.s`) from the beginning of the instruction following the current instruction.

If the target instruction has one or more prefix codes, control can only be transferred to the first of these prefixes.

Control transfers into and out of `try`, `catch`, `filter`, and `finally` blocks cannot be performed by this instruction. (Such transfers are severely restricted and must use the `leave` instruction instead; see Partition I [sections 12.4.2.5 through 12.4.2.8] for details.)

Exceptions:

None.

Verifiability:

Correct CIL must observe all of the control transfer rules specified above and must guarantee that there is a minimum of one item on the stack.

In addition, verifiable code requires the type-consistency of the stack, locals, and arguments for every possible path to the destination instruction. See Partition III, section 1.5 for more details.

3.18 brtrue.<length> – Branch on Non-false or Non-null

Format	Assembly Format	Description
3A <int32>	brtrue *target*	Branch to *target* if *value* is non-zero (true).
2D <int8>	brtrue.s *target*	Branch to *target* if *value* is non-zero (true), short form.
3A <int32>	brinst *target*	Branch to *target* if *value* is a non-null object reference (alias for `brtrue`).
2D <int8>	brinst.s *target*	Branch to *target* if *value* is a non-null object reference, short form (alias for `brtrue.s`).

Stack Transition:

…, value → …

Description:

The `brtrue` instruction transfers control to *target* if *value* (of type `native int`) is non-zero (true). If *value* is zero (false), execution continues at the next instruction.

If the *value* is an object reference (type `O`), then `brinst` (an alias for `brtrue`) transfers control if it represents an instance of an object (i.e., isn't the null object reference; see `ldnull` [Partition III, section 3.45]).

target is represented as a signed offset (4 bytes for `brtrue`, 1 byte for `brtrue.s`) from the beginning of the instruction following the current instruction.

If the target instruction has one or more prefix codes, control can only be transferred to the first of these prefixes.

Control transfers into and out of `try`, `catch`, `filter`, and `finally` blocks cannot be performed by this instruction. (Such transfers are severely restricted and must use the `leave` instruction instead; see Partition I [sections 12.4.2.5 through 12.4.2.8] for details.)

Exceptions:

None.

Verifiability:

Correct CIL must observe all of the control transfer rules specified above and must guarantee that there is a minimum of one item on the stack.

In addition, verifiable code requires the type-consistency of the stack, locals, and arguments for every possible path to the destination instruction. See Partition III, section 1.5 for more details.

3.19 call – Call a Method

Format	Assembly Format	Description
28 ‹T›	call *method*	Call method described by *method*.

Stack Transition:

…, arg1, arg2 … argn ➔ …, retVal (not always returned)

Description:

The `call` instruction calls the method indicated by the descriptor *method*. *method* is a metadata token (either a `methodref` or `methoddef`; see Partition II) that indicates the method to call and the number, type, and order of the arguments that have been placed on the stack to be passed to that method, as well as the calling convention to be used. See Partition I [section 12.4 and its subsections] for a detailed description of the CIL calling sequence. The `call` instruction may be immediately preceded by a `tail.` prefix to specify that the current method state should be released before transferring control (see Partition III, section 2.1).

The metadata token carries sufficient information to determine whether the call is to a static method, an instance method, a virtual method, or a global function. In all of these cases the destination address is determined entirely from the metadata token. (Contrast with the `callvirt` instruction for calling virtual methods, where the destination address also depends upon the runtime type of the instance reference pushed before the `callvirt`; see below).

If the method does not exist in the class specified by the metadata token, the base classes are searched to find the most derived class which defines the method, and that method is called.

> **RATIONALE**
> This implements "call superclass" behavior.

The arguments are placed on the stack in left-to-right order. That is, the first argument is computed and placed on the stack, then the second argument, etc. There are three important special cases:

1. Calls to an instance (or virtual; see the following paragraph) method must push that instance reference (the `this` pointer) before any of the user-visible arguments. The signature carried in the metadata does not contain an entry in the parameter list for

the `this` pointer but uses a bit (called `HASTHIS`) to indicate whether the method requires passing the `this` pointer (see Partition II, sections 22.2.1 and 22.2.2).

ANNOTATION: For calls to methods on value types, the `this` pointer is a managed pointer, not an instance reference.

---

2. It is legal to call a virtual method using `call` (rather than `callvirt`); this indicates that the method is to be resolved using the class specified by *method* rather than as specified dynamically from the object being invoked. This is used, for example, to compile calls to "methods on `super`" (i.e., the statically known parent class).
3. Note that a delegate's `Invoke` method may be called with either the `call` or `callvirt` instruction.

Exceptions:

`SecurityException` may be thrown if system security does not grant the caller access to the called method. The security check may occur when the CIL is converted to native code rather than at runtime.

Verifiability:

Correct CIL ensures that the stack contains the correct number and type of arguments for the method being called.

For a typical use of the `call` instruction, verification checks that (a) *method* refers to a valid `methodref` or `methoddef` token; (b) the types of the objects on the stack are consistent with the types expected by the method call, and (c) the method is accessible from the call site, and (d) the method is not abstract (i.e., it has an implementation).

The `call` instruction may also be used to call an object's superclass constructor, or to initialize a value type location by calling an appropriate constructor, both of which are treated as special cases by verification. A `call` annotated by `tail.` is also a special case.

If the target method is global (defined outside of any type), then the method must be static.

3.20 calli – Indirect Method Call

Format	Assembly Format	Description
29 <T>	calli *callsitedescr*	Call method indicated on the stack with arguments described by *callsitedescr*.

Stack Transition:

…, arg1, arg2 … argn, ftn → …, retVal (not always returned)

Description:

The `calli` instruction calls *ftn* (a pointer to a method entry point) with the arguments `arg1` … `argn`. The types of these arguments are described by the signature `callsite-descr`. See Partition I [section 12.4 and its subsections] for a description of the CIL calling sequence. The `calli` instruction may be immediately preceded by a `tail.` prefix to specify that the current method state should be released before transferring control. If the call would transfer control to a method of higher trust than the origin method, the stack frame would not be released; instead, the execution would continue silently as if the `tail.` prefix had not been supplied.

(A callee of "higher trust" is defined as one whose permission grant-set is a strict superset of the grant-set of the caller.)

The *ftn* argument is assumed to be a pointer to native code (of the target machine) that can be legitimately called with the arguments described by *callsitedescr* (a metadata token for a stand-alone signature). Such a pointer can be created using the `ldftn` or `ldvirtftn` instruction, or have been passed in from native code.

The stand-alone signature specifies the number and type of parameters being passed, as well as the calling convention (see Partition II [section 14.3]). The calling convention is not checked dynamically, so code that uses a `calli` instruction will not work correctly if the destination does not actually use the specified calling convention.

The arguments are placed on the stack in left-to-right order. That is, the first argument is computed and placed on the stack, then the second argument, etc. The argument-building code sequence for an instance or virtual method must push that instance reference (the `this` pointer, which must not be null) before any of the user-visible arguments.

ANNOTATION: For calls to methods on value types, the `this` pointer is a managed pointer, not an instance reference.

Exceptions:

`SecurityException` may be thrown if the system security does not grant the caller access to the called method. The security check may occur when the CIL is converted to native code rather than at runtime.

Verifiability:
Correct CIL requires that the function pointer contains the address of a method whose signature matches that specified by *callsitedescr* and that the arguments correctly correspond to the types of the destination function's parameters.

Verification checks that *ftn* is a pointer to a function generated by `ldftn` or `ldvirtfn`.

ANNOTATION:
Implementation-Specific (Microsoft): In the first release of Microsoft's implementation of the CLI, the `calli` instruction is never verifiable.

3.21 ceq – Compare Equal

Format	Assembly Format	Description
FE 01	ceq	Push 1 (of type `int32`) if *value1* equals *value2*, else 0.

Stack Transition:
…, value1, value2 → …, result

Description:
The `ceq` instruction compares *value1* and *value2*. If *value1* is equal to *value2*, then 1 (of type `int32`) is pushed onto the stack. Otherwise 0 (of type `int32`) is pushed onto the stack.

For floating point numbers, `ceq` will return 0 if the numbers are unordered (either or both are NaN). The infinite values are equal to themselves.

The acceptable operand types are encapsulated inTable 6-4, Binary Comparison or Branch Operations.

Exceptions:
None.

Verifiability:
Correct CIL provides two values on the stack whose types match those specified in Table 6-4, Binary Comparison or Branch Operations. There are no additional verification requirements.

3.22 cgt – Compare Greater Than

Format	Assembly Format	Description
FE 02	cgt	Push 1 (of type `int32`) if *value1* > *value2*, else 0.

Stack Transition:
…, value1, value2 → …, result

Description:
The `cgt` instruction compares *value1* and *value2*. If *value1* is strictly greater than *value2*, then 1 (of type `int32`) is pushed onto the stack. Otherwise 0 (of type `int32`) is pushed onto the stack.

For floating point numbers, `cgt` returns 0 if the numbers are unordered (that is, if one or both of the arguments are NaN).

As per IEC 60559:1989, infinite values are ordered with respect to normal numbers (e.g., +infinity > 5.0 > –infinity).

The acceptable operand types are encapsulated in Table 6-4, Binary Comparison or Branch Operations.

Exceptions:
None.

Verifiability:
Correct CIL provides two values on the stack whose types match those specified in Table 6-4, Binary Comparison or Branch Operations. There are no additional verification requirements.

3.23 cgt.un – Compare Greater Than, Unsigned or Unordered

Format	Assembly Format	Description
FE 03	cgt.un	Push 1 (of type `int32`) if *value1* > *value2*, unsigned or unordered, else 0.

Stack Transition:
…, value1, value2 → …, result

Description:
The `cgt.un` instruction compares *value1* and *value2*. A value of 1 (of type `int32`) is pushed onto the stack if

- For floating point numbers, either *value1* is strictly greater than *value2*, or *value1* is not ordered with respect to *value2*.
- For integer values, *value1* is strictly greater than *value2* when considered as unsigned numbers.

Otherwise 0 (of type `int32`) is pushed onto the stack.

As per IEC 60559:1989, infinite values are ordered with respect to normal numbers (e.g., +infinity > 5.0 > –infinity).

The acceptable operand types are encapsulated inTable 6-4, Binary Comparison or Branch Operations.

Exceptions:
None.

Verifiability:
Correct CIL provides two values on the stack whose types match those specified in Table 6-4, Binary Comparison or Branch Operations. There are no additional verification requirements.

3.24 ckfinite – Check for a Finite Real Number

Format	Assembly Format	Description
C3	ckfinite	Throw `ArithmeticException` if value is not a finite number.

Stack Transition:
…, value → …, value

Description:
The `ckfinite` instruction throws `ArithmeticException` if *value* (a floating point number) is either a "not a number" value (NaN) or a +/– infinity value. `ckfinite` leaves the value on the stack if no exception is thrown. Execution is unspecified if*value* is not a floating point number.

Exceptions:
`ArithmeticException` is thrown if *value* is not a "normal" number.

Verifiability:
Correct CIL guarantees that *value* is a floating point number. There are no additional verification requirements.

3.25 clt – Compare Less Than

Format	Assembly Format	Description
FE 04	clt	Push 1 (of type `int32`) if *value1* < *value2*, else 0.

Stack Transition:
…, value1, value2 → …, result

Description:
The `clt` instruction compares *value1* and *value2*. If *value1* is strictly less than *value2*, then 1 (of type `int32`) is pushed onto the stack. Otherwise 0 (of type `int32`) is pushed onto the stack.

For floating point numbers, `clt` will return 0 if the numbers are unordered (that is, one or both of the arguments are NaN).

As per IEC 60559:1989, infinite values are ordered with respect to normal numbers (e.g., +infinity > 5.0 > –infinity).

The acceptable operand types are encapsulated in Table 6-4, Binary Comparison or Branch Operations.

Exceptions:
None.

Verifiability:
Correct CIL provides two values on the stack whose types match those specified in Table 6-4, Binary Comparison or Branch Operations. There are no additional verification requirements.

3.26 clt.un – Compare Less Than, Unsigned or Unordered

Format	Assembly Format	Description
FE 05	clt.un	Push 1 (of type `int32`) if *value1* < *value2*, unsigned or unordered, else 0.

Stack Transition:
…, value1, value2 → …, result

Description:
The `clt.un` instruction compares *value1* and *value2*. A value of 1 (of type `int32`) is pushed onto the stack if

- For floating point numbers, either *value1* is strictly less than *value2*, or *value1* is not ordered with respect to *value2*.
- For integer values, *value1* is strictly less than *value2* when considered as unsigned numbers.

Otherwise 0 (of type `int32`) is pushed onto the stack.

As per IEC 60559:1989, infinite values are ordered with respect to normal numbers (e.g., +infinity > 5.0 > –infinity).

The acceptable operand types are encapsulated inTable 6-4, Binary Comparison or Branch Operations.

Exceptions:
None.

Verifiability:
Correct CIL provides two values on the stack whose types match those specified in Table 6-4, Binary Comparison or Branch Operations. There are no additional verification requirements.

3.27 conv.<to type> – Data Conversion

Format	Assembly Format	Description
67	conv.i1	Convert to `int8`, pushing `int32` onto stack.
68	conv.i2	Convert to `int16`, pushing `int32` onto stack.
69	conv.i4	Convert to `int32`, pushing `int32` onto stack.
6A	conv.i8	Convert to `int64`, pushing `int64` onto stack.
6B	conv.r4	Convert to `float32`, pushing `F` onto stack.
6C	conv.r8	Convert to `float64`, pushing `F` onto stack.
D2	conv.u1	Convert to `unsigned int8`, pushing `int32` onto stack.

Format	Assembly Format	Description
D1	conv.u2	Convert to unsigned int16, pushing int32 onto stack.
6D	conv.u4	Convert to unsigned int32, pushing int32 onto stack.
6E	conv.u8	Convert to unsigned int64, pushing int64 onto stack.
D3	conv.i	Convert to native int, pushing native int onto stack.
E0	conv.u	Convert to native unsigned int, pushing native int onto stack.
76	conv.r.un	Convert unsigned integer to floating point, pushing F onto stack.

Stack Transition:

..., value → ..., result

Description:

Convert the value on top of the stack to the type specified in the opcode, and leave that converted value on the top of the stack. Note that integer values of less than 4 bytes are extended to int32 (not native int) when they are loaded onto the evaluation stack, and floating point values are converted to the F type.

Conversion from floating point numbers to integral values truncates the number toward zero. When converting from a float64 to a float32, precision may be lost. If *value* is too large to fit in a float32, the IEC 60559:1989 positive infinity (if *value* is positive) or IEC 60559:1989 negative infinity (if *value* is negative) is returned. If overflow occurs converting one integer type to another, the high-order bits are silently truncated. If the result is smaller than an int32, then the value is sign-extended to fill the slot.

If overflow occurs converting a floating point type to an integer, the value returned is unspecified. The conv.r.un operation takes an integer off the stack, interprets it as unsigned, and replaces it with a floating point number to represent the integer; either a float32, if this is wide enough to represent the integer without loss of precision, else a float64.

No exceptions are ever thrown. See conv.ovf [Partition III, section 3.28] for instructions that will throw an exception when the result type cannot properly represent the result value.

The acceptable operand types and their corresponding result data type are encapsulated in Table 6-8, Conversion Operations.

Exceptions:
None.

Verifiability:
Correct CIL has at least one value, of a type specified in Table 6-8, Conversion Operations, on the stack. The same table specifies a restricted set of types that are acceptable in verified code.

3.28 conv.ovf.<to type> – Data Conversion with Overflow Detection

Format	Assembly Format	Description
B3	conv.ovf.i1	Convert to an `int8` (on the stack as `int32`) and throw an exception on overflow.
B5	conv.ovf.i2	Convert to an `int16` (on the stack as `int32`) and throw an exception on overflow.
B7	conv.ovf.i4	Convert to an `int32` (on the stack as `int32`) and throw an exception on overflow.
B9	conv.ovf.i8	Convert to an `int64` (on the stack as `int64`) and throw an exception on overflow.
B4	conv.ovf.u1	Convert to a `unsigned int8` (on the stack as `int32`) and throw an exception on overflow.
B6	conv.ovf.u2	Convert to a `unsigned int16` (on the stack as `int32`) and throw an exception on overflow.
B8	conv.ovf.u4	Convert to a `unsigned int32` (on the stack as `int32`) and throw an exception on overflow.
BA	conv.ovf.u8	Convert to a `unsigned int64` (on the stack as `int64`) and throw an exception on overflow.
D4	conv.ovf.i	Convert to an `native int` (on the stack as `native int`) and throw an exception on overflow.
D5	conv.ovf.u	Convert to a `native unsigned int` (on the stack as `native int`) and throw an exception on overflow.

Stack Transition:
…, value → …, result

Description:
Convert the value on top of the stack to the type specified in the opcode, and leave that converted value on the top of the stack. If the value is too large or too small to be represented by the target type, an exception is thrown.

Conversions from floating point numbers to integral values truncate the number toward zero. Note that integer values of less than 4 bytes are extended to `int32` (not `native int`) on the evaluation stack.

The acceptable operand types and their corresponding result data type are encapsulated in Table 6-8, Conversion Operations.

Exceptions:
`OverflowException` is thrown if the result cannot be represented in the result type.

Verifiability:
Correct CIL has at least one value, of a type specified in Table 6-8, Conversion Operations, on the stack. The same table specifies a restricted set of types that are acceptable in verified code.

3.29 conv.ovf.<to type>.un – Unsigned Data Conversion with Overflow Detection

Format	Assembly Format	Description
82	conv.ovf.i1.un	Convert unsigned to an `int8` (on the stack as `int32`) and throw an exception on overflow.
83	conv.ovf.i2.un	Convert unsigned to an `int16` (on the stack as `int32`) and throw an exception on overflow.
84	conv.ovf.i4.un	Convert unsigned to an `int32` (on the stack as `int32`) and throw an exception on overflow.
85	conv.ovf.i8.un	Convert unsigned to an `int64` (on the stack as `int64`) and throw an exception on overflow.
86	conv.ovf.u1.un	Convert unsigned to an `unsigned int8` (on the stack as `int32`) and throw an exception on overflow.
87	conv.ovf.u2.un	Convert unsigned to an `unsigned int16` (on the stack as `int32`) and throw an exception on overflow.
88	conv.ovf.u4.un	Convert unsigned to an `unsigned int32` (on the stack as `int32`) and throw an exception on overflow.

Format	Assembly Format	Description
89	conv.ovf.u8.un	Convert unsigned to an `unsigned int64` (on the stack as `int64`) and throw an exception on overflow.
8A	conv.ovf.i.un	Convert unsigned to a `native int` (on the stack as `native int`) and throw an exception on overflow.
8B	conv.ovf.u.un	Convert unsigned to a `native unsigned int` (on the stack as `native int`) and throw an exception on overflow.

Stack Transition:

..., value ➔ ..., result

Description:

Convert the value on top of the stack to the type specified in the opcode, and leave that converted value on the top of the stack. If the value cannot be represented, an exception is thrown. The item at the top of the stack is treated as an unsigned value.

Conversions from floating point numbers to integral values truncate the number toward zero. Note that integer values of less than 4 bytes are extended to `int32` (not `native int`) on the evaluation stack.

The acceptable operand types and their corresponding result data type are encapsulated in Table 6-8, Conversion Operations.

Exceptions:

`OverflowException` is thrown if the result cannot be represented in the result type.

Verifiability:

Correct CIL has at least one value, of a type specified in Table 6-8, Conversion Operations, on the stack. The same table specifies a restricted set of types that are acceptable in verified code.

3.30 cpblk – Copy Data from Memory to Memory

Format	Instruction	Description
FE 17	cpblk	Copy data from memory to memory.

Stack Transition:

..., destaddr, srcaddr, size ➔ ...

Description:
The `cpblk` instruction copies *size* (of type `unsigned int32`) bytes from address *srcaddr* (of type `native int`, or `&`) to address *destaddr* (of type `native int`, or `&`). The behavior of `cpblk` is unspecified if the source and destination areas overlap.

`cpblk` assumes that both *destaddr* and *srcaddr* are aligned to the natural size of the machine (but see the `unaligned.` prefix instruction). The `cpblk` instruction may be immediately preceded by the `unaligned.` prefix instruction to indicate that either the source or the destination is unaligned.

> **RATIONALE**
> `cpblk` is intended for copying structures (rather than arbitrary byte-runs). All such structures, allocated by the CLI, are naturally aligned for the current platform. Therefore, there is no need for the compiler that generates `cpblk` instructions to be aware of whether the code will eventually execute on a 32-bit or 64-bit platform.

The operation of the `cpblk` instruction may be altered by an immediately preceding `volatile.` or `unaligned.` prefix instruction.

Exceptions:
`NullReferenceException` may be thrown if an invalid address is detected.

Verifiability:
The `cpblk` instruction is never verifiable. Correct CIL ensures the conditions specified above.

3.31 div – Divide Values

Format	Assembly Format	Description
5B	div	Divide two values to return a quotient or floating point result.

Stack Transition:
…, value1, value2 → …, result

Description:
result = *value1* ***div*** *value2* satisfies the following conditions:

| *result* | = | *value1* | / | *value2* |, and

sign(result) = +, *if sign(value1)* = *sign(value2)*, or
–, *if sign(value1)* ~= *sign(value2)*

The `div` instruction computes *result* and pushes it onto the stack.

Integer division truncates toward zero.

Floating point division is per IEC 60559:1989. In particular, division of a finite number by 0 produces the correctly signed infinite value and

```
0 / 0 = NaN
infinity / infinity = NaN
X / infinity = 0
```

The acceptable operand types and their corresponding result data type are encapsulated in Table 6-2, Binary Numeric Operations.

Exceptions:
Integral operations throw `ArithmeticException` if the result cannot be represented in the result type. This can happen if *value1* is the smallest representable integer value, and *value2* is –1.

Integral operations throw `DivideByZeroException` if *value2* is zero.

ANNOTATION:
Implementation-Specific (Microsoft): On the x86, an `OverflowException` is thrown when computing (*minint* `div` –1).

Floating point operations never throw an exception (they produce NaNs or infinities instead; see Partition I [section 12.1.3]).

Example:
```
+14 div +3 is 4
+14 div -3 is -4
-14 div +3 is -4
-14 div -3 is 4
```

Verifiability:
See Table 6-2, Binary Numeric Operations.

3.32 div.un – Divide Integer Values, Unsigned

Format	Assembly Format	Description
5C	div.un	Divide two values, unsigned, returning a quotient.

Stack Transition:
…, value1, value2 → …, result

Description:
The `div.un` instruction computes *value1* divided by *value2*, both taken as unsigned integers, and pushes the result on the stack.

The acceptable operand types and their corresponding result data type are encapsulated in Table 6-5, Integer Operations.

Exceptions:
`DivideByZeroException` is thrown if *value2* is zero.

Example:

```
+5 div.un +3    is 1
+5 div.un -3    is 0
-5 div.un +3    is 14316557630 or 0x55555553
-5 div.un -3    is 0
```

Verifiability:
See Table 6-5, Integer Operations.

3.33 dup – Duplicate the Top Value of the Stack

Format	Assembly Format	Description
25	dup	Duplicate value on the top of the stack.

Stack Transition:
…, value → …, value, value

Description:
The dup instruction duplicates the top element of the stack.

Exceptions:
None.

Verifiability:
No additional requirements.

3.34 endfilter – End filter Clause of SEH

Format	Assembly Format	Description
FE 11	endfilter	End exception handling `filter` clause.

Stack Transition:
…, value → …

Description:
Return from `filter` clause of an exception (see the Exception Handling section of Partition I [section 12.4.2] for a discussion of exceptions). *Value* (which must be of type `int32` and is one of a specific set of values) is returned from the `filter` clause. It should be one of:

- `exception_continue_search` (0) to continue searching for an exception handler.
- `exception_execute_handler` (1) to start the second phase of exception handling where `finally` blocks are run until the handler associated with this `filter` clause is located. Then the handler is executed.

Other integer values will produce unspecified results.

The entry point of a filter, as shown in the method's exception table, must be the (lexically) first instruction in the filter's code block. The `endfilter` must be the (lexically) last instruction in the filter's code block (hence there can only be one `endfilter` for any single `filter` block). After executing the `endfilter` instruction, control logically flows back to the CLI exception handling mechanism.

Control cannot be transferred into a `filter` block except through the exception mechanism. Control cannot be transferred out of a `filter` block except through the use of a `throw` instruction or executing the final `endfilter` instruction. In particular, it is not legal to execute a `ret` or `leave` instruction within a `filter` block. It is not legal to embed a `try` block within a `filter` block. If an exception is thrown inside the `filter` block, it is intercepted and a value of `exception_continue_search` is returned.

Exceptions:
None.

Verifiability:
Correct CIL guarantees the control transfer restrictions specified above. Also, the stack must contain exactly one item (of type `int32`).

3.35 endfinally – End the finally or fault Clause of an Exception Block

Format	Assembly Format	Description
DC	endfault	End `fault` clause of an exception block.
DC	endfinally	End `finally` clause of an exception block.

Stack Transition:

Description:
Return from the `finally` or `fault` clause of an exception block; see the Exception Handling section of Partition I [section 12.4.2] for details.

Signals the end of the `finally` or `fault` clause so that stack unwinding can continue until the exception handler is invoked. The `endfinally` or `endfault` instruction transfers control back to the CLI exception mechanism. This then searches for the next `finally` clause in the chain if the protected block was exited with a `leave` instruction. If the protected block was exited with an exception, the CLI will search for the next `finally` or `fault`, or enter the exception handler chosen during the first pass of exception handling.

An `endfinally` instruction may only appear lexically within a `finally` block. Unlike the `endfilter` instruction, there is no requirement that the block end with an `endfinally` instruction, and there can be as many `endfinally` instructions within the block as required. These same restrictions apply to the `endfault` instruction and the `fault` block, *mutatis mutandis*.

Control cannot be transferred into a `finally` (or `fault` block) except through the exception mechanism. Control cannot be transferred out of a `finally` (or `fault`) block except through the use of a `throw` instruction or executing the `endfinally` (or `endfault`) instruction. In particular, it is not legal to "fall out" of a `finally` (or `fault`) block or to execute a `ret` or `leave` instruction within a `finally` (or `fault`) block.

Note that the `endfault` and `endfinally` instructions are aliases—they correspond to the same opcode.

Exceptions:
None.

Verifiability:
Correct CIL guarantees the control transfer restrictions specified above. There are no additional verification requirements.

3.36 initblk – Initialize a Block of Memory to a Value

Format	Assembly Format	Description
FE 18	initblk	Set a block of memory to a given byte.

Stack Transition:
…, addr, value, size → …

Description:
The `initblk` instruction sets *size* (of type `unsigned int32`) bytes starting at *addr* (of type `native int`, or `&`) to *value* (of type `unsigned int8`). `initblk` assumes that *addr* is aligned to the natural size of the machine (but see the `unaligned.` prefix instruction [Partition III, section 2.2]).

RATIONALE
`initblk` is intended for initializing structures (rather than arbitrary byte-runs). All such structures, allocated by the CLI, are naturally aligned for the current platform. Therefore, there is no need for the compiler that generates `initblk` instructions to be aware of whether the code will eventually execute on a 32-bit or 64-bit platform.

The operation of the `initblk` instructions may be altered by an immediately preceding `volatile.` or `unaligned.` prefix instruction.

Exceptions:
`NullReferenceException` may be thrown if an invalid address is detected.

Verifiability:
The `initblk` instruction is never verifiable. Correct CIL code ensures the restrictions specified above.

3.37 jmp – Jump to Method

Format	Assembly Format	Description
27 <T>	jmp *method*	Exit current method and jump to specified method.

Stack Transition:

Description:

Transfer control to the method specified by *method*, which is a metadata token (either a `methodref` or `methoddef`; see Partition II). The current arguments are transferred to the destination method.

The evaluation stack must be empty when this instruction is executed. The calling convention, number, and type of arguments at the destination address must match those of the current method.

The `jmp` instruction cannot be used to transferred control out of a `try`, `filter`, `catch`, `fault`, or `finally` block; or out of a synchronized region. If this is done, results are undefined. See Partition I [sections 12.4.2.5 through 12.4.2.8].

Exceptions:

None.

Verifiability:

The `jmp` instruction is never verifiable. Correct CIL code obeys the control flow restrictions specified above.

3.38 ldarg.<length> – Load Argument onto the Stack

Format	Assembly Format	Description
FE 09 <**unsigned int16**>	ldarg *num*	Load argument numbered num onto stack.
0E <**unsigned int8**>	ldarg.s *num*	Load argument numbered num onto stack, short form.
02	ldarg.0	Load argument 0 onto stack.
03	ldarg.1	Load argument 1 onto stack.
04	ldarg.2	Load argument 2 onto stack.
05	ldarg.3	Load argument 3 onto stack.

Stack Transition:
… → …, value

Description:
The `ldarg` *num* instruction pushes the *num*'th incoming argument, where arguments are numbered 0 onward onto the evaluation stack. The `ldarg` instruction can be used to load a value type or a built-in value onto the stack by copying it from an incoming argument. The type of the value is the same as the type of the argument, as specified by the current method's signature.

The `ldarg.0`, `ldarg.1`, `ldarg.2`, and `ldarg.3` instructions are efficient encodings for loading any of the first four arguments. The `ldarg.s` instruction is an efficient encoding for loading argument numbers 4 through 255.

For procedures that take a variable-length argument list, the `ldarg` instructions can be used only for the initial fixed arguments, not those in the variable part of the signature. (See the `arglist` instruction.)

Arguments that hold an integer value smaller than 4 bytes long are expanded to type `int32` when they are loaded onto the stack. Floating point values are expanded to their native size (type `F`).

Exceptions:
None.

Verifiability:
Correct CIL guarantees that *num* is a valid argument index. See Partition III, section 1.5 for more details on how verification determines the type of the value loaded onto the stack.

3.39 ldarga.<length> – Load an Argument Address

Format	Assembly Format	Description
FE 0A <unsigned int16>	ldarga *argNum*	Fetch the address of argument *argNum*.
0F <unsigned int8>	ldarga.s *argNum*	Fetch the address of argument *argNum*, short form.

Stack Transition:
…, → …, address of argument number argNum

Description:
The `ldarga` instruction fetches the address (of type `&`—i.e., managed pointer) of the *argNum*'th argument, where arguments are numbered 0 onward. The address will always

be aligned to a natural boundary on the target machine (cf. `cpblk` and `initblk` [see Partition III, sections 3.30 and 3.36, respectively]). The short form (`ldarga.s`) should be used for argument numbers 0 through 255.

For procedures that take a variable-length argument list, the `ldarga` instructions can be used only for the initial fixed arguments, not those in the variable part of the signature.

> **RATIONALE**
> `ldarga` is used for by-ref parameter passing (see Partition I [section 12.4.1.5.2]). In other cases, `ldarg` and `starg` should be used.

Exceptions:
None.

Verifiability:
Correct CIL ensures that *argNum* is a valid argument index. See Partition III, section 1.5 for more details on how verification determines the type of the value loaded onto the stack.

3.40 ldc.<type> – Load Numeric Constant

Format	Assembly Format	Description
20 <int32>	ldc.i4 *num*	Push *num* of type `int32` onto the stack as `int32`.
21 <int64>	ldc.i8 *num*	Push *num* of type `int64` onto the stack as `int64`.
22 <float32>	ldc.r4 *num*	Push *num* of type `float32` onto the stack as `F`.
23 <float32>	ldc.r8 *num*	Push *num* of type `float64` onto the stack as `F`.
16	ldc.i4.0	Push 0 onto the stack as `int32`.
17	ldc.i4.1	Push 1 onto the stack as `int32`.
18	ldc.i4.2	Push 2 onto the stack as `int32`.
19	ldc.i4.3	Push 3 onto the stack as `int32`.
1A	ldc.i4.4	Push 4 onto the stack as `int32`.
1B	ldc.i4.5	Push 5 onto the stack as `int32`.

Format	Assembly Format	Description
1C	ldc.i4.6	Push 6 onto the stack as `int32`.
1D	ldc.i4.7	Push 7 onto the stack as `int32`.
1E	ldc.i4.8	Push 8 onto the stack as `int32`.
15	ldc.i4.m1	Push –1 onto the stack as `int32`.
15	ldc.i4.M1	Push –1 of type `int32` onto the stack as `int32` (alias for `ldc.i4.m1`).
1F <int8>	ldc.i4.s num	Push num onto the stack as `int32`, short form.

Stack Transition:

… → …, num

Description:

The `ldc` *num* instruction pushes number *num* onto the stack. There are special short encodings for the integers –128 through 127 (with especially short encodings for –1 through 8). All short encodings push 4-byte integers onto the stack. Longer encodings are used for 8-byte integers and 4- and 8-byte floating point numbers, as well as 4-byte values that do not fit in the short forms.

There are three ways to push an 8-byte integer constant onto the stack:

1. Use the `ldc.i8` instruction for constants that must be expressed in more than 32 bits.
2. Use the `ldc.i4` instruction followed by a `conv.i8` for constants that require 9 to 32 bits.
3. Use a short form instruction followed by a `conv.i8` for constants that can be expressed in 8 or fewer bits.

There is no way to express a floating point constant that has a larger range or greater precision than a 64-bit IEC 60559:1989 number, since these representations are not portable across architectures.

Exceptions:

None.

Verifiability:

The `ldc` instruction is always verifiable.

3.41 ldftn – Load Method Pointer

Format	Assembly Format	Description
FE 06 <T>	ldftn *method*	Push a pointer to a method referenced by *method* onto the stack.

Stack Transition:
… → …, ftn

Description:
The `ldftn` instruction pushes an unmanaged pointer (type `native int`) to the native code implementing the method described by *method* (a metadata token, either a `method-def` or `methodref`; see Partition II) onto the stack. The value pushed can be called using the `calli` instruction if it references a managed method (or a stub that transitions from managed to unmanaged code).

The value returned points to native code using the calling convention specified by *method*. Thus a method pointer can be passed to unmanaged native code (e.g., as a callback routine). Note that the address computed by this instruction may be to a thunk produced specially for this purpose (for example, to re-enter the CIL interpreter when a native version of the method isn't available).

ANNOTATION: There are many options for implementing this instruction. Conceptually, this instruction places on the virtual machine's evaluation stack a representation of the address of the method specified. In terms of native code this may be an address (as specified), a data structure that contains the address, or any value that can be used to compute the address, depending on the architecture of the underlying machine, the native calling conventions, and the implementation technology of the VES (JIT, interpreter, threaded code, etc.).

Exceptions:
None.

Verifiability:
Correct CIL requires that *method* is a valid `methoddef` or `methodref` token. Verification tracks the type of the value pushed in more detail than the `native int` type, remembering that it is a method pointer. Such a method pointer can then be used with `calli` or to construct a delegate.

3.42 ldind.<type> – Load Value Indirect onto the Stack

Format	Assembly Format	Description
46	ldind.i1	Indirect load value of type `int8` as `int32` onto the stack.
48	ldind.i2	Indirect load value of type `int16` as `int32` onto the stack.
4A	ldind.i4	Indirect load value of type `int32` as `int32` onto the stack.
4C	ldind.i8	Indirect load value of type `int64` as `int64` onto the stack.
47	ldind.u1	Indirect load value of type `unsigned int8` as `int32` onto the stack.
49	ldind.u2	Indirect load value of type `unsigned int16` as `int32` onto the stack.
4B	ldind.u4	Indirect load value of type `unsigned int32` as `int32` onto the stack.
4E	ldind.r4	Indirect load value of type `float32` as `F` onto the stack.
4C	ldind.u8	Indirect load value of type `unsigned int64` as `int64` onto the stack (alias for `ldind.i8`).
4F	ldind.r8	Indirect load value of type `float64` as `F` onto the stack.
4D	ldind.i	Indirect load value of type `native int` as `native int` onto the stack.
50	ldind.ref	Indirect load value of type `object ref` as `O` onto the stack.

Stack Transition:

…, addr → …, value

Description:

The `ldind` instruction indirectly loads a value from address *addr* (an unmanaged pointer, `native int`, or managed pointer, `&`) onto the stack. The source value is indicated by the instruction suffix. All of the `ldind` instructions are shortcuts for a `ldobj` instruction that specifies the corresponding built-in value class.

Note that integer values of less than 4 bytes are extended to `int32` (not `native int`) when they are loaded onto the evaluation stack. Floating point values are converted to `F` type when loaded onto the evaluation stack.

Correct CIL ensures that the `ldind` instructions are used in a manner consistent with the type of the pointer.

The address specified by addr must be aligned to a location with the natural alignment of `<type>`, or a `NullReferenceException` may occur (but see the `unaligned.` prefix instruction [Partition III, section 2.2, and the Memory Model section (Partition I, Section 12.6) for a definition of natural alignment]). The results of all CIL instructions that return addresses (e.g., `ldloca` and `ldarga`) are safely aligned. For data types larger than 1 byte, the byte ordering is dependent on the target CPU. Code that depends on byte ordering may not run on all platforms.

The operation of the `ldind` instructions may be altered by an immediately preceding `volatile.` or `unaligned.` prefix instruction.

RATIONALE

Signed and unsigned forms for the small integer types are needed so that the CLI can know whether to sign-extend or zero-extend. The `ldind.u8` and `ldind.u4` variants are provided for convenience; `ldind.u8` is an alias for `ldind.i8`; `ldind.u4` and `ldind.i4` have different opcodes, but their effect is identical.

Exceptions:

`NullReferenceException` may be thrown if an invalid address is detected.

Verifiability:

Correct CIL only uses an `ldind` instruction in a manner consistent with the type of the pointer.

3.43 ldloc – Load Vocal Variable onto the Stack

Format	Assembly Format	Description
FE 0C <unsigned int16>	ldloc *indx*	Load local variable of index *indx* onto stack.
11 <unsigned int8>	ldloc.s *indx*	Load local variable of index *indx* onto stack, short form.
06	ldloc.0	Load local variable 0 onto stack.
07	ldloc.1	Load local variable 1 onto stack.

Format	Assembly Format	Description
08	ldloc.2	Load local variable 2 onto stack.
09	ldloc.3	Load local variable 3 onto stack.

Stack Transition:

… → …, value

Description:

The `ldloc` *indx* instruction pushes the contents of the local variable number *indx* onto the evaluation stack, where local variables are numbered 0 onward. Local variables are initialized to 0 before entering the method only if the initialize flag on the method is true (see Partition I). The `ldloc.0`, `ldloc.1`, `ldloc.2`, and `ldloc.3` instructions provide an efficient encoding for accessing the first four local variables. The `ldloc.s` instruction provides an efficient encoding for accessing local variables 4 through 255.

ANNOTATION: The "zero init flag" syntax in the assembler syntax is the **.local init** directive; and in the file format, it is the flag **CorILMethod_InitLocals** (see Partition II, section 24.4.4).

The type of the value is the same as the type of the local variable, which is specified in the method header. See Partition I [section 12.1.6.1].

Local variables that are smaller than 4 bytes long are expanded to type `int32` when they are loaded onto the stack. Floating point values are expanded to their native size (type `F`).

Exceptions:

`VerificationException` is thrown if the "zero initialize" bit for this method has not been set, and the assembly containing this method has not been granted *SecurityPermission.SkipVerification* (and the CIL does not perform automatic definite-assignment analysis).

Verifiability:

Correct CIL ensures that *indx* is a valid local index. See Partition III, section 1.5 for more details on how verification determines the type of a local variable. For the *ldloca indx* instruction, *indx* must lie in the range 0 to 65534 inclusive (specifically, 65535 is not valid).

> **RATIONALE**
> The reason for excluding 65535 is pragmatic: likely implementations will use a 2-byte integer to track both a local's index, as well as the total number of locals for a given method. If an index of 65535 had been made legal, it would require a wider integer to track the number of locals in such a method.

Also, for verifiable code, this instruction must guarantee that it is not loading an uninitialized value—whether that initialization is done explicitly by having set the "zero initialize" bit for the method, or by previous instructions (where the CLI performs definite-assignment analysis).

3.44 ldloca.<length> – Load Local Variable Address

Format	Assembly Format	Description
FE 0D <**unsigned int16**>	ldloca *index*	Load address of local variable with index *indx*.
12 <**unsigned int8**>	ldloca.s *index*	Load address of local variable with index *indx*, short form.

Stack Transition:

… → …, address

Description:

The `ldloca` instruction pushes the address of the local variable number *index* onto the stack, where local variables are numbered 0 onward. The value pushed onto the stack is already aligned correctly for use with instructions like `ldind` and `stind`. The result is a managed pointer (type `&`). The `ldloca.s` instruction provides an efficient encoding for use with the local variables 0 through 255.

ANNOTATION: Local variables for which `ldloca` is executed must be aligned as described in Partition III, section 3.42, because the address obtained by `ldloca` may be used as an argument to `ldind`.

Exceptions:

`VerificationException` is thrown if the the "zero initialize" bit for this method has not been set, and the assembly containing this method has not been granted *Security-*

Permission.SkipVerification (and the CIL does not perform automatic definite-assignment analysis).

Verifiability:
Correct CIL ensures that *indx* is a valid local index. See Partition III, section 1.5 for more details on how verification determines the type of a local variable. For the *ldloca indx* instruction, *indx* must lie in the range 0 to 65534 inclusive (specifically, 65535 is not valid).

> **RATIONALE**
> The reason for excluding 65535 is pragmatic: likely implementations will use a 2-byte integer to track both a local's index, as well as the total number of locals for a given method. If an index of 65535 had been made legal, it would require a wider integer to track the number of locals in such a method.

Also, for verifiable code, this instruction must guarantee that it is not loading an uninitialized value—whether that initialization is done explicitly by having set the "zero initialize" bit for the method, or by previous instructions (where the CLI performs definite-assignment analysis).

3.45 ldnull – Load a Null Pointer

Format	Assembly Format	Description
14	ldnull	Push null reference onto the stack.

Stack Transition:
… → …, null value

Description:
The `ldnull` pushes a null reference (type `O`) onto the stack. This is used to initialize locations before they become live or when they become dead.

> **RATIONALE**
> It might be thought that `ldnull` is redundant: why not use `ldc.i4.0` or `ldc.i8.0` instead? The answer is that `ldnull` provides a size-agnostic null—analogous to a `ldc.i` instruction, which does not exist. However, even if CIL were to include a `ldc.i` instruction, it would still benefit verification algorithms to retain the `ldnull` instruction because it makes type tracking easier.

Exceptions:
None.

Verifiability:
The `ldnull` instruction is always verifiable, and produces a value that verification considers compatible with any other reference type.

3.46 leave.<length> – Exit a Protected Region of Code

Format	Assembly Format	Description
DD <int32>	leave *target*	Exit a protected region of code.
DE <int8>	leave.s *target*	Exit a protected region of code, short form.

Stack Transition:
…, →

Description:
The `leave` instruction unconditionally transfers control to *target*. *target* is represented as a signed offset (4 bytes for `leave`, 1 byte for `leave.s`) from the beginning of the instruction following the current instruction.

The `leave` instruction is similar to the br instruction, but it can be used to exit a `try`, `filter`, or `catch` block, whereas the ordinary branch instructions can only be used in such a block to transfer control within it. The `leave` instruction empties the evaluation stack and ensures that the appropriate surrounding `finally` blocks are executed.

It is not legal to use a `leave` instruction to exit a `finally` block. To ease code generation for exception handlers, it is legal from within a `catch` block to use a `leave` instruction to transfer control to any instruction within the associated `try` block.

If an instruction has one or more prefix codes, control can only be transferred to the first of these prefixes.

Exceptions:
None.

Verifiability:
Correct CIL requires that the computed destination lie within the current method. See Partition III, section 1.5 for more details.

3.47 localloc – Allocate Space in the Local Dynamic Memory Pool

Format	Assembly Format	Description
FE 0F	localloc	Allocate space from the local memory pool.

Stack Transition:
size → address

Description:
The `localloc` instruction allocates *size* (type `native unsigned int`) bytes from the local dynamic memory pool and returns the address (a managed pointer, type `&`) of the first allocated byte. The block of memory returned is initialized to 0 only if the initialize flag on the method is true (see Partition I). The area of memory is newly allocated. When the current method returns, the local memory pool is available for reuse.

ANNOTATION: The standard appears to be in error on the return type. A managed pointer is always a pointer to a specific type. The probable correct return type is an unmanaged pointer, although this is a point that has not been approved at this time through the ECMA committee. In any case, the `localloc` instruction isn't verifiable, so, from the point of view of the Standard, the precise type doesn't matter too much.

ANNOTATION: The "zero init flag" syntax in the assembler syntax is the **.local init** directive; and in the file format, it is the flag **CorILMethod_InitLocals** (see Partition II, section 24.4.4).

address is aligned so that any built-in data type can be stored there using the `stind` instructions and loaded using the `ldind` instructions.

The `localloc` instruction cannot occur within an exception block: `filter`, `catch`, `finally`, or `fault`.

RATIONALE

`localloc` is used to create local aggregates whose size must be computed at runtime. It can be used for C's intrinsic `alloca` method.

6. CIL Instruction Set

Exceptions:
`StackOverflowException` is thrown if there is insufficient memory to service the request.

Verifiability:
Correct CIL requires that the evaluation stack be empty, apart from the *size* item. This instruction is never verifiable.

3.48 mul – Multiply Values

Format	Assembly Format	Description
5A	mul	Multiply values.

Stack Transition:
…, value1, value2 → …, result

Description:
The `mul` instruction multiplies *value1* by *value2* and pushes the result onto the stack. Integral operations silently truncate the upper bits on overflow (see `mul.ovf` [Partition III, section 3.49]).

For floating point types, 0 × `infinity` = `NaN`.

The acceptable operand types and their corresponding result data types are encapsulated in Table 6-2, Binary Numeric Operations.

Exceptions:
None.

Verifiability:
See Table 6-2, Binary Numeric Operations.

3.49 mul.ovf.<type> – Multiply Integer Values with Overflow Check

Format	Assembly Format	Description
D8	mul.ovf	Multiply signed integer values. Signed result must fit in same size.
D9	mul.ovf.un	Multiply unsigned integer values. Unsigned result must fit in same size.

Stack Transition:

..., value1, value2 → ..., result

Description:

The `mul.ovf` instruction multiplies integers, *value1* and *value2*, and pushes the result onto the stack. An exception is thrown if the result will not fit in the result type.

The acceptable operand types and their corresponding result data types are encapsulated in Table 6-7, Overflow Arithmetic Operations.

Exceptions:

`OverflowException` is thrown if the result cannot be represented in the result type.

Verifiability:

See Table 6-7, Overflow Arithmetic Operations.

3.50 neg – Negate

Format	Assembly Format	Description
65	neg	Negate value.

Stack Transition:

..., value → ..., result

Description:

The `neg` instruction negates *value* and pushes the result on top of the stack. The return type is the same as the operand type.

Negation of integral values is standard twos complement negation. In particular, negating the most negative number (which does not have a positive counterpart) yields the most negative number. To detect this overflow, use the `sub.ovf` instruction instead (i.e., subtract from 0) [see Partition III, section 3.65].

Negating a floating point number cannot overflow; negating `NaN` returns `NaN`.

The acceptable operand types and their corresponding result data types are encapsulated in Table 6-3, Unary Numeric Operations.

Exceptions:

None.

Verifiability:

See Table 6-3, Unary Numeric Operations.

3.51 nop – No Operation

Format	Assembly Format	Description
00	nop	Do nothing.

Stack Transition:
…, → …,

Description:
The nop operation does nothing. It is intended to fill in space if bytecodes are patched.

Exceptions:
None.

Verifiability:
The nop instruction is always verifiable.

3.52 not – Bitwise Complement

Format	Assembly Format	Description
66	not	Bitwise complement

Stack Transition:
…, value → …, result

Description:
Compute the bitwise complement of the integer value on top of the stack and leave the result on top of the stack. The return type is the same as the operand type.

The acceptable operand types and their corresponding result data type are encapsulated in Table 6-5, Integer Operations.

Exceptions:
None.

Verifiability:
See Table 6-5, Integer Operations.

3.53 or – Bitwise OR

Format	Instruction	Description
60	or	Bitwise OR of two integer values, returns an integer.

Stack Transition:
…, value1, value2 → …, result

Description:
The `or` instruction computes the bitwise OR of the top two values on the stack and leaves the result on the stack.

The acceptable operand types and their corresponding result data type are encapsulated in Table 6-5, Integer Operations.

Exceptions:
None.

Verifiability:
See Table 6-5, Integer Operations.

3.54 pop – Remove the Top Element of the Stack

Format	Assembly Format	Description
26	pop	Pop a value from the stack.

Stack Transition:
…, value → …

Description:
The pop instruction removes the top element from the stack.

Exceptions:
None.

Verifiability:
No additional requirements.

3.55 rem – Compute Remainder

Format	Assembly Format	Description
5D	rem	Remainder of dividing *value1* by *value2*.

Stack Transition:

…, value1, value2 → …, result

Description:

The acceptable operand types and their corresponding result data type are encapsulated in Table 6-2, Binary Numeric Operations.

For Integer Operands:

result = *value1* ***rem*** *value2* satisfies the following conditions:

> *result* = *value1* – *value2*×(*value1* ***div*** *value2*), and
>
> *0* _ | *result* | < | *value2* |, and
>
> *sign*(*result*) = *sign*(*value1*),

where `div` is the division instruction, which truncates toward zero.

The `rem` instruction computes *result* and pushes it onto the stack.

For Floating Point Operands:

`rem` is defined similarly, except that if *value2* is zero or *value1* is infinity, the result is NaN. If *value2* is `infinity`, the result is *value1* (negated for `-infinity`). This definition is different from the one for floating point remainders in the IEC 60559:1989 Standard. That standard specifies that *value1* ***div*** *value2* is the nearest integer instead of truncating toward zero. `System.Math.IEEERemainder` (see the *.NET Framework Standard Library Annotated Reference*) provides the IEC 60559:1989 behavior.

ANNOTATION

Implementation-Specific (Microsoft): In the Microsoft CLI, where *value2* is `+infinity` or `-infinity`, the result is simply *value1*. In effect, delete the phrase "(negated for `-infinity`)" immediately above. This amendment will be proposed for incorporation into the standard.

Exceptions:

Integral operations throw `DivideByZeroException` if *value2* is zero.

Integral operations may throw `ArithmeticException` if *value1* is the smallest representable integer value and *value2* is –1.

ANNOTATION

Implementation-Specific (Microsoft): On the x86, an `OverflowException` is thrown when computing (*System.Int32.MaxValue* `rem -1`).

Example:

```
+10 rem +6      is 4        (+10 div +6  = 1)
+10 rem -6      is 4        (+10 div -6  = -1)
-10 rem +6      is -4       (-10 div +6  = -1)
-10 rem -6      is -4       (-10 div -6  = 1)
```

For the various floating point values of 10.0 and 6.0, `rem` gives the same values; `System.Math.IEEERemainder`, however, gives the following values:

```
System.Math.IEEERemainder(+10.0,+6.0) is  -2 (+10.0 div +6.0 =  1.666…7)
System.Math.IEEERemainder(+10.0,-6.0) is  -2 (+10.0 div -6.0 = -1.666…7)
System.Math.IEEERemainder(-10.0,+6.0) is   2 (-10.0 div +6.0 = -1.666…7)
System.Math.IEEERemainder(-10.0,-6.0) is   2 (-10.0 div -6.0 =  1.666…7)
```

Verifiability:

See Table 6-2, Binary Numeric Operations.

3.56 rem.un – Compute Integer Remainder, Unsigned

Format	Assembly Format	Description
5E	rem.un	Remainder of unsigned dividing *value1* by *value2*

Stack Transition:

…, value1, value2 → …, result

Description:

result = *value1* ***rem.un*** *value2* satisfies the following conditions:

result = *value1* – *value2*×(*value1* ***div.un*** *value2*), and

0 _*result* < *value2*,

where `div.un` is the unsigned division instruction. The `rem.un` instruction computes *result* and pushes it onto the stack. `Rem.un` treats its arguments as unsigned integers, while `rem` treats them as signed integers. `rem.un` is unspecified for floating point numbers.

The acceptable operand types and their corresponding result data type are encapsulated in Table 6-5, Integer Operations.

Exceptions:
Integral operations throw `DivideByZeroException` if *value2* is zero.

Example:

```
+5 rem.un +3 is 2                    (+5 div.un +3 = 1)
+5 rem.un -3 is 5                    (+5 div.un -3 = 0)
-5 rem.un +3 is 2                    ( -5 div.un +3 = 1431655763 or 0x55555553)
-5 rem.un -3 is -5 or 0xfffffffb     ( -5 div.un -3 = 0)
```

Verifiability:
See Table 6-5, Integer Operations.

3.57 ret – Return from Method

Format	Assembly Format	Description
2A	ret	Return from method, possibly returning a value.

Stack Transition:
retVal on callee evaluation stack (not always present) →

…, retVal on caller evaluation stack (not always present)

Description:
Return from the current method. The return type, if any, of the current method determines the type of value to be fetched from the top of the stack and copied onto the stack of the method that called the current method. The evaluation stack for the current method must be empty except for the value to be returned.

The `ret` instruction cannot be used to transfer control out of a `try`, `filter`, `catch`, or `finally` block. From within a `try` or `catch` [block], use the `leave` instruction with a destination of a `ret` instruction that is outside all enclosing exception blocks. Because the `filter` and `finally` blocks are logically part of exception handling, not the method in which their code is embedded, correctly generated CIL does not perform a method return from within a `filter` or `finally` [block]. See Partition I [sections 12.4.2.5 through 12.4.2.8].

Exceptions:

None.

Verifiability:

Correct CIL obeys the control constraints described above. Verification requires that the type of *retVal* is compatible with the declared return type of the current method.

3.58 shl – Shift Integer Left

Format	Assembly Format	Description
62	shl	Shift an integer left (shifting in zeros), return an integer.

Stack Transition:

…, value, shiftAmount → …, result

Description:

The `shl` instruction shifts *value* (`int32`, `int64`, or `native int`) left by the number of bits specified by *shiftAmount*. *shiftAmount* is of type `int32`, `int64`, or `native int`. The return value is unspecified if *shiftAmount* is greater than or equal to the width of *value*. See Table 6-6, Shift Operations, for details of which operand types are allowed, and their corresponding result type.

Exceptions:

None.

Verifiability:

See Table 6-6, Shift Operations.

3.59 shr – Shift Integer Right

Format	Assembly Format	Description
63	shr	Shift an integer right (shift in sign), return an integer.

Stack Transition:

…, value, shiftAmount → …, result

Description:

The `shr` instruction shifts *value* (`int32`, `int64`, or `native int`) right by the number of bits specified by *shiftAmount*. *shiftAmount* is of type `int32`, `int64`, or `native int`. The return value is unspecified if *shiftAmount* is greater than or equal to the width of *value*. `shr` replicates the high-order bit on each shift, preserving the sign of the original value in the result. See Table 6-6, Shift Operations, for details of which operand types are allowed, and their corresponding result type.

Exceptions:
None.

Verifiability:
See Table 6-6, Shift Operations.

3.60 shr.un – Shift Integer Right, Unsigned

Format	Assembly Format	Description
64	shr.un	Shift an integer right (shift in zero), return an integer.

Stack Transition:
…, value, shiftAmount → …, result

Description:
The `shr.un` instruction shifts *value* (`int32`, `int 64`, or `native int`) right by the number of bits specified by *shiftAmount*. *shiftAmount* is of type `int32` or `native int`. The return value is unspecified if *shiftAmount* is greater than or equal to the width of *value*. `shr.un` inserts a zero bit on each shift. See Table 6-6, Shift Operations, for details of which operand types are allowed, and their corresponding result type.

Exceptions:
None.

Verifiability:
See Table 6-6, Shift Operations.

3.61 starg.<length> – Store a Value in an Argument Slot

Format	Assembly Format	Description
FE 0B <unsigned int16>	starg *num*	Store a value to the argument numbered *num*.
10 <unsigned int8>	starg.s *num*	Store a value to the argument numbered *num*, short form.

Stack Transition:

…, value → …,

Description:

The `starg` *num* instruction pops a value from the stack and places it in argument slot *num* (see Partition I [sections 12.1.5 and 12.6.2.2]). The type of the value must match the type of the argument, as specified in the current method's signature. The `starg.s` instruction provides an efficient encoding for use with the first 256 arguments.

For procedures that take a variable[-length] argument list, the `starg` instructions can be used only for the initial fixed arguments, not those in the variable part of the signature.

Storing into arguments that hold an integer value smaller than 4 bytes long truncates the value as it moves from the stack to the argument. Floating point values are rounded from their native size (type `F`) to the size associated with the argument.

Exceptions:

None.

Verifiability:

Correct CIL requires that *num* is a valid argument slot.

Verification also checks that the verification type of *value* matches the type of the argument, as specified in the current method's signature (verification types are less detailed than CLI types).

3.62 stind.<type> – Store Value Indirect from Stack

Format	Assembly Format	Description
52	stind.i1	Store value of type `int8` into memory at address.
53	stind.i2	Store value of type `int16` into memory at address.
54	stind.i4	Store value of type `int32` into memory at address.
55	stind.i8	Store value of type `int64` into memory at address.
56	stind.r4	Store value of type `float32` into memory at address.
57	stind.r8	Store value of type `float64` into memory at address.
DF	stind.i	Store value of type `native int` into memory at address.
51	stind.ref	Store value of type `object ref` (type `O`) into memory at address.

Stack Transition:

…, addr, val → …

Description:

The `stind` instruction stores a value *val* at address *addr* (an unmanaged pointer, type `native int`, or managed pointer, type `&`). The address specified by *addr* must be aligned to the natural size of *val* or a `NullReferenceException` may occur (but see the `unaligned`. prefix instruction [Partition III, section 2.2]). The results of all CIL instructions that return addresses (e.g., `ldloca` and `ldarga`) are safely aligned. For data types larger than 1 byte, the byte ordering is dependent on the target CPU. Code that depends on byte ordering may not run on all platforms.

Typesafe operation requires that the `stind` instruction be used in a manner consistent with the type of the pointer.

The operation of the `stind` instruction may be altered by an immediately preceding `volatile.` or `unaligned.` prefix instruction.

Exceptions:

`NullReferenceException` is thrown if *addr* is not naturally aligned for the argument type implied by the instruction suffix.

Verifiability:

Correct CIL ensures that *addr* be a pointer whose type is known and is assignment compatible with that of *val*.

3.63 stloc – Pop Value from Stack to Local Variable

Format	Assembly Format	Description
FE 0E <**unsigned int16**>	stloc *indx*	Pop value from stack into local variable *indx*.
13 <**unsigned int8**>	stloc.s *indx*	Pop value from stack into local variable *indx*, short form.
0A	stloc.0	Pop value from stack into local variable 0.
0B	stloc.1	Pop value from stack into local variable 1.
0C	stloc.2	Pop value from stack into local variable 2.
0D	stloc.3	Pop value from stack into local variable 3.

Stack Transition:

..., value → ...

Description:

The `stloc` *indx* instruction pops the top value off the evalution stack and moves it into local variable number *indx* (see Partition I [sections 12.1.5 and 12.6.2.2]), where local variables are numbered 0 onward. The type of *value* must match the type of the local variable as specified in the current method's locals signature. The `stloc.0`, `stloc.1`, `stloc.2`, and `stloc.3` instructions provide an efficient encoding for the first four local variables; the `stloc.s` instruction provides an efficient encoding for local variables 4 through 255.

Storing into locals that hold an integer value smaller than 4 bytes long truncates the value as it moves from the stack to the local variable. Floating point values are rounded from their native size (type `F`) to the size associated with the argument.

Exceptions:

None.

Verifiability:

Correct CIL requires that *indx* is a valid local index. For the `stloc` *indx* instruction, *indx* must lie in the range 0 to 65534 inclusive (specifically, 65535 is not valid).

> **RATIONALE**
>
> The reason for excluding 65535 is pragmatic: likely implementations will use a 2-byte integer to track both a local's index, as well as the total number of locals for a given method. If an index of 65535 had been made legal, it would require a wider integer to track the number of locals in such a method.

Verification also checks that the verification type of *value* matches the type of the local, as specified in the current method's locals signature.

3.64 sub – Subtract Numeric Values

Format	Assembly Format	Description
59	sub	Subtract *value2* from *value1*, returning a new value.

Stack Transition:

..., value1, value2 → ..., result

Description:
The `sub` instruction subtracts *value2* from *value1* and pushes the result onto the stack. Overflow is not detected for the integral operations (see `sub.ovf` [Partition III, section 3.65]); for floating point operands, `sub` returns `+inf` on positive overflow, `-inf` on negative overflow, and zero on floating point underflow.

The acceptable operand types and their corresponding result data type are encapsulated in Table 6-2, Binary Numeric Operations.

Exceptions:
None.

Verifiability:
See Table 6-2, Binary Numeric Operations.

3.65 sub.ovf.<type> – Subtract Integer Values, Checking for Overflow

Format	Assembly Format	Description
DA	sub.ovf	Subtract `native int` from a `native int`. Signed result must fit in same size.
DB	sub.ovf.un	Subtract native `unsigned int` from a `native unsigned int`. Unsigned result must fit in same size.

Stack Transition:
…, value1, value2 → …, result

Description:
The `sub.ovf` instruction subtracts *value2* from *value1* and pushes the result onto the stack. The type of the values and the return type are specified by the instruction. An exception is thrown if the result does not fit in the result type.

The acceptable operand types and their corresponding result data type are encapsulated in Table 6-7, Overflow Arithmetic Operations.

Exceptions:
`OverflowException` is thrown if the result cannot be represented in the result type.

Verifiability:
See Table 6-7, Overflow Arithmetic Operations.

3.66 switch – Table Switch on Value

Format	Assembly Format	Description
45 <unsigned int32> <int32>... <int32>	switch (*t1*, *t2* ... *tn*)	Jump to one of *n* values.

Stack Transition:

..., value → ...,

Description:

The `switch` instruction implements a jump table. The format of the instruction is an `unsigned int32` representing the number of targets *n*, followed by *n* `int32` values specifying jump targets; these targets are represented as offsets (positive or negative) from the beginning of the instruction following this switch instruction.

The switch instruction pops *value* off the stack and compares it, as an unsigned integer, to *n*. If *value* is less than *n*, execution is transferred to the *value*'th target, where targets are numbered from 0 (i.e., a *value* of 0 takes the first target, a *value* of 1 takes the second target, etc.). If *value* is not less than *n*, execution continues at the next instruction (fall through).

If the target instruction has one or more prefix codes, control can only be transferred to the first of these prefixes.

Control transfers into and out of `try`, `catch`, `filter`, and `finally` blocks cannot be performed by this instruction. (Such transfers are severely restricted and must use the `leave` instruction instead; see Partition I [sections 12.4.2.5 through 12.4.2.8] for details.)

Exceptions:

None.

Verifiability:

Correct CIL obeys the control transfer constraints listed above. In addition, verification requires the type-consistency of the stack, locals, and arguments for every possible way of reaching all destination instructions. See Partition III, section 1.5 for more details.

3.67 xor – Bitwise XOR

Format	Assembly Format	Description
61	xor	Bitwise XOR of integer values; returns an integer.

Stack Transition:

..., value1, value2 → ..., result

Description:
The `xor` instruction computes the bitwise XOR of *value1* and *value2* and leaves the result on the stack.

The acceptable operand types and their corresponding result data type are encapsulated in Table 6-5, Integer Operations.

Exceptions:
None.

Verifiability:
See Table 6-5, Integer Operations.

4 Object Model Instructions

The instructions described in the base instruction set are independent of the object model being executed. Those instructions correspond closely to what would be found on a real CPU. The object model instructions are less built-in than the base instructions in the sense that they could be built out of the base instructions and calls to the underlying operating system.

RATIONALE

The object model instructions provide a common, efficient implementation of a set of services used by many (but by no means all) higher-level languages. They embed in their operation a set of conventions defined by the Common Type System. This includes (among other things):

Field layout within an object

Layout for late-bound method calls (vtables)

Memory allocation and reclamation

Exception handling

Boxing and unboxing to convert between reference-based Objects and Value Types

For more details, see Partition I [section 8 and its subsections].

4.1 box – Convert Value Type to Object Reference

Format	Assembly Format	Description
8C <T>	box *valTypeTok*	Convert *valueType* to a true object reference.

Stack Transition:
…, valueType → …, obj

Description:
A value type has two separate representations (see Partition I [section 8.2 and its subsections]) within the CLI:

- A "raw" form used when a value type is embedded within another object or on the stack
- A "boxed" form, where the data in the value type is wrapped (boxed) into an object so it can exist as an independent entity

The `box` instruction converts the "raw" *valueType* (an unboxed value type) into an instance of type Object (of type `O`). This is accomplished by creating a new object and copying the data from *valueType* into the newly allocated object. *valTypeTok* is a metadata token (a `typeref` or `typedef`) indicating the type of *valueType* (see Partition II).

Exceptions:
`OutOfMemoryException` is thrown if there is insufficient memory to satisfy the request.

`TypeLoadException` is thrown if *class* cannot be found. This is typically detected when CIL is converted to native code rather than at runtime.

Verifiability:
Correct CIL ensures that *valueType* is of the correct value type, and that *valTypeTok* is a `typeref` or `typedef` metadata token for that value type.

4.2 callvirt – Call a Method Associated, at Runtime, with an Object

Format	Assembly Format	Description
6F <T>	callvirt *method*	Call a method associated with *obj*.

Stack Transition:
…, obj, arg1, … argN → …, returnVal (not always returned)

Description:

The `callvirt` instruction calls a late-bound method on an object. That is, the method is chosen based on the runtime type of *obj* rather than the compile-time class visible in the *method* metadata token. `callvirt` can be used to call both virtual and instance methods. See Partition I [section 12.4 and its subsections] for a detailed description of the CIL calling sequence. The `callvirt` instruction may be immediately preceded by a `tail.` prefix to specify that the current stack frame should be released before transferring control. If the call would transfer control to a method of higher trust than the original method, the stack frame would not be released.

(A callee of "higher trust" is defined as one whose permission grant-set is a strict superset of the grant-set of the caller.)

method is a metadata token (a `methoddef` or `methodref`; see Partition II) that provides the name, class, and signature of the method to call. In more detail, `callvirt` can be thought of as follows. Associated with *obj* is the class of which it is an instance. If *obj*'s class defines a non-static method that matches the indicated method name and signature, this method is called. Otherwise all classes in the superclass chain of *obj*'s class are checked in order. It is an error if no method is found.

`callvirt` pops the object and the arguments off the evaluation stack before calling the method. If the method has a return value, it is pushed onto the stack upon method completion. On the callee side, the *obj* parameter is accessed as argument 0, *arg1* as argument 1, etc.

The arguments are placed on the stack in left-to-right order. That is, the first argument is computed and placed on the stack, then the second argument, etc. The `this` pointer (always required for `callvirt`) must be pushed before any of the user-visible arguments. The signature carried in the metadata does not contain an entry in the parameter list for the `this` pointer, but uses a bit (called `HASTHIS`) to indicate whether the method requires passing the `this` pointer (see Partition II [sections 22.2.1 and 22.2.2]).

Note that a virtual method may also be called using the `call` instruction.

Exceptions:

`MissingMethodException` is thrown if a non-static method with the indicated name and signature could not be found in *obj*'s class or any of its superclasses. This is typically detected when CIL is converted to native code, rather than at runtime.

`NullReferenceException` is thrown if *obj* is null.

`SecurityException` is thrown if system security does not grant the caller access to the called method. The security check may occur when the CIL is converted to native code rather than at runtime.

Verifiability:
Correct CIL ensures that the destination method exists and the values on the stack correspond to the types of the parameters of the method being called.

In its typical use, `callvirt` is verifiable if (a) the above restrictions are met, (b) the verification type of *obj* is consistent with the method being called, (c) the verification types of the arguments on the stack are consistent with the types expected by the method call, and (d) the method is accessible from the call site. A `callvirt` annotated by `tail.` has additional considerations—see Partition III, section 2.1.

4.3 castclass – Cast an Object to a Class

Format	Assembly Format	Description
74 <T>	castclass *class*	Cast *obj* to *class*.

Stack Transition:
…, obj → …, obj2

Description:
The `castclass` instruction attempts to cast *obj* (an `O`) to the *class*. *class* is a metadata token (a `typeref` or `typedef`) indicating the desired class. If the class of the object on the top of the stack does not implement *class* (if *class* is an interface), and is not a subclass of *class* (if *class* is a regular class), then an `InvalidCastException` is thrown.

Note that:

1. Arrays inherit from `System.Array`.
2. If Foo can be cast to Bar, then Foo[] can be cast to Bar[].
3. For the purposes of 2, enums are treated as their underlying type: thus E1[] can cast to E2[] if E1 and E2 share an underlying type.

If *obj* is null, `castclass` succeeds and returns null. This behavior differs from `isInst`.

Exceptions:
`InvalidCastException` is thrown if *obj* cannot be cast to *class*.

`TypeLoadException` is thrown if *class* cannot be found. This is typically detected when CIL is converted to native code rather than at runtime.

Verifiability:
Correct CIL ensures that *class* is a valid `typeref` or `typedef` token, and that *obj* is always either null or an object reference.

4.4 cpobj – Copy a Value Type

Format	Assembly Format	Description
70 <T>	Cpobj *classTok*	Copy a value type from *srcValObv* to *destValObj*.

Stack Transition:
…, destValObj, srcValObj → …,

Description:
The `cpobj` instruction copies the value type located at the address specified by *srcValObj* (an unmanaged pointer, `native int`, or a managed pointer, &) to the address specified by *destValObj* (also a pointer). Behavior is unspecified if *srcValObj* and *dstValObj* are not pointers to instances of the class represented by *classTok* (a `typeref` or `typedef`), or if *classTok* does not represent a value type.

Exceptions:
`NullReferenceException` may be thrown if an invalid address is detected.

Verifiability:
Correct CIL ensures that *classTok* is a valid `typeref` or `typedef` token for a value type, as well as that *srcValObj* and *destValObj* are both pointers to locations of that type.

Verification requires, in addition, that *srcValObj* and *destValObj* are both managed pointers (not unmanaged pointers).

4.5 initobj – Initialize a Value Type

Format	Assembly Format	Description
FE 15 <T>	initobj *classTok*	Initialize a value type.

Stack Transition:
…, addrOfValObj → …,

Description:
The `initobj` instruction initializes all the fields of the object represented by the address *addrOfValObj* (of type `native int`, or &) to `null` or a 0 of the appropriate built-in type. After this method is called, the instance is ready for the constructor method to be called. Behavior is unspecified if either *addrOfValObj* is not a pointer to an instance of the class represented by *classTok* (a `typeref` or `typedef`; see Partition II), or *classTok* does not represent a value type.

Notice that, unlike `newobj`, the constructor method is not called by `initobj`. `initobj` is intended for initializing value types, while `newobj` is used to allocate and initialize objects.

Exceptions:
None.

Verifiability:
Correct CIL ensures that *classTok* is a valid `typeref` or `typedef` token specifying a value type, and that *valObj* is a managed pointer to an instance of that value type.

4.6 isinst – Test If an Object Is an Instance of a Class or Interface

Format	Assembly Format	Description
75 <T>	isinst *class*	Test if *obj* is an instance of *class*, returning null or an instance of that class or interface.

Stack Transition:
…, obj → …, result

Description:
The `isinst` instruction tests whether *obj* (type `O`) is an instance of *class*. *class* is a metadata token (a `typeref` or `typedef`; see Partition II) indicating the desired class. If the class of the object on the top of the stack implements *class* (if *class* is an interface) or is a subclass of *class* (if *class* is a regular class), then it is cast to the type *class* and the result is pushed onto the stack, exactly as though `castclass` had been called. Otherwise null is pushed onto the stack. If *obj* is null, `isinst` returns null.

Note that:

1. Arrays inherit from `System.Array`.
2. If Foo can be cast to Bar, then Foo[] can be cast to Bar[].
3. For the purposes of 2, enums are treated as their underlying type: thus E1[] can cast to E2[] if E1 and E2 share an underlying type.

Exceptions:
`TypeLoadException` is thrown if *class* cannot be found. This is typically detected when CIL is converted to native code rather than at runtime.

Verifiability:
Correct CIL ensures that *class* is a valid `typeref` or `typedef` token indicating a class, and that *obj* is always either null or an object reference.

4.7 ldelem.<type> – Load an Element of an Array

Format	Assembly Format	Description
90	ldelem.i1	Load the element with type `int8` at *index* onto the top of the stack as an `int32`.
92	ldelem.i2	Load the element with type `int16` at *index* onto the top of the stack as an `int32`.
94	ldelem.i4	Load the element with type `int32` at *index* onto the top of the stack as an `int32`.
96	ldelem.i8	Load the element with type `int64` at *index* onto the top of the stack as an `int64`.
91	ldelem.u1	Load the element with type `unsigned int8` at *index* onto the top of the stack as an `int32`.
93	ldelem.u2	Load the element with type `unsigned int16` at *index* onto the top of the stack as an `int32`.
95	ldelem.u4	Load the element with type `unsigned int32` at *index* onto the top of the stack as an `int32`.
96	ldelem.u8	Load the element with type `unsigned int64` at *index* onto the top of the stack as an `int64` (alias for `ldelem.i8`).
98	ldelem.r4	Load the element with type `float32` at *index* onto the top of the stack as an `F`.
99	ldelem.r8	Load the element with type `float64` at *index* onto the top of the stack as an `F`.
97	ldelem.i	Load the element with type `native int` at *index* onto the top of the stack as a `native int`.
9A	ldelem.ref	Load the element of type object, at *index* onto the top of the stack as an `O`.

Stack Transition:

…, array, index → …, value

Description:

The `ldelem` instruction loads the value of the element with index *index* (of type `int32` or `native int`) in the zero-based, one-dimensional array *array* and places it on the top of the stack. Arrays are objects and hence represented by a value of type `O`. The return value is indicated by the instruction.

For one-dimensional arrays that aren't zero-based, and for multi-dimensional arrays, the array class provides a `Get` method.

Note that integer values of less than 4 bytes are extended to `int32` (not `native int`) when they are loaded onto the evaluation stack. Floating point values are converted to `F` type when loaded onto the evaluation stack.

Exceptions:
`NullReferenceException` is thrown if *array* is null.

`IndexOutOfRangeException` is thrown if *index* is negative, or larger than the bound of *array*.

`ArrayTypeMismatchException` is thrown if *array* doesn't hold elements of the required type.

Verifiability:
Correct CIL code requires that *array* is either null or a zero-based, one-dimensional array whose declared element type matches exactly the type for this particular instruction suffix (e.g., `ldelem.r4` can only be applied to a zero-based, one-dimensional array of `float32`s).

4.8 ldelema – Load Address of an Element of an Array

Format	Assembly Format	Description
8F <T>	ldelema *class*	Load the address of element at *index* onto the top of the stack.

Stack Transition:
…, array, index → …, address

Description:
The `ldelema` instruction loads the address of the element with index *index* (of type `int32` or `native int`) in the zero-based, one-dimensional array *array* (of element type *class*) and places it on the top of the stack. Arrays are objects and hence represented by a value of type `O`. The return address is a managed pointer (type `&`).

For one-dimensional arrays that aren't zero-based, and for multi-dimensional arrays, the array class provides a `Address` method.

Exceptions:

`NullReferenceException` is thrown if *array* is null.

`IndexOutOfRangeException` is thrown if *index* is negative, or larger than the bound of *array*.

`ArrayTypeMismatchException` is thrown if *array* doesn't hold elements of the required type.

Verifiability:

Correct CIL ensures that *class* is a `typeref` or `typedef` token to a class, and that *array* is indeed always either null or a zero-based, one-dimensional array whose declared element type matches *class* exactly.

4.9 ldfld – Load Field of an Object

Format	Assembly Format	Description
7B <T>	ldfld *field*	Push the value of *field* of object, or value type, *obj*, onto the stack.

Stack Transition:

…, obj → …, value

Description:

The `ldfld` instruction pushes onto the stack the value of a field of *obj*. *obj* must be an object (type `O`), a managed pointer (type `&`), an unmanaged pointer (type `native int`), or an instance of a value type. The use of an unmanaged pointer is not permitted in verifiable code. *field* is a metadata token (a `fieldref` or `fielddef`; see Partition II) that must refer to a field member. The return type is that associated with *field*. `ldfld` pops the object reference off the stack and pushes the value for the field in its place. The field may be either an instance field (in which case *obj* must not be null) or a static field.

The `ldfld` instruction may be preceded by either or both of the `unaligned.` and `volatile.` prefixes.

Exceptions:

`NullReferenceException` is thrown if *obj* is null and the field is not static.

`MissingFieldException` is thrown if *field* is not found in the metadata. This is typically checked when CIL is converted to native code, not at runtime.

Verifiability:
Correct CIL ensures that *field* is a valid token referring to a field, and that *obj* will always have a type compatible with that required for the lookup being performed. For verifiable code, *obj* may not be an unmanaged pointer.

4.10 ldflda – Load Field Address

Format	Assembly Format	Description
7C <T>	ldflda *field*	Push the address of *field* of object *obj* onto the stack.

Stack Transition:
…, obj → …, address

Description:
The `ldflda` instruction pushes the address of a field of *obj*. *obj* is either an object, type `O`; a managed pointer, type `&`; or an unmanaged pointer, type `native int`. The use of an unmanaged pointer is not allowed in verifiable code. The value returned by `ldflda` is a managed pointer (type `&`) unless *obj* is an unmanaged pointer, in which case it is an unmanaged pointer (type `native int`).

field is a metadata token (a `fieldref` or `fielddef`; see Partition II) that must refer to a field member. The field may be either an instance field (in which case *obj* must not be null) or a static field.

Exceptions:
`InvalidOperationException` is thrown if the *obj* is not within the application domain from which it is being accessed. The address of a field that is not inside the accessing application domain cannot be loaded.

`MissingFieldException` is thrown if *field* is not found in the metadata. This is typically checked when CIL is converted to native code, not at runtime.

`NullReferenceException` is thrown if *obj* is null and the field isn't static.

Verifiability:
Correct CIL ensures that *field* is a valid `fieldref` token and that *obj* will always have a type compatible with that required for the lookup being performed.

NOTE

Using `ldflda` to compute the address of a static, init-only field and then using the resulting pointer to modify that value outside the body of the class initializer may lead to unpredictable behavior. It cannot, however, compromise memory integrity or type safety, so it is not tested by verification.

4.11 ldlen – Load the Length of an Array

Format	Assembly Format	Description
8E	ldlen	Push the length (of type `native unsigned int`) of *array* onto the stack.

Stack Transition:

…, array → …, length

Description:

The `ldlen` instruction pushes the number of elements of *array* (a zero-based, one-dimensional array) onto the stack.

Arrays are objects and hence represented by a value of type `O`. The return value is a `native unsigned int`.

Exceptions:

`NullReferenceException` is thrown if *array* is null.

Verifiability:

Correct CIL ensures that *array* is indeed always either null or a zero-based, one-dimensional array.

4.12 ldobj – Copy Value Type to the Stack

Format	Assembly Format	Description
71 <T>	ldobj *classTok*	Copy instance of value type *classTok* to the stack.

Stack Transition:

…, addrOfValObj → …, valObj

6. CIL Instruction Set

Description:
The `ldobj` instruction copies the value pointed to by *addrOfValObj* (of type managed pointer, `&`, or unmanaged pointer, `native unsigned int`) to the top of the stack. The number of bytes copied depends on the size of the class represented by *classTok*. *classTok* is a metadata token (a `typeref` or `typedef`; see Partition II) representing a value type.

> **RATIONALE**
> The `ldobj` instruction is used to pass a value type as a parameter. See Partition I [section 12.1.6.2.2].

It is unspecified what happens if *addrOfValObj* is not an instance of the class represented by *classTok* or if *classTok* does not represent a value type.

The operation of the `ldobj` instruction may be altered by an immediately preceding `volatile.` or `unaligned.` prefix instruction.

Exceptions:
`TypeLoadException` is thrown if *class* cannot be found. This is typically detected when CIL is converted to native code rather than at runtime.

Verifiability:
Correct CIL ensures that *classTok* is a metadata token representing a value type and that *addrOfValObj* is a pointer to a location containing a value of the type specified by *classTok*. Verifiable code additionally requires that *addrOfValObj* is a managed pointer of a matching type.

4.13 ldsfld – Load Static Field of a Class

Format	Assembly Format	Description
7E <T>	ldsfld *field*	Push the value of *field* onto the stack.

Stack Transition:
…, → …, value

Description:
The `ldsfld` instruction pushes the value of a static (shared among all instances of a class) field onto the stack. *field* is a metadata token (a `fieldref` or `fielddef`; see Partition II) referring to a static field member. The return type is that associated with *field*.

The `ldsfld` instruction may have a `volatile.` prefix.

Exceptions:
None.

Verifiability:
Correct CIL ensures that *field* is a valid metadata token referring to a static field member.

4.14 ldsflda – Load Static Field Address

Format	Assembly Format	Description
7F <T>	ldsflda *field*	Push the address of the static field, *field*, onto the stack.

Stack Transition:
…, → …, address

Description:
The `ldsflda` instruction pushes the address (a managed pointer, type `&`, if *field* refers to a type whose memory is managed; otherwise an unmanaged pointer, type `native int`) of a static field onto the stack. *field* is a metadata token (a `fieldref` or `fielddef`; see Partition II) referring to a static field member. (Note that *field* may be a static global with assigned RVA, in which case its memory is *un*managed—where RVA stands for Relative Virtual Address, the offset of the field from the base address at which its containing PE file is loaded into memory.)

Exceptions:
`MissingFieldException` is thrown if *field* is not found in the metadata. This is typically checked when CIL is converted to native code, not at runtime.

Verifiability:
Correct CIL ensures that *field* is a valid metadata token referring to a static field member if *field* refers to a type whose memory is managed.

> **NOTE**
> Using `ldsflda` to compute the address of a static, init-only field and then using the resulting pointer to modify that value outside the body of the class initializer may lead to unpredictable behavior. It cannot, however, compromise memory integrity or type safety, so it is not tested by verification.

4.15 ldstr – Load a Literal String

Format	Assembly Format	Description
72 <T>	ldstr *string*	Push a string object for the literal *string*.

Stack Transition:
…, → …, string

Description:
The `ldstr` instruction pushes a new string object representing the literal stored in the metadata as *string* (that must be a string literal).

The `ldstr` instruction allocates memory and performs any format conversion required to convert from the form used in the file to the string format required at runtime. The CLI guarantees that the result of two `ldstr` instructions referring to two metadata tokens that have the same sequence of characters return precisely the same string object (a process known as "string interning").

Exceptions:
None.

Verifiability:
Correct CIL requires that *string* is a valid string literal metadata token.

4.16 ldtoken – Load the Runtime Representation of a Metadata Token

Format	Assembly Format	Description
D0 <T>	ldtoken *token*	Convert metadata *token* to its runtime representation.

Stack Transition:
… → …, RuntimeHandle

Description:
The `ldtoken` instruction pushes a *RuntimeHandle* for the specified metadata token. The token must be one of:

A `methoddef` or `methodref`: pushes a `RuntimeMethodHandle`

A `typedef` or `typeref`: pushes a `RuntimeTypeHandle`

A `fielddef` or `fieldref`: pushes a `RuntimeFieldHandle`

The value pushed onto the stack can be used in calls to Reflection methods in the system class library.

Exceptions:
None.

Verifiability:
Correct CIL requires that *token* describes a valid metadata token.

4.17 ldvirtftn – Load a Virtual Method Pointer

Format	Assembly Format	Description
FE 07 <T>	ldvirtftn *mthd*	Push address of virtual method *mthd* onto the stack.

Stack Transition:
… object → …, ftn

Description:
The `ldvirtftn` instruction pushes an unmanaged pointer (type `native int`) to the native code implementing the virtual method associated with *object* and described by the method reference *mthd* (a metadata token, either a `methoddef` or `methodref`; see Partition II) onto the stack. The value pushed can be called using the `calli` instruction if it references a managed method (or a stub that transitions from managed to unmanaged code).

The value returned points to native code using the calling convention specified by *mthd*. Thus a method pointer can be passed to unmanaged native code (e.g., as a callback routine) if that routine expects the corresponding calling convention. Note that the address computed by this instruction may be to a thunk produced specially for this purpose (for example, to re-enter the CLI when a native version of the method isn't available).

Exceptions:
None.

Verifiability:
Correct CIL ensures that *mthd* is a valid `methoddef` or `methodref` token, and also that *mthd* references a non-static method that is defined for *object*. Verification tracks the type of the value pushed in more detail than the `native int` type, remembering that it is a method pointer. Such a method pointer can then be used in verified code with `calli` or to construct a delegate.

ANNOTATION:

Implementation-Specific (Microsoft): In the first release of Microsoft's implementation of the CLI, the `calli` instruction is never verifiable.

4.18 mkrefany – Push a Typed Reference onto the Stack

Format	Assembly Format	Description
C6 <T>	mkrefany *class*	Push a typed reference to *ptr* of type *class* onto the stack.

Stack Transition:

…, ptr → …, typedRef

Description:

The `mkrefany` instruction supports the passing of dynamically typed references. *ptr* must be a pointer (type `&`, or `native int`) that holds the address of a piece of data. *class* is the class token (a `typeref` or `typedef`; see Partition II) describing the type of *ptr*. `mkrefany` pushes a typed reference onto the stack that is an opaque descriptor of *ptr* and *class*. The only legal operation on a typed reference on the stack is to pass it to a method that requires a typed reference as a parameter. The callee can then use the `refanytype` and `refanyval` instructions to retrieve the type (*class*) and address (*ptr*), respectively.

Exceptions:

`TypeLoadException` is thrown if *class* cannot be found. This is typically detected when CIL is converted to native code rather than at runtime.

Verifiability:

Correct CIL ensures that *class* is a valid `typeref` or `typedef` token describing some type, and that *ptr* is a pointer to exactly that type. Verification additionally requires that *ptr* be a managed pointer. Verification will fail if it cannot deduce that *ptr* is a pointer to an instance of *class*.

4.19 newarr – Create a Zero-Based, One-Dimensional Array

Format	Assembly Format	Description
8D <T>	newarr *etype*	Create a new array with elements of type *etype*.

Stack Transition:
…, numElems → …, array

Description:
The `newarr` instruction pushes a reference to a new zero-based, one-dimensional array whose elements are of type *elemtype*, a metadata token (a `typeref` or `typedef`; see Partition II). *numElems* (of type `native int`) specifies the number of elements in the array. Valid array indexes are 0 ≤ index < *numElems*. The elements of an array can be any type, including value types.

Zero-based, one-dimensional arrays of numbers are created using a metadata token referencing the appropriate value type (`System.Int32`, etc.). Elements of the array are initialized to 0 of the appropriate type.

One-dimensional arrays that aren't zero-based, and multi-dimensional arrays, are created using `newobj` rather than `newarr`. More commonly, they are created using the methods of `System.Array` class in the Base Framework.

Exceptions:
`OutOfMemoryException` is thrown if there is insufficient memory to satisfy the request.

`OverflowException` is thrown if *numElems* is < 0.

Verifiability:
Correct CIL ensures that *etype* is a valid `typeref` or `typedef` token.

4.20 newobj – Create a New Object

Format	Assembly Format	Description
73 <T>	newobj *ctor*	Allocate an uninitialized object or value type and call *ctor*.

Stack Transition:
…, arg1, … argN → …, obj

Description:
The `newobj` instruction creates a new object or a new instance of a value type. *ctor* is a metadata token (a `methodref` or `methodef` that must be marked as a constructor; see Partition II) that indicates the name, class, and signature of the constructor to call. If a constructor exactly matching the indicated name, class, and signature cannot be found, `MissingMethodException` is thrown.

The `newobj` instruction allocates a new instance of the class associated with *constructor* and initializes all the fields in the new instance to 0 (of the proper type) or *null* as appropriate. It then calls the constructor with the given arguments along with the newly created instance. After the constructor has been called, the now initialized object reference is pushed onto the stack.

From the constructor's point of view, the uninitialized object is argument 0 and the other arguments passed to `newobj` follow in order.

All zero-based, one-dimensional arrays are created using `newarr`, not `newobj`. On the other hand, all other arrays (more than one dimension, or one-dimensional but not zero-based) are created using `newobj`.

Value types are not usually created using `newobj`. They are usually allocated either as arguments or local variables, using `newarr` (for zero-based, one-dimensional arrays), or as fields of objects. Once allocated, they are initialized using `initobj`. However, the `newobj` instruction can be used to create a new instance of a value type on the stack, that can then be passed as an argument, stored in a local, etc.

Exceptions:
`OutOfMemoryException` is thrown if there is insufficient memory to satisfy the request.

`MissingMethodException` is thrown if a constructor method with the indicated name, class, and signature could not be found. This is typically detected when CIL is converted to native code, rather than at runtime.

Verifiability:
Correct CIL ensures that `constructor` is a valid `methodref` or `methoddef` token, and that the arguments on the stack are compatible with those expected by the constructor. Verification considers a delegate constructor as a special case, checking that the method pointer passed in as the second argument, of type `native int`, does indeed refer to a method of the correct type.

4.21 **refanytype – Load the Type Out of a Typed Reference**

Format	Assembly Format	Description
FE 1D	refanytype	Push the type token stored in a typed reference.

Stack Transition:
…, TypedRef → …, type

Description:
Retrieves the type token embedded in *TypedRef*. See the `mkrefany` instruction [Partition III, section 4.18].

Exceptions:
None.

Verifiability:
Correct CIL ensures that *TypedRef* is a valid typed reference (created by a previous call to `mkrefany`). The `refanytype` instruction is always verifiable.

4.22 refanyval – Load the Address Out of a Typed Reference

Format	Assembly Format	Description
C2 <T>	refanyval *type*	Push the address stored in a typed reference.

Stack Transition:
…, TypedRef → …, address

Description:
Retrieves the address (of type `&`) embedded in *TypedRef*. The type of reference in *TypedRef* must match the type specified by `type` (a metadata token, either a `typedef` or a `typeref`; see Partition II). See the `mkrefany` instruction [Partition III, section 4.18].

Exceptions:
`InvalidCastException` is thrown if *type* is not identical to the type stored in the *TypedRef* (i.e., the *class* supplied to the `mkrefany` instruction that constructed that *TypedRef*).

`TypeLoadException` is thrown if *type* cannot be found.

Verifiability:
Correct CIL ensures that *TypedRef* is a valid typed reference (created by a previous call to `mkrefany`). The `refanyval` instruction is always verifiable.

4.23 rethrow – Rethrow the Current Exception

Format	Assembly Format	Description
FE 1A	rethrow	Rethrow the current exception.

Stack Transition:
…, → …,

Description:

The `rethrow` instruction is only permitted within the body of a `catch` handler (see Partition I [sections 12.4.2.5 through 12.4.2.8]). It throws the same exception that was caught by this handler.

ANNOTATION: A `rethrow` does not change the stack trace in the object. `rethrow` means that you caught an exception and then decided to resume processing it. This would not, then, change the captured trace information.

Exceptions:

The original exception is thrown.

Verifiability:

Correct CIL uses this instruction only within the body of a `catch` handler (not of any exception handlers embedded within that `catch` handler). If a rethrow occurs elsewhere, then an exception will be thrown, but precisely which exception is undefined.

4.24 sizeof – Load the Size in Bytes of a Value Type

Format	Assembly Format	Description
FE 1C <T>	sizeof *valueType*	Push the size, in bytes, of a value type as a `unsigned int32`.

Stack Transition:

…, → …, size (4 bytes, unsigned)

Description:

Returns the size, in bytes, of a value type. *valueType* must be a metadata token (a `typeref` or `typedef`; see Partition II) that specifies a value type.

RATIONALE

The definition of a value type can change between the time the CIL is generated and the time that it is loaded for execution. Thus, the size of the type is not always known when the CIL is generated. The `sizeof` instruction allows CIL code to determine the size at runtime without the need to call into the Framework class library. The computation can occur entirely at runtime or at CIL-to-native-code compilation time. `sizeof` returns the total size that would be occupied by each element in an array of this value type—including any padding the implementation chooses to add. Specifically, array elements lie `sizeof` bytes apart.

ANNOTATION: Even if the definition of a value type does not change, the application cannot assume anything about the size of the instance unless one of the restrictive layouts was chosen.

Exceptions:
None.

Verifiability:
Correct CIL ensures that `valueType` is a `typeref` or `typedef` referring to a value type. It is always verifiable.

4.25 stelem.<type> – Store an Element of an Array

Format	Assembly Format	Description
9C	stelem.i1	Replace array element at *index* with the `int8` value on the stack.
9D	stelem.i2	Replace array element at *index* with the `int16` value on the stack.
9E	stelem.i4	Replace array element at *index* with the `int32` value on the stack.
9F	stelem.i8	Replace array element at *index* with the `int64` value on the stack.
A0	stelem.r4	Replace array element at *index* with the `float32` value on the stack.
A1	stelem.r8	Replace array element at *index* with the `float64` value on the stack.
9B	stelem.i	Replace array element at *index* with the `i` value on the stack.
A2	stelem.ref	Replace array element at *index* with the `ref` value on the stack.

Stack Transition:
…, array, index, value → …,

Description:

The `stelem` instruction replaces the value of the element with zero-based index *index* (of type `int32` or `native int`) in the one-dimensional array *array* with *value*. Arrays are objects and hence represented by a value of type `O`.

Note that `stelem.ref` implicitly casts *value* to the element type of *array* before assigning the value to the array element. This cast can fail, even for verified code. Thus the `stelem.ref` instruction may throw the `ArrayTypeMismatchException`.

For one-dimensional arrays that aren't zero-based, and for multi-dimensional arrays, the array class provides a *StoreElement* method.

Exceptions:

`NullReferenceException` is thrown if *array* is null.

`IndexOutOfRangeException` is thrown if *index* is negative, or larger than the bound of *array*.

`ArrayTypeMismatchException` is thrown if *array* doesn't hold elements of the required type.

Verifiability:

Correct CIL requires that *array* be a zero-based, one-dimensional array whose declared element type matches exactly the type for this particular instruction suffix (e.g., `stelem.r4` can only be applied to a zero-based, one-dimensional array of `float32s`), and also that *index* lies within the bounds of *array*.

4.26 stfld – Store into a Field of an Object

Format	Assembly Format	Description
7D <T>	stfld *field*	Replace the value of *field* of the object *obj* with *val*.

Stack Transition:

…, obj, value → …,

Description:

The `stfld` instruction replaces the value of a field of an *obj* (an **O**) or via a pointer (type `native int`, or `&`) with `value`. `field` is a metadata token (a `fieldref` or `fielddef`; see Partition II) that refers to a field member reference. `stfld` pops the value and the object reference off the stack and updates the object.

The `stfld` instruction may have a prefix of either or both of `unaligned.` and `volatile.`.

6. CIL Instruction Set

Exceptions:

`NullReferenceException` is thrown if *obj* is null and the field isn't static.

`MissingFieldException` is thrown if *field* is not found in the metadata. This is typically checked when CIL is converted to native code, not at runtime.

Verifiability:

Correct CIL ensures that *field* is a valid token referring to a field, and that *obj* and *value* will always have types appropriate for the assignment being performed. For verifiable code, *obj* may not be an unmanaged pointer.

> **NOTE**
>
> Using `stfld` to change the value of a static, init-only field outside the body of the class initializer may lead to unpredictable behavior. It cannot, however, compromise memory integrity or type safety, so it is not tested by verification.

4.27 stobj – Store a Value Type from the Stack into Memory

Format	Assembly Format	Description
81 <T>	stobj *classTok*	Store a value of type *classTok* from the stack into memory.

Stack Transition:

…, addr, valObj → …,

Description:

The `stobj` instruction copies the value type *valObj* into the address specified by *addr* (a pointer of type `native int`, or `&`). The number of bytes copied depends on the size of the class represented by *classTok*. *classTok* is a metadata token (a `typeref` or `typedef`; see Partition II) representing a value type.

It is unspecified what happens if *valObj* is not an instance of the class represented by *classTok* or if *classTok* does not represent a value type.

The operation of the `stobj` instruction may be altered by an immediately preceding `volatile.` or `unaligned.` prefix instruction.

Exceptions:

`TypeLoadException` is thrown if *class* cannot be found. This is typically detected when CIL is converted to native code rather than at runtime.

Verifiability:
Correct CIL ensures that *classTok* is a metadata token representing a value type and that *valObj* is a pointer to a location containing an initialized value of the type specified by *classTok*. In addition, verifiable code requires that *addr* be a managed pointer to the type specified by *classTok*.

4.28 stsfld – Store a Static Field of a Class

Format	Assembly Format	Description
80 <T>	stsfld *field*	Replace the value of *field* with *val*.

Stack Transition:
…, val → …,

Description:
The `stsfld` instruction replaces the value of a static field with a value from the stack. *field* is a metadata token (a `fieldref` or `fielddef`; see Partition II) that must refer to a static field member. `stsfld` pops the value off the stack and updates the static field with that value.

The `stsfld` instruction may be prefixed by `volatile.`.

Exceptions:
`MissingFieldException` is thrown if *field* is not found in the metadata. This is typically checked when CIL is converted to native code, not at runtime.

Verifiability:
Correct CIL ensures that *field* is a valid token referring to a static field, and that *value* will always have a type appropriate for the assignment being performed.

> **NOTE**
> Using `stsfld` to change the value of a static, init-only field outside the body of the class initializer may lead to unpredictable behavior. It cannot, however, compromise memory integrity or type safety, so it is not tested by verification.

4.29 throw – Throw an Exception

Format	Assembly Format	Description
7A	throw	Throw an exception.

Stack Transition:
…, object → …,

Description:
The `throw` instruction throws the exception *object* (type `O`) on the stack. For details of the exception mechanism, see Partition I [sections 12.4.2.5 through 12.4.2.8].

> **NOTE**
> While the CLI permits any object to be thrown, the Common Language Specification (CLS) describes a specific exception class that must be used for language interoperability.

Exceptions:
`NullReferenceException` is thrown if *obj* is null.

Verifiability:
Correct CIL ensures that *class* is a valid `typeref` token indicating a class, and that *obj* is always either null or an object reference—i.e., of type `O`.

4.30 unbox – Convert Boxed Value Type to Its Raw Form

Format	Assembly Format	Description
79 <T>	unbox *valuetype*	Extract the value type data from *obj*, its boxed representation.

Stack Transition:
…, obj → …, valueTypePtr

Description:
A value type has two separate representations (see Partition I [section 8.2 and its subsections]) within the CLI:

- A "raw" form used when a value type is embedded within another object

- A "boxed" form, where the data in the value type is wrapped (boxed) into an object so it can exist as an independent entity

The `unbox` instruction converts *obj* (of type `O`), the boxed representation of a value type, to *valueTypePtr* (a managed pointer, type `&`), its unboxed form. *valuetype* is a metadata token (a `typeref` or `typedef`) indicating the type of value type contained within *obj*. If obj is not a boxed instance of *valuetype*, or if *obj* is a boxed enum and *valuetype* is not its underlying type, then this instruction will throw an `InvalidCastException`.

Unlike `box`, which is required to make a copy of a value type for use in the object, `unbox` is *not* required to copy the value type from the object. Typically it simply computes the address of the value type that is already present inside of the boxed object.

Exceptions:

`InvalidCastException` is thrown if *obj* is not a boxed *valuetype* (or if *obj* is a boxed enum and *valuetype* is not its underlying type).

`NullReferenceException` is thrown if obj is null.

`TypeLoadException` is thrown if *class* cannot be found. This is typically detected when CIL is converted to native code rather than at runtime.

Verifiability:

Correct CIL ensures that *valueType* is a `typeref` or `typedef` metadata token for some value type, and that *obj* is always an object reference—i.e., of type `O`—and represents a boxed instance of a *valuetype* value type.

COMMON LANGUAGE INFRASTRUCTURE (CLI)

7. Partition IV: Profiles and Libraries

1 Overview

NOTE

While compiler writers are most concerned with issues of file format, instruction set design, and a common type system, application programmers are most interested in the programming library that is available to them in the language they are using. The Common Language Infrastructure (CLI) specifies a Common Language Specification (CLS; see Partition I, sections 8, 10, and 11) that shall be used to define the externally visible aspects (method signatures, etc.) when they are intended to be used from a wide range of programming languages. Since it is the goal of the CLI Libraries to be available from as many programming languages as possible, all of the library functionality is available through CLS-compliant types and type members.

The CLI Libraries are designed with the following goals in mind:

- Wide reach across programming languages
- Consistent design patterns throughout
- Features on parity with the ISO/IEC C Standard library of 1990
- Features for more recent programming paradigms, notably networking, XML, runtime type inspection, instance creation, and dynamic method dispatch
- Factoring into self-consistent libraries with minimal interdependence

This document provides an overview of the CLI Libraries and a specification of their factoring into Profiles and Libraries. A companion document, considered to be part of this Partition but distributed in XML format, provides details of each class, value type, and interface in the CLI Libraries. While the normative specification of the CLI Libraries is in XML form, it can be processed using an XSL transform to produce easily browsed information about the class libraries.

ANNOTATION: The class libraries are also published in this series as the *.NET Framework Standard Library Annotated Reference*.

Partition V contains an informative annex [Annex D] describing programming conventions used in defining the CLI Libraries. These conventions, while not normative, can significantly simplify the use of libraries. Implementers are encouraged to follow them when creating additional (non-Standard) Libraries.

2 Libraries and Profiles

Libraries and Profiles, defined below, are constructs created for the purpose of standards conformance/compliance. They specify a set of features that shall be present in an implementation of the Common Language Infrastructure (CLI) and a set of types that shall be available to programs run by that CLI.

NOTE

There need not be any direct support for Libraries and Profiles in the Virtual Execution System (VES). They are not represented in the metadata, and they have no impact on the structure or performance of an implementation of the CLI. Libraries and Profiles may span assemblies (the deployment unit), and the names of types in a single Library or Profile are not required to have a common prefix ("namespace").

There is, in general, no way to test whether a feature is available at runtime, nor is there a way to enquire whether a particular Profile or Library is available. If present, however, the Reflection Library makes it possible to test at runtime for the existence of particular methods and types.

2.1 Libraries

A Library specifies three things:

- A set of types that shall be available, including their grouping into assemblies.
- A set of features of the CLI that shall be available.

> **NOTE**
> The set of features required for any particular Library is a subset of the complete set of CLI features. Each Library described in Partition IV, section 5 has text that defines what CLI features are required for implementations that support the Library.

- Modifications to types defined in *other* Libraries. These modifications are typically the addition of methods and interfaces to types belonging to the other Library, and additional exceptions that may be thrown by methods of the other Library's types. These modifications shall provide only additional functionality or specify behavior where it was previously unspecified; they shall not be used to alter previously specified behavior.

  Example (informative): Consider the Extended Numerics Library. Since it provides a new base data type, Double, it also specifies that the method ToDouble be added to the System.Convert class that is part of the Base Class Library. It also defines a new exception, System.NotFiniteNumberException, and specifies existing methods in other Libraries' methods that throw it (as it happens, there are no such methods).

In the XML specification of the Libraries, each type specifies the Library to which it belongs. For those members (e.g., `Console.WriteLine(float)`) that are part of one Library (Extended Numerics) but whose type is in another Library (BCL [Base Class Library]), the XML specifies the Library that defines the method. [The class libraries are also published in this series as the .NET Framework Standard Library Annotated Reference.]

ANNOTATION: Partition I of the standard describes framework developers as one of the audiences of this standard. The term "framework" was used to denote what is traditionally thought of as a library—that is a set of data types and the operations upon them. In this section, "library" is more broadly defined. In terms of the CLI, a library definition has three parts: (1) the data types and operations that the programmer sees, (2) the impact of that library on other libraries, and (3) additions to the VES required to support that library.

For example, if you add a library like the Extended Numerics Library, which adds the floating point data type, new data converters for that type must be added to the Base Class Library, along with new exceptions for those operations. In addition, floating point instructions must be added to the VES.

If you are implementing a VES, you need only implement the parts of the VES that support the libraries you choose to support. A conforming implementation of the CLI must support the CLI, which requires a minimum set of libraries, as shown in the diagram in Partition IV, section 2.3. If you add a library, all you add is functionality in the

VES, not user programming libraries. Often what programmers see is not changes to the libraries, but syntax changes that their programming languages provide. For example, if support for multi-dimensional arrays is added, and the languages support it as well, programmers see that the languages allow commas in the brackets for array indexing. If languages do not have the syntax for something, programmers cannot use that thing.

However, putting functionality into CLS-compliant frameworks with new classes makes this functionality visible in all programming languages, without requiring languages to add syntax for each addition of new functionality. Certainly, calling base classes from the library is less convenient than if there were supporting language syntax, but it is possible.

For a VES developer, deciding to add support for a new library requires several kinds of tasks. For example, if you built a VES that originally supported only the kernel, and then add extended numerics, you would need to add a data type to the verifier, add a set of new rules to the verifier, add a set of instructions to the VES, make sure that all the marshal conventions on the native code side can handle passing floating point numbers, learn how the underlying platform handles floating point numbers, etc.

For a compiler writer with a CLI-compliant language, there is no new work in supporting the framework part of the library, because the library is CLS-compliant. But some libraries have a component that requires a new instruction. In this case there are two possibilities. One is that the instruction will be needed for a library that the VES developers are responsible for building. On the other hand, sometimes the language must either add new syntax or modify old syntax to support it. One example is type conversions in C#. If you are adding floating point capability, you must now be able to convert from an integer to a float, and the language will need new syntax not previously required.

2.2 Profiles

A Profile is simply a set of Libraries, grouped together to form a consistent whole that provides a fixed level of functionality. A conforming implementation of the CLI shall specify a Profile it implements, as well as any additional Libraries that it provides. The Kernel Profile (see Partition IV, section 3.1) shall be included in all conforming implementations of the CLI. Thus, all Libraries and CLI features that are part of the Kernel Profile are available in all conforming implementations. This minimal feature set is described in Partition IV, section 4.

RATIONALE

The rules for combining Libraries together are complex, since each Library may add members to types defined in other libraries. By standardizing a small number of Profiles, we specify completely the interaction of the Libraries that are part of each Profile. A Profile provides a consistent target for vendors of devices, compilers, tools, and applications. Each Profile specifies a trade-off of CLI feature and implementation complexity against resource constraints. By defining a very small number of Profiles, we increase the market for each Profile, making each a desirable target for a class of applications across a wide range of implementations and tool sets.

2.3 Structure of the Standard

This standard specifies two Standard Profiles (see Partition IV, section 3) and seven Standard Libraries (see Partition IV, section 5). The following diagram shows the relationship between the Libraries and the Profiles:

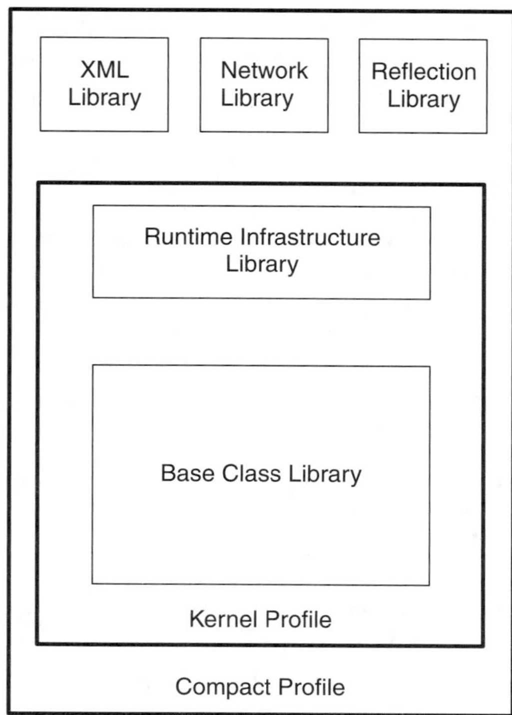

The Extended Array Library and the Extended Numerics Library are not part of either Profile, but may be combined with either of them. Doing so adds the appropriate methods, exceptions, and interfaces to the types specified in the Profile.

ANNOTATION: The diagram above provides an excellent road map for VES developers, showing the libraries required for a basic VES, and what can be added later in development. A minimal conforming implementation of the CLI includes both Libraries (Base Class and Runtime Infrastructure) in the Kernel Profile.

---

3 The Standard Profiles

There are two Standard Profiles. The smallest conforming implementation of the CLI is the Kernel Profile, while the Compact Profile contains additional features useful for applications targeting a more resource-rich set of devices.

A conforming implementation of the CLI shall throw an appropriate exception (e.g., `System.Not-ImplementedException`, `System.MissingMethodException`, or `System.ExecutionEngineException`) when it encounters a feature specified in this Standard but not supported by the particular Profile (see Partition III).

> **NOTE**
> Implementers should consider providing tools that statically detect features they do not support so users have an option of checking programs for the presence of such features before running them.

> **NOTE**
> Vendors of compliant CLI implementations should specify exactly which configurations of Standard Libraries and Standard Profiles they support.

> **NOTE**
> "Features" may be something like the use of a floating point CIL instruction in the implementation of a method when the CLI upon which it is running does not support the Extended Numerics Library. Or, the "feature" might be a call to a method that

this Standard specifies exists only when a particular Library is implemented and yet the code making the call is running on an implementation of the CLI that does not support that particular library.

3.1 The Kernel Profile

This profile is the minimal possible conforming implementation of the CLI. It contains the types commonly found in a modern programming language class library plus the classes needed by compilers targeting the CLI.

Contents: Base Class Library, Runtime Infrastructure Library

ANNOTATION: Whereas the Base Class Library is what programmers code with, the Runtime Infrastructure Library is used by compiler writers to support common syntax in languages. For example, certain classes enable array copying, but in a language like C#, that shows up as simple assignment statements, with no calls to the Base Class Library.

3.2 The Compact Profile

This Profile is designed to allow implementation on devices with only modest amounts of physical memory yet provides more functionality than the Kernel Profile alone.

Contents: Kernel Profile, XML Library, Network Library, Reflection Library

4 Kernel Profile Feature Requirements

All conforming implementations of the CLI support at least the Kernel Profile, and consequently all CLI features required by the Kernel Profile must be implemented by all conforming implementations. This section defines that minimal feature set by enumerating the set of features that are not required—i.e., a minimal conforming implementation must implement all CLI features except those specified in the remainder of this section. The feature requirements of individual Libraries as specified in Partition IV, section 5 are defined by reference to restricted items described in this section. For ease of reference, each feature has a name indicated by the name of the section heading. Where Libraries do not specify any additional feature requirement, it shall be assumed that only the features of the Kernel Profile as described in this section are required.

4.1 Features Excluded from Kernel Profile

The following internal data types and constructs, specified elsewhere in this Standard, are *not* required of CLI implementations that conform only to the Kernel Profile. All other CLI features are required.

ANNOTATION: As stated, the features in this section are not required for Kernel Profile implementations. Choosing what to support depends on the languages that you intend to support and other features that you decide you require. For example, some languages, like Microsoft Visual Basic, have filtered exceptions, while C# does not. If your VES runs Microsoft Visual Basic, it needs to support filtered exceptions.

4.1.1 *Floating Point*

The **floating point feature set** consists of the user-visible floating point data types `float32` and `float64`, and support for an internal representation of floating point numbers.

If omitted: The CIL instructions that deal specifically with these data types throw the `System.NotImplementedException` exception. These instructions are: `ckfinite`, `conv.r.un`, `conv.r4`, `conv.r8`, `ldc.r4`, `ldc.r8`, `ldelem.r4`, `ldelem.r8`, `ldind.r4`, `ldind.r8`, `stelem.r4`, `stelem.r8`, `stind.r4`, `stind.r8`. Any attempt to reference a signature including the floating point data types shall throw the `System.NotImplementedException` exception. The precise timing of the exception is not specified.

> **NOTE**
> These restrictions guarantee that the VES will not encounter any floating point data. Hence the implementation of the arithmetic instructions (`add`, etc.) need not handle those types.

Part of Library: Extended Numerics (see Partition IV, section 5.6).

4.1.2 *Non-vector Arrays*

The **non-vector arrays feature set** includes the support for arrays with more than one dimension or with lower bounds other than zero. This includes support for signatures referencing such arrays, runtime representations of such arrays, and marshalling of such arrays to and from native data types.

If omitted: Any attempt to reference a signature including a non-vector array shall throw the `System.NotImplementedException` exception. The precise timing of the exception is not specified.

> **NOTE**
> The generic type `System.Array` is part of the Kernel Profile and is available in all conforming implementations of the CLI. An implementation that does not provide the non-vector array feature set can correctly assume that all instances of that class are vectors.

Part of Library: Extended Arrays (see Partition IV, section 5.7).

4.1.3 *Reflection*

The **reflection feature set** supports full reflection on data types. All of its functionality is exposed through methods in the Reflection Library.

If omitted: The Kernel Profile specifies an opaque type, `System.Type`, instances of which uniquely represent any type in the system and provide access to the name of the type.

> **NOTE**
> With just the Kernel Profile there is no requirement, for example, to determine the members of the type, dynamically create instances of the type, or invoke methods of the type given an instance of `System.Type`. This can simplify the implementation of the CLI compared to that required when the Reflection Library is available.

Part of Library: Reflection (see Partition IV, section 5.4).

4.1.4 *Application Domains*

The **application domain feature set** supports multiple application domains. The Kernel Profile requires that a single application domain exist.

If omitted: Methods for creating application domains (part of the Base Class Library; see Partition IV, section 5.2) throw the `System.NotImplementedException` exception.

Part of Library: (none)

4.1.5 *Remoting*

The **remoting feature set** supports remote method invocation. It is provided primarily through special semantics of the class `System.MarshalByRefObject` as described in the *.NET Framework Standard Library Annotated Reference.*

If omitted: The class `System.MarshalByRefObject` shall be treated as a simple class with no special meaning.

Part of Library: (none)

4.1.6 *Varargs*

The **varargs feature set** supports variable-length argument lists and runtime typed pointers.

If omitted: Any attempt to reference a method with the `varargs` calling convention or the signature encodings associated with varargs methods (see Partition II [section 7]) shall throw the `System.NotImplementedException` exception. Methods using the CIL instructions `arglist`, `refanytype`, `mkrefany`, and `refanyval` shall throw the `System.NotImplementedException` exception. The precise timing of the exception is not specified. The type `System.TypedReference` need not be defined.

Part of Library: (none)

4.1.7 *[Varargs] Frame Growth*

The **frame growth feature set** supports dynamically extending a stack frame.

If omitted: Methods using the CIL `localloc` instruction shall throw the `System.NotImplementedException` exception. The precise timing of the exception is not specified.

Part of Library: (none)

4.1.8 *Filtered Exceptions*

The **filtered exceptions feature set** supports user-supplied filters for exceptions.

If omitted: Methods using the CIL `endfilter` instruction or with an `exceptionentry` that contains a non-null `filterstart` (see Partition I, sections 12.4.2.5 through 12.4.2.8) shall throw the `System.NotImplementedException` exception. The precise timing of the exception is not specified.

Part of Library: (none)

5 The Standard Libraries

The detailed content of each Library, in terms of the types it provides and the changes it makes to types in other Libraries, is provided in XML form. This section provides a brief description of each Library's purpose, as well as specifying the features of the CLI required by each Library beyond those required by the Kernel Profile.

ANNOTATION: The class libraries are also published in this series as the *.NET Framework Standard Library Annotated Reference*.

5.1 Runtime Infrastructure Library

The Runtime Infrastructure Library is part of the Kernel Profile. It provides the services needed by a compiler to target the CLI and the facilities needed to dynamically load types from a stream in the file format specified in Partition II, section 23. For example, it provides `System.BadImageFormatException`, which is thrown when a stream that does not have the correct format is loaded.

Name used in XML: RuntimeInfrastructure

CLI Feature Requirement: None

5.2 Base Class Library

The Base Class Library is part of the Kernel Profile. It is a simple runtime library for modern programming languages. It serves as the Standard for the runtime library for the language C# as well as one of the CLI Standard Libraries. It provides types to represent the built-in data types of the CLI, simple file access, custom attributes, security attributes, string manipulation, formatting, streams, collections, and so forth.

Name used in XML: BCL

CLI Feature Requirement: None

ANNOTATION: The CLI specification requires that all string objects embed characters directly in the object at a constant offset from the start of the object. This requirement is not specified in the text of the five partitions, but it is implied by the definition of the `System.Runtime.CompilerServices.RuntimeHelpers.OffsetToStringData` property. This requirement restricts the flexibility by not allowing multiple strings to share a character array and identify the string by offset and length of a substring in that array. Figure 7-1 shows the required layout for three strings: "LAN", "LANGUAGE", and "AGE". It would be desirable to allow flexibility so that the implementation could choose between the layout of Figure 7-1 and the shared layout of Figure 7-2. The lack of such flexibility was noted during the work of the ECMA technical committee responsible for this standard, and the description of `System.Runtime.CompilerServices.RuntimeHelpers.OffsetToStringData` states that this property is deprecated.

5.3 Network Library

The Network Library is part of the Compact Profile. It provides simple networking services, including direct access to network ports as well as HTTP support.

Name used in XML: Networking

CLI Feature Requirement: None

5.4 Reflection Library

The Reflection Library is part of the Compact Profile. It provides the ability to examine the structure of types, create instances of types, and invoke methods on types, all based on a description of the type.

Name used in XML: Reflection

CLI Feature Requirement: Must support Runtime Infrastructure; see Partition IV, section 5.1.

5.5 XML Library

The XML Library is part of the Compact Profile. It provides a simple "pull-style" parser for XML. It is designed for resource-constrained devices, yet provides a simple user model. A conforming implementation of the CLI that includes the XML Library shall also implement the Network Library (see Partition IV, section 5.3).

Name used in XML: XML

CLI Feature Requirement: None

5.6 Extended Numerics Library

The Extended Numerics Library is not part of any Profile but can be supplied as part of any CLI implementation. It provides the support for floating point (`System.Single`, `System.Double`) and extended-precision (`System.Decimal`) data types. Like the Base Class Library, this Library is directly referenced by the C# Standard.

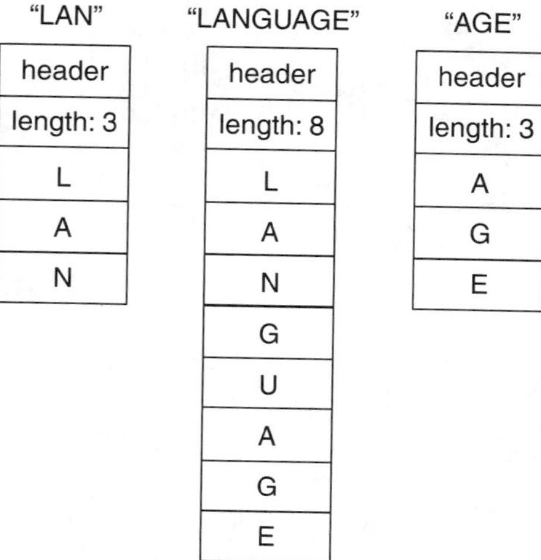

Figure 7-1 String Objects with Private Copies of Character

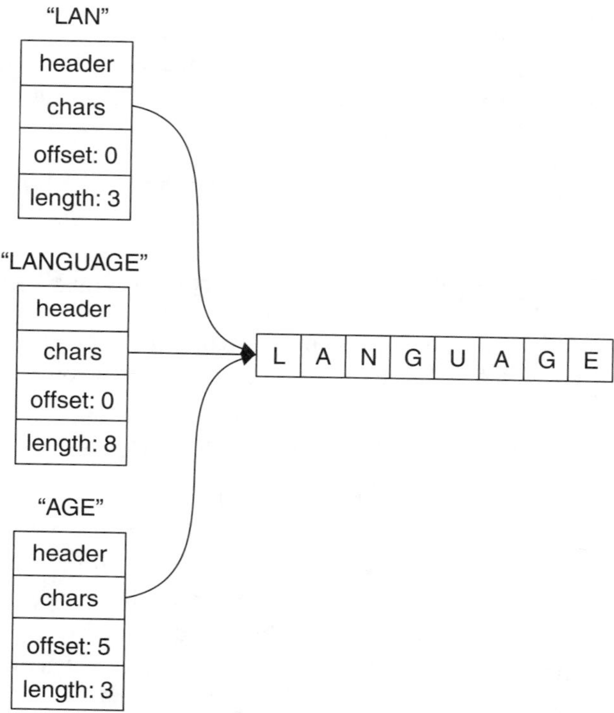

Figure 7-2 Sting Objects with Shared Character

NOTE

Programmers who use this library will benefit if implementations specify which arithmetic operations on these data types are implemented primarily through hardware support.

RATIONALE

The Extended Numerics Library is kept separate because some commonly available processors do not provide direct support for the data types. While software emulation can be provided, the performance difference is often so large (1,000-fold or more) that it is unreasonable to build software using floating point operations without being aware of whether the underlying implementation is hardware-based.

CLI Feature Requirement: Floating Point; see Partition IV, section 4.1.1.

5.7 Extended Array Library

This Library is not part of any Profile but can be supplied as part of any CLI implementation. It provides support for non-vector arrays—that is, arrays that have more than one dimension, and arrays that have non-zero lower bounds.

CLI Feature Requirement: Non-vector Arrays; see Partition IV, section 4.1.2.

6 Implementation-Specific Modifications to the System Libraries

Implementers are encouraged to extend or modify the types specified in this standard to provide additional functionality. Implementers should notice, however, that type names beginning with "`System.`" and bearing the special Standard Public Key are intended for use by the Standard Libraries; such names not currently in use may be defined in a future version of this standard.

ANNOTATION: This standard is intended to describe a minimum set of programming libraries. It is the explicit intention of the standard that it be extended. However, arbitrary extensions would make it impossible to write portable programs. Therefore, this section explicitly states both legitimate extensions and restrictions.

Among the restrictions are that you cannot put new interfaces and virtual methods on existing interfaces, and you cannot add them to abstract classes unless you provide implementations. You cannot take an instance method and make it a virtual method. If this were not forbidden and you compiled against a library that had done this for a method, then your program would be able to successfully override that method. However, the same program would not work on a standard conforming library implementation, because you cannot override instance methods.

To allow programs compiled against the Standard Libraries to work when run on implementations that have extended or modified the Standard Libraries, such extensions or modifications shall obey the following rules:

- The contract specified by virtual methods shall be maintained in new classes that override them.
- New exceptions may be thrown, but where possible these should be subclasses of the exceptions already specified as thrown rather than entirely new exception types. Exceptions initiated by methods of types defined in the Standard Libraries shall be derived from `System.Exception`.

ANNOTATION: The second bullet in this section is important to programmers and VES implementers, although of less concern to compilers. It says that it is legitimate (and important) for a VES implementer to throw a new exception, and it should be documented. For example, suppose a class that formerly would take only integers is extended to take floating point numbers too. In this case, current exceptions may need to be extended to include things like floating underflow.

- Interfaces and virtual methods shall not be added to an existing interface. Nor shall they be added to an abstract class unless the class provides an implementation.

RATIONALE

An interface or virtual method may be added only where it carries an implementation. This allows programs written when the interface or method was not present to continue to work.

- Instance methods shall not be implemented as virtual methods.

> **RATIONALE**
>
> Methods specified as instance (non-static, non-virtual) in this standard are not permitted to be implemented as virtual methods in order to reduce the likelihood of creating non-portable files by using implementation-supplied libraries at compile time. Even though a compiler need not take a dependence on the distinction between virtual and instance methods, it is easy for a user to inadvertently override a virtual method and thus create non-portable code. The alternative of providing special files corresponding to this standard for use at compile time is prone to user error.

- The accessibility of fields and non-virtual methods may be widened from that specified in this Standard.

> **NOTE**
>
> The following common extensions are permitted by these rules.
>
> - Adding new members to existing types.
> - Concrete (non-abstract) classes may implement interfaces not defined in this standard.
> - Adding fields (values) to enumerations.
> - An implementation may insert a new type into the hierarchy between a type specified in this standard and the type specified as its base type. That is, this standard specifies an inheritance relation between types but does not specify the immediate base type.

> **RATIONALE**
>
> An implementation may wish to split functionality across several types in order to provide non-standard extension mechanisms, or may wish to provide additional non-standard functionality through the new base type. As long as programs do not reference these non-standard types, they will remain portable across conforming implementations of the CLI.

7 Semantics of the XML Specification

The XML specification conforms to the Document Type Definition (DTD) in Figure 7-3. Only types that are included in a specified library are included in the XML.

ANNOTATION: The libraries are a part of the standard, and are described using XML. The XML DTD included in this section allows interpretation of the XML form, available online. The standardized libraries are also published in the *.NET Framework Standard Library Annotated Reference.*

There are three types of elements/attributes:

- **Normative:** An element or attribute is normative such that the XML specification would be incomplete without it.
- **Informative:** An element or attribute is informative if it specifies information that helps clarify the XML specification, but without it the specification still stands alone.
- **Rendering/Formatting:** An element or attribute is for rendering or formatting if it specifies information to help an XML rendering tool.

The text associated with an element or an attribute (e.g., #PCDATA, #CDATA) is, unless explicitly stated otherwise, normative or informative depending on the element or attribute with which it is associated, as described in Figure 7-3.

(**Note:** Many of the elements and attributes in the DTD are for rendering purposes.)

Figure 7-3 XML DTD

```
<?xml version="1.0" encoding="UTF-8"?>
```

```
<!ELEMENT AssemblyCulture (#PCDATA)>
```

(Normative) Specifies the culture of the assembly that defines the current type. Currently this value is always "none". It is reserved for future use.

```
<!ELEMENT AssemblyInfo (AssemblyName, AssemblyPublicKey, AssemblyVersion,
AssemblyCulture, Attributes)>
```

(Normative) Specifies information about the assembly of a given type. These correspond to sections of the metadata of an assembly as described in Partition II and include information from the AssemblyName, AssemblyPublicKey, AssemblyVersion, AssemblyCulture, and Attributes elements.

```
<!ELEMENT AssemblyName (#PCDATA)>
```

(Normative) Specifies the name of the assembly of which a given type is a member. For example, all of the types in the BCL are members of the "mscorlib" assembly.

Figure 7-3 XML DTD (*continued*)

```
<!ELEMENT AssemblyPublicKey (#PCDATA)>
```

(Normative) Specifies the public key of the assembly. The public key is represented as a 128-bit value.

```
<!ELEMENT AssemblyVersion (#PCDATA)>
```

(Normative) Specifies the version of the assembly in the form 1.0.x.y, where x is a build number and y is a revision number.

```
<!ELEMENT Attribute (AttributeName, Excluded, ExcludedTypeName?,
ExcludedLibraryName?)>
```

(Normative) Specifies the text for a custom attribute on a type or a member of a type. This includes the attribute name and whether or not the attribute type itself is contained in another library.

```
<!ELEMENT AttributeName (#PCDATA)>
```

(Normative) Specifies the name of the custom attribute associated with a type or member of a type. Also contains the data needed to instantiate the attribute.

```
<!ELEMENT Attributes (Attribute*)>
```

(Normative) Specifies the list of the attributes on a given type or member of a type.

```
<!ELEMENT Base (BaseTypeName?, ExcludedBaseTypeName?, ExcludedLibraryName?)>
```

(Normative) Specifies the information related to the base type of the current type. Although the **ExcludedBaseTypeName** and **ExcludedLibraryName** elements are rarely found within this element, they are required when a type inherits from a type not found in the current library.

```
<!ELEMENT BaseTypeName (#PCDATA)>
```

(Normative) Specifies the fully qualified name of the class from which a type inherits (i.e., the type's base class).

```
<!ELEMENT Docs (summary?, altmember?, altcompliant?, param*, returns?, value?,
exception*, threadsafe?, remarks?, example?, permission?, example?)>
```

(Normative) Specifies the textual documentation of a given type or member of a type.

```
<!ELEMENT Excluded (#PCDATA)>
```

(Normative) Specifies, by a "0" or "1", whether a given member can be excluded from the current type in the absence of a given library. "0" specifies that it cannot be excluded.

```
<!ELEMENT ExcludedBaseTypeName (#PCDATA)>
```

(Normative) Specifies the fully qualified name of the type that the current type must inherit from if a given library is present in an implementation. The library name is specified in the **ExcludedLibraryName** element. An example is the System.Type class that inherits from System.Object, but if the Reflection library is present, it must inherit from System.Reflection.MemberInfo.

```
<!ELEMENT ExcludedLibrary (#PCDATA)>
```

(Normative) Specifies the library that must be present in order for a given member of a type to be required to be implemented. For example, System.Console.WriteLine(double) need only be implemented if the ExtendedNumerics library is available.

```
<!ELEMENT ExcludedLibraryName (#PCDATA)>
```

(Normative) This element appears only in the description of custom attributes. It specifies the name of the library that defines the described attribute. For example, the member that is invoked when no member name is specified for System.Text.StringBuilder (in C#, this is the indexer) is called "chars". The attribute needed for this is System.Reflection.DefaultMemberAttribute. This is found in the RuntimeInfrastructure library. This element is used with the **ExcludedTypeName** element.

```
<!ELEMENT ExcludedTypeName (#PCDATA)>
```

(Normative) Specifies the fully qualified name of the attribute that is needed for a member to succesfully specify the given attribute. This element is related to the **ExcludedLibraryName** element and is used for attributes.

```
<!ELEMENT Interface (InterfaceName, Excluded)>
```

(Normative) Specifies information about an interface that a type implements. This element contains sub-elements specifying the interface name and whether another library is needed for the interface to be required in the current library.

```
<!ELEMENT InterfaceName (#PCDATA)>
```

(Normative) Represents the fully qualified interface name that a type implements.

```
<!ELEMENT Interfaces (Interface*)>
```

(Normative) Specifies information on the interfaces, if any, a type implements. There is one **Interface** element for each interface implemented by the type.

```
<!ELEMENT Libraries (Types+)>
```

(Normative) This is the root element. Specifies all of the information necessary for all of the class libraries of the standard. This includes all of the types and all children elements underneath.

```
<!ELEMENT Member (MemberSignature+, MemberType, Attributes?, ReturnValue,
Parameters, MemberValue?, Docs, Excluded, ExcludedLibrary*)>
```

(Normative) Specifies information about a member of a type. This information includes the signatures, type of the member, parameters, etc., all of which are elements in the XML specification.

```
<!ATTLIST Member

MemberName NMTOKEN #REQUIRED
```

(Normative) **MemberName** specifies the name of the current member.

```
>
```

```
<!ELEMENT MemberOfLibrary (#PCDATA)>
```

(Normative) **PCDATA** is the name of the library containing the type.

```
<!ELEMENT MemberSignature EMPTY>
```

(Normative) Specifies the text (in source code format) for the signature of a given member of a type.

```
<!ATTLIST MemberSignature

Language CDATA #REQUIRED
```

(Normative) **CDATA** is the programming language the signature is written in. All members are described in both ilasm and C#.

Figure 7-3 XML DTD *(continued)*

```
Value CDATA #REQUIRED
```

(Normative) **CDATA** is the text of the member signature in a given language.

```
>
<!ELEMENT MemberType (#PCDATA)>
```

(Normative) Specifies the kind of the current member. The member kinds are: method, property, constructor, field, and event.

```
<!ELEMENT MemberValue (#PCDATA)>
```

(Normative) Specifies the value of a static literal field.

```
<!ELEMENT Members (Member*)>
```

(Normative) Specifies information about all of the members of a given type.

```
<!ELEMENT PRE EMPTY>
```

(Rendering/Formatting) This element exists for rendering purposes only to specify, for example, that future text should be separated from the previous text.

```
<!ELEMENT Parameter (Attributes?)>
```

(Normative) Specifies the information about a specific parameter of a method or property.

```
<!ATTLIST Parameter
      Name NMTOKEN #REQUIRED
```

(Normative) Specifies the name of the parameter.

```
Type CDATA #REQUIRED
```

(Normative) Specifies the fully qualified name of the type of the parameter.

```
>
<!ELEMENT Parameters (Parameter*)>
```

(Normative) Specifies information for the parameters of a given method or property. The information specified is included in each **Parameter** element of this element. This element will contain one **Parameter** for each parameter of the method or property.

```
<!ELEMENT ReturnType (#PCDATA)>
```

(Normative) Specifies the fully qualified name of the type that the current member returns.

```
<!ELEMENT ReturnValue (ReturnType?)>
```

(Normative) Specifies the return type of a member. s**ReturnType** shall be present for all kinds of members except constructors.

```
<!ELEMENT SPAN (#PCDATA | para | paramref | SPAN | see | block)*>
```

(Rendering/Formatting) This element specifies that the text should be segmented from other text (e.g., with a carriage return). References to parameters, other types, and even blocks of text can be included within a **SPAN** element.

```
<!ELEMENT ThreadingSafetyStatement (#PCDATA)>
```

(Normative) Specifies a thread safety statement for a given type.

```
<!ELEMENT Type (TypeSignature+, MemberOfLibrary, AssemblyInfo,
ThreadingSafetyStatement?, Docs, Base, Interfaces, Attributes?, Members,
TypeExcluded)>
```

(Normative) Specifies all of the information for a given type.

```
<!ATTLIST Type
```

```
    Name NMTOKEN #REQUIRED
```

(Informative) Specifies the simple name (e.g., "String" rather than "System.String") of a given type.

```
    FullName NMTOKEN #REQUIRED
```

(Normative) Specifies the fully qualified name of a given type.

```
FullNameSP NMTOKEN #REQUIRED
```

(Informative) Specifies the fully qualified name with each "." of the fully qualified name replaced by an "_".

```
>
```

```
<!ELEMENT TypeExcluded (#PCDATA)>
```

(Normative) **PCDATA** shall be "0".

```
<!ELEMENT TypeSignature EMPTY>
```

(Normative) Specifies the text for the signature (in code representation) of a given type.

```
<!ATTLIST TypeSignature
```

```
    Language CDATA #REQUIRED
```

(Normative) Specifies the language the specified type signature is written in. All type signatures are specified in both ilasm and C#.

```
    Value CDATA #REQUIRED
```

(Normative) **CDATA** is the type signature in the specified language.

```
>
```

```
<!ELEMENT Types (Type+)>
```

(Normative) Specifies information about all of the types of a library.

```
<!ATTLIST Types
```

```
    Library NMTOKEN #REQUIRED
```

Figure 7-3 XML DTD (*continued*)

(Normative) Specifies the library in which all of the types are defined. An example of such a library is "BCL".

```
>

<!ELEMENT altcompliant EMPTY>
```

(Informative) Specifies that an alternative, CLS-compliant method call exists for the current non-CLS-compliant method. For example, this element exists in the System.IO.TextWriter.WriteLine(ulong) method to show that System.IO.TextWriter.WriteLine(long) is an alternative, CLS-compliant method.

```
<!ATTLIST altcompliant

     cref CDATA #REQUIRED
```

(Informative) Specifies the link to the actual documentation for the alternative CLS-compliant method. (**Note:** In this specification, **CDATA** matches the documentation comment format specified in Appendix E of the C# Language specification.)

```
>

<!ELEMENT altmember EMPTY>
```

(Informative) Specifies that an alternative, equivalent member call exists for the current method. This element is used for operator overloads.

```
<!ATTLIST altmember

     cref CDATA #REQUIRED
```

(Informative) Specifies the link to the actual documentation for the alternative member call. (**Note:** In this specification, **CDATA** matches the documentation comment format specified in Appendix E of the C# Language specification.)

```
>

<!ELEMENT block (#PCDATA | see | para | paramref | list | block | c | subscript
| code | sup | pi)*>
```

(Rendering/Formatting) Specifies that the children should be formatted according to the **type** specified as an attribute.

```
<!ATTLIST block

     subset CDATA #REQUIRED
```

(Rendering/Formatting) This attribute is reserved for future use and currently only has the value of "none".

```
     type NMTOKEN #REQUIRED
```

(Rendering/Formatting) Specifies the type of block that follows, one of: usage, overrides, note, example, default, behaviors.

```
>

<!ELEMENT c (#PCDATA | para | paramref | code | see)*>
```

(Rendering/Formatting) Specifies that the text is the output of a code sample.

```
<!ELEMENT code (#PCDATA)>
```

(Informative) Specifies the text is a code sample.

```
<!ATTLIST code

     lang CDATA #IMPLIED
```

(Informative) Specifies the programming language of the code sample. This specification uses C# as the language for the samples.

```
>

<!ELEMENT codelink EMPTY>
```

(Informative) Specifies a piece of code to which a link may be made from another sample. (**Note:** The XML format specified here does not provide a means of creating such a link.)

```
<!ATTLIST codelink

     SampleID CDATA #REQUIRED
```

(Informative) SampleID is the unique ID assigned to this code sample.

```
     SnippetID CDATA #REQUIRED
```

(Informative) SnippetID is the unique ID assigned to a section of text within the sample code.

```
>

<!ELEMENT description (#PCDATA | SPAN | paramref | para | see | c | permille |
block | sub)*>
```

(Normative) Specifies the text for a description for a given term element in a list or table. This element also specifies the text for a column header in a table.

```
<!ELEMENT example (#PCDATA | para | code | c | codelink | see)*>
```

(Informative) Specifies that the text will be an example of the usage of a type or a member of a given type.

```
<!ELEMENT exception (#PCDATA | paramref | see | para | SPAN | block)*>
```

(Normative) Specifies text that provides the information for an exception that can be thrown by a member of a type. This element can contain just text or other rendering options, such as blocks, etc.

```
<!ATTLIST exception

     cref CDATA #REQUIRED
```

(Rendering/Formatting) Specifies a link to the documentation of the exception. (**Note:** In this specification, **CDATA** matches the documentation comment format specified in Appendix E of the C# Language specification.)

```
>

<!ELEMENT i (#PCDATA)>
```

(Rendering/Formatting) Specifies that the text should be italicized.

Figure 7-3 XML DTD (*continued*)

```
<!ELEMENT item (term, description*)>
```

(Rendering/Formatting) Specifies a specific item of a list or a table.

```
<!ELEMENT list (listheader?, item*)>
```

(Rendering/Formatting) Specifies that the text should be displayed in a list format.

```
<!ATTLIST list

     type NMTOKEN #REQUIRED
```

(Rendering/Formatting) Specifies the type of list in which the following text will be represented. Values in the specification are: bullet, number, and table.

```
>

<!ELEMENT listheader (term, description+)>
```

(Rendering/Formatting) Specifies the header of all columns in a given list or table.

```
<!ELEMENT onequarter EMPTY>
```

(Rendering/Formatting) Specifies that text, in the form of "¼", is to be displayed.

```
<!ELEMENT para (#PCDATA | see | block | paramref | c | onequarter | superscript
| sup | permille | SPAN | list | pi | theta | sub)*>
```

(Rendering/Formatting) Specifies that the text is part of what can be considered a paragraph of its own.

```
<!ELEMENT param (#PCDATA | c | paramref | see | block | para | SPAN)*>
```

(Normative) Specifies the information on the meaning or purpose of a parameter. The name of the parameter and a textual description will be associated with this element.

```
<!ATTLIST param

     name CDATA #REQUIRED
```

(Normative) Specifies the name of the parameter being described.

```
>

<!ELEMENT paramref EMPTY>
```

(Rendering/Formatting) Specifies a reference to a parameter of a member of a type.

```
<!ATTLIST paramref

     name CDATA #REQUIRED
```

(Rendering/Formatting) Specifies the name of the parameter to which the **paramref** element is referring.

```
>

<!ELEMENT permille EMPTY>
```

(Rendering/Formatting) Specifies that the current text is to be displayed as the "‰" symbol.

```
<!ELEMENT permission (#PCDATA | see | paramref | para | block)*>
```

(Normative) Specifies the permission, given as a fully qualified type name and supportive text, needed to call a member of a type.

```
<!ATTLIST permission

      cref CDATA #REQUIRED
```

(Rendering/Formatting) Specifies a link to the documentation of the permission. (**Note:** In this specification, **CDATA** matches the documentation comment format specified in Appendix E of the C# Language specification.)

```
>

<!ELEMENT pi EMPTY>
```

(Rendering/Fomatting) Specifies that the current text is to be displayed as the "π" symbol.

```
<!ELEMENT pre EMPTY>
```

(Rendering/Formatting) Specifies a break between the preceding and following text.

```
<!ELEMENT remarks (#PCDATA | para | block | list | c | paramref | see | pre |
SPAN | code | PRE)*>
```

(Normative) Specifies additional information, beyond that supplied by the **summary**, on a type or member of a type.

```
<!ELEMENT returns (#PCDATA | para | list | paramref | see)*>
```

(Normative) Specifies text that describes the return value of a given type member.

```
<!ELEMENT see EMPTY>
```

(Informative) Specifies a link to another type or member.

```
<!ATLIST see

      cref CDATA #IMPLIED
```

(Informative) **cref** specifies the fully qualified name of the type or member to link to. (**Note:** In this specification, **CDATA** matches the documentation comment format specified in Appendix E of the C# Language specification.)

```
      langword CDATA #IMPLIED
```

(Informative) **langword** specifies that the link is to a language-agnostic keyword such as "null".

```
      qualify CDATA #IMPLIED
```

(Informative) **qualify** indicates that the type or member specified in the link must be displayed as fully qualified. Value of this attribute is "true" or "false", with a default value of "false".

```
>

<!ELEMENT sub (#PCDATA | paramref)*>
```

(Rendering/Formatting) Specifies that the current piece of text is to be displayed in subscript notation.

Figure 7-3 XML DTD *(continued)*

```
<!ELEMENT subscript EMPTY>
```

(Rendering/Formatting) Specifies that the current piece of text is to be displayed in subscript notation.

```
<!ATTLIST subscript
     term CDATA #REQUIRED
```

(Rendering/Formatting) Specifies the value to be rendered as a subscript.

```
>
```

```
<!ELEMENT summary (#PCDATA | para | see | block | list)*>
```

(Normative) Specifies a summary description of a given type or member of a type.

```
<!ELEMENT sup (#PCDATA | i | paramref)*>
```

(Rendering/Formatting) Specifies that the current piece of text is to be displayed in superscript notation.

```
<!ELEMENT superscript EMPTY>
```

(Rendering/Formatting) Specifies that the current piece of text is to be displayed in superscript notation.

```
<!ATTLIST superscript
     term CDATA #REQUIRED
```

(Rendering/Formatting) Specifies the value to be rendered as a superscript.

```
>
```

```
<!ELEMENT term (#PCDATA | block | see | paramref | para | c | sup | pi |
theta)*>
```

(Rendering/Formatting) Specifies the text is a list item or an item in the primary column of a table.

```
<!ELEMENT theta EMPTY>
```

(Rendering/Formatting) Specifies that text, in the form of "θ", is to be displayed.

```
<!ELEMENT threadsafe (para+)>
```

(Normative) Specifies that the text describes additional detail, beyond that specified by **ThreadingSafetyStatement**, the thread safety implications of the current type. For example, the text will describe what an implementation must do in terms of synchronization.

```
<!ELEMENT value (#PCDATA | para | list | see)*>
```

(Normative) Specifies description information on the "value" passed into the set method of a property.

7.1 Value Types as Objects

Throughout the textual descriptions of methods in the XML, there are places where a parameter of type **object** or an interface type is expected, but the description refers to passing a value type for that parameter. In these cases, the caller shall box the value type before making the call.

COMMON LANGUAGE INFRASTRUCTURE (CLI)

8. Partition V: Annexes

Annex A Scope

Annex A is this high-level overview of the other annexes.

Annex B contains sample programs written in CIL Assembly Language (ilasm).

Annex C contains information about a particular implementation of an assembler, which provides a superset of the functionality of the syntax described in Partition II, sections 1–20. It also provides a machine-readable description of the CIL instruction set which may be used to derive parts of the grammar used by this assembler as well as other tools that manipulate CIL.

Annex D contains a set of guidelines used in the design of the libraries of Partition IV. The rules are provided here, since they have proven themselves effective in designing cross-language APIs. They also serve as guidelines for those intending to supply additional functionality in a way that meshes seamlessly with the standardized libraries.

Annex E contains information of interest to implementers with respect to the latitude they have in implementing the CLI.

ANNOTATION: Annexes B, C, and D are primarily of interest to language developers, but Annex E also contains information of interest to VES developers.

Annex B Sample Programs

This section contains only informative text.

This Annex shows two complete examples written using ilasm.

ANNOTATION: To illustrate how CIL maps to high-level languages, these examples are annotated with near-equivalent programs in high-level languages. The program in section B.1 was written in Microsoft C#, and the program in section B.2 was written in Visual Basic.

B.1 Mutually Recursive Program (with tail. Calls)

The following is an example of a mutually recursive program that uses `tail.` calls. The methods below determine whether a number is even or odd.

```
.assembly extern mscorlib { }
.assembly test.exe { }
.class EvenOdd
{ .method private static bool IsEven(int32 N) cil managed
  { .maxstack   2
    ldarg.0              // N
    ldc.i4.0
    bne.un      NonZero
    ldc.i4.1
    ret
NonZero:
    ldarg.0
    ldc.i4.1
    sub
    tail.
    call bool EvenOdd::IsOdd(int32)
    ret
  } // end of method "EvenOdd::IsEven"

  .method private static bool IsOdd(int32 N) cil managed
  { .maxstack   2
    // Demonstrates use of argument names and labels
    // Notice that the assembler does not convert these
    // automatically to their short versions
    ldarg       N
    ldc.i4.0
    bne.un      NonZero
```

```
      ldc.i4.0
      ret
 NonZero:
      ldarg       N
      ldc.i4.1
      sub
      tail.
      call bool EvenOdd::IsEven(int32)
      ret
   } // end of method "EvenOdd::IsOdd"

   .method public static void Test(int32 N) cil managed
   { .maxstack   1
     ldarg        N
     call         void [mscorlib]System.Console::Write(int32)
     ldstr        " is "
     call         void [mscorlib]System.Console::Write(string)
     ldarg        N
     call         bool EvenOdd::IsEven(int32)
     brfalse      LoadOdd
     ldstr        "even"
Print:
     call         void [mscorlib]System.Console::WriteLine(string)
     ret
LoadOdd:
     ldstr        "odd"
     br           Print
  } // end of method "EvenOdd::Test"
} // end of class "EvenOdd"

//Global method

.method public static void main() cil managed
{ .entrypoint
  .maxstack     1
  ldc.i4.5
  call           void EvenOdd::Test(int32)
  ldc.i4.2
```

```
    call          void EvenOdd::Test(int32)
    ldc.i4        100
    call          void EvenOdd::Test(int32)
    ldc.i4        1000001
    call          void EvenOdd::Test(int32)
    ret
  } // end of global method "main"
```

ANNOTATION: The following code simulates in C# the operations of the above program, although C# does not generate `tail.` for the calls, so the program fails on the final line with an out-of-stack exception.

```
class EvenOdd
{ private static bool IsEven(int N)
  { if (N==0) return true;
         else return IsOdd(N-1);  /* Should be tail. call */
  }
  private static bool IsOdd(int N)
  { if (N==0) return false;
          else return IsEven(N-1);       /* Should be tail. call */
  }
  public static void Test(int N)
  { System.Console.Write(N);
        System.Console.Write(" is ");
        System.Console.WriteLine(EvenOdd.IsEven(N) ? "even" : "odd");
  }
  static void Main(string[] args)
  { EvenOdd.Test(5);
    EvenOdd.Test(2);
        EvenOdd.Test(100);
    EvenOdd.Test(1000001);
  }
}
```

B.2 Using Value Types

The following program shows how rational numbers can be implemented using value types.

```
.assembly extern mscorlib { }
.assembly rational.exe { }
.class private sealed Rational extends [mscorlib]System.ValueType
                                implements [mscorlib]System.IComparable
```

```
{ .field public int32 Numerator
  .field public int32 Denominator

  .method virtual public int32 CompareTo(object o)
  // Implements IComparable::CompareTo(Object)
  { ldarg.0     // "this" as a managed pointer
    ldfld int32 value class Rational::Numerator
    ldarg.1     // "o" as an object
    unbox value class Rational
    ldfld int32 value class Rational::Numerator
    beq.s TryDenom
    ldc.i4.0
    ret
TryDenom:
    ldarg.0     // "this" as a managed pointer
    ldfld int32 value class Rational::Denominator
    ldarg.1     // "o" as an object
    unbox value class Rational
    ldfld int32 class Rational::Denominator
    ceq
    ret
  }

  .method virtual public string ToString()
  // Implements Object::ToString
  { .locals init (class [mscorlib]System.Text.StringBuilder SB,
                  string S, object N, object D)
    newobj void [mscorlib]System.Text.StringBuilder::.ctor()
    stloc.s SB
    ldstr "The value is: {0}/{1}"
    stloc.s S
    ldarg.0     // managed pointer to self
    dup
    ldfld int32 value class Rational::Numerator
    box [mscorlib]System.Int32
    stloc.s N
    ldfld int32 value class Rational::Denominator
    box [mscorlib]System.Int32
```

8. Annexes

```
    stloc.s D
    ldloc.s SB
    ldloc.s S
    ldloc.s N
    ldloc.s D
    call instance class [mscorlib]System.Text.StringBuilder
      [mscorlib]System.Text.StringBuilder::AppendFormat(string,
                object, object)
    callvirt instance string [mscorlib]System.Object::ToString()
    ret
  }
  .method public value class Rational Mul(value class Rational)
  {
    .locals init (value class Rational Result)
    ldloca.s Result
    dup
    ldarg.0     // "this"
    ldfld int32 value class Rational::Numerator
    ldarga.s    1     // arg
    ldfld int32 value class Rational::Numerator
    mul
    stfld int32 value class Rational::Numerator
    ldarg.0     // "this"
    ldfld int32 value class Rational::Denominator
    ldarga.s    1     // arg
    ldfld int32 value class Rational::Denominator
    mul
    stfld int32 value class Rational::Denominator
    ldloc.s Result
    ret
  }
}
.method static void main()
{
```

```
.entrypoint
.locals init (value class Rational Half,
              value class Rational Third,
              value class Rational Temporary,
              object H, object T)
// Initialize Half, Third, H, and T
ldloca.s Half
dup
ldc.i4.1
stfld int32 value class Rational::Numerator
ldc.i4.2
stfld  int32 value class Rational::Denominator
ldloca.s Third
dup
ldc.i4.1
stfld int32 value class Rational::Numerator
ldc.i4.3
stfld int32 value class Rational::Denominator
ldloc.s Half
box value class Rational
stloc.s H
ldloc.s Third
box value class Rational
stloc.s T
// WriteLine(H.IComparable::CompareTo(H))
// Call CompareTo via interface using boxed instance
ldloc H
dup
callvirt int32 [mscorlib]System.IComparable::CompareTo(object)
call void [mscorlib]System.Console::WriteLine(bool)
// WriteLine(Half.CompareTo(T))
// Call CompareTo via value type directly
ldloca.s Half
ldloc T
call instance int32
value class Rational::CompareTo(object)
```

8. Annexes

```
  call void [mscorlib]System.Console::WriteLine(bool)
  // WriteLine(Half.ToString())
  // Call virtual method via value type directly
  ldloca.s Half
  call instance string class Rational::ToString()
  call void [mscorlib]System.Console::WriteLine(string)
  // WriteLine(T.ToString)
  // Call virtual method inherited from Object, via boxed instance
  ldloc T
  callvirt string [mscorlib]System.Object::ToString()
  call void [mscorlib]System.Console::WriteLine(string)
  // WriteLine((Half.Mul(T)).ToString())
  // Mul is called on two value types, returning a value type
  // ToString is then called directly on that value type
  // Note that we are required to introduce a temporary variable
  //   since the call to ToString requires
  //   a managed pointer (address)
  ldloca.s Half
  ldloc.s Third
  call instance value class Rational
         Rational::Mul(value class Rational)
  stloc.s Temporary
  ldloca.s Temporary
  call instance string Rational::ToString()
  call void [mscorlib]System.Console::WriteLine(string)
  ret
}
```

ANNOTATION: An interesting part of this example is its use of boxing and unboxing. In the method `CompareTo`, the third and fourth instructions are `ldarg` and `unbox`. That's because `ldarg.1` is the argument *o*, which is a boxed object. To be able to use the `ldfld` instruction, you need the value type contained in the boxed object, so you need to call `unbox` to get a reference to the value type. If what you were passing were not of type `Rational`, `unbox` would give you an exception; otherwise it would give you the unboxed value and you could fetch the field out of it. Similarly, after the label `TryDenom`, there's another `unbox`, to get the denominator.

Next, in the method ToString, there are two boxed int32s. We have loaded the numerator and denominator fields, which are 32-bit integers, Then we want to store the numerator in the variable N and the denominator in the variable D, which are of type **object**, so we have to box them.

The next box operations are in main(). We want to take the Rational value Half and store it in H, which is of type object, so it must be boxed. Similarly, the Rational value Third must be boxed to store it in the object type T.

In a high-level language, boxing and unboxing are handled by the compiler, as shown in the following equivalent Visual Basic code:

```
Option Explicit On
Option Strict On

Module Module1

    Private Structure Rational
        Implements System.IComparable
        Public Numerator As Integer
        Public Denominator As Integer

        Public Function CompareTo(ByVal o As Object) As Integer _
           Implements System.IComparable.CompareTo
            'Return 0 if I'm different from o, 1 if we're the same
            'Assumes that rationals are stored in a canonical format
            If Me.Numerator <> CType(o, Rational).Numerator Then Return 0
            If Me.Denominator <> CType(o, Rational).Denominator Then Return 0
            Return 1
        End Function

        Public Overrides Function ToString() As String
            Dim SB As New System.Text.StringBuilder, S As String, N As Object,
D As Object
            S = "The value is: {0}/{1}"
            N = Me.Numerator
            D = Me.Denominator
            SB.AppendFormat(S, N, D)
            Return SB.ToString()
        End Function

        Public Function Mul(ByVal R As Rational) As Rational
            'Multiplies two rationals, but does NOT put into canonical form
            Dim Result As Rational
            Result.Numerator = Me.Numerator * R.Numerator
            Result.Denominator = Me.Denominator * R.Denominator
            Return Result
        End Function
    End Structure

    Sub Main()
        Dim Half As Rational, Third As Rational, Temporary As Rational
        Dim H As Object, T As Object
        Half.Numerator = 1
        Half.Denominator = 2
```

8. Annexes

```
            Third.Numerator = 1
            Third.Denominator = 3
            H = Half
            T = Third
            System.Console.WriteLine(CBool(CType(H, Rational).CompareTo(H)))
            System.Console.WriteLine(CBool(Half.CompareTo(T)))
            System.Console.WriteLine(Half.ToString())
            System.Console.WriteLine(T.ToString())
            Temporary = Half.Mul(Third)
            System.Console.WriteLine(Temporary.ToString())
        End Sub
    End Module
```

Annex C CIL Assembler Implementation

This section contains only informative text.

This section provides information about a particular assembler for CIL, called ilasm. It supports a superset of the syntax defined normatively in Partition II, sections 1–20, and it provides a concrete syntax for the CIL instructions specified in Partition III.

Even for those who have no interest in this particular assembler, Partition V, sections C.1 and C.2 may prove of interest. The former is a machine-readable file (ready for input to a C or C++ preprocessor) that partially describes the CIL instructions. It can be used to generate tables for use by a wide variety of tools that deal with CIL. The latter contains a concrete syntax for CIL instructions, which is not described elsewhere.

C.1 ilasm Keywords

This section provides a complete list of the keywords used by ilasm. If users wish to use any of these as simple identifiers within programs, they just make use of the appropriate escape notation (single or double quotation marks as specified in the grammar). This assembler is case-sensitive.

ANNOTATION

Implementation-Specific (Microsoft): The table below consists of the contents of the file **include\il_kywd.h** from the SDK and the names of all opcodes mentioned in **include\opcode.def** from the Microsoft .NET SDK.

#line
.addon
.assembly
.cctor
.class
.corflags
.ctor
.custom
.data
.emitbyte
.entrypoint
.event
.export
.field
.file
.fire
.get
.hash
.imagebase
.import
.language
.line
.locale
.localized
.locals
.manifestres
.maxstack
.method
.module
.mresource
.namespace
.other
.override
.pack
.param
.pdirect
.permission
.permissionset
.property
.publickey
.publickeytoken
.removeon
.set
.size
.subsystem
.try
.ver
.vtable
.vtentry
.vtfixup
.zeroinit
^THE_END^
abstract
add
add.ovf
add.ovf.un
algorithm
alignment
and
ansi
any
arglist
array
as
assembly
assert
at
auto
autochar
beforefieldinit
beq
beq.s
bge
bge.s
bge.un
bge.un.s
bgt
bgt.s
bgt.un
bgt.un.s
ble
ble.s
ble.un
ble.un.s
blob
blob_object
blt
blt.s
blt.un
blt.un.s
bne.un
bne.un.s
bool
box
br
br.s
break
brfalse
brfalse.s
brinst
brinst.s
brnull
brnull.s
brtrue
brtrue.s
brzero
brzero.s
bstr
bytearray
byvalstr
call
calli

callmostderived	conv.ovf.i2.un	decimal	finally
callvirt	conv.ovf.i4	default	fixed
carray	conv.ovf.i4.un	default	float
castclass	conv.ovf.i8	demand	float32
catch	conv.ovf.i8.un	deny	float64
cdecl	conv.ovf.u	div	forwardref
ceq	conv.ovf.u.un	div.un	fromunmanaged
cf	conv.ovf.u1	dup	handler
cgt	conv.ovf.u1.un	endfault	hidebysig
cgt.un	conv.ovf.u2	endfilter	hresult
char	conv.ovf.u2.un	endfinally	idispatch
cil	conv.ovf.u4	endmac	il
ckfinite	conv.ovf.u4.un	enum	illegal
class	conv.ovf.u8	error	implements
clsid	conv.ovf.u8.un	explicit	implicitcom
clt	conv.r.un	extends	implicitres
clt.un	conv.r4	extern	import
const	conv.r8	false	in
conv.i	conv.u	famandassem	inheritcheck
conv.i1	conv.u1	family	init
conv.i2	conv.u2	famorassem	initblk
conv.i4	conv.u4	fastcall	initobj
conv.i8	conv.u8	fastcall	initonly
conv.ovf.i	cpblk	fault	instance
conv.ovf.i.un	cpobj	field	int
conv.ovf.i1	currency	filetime	int16
conv.ovf.i1.un	custom	filter	int32
conv.ovf.i2	date	final	int64

int8
interface
internalcall
isinst
iunknown
jmp
lasterr
lcid
ldarg
ldarg.0
ldarg.1
ldarg.2
ldarg.3
ldarg.s
ldarga
ldarga.s
ldc.i4
ldc.i4.0
ldc.i4.1
ldc.i4.2
ldc.i4.3
ldc.i4.4
ldc.i4.5
ldc.i4.6
ldc.i4.7
ldc.i4.8
ldc.i4.M1
ldc.i4.m1
ldc.i4.s
ldc.i8
ldc.r4
ldc.r8
ldelem.i
ldelem.i1
ldelem.i2
ldelem.i4
ldelem.i8
ldelem.r4
ldelem.r8
ldelem.ref
ldelem.u1
ldelem.u2
ldelem.u4
ldelem.u8
ldelema
ldfld
ldflda
ldftn
ldind.i
ldind.i1
ldind.i2
ldind.i4
ldind.i8
ldind.r4
ldind.r8
ldind.ref
ldind.u1
ldind.u2
ldind.u4
ldind.u8
ldlen
ldloc
ldloc.0
ldloc.1
ldloc.2
ldloc.3
ldloc.s
ldloca
ldloca.s
ldnull
ldobj
ldsfld
ldsflda
ldstr
ldtoken
ldvirtftn
leave
leave.s
linkcheck
literal
localloc
lpstr
lpstruct
lptstr
lpvoid
lpwstr
managed
marshal
method
mkrefany
modopt
modreq
mul
mul.ovf
mul.ovf.un
native
neg
nested
newarr
newobj
newslot
noappdomain
noinlining
nomachine
nomangle
nometadata
noncasdemand
noncasinheritance
noncaslinkdemand
nop
noprocess
not

not_in_gc_heap	privatescope	sizeof	stloc.1
notremotable	protected	special	stloc.2
notserialized	public	specialname	stloc.3
null	readonly	starg	stloc.s
nullref	record	starg.s	stobj
object	refany	static	storage
objectref	refanytype	stdcall	stored_object
opt	refanyval	stdcall	stream
optil	rem	stelem.i	streamed_object
or	rem.un	stelem.i1	string
out	reqmin	stelem.i2	struct
permitonly	reqopt	stelem.i4	stsfld
pinned	reqrefuse	stelem.i8	sub
pinvokeimpl	reqsecobj	stelem.r4	sub.ovf
pop	request	stelem.r8	sub.ovf.un
prefix1	ret	stelem.ref	switch
prefix2	rethrow	stfld	synchronized
prefix3	retval	stind.i	syschar
prefix4	rtspecialname	stind.i1	sysstring
prefix5	runtime	stind.i2	tail.
prefix6	safearray	stind.i4	tbstr
prefix7	sealed	stind.i8	thiscall
prefixref	sequential	stind.r4	thiscall
prejitdeny	serializable	stind.r8	throw
prejitgrant	shl	stind.ref	tls
preservesig	shr	stloc	to
private	shr.un	stloc.0	true

typedref	unsigned	variant	winapi
unaligned.	unused	vector	with
unbox	userdefined	virtual	wrapper
unicode	value	void	xor
unmanaged	valuetype	volatile.	
unmanagedexp	vararg	wchar	

C.2 CIL Opcode Descriptions

This section contains text which is intended for use with the C or C++ preprocessor. By appropriately defining the macros `OPDEF` and `OPALIAS` before including this text, it is possible to use this to produce tables or code for handling CIL instructions.

ANNOTATION: Both the previous section and this one were derived from the public headers of the Microsoft implementation of ilasm. Section C.2 is the only public description of this file. The information in C.2 and the contents of that file are used throughout the Microsoft implementations to describe almost all the information on the operation of the IL instructions, which are encoded using these macros.

Because it is very difficult to add new opcode formats, it is not expected over time that many new opcode formats will be created. So if you want to design extensions to the VES, it would be best to ensure that your opcodes have one of these encodings, and that what it pops off of and pushes onto the stack follow these guidelines. Thus, in designing new machine instructions, Microsoft tries to keep within this set, extending it as little as possible. Similarly, it uses this information to handle control flow issues.

This information can be used for building other tools. Microsoft uses it to build one of the verifiers.

– Jim Miller

The `OPDEF` macro is passed ten arguments, in the following order:

1. A symbolic name for the opcode, beginning with "CEE_".
2. A string that constitutes the name of the opcode and corresponds to the names given in Partition III.

3. Data removed from the stack to compute this operations result. The possible values here are the following:
   a. **Pop0** – no inputs.
   b. **Pop1** – one value type specified by data flow.
   c. **Pop1+Pop1** – two input values, types specified by data flow.
   d. **PopI** – one machine-sized integer.
   e. **PopI+Pop1** – top of stack is described by data flow; next item is a native pointer.
   f. **PopI+PopI** – top two items on stack are integers (size may vary by instruction).
   g. **PopI+PopI+PopI** – top three items on stack are machine-sized integers.
   h. **PopI8+Pop8** – top of stack is an 8-byte integer; next is a native pointer.
   i. **PopI+PopR4** – top of stack is a 4-byte floating point number; next is a native pointer.
   j. **PopI+PopR8** – top of stack is an 8-byte floating point number; next is a native pointer.
   k. **PopRef** – top of stack is an object reference.
   l. **PopRef+PopI** – top of stack is an integer (size may vary by instruction); next is an object reference.
   m. **PopRef+PopI+PopI** – top of stack has two integers (size may vary by instruction); next is an object reference.
   n. **PopRef+PopI+PopI8** – top of stack is an 8-byte integer, then a native-sized integer, then an object reference.
   o. **PopRef+PopI+PopR4** – top of stack is a 4-byte floating point number, then a native-sized integer, then an object reference.
   p. **PopRef+PopI+PopR8** – Top of stack is an 8-byte floating point number, then a native-sized integer, then an object reference.
   q. **VarPop** – variable number of items used; see Partition III for details.
4. Amount and type of data pushed as a result of the instruction. The possible values here are the following:
   a. **Push0** – no output value.
   b. **Push1** – one output value, type defined by data flow.
   c. **Push1+Push1** – two output values, type defined by data flow.
   d. **PushI** – push one native integer or pointer.
   e. **PushI8** – push one 8-byte integer.

   f. **PushR4** – push one 4-byte floating point number.
   g. **PushR8** – push one 8-byte floating point number.
   h. **PushRef** – push one object reference.
   i. **VarPush** – variable number of items pushed; see Partition III for details.
5. Type of in-line argument to instruction. The in-line argument is stored with least significant byte first ("little-endian"). The possible values here are the following:
   a. **InlineBrTarget** – branch target, represented as a 4-byte signed integer from the beginning of the instruction following the current instruction.
   b. **InlineField** – metadata token (4 bytes) representing a *FieldRef* (i.e., a *MemberRef* to a field) or *FieldDef*.
   c. **InlineI** – 4-byte integer.
   d. **InlineI8** – 8-byte integer.
   e. **InlineMethod** – metadata token (4 bytes) representing a *MethodRef* (i.e., a *MemberRef* to a method) or *MethodDef*.
   f. **InlineNone** – no in-line argument.
   g. **InlineR** – 8-byte floating point number.
   h. **InlineSig** – metadata token (4 bytes) representing a stand-alone signature.
   i. **InlineString** – metadata token (4 bytes) representing a UserString.
   j. **InlineSwitch** – special for the switch instructions; see Partition III [section 3.66] for details.
   k. **InlineTok** – arbitrary metadata token (4 bytes), used for `ldtoken` instruction; see Partition III [section 4.16] for details.
   l. **InlineType** – metadata token (4 bytes) representing a *TypeDef*, *TypeRef*, or *TypeSpec*.
   m. **InlineVar** – 2-byte integer representing an argument or local variable.
   n. **ShortInlineBrTarget** – short branch target, represented as 1 signed byte from the beginning of the instruction following the current instruction.
   o. **ShortInlineI** – 1-byte integer, signed or unsigned depending on instruction.
   p. **ShortInlineR** – 4-byte floating point number.
   q. **ShortInlineVar** – 1-byte integer representing an argument or local variable.
6. Type of opcode. The current classification is of no current value, but is retained for historical reasons.
7. Number of bytes for the opcode. Currently 1 or 2; can be 4 in future.
8. First byte of 2-byte encoding, or 0xFF if single-byte instruction.

9. 1-byte encoding, or second byte of 2-byte encoding.
10. Control flow implications of instruction. The possible values here are the following:
    a. **BRANCH** – unconditional branch
    b. **CALL** – method call
    c. **COND_BRANCH** – conditional branch
    d. **META** – unused operation or prefix code
    e. **NEXT** – control flow unaltered ("fall through")
    f. **RETURN** – return from method
    g. **THROW** – throw or rethrow an exception

The `OPALIAS` macro takes three arguments:

1. A symbolic name for a "new instruction" which is simply an alias (renaming for the assembler) of an existing instruction.
2. A string name for the "new instruction."
3. The symbolic name for an instruction introduced using the `OPDEF` macro. The "new instruction" is really just an alternative name for this instruction.

ANNOTATION

Implementation-Specific (Microsoft): This file is available as **include\opcode.def** in the Microsoft .NET SDK.

```
#ifndef __OPCODE_DEF_
#define __OPCODE_DEF_

#define MOOT    0x00    // Marks unused second byte when encoding single
#define STP1    0xFE    // Prefix code 1 for Standard Map
#define REFPRE  0xFF    // Prefix for Reference Code Encoding
#define RESERVED_PREFIX_START 0xF7

#endif

// If the first byte of the standard encoding is 0xFF, then
// the second byte can be used as 1-byte encoding. Otherwise
l   b         b
```

```
// the encoding is 2 bytes.
e   y        y
//
n   t        t
//
g   e        e
//
(unused)     t
//  Canonical Name                          String Name                     Stack Behaviour
Operand Params    Opcode Kind       h    1         2     Control Flow
// --------------------------------------------------------------------------------
--------------------------------------------------------------------
OPDEF(CEE_NOP,                     "nop",              Pop0,                 Push0,
InlineNone,            IPrimitive,  1,   0xFF,     0x00,     NEXT)

OPDEF(CEE_BREAK,                   "break",            Pop0,                 Push0,
InlineNone,            IPrimitive,  1,   0xFF,     0x01,     BREAK)

OPDEF(CEE_LDARG_0,                 "ldarg.0",          Pop0,                 Push1,
InlineNone,            IMacro,      1,   0xFF,     0x02,     NEXT)

OPDEF(CEE_LDARG_1,                 "ldarg.1",          Pop0,                 Push1,
InlineNone,            IMacro,      1,   0xFF,     0x03,     NEXT)

OPDEF(CEE_LDARG_2,                 "ldarg.2",          Pop0,                 Push1,
InlineNone,            IMacro,      1,   0xFF,     0x04,     NEXT)

OPDEF(CEE_LDARG_3,                 "ldarg.3",          Pop0,                 Push1,
InlineNone,            IMacro,      1,   0xFF,     0x05,     NEXT)

OPDEF(CEE_LDLOC_0,                 "ldloc.0",          Pop0,                 Push1,
InlineNone,            IMacro,      1,   0xFF,     0x06,     NEXT)

OPDEF(CEE_LDLOC_1,                 "ldloc.1",          Pop0,                 Push1,
InlineNone,            IMacro,      1,   0xFF,     0x07,     NEXT)

OPDEF(CEE_LDLOC_2,                 "ldloc.2",          Pop0,                 Push1,
InlineNone,            IMacro,      1,   0xFF,     0x08,     NEXT)

OPDEF(CEE_LDLOC_3,                 "ldloc.3",          Pop0,                 Push1,
InlineNone,            IMacro,      1,   0xFF,     0x09,     NEXT)
```

```
OPDEF(CEE_STLOC_0,              "stloc.0",        Pop1,           Push0,
InlineNone,           IMacro,       1,   0xFF,    0x0A,     NEXT)

OPDEF(CEE_STLOC_1,              "stloc.1",        Pop1,           Push0,
InlineNone,           IMacro,       1,   0xFF,    0x0B,     NEXT)

OPDEF(CEE_STLOC_2,              "stloc.2",        Pop1,           Push0,
InlineNone,           IMacro,       1,   0xFF,    0x0C,     NEXT)

OPDEF(CEE_STLOC_3,              "stloc.3",        Pop1,           Push0,
InlineNone,           IMacro,       1,   0xFF,    0x0D,     NEXT)

OPDEF(CEE_LDARG_S,              "ldarg.s",        Pop0,           Push1,
ShortInlineVar,       IMacro,       1,   0xFF,    0x0E,     NEXT)

OPDEF(CEE_LDARGA_S,             "ldarga.s",       Pop0,           PushI,
ShortInlineVar,       IMacro,       1,   0xFF,    0x0F,     NEXT)
OPDEF(CEE_STARG_S,              "starg.s",        Pop1,           Push0,
ShortInlineVar,       IMacro,       1,   0xFF,    0x10,     NEXT)

OPDEF(CEE_LDLOC_S,              "ldloc.s",        Pop0,           Push1,
ShortInlineVar,       IMacro,       1,   0xFF,    0x11,     NEXT)

OPDEF(CEE_LDLOCA_S,             "ldloca.s",       Pop0,           PushI,
ShortInlineVar,       IMacro,       1,   0xFF,    0x12,     NEXT)

OPDEF(CEE_STLOC_S,              "stloc.s",        Pop1,           Push0,
ShortInlineVar,       IMacro,       1,   0xFF,    0x13,     NEXT)

OPDEF(CEE_LDNULL,               "ldnull",         Pop0,           PushRef,
InlineNone,           IPrimitive,   1,   0xFF,    0x14,     NEXT)

OPDEF(CEE_LDC_I4_M1,            "ldc.i4.m1",      Pop0,           PushI,
InlineNone,           IMacro,       1,   0xFF,    0x15,     NEXT)

OPDEF(CEE_LDC_I4_0,             "ldc.i4.0",       Pop0,           PushI,
InlineNone,           IMacro,       1,   0xFF,    0x16,     NEXT)

OPDEF(CEE_LDC_I4_1,             "ldc.i4.1",       Pop0,           PushI,
InlineNone,           IMacro,       1,   0xFF,    0x17,     NEXT)
```

8. Annexes

```
OPDEF(CEE_LDC_I4_2,            "ldc.i4.2",        Pop0,                PushI,
InlineNone,          IMacro,        1,   0xFF,    0x18,     NEXT)

OPDEF(CEE_LDC_I4_3,            "ldc.i4.3",        Pop0,                PushI,
InlineNone,          IMacro,        1,   0xFF,    0x19,     NEXT)

OPDEF(CEE_LDC_I4_4,            "ldc.i4.4",        Pop0,                PushI,
InlineNone,          IMacro,        1,   0xFF,    0x1A,     NEXT)

OPDEF(CEE_LDC_I4_5,            "ldc.i4.5",        Pop0,                PushI,
InlineNone,          IMacro,        1,   0xFF,    0x1B,     NEXT)

OPDEF(CEE_LDC_I4_6,            "ldc.i4.6",        Pop0,                PushI,
InlineNone,          IMacro,        1,   0xFF,    0x1C,     NEXT)

OPDEF(CEE_LDC_I4_7,            "ldc.i4.7",        Pop0,                PushI,
InlineNone,          IMacro,        1,   0xFF,    0x1D,     NEXT)
OPDEF(CEE_LDC_I4_8,            "ldc.i4.8",        Pop0,                PushI,
InlineNone,          IMacro,        1,   0xFF,    0x1E,     NEXT)

OPDEF(CEE_LDC_I4_S,            "ldc.i4.s",        Pop0,                PushI,
ShortInlineI,        IMacro,        1,   0xFF,    0x1F,     NEXT)

OPDEF(CEE_LDC_I4,              "ldc.i4",          Pop0,                PushI,
InlineI,             IPrimitive,    1,   0xFF,    0x20,     NEXT)

OPDEF(CEE_LDC_I8,              "ldc.i8",          Pop0,                PushI8,
InlineI8,            IPrimitive,    1,   0xFF,    0x21,     NEXT)

OPDEF(CEE_LDC_R4,              "ldc.r4",          Pop0,                PushR4,
ShortInlineR,        IPrimitive,    1,   0xFF,    0x22,     NEXT)

OPDEF(CEE_LDC_R8,              "ldc.r8",          Pop0,                PushR8,
InlineR,             IPrimitive,    1,   0xFF,    0x23,     NEXT)

OPDEF(CEE_UNUSED49,            "unused",          Pop0,                Push0,
InlineNone,          IPrimitive,    1,   0xFF,    0x24,     NEXT)

OPDEF(CEE_DUP,                 "dup",             Pop1,                Push1+Push1,
InlineNone,          IPrimitive,    1,   0xFF,    0x25,     NEXT)
```

8. Annexes

```
OPDEF(CEE_POP,                "pop",            Pop1,             Push0,
InlineNone,          IPrimitive,  1,  0xFF,    0x26,    NEXT)

OPDEF(CEE_JMP,                "jmp",            Pop0,             Push0,
InlineMethod,        IPrimitive,  1,  0xFF,    0x27,    CALL)

OPDEF(CEE_CALL,               "call",           VarPop,           VarPush,
InlineMethod,        IPrimitive,  1,  0xFF,    0x28,    CALL)

OPDEF(CEE_CALLI,              "calli",          VarPop,           VarPush,
InlineSig,           IPrimitive,  1,  0xFF,    0x29,    CALL)

OPDEF(CEE_RET,                "ret",            VarPop,           Push0,
InlineNone,          IPrimitive,  1,  0xFF,    0x2A,    RETURN)

OPDEF(CEE_BR_S,               "br.s",           Pop0,             Push0,
ShortInlineBrTarget,IMacro,       1,  0xFF,    0x2B,    BRANCH)

OPDEF(CEE_BRFALSE_S,          "brfalse.s",      PopI,             Push0,
ShortInlineBrTarget,IMacro,       1,  0xFF,    0x2C,    COND_BRANCH)

OPDEF(CEE_BRTRUE_S,           "brtrue.s",       PopI,             Push0,
ShortInlineBrTarget,IMacro,       1,  0xFF,    0x2D,    COND_BRANCH)

OPDEF(CEE_BEQ_S,              "beq.s",          Pop1+Pop1,        Push0,
ShortInlineBrTarget,IMacro,       1,  0xFF,    0x2E,    COND_BRANCH)

OPDEF(CEE_BGE_S,              "bge.s",          Pop1+Pop1,        Push0,
ShortInlineBrTarget,IMacro,       1,  0xFF,    0x2F,    COND_BRANCH)

OPDEF(CEE_BGT_S,              "bgt.s",          Pop1+Pop1,        Push0,
ShortInlineBrTarget,IMacro,       1,  0xFF,    0x30,    COND_BRANCH)

OPDEF(CEE_BLE_S,              "ble.s",          Pop1+Pop1,        Push0,
ShortInlineBrTarget,IMacro,       1,  0xFF,    0x31,    COND_BRANCH)

OPDEF(CEE_BLT_S,              "blt.s",          Pop1+Pop1,        Push0,
ShortInlineBrTarget,IMacro,       1,  0xFF,    0x32,    COND_BRANCH)

OPDEF(CEE_BNE_UN_S,           "bne.un.s",       Pop1+Pop1,        Push0,
ShortInlineBrTarget,IMacro,       1,  0xFF,    0x33,    COND_BRANCH)
```

```
OPDEF(CEE_BGE_UN_S,           "bge.un.s",        Pop1+Pop1,         Push0,
ShortInlineBrTarget,IMacro,       1,   0xFF,     0x34,      COND_BRANCH)

OPDEF(CEE_BGT_UN_S,           "bgt.un.s",        Pop1+Pop1,         Push0,
ShortInlineBrTarget,IMacro,       1,   0xFF,     0x35,      COND_BRANCH)

OPDEF(CEE_BLE_UN_S,           "ble.un.s",        Pop1+Pop1,         Push0,
ShortInlineBrTarget,IMacro,       1,   0xFF,     0x36,      COND_BRANCH)

OPDEF(CEE_BLT_UN_S,           "blt.un.s",        Pop1+Pop1,         Push0,
ShortInlineBrTarget,IMacro,       1,   0xFF,     0x37,      COND_BRANCH)

OPDEF(CEE_BR,                 "br",              Pop0,              Push0,
InlineBrTarget,     IPrimitive,  1,   0xFF,     0x38,      BRANCH)

OPDEF(CEE_BRFALSE,            "brfalse",         PopI,              Push0,
InlineBrTarget,     IPrimitive,  1,   0xFF,     0x39,      COND_BRANCH)

OPDEF(CEE_BRTRUE,             "brtrue",          PopI,              Push0,
InlineBrTarget,     IPrimitive,  1,   0xFF,     0x3A,      COND_BRANCH)

OPDEF(CEE_BEQ,                "beq",             Pop1+Pop1,         Push0,
InlineBrTarget,     IMacro,       1,   0xFF,     0x3B,      COND_BRANCH)

OPDEF(CEE_BGE,                "bge",             Pop1+Pop1,         Push0,
InlineBrTarget,     IMacro,       1,   0xFF,     0x3C,      COND_BRANCH)

OPDEF(CEE_BGT,                "bgt",             Pop1+Pop1,         Push0,
InlineBrTarget,     IMacro,       1,   0xFF,     0x3D,      COND_BRANCH)

OPDEF(CEE_BLE,                "ble",             Pop1+Pop1,         Push0,
InlineBrTarget,     IMacro,       1,   0xFF,     0x3E,      COND_BRANCH)

OPDEF(CEE_BLT,                "blt",             Pop1+Pop1,         Push0,
InlineBrTarget,     IMacro,       1,   0xFF,     0x3F,      COND_BRANCH)

OPDEF(CEE_BNE_UN,             "bne.un",          Pop1+Pop1,         Push0,
InlineBrTarget,     IMacro,       1,   0xFF,     0x40,      COND_BRANCH)

OPDEF(CEE_BGE_UN,             "bge.un",          Pop1+Pop1,         Push0,
InlineBrTarget,     IMacro,       1,   0xFF,     0x41,      COND_BRANCH)
```

```
OPDEF(CEE_BGT_UN,             "bgt.un",        Pop1+Pop1,        Push0,
InlineBrTarget,    IMacro,       1,   0xFF,    0x42,     COND_BRANCH)

OPDEF(CEE_BLE_UN,             "ble.un",        Pop1+Pop1,        Push0,
InlineBrTarget,    IMacro,       1,   0xFF,    0x43,     COND_BRANCH)

OPDEF(CEE_BLT_UN,             "blt.un",        Pop1+Pop1,        Push0,
InlineBrTarget,    IMacro,       1,   0xFF,    0x44,     COND_BRANCH)

OPDEF(CEE_SWITCH,             "switch",        PopI,             Push0,
InlineSwitch,      IPrimitive,   1,   0xFF,    0x45,     COND_BRANCH)

OPDEF(CEE_LDIND_I1,           "ldind.i1",      PopI,             PushI,
InlineNone,        IPrimitive,   1,   0xFF,    0x46,     NEXT)

OPDEF(CEE_LDIND_U1,           "ldind.u1",      PopI,             PushI,
InlineNone,        IPrimitive,   1,   0xFF,    0x47,     NEXT)

OPDEF(CEE_LDIND_I2,           "ldind.i2",      PopI,             PushI,
InlineNone,        IPrimitive,   1,   0xFF,    0x48,     NEXT)

OPDEF(CEE_LDIND_U2,           "ldind.u2",      PopI,             PushI,
InlineNone,        IPrimitive,   1,   0xFF,    0x49,     NEXT)

OPDEF(CEE_LDIND_I4,           "ldind.i4",      PopI,             PushI,
InlineNone,        IPrimitive,   1,   0xFF,    0x4A,     NEXT)

OPDEF(CEE_LDIND_U4,           "ldind.u4",      PopI,             PushI,
InlineNone,        IPrimitive,   1,   0xFF,    0x4B,     NEXT)

OPDEF(CEE_LDIND_I8,           "ldind.i8",      PopI,             PushI8,
InlineNone,        IPrimitive,   1,   0xFF,    0x4C,     NEXT)

OPDEF(CEE_LDIND_I,            "ldind.i",       PopI,             PushI,
InlineNone,        IPrimitive,   1,   0xFF,    0x4D,     NEXT)

OPDEF(CEE_LDIND_R4,           "ldind.r4",      PopI,             PushR4,
InlineNone,        IPrimitive,   1,   0xFF,    0x4E,     NEXT)

OPDEF(CEE_LDIND_R8,           "ldind.r8",      PopI,             PushR8,
InlineNone,        IPrimitive,   1,   0xFF,    0x4F,     NEXT)
```

```
OPDEF(CEE_LDIND_REF,          "ldind.ref",        PopI,                 PushRef,
InlineNone,          IPrimitive,  1,  0xFF,    0x50,     NEXT)

OPDEF(CEE_STIND_REF,          "stind.ref",        PopI+PopI,            Push0,
InlineNone,          IPrimitive,  1,  0xFF,    0x51,     NEXT)

OPDEF(CEE_STIND_I1,           "stind.i1",         PopI+PopI,            Push0,
InlineNone,          IPrimitive,  1,  0xFF,    0x52,     NEXT)

OPDEF(CEE_STIND_I2,           "stind.i2",         PopI+PopI,            Push0,
InlineNone,          IPrimitive,  1,  0xFF,    0x53,     NEXT)

OPDEF(CEE_STIND_I4,           "stind.i4",         PopI+PopI,            Push0,
InlineNone,          IPrimitive,  1,  0xFF,    0x54,     NEXT)

OPDEF(CEE_STIND_I8,           "stind.i8",         PopI+PopI8,           Push0,
InlineNone,          IPrimitive,  1,  0xFF,    0x55,     NEXT)

OPDEF(CEE_STIND_R4,           "stind.r4",         PopI+PopR4,           Push0,
InlineNone,          IPrimitive,  1,  0xFF,    0x56,     NEXT)

OPDEF(CEE_STIND_R8,           "stind.r8",         PopI+PopR8,           Push0,
InlineNone,          IPrimitive,  1,  0xFF,    0x57,     NEXT)

OPDEF(CEE_ADD,                "add",              Pop1+Pop1,            Push1,
InlineNone,          IPrimitive,  1,  0xFF,    0x58,     NEXT)

OPDEF(CEE_SUB,                "sub",              Pop1+Pop1,            Push1,
InlineNone,          IPrimitive,  1,  0xFF,    0x59,     NEXT)

OPDEF(CEE_MUL,                "mul",              Pop1+Pop1,            Push1,
InlineNone,          IPrimitive,  1,  0xFF,    0x5A,     NEXT)

OPDEF(CEE_DIV,                "div",              Pop1+Pop1,            Push1,
InlineNone,          IPrimitive,  1,  0xFF,    0x5B,     NEXT)

OPDEF(CEE_DIV_UN,             "div.un",           Pop1+Pop1,            Push1,
InlineNone,          IPrimitive,  1,  0xFF,    0x5C,     NEXT)

OPDEF(CEE_REM,                "rem",              Pop1+Pop1,            Push1,
InlineNone,          IPrimitive,  1,  0xFF,    0x5D,     NEXT)
```

```
OPDEF(CEE_REM_UN,            "rem.un",            Pop1+Pop1,         Push1,
InlineNone,          IPrimitive,  1,  0xFF,     0x5E,     NEXT)

OPDEF(CEE_AND,               "and",               Pop1+Pop1,         Push1,
InlineNone,          IPrimitive,  1,  0xFF,     0x5F,     NEXT)

OPDEF(CEE_OR,                "or",                Pop1+Pop1,         Push1,
InlineNone,          IPrimitive,  1,  0xFF,     0x60,     NEXT)

OPDEF(CEE_XOR,               "xor",               Pop1+Pop1,         Push1,
InlineNone,          IPrimitive,  1,  0xFF,     0x61,     NEXT)

OPDEF(CEE_SHL,               "shl",               Pop1+Pop1,         Push1,
InlineNone,          IPrimitive,  1,  0xFF,     0x62,     NEXT)

OPDEF(CEE_SHR,               "shr",               Pop1+Pop1,         Push1,
InlineNone,          IPrimitive,  1,  0xFF,     0x63,     NEXT)

OPDEF(CEE_SHR_UN,            "shr.un",            Pop1+Pop1,         Push1,
InlineNone,          IPrimitive,  1,  0xFF,     0x64,     NEXT)

OPDEF(CEE_NEG,               "neg",               Pop1,              Push1,
InlineNone,          IPrimitive,  1,  0xFF,     0x65,     NEXT)

OPDEF(CEE_NOT,               "not",               Pop1,              Push1,
InlineNone,          IPrimitive,  1,  0xFF,     0x66,     NEXT)

OPDEF(CEE_CONV_I1,           "conv.i1",           Pop1,              PushI,
InlineNone,          IPrimitive,  1,  0xFF,     0x67,     NEXT)

OPDEF(CEE_CONV_I2,           "conv.i2",           Pop1,              PushI,
InlineNone,          IPrimitive,  1,  0xFF,     0x68,     NEXT)

OPDEF(CEE_CONV_I4,           "conv.i4",           Pop1,              PushI,
InlineNone,          IPrimitive,  1,  0xFF,     0x69,     NEXT)

OPDEF(CEE_CONV_I8,           "conv.i8",           Pop1,              PushI8,
InlineNone,          IPrimitive,  1,  0xFF,     0x6A,     NEXT)

OPDEF(CEE_CONV_R4,           "conv.r4",           Pop1,              PushR4,
InlineNone,          IPrimitive,  1,  0xFF,     0x6B,     NEXT)
```

```
OPDEF(CEE_CONV_R8,            "conv.r8",          Pop1,              PushR8,
InlineNone,         IPrimitive,  1,  0xFF,     0x6C,     NEXT)

OPDEF(CEE_CONV_U4,            "conv.u4",          Pop1,              PushI,
InlineNone,         IPrimitive,  1,  0xFF,     0x6D,     NEXT)

OPDEF(CEE_CONV_U8,            "conv.u8",          Pop1,              PushI8,
InlineNone,         IPrimitive,  1,  0xFF,     0x6E,     NEXT)

OPDEF(CEE_CALLVIRT,           "callvirt",         VarPop,            VarPush,
InlineMethod,       IObjModel,   1,  0xFF,     0x6F,     CALL)

OPDEF(CEE_CPOBJ,              "cpobj",            PopI+PopI,         Push0,
InlineType,         IObjModel,   1,  0xFF,     0x70,     NEXT)

OPDEF(CEE_LDOBJ,              "ldobj",            PopI,              Push1,
InlineType,         IObjModel,   1,  0xFF,     0x71,     NEXT)

OPDEF(CEE_LDSTR,              "ldstr",            Pop0,              PushRef,
InlineString,       IObjModel,   1,  0xFF,     0x72,     NEXT)

OPDEF(CEE_NEWOBJ,             "newobj",           VarPop,            PushRef,
InlineMethod,       IObjModel,   1,  0xFF,     0x73,     CALL)

OPDEF(CEE_CASTCLASS,          "castclass",        PopRef,            PushRef,
InlineType,         IObjModel,   1,  0xFF,     0x74,     NEXT)

OPDEF(CEE_ISINST,             "isinst",           PopRef,            PushI,
InlineType,         IObjModel,   1,  0xFF,     0x75,     NEXT)

OPDEF(CEE_CONV_R_UN,          "conv.r.un",        Pop1,              PushR8,
InlineNone,         IPrimitive,  1,  0xFF,     0x76,     NEXT)

OPDEF(CEE_UNUSED58,           "unused",           Pop0,              Push0,
InlineNone,         IPrimitive,  1,  0xFF,     0x77,     NEXT)

OPDEF(CEE_UNUSED1,            "unused",           Pop0,              Push0,
InlineNone,         IPrimitive,  1,  0xFF,     0x78,     NEXT)

OPDEF(CEE_UNBOX,              "unbox",            PopRef,            PushI,
InlineType,         IPrimitive,  1,  0xFF,     0x79,     NEXT)
```

8. Annexes

```
OPDEF(CEE_THROW,              "throw",           PopRef,          Push0,
InlineNone,          IObjModel,   1,   0xFF,     0x7A,     THROW)

OPDEF(CEE_LDFLD,              "ldfld",           PopRef,          Push1,
InlineField,         IObjModel,   1,   0xFF,     0x7B,     NEXT)

OPDEF(CEE_LDFLDA,             "ldflda",          PopRef,          PushI,
InlineField,         IObjModel,   1,   0xFF,     0x7C,     NEXT)

OPDEF(CEE_STFLD,              "stfld",           PopRef+Pop1,     Push0,
InlineField,         IObjModel,   1,   0xFF,     0x7D,     NEXT)

OPDEF(CEE_LDSFLD,             "ldsfld",          Pop0,            Push1,
InlineField,         IObjModel,   1,   0xFF,     0x7E,     NEXT)

OPDEF(CEE_LDSFLDA,            "ldsflda",         Pop0,            PushI,
InlineField,         IObjModel,   1,   0xFF,     0x7F,     NEXT)

OPDEF(CEE_STSFLD,             "stsfld",          Pop1,            Push0,
InlineField,         IObjModel,   1,   0xFF,     0x80,     NEXT)

OPDEF(CEE_STOBJ,              "stobj",           PopI+Pop1,       Push0,
InlineType,          IPrimitive,  1,   0xFF,     0x81,     NEXT)

OPDEF(CEE_CONV_OVF_I1_UN,     "conv.ovf.i1.un",  Pop1,            PushI,
InlineNone,          IPrimitive,  1,   0xFF,     0x82,     NEXT)

OPDEF(CEE_CONV_OVF_I2_UN,     "conv.ovf.i2.un",  Pop1,            PushI,
InlineNone,          IPrimitive,  1,   0xFF,     0x83,     NEXT)

OPDEF(CEE_CONV_OVF_I4_UN,     "conv.ovf.i4.un",  Pop1,            PushI,
InlineNone,          IPrimitive,  1,   0xFF,     0x84,     NEXT)

OPDEF(CEE_CONV_OVF_I8_UN,     "conv.ovf.i8.un",  Pop1,            PushI8,
InlineNone,          IPrimitive,  1,   0xFF,     0x85,     NEXT)

OPDEF(CEE_CONV_OVF_U1_UN,     "conv.ovf.u1.un",  Pop1,            PushI,
InlineNone,          IPrimitive,  1,   0xFF,     0x86,     NEXT)

OPDEF(CEE_CONV_OVF_U2_UN,     "conv.ovf.u2.un",  Pop1,            PushI,
InlineNone,          IPrimitive,  1,   0xFF,     0x87,     NEXT)
```

```
OPDEF(CEE_CONV_OVF_U4_UN,     "conv.ovf.u4.un",   Pop1,                 PushI,
InlineNone,           IPrimitive,  1,   0xFF,     0x88,     NEXT)

OPDEF(CEE_CONV_OVF_U8_UN,     "conv.ovf.u8.un",   Pop1,                 PushI8,
InlineNone,           IPrimitive,  1,   0xFF,     0x89,     NEXT)

OPDEF(CEE_CONV_OVF_I_UN,      "conv.ovf.i.un",    Pop1,                 PushI,
InlineNone,           IPrimitive,  1,   0xFF,     0x8A,     NEXT)

OPDEF(CEE_CONV_OVF_U_UN,      "conv.ovf.u.un",    Pop1,                 PushI,
InlineNone,           IPrimitive,  1,   0xFF,     0x8B,     NEXT)

OPDEF(CEE_BOX,                "box",              Pop1,                 PushRef,
InlineType,           IPrimitive,  1,   0xFF,     0x8C,     NEXT)

OPDEF(CEE_NEWARR,             "newarr",           PopI,                 PushRef,
InlineType,           IObjModel,   1,   0xFF,     0x8D,     NEXT)

OPDEF(CEE_LDLEN,              "ldlen",            PopRef,               PushI,
InlineNone,           IObjModel,   1,   0xFF,     0x8E,     NEXT)

OPDEF(CEE_LDELEMA,            "ldelema",          PopRef+PopI,          PushI,
InlineType,           IObjModel,   1,   0xFF,     0x8F,     NEXT)

OPDEF(CEE_LDELEM_I1,          "ldelem.i1",        PopRef+PopI,          PushI,
InlineNone,           IObjModel,   1,   0xFF,     0x90,     NEXT)

OPDEF(CEE_LDELEM_U1,          "ldelem.u1",        PopRef+PopI,          PushI,
InlineNone,           IObjModel,   1,   0xFF,     0x91,     NEXT)

OPDEF(CEE_LDELEM_I2,          "ldelem.i2",        PopRef+PopI,          PushI,
InlineNone,           IObjModel,   1,   0xFF,     0x92,     NEXT)

OPDEF(CEE_LDELEM_U2,          "ldelem.u2",        PopRef+PopI,          PushI,
InlineNone,           IObjModel,   1,   0xFF,     0x93,     NEXT)

OPDEF(CEE_LDELEM_I4,          "ldelem.i4",        PopRef+PopI,          PushI,
InlineNone,           IObjModel,   1,   0xFF,     0x94,     NEXT)

OPDEF(CEE_LDELEM_U4,          "ldelem.u4",        PopRef+PopI,          PushI,
InlineNone,           IObjModel,   1,   0xFF,     0x95,     NEXT)
```

```
OPDEF(CEE_LDELEM_I8,          "ldelem.i8",        PopRef+PopI,          PushI8,
InlineNone,          IObjModel,   1,   0xFF,     0x96,     NEXT)

OPDEF(CEE_LDELEM_I,           "ldelem.i",         PopRef+PopI,          PushI,
InlineNone,          IObjModel,   1,   0xFF,     0x97,     NEXT)

OPDEF(CEE_LDELEM_R4,          "ldelem.r4",        PopRef+PopI,          PushR4,
InlineNone,          IObjModel,   1,   0xFF,     0x98,     NEXT)

OPDEF(CEE_LDELEM_R8,          "ldelem.r8",        PopRef+PopI,          PushR8,
InlineNone,          IObjModel,   1,   0xFF,     0x99,     NEXT)

OPDEF(CEE_LDELEM_REF,         "ldelem.ref",       PopRef+PopI,          PushRef,
InlineNone,          IObjModel,   1,   0xFF,     0x9A,     NEXT)

OPDEF(CEE_STELEM_I,           "stelem.i",         PopRef+PopI+PopI,     Push0,
InlineNone,          IObjModel,   1,   0xFF,     0x9B,     NEXT)

OPDEF(CEE_STELEM_I1,          "stelem.i1",        PopRef+PopI+PopI,     Push0,
InlineNone,          IObjModel,   1,   0xFF,     0x9C,     NEXT)

OPDEF(CEE_STELEM_I2,          "stelem.i2",        PopRef+PopI+PopI,     Push0,
InlineNone,          IObjModel,   1,   0xFF,     0x9D,     NEXT)

OPDEF(CEE_STELEM_I4,          "stelem.i4",        PopRef+PopI+PopI,     Push0,
InlineNone,          IObjModel,   1,   0xFF,     0x9E,     NEXT)

OPDEF(CEE_STELEM_I8,          "stelem.i8",        PopRef+PopI+PopI8,    Push0,
InlineNone,          IObjModel,   1,   0xFF,     0x9F,     NEXT)

OPDEF(CEE_STELEM_R4,          "stelem.r4",        PopRef+PopI+PopR4,    Push0,
InlineNone,          IObjModel,   1,   0xFF,     0xA0,     NEXT)

OPDEF(CEE_STELEM_R8,          "stelem.r8",        PopRef+PopI+PopR8,    Push0,
InlineNone,          IObjModel,   1,   0xFF,     0xA1,     NEXT)

OPDEF(CEE_STELEM_REF,         "stelem.ref",       PopRef+PopI+PopRef,   Push0,
InlineNone,          IObjModel,   1,   0xFF,     0xA2,     NEXT)

OPDEF(CEE_UNUSED2,            "unused",           Pop0,                 Push0,
InlineNone,          IPrimitive,  1,   0xFF,     0xA3,     NEXT)
```

8. Annexes

```
OPDEF(CEE_UNUSED3,          "unused",          Pop0,            Push0,
InlineNone,           IPrimitive,  1,  0xFF,    0xA4,    NEXT)

OPDEF(CEE_UNUSED4,          "unused",          Pop0,            Push0,
InlineNone,           IPrimitive,  1,  0xFF,    0xA5,    NEXT)

OPDEF(CEE_UNUSED5,          "unused",          Pop0,            Push0,
InlineNone,           IPrimitive,  1,  0xFF,    0xA6,    NEXT)

OPDEF(CEE_UNUSED6,          "unused",          Pop0,            Push0,
InlineNone,           IPrimitive,  1,  0xFF,    0xA7,    NEXT)

OPDEF(CEE_UNUSED7,          "unused",          Pop0,            Push0,
InlineNone,           IPrimitive,  1,  0xFF,    0xA8,    NEXT)

OPDEF(CEE_UNUSED8,          "unused",          Pop0,            Push0,
InlineNone,           IPrimitive,  1,  0xFF,    0xA9,    NEXT)

OPDEF(CEE_UNUSED9,          "unused",          Pop0,            Push0,
InlineNone,           IPrimitive,  1,  0xFF,    0xAA,    NEXT)

OPDEF(CEE_UNUSED10,         "unused",          Pop0,            Push0,
InlineNone,           IPrimitive,  1,  0xFF,    0xAB,    NEXT)

OPDEF(CEE_UNUSED11,         "unused",          Pop0,            Push0,
InlineNone,           IPrimitive,  1,  0xFF,    0xAC,    NEXT)

OPDEF(CEE_UNUSED12,         "unused",          Pop0,            Push0,
InlineNone,           IPrimitive,  1,  0xFF,    0xAD,    NEXT)

OPDEF(CEE_UNUSED13,         "unused",          Pop0,            Push0,
InlineNone,           IPrimitive,  1,  0xFF,    0xAE,    NEXT)

OPDEF(CEE_UNUSED14,         "unused",          Pop0,            Push0,
InlineNone,           IPrimitive,  1,  0xFF,    0xAF,    NEXT)

OPDEF(CEE_UNUSED15,         "unused",          Pop0,            Push0,
InlineNone,           IPrimitive,  1,  0xFF,    0xB0,    NEXT)

OPDEF(CEE_UNUSED16,         "unused",          Pop0,            Push0,
InlineNone,           IPrimitive,  1,  0xFF,    0xB1,    NEXT)
```

```
OPDEF(CEE_UNUSED17,          "unused",          Pop0,          Push0,
InlineNone,          IPrimitive,  1,  0xFF,     0xB2,     NEXT)

OPDEF(CEE_CONV_OVF_I1,       "conv.ovf.i1",     Pop1,          PushI,
InlineNone,          IPrimitive,  1,  0xFF,     0xB3,     NEXT)

OPDEF(CEE_CONV_OVF_U1,       "conv.ovf.u1",     Pop1,          PushI,
InlineNone,          IPrimitive,  1,  0xFF,     0xB4,     NEXT)

OPDEF(CEE_CONV_OVF_I2,       "conv.ovf.i2",     Pop1,          PushI,
InlineNone,          IPrimitive,  1,  0xFF,     0xB5,     NEXT)

OPDEF(CEE_CONV_OVF_U2,       "conv.ovf.u2",     Pop1,          PushI,
InlineNone,          IPrimitive,  1,  0xFF,     0xB6,     NEXT)

OPDEF(CEE_CONV_OVF_I4,       "conv.ovf.i4",     Pop1,          PushI,
InlineNone,          IPrimitive,  1,  0xFF,     0xB7,     NEXT)

OPDEF(CEE_CONV_OVF_U4,       "conv.ovf.u4",     Pop1,          PushI,
InlineNone,          IPrimitive,  1,  0xFF,     0xB8,     NEXT)

OPDEF(CEE_CONV_OVF_I8,       "conv.ovf.i8",     Pop1,          PushI8,
InlineNone,          IPrimitive,  1,  0xFF,     0xB9,     NEXT)

OPDEF(CEE_CONV_OVF_U8,       "conv.ovf.u8",     Pop1,          PushI8,
InlineNone,          IPrimitive,  1,  0xFF,     0xBA,     NEXT)

OPDEF(CEE_UNUSED50,          "unused",          Pop0,          Push0,
InlineNone,          IPrimitive,  1,  0xFF,     0xBB,     NEXT)

OPDEF(CEE_UNUSED18,          "unused",          Pop0,          Push0,
InlineNone,          IPrimitive,  1,  0xFF,     0xBC,     NEXT)

OPDEF(CEE_UNUSED19,          "unused",          Pop0,          Push0,
InlineNone,          IPrimitive,  1,  0xFF,     0xBD,     NEXT)

OPDEF(CEE_UNUSED20,          "unused",          Pop0,          Push0,
InlineNone,          IPrimitive,  1,  0xFF,     0xBE,     NEXT)

OPDEF(CEE_UNUSED21,          "unused",          Pop0,          Push0,
InlineNone,          IPrimitive,  1,  0xFF,     0xBF,     NEXT)
```

```
OPDEF(CEE_UNUSED22,           "unused",         Pop0,             Push0,
InlineNone,          IPrimitive,  1,  0xFF,     0xC0,     NEXT)

OPDEF(CEE_UNUSED23,           "unused",         Pop0,             Push0,
InlineNone,          IPrimitive,  1,  0xFF,     0xC1,     NEXT)

OPDEF(CEE_REFANYVAL,          "refanyval",      Pop1,             PushI,
InlineType,          IPrimitive,  1,  0xFF,     0xC2,     NEXT)

OPDEF(CEE_CKFINITE,           "ckfinite",       Pop1,             PushR8,
InlineNone,          IPrimitive,  1,  0xFF,     0xC3,     NEXT)

OPDEF(CEE_UNUSED24,           "unused",         Pop0,             Push0,
InlineNone,          IPrimitive,  1,  0xFF,     0xC4,     NEXT)

OPDEF(CEE_UNUSED25,           "unused",         Pop0,             Push0,
InlineNone,          IPrimitive,  1,  0xFF,     0xC5,     NEXT)

OPDEF(CEE_MKREFANY,           "mkrefany",       PopI,             Push1,
InlineType,          IPrimitive,  1,  0xFF,     0xC6,     NEXT)

OPDEF(CEE_UNUSED59,           "unused",         Pop0,             Push0,
InlineNone,          IPrimitive,  1,  0xFF,     0xC7,     NEXT)

OPDEF(CEE_UNUSED60,           "unused",         Pop0,             Push0,
InlineNone,          IPrimitive,  1,  0xFF,     0xC8,     NEXT)

OPDEF(CEE_UNUSED61,           "unused",         Pop0,             Push0,
InlineNone,          IPrimitive,  1,  0xFF,     0xC9,     NEXT)

OPDEF(CEE_UNUSED62,           "unused",         Pop0,             Push0,
InlineNone,          IPrimitive,  1,  0xFF,     0xCA,     NEXT)

OPDEF(CEE_UNUSED63,           "unused",         Pop0,             Push0,
InlineNone,          IPrimitive,  1,  0xFF,     0xCB,     NEXT)

OPDEF(CEE_UNUSED64,           "unused",         Pop0,             Push0,
InlineNone,          IPrimitive,  1,  0xFF,     0xCC,     NEXT)

OPDEF(CEE_UNUSED65,           "unused",         Pop0,             Push0,
InlineNone,          IPrimitive,  1,  0xFF,     0xCD,     NEXT)
```

```
OPDEF(CEE_UNUSED66,          "unused",          Pop0,               Push0,
InlineNone,          IPrimitive,  1,  0xFF,     0xCE,      NEXT)

OPDEF(CEE_UNUSED67,          "unused",          Pop0,               Push0,
InlineNone,          IPrimitive,  1,  0xFF,     0xCF,      NEXT)

OPDEF(CEE_LDTOKEN,           "ldtoken",         Pop0,               PushI,
InlineTok,           IPrimitive,  1,  0xFF,     0xD0,      NEXT)

OPDEF(CEE_CONV_U2,           "conv.u2",         Pop1,               PushI,
InlineNone,          IPrimitive,  1,  0xFF,     0xD1,      NEXT)

OPDEF(CEE_CONV_U1,           "conv.u1",         Pop1,               PushI,
InlineNone,          IPrimitive,  1,  0xFF,     0xD2,      NEXT)

OPDEF(CEE_CONV_I,            "conv.i",          Pop1,               PushI,
InlineNone,          IPrimitive,  1,  0xFF,     0xD3,      NEXT)

OPDEF(CEE_CONV_OVF_I,        "conv.ovf.i",      Pop1,               PushI,
InlineNone,          IPrimitive,  1,  0xFF,     0xD4,      NEXT)

OPDEF(CEE_CONV_OVF_U,        "conv.ovf.u",      Pop1,               PushI,
InlineNone,          IPrimitive,  1,  0xFF,     0xD5,      NEXT)

OPDEF(CEE_ADD_OVF,           "add.ovf",         Pop1+Pop1,          Push1,
InlineNone,          IPrimitive,  1,  0xFF,     0xD6,      NEXT)

OPDEF(CEE_ADD_OVF_UN,        "add.ovf.un",      Pop1+Pop1,          Push1,
InlineNone,          IPrimitive,  1,  0xFF,     0xD7,      NEXT)

OPDEF(CEE_MUL_OVF,           "mul.ovf",         Pop1+Pop1,          Push1,
InlineNone,          IPrimitive,  1,  0xFF,     0xD8,      NEXT)

OPDEF(CEE_MUL_OVF_UN,        "mul.ovf.un",      Pop1+Pop1,          Push1,
InlineNone,          IPrimitive,  1,  0xFF,     0xD9,      NEXT)

OPDEF(CEE_SUB_OVF,           "sub.ovf",         Pop1+Pop1,          Push1,
InlineNone,          IPrimitive,  1,  0xFF,     0xDA,      NEXT)

OPDEF(CEE_SUB_OVF_UN,        "sub.ovf.un",      Pop1+Pop1,          Push1,
InlineNone,          IPrimitive,  1,  0xFF,     0xDB,      NEXT)
```

```
OPDEF(CEE_ENDFINALLY,         "endfinally",         Pop0,                  Push0,
InlineNone,           IPrimitive,  1,   0xFF,     0xDC,     RETURN)

OPDEF(CEE_LEAVE,              "leave",              Pop0,                  Push0,
InlineBrTarget,       IPrimitive,  1,   0xFF,     0xDD,     BRANCH)

OPDEF(CEE_LEAVE_S,            "leave.s",            Pop0,                  Push0,
ShortInlineBrTarget,IPrimitive,  1,   0xFF,     0xDE,     BRANCH)

OPDEF(CEE_STIND_I,            "stind.i",            PopI+PopI,             Push0,
InlineNone,           IPrimitive,  1,   0xFF,     0xDF,     NEXT)

OPDEF(CEE_CONV_U,             "conv.u",             Pop1,                  PushI,
InlineNone,           IPrimitive,  1,   0xFF,     0xE0,     NEXT)

OPDEF(CEE_UNUSED26,           "unused",             Pop0,                  Push0,
InlineNone,           IPrimitive,  1,   0xFF,     0xE1,     NEXT)

OPDEF(CEE_UNUSED27,           "unused",             Pop0,                  Push0,
InlineNone,           IPrimitive,  1,   0xFF,     0xE2,     NEXT)

OPDEF(CEE_UNUSED28,           "unused",             Pop0,                  Push0,
InlineNone,           IPrimitive,  1,   0xFF,     0xE3,     NEXT)

OPDEF(CEE_UNUSED29,           "unused",             Pop0,                  Push0,
InlineNone,           IPrimitive,  1,   0xFF,     0xE4,     NEXT)

OPDEF(CEE_UNUSED30,           "unused",             Pop0,                  Push0,
InlineNone,           IPrimitive,  1,   0xFF,     0xE5,     NEXT)

OPDEF(CEE_UNUSED31,           "unused",             Pop0,                  Push0,
InlineNone,           IPrimitive,  1,   0xFF,     0xE6,     NEXT)

OPDEF(CEE_UNUSED32,           "unused",             Pop0,                  Push0,
InlineNone,           IPrimitive,  1,   0xFF,     0xE7,     NEXT)

OPDEF(CEE_UNUSED33,           "unused",             Pop0,                  Push0,
InlineNone,           IPrimitive,  1,   0xFF,     0xE8,     NEXT)

OPDEF(CEE_UNUSED34,           "unused",             Pop0,                  Push0,
InlineNone,           IPrimitive,  1,   0xFF,     0xE9,     NEXT)
```

```
OPDEF(CEE_UNUSED35,          "unused",          Pop0,               Push0,
InlineNone,          IPrimitive,  1,  0xFF,    0xEA,     NEXT)

OPDEF(CEE_UNUSED36,          "unused",          Pop0,               Push0,
InlineNone,          IPrimitive,  1,  0xFF,    0xEB,     NEXT)

OPDEF(CEE_UNUSED37,          "unused",          Pop0,               Push0,
InlineNone,          IPrimitive,  1,  0xFF,    0xEC,     NEXT)

OPDEF(CEE_UNUSED38,          "unused",          Pop0,               Push0,
InlineNone,          IPrimitive,  1,  0xFF,    0xED,     NEXT)

OPDEF(CEE_UNUSED39,          "unused",          Pop0,               Push0,
InlineNone,          IPrimitive,  1,  0xFF,    0xEE,     NEXT)

OPDEF(CEE_UNUSED40,          "unused",          Pop0,               Push0,
InlineNone,          IPrimitive,  1,  0xFF,    0xEF,     NEXT)

OPDEF(CEE_UNUSED41,          "unused",          Pop0,               Push0,
InlineNone,          IPrimitive,  1,  0xFF,    0xF0,     NEXT)

OPDEF(CEE_UNUSED42,          "unused",          Pop0,               Push0,
InlineNone,          IPrimitive,  1,  0xFF,    0xF1,     NEXT)

OPDEF(CEE_UNUSED43,          "unused",          Pop0,               Push0,
InlineNone,          IPrimitive,  1,  0xFF,    0xF2,     NEXT)

OPDEF(CEE_UNUSED44,          "unused",          Pop0,               Push0,
InlineNone,          IPrimitive,  1,  0xFF,    0xF3,     NEXT)

OPDEF(CEE_UNUSED45,          "unused",          Pop0,               Push0,
InlineNone,          IPrimitive,  1,  0xFF,    0xF4,     NEXT)

OPDEF(CEE_UNUSED46,          "unused",          Pop0,               Push0,
InlineNone,          IPrimitive,  1,  0xFF,    0xF5,     NEXT)

OPDEF(CEE_UNUSED47,          "unused",          Pop0,               Push0,
InlineNone,          IPrimitive,  1,  0xFF,    0xF6,     NEXT)

OPDEF(CEE_UNUSED48,          "unused",          Pop0,               Push0,
InlineNone,          IPrimitive,  1,  0xFF,    0xF7,     NEXT)
```

```
OPDEF(CEE_PREFIX7,              "prefix7",              Pop0,                   Push0,
InlineNone,             IInternal,   1,   0xFF,     0xF8,     META)

OPDEF(CEE_PREFIX6,              "prefix6",              Pop0,                   Push0,
InlineNone,             IInternal,   1,   0xFF,     0xF9,     META)

OPDEF(CEE_PREFIX5,              "prefix5",              Pop0,                   Push0,
InlineNone,             IInternal,   1,   0xFF,     0xFA,     META)

OPDEF(CEE_PREFIX4,              "prefix4",              Pop0,                   Push0,
InlineNone,             IInternal,   1,   0xFF,     0xFB,     META)

OPDEF(CEE_PREFIX3,              "prefix3",              Pop0,                   Push0,
InlineNone,             IInternal,   1,   0xFF,     0xFC,     META)

OPDEF(CEE_PREFIX2,              "prefix2",              Pop0,                   Push0,
InlineNone,             IInternal,   1,   0xFF,     0xFD,     META)

OPDEF(CEE_PREFIX1,              "prefix1",              Pop0,                   Push0,
InlineNone,             IInternal,   1,   0xFF,     0xFE,     META)

OPDEF(CEE_PREFIXREF,            "prefixref",            Pop0,                   Push0,
InlineNone,             IInternal,   1,   0xFF,     0xFF,     META)


OPDEF(CEE_ARGLIST,              "arglist",              Pop0,                   PushI,
InlineNone,             IPrimitive,  2,   0xFE,     0x00,     NEXT)

OPDEF(CEE_CEQ,                  "ceq",                  Pop1+Pop1,              PushI,
InlineNone,             IPrimitive,  2,   0xFE,     0x01,     NEXT)

OPDEF(CEE_CGT,                  "cgt",                  Pop1+Pop1,              PushI,
InlineNone,             IPrimitive,  2,   0xFE,     0x02,     NEXT)

OPDEF(CEE_CGT_UN,               "cgt.un",               Pop1+Pop1,              PushI,
InlineNone,             IPrimitive,  2,   0xFE,     0x03,     NEXT)

OPDEF(CEE_CLT,                  "clt",                  Pop1+Pop1,              PushI,
InlineNone,             IPrimitive,  2,   0xFE,     0x04,     NEXT)
```

8. Annexes

```
OPDEF(CEE_CLT_UN,              "clt.un",          Pop1+Pop1,          PushI,
InlineNone,         IPrimitive,  2,   0xFE,     0x05,     NEXT)

OPDEF(CEE_LDFTN,               "ldftn",           Pop0,               PushI,
InlineMethod,       IPrimitive,  2,   0xFE,     0x06,     NEXT)

OPDEF(CEE_LDVIRTFTN,           "ldvirtftn",       PopRef,             PushI,
InlineMethod,       IPrimitive,  2,   0xFE,     0x07,     NEXT)

OPDEF(CEE_UNUSED56,            "unused",          Pop0,               Push0,
InlineNone,         IPrimitive,  2,   0xFE,     0x08,     NEXT)

OPDEF(CEE_LDARG,               "ldarg",           Pop0,               Push1,
InlineVar,          IPrimitive,  2,   0xFE,     0x09,     NEXT)

OPDEF(CEE_LDARGA,              "ldarga",          Pop0,               PushI,
InlineVar,          IPrimitive,  2,   0xFE,     0x0A,     NEXT)

OPDEF(CEE_STARG,               "starg",           Pop1,               Push0,
InlineVar,          IPrimitive,  2,   0xFE,     0x0B,     NEXT)

OPDEF(CEE_LDLOC,               "ldloc",           Pop0,               Push1,
InlineVar,          IPrimitive,  2,   0xFE,     0x0C,     NEXT)

OPDEF(CEE_LDLOCA,              "ldloca",          Pop0,               PushI,
InlineVar,          IPrimitive,  2,   0xFE,     0x0D,     NEXT)

OPDEF(CEE_STLOC,               "stloc",           Pop1,               Push0,
InlineVar,          IPrimitive,  2,   0xFE,     0x0E,     NEXT)

OPDEF(CEE_LOCALLOC,            "localloc",        PopI,               PushI,
InlineNone,         IPrimitive,  2,   0xFE,     0x0F,     NEXT)

OPDEF(CEE_UNUSED57,            "unused",          Pop0,               Push0,
InlineNone,         IPrimitive,  2,   0xFE,     0x10,     NEXT)

OPDEF(CEE_ENDFILTER,           "endfilter",       PopI,               Push0,
InlineNone,         IPrimitive,  2,   0xFE,     0x11,     RETURN)

OPDEF(CEE_UNALIGNED,           "unaligned.",      Pop0,               Push0,
ShortInlineI,       IPrefix,     2,   0xFE,     0x12,     META)
```

```
OPDEF(CEE_VOLATILE,            "volatile.",         Pop0,                Push0,
InlineNone,           IPrefix,      2,   0xFE,    0x13,     META)

OPDEF(CEE_TAILCALL,            "tail.",             Pop0,                Push0,
InlineNone,           IPrefix,      2,   0xFE,    0x14,     META)

OPDEF(CEE_INITOBJ,             "initobj",           PopI,                Push0,
InlineType,           IObjModel,    2,   0xFE,    0x15,     NEXT)

OPDEF(CEE_UNUSED68,            "unused",            Pop0,                Push0,
InlineNone,           IPrimitive,   2,   0xFE,    0x16,     NEXT)

OPDEF(CEE_CPBLK,               "cpblk",             PopI+PopI+PopI,      Push0,
InlineNone,           IPrimitive,   2,   0xFE,    0x17,     NEXT)

OPDEF(CEE_INITBLK,             "initblk",           PopI+PopI+PopI,      Push0,
InlineNone,           IPrimitive,   2,   0xFE,    0x18,     NEXT)

OPDEF(CEE_UNUSED69,            "unused",            Pop0,                Push0,
InlineNone,           IPrimitive,   2,   0xFE,    0x19,     NEXT)

OPDEF(CEE_RETHROW,             "rethrow",           Pop0,                Push0,
InlineNone,           IObjModel,    2,   0xFE,    0x1A,     THROW)

OPDEF(CEE_UNUSED51,            "unused",            Pop0,                Push0,
InlineNone,           IPrimitive,   2,   0xFE,    0x1B,     NEXT)

OPDEF(CEE_SIZEOF,              "sizeof",            Pop0,                PushI,
InlineType,           IPrimitive,   2,   0xFE,    0x1C,     NEXT)

OPDEF(CEE_REFANYTYPE,          "refanytype",        Pop1,                PushI,
InlineNone,           IPrimitive,   2,   0xFE,    0x1D,     NEXT)

OPDEF(CEE_UNUSED52,            "unused",            Pop0,                Push0,
InlineNone,           IPrimitive,   2,   0xFE,    0x1E,     NEXT)

OPDEF(CEE_UNUSED53,            "unused",            Pop0,                Push0,
InlineNone,           IPrimitive,   2,   0xFE,    0x1F,     NEXT)

OPDEF(CEE_UNUSED54,            "unused",            Pop0,                Push0,
InlineNone,           IPrimitive,   2,   0xFE,    0x20,     NEXT)
```

```
OPDEF(CEE_UNUSED55,           "unused",          Pop0,              Push0,
InlineNone,         IPrimitive,  2,   0xFE,    0x21,    NEXT)

OPDEF(CEE_UNUSED70,           "unused",          Pop0,              Push0,
InlineNone,         IPrimitive,  2,   0xFE,    0x22,    NEXT)

// These are not real opcodes, but they are handy internally in the EE

OPDEF(CEE_ILLEGAL,            "illegal",         Pop0,              Push0,
InlineNone,         IInternal,   0,   MOOT,    MOOT,    META)
OPDEF(CEE_MACRO_END,          "endmac",          Pop0,              Push0,
InlineNone,         IInternal,   0,   MOOT,    MOOT,    META)


#ifndef OPALIAS
#define _OPALIAS_DEFINED_
#define OPALIAS(canonicalName, stringName, realOpcode)
#endif

OPALIAS(CEE_BRNULL,         "brnull",          CEE_BRFALSE)
OPALIAS(CEE_BRNULL_S,       "brnull.s",        CEE_BRFALSE_S)
OPALIAS(CEE_BRZERO,         "brzero",          CEE_BRFALSE)
OPALIAS(CEE_BRZERO_S,       "brzero.s",        CEE_BRFALSE_S)
OPALIAS(CEE_BRINST,         "brinst",          CEE_BRTRUE)
OPALIAS(CEE_BRINST_S,       "brinst.s",        CEE_BRTRUE_S)
OPALIAS(CEE_LDIND_U8,       "ldind.u8",        CEE_LDIND_I8)
OPALIAS(CEE_LDELEM_U8,      "ldelem.u8",       CEE_LDELEM_I8)
OPALIAS(CEE_LDC_I4_M1x,     "ldc.i4.M1",       CEE_LDC_I4_M1)
OPALIAS(CEE_ENDFAULT,       "endfault",        CEE_ENDFINALLY)

#ifdef _OPALIAS_DEFINED_
#undef OPALIAS
#undef _OPALIAS_DEFINED_
#endif
```

C.3 Complete Grammar

This grammar provides a number of ease-of-use features not provided in the grammar of Partition II, sections 1–20, as well as supporting some features which are not portable across implementations and hence are not part of this standard. Unlike the grammar of Partition II, this one is designed for ease of programming rather than ease of reading; it can be converted directly into a YACC grammar.

ANNOTATION:

Implementation-Specific (Microsoft): This file is available as **include\asmparse.grammar** in the Microsoft .NET SDK.

ANNOTATION: The normative ilasm syntax in Partition II was largely derived from the syntax part of the productions in this file, which ships as part of Microsoft's shared source implementation of the CLI ("Rotor"). Studying these rules made it straightforward to determine which parts of the metadata were affected by which parts of the grammar. This analysis led directly to much of the information in Partition II.

– Jim Miller

```
Lexical tokens
    ID - C style alphaNumeric identifier (e.g. Hello_There2)
    QSTRING  - C style quoted string (e.g.  "hi\n")
    SQSTRING - C style singlely quoted string(e.g.  'hi')
    INT32    - C style 32 bit integer (e.g.  235,  03423, 0x34FFF)
    INT64    - C style 64 bit integer (e.g.  -2353453636235234,  0x34FFFFFFFFFF)
    FLOAT64  - C style floating point number (e.g.  -0.2323, 354.3423, 3435.34E-5)
    INSTR_*  - IL instructions of a particular class (see opcode.def).
----------------------------------------------------------------------------------
START             : decls
                  ;

decls                       : /* EMPTY */
                            | decls decl
                            ;

decl                        : classHead '{' classDecls '}'
                            | nameSpaceHead '{' decls '}'
```

```
                        | methodHead  methodDecls '}'
                        | fieldDecl
                        | dataDecl
                        | vtableDecl
                        | vtfixupDecl
                        | extSourceSpec
                        | fileDecl
                        | assemblyHead '{' assemblyDecls '}'
                        | assemblyRefHead '{' assemblyRefDecls '}'
                        | comtypeHead '{' comtypeDecls '}'
                        | manifestResHead '{' manifestResDecls '}'
                        | moduleHead
                        | secDecl
                        | customAttrDecl
                                     | '.subsystem' int32
                                     | '.corflags' int32
                                     | '.file' 'alignment' int32
                                     | '.imagebase' int64
                                     | languageDecl
                        ;

compQstring             : QSTRING
                        | compQstring '+' QSTRING
                                     ;

languageDecl                : '.language' SQSTRING
                        | '.language' SQSTRING ',' SQSTRING
                        | '.language' SQSTRING ',' SQSTRING ',' SQSTRING
                                     ;

customAttrDecl          : '.custom' customType
                        | '.custom' customType '=' compQstring
                        | customHead bytes ')'
                        | '.custom' '(' ownerType ')' customType
                        | '.custom' '(' ownerType ')' customType '=' compQstring
                        | customHeadWithOwner bytes ')'
                        ;
```

```
moduleHead              : '.module'
                        | '.module' name1
                        | '.module' 'extern' name1
                        ;

vtfixupDecl             : '.vtfixup' '[' int32 ']' vtfixupAttr 'at' id
                        ;

vtfixupAttr             : /* EMPTY */
                        | vtfixupAttr 'int32'
                        | vtfixupAttr 'int64'
                        | vtfixupAttr 'fromunmanaged'
                        | vtfixupAttr 'callmostderived'
                        ;

vtableDecl              : vtableHead bytes ')'
                        ;

vtableHead              : '.vtable' '=' '('
                        ;

nameSpaceHead           : '.namespace' name1
                        ;

classHead               : '.class' classAttr id extendsClause implClause
                        ;

classAttr               : /* EMPTY */
                        | classAttr 'public'
                        | classAttr 'private'
                        | classAttr 'value'
                        | classAttr 'enum'
                        | classAttr 'interface'
                        | classAttr 'sealed'
                        | classAttr 'abstract'
```

```
                                | classAttr 'auto'
                                | classAttr 'sequential'
                                | classAttr 'explicit'
                                | classAttr 'ansi'
                                | classAttr 'unicode'
                                | classAttr 'autochar'
                                | classAttr 'import'
                                | classAttr 'serializable'
                                | classAttr 'nested' 'public'
                                | classAttr 'nested' 'private'
                                | classAttr 'nested' 'family'
                                | classAttr 'nested' 'assembly'
                                | classAttr 'nested' 'famandassem'
                                | classAttr 'nested' 'famorassem'
                                | classAttr 'beforefieldinit'
                                | classAttr 'specialname'
                                | classAttr 'rtspecialname'
                                ;

extendsClause                   : /* EMPTY */
                                | 'extends' className
                                ;

implClause                      : /* EMPTY */
                                | 'implements' classNames
                                                    ;

classNames                      : classNames ',' className
                                | className
                                ;

classDecls                      : /* EMPTY */
                                | classDecls classDecl
                                ;

classDecl                       : methodHead  methodDecls '}'
                                | classHead '{' classDecls '}'
```

```
                        | eventHead '{' eventDecls '}'
                        | propHead '{' propDecls '}'
                        | fieldDecl
                        | dataDecl
                        | secDecl
                        | extSourceSpec
                        | customAttrDecl
                        | '.size' int32
                        | '.pack' int32
                        | exportHead '{' comtypeDecls '}'
                        | '.override' typeSpec '::' methodName 'with' callConv
                          type typeSpec '::' methodName '(' sigArgs0 ')'
                        | languageDecl
                        ;

fieldDecl               : '.field' repeatOpt fieldAttr type id atOpt initOpt
                        ;


atOpt                   : /* EMPTY */
                        | 'at' id
                        ;

initOpt                 : /* EMPTY */
                        | '=' fieldInit
                                          ;

repeatOpt                          : /* EMPTY */
                        | '[' int32 ']'
                                          ;

customHead              : '.custom' customType '=' '('
                        ;

customHeadWithOwner     : '.custom' '(' ownerType ')' customType '=' '('
                        ;
```

8. Annexes

```
memberRef         : methodSpec callConv type typeSpec '::' methodName '('
                      sigArgs0 ')'
                  | methodSpec callConv type methodName '(' sigArgs0 ')'
                  | 'field' type typeSpec '::' id
                  | 'field' type id
                  ;

customType        : callConv type typeSpec '::' '.ctor' '(' sigArgs0 ')'
                  | callConv type '.ctor' '(' sigArgs0 ')'
                  ;

ownerType         : typeSpec
                  | memberRef
                  ;

eventHead         : '.event' eventAttr typeSpec id
                  | '.event' eventAttr id
                  ;

eventAttr         : /* EMPTY */
                  | eventAttr 'rtspecialname' /**/
                  | eventAttr 'specialname'
                  ;

eventDecls        : /* EMPTY */
                  | eventDecls eventDecl
                  ;

eventDecl         : '.addon' callConv type typeSpec '::' methodName '('
                      sigArgs0 ')'
                  | '.addon' callConv type methodName '(' sigArgs0 ')'
                  | '.removeon' callConv type typeSpec '::' methodName '('
                      sigArgs0 ')'
                  | '.removeon' callConv type methodName '(' sigArgs0 ')'
                  | '.fire' callConv type typeSpec '::' methodName '('
                      sigArgs0 ')'
                  | '.fire' callConv type methodName '(' sigArgs0 ')'
```

```
                        | '.other' callConv type typeSpec '::' methodName '('
                            sigArgs0 ')'
                        | '.other' callConv type methodName '(' sigArgs0 ')'
                        | extSourceSpec
                        | customAttrDecl
                        | languageDecl
                        ;

propHead                : '.property' propAttr callConv type id '(' sigArgs0 ')'
initOpt
                        ;

propAttr                : /* EMPTY */
                        | propAttr 'rtspecialname' /**/
                        | propAttr 'specialname'
                        ;

propDecls               : /* EMPTY */
                        | propDecls propDecl
                        ;

propDecl                : '.set' callConv type typeSpec '::' methodName '('
                            sigArgs0 ')'
                        | '.set' callConv type methodName '(' sigArgs0 ')'
                        | '.get' callConv type typeSpec '::' methodName '('
                            sigArgs0 ')'
                        | '.get' callConv type methodName '(' sigArgs0 ')'
                        | '.other' callConv type typeSpec '::' methodName '('
                            sigArgs0 ')'
                        | '.other' callConv type methodName '(' sigArgs0 ')'
                        | customAttrDecl
                        | extSourceSpec
                        | languageDecl
                        ;
```

```
methodHeadPart1        : '.method'
                       ;

methodHead             : methodHeadPart1 methAttr callConv paramAttr type
                           methodName '(' sigArgs0 ')' implAttr '{'
                       | methodHeadPart1 methAttr callConv paramAttr type
                           'marshal' '(' nativeType ')' methodName '(' sigArgs0
                           ')' implAttr '{'
                       ;

methAttr               : /* EMPTY */

                       | methAttr 'static'
                       | methAttr 'public'
                       | methAttr 'private'
                       | methAttr 'family'
                       | methAttr 'final'
                       | methAttr 'specialname'
                       | methAttr 'virtual'
                       | methAttr 'abstract'
                       | methAttr 'assembly'
                       | methAttr 'famandassem'
                       | methAttr 'famorassem'
                       | methAttr 'privatescope'
                       | methAttr 'hidebysig'
                       | methAttr 'newslot'
                       | methAttr 'rtspecialname' /**/
                       | methAttr 'unmanagedexp'
                       | methAttr 'reqsecobj'

                       | methAttr 'pinvokeimpl' '(' compQstring 'as' compQstring
  pinvAttr ')'
                       | methAttr 'pinvokeimpl' '(' compQstring  pinvAttr ')'
                       | methAttr 'pinvokeimpl' '(' pinvAttr ')'
                       ;

pinvAttr               : /* EMPTY */
                       | pinvAttr 'nomangle'
```

```
                        | pinvAttr 'ansi'
                        | pinvAttr 'unicode'
                        | pinvAttr 'autochar'
                        | pinvAttr 'lasterr'
                        | pinvAttr 'winapi'
                        | pinvAttr 'cdecl'
                        | pinvAttr 'stdcall'
                        | pinvAttr 'thiscall'
                        | pinvAttr 'fastcall'
                        ;

methodName              : '.ctor'
                        | '.cctor'
                        | name1
                        ;

paramAttr               : /* EMPTY */
                        | paramAttr '[' 'in' ']'
                        | paramAttr '[' 'out' ']'
                        | paramAttr '[' 'opt' ']'
                        | paramAttr '[' int32 ']'
                        ;

fieldAttr               : /* EMPTY */
                        | fieldAttr 'static'
                        | fieldAttr 'public'
                        | fieldAttr 'private'
                        | fieldAttr 'family'
                        | fieldAttr 'initonly'
                        | fieldAttr 'rtspecialname'  /**/
                        | fieldAttr 'specialname'
                       /* commented out because PInvoke for fields is not
supported by EE
                        | fieldAttr 'pinvokeimpl' '(' compQstring 'as' compQstring
pinvAttr ')'
                        | fieldAttr 'pinvokeimpl' '(' compQstring  pinvAttr ')'
                        | fieldAttr 'pinvokeimpl' '(' pinvAttr ')'
                                      */
```

8. Annexes

```
                        | fieldAttr 'marshal' '(' nativeType ')'
                        | fieldAttr 'assembly'
                        | fieldAttr 'famandassem'
                        | fieldAttr 'famorassem'
                        | fieldAttr 'privatescope'
                        | fieldAttr 'literal'
                        | fieldAttr 'notserialized'
                        ;

implAttr                : /* EMPTY */
                        | implAttr 'native'
                        | implAttr 'cil'
                        | implAttr 'optil'
                        | implAttr 'managed'
                        | implAttr 'unmanaged'
                        | implAttr 'forwardref'
                        | implAttr 'preservesig'
                        | implAttr 'runtime'
                        | implAttr 'internalcall'
                        | implAttr 'synchronized'
                        | implAttr 'noinlining'
                        ;

localsHead              : '.locals'
                        ;

methodDecl              : '.emitbyte' int32
                        | sehBlock
                        | '.maxstack' int32
                        | localsHead '(' sigArgs0 ')'
                        | localsHead 'init' '(' sigArgs0 ')'
                        | '.entrypoint'
                        | '.zeroinit'
                        | dataDecl
                        | instr
```

```
                          | id ':'
                          | secDecl
                          | extSourceSpec
                          | languageDecl
                          | customAttrDecl
                                    | '.export' '[' int32 ']'
                                    | '.export' '[' int32 ']''as' id
                          | '.vtentry' int32 ':' int32
                          | '.override' typeSpec '::' methodName
                          | scopeBlock
                          | '.param' '[' int32 ']' initOpt
                          ;

scopeBlock                : scopeOpen methodDecls '}'
                          ;

scopeOpen                 : '{'
                          ;

sehBlock                  : tryBlock sehClauses
                          ;

sehClauses                : sehClause sehClauses
                          | sehClause
                          ;

tryBlock                  : tryHead scopeBlock
                          | tryHead id 'to' id
                          | tryHead int32 'to' int32
                          ;

tryHead                   : '.try'
                          ;

sehClause                 : catchClause handlerBlock
                          | filterClause handlerBlock
```

```
                    | finallyClause handlerBlock
                    | faultClause handlerBlock
                    ;

filterClause        : filterHead scopeBlock
                    | filterHead id
                    | filterHead int32
                    ;

filterHead          : 'filter'
                    ;

catchClause         : 'catch' className
                    ;

finallyClause       : 'finally'
                    ;

faultClause         : 'fault'
                    ;

handlerBlock        : scopeBlock
                    | 'handler' id 'to' id
                    | 'handler' int32 'to' int32
                    ;

methodDecls         : /* EMPTY */
                    | methodDecls methodDecl
                    ;

dataDecl            : ddHead ddBody
                    ;
```

```
ddHead          : '.data' tls id '='
                | '.data' tls
                ;

tls             : /* EMPTY */
                | 'tls'
                ;

ddBody          : '{' ddItemList '}'
                | ddItem
                ;

ddItemList      : ddItem ',' ddItemList
                | ddItem
                ;

ddItemCount     : /* EMPTY */
                | '[' int32 ']'
                ;

ddItem          : 'char' '*' '(' compQstring ')'
                | '&' '(' id ')'
                | bytearrayhead bytes ')'
                | 'float32' '(' float64 ')' ddItemCount
                | 'float64' '(' float64 ')' ddItemCount
                | 'int64' '(' int64 ')' ddItemCount
                | 'int32' '(' int32 ')' ddItemCount
                | 'int16' '(' int32 ')' ddItemCount
                | 'int8' '(' int32 ')' ddItemCount
                | 'float32' ddItemCount
                | 'float64' ddItemCount
                | 'int64' ddItemCount
                | 'int32' ddItemCount
                | 'int16' ddItemCount
                | 'int8' ddItemCount
                ;
```

8. Annexes

```
fieldInit               : 'float32' '(' float64 ')'
                        | 'float64' '(' float64 ')'
                        | 'float32' '(' int64 ')'
                        | 'float64' '(' int64 ')'
                        | 'int64' '(' int64 ')'
                        | 'int32' '(' int64 ')'
                        | 'int16' '(' int64 ')'
                        | 'char' '(' int64 ')'
                        | 'int8' '(' int64 ')'
                        | 'bool' '(' truefalse ')'
                        | compQstring
                        | bytearrayhead bytes ')'
                                          | 'nullref'
                        ;

bytearrayhead           : 'bytearray' '('
                        ;

bytes                   : /* EMPTY */
                        | hexbytes
                        ;

hexbytes                : HEXBYTE
                        | hexbytes HEXBYTE
                        ;

instr_r_head            : INSTR_R '('
                        ;

instr_tok_head          : INSTR_TOK
                        ;

methodSpec              : 'method'
                        ;

instr                   : INSTR_NONE
                        | INSTR_VAR int32
```

```
                        | INSTR_VAR id
                        | INSTR_I int32
                        | INSTR_I8 int64
                        | INSTR_R float64
                        | INSTR_R int64
                        | instr_r_head bytes ')'
                        | INSTR_BRTARGET int32
                        | INSTR_BRTARGET id
                        | INSTR_METHOD callConv type typeSpec '::' methodName '('
sigArgs0 ')'
                        | INSTR_METHOD callConv type methodName '(' sigArgs0 ')'
                        | INSTR_FIELD type typeSpec '::' id
                        | INSTR_FIELD type id
                        | INSTR_TYPE typeSpec
                        | INSTR_STRING compQstring
                        | INSTR_STRING bytearrayhead bytes ')'
                        | INSTR_SIG callConv type '(' sigArgs0 ')'
                        | INSTR_RVA id
                        | INSTR_RVA int32
                        | instr_tok_head ownerType /* ownerType ::= memberRef |
typeSpec */
                        | INSTR_SWITCH '(' labels ')'
                        | INSTR_PHI int16s
                        ;

sigArgs0                : /* EMPTY */
                        | sigArgs1
                        ;

sigArgs1                : sigArg
                        | sigArgs1 ',' sigArg
                        ;

sigArg                  : '...'
                        | paramAttr type
                        | paramAttr type id
                        | paramAttr type 'marshal' '(' nativeType ')'
```

8. Annexes

```
                        | paramAttr type 'marshal' '(' nativeType ')' id
                        ;

name1                   : id
                        | DOTTEDNAME
                        | name1 '.' name1
                        ;

className               : '[' name1 ']' slashedName
                        | '[' '.module' name1 ']' slashedName
                        | slashedName
                        ;

slashedName             : name1
                        | slashedName '/' name1
                        ;

typeSpec                : className
                        | '[' name1 ']'
                        | '[' '.module' name1 ']'
                        | type
                        ;

callConv                : 'instance' callConv
                        | 'explicit' callConv
                        | callKind
                        ;

callKind                : /* EMPTY */
                        | 'default'
                        | 'vararg'
                        | 'unmanaged' 'cdecl'
                        | 'unmanaged' 'stdcall'
                        | 'unmanaged' 'thiscall'
                        | 'unmanaged' 'fastcall'
                        ;
```

```
nativeType              : /* EMPTY */
                        | 'custom' '(' compQstring ',' compQstring ',' compQstring
                            ',' compQstring ')'
                        | 'custom' '(' compQstring ',' compQstring ')'
                        | 'fixed' 'sysstring' '[' int32 ']'
                        | 'fixed' 'array' '[' int32 ']'
                        | 'variant'
                        | 'currency'
                        | 'syschar'
                        | 'void'
                        | 'bool'
                        | 'int8'
                        | 'int16'
                        | 'int32'
                        | 'int64'
                        | 'float32'
                        | 'float64'
                        | 'error'
                        | 'unsigned' 'int8'
                        | 'unsigned' 'int16'
                        | 'unsigned' 'int32'
                        | 'unsigned' 'int64'
                        | nativeType '*'
                        | nativeType '[' ']'
                        | nativeType '[' int32 ']'
                        | nativeType '[' int32 '+' int32 ']'
                        | nativeType '[' '+' int32 ']'
                                    | 'decimal'
                        | 'date'
                        | 'bstr'
                        | 'lpstr'
                        | 'lpwstr'
                        | 'lptstr'
                        | 'objectref'
                        | 'iunknown'
                        | 'idispatch'
                        | 'struct'
```

8. Annexes

```
                         | 'interface'
                         | 'safearray' variantType
                         | 'safearray' variantType ',' compQstring

                         | 'int'
                         | 'unsigned' 'int'
                         | 'nested' 'struct'
                         | 'byvalstr'
                         | 'ansi' 'bstr'
                         | 'tbstr'
                         | 'variant' 'bool'
                         | methodSpec
                         | 'as' 'any'
                         | 'lpstruct'
                         ;

variantType              : /* EMPTY */
                         | 'null'
                         | 'variant'
                         | 'currency'
                         | 'void'
                         | 'bool'
                         | 'int8'
                         | 'int16'
                         | 'int32'
                         | 'int64'
                         | 'float32'
                         | 'float64'
                         | 'unsigned' 'int8'
                         | 'unsigned' 'int16'
                         | 'unsigned' 'int32'
                         | 'unsigned' 'int64'
                         | '*'
                         | variantType '[' ']'
                         | variantType 'vector'
                         | variantType '&'
```

```
                    | 'decimal'
                    | 'date'
                    | 'bstr'
                    | 'lpstr'
                    | 'lpwstr'
                    | 'iunknown'
                    | 'idispatch'
                    | 'safearray'
                    | 'int'
                    | 'unsigned' 'int'
                    | 'error'
                    | 'hresult'
                    | 'carray'
                    | 'userdefined'
                    | 'record'
                    | 'filetime'
                    | 'blob'
                    | 'stream'
                    | 'storage'
                    | 'streamed_object'
                    | 'stored_object'
                    | 'blob_object'
                    | 'cf'
                    | 'clsid'
                    ;

type                : 'class' className
                                 | 'object'
                                 | 'string'
                    | 'value' 'class' className
                    | 'valuetype' className
                    | type '[' ']'
                    | type '[' bounds1 ']'
                    /* uncomment when and if this type is supported by the
Runtime
                    | type 'value' '[' int32 ']'
                    */
```

```
                    | type '&'
                    | type '*'
                    | type 'pinned'
                    | type 'modreq' '(' className ')'
                    | type 'modopt' '(' className ')'
                    | '!' int32
                    | methodSpec callConv type '*' '(' sigArgs0 ')'
                    | 'typedref'
                    | 'char'
                    | 'void'
                    | 'bool'
                    | 'int8'
                    | 'int16'
                    | 'int32'
                    | 'int64'
                    | 'float32'
                    | 'float64'
                    | 'unsigned' 'int8'
                    | 'unsigned' 'int16'
                    | 'unsigned' 'int32'
                    | 'unsigned' 'int64'
                    | 'native' 'int'
                    | 'native' 'unsigned' 'int'
                    | 'native' 'float'
                    ;

bounds1             : bound
                    | bounds1 ',' bound
                    ;

bound               : /* EMPTY */
                    | '...'
                    | int32
                    | int32 '...' int32
                    | int32 '...'
                    ;
```

```
labels              : /* empty */
                    | id ',' labels
                    | int32 ',' labels
                    | id
                    | int32
                    ;

id                  : ID
                    | SQSTRING
                    ;

int16s              : /* EMPTY */
                    | int16s int32
                    ;

int32               : INT64
                    ;

int64               : INT64
                    ;

float64             : FLOAT64
                    | 'float32' '(' int32 ')'
                    | 'float64' '(' int64 ')'
                    ;

secDecl             : '.permission' secAction typeSpec '(' nameValPairs ')'
                    | '.permission' secAction typeSpec
                    | psetHead bytes ')'
                    ;

psetHead            : '.permissionset' secAction '=' '('
                    ;
```

```
nameValPairs            : nameValPair
                        | nameValPair ',' nameValPairs
                        ;

nameValPair             : compQstring '=' caValue
                        ;

truefalse               : 'true'
                        | 'false'
                        ;

caValue                 : truefalse
                        | int32
                        | 'int32' '(' int32 ')'
                        | compQstring
                        | className '(' 'int8' ':' int32 ')'
                        | className '(' 'int16' ':' int32 ')'
                        | className '(' 'int32' ':' int32 ')'
                        | className '(' int32 ')'
                        ;

secAction               : 'request'
                        | 'demand'
                        | 'assert'
                        | 'deny'
                        | 'permitonly'
                        | 'linkcheck'
                        | 'inheritcheck'
                        | 'reqmin'
                        | 'reqopt'
                        | 'reqrefuse'
                        | 'prejitgrant'
                        | 'prejitdeny'
                        | 'noncasdemand'
                        | 'noncaslinkdemand'
                        | 'noncasinheritance'
                        ;
```

```
extSourceSpec          : '.line' int32 SQSTRING
                       | '.line' int32
                       | '.line' int32 ':' int32 SQSTRING
                       | '.line' int32 ':' int32
                       | P_LINE int32 QSTRING
                       ;

fileDecl               : '.file' fileAttr name1 fileEntry hashHead bytes ')'
                           fileEntry
                       | '.file' fileAttr name1 fileEntry
                       ;

fileAttr               : /* EMPTY */
                       | fileAttr 'nometadata'
                       ;

fileEntry              : /* EMPTY */
                       | '.entrypoint'
                       ;

hashHead               : '.hash' '=' '('
                       ;

assemblyHead           : '.assembly' asmAttr name1
                       ;

asmAttr                : /* EMPTY */
                       | asmAttr 'noappdomain'
                       | asmAttr 'noprocess'
                       | asmAttr 'nomachine'
                       ;

assemblyDecls          : /* EMPTY */
                       | assemblyDecls assemblyDecl
                       ;
```

```
assemblyDecl            : '.hash' 'algorithm' int32
                        | secDecl
                        | asmOrRefDecl

                        ;

asmOrRefDecl            : publicKeyHead bytes ')'
                        | '.ver' int32 ':' int32 ':' int32 ':' int32
                        | '.locale' compQstring
                        | localeHead bytes ')'
                        | customAttrDecl
                        ;

publicKeyHead           : '.publickey' '=' '('
                        ;

publicKeyTokenHead      : '.publickeytoken' '=' '('
                        ;

localeHead              : '.locale' '=' '('
                        ;

assemblyRefHead         : '.assembly' 'extern' name1
                        | '.assembly' 'extern' name1 'as' name1
                        ;

assemblyRefDecls        : /* EMPTY */
                        | assemblyRefDecls assemblyRefDecl
                        ;

assemblyRefDecl         : hashHead bytes ')'
                        | asmOrRefDecl
                        | publicKeyTokenHead bytes ')'
                        ;

comtypeHead             : '.class' 'extern' comtAttr name1
                        ;
```

```
exportHead              : '.export' comtAttr name1
                        ;

comtAttr                : /* EMPTY */
                        | comtAttr 'private'
                        | comtAttr 'public'
                        | comtAttr 'nested' 'public'
                        | comtAttr 'nested' 'private'
                        | comtAttr 'nested' 'family'
                        | comtAttr 'nested' 'assembly'
                        | comtAttr 'nested' 'famandassem'
                        | comtAttr 'nested' 'famorassem'
                        ;

comtypeDecls            : /* EMPTY */
                        | comtypeDecls comtypeDecl
                        ;

comtypeDecl             : '.file' name1
                        | '.class' 'extern' name1
                        | '.class'  int32
                        | customAttrDecl
                        ;

manifestResHead         : '.mresource' manresAttr name1
                        ;

manresAttr              : /* EMPTY */
                        | manresAttr 'public'
                        | manresAttr 'private'
                        ;

manifestResDecls        : /* EMPTY */
                        | manifestResDecls manifestResDecl
                        ;
```

```
manifestResDecl          : '.file' name1 'at' int32
                         | '.assembly' 'extern' name1
                         | customAttrDecl
                         ;
```

C.4 Instruction Syntax

While each section specifies the exact list of instructions that are included in a grammar class, this information is subject to change over time. The precise format of an instruction can be found by combining the information in Partition V, section C.1 with the information in the following Table 8-1.

Table 8-1 Instruction Syntax Classes

Grammar Class	Format(s) Specified in Partition V, Section C.1 Ilasm Keywords
<instr_brtarget>	InlineBrTarget, ShortInlineBrTarget
<instr_field>	InlineField
<instr_i>	InlineI, ShortInlineI
<instr_i8>	InlineI8
<instr_method>	InlineMethod
<instr_none>	InlineNone
<instr_phi>	InlinePhi
<instr_r>	InlineR, ShortInlineR
<instr_rva>	InlineRVA
<instr_sig>	InlineSig
<instr_string>	InlineString
<instr_switch>	InlineSwitch
<instr_tok>	InlineTok
<instr_type>	InlineType
<instr_var>	InlineVar, ShortInlineVar

ANNOTATION: The information in this section is derived from the file **opcode.def**. It shows all the instructions broken out by argument type.

C.4.1 *Top-Level Instruction Syntax*

```
<instr> ::=
    <instr_brtarget> <int32>
  | <instr_brtarget> <label>
  | <instr_field> <type> [ <typeSpec> :: ] <id>
  | <instr_i> <int32>
  | <instr_i8> <int64>
  | <instr_method>
      <callConv> <type> [ <typeSpec> :: ]
          <methodName> ( <parameters> )
  | <instr_none>
  | <instr_phi> <int16>*
  | <instr_r> ( <bytes> )      // <bytes> represent the binary image of
                               // float or double (4 or 8 bytes,
                               // respectively)
  | <instr_r> <float64>
  | <instr_r> <int64>  // integer is converted to float
                               // with possible
                               // loss of precision
  | <instr_sig> <callConv> <type> ( <parameters> )
  | <instr_string> bytearray ( <bytes> )
  | <instr_string> <QSTRING>
  | <instr_switch> ( <labels> )
  | <instr_tok> field <type> [ <typeSpec> :: ] <id>
  | <instr_tok> b
      <callConv> <type> [ <typeSpec> :: ]
          <methodName> ( <parameters> )
  | <instr_tok> <typeSpec>
  | <instr_type> <typeSpec>
  | <instr_var> <int32>
  | <instr_var> <localname>
```

8. Annexes

C.4.2 *Instructions with No Operand*

These instructions require no operands, so they simply appear by themselves.

```
<instr> ::= <instr_none>
<instr_none> ::= // Derived from opcode.def
        add            | add.ovf       | add.ovf.un     | and           |
        arglist        | break         | ceq            | cgt           |
        cgt.un         | ckfinite      | clt            | clt.un        |
        conv.i         | conv.i1       | conv.i2        | conv.i4       |
        conv.i8        | conv.ovf.i    | conv.ovf.i.un  | conv.ovf.i1|
        conv.ovf.i1.un | conv.ovf.i2   | conv.ovf.i2.un | conv.ovf.i4|
        conv.ovf.i4.un | conv.ovf.i8   | conv.ovf.i8.un | conv.ovf.u |
        conv.ovf.u.un  | conv.ovf.u1   | conv.ovf.u1.un | conv.ovf.u2|
        conv.ovf.u2.un | conv.ovf.u4   | conv.ovf.u4.un | conv.ovf.u8|
        conv.ovf.u8.un | conv.r.un     | conv.r4        | conv.r8       |
        conv.u         | conv.u1       | conv.u2        | conv.u4       |
        conv.u8        | cpblk         | div            | div.un        |
        dup            | endfault      | endfilter      | endfinally    |
        initblk        |               | ldarg.0        | ldarg.1       |
        ldarg.2        | ldarg.3       | ldc.i4.0       | ldc.i4.1      |
        ldc.i4.2       | ldc.i4.3      | ldc.i4.4       | ldc.i4.5      |
        ldc.i4.6       | ldc.i4.7      | ldc.i4.8       | ldc.i4.M1     |
        ldelem.i       | ldelem.i1     | ldelem.i2      | ldelem.i4     |
        ldelem.i8      | ldelem.r4     | ldelem.r8      | ldelem.ref    |
        ldelem.u1      | ldelem.u2     | ldelem.u4      | ldind.i       |
        ldind.i1       | ldind.i2      | ldind.i4       | ldind.i8      |
        ldind.r4       | ldind.r8      | ldind.ref      | ldind.u1      |
        ldind.u2       | ldind.u4      | ldlen          | ldloc.0       |
        ldloc.1        | ldloc.2       | ldloc.3        | ldnull        |
        localloc       | mul           | mul.ovf        | mul.ovf.un    |
        neg            | nop           | not            | or            |
        pop            | refanytype    | rem            | rem.un        |
        ret            | rethrow       | shl            | shr           |
        shr.un         | stelem.i      | stelem.i1      | stelem.i2     |
        stelem.i4      | stelem.i8     | stelem.r4      | stelem.r8     |
        stelem.ref     | stind.i       | stind.i1       | stind.i2      |
        stind.i4       | stind.i8      | stind.r4       | stind.r8      |
```

```
stind.ref     | stloc.0    | stloc.1      | stloc.2     |
stloc.3       | sub        | sub.ovf      | sub.ovf.un  |
tail.         | throw      | volatile.    | xor
```

Examples:

```
ldlen
not
```

C.4.3 *Instructions That Refer to Parameters or Local Variables*

These instructions take one operand, which references a parameter or local variable of the current method. The variable can be referenced by its number (starting with variable 0) or by name (if the names are supplied as part of a signature using the form that supplies both a type and a name).

```
<instr> ::= <instr_var> <int32> |
            <instr_var> <localname>
<instr_var> ::= // Derived from opcode.def
              | ldarg    | ldarg.s  | ldarga
    ldarga.s  | ldloc    | ldloc.s  | ldloca
    ldloca.s  | starg    | starg.s  | stloc
    stloc.s
```

Examples:

```
stloc 0          // store into 0th local
ldarg X3       // load from argument named X3
```

C.4.4 *Instructions That Take a Single 32-Bit Integer Argument*

These instructions take one operand, which must be a 32-bit integer.

```
<instr> ::= <instr_i> <int32>
<instr_i> ::= // Derived from opcode.def
    ldc.i4 | ldc.i4.s | unaligned.
```

Examples:

```
ldc.i4 123456  // Load the number 123456
ldc.i4.s 10    // Load the number 10
```

C.4.5 *Instructions That Take a Single 64-Bit Integer Argument*

These instructions take one operand, which must be a 64-bit integer.

```
<instr> ::= <instr_i8> <int64>
<instr_i8> ::= // Derived from opcode.def
    ldc.i8
```

Examples:

```
ldc.i8 0x123456789AB

ldc.i8 12
```

C.4.6 *Instructions That Take a Single Floating Point Argument*

These instructions take one operand, which must be a floating point number.

```
<instr> ::= <instr_r> <float64> |
            <instr_r> <int64>   |
            <instr_r> ( <bytes> )  // <bytes> is binary image

<instr_r> ::= // Derived from opcode.def
ldc.r4 | ldc.r8
```

Examples:

```
ldc.r4 10.2

ldc.r4 10

ldc.r4 0x123456789ABCDEF

ldc.r8 (00 00 00 00 00 00 F8 FF)
```


C.4.7 *Branch Instructions*

The assembler does not optimize branches. The branch must be specified explicitly as using either the short or the long form of the instruction. If the displacement is too large for the short form, then the assembler will display an error.

```
<instr> ::=
    <instr_brtarget> <int32> |
    <instr_brtarget> <label>
<instr_brtarget> ::= // Derived from opcode.def
                            | beq     | beq.s     | bge     | bge.s     |
    bge.un      | bge.un.s    | bgt     | bgt.s     | bgt.un  | bgt.un.s  |
    ble         | ble.s       | ble.un  | ble.un.s  | blt     | blt.s     |
    blt.un      | blt.un.s    | bne.un  | bne.un.s  | br      | br.s      |
    brfalse     | brfalse.s   | brtrue  | brtrue.s  | leave   | leave.s
```

Example:

```
br.s 22

br foo
```

C.4.8 *Instructions That Take a Method as an Argument*

These instructions reference a method, either in another class (first instruction format) or in the current class (second instruction format).

```
<instr> ::=
   <instr_method>
      <callConv> <type> [ <typeSpec> :: ] <methodName> ( <parameters> )
<instr_method> ::= // Derived from opcode.def
      call   | callvirt | jmp | ldftn    | ldvirtftn         | newobj
```

Examples:

```
call instance int32 C.D.E::X(class W, native int)
ldftn vararg char F(...) // Global Function F
```

C.4.9 *Instructions That Take a Field of a Class as an Argument*

These instructions reference a field of a class.

```
<instr> ::=
     <instr_field> <type> <typeSpec> :: <id>
<instr_field> ::= // Derived from opcode.def
     ldfld | ldflda | ldsfld | ldsflda | stfld | stsfld
```

Examples:

```
ldfld native int X::IntField
stsfld int32 Y::AnotherField
```

C.4.10 *Instructions That Take a Type as an Argument*

These instructions reference a type.

```
<instr> ::= <instr_type> <typeSpec>
<instr_type> ::= // Derived from opcode.def
     box     | castclass | cpobj    | initobj | isinst    |
     ldelema | ldobj     | mkrefany | newarr  | refanyval |
     sizeof  | stobj     | unbox
```

Examples:

```
initobj [mscorlib]System.Console
sizeof class X
```

C.4.11 *Instructions That Take a String as an Argument*

These instructions take a string as an argument.

```
<instr> ::= <instr_string> <QSTRING>
<instr_string> ::= // Derived from opcode.def
     ldstr
```

8. Annexes

Examples:

```
ldstr "This is a string"
ldstr "This has a\nnewline in it"
```

C.4.12 *Instructions That Take a Signature as an Argument*

These instructions take a stand-alone signature as an argument.

```
<instr> ::= <instr_sig> <callConv> <type> ( <parameters> )
<instr_sig> ::= // Derived from opcode.def
      calli
```

Examples:

```
calli class A.B(wchar *)
calli vararg bool(int32[,] X, ...)
// Returns a boolean, takes at least one argument. The first
// argument, named X, must be a two-dimensional array of
// 32-bit ints.
```

C.4.13 *Instructions That Take a Metadata Token as an Argument*

This instruction takes a metadata token as an argument. The token can reference a type, a method, or a field of a class.

```
<instr> ::= <instr_tok> <typeSpec> |
            <instr_tok> method
               <callConv> <type> <typeSpec> :: <methodName>
                          ( <parameters> ) |
            <instr_tok> method
               <callConv> <type> <methodName>
                          ( <parameters> ) |
            <instr_tok> field <type> <typeSpec> :: <id>
<instr_tok> ::= // Derived from opcode.def
ldtoken
```

Examples:

```
ldtoken class [mscorlib]System.Console
ldtoken method int32 X::Fn()
ldtoken method bool GlobalFn(int32 &)
ldtoken field class X.Y Class::Field
```

C.4.14 *Switch Instruction*

The switch instruction takes a set of labels or decimal relative values.

```
<instr> ::= <instr_switch> ( <labels> )
<instr_switch> ::= // Derived from opcode.def
     switch
```

Examples:

```
switch (0x3, -14, Label1)
switch (5, Label2)
```

Annex D Class Library Design Guidelines

This section contains only informative text.

This section describes the guidelines that were used in the design of the class libraries, including naming conventions and coding patterns. They are intended to give guidance to anyone who is extending the libraries, including:

- Implementers of the CLI who wish to extend the libraries beyond those specified in this standard
- Implementers of libraries that will run on top of the CLI and wish their libraries to be consistent with the standard libraries
- Future standards efforts aimed at refining the existing libraries or defining additional libraries

As with any set of guidelines, they should be applied with an eye toward the end goal of consistency but understanding that for functionality, performance, or external compatibility reasons they may require modification or simply prove inappropriate in particular cases. The guidelines should not be applied blindly, and they should be revisited periodically to ensure that they remain viable.

Throughout this chapter, we use the following conventions:

- ***Do*** means that the described practice should be followed where possible.
- ***Do not*** means that the described practice should be avoided where possible.
- ***Consider*** means that the described practice is often helpful, but there are common cases where it is impractical or inadvisable; thus, the practice should be carefully considered but may not be appropriate.

ANNOTATION: Although the ECMA technical committee responsible for this standard started with the Microsoft rules for designing class frameworks, the committee carefully selected a subset for the standard. The selected guidelines did not reflect any internal Microsoft ways of doing things and were generally good ideas. So the committee intends to follow these guidelines when it adds more to the standard, although it is likely to update these guidelines as well.

D.1 Naming Guidelines

One of the most important elements of predictability and discoverability in a managed class library is the use of a consistent naming pattern. Many of the most common user questions should not arise once these conventions are understood and widely used.

There are three elements of naming guidelines.

- **Case:** Use the correct capitalization style.
- **Mechanics:** Use nouns for classes, verbs for methods, etc.
- **Word Choice:** Use terms consistently across libraries.

The following section describes rules for case and mechanics, and some philosophy regarding word choice.

D.1.1 *Capitalization Styles*

The following section describes different ways of capitalizing identifiers. These terms will be referred to throughout the rest of this document.

D.1.1.1 Pascal Casing

This convention capitalizes the first character of each word, as in the following example:

```
BackColor
```

D.1.1.2 Camel Casing

This convention capitalizes the first character of each word except the first word, as in the following example:.

```
backColor
```

D.1.1.3 Upper Case

Only use all uppercase letters for identifiers if it contains an abbreviation that is two characters long or less. Identifiers of three or more characters should use PascalCasing.

```
System.IO
System.Web.UI
System.CodeDom
```

D.1.1.4 Capitalization Summary

The following table describes the capitalization rules for different types of identifiers.

Type	Case	Notes
Class	PascalCase	
Enum values	PascalCase	
Enum type	PascalCase	
Events	PascalCase	
Exception class	PascalCase	Ends with the suffix "Exception".
Final Static field	PascalCase	
Interface	PascalCase	Begins with the prefix "I".
Method	PascalCase	
Namespace	PascalCase	
Property	PascalCase	
Public Instance Field	PascalCase	Rarely used; prefer properties.
Protected Instance Field	camelCase	Rarely used; prefer properties.
Parameter	camelCase	

D.1.2 *Word Choice*

- ***Do*** avoid using class names duplicated in heavily used namespaces. For example, do not use any of the following for a class name:

  System

  Collections

  Forms

  UI

- *Do* avoid using identifiers that conflict with the following keywords:

ANNOTATION: To get the keywords in this table, the ECMA committee did a survey of programming languages in use and pulled out these keywords as likely to be used as identifiers in a program. This is not a complete list of keywords.

alias	and	ansi	as	assembly
auto	base	bool	boolean	byte
call	case	catch	char	class
const	current	date	decimal	declare
default	delegate	dim	do	double
each	else	elseif	end	enum
erase	error	eval	event	exit
extends	finalize	finally	float	for
friend	function	get	goto	handles
if	implements	import	imports	in
inherit	inherits	instanceof	int	integer
interface	is	let	lib	like
lock	long	loop	me	mod
module	namespace	new	next	not
nothing	null	object	on	or
overloads	override	overrides	package	private
property	protected	public	raise	readonly
redim	rem	resume	return	select
self	set	shared	short	single

static	step	stop	string	structure
sub	synchronize	synchronized	then	this
throw	to	try	typeof	unlock
until	use	uses	using	var
void	volatile	when	while	with
xor	FALSE	TRUE		

- ***Do not*** use abbreviations in identifiers (including parameter names).
- If you must use abbreviations, ***do*** use camelCasing for any abbreviation over two characters long, even if this is not the standard abbreviation.

D.1.3 *Case Sensitivity*

Do not use names that require case sensitivity. Components must be fully usable in both case-sensitive and case-insensitive languages. Since case-insensitive languages cannot distinguish between two names within the same context that differ only by case, components must avoid this situation.

- ***Do not*** have two namespaces whose names differ only by case:

```
namespace ee.cummings;
namespace Ee.Cummings;
```

- ***Do not*** have a function with two parameters whose names differ only by case:

```
void foo(string a, string A)
```

- ***Do not*** have a namespace with two types whose names differ only by case:

```
System.Drawing.Point p;
System.Drawing.POINT pp;
```

- ***Do not*** have a type with two properties whose names differ only by case:

```
int Foo {get, set};
int FOO {get, set};
```

- ***Do not*** have a type with two methods whose names differ only by case:

```
void foo();
void Foo();
```

8. Annexes

D.1.4 *Avoiding Type Name Confusion*

Different languages use different terms to identify the fundamental managed types. Designers must avoid using language-specific terminology. Follow the rules described in this section to avoid type name confusion.

- ***Do*** use semantically interesting names rather than type names.
- In the rare case that a parameter has no semantic meaning beyond its type, use a generic name. For example, a class that supports writing a variety of data types into a stream might have the following methods.

```
void Write(double value);
void Write(float value);
void Write(long value);
void Write(int value);
void Write(short value);
```

- The above example is preferred to the following language-specific alternative:

```
void Write(double doubleValue);
void Write(float floatValue);
void Write(long longValue);
void Write(int intValue);
void Write(short shortValue);
```

In the extremely rare case that it is necessary to have a uniquely named method for each fundamental data type, ***do*** use the following **universal type** names:

C# Type Name	ilasm Representation	Universal Type Name
sbyte	int8	SByte
byte	unsigned int8	Byte
short	int16	Int16
ushort	unsigned int16	UInt16
int	int32	Int32
uint	unsigned int32	UInt32
long	int64	Int64
ulong	unsigned int64	UInt64

C# Type Name	ilasm Representation	Universal Type Name
float	float32	Single
double	float64	Double
bool	int32	Boolean
char	unsigned int16	Char
string	System.String	String
object	System.Object	Object

A class that supports reading a variety of data types from a stream might have the following methods:

```
double ReadDouble();
float ReadSingle();
long ReadInt64();
int ReadInt32();
short ReadInt16();
```

The above example is preferred to the following language-specific alternative:

```
double ReadDouble();
float ReadFloat();
long ReadLong();
int ReadInt();
short ReadShort();
```

D.1.5 *Namespaces*

The following example illustrates the general rule for naming namespaces:

```
CompanyName.TechnologyName
```

Therefore, we should expect to see namespaces like the following:

```
Microsoft.Office
PowerSoft.PowerBuilder
```

- ***Do*** avoid the possibility of two published namespaces having the same name, by prefixing namespace names with a company name or other well-established brand. For example, `Microsoft.Office` for the Office Automation Classes provided by Microsoft.

- *Do* use PascalCasing, and separate logical components with periods (for example, `Microsoft.Office.PowerPoint`). If your brand employs non-traditional casing, *do* follow the casing defined by your brand, even if it deviates from normal namespace casing (for example, `NeXT.WebObjects` and `ee.cummings`).
- *Do* use plural namespace names where appropriate. For example, use `System.Collections` not `System.Collection`. Exceptions to this rule are brand names and abbreviations. For example, use `System.IO` not `System.IOs`.
- *Do not* specify the same name for namespaces and classes. For example, do not use `Debug` for a namespace name and also provide a class named `Debug`.

D.1.6 *Classes*

- *Do* name classes with nouns or noun phrases.
- *Do* use PascalCasing.
- *Do* use abbreviations in class names sparingly.
- *Do not* use any type of class prefix (such as "C").
- *Do not* use the underscore character.
- Occasionally, it is necessary to have a class name that begins with "I", that is not an interface. This is acceptable as long as the character that follows "I" is lower case (for example, `IdentityStore`).

The following are examples of correctly named classes:

```
public class FileStream
{
}
public class Button
{
}
public class String
{
}
```

D.1.7 *Interfaces*

- *Do* name interfaces with nouns or noun phrases, or adjectives describing behavior. For example, `IComponent` (descriptive noun), `ICustomAttributeProvider` (noun phrase), and `IPersistable` (adjective) are appropriate interface names.
- *Do* use PascalCasing.

- *Do* use abbreviations in interface names sparingly.
- *Do not* use the underscore character.
- *Do* prefix interface names with the letter "I", to indicate that the type is an interface.
- *Do* use similar names when defining a class/interface pair where the class is a standard implementation of the interface. The names should differ only by the letter "I" prefix on the interface name.

The following example illustrates these guidelines for the interface `IComponent` and its standard implementation, the class `Component`:

```
public interface IComponent
{
}
public class Component : IComponent
{
}
public interface IServiceProvider
{
}
public interface IFormattable
{
}
```


D.1.8 *Attributes*

- *Do* add the **Attribute** suffix to custom attribute classes as in the following example:

```
public class ObsoleteAttribute
{
}
```

D.1.9 *Enums*

- *Do* use PascalCasing for an `enum` type.
- *Do* use PascalCasing for an `enum` value name.
- *Do* use abbreviations in `enum` names sparingly.
- *Do not* use a prefix on `enum` names (for example, "adXXX" for ADO enums, "rtfXXX" for rich text enums, etc.).
- *Do not* use an "Enum" suffix on `enum` types.

- *Do* use a singular name for an enum.
- *Do* use a plural name for bit fields.

D.1.10 *Fields*

- *Do* use camelCasing (except for static fields; see Partition V, section D.1.10.1).
- *Do not* abbreviate field names.

  Spell out all the words used in a field name. Only use abbreviations if developers generally understand them. *Do not* use uppercase letters for field names. For example:

  ```
  class Foo
  {
     string url;
     string destinationUrl;
  }
  ```

- *Do not* use Hungarian notation for field names. Good names describe semantics, not type.
- *Do not* use a prefix for field names.
- *Do not* include a prefix on a field name—for example, "g_" or "s_"—to distinguish static versus non-static fields.

D.1.10.1 Static Fields

- *Do* name static fields with nouns, noun phrases, or abbreviations for nouns.
- *Do not* use a prefix for static field names.
- *Do* name static fields with PascalCasing.
- *Do not* prefix static field names with Hungarian type notation.

D.1.11 *Parameter Names*

- *Do* use descriptive parameter names. Parameter names should be descriptive enough that in most scenarios the name of the parameter and its type can be used to determine its meaning.
- *Do* name parameters with camelCasing.
- *Do* use names based on a parameter's meaning rather than names based on the parameter's type. We expect development tools to provide the information about type in a useful manner, so the parameter name can be put to better use describing semantics rather than type. Occasional use of type-based parameter names is entirely appropriate.
- *Do not* use **reserved** parameters. If more data is needed in the next version, a new overload can be added.

- ***Do not*** prefix parameter names with Hungarian type notation.

```
Type GetType (string typeName)
string Format (string format, object [] args)
```

D.1.12 *Method Names*

- ***Do*** name methods with PascalCasing as in the following examples:

```
RemoveAll()
GetCharArray()
Invoke()
```

- ***Do not*** use Hungarian notation.
- ***Do*** name methods with verbs or verb phrases.

D.1.13 *Property Names*

- ***Do*** name properties using a noun or noun phrase.
- ***Do*** name properties with PascalCasing.
- ***Do not*** use Hungarian notation.

D.1.14 *Event Names*

- ***Do*** name events using PascalCasing.
- ***Do not*** use Hungarian notation.
- ***Do*** name event handlers (delegate types) with the "EventHandler" suffix, as in the following example:

```
public delegate void MouseEventHandler(object sender, MouseEvent e);
```

- ***Consider*** using two parameters named `sender and e.`

  The `sender` parameter represents the object that raised the event. The `sender` parameter is always of type `object`, even if it is possible to employ a more specific type.

  The state associated with the event is encapsulated in an instance of an event class named `e`. Use an appropriate and specific event class for its type.

```
public delegate void MouseEventHandler(object sender, MouseEvent e);
```

- ***Do*** name event argument classes with the "EventArgs" suffix, as in the following example:

```
public class MouseEventArgs : EventArgs
{
   int x;
```

8. Annexes

```
    int y;
    public MouseEventArgs(int x, int y)
        { this.x = x; this.y = y; }
    public int X { get { return x; } }
    public int Y { get { return y; } }
}
```

- ***Do*** name event names that have a concept of pre and post using the present and past tense (do not use the BeforeXxx\AfterXxx pattern). For example, a close event that can be canceled would have a Closing and Closed event.
- ***Consider*** naming events with a verb.

D.2 Type Member Usage Guidelines

D.2.1 *Property Usage Guidelines*

- ***Do*** see Partition V, section D.2.1.1 on choosing between properties and methods.
- ***Do not*** use properties and types with the same name.

  Defining a property with the same name as a type can cause ambiguity in some programming languages. It is best to avoid this ambiguity unless there is a clear justification for not doing so.
- ***Do*** preserve the previous value if a property set throws an exception.
- ***Do*** allow properties to be set in any order. Properties should be stateless with respect to other properties.

  It is often the case that a particular feature of an object will not take effect until the developer specifies a particular set of properties, or until an object has a particular state. Until the object is in the correct state, the feature is not active. When the object is in the correct state, the feature automatically activates itself without requiring an explicit call. The semantics are the same regardless of the order in which the developer sets the property values or how the developer gets the object into the active state.

D.2.1.1 Properties vs. Methods

Library designers sometimes face a decision between a property and a method. Use the following guidelines to help you choose between these options. The philosophy here is that users will think of properties as though they were fields, hence methods are preferred where the intuitive semantics or performance differ from those of fields.

- ***Do*** use a property if the member has a logical backing store.
- ***Do*** use a method in the following situations.
  - The operation is a conversion (such as `Object.ToString()`).

- The operation is expensive (orders of magnitude slower than a field set would be).
- Obtaining a property value using the `Get` accessor has an observable side effect.
- Calling the member twice in succession results in different results.
- The order of execution relative to other properties is important.
- The member is static but returns a mutable value.
- The member returns an array.

  Properties that return arrays can be very misleading. Usually it is necessary to return a copy of the internal array so that the user cannot change internal state. This, coupled with the fact that a user could easily assume it is an indexed property, leads to inefficient code. In the following example, each call to the Methods property creates a copy of the array. That would be 2n+1 copies for this loop.

```
Type type = //get a type somehow
for (int i = 0; i < type.Methods.Length; i++)
{
   if (type.Methods[i].Name.Equals ("foo"))
   {...}
}
```


D.2.1.2 Read-Only and Write-Only Properties

- ***Do*** use read-only properties when the user cannot change the logical backing data field.
- ***Do not*** use write-only properties.

D.2.1.3 Indexed Property Usage

- ***Do*** use only one indexed property per class, and make it the default indexed property for that class.
- ***Do not*** use non-default indexed properties.
- ***Do*** use the name "Item" for indexed properties unless there is an obviously better name (for example, a `Chars` property on `string` is better than `Item`).
- ***Do*** use indexed properties when the logical backing store is an array.
- ***Do not*** provide both indexed properties and methods that are semantically equivalent to two or more overloaded methods.

```
MethodInfo Type.Method[string name]        ;; Should be method
MethodInfo Type.GetMethod (string name, boolean ignoreCase)
```

D.2.2 *Event Usage Guidelines*

- ***Do*** use the "raise" terminology for events rather than "fire" or "trigger" terminology.
- ***Do*** use a return type of void for event handlers.

- *Do* make event classes extend the class `System.EventArgs`.
- *Do* implement `AddOn<EventName>` and `RemoveOn<EventName>` for each event.
- *Do* use a `family virtual` method to raise each event.

  This is not appropriate for sealed classes, because classes cannot be derived from them. The purpose of the method is to provide a way for a derived class to handle the event using an override. This is more natural than using delegates in the case where the developer is creating a derived class.

  The derived class can choose not to call the base during the processing of `On<EventName>`. Be prepared for this by not including any processing in the `On<EventName>` method that is required for the base class to work correctly.

- *Do* assume that anything can go in an event handler.

  Classes are ready for the handler of the event to do almost anything, and in all cases the object is left in a good state after the event has been raised. Consider using a `try/finally` block at the point where the event is raised. Since the developer can call back on the object to perform other actions, do not assume anything about the object state when control returns to the point at which the event was raised

D.2.3 *Method Usage Guidelines*

- *Do* use non-virtual methods unless overriding is intended by the design. Providing the ability to override a method (i.e., making the method virtual) implies that the design of the type is independent of details of the method's implementation; this is rarely true without careful design of the type.
- *Do* use method overloading when you provide different methods that do semantically the same thing.
- *Do* favor method overloading to default arguments. Default arguments are not allowed in the Common Language Specification (CLS).

```
int String.IndexOf (String name);
int String.IndexOf (String name, int startIndex);
```

- *Do* use default values correctly.

  In a family of overloaded methods the complex method should use parameter names that indicate a change from the default state assumed in the simple method.

  For example, in the code below, the first method assumes the look-up will not be case-sensitive. In method two, we use the name *ignoreCase* rather than *caseSensitive* because the former indicates how we are changing the default behavior.

```
MethodInfo Type.GetMethod(String name);   //ignoreCase = false
MethodInfo Type.GetMethod (String name, boolean ignoreCase);
```

It is very common to use a zeroed state for the default value (such as: 0, 0.0, false, "", etc.).

- *Do* be consistent in the ordering and naming of method parameters.

  It is common to have a set of overloaded methods with an increasing number of parameters to allow the developer to specify a desired level of information. The more parameters specified, the more detail that is specified. All the related methods have a consistent parameter order and naming pattern. Each of the method variations has the same semantics for their shared set of parameters.

  This consistency is useful even if the parameters have different types.

  The only method in such a group that should be virtual is the one that has the most parameters.

- *Do* use method overloading for variable numbers of parameters.

  Where it is appropriate to have variable numbers of parameters to a method, use the convention of declaring N methods with increasing numbers of parameters, and also provide a method which takes an array of values for numbers greater than N. $N = 3$ or $N = 4$ is appropriate for most cases. Only the method that takes the array should be virtual.

- *Do* make only the most complete overload virtual (if extensibility is needed) and define the other operations in terms of it.

```
public int IndexOf (string s)
{ return IndexOf (s, 0); }
public int IndexOf (string s, int start)
{ return IndexOf (s, startIndex, s.Length); }
public virtual int IndexOf (string s, int start, int count)
{ //do real work }
```

- *Do* use the `ParamsAttribute` pattern for defining methods with a variable number of arguments.

```
void Format (string formatString, params object [] args)
```

- *Consider* using the varargs ("...") calling convention to provide a variable number of arguments, but ***do not*** use this without providing an alternative mechanism to accomplish the same thing, since it is not CLS-compliant.

- *Consider* providing special-case code for a small number of arguments to a method that takes a variable number of arguments, but only where the performance gained is significant. When this approach is taken, it becomes difficult to allow the method to be overridden because all the special cases must be overridden as well.

D.2.4 *Constructor Usage Guidelines*

- ***Do*** have only a default `private` constructor (or no constructor at all) if there are only static methods and properties on a class.
- ***Do*** minimal work in the constructor.
- ***Do*** provide a `family` constructor that can be used by types in a derived class.
- ***Do not*** provide an empty default constructor for value types.
- ***Do*** use parameters in constructors as shortcuts for setting properties.

  There should be no difference in semantics between using the empty constructor followed by some calls to property setters, and using a constructor with multiple arguments.

- ***Do*** be consistent in the ordering and naming of constructor parameters.

  A common pattern for constructor parameters is to provide an increasing number of parameters to allow the developer to specify a desired level of information. The more parameters that are specified, the more detail that is specified. For all of the following constructors, there is a consistent order and naming of the parameters.

D.2.5 *Field Usage Guidelines*

- ***Do not*** use instance fields that are `public` or `family`.
- ***Consider*** providing `get` and `set` property accessors for fields instead of making them `public`.
- ***Do*** use a `family` property that returns the value of a `private` field to expose a field to a derived class.

  By not exposing fields directly to the developer, the class can be versioned more easily for the following reasons:

  a. A field cannot be changed to a property while maintaining binary compatibility.

  b. The presence of executable code in `get` and `set` property accessors allows later improvements, such as demand-creation of an object upon usage of the property, or a property change notification.

- ***Do*** use `readonly static` fields instead of properties where the value is a global constant.
- ***Do not*** use `literal static` fields if the value can change between versions.
- ***Do*** use `public static` readonly fields for predefined object instances.

D.2.6 *Parameter Usage Guidelines*

- *Do* check arguments for validity.

  Perform argument validation for every `public` or `family` method and property `set` accessor, and throw meaningful exceptions to the developer. The `System.ArgumentException` exception, or one of its subclasses, is used in these cases.

  Note that the actual checking does not necessarily have to happen in the `public`/`family` method itself. It could happen at a lower level in some `private` routines. The main point is that the entire surface area that is exposed to developers checks for valid arguments.

  Parameter validation should be performed before any side-effects occur.

D.3 Type Usage Guidelines

D.3.1 *Class Usage Guidelines*

- *Do* favor using classes over any other type (i.e., interfaces or value types).

D.3.1.1 Base Class Usage Guidelines

Base classes are a useful way to group objects that share a common set of functionality. Base classes can provide a default set of functionality, while allowing customization though extension.

Add extensibility or polymorphism to your design only if you have a clear customer scenario for it.

- *Do* use base classes rather than interfaces.

  From a versioning perspective, interfaces are less flexible than classes. With a class, you can ship Version 1.0 and then in Version 2.0 decide to add another method. As long as the method is not abstract (that is, as long as you provide a default implementation of the method), any existing derived classes continue to function unchanged.

  Because interfaces do not support implementation inheritance, the pattern that applies to classes does not apply to interfaces. Adding a method to an interface is like adding an abstract method to a base class: any class that implements the interface will break because the class does not implement the interface's new method.

  Interfaces are appropriate in the following situations:

  - Several unrelated classes want to support the protocol.
  - These classes already have established base classes.
  - Aggregation is not appropriate or practical.

For all other cases, class inheritance is a better model. For example, make `IByteStream` an interface so a class can implement multiple stream types. Make `ValueEditor` an abstract class because classes derived from `ValueEditor` have no other purpose than to edit values.

- ***Do*** provide customization through `family` methods.

  The public interface of a base class should provide a rich set of functionality for the consumer of that class. However, customizers of that class often want to implement the fewest methods possible to provide that rich set of functionality to the consumer. To meet this goal, provide a set of non-virtual or final public methods that call through to a single family method with the "Impl" suffix that provides implementations for such a method. This pattern is also known as the "Template Method."

```
Public Control
{ public void SetBounds(int x, int y, int width, int height)
  { . . .
    SetBoundsImpl (…);
  }

  public void SetBounds(int x, int y,
                        int width, int height,
                        BoundsSpecified specified)
  { . . .
    SetBoundsImpl (…);
  }

  protected virtual void SetBoundsImpl
                         (int x, int y,
                          int width, int height,
                          BoundsSpecified specified)
   { // Do the real work here.
    }
  }
```

- ***Do*** define a `family` constructor on all `abstract` classes. Many compilers will insert a `public` constructor if you do not. This can be very misleading to users, as it can only be called from derived classes.

D.3.1.2 Sealed Class Usage Guidelines

- ***Do*** use `sealed` classes if creating derived classes will not be required.
- ***Do*** use `sealed` classes if there are only `static` methods and properties on a class.

D.3.2 *Value Type Usage Guidelines*

- ***Do*** use a value type for types that meet all of the following criteria:
  - Act like built-in types.
  - Have an instance size under 16 bytes.
  - Value semantics are desirable.
- ***Do not*** provide a default constructor.
- ***Do*** program assuming a state where all instance data [that] is set to zero, false, or null (as appropriate) is valid, since this will be the state if no constructor is run and there is no guarantee that a constructor will be run (unlike for classes).

D.3.2.1 Enum Usage Guidelines

- ***Do*** use an `Enum` to strongly type parameters, property, and return type. This allows development tools to know the possible values for a property or parameter.
- ***Do*** use the `System.Flags` custom attribute for an enum if a bitwise OR operation is to be performed on the numeric values.
- ***Do*** use `int32` as the underlying type of an `enum`.

  An exception to this rule is if the `enum` represents flags and there are many flags (>32) or the `enum` may grow to many flags in the future or the type needs to be different from type `int32` for backward compatibility.
- ***Do*** use an `enum` with flags attributes only if the value can be completely expressed as a set of bitflags. Do not use an enum for open sets (e.g., a version number).
- ***Do not*** assume `enum` arguments will be in the defined range. ***Do*** argument validation.
- ***Do*** favor using an `enum` over static final constants.
- ***Do*** use `int32` as the underlying type of an enum unless either of the following is true:
  a. The `enum` represents flags, and there are currently many flags (>32), or the enum may grow to many flags in the future.
  b. The type needs to be different from `int` for backward compatibility.
- ***Do not*** use a non-integral `enum` type. Only use `int8`, `int16`, `int32`, or `int64`.
- ***Do not*** define methods, properties, or events on an `enum`.
- ***Do not*** use any suffix on `enum` types.

D.3.3 *Interface Usage Guidelines*

- ***Do*** favor using classes over any other type (i.e., interfaces or value types).
- ***Do*** use a class or abstract class in preference to an interface, where possible.

- *Do* use interfaces to provide extensibility and the ability to customize.
- *Do* provide a default implementation of an interface where it is appropriate. For example, `System.Collections.DictionaryBase` is the default implementation of the `System.Collections.IDictionary` interface.
- *Do* see Partition V, section D.3.1.1 on the versioning issues with interfaces and abstract classes.
- *Do not* use interfaces as empty markers. Use custom attributes instead.

  If you need to mark a class as having a specific attribute (such as immutable or serializable), use a custom attribute rather than an interface.
- *Do* implement interfaces using *MethodImpls* (see Partition II [section 21.25]) and `private virtual` methods if you only want the interface methods available when cast to that interface. This is particularly useful when a class or value type implements an internal interface that is of no interest to a consumer of the class or value type.

D.3.4 *Delegate Usage Guidelines*

Delegates are a powerful tool that allow the managed code object model designer to encapsulate method calls. They are used in two basic areas.

`Event Notifications:`
See Partition V, section D.2.2 on event usage guidelines.

`Callbacks:`
Passed to a method so that user code can be called multiple times during execution to provide customization. The classic example of this is passing a Compare callback to a sort routine. These methods should use the Callback conventions

- *Do* use an Event design pattern for events (even if it is not user interface related).

D.3.5 *Attribute Classes*

The CLI enables developers to invent new kinds of declarative information, to specify declarative information for various program entities, and to retrieve attribute information in a runtime environment. New kinds of declarative information are defined through the declaration of attribute classes, which may have positional and named parameters.

- *Do* specify an `AttributeUsage` on your attributes to define their usage precisely.
- *Do* seal attribute classes if possible.
- *Do* provide a single constructor for the attribute.
- *Do* use a parameter to the attribute's constructor when the value of that parameter is always required to make the attribute.

- *Do* use a field on an attribute when the value of that property can be optionally specified to make the attribute.
- *Do not* name a parameter to the constructor with the same name as a field or property of the attribute.
- *Do* provide a read-only property with the same name (different casing) as each parameter to the constructor.
- *Do* provide a read-write property with the same name (different casing) as each field of the attribute.

D.3.6 *Nested Types*

A nested type is a type defined within the scope of another type. Nested types are very useful for encapsulating implementation details of a type, such as an enumerator over a collection, because they can have access to private state. Public nested types are rarely used.

Do not use public nested types unless all of the following are true:

- The nested type logically belongs to the containing type.
- The nested type is not used very often, or at least not directly.

D.4 Error Raising and Handling

- *Do* end Exception class names with the "Exception" suffix.
- *Do* use these common constructors.

```
public class XxxException : Exception
{
    XxxException() { }
    XxxException(string message) { }
    XxxException(string message, Exception inner) { }
}
```

- *Do* use the predefined exception types. Only define new exception types for programmatic scenarios, meaning you expect users of your library to catch exceptions of this new type and perform a programmatic action based on the exception type.
- *Do* not derive new exceptions directly from the base class `Exception`. Use one of its predefined subclasses instead.
- *Do* use a localized description string. When the user sees an error message, it will be derived from the description string of the exception that was thrown, and never from the exception class. Include a description string in every exception.

- *Do* use grammatically correct error messages, including ending punctuation.

  Each sentence in a description string of an exception should end in a period. This way, code that generically displays an exception message to the user does not have to handle the case where a developer forgot the final period, which is relatively cumbersome and expensive.

- *Do* provide exception properties for programmatic access. Include extra information (besides the description string) in an exception only when there is a programmatic scenario where that additional information is useful.

- *Do* throw exceptions only in exceptional cases.
  - *Do not* use exceptions for normal or expected errors.
  - *Do not* use exceptions for normal flow of control.

- *Do* return null for extremely common error cases. For example, `File.Open` returns a null if the file is not found, but throws an exception if the file is locked.

- *Do* design classes such that in the normal course of use there will never be an exception thrown. For example, a `FileStream` class might expose a way of determining if the end of the file has been reached to avoid the exception that will be thrown if the developer reads past the end of the file.

- *Do* throw an `InvalidOperationException` if in an inappropriate state.

  The `System.InvalidOperationException` exception should be thrown if the property set or method call is not appropriate given the object's current state.

- *Do* throw an `ArgumentException` or create an exception derived from this class if bad parameters are passed or detected.

- *Do* realize that the stack trace starts at the point where an exception is thrown, not where it is created with the `new` operator. You should consider this when deciding where to throw an exception.

- *Do* throw exceptions rather than return an error code.

- *Do* throw the most specific exception possible.

- *Do* set all the fields on the exception you use.

- *Do* use Inner exceptions (chained exceptions).

- *Do* clean up side-effects when throwing an exception. Clearly document cases where an exception may occur after a side-effect has already taken place and cannot be retracted.

- *Do not* assume that side-effects do not occur before an exception is thrown, but rather that the state is restored if one is thrown. That is, another thread may see the side-effect, but will then see an additional one to restore the state.

D.4.1 *Standard Exception Types*

The following table breaks down the standard exceptions and the conditions for which you should create a derived class.

Exception Type	Base Type	Description	Example
Exception	Object	Base class for all exceptions.	None (use a derived class of this exception)
SystemException	Exception	Base class for all runtime-generated errors.	None (use a derived class of this exception)
IndexOutOfRange-Exception	SystemException	Thrown only by the runtime when an array is indexed improperly.	Indexing an array outside of its valid range: arr[arr.Length+1]
NullReference-Exception	SystemException	Thrown only by the runtime when a null object is referenced.	object o = null; o.ToString();
InvalidOperation-Exception	SystemException	Thrown by methods when in an invalid state.	Calling Enumerator.GetNext() after removing an item from the underlying collection.
ArgumentException	SystemException	Base class for all argument exceptions. Derived classes of this exception should be thrown where applicable.	None (use a derived class of this exception)
ArgumentNull-Exception	ArgumentException	Thrown by methods that do not allow an argument to be null.	String s = null; "foo".IndexOf (s);
ArgumentOutOf-RangeException	ArgumentException	Thrown by methods that verify that arguments are in a given range.	String s = "string"; s.Chars[9];
InteropException	SystemException	Base class for exceptions that occur or are targeted at environments outside of the runtime.	None (use a derived class of this exception)

D.5 Array Usage Guidelines

- ***Do*** use a collection when `Add`, `Remove`, or other methods for manipulating the collection are supported. This scopes all related methods to the collection.
- ***Do*** use collections to add read-only wrappers around internal arrays.
- ***Do*** use collections to avoid the inefficiencies in the following code.

  ```
  for (int i = 0; i < obj.myObj.Count; i++)
        DoSomething(obj.myObj[i])
  ```

  Also see Partition V, section D.2.1.1.
- ***Do*** return an Empty array instead of a null.

  Users assume that the following code will work:

  ```
  public void DoSomething(…)
  { int a[] = SomeOtherFunc();
    if (a.Length > 0)// Don't expect NULL here!
    { // do something
    }
  }
  ```

D.6 Operator Overloading Usage Guidelines

- ***Do*** define operators on Value types that are logically a built-in language type.
- ***Do*** provide operator-overloading methods only involving the class in which the methods are defined.
- ***Do*** use the names and signature conventions described in the Common Language Specification.
- ***Do not*** be cute.

  Operator overloading is useful in cases where it is immediately obvious what the result of the operation will be. For example, it makes sense to be able to subtract one `Time` value from another `Time` value and get a `TimeSpan`. However, it is not appropriate to use `shift` to write to a stream.
- ***Do*** overload operators in a symmetric fashion. For example, if you overload the `Equal` operator (`==`), you should also overload the not equal (`!=`) operator.
- ***Do*** provide alternative signatures.

  Most languages do not support operator overloading. For this reason it is a CLS requirement that you include a method with an appropriate domain-specific name that has the equivalent functionality, as in the following example.

```
class Time {
   TimeSpan operator -(Time t1, Time t2) { }
   TimeSpan Difference(Time t1, Time t2) { }
}
```

See Partition I, section 10.3.

D.6.1 *Implementing Equals and operator==*

- *Do* see the section on implementing the `Equals` method in Partition V, section D.7.
- *Do* implement `GetHashCode()` whenever you implement `Equals()`. This keeps `Equals()` and `GetHashCode()` synchronized.
- *Do* override `Equals` whenever you implement `operator==` and make them do the same thing. This allows infrastructure code such as `Hashtable` and `ArrayList`, which use `Equals()`, to behave the same way as user code written using `operator==`.
- *Do* override `Equals` anytime you implement `IComparable`.
- *Consider* implementing operator overloading for `==`, `!=` , `<`, and `>` when you implement `IComparable`.
- *Do not* throw exceptions from `Equals()`, `GetHashCode()`, or `operator==` methods.

D.6.1.1 Implementing operator== on Value Types

- *Do* overload `operator==` anytime equality is meaningful, because in most programming languages there is no default implementation of `operator==` for value types.
- *Consider* implementing `Equals()` on ValueTypes because the default implementation on `System.ValueType` will not perform as well as your custom implementation.
- *Do* implement `operator==` anytime you override `Equals()`.

D.6.1.2 Implementing operator== on Reference Types

- *Do* use care when implementing `operator==` on reference types. Most languages do provide a default implementation of `operator==` for reference types; therefore, overriding the default implementation should be done with care. Most reference types, even those that implement `Equals()` should not override `operator==`.
- *Do* override `operator==` if your type has value semantics (that is, if it looks like a base type such as a Point, String, BigNumber, etc.). Anytime you are tempted to overload + and –, you also should consider overloading `operator==`.

D.6.2 *Cast Operations (op_Explicit and op_Implicit)*

- *Do not* lose precision in implicit casts.

  For example, there should not be an implicit cast from `Double` to `Int32`, but there may be one from `Int32` to `Int64`.

8. Annexes

- ***Do not*** throw exceptions from implicit casts because it is very difficult for the developer to understand what is happening.
- ***Do*** provide cast operations that operate on the whole object. The value that is cast represents the whole value being cast, not one sub-part. For example, it is not appropriate for a Button to cast to a string by returning its caption.
- ***Do not*** generate a semantically different value.

  For example, it is appropriate to convert a `Time` or `TimeSpan` into an `Int`. The `Int` still represents the time or duration. It does not make sense to convert a file name string such as, "c:\mybitmap.gif" into a Bitmap object.
- ***Do not*** provide cast operations for values between different semantic domains. For example, it makes sense that an `Int32` can cast to a `Double`. It does not make sense for an `Int` to cast to a `String`, because they are in different domains.

D.7 Equals

Do see Partition V, section D.6.1 on implementing `operator==`.

Do override `GetHashCode()` in order for the type to behave correctly in a hashtable.

Do not throw an exception in your `Equals` implementation. Return false for a null argument, etc.

Do follow the contract defined on `Object.Equals`.

- `x.Equals(x)` returns true.
- `x.Equals(y)` returns the same value as `y.Equals(x)`.
- `(x.Equals(y) && y.Equals(z))` returns true if and only if `x.Equals(z)` returns true.
- Successive invocations of `x.Equals(y)` return the same value as long as the objects referenced by `x` and `y` are not modified.
- `x.Equals(null)` returns false.

For some kinds of objects, it is desirable to have `Equals` test for *value equality* instead of referential equality. Such implementations of `Equals` return true if the two objects have the same value, even if they are not the same instance. The definition of what constitutes an object's value is up to the implementer of the type, but it is typically some or all of the data stored in the instance variables of the object. For example, the value of a string is based on the characters of the string; the `Equals` method of the `String` class returns true for any two string instances that contain exactly the same characters in the same order.

When the `Equals` method of a base class provides value equality, an override of `Equals` in a class derived from that base class should invoke the inherited implementation of `Equals`.

If you choose to overload the equality operator for a given type, that type should override the `Equals` method. Such implementations of the `Equals` method should return the same results as the equality operator. Following this guideline will help ensure that class library code using `Equals` (such as `ArrayList` and `Hashtable`) behaves in a manner that is consistent with the way the equality operator is used by application code.

If you are implementing a value type, you should follow these guidelines:

- Consider overriding `Equals` to gain increased performance over that provided by the default implementation of `Equals on System.ValueType`.
- If you override `Equals` and the language supports operator overloading, you should overload the equality operator for your value type.

If you are implementing reference types, you should follow these guidelines:

- Consider overriding `Equals` on a reference type if the semantics of the type are based on the fact that the type represents some value(s). For example, reference types such as Point and BigNumber should override `Equals`.
- Most reference types should not overload the equality operator, even if they override `Equals`. However, if you are implementing a reference type that is intended to have value semantics, such as a complex number type, you should override the equality operator.

If you implement `IComparable` on a given type, you should override `Equals` on that type.

8. Annexes

ANNOTATION: This section on `Equals` is very worth a careful reading by anyone who is adding new data types to the system. Equality is very complicated, the rules are confusing, and violating them leads to unusual behavior in unexpected places. In C#, for example, `a==b` checks the identity of the two reference types, but if you overloaded the values, it checks those overloaded types. If you need to check object identity, you must use "`object.reference =`", which will work, where "==" will not. Not all are enthusiastic about these rules.

D.8 Callbacks

Delegates, Interfaces, and Events can each be used to provide callback functionality. Each has its own specific usage characteristics that make it better suited to particular situations.

Use Events if the following are true:

- One signs up for the callback up front (typically through separate `Add` and `Remove` methods).
- Typically more than one object will care.

Use a Delegate if the following are true:

- You want a C-style function pointer.
- Single callback.
- Registered in the call or at construction time (not through separate `Add` method).

Use an Interface if the following is true:

- The callback entails complex behavior.

D.9 Security in Class Libraries

Class library authors need to consider two perspectives with respect to security. Whether these perspectives are applicable will depend upon the class itself. Some classes, such as `System.IO.FileStream` represent objects that need protection with permissions; the implementation of these classes is responsible for checking the appropriate permissions of the caller required for each action and only allowing authorized callers to perform the actions for which they have permission. The `System.Security` namespace contains some classes to help make these checks easier. Additionally, class library code often is fully trusted, or at least highly trusted, code. Any flaws in the code represent a serious threat to the integrity of the entire security system. Therefore, extra care is required when writing class library code, as detailed below.

- ***Do*** access protected resources only after checking the permissions of your callers, through either a declarative security attribute or an explicit call to `Demand` on an appropriate security permission object.
- ***Do*** assert a permission only when necessary, and always precede it by the necessary checks.
- ***Do not*** assume that code will only be called by callers with certain permissions.
- ***Do not*** define non-typesafe interfaces that might be used to bypass security.
- ***Do not*** expose functionality that allows a semi-trusted caller to take advantage of higher trust of the class.

D.10 Threading Design Guidelines

- ***Do not*** provide static methods that mutate static state.

  In common server scenarios, static state is shared across requests, which means multiple threads can execute that code at the same time. This opens up the possibility for threading bugs. ***Consider*** using a design pattern that encapsulates data into instances that are not shared.

- ***Do not*** normally provide thread-safe instance state.

  By default, the library is not thread-safe. Adding locks to create thread-safe code decreases performance and increases lock contention (as well as opening up deadlock bugs). In common application models, only one thread at a time executes user code, which minimizes the need for thread safety. In cases where it is interesting to provide a thread-safe version, a `GetSynchronized()` method can be used to return a thread-safe instance of that type. (See `System.Collections`, which is described in the *.NET Framework Standard Library Annotated Reference*, for examples.)

- ***Do*** make all static state thread-safe.

  If you must use static state, make it thread-safe. In common server scenarios, static data is shared across requests, which means multiple threads can execute that code at the same time. For this reason it is necessary to protect static state.

- ***Do*** be aware of non-atomic operations.

  Value types whose underlying representations are greater than 32 bits may have non-atomic operations. Specifically, because value types are copied bitwise (by value as opposed to by reference), race conditions can occur in what appear to be straightforward assignments within code.

  For example, consider the following code (executing on two separate threads), where the variable x has been declared as type `Int64`.

```
// Code executing on Thread "A".
x = 54343343433;


// Code executing on Thread "B".
x = 934343434343;
```

  At first glance it seems to indicate that there is no possibility of race conditions (since each line looks like a straight assignment operation). However, because the underlying variable is a 64-bit value type, the actual code is not doing an atomic assignment operation. Instead, it is doing a bitwise copy of two 32-bit halves. In the event of a context switch, halfway during the value type assignment operation on one of the threads, the resulting `x` variable can have corrupt data (for example, the resulting value will be composed of 32 bits of the first number, and 32 bits of the second number).

8. Annexes

- *Do* be aware of method calls in locked sections.

  Deadlocks can result when a static method in class A calls static methods in class B, and vice versa. If A and B both synchronize their static methods, this will cause a deadlock. You might only discover this deadlock under heavy threading stress.

  Performance issues can result when a static method in class A calls a static method in class A. If these methods are not factored correctly, performance will suffer because there will be a large amount of redundant synchronization. Excessive use of fine-grained synchronization might negatively impact performance. In addition, it might have a significant negative impact on scalability.

- *Do* be aware of issues with the `lock` statement and ***consider*** using `System.Threading.Interlocked` instead.

  It's tempting to use the `lock` statement in C# to solve all threading problems. But the `System.Threading.Interlocked` class is superior for updates that must be made automically.

- *Do* avoid the need for synchronization if possible.

  Obviously for high-traffic pathways it is nice to avoid synchronization. Sometimes the algorithm can be adjusted to tolerate races rather than eliminating them.

ANNOTATION: It is important to understand the threading guidelines. The design philosophy in this regard of the CLI is dfferent for some other libraries. For the most part, the CLI class libraries are not written to do locking, because general-purpose locking leads to inefficiencies that are imposed on everyone for programs that work in a multi-threaded environment. Instead, it was determined to first ensure that the libraries are efficient, and to provide simple ways to use locks. Thus, those who are in multi-threaded environments can use locks without building locking into the libraries.

Annex E Portability Considerations

This section gathers together information about areas where this standard deliberately gives leeway to implementations. This leeway is intended to allow compliant implementations to make choices that provide better performance or add value in other ways. But this leeway inherently makes programs non-portable. This section describes the techniques that can be used to ensure that programs operate the same way independent of the particular implementation of the CLI.

Note that code may be portable even though the data is not, because of both size of integer type and direction of bytes in words. Read-write invariance holds, provided the read method corresponds to the write method (i.e., "write as int, read as int" works, but "write as string, read as int" might not).

E.1 Uncontrollable Behavior

The following aspects of program behavior are implementation-dependent. Many of these items will be familiar to programmers used to writing code designed for portability (for example, the fact that the CLI does not impose a minimum size for heap or stack).

1. The heap and stack aren't required to have minimum sizes.
2. Behavior [is] relative to asynchronous exceptions (see `System.Thread.Abort`).
3. Globalization is not supported, so every implementation specifies its culture information, including such user-visible features as sort order for strings.
4. Threads cannot be assumed to be either pre-emptively or non-pre-emptively scheduled. This decision is implementation-specific.
5. Locating assemblies is an implementation-specific mechanism.
6. Security policy is an implementation-specific mechanism.
7. File names are implementation-specific.
8. Timer resolution (granularity) is implementation-specific, although the unit is specified.

E.2 Language- and Compiler-Controllable Behavior

The following aspects of program behavior can be controlled through language design or careful generation of CIL by a language-specific compiler. The CLI provides all the support necessary to control the behavior, but the default is to allow implementation-specific optimizations.

1. Unverifiable code can access arbitrary memory and cannot be guaranteed to be portable.
2. Floating point – compiler can force all intermediate values to known precision.
3. Integer overflow – compiler can force overflow checking.
4. Native integer type need not be exposed, or can be exposed for opaque handles only, or can reliably recast with overflow check to known size values before use. Note that "free conversion" between native integer and fixed-size integer without overflow checks will not be portable.

5. Deterministic initialization of types is portable, but "before first reference to static variable" is not. Language design either can force all initialization to be deterministic (cf. Java) or can restrict initialization to deterministic cases (i.e., simple static assignments).

E.3 Programmer-Controllable Behavior

The following aspects of program behavior can be controlled directly by the programmer.

1. Code that is not thread-safe may operate differently even on a single implementation. In particular, the atomicity guarantees [that] around 64-bit must be adhered to, and testing on 64-bit implementations may not be sufficient to find all such problems. The key is never to use both normal read-write and interlocked access to the same 64-bit datum.
2. [Be careful with] calls to unmanaged code or calls to non-standardized extensions to libraries.
3. Do not depend on the relative order of finalization of objects.
4. Do not use explicit layout of data.
5. Do not rely on the relative order of exceptions within a single CIL instruction or a given library method call.

APPENDIX

Microsoft Portable Executable and Object File Format Specification

VISUAL C++® BUSINESS UNIT
MICROSOFT CORPORATION

REVISION 7.1 JUNE 2003

Note: This document is provided to aid in the development of tools and applications for Microsoft Windows® but is not guaranteed to be a complete specification in all respects. Microsoft reserves the right to alter this document without notice.

1 General Concepts

This document specifies the structure of executable (image) files and object files under Microsoft Windows. These files are referred to as Portable Executable (PE) and Common Object File Format (COFF) files, respectively. The name "Portable Executable" refers to the fact that the format is not architecture-specific.

Certain concepts appear throughout this specification and are described in the following table:

Name	Description
Image file	Executable file: either an .EXE file or a .DLL. An image file can be thought of as a "memory image." The term "image file" is usually used instead of "executable file," because the latter sometimes is taken to mean only an .EXE file.
Object file	A file given as input to the linker. The linker produces an image file, which in turn is used as input by the loader. The term "object file" does not necessarily imply any connection to object-oriented programming.
RVA	Relative Virtual Address. In an image file, an RVA is always the address of an item *once loaded into memory*, with the base address of the image file subtracted from it. The RVA of an item will almost always differ from its position within the file on disk (File Pointer). In an object file, an RVA is less meaningful because memory locations are not assigned. In this case, an RVA would be an address within a section (see below), to which a relocation is later applied during linking. For simplicity, compilers should just set the first RVA in each section to zero.
Virtual Address (VA)	Same as RVA (see above), except that the base address of the image file is not subtracted. The address is called a "Virtual Address" because Windows creates a distinct virtual address space for each process, independent of physical memory. For almost all purposes, a virtual address should be considered just an address. A virtual address is not as predictable as an RVA, because the loader might not load the image at its preferred location.
The linker	Refers to Microsoft Corporation's Linker.

Name	Description
File pointer	Location of an item within the file itself, before being processed by the linker (in the case of object files) or the loader (in the case of image files). In other words, this is a position within the file as stored on disk.
Date/Time Stamp	Date/time stamps are used in a number of places in a PE/COFF file, and for different purposes. The format of each such stamp, however, is always the same: that used by the time functions in the C run-time library.
Section	A section is the basic unit of code or data within a PE/COFF file. In an object file, for example, all code can be combined within a single section, or (depending on compiler behavior) each function can occupy its own section. With more sections, there is more file overhead, but the linker is able to link in code more selectively. A section is somewhat similar to a segment in Intel 8086 architecture. All the raw data in a section must be loaded contiguously. In addition, an image file can contain a number of sections, such as .tls or .reloc, which have special purposes.
Attribute Certificate	Attribute certificates are used to associate verifiable statements with an image. There are a number of different verifiable statements that can be associated with a file, but one of the most useful ones is a statement by a software manufacturer indicating what the message digest of the image is expected to be. A message digest is similar to a checksum except that it is extremely difficult to forge, and, therefore it is very difficult to modify a file in such a way as to have the same message digest as the original file. The statement may be verified as being made by the manufacturer by use of public/private key cryptography schemes. This document does not go into details of attribute certificates other than to allow for their insertion into image files.

2 Overview

Figures A-1 and A-2 illustrate the Microsoft PE executable format and the Microsoft COFF object-module format.

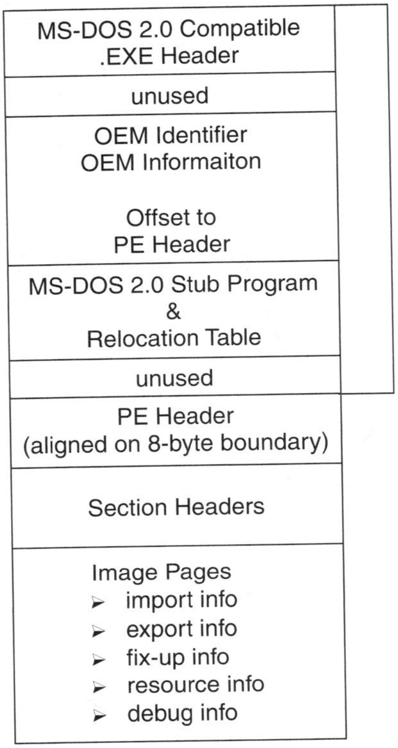

Figure A-1 Typical 32-Bit Portable .EXE File Layout

MS COFF Header

Section Headers

Image Pages
- fix-up info
- debug info

Figure A-2 Typical 32- and 64-Bit COFF Object Module Layout

3 File Headers

The PE file header consists of an MS-DOS stub, the PE signature, the COFF File Header, and an Optional header. A COFF object file header consists of a COFF File Header and an Optional Header. In both cases, the file headers are followed immediately by section headers.

3.1 MS-DOS Stub (Image Only)

The MS-DOS Stub is a valid application that runs under MS-DOS and is placed at the front of the .EXE image. The linker places a default stub here, which prints out the message "This program cannot be run in DOS mode" when the image is run in MS-DOS. The user can specify another stub by using the /STUB linker option.

At location 0x3c, the stub has the file offset to the Portable Executable (PE) signature. This information enables Windows to properly execute the image file, even though it has a DOS Stub. This file offset is placed at location 0x3c during linking.

3.2 Signature (Image Only)

After the MS-DOS stub, at the file offset specified at offset 0x3c, there is a 4-byte signature identifying the file as a PE formatimage file. Currently, this signature is "PE\0\0" (the letters "P" and "E" followed by two null bytes).

3.3 COFF File Header (Object & Image)

At the beginning of an object file, or immediately after the signature of an image file, there is a standard COFF header of the following format. Note that the Windows loader limits the Number of Sections to 96.

Offset	Size	Field	Description
0	2	Machine	Number identifying type of target machine. See Section 3.3.1, "Machine Types," for more information.
2	2	NumberOfSections	Number of sections; indicates size of the Section Table, which immediately follows the headers.
4	4	TimeDateStamp	The low 32-bits of the number of seconds since 00:00 January 1, 1970 (a C Runtime time_t value) when the file was created.
8	4	PointerToSymbolTable	File offset of the COFF symbol table or 0 if none is present. Should be zero for an image as COFF debugging information is deprecated.

Offset	Size	Field	Description
12	4	NumberOfSymbols	Number of entries in the symbol table. This data can be used in locating the string table, which immediately follows the symbol table. Should be zero for an image as COFF debugging information is deprecated.
16	2	SizeOfOptionalHeader	Size of the optional header, which is required for executable files but not for object files. An object file should have a value of 0 here. The format is described in the section "Optional Header."
18	2	Characteristics	Flags indicating attributes of the file. See Section 3.3.2, "Characteristics," for specific flag values.

3.3.1 Machine Types

The Machine field has one of the following values, defined below, which specify its machine (CPU) type. An image file can be run only on the specified machine, or a system emulating it.

Constant	Value	Description
IMAGE_FILE_MACHINE_UNKNOWN	0x0	Contents assumed to be applicable to any machine type.
IMAGE_FILE_MACHINE_AM33	0x1d3	Matsushita AM33
IMAGE_FILE_MACHINE_AMD64	0x8664	AMD AMD64
IMAGE_FILE_MACHINE_ARM	0x1c0	ARM little endian
IMAGE_FILE_MACHINE_CEE	0xc0ee	clr pure MSIL (object only)
IMAGE_FILE_MACHINE_EBC	0xebc	EFI Byte Code
IMAGE_FILE_MACHINE_I386	0x14c	Intel 386 or later, and compatible processors
IMAGE_FILE_MACHINE_IA64	0x200	Intel IA64
IMAGE_FILE_MACHINE_M32R	0x9041	Mitsubishi M32R little endian
IMAGE_FILE_MACHINE_MIPS16	0x266	

Constant	Value	Description
IMAGE_FILE_MACHINE_MIPSFPU	0x366	MIPS with FPU
IMAGE_FILE_MACHINE_MIPSFPU16	0x466	MIPS16 with FPU
IMAGE_FILE_MACHINE_POWERPC	0x1f0	Power PC, little endian
IMAGE_FILE_MACHINE_POWERPCFP	0x1f1	Power PC with floating point support
IMAGE_FILE_MACHINE_R4000	0x166	MIPS little endian
IMAGE_FILE_MACHINE_SH3	0x1a2	Hitachi SH3
IMAGE_FILE_MACHINE_SH3DSP	0x1a3	Hitachi SH3 DSP
IMAGE_FILE_MACHINE_SH4	0x1a6	Hitachi SH4
IMAGE_FILE_MACHINE_SH5	0x1a8	Hitachi SH5
IMAGE_FILE_MACHINE_THUMB	0x1c2	Thumb
IMAGE_FILE_MACHINE_WCEMIPSV2	0x169	MIPS little endian WCE v2

3.3.2 Characteristics

The Characteristics field contains flags that indicate attributes of the object or image file. The following flags are currently defined:

Flag	Value	Description
IMAGE_FILE_RELOCS_STRIPPED	0x0001	Image only, Windows CE, Windows NT and above. Indicates that the file does not contain base relocations and must therefore be loaded at its preferred base address. If the base address is not available, the loader reports an error. The default behavior of the linker is to strip base relocations from EXEs.
IMAGE_FILE_EXECUTABLE_IMAGE	0x0002	Image only. Indicates that the image file is valid and can be run. If this flag is not set, it indicates a linker error.

Flag	Value	Description
IMAGE_FILE_LINE_NUMS_STRIPPED	0x0004	COFF line numbers have been removed. Deprecated and should be zero.
IMAGE_FILE_LOCAL_SYMS_STRIPPED	0x0008	COFF symbol table entries for local symbols have been removed. Deprecated and should be zero.
IMAGE_FILE_AGGRESSIVE_WS_TRIM	0x0010	Obsolete. Aggressively trim working set. Deprecated in Windows 2000 and later. Must be zero.
IMAGE_FILE_LARGE_ADDRESS_AWARE	0x0020	App can handle > 2gb addresses.
	0x0040	Use of this flag is reserved for future use.
IMAGE_FILE_BYTES_REVERSED_LO	0x0080	Little endian: LSB precedes MSB in memory. Deprecated and should be zero.
IMAGE_FILE_32BIT_MACHINE	0x0100	Machine based on 32-bit-word architecture.
IMAGE_FILE_DEBUG_STRIPPED	0x0200	Debugging information removed from image file.
IMAGE_FILE_REMOVABLE_RUN_FROM_SWAP	0x0400	If image is on removable media, fully load it and copy it to the swap file.
IMAGE_FILE_NET_RUN_FROM_SWAP	0x0800	If image is on network media, fully load it and copy it to the swap file.
IMAGE_FILE_SYSTEM	0x1000	The image file is a system file, not a user program.
IMAGE_FILE_DLL	0x2000	The image file is a dynamic-link library (DLL). Such files are considered executable files for almost all purposes, although they cannot be directly run.
IMAGE_FILE_UP_SYSTEM_ONLY	0x4000	File should be run only on a UP machine.
IMAGE_FILE_BYTES_REVERSED_HI	0x8000	Big endian: MSB precedes LSB in memory. Deprecated and should be zero.

3.4 Optional Header (Image Only)

Every image file has an Optional Header that provides information to the loader. This header is optional in the sense that some files (specifically, object files) do not have it. For image files, this header is required. An object file may have an optional header, but generally this header has no function in an object file except to increase size.

Note that the size of the optional header is not fixed. The SizeOfOptionalHeader field in the COFF Header (see Section 3.3, "COFF File Header (Object & Image)") must be used to validate that a probe into the file for a particular Data Directory does not go beyond the SizeOfOptionalHeader. The NumberOfRvaAndSizes field of the Optional Header should also be used to ensure that no probe for a particular Data Directory entry goes beyond the Optional Header. In addition, it is important to validate the Optional Header's Magic number for format compatibility.

The Optional Header's Magic number determines whether an image is a PE32 or PE32+ executable:

Magic Number	PE Format
0x10b	PE32
0x20b	PE32+

PE32+ images allow for a 64-bit address space while limiting the image size to 2 Gigabytes. Other PE32+ modifications are addressed in their respective sections.

The Optional Header itself has three major parts:

Offset (PE32/PE32+)	Size (PE32/PE32+)	Header Part	Description
0	28/24	Standard fields	These are defined for all implementations of COFF, including UNIX.
28/24	68 / 88	Windows specific fields	These include additional fields to support specific features of Windows (for example, subsystem).
96/112	Variable	Data directories	These fields are address/size pairs for special tables, found in the image file and used by the operating system (for example, Import Table and Export Table).

Appendix

3.4.1 *Optional Header Standard Fields (Image Only)*

The first eight fields of the Optional Header are standard fields, defined for every implementation of COFF. These fields contain general information useful for loading and running an executable file, and are unchanged for the PE32+ format.

Offset	Size	Field	Description
0	2	Magic	Unsigned integer identifying the state of the image file. The most common number is 0x10B, identifying it as a normal executable file, 0x107 identifies a ROM image, and 0x20B identifies it as a PE32+ executable.
2	1	MajorLinkerVersion	Linker major version number.
3	1	MinorLinkerVersion	Linker minor version number.
4	4	SizeOfCode	Size of the code (text) section, or the sum of all code sections if there are multiple sections.
8	4	SizeOfInitializedData	Size of the initialized data section, or the sum of all such sections if there are multiple data sections.
12	4	SizeOfUninitializedData	Size of the uninitialized data section (BSS), or the sum of all such sections if there are multiple BSS sections.
16	4	AddressOfEntryPoint	Address of entry point, relative to image base, when executable file is loaded into memory. For program images, this is the starting address. For device drivers, this is the address of the initialization function. An entry point is optional for DLLs. When none is present this field must be 0.
20	4	BaseOfCode	Address, relative to image base, of beginning of code section, when loaded into memory.

PE32 contains this additional field, absent in PE32+, following BaseOfCode:

24	4	BaseOfData	Address, relative to image base, of beginning of data section, when loaded into memory.

3.4.2 Optional Header Windows-Specific Fields (Image Only)

The next twenty-one fields are an extension to the COFF Optional Header format and contain additional information needed by the linker and loader in Windows.

Offset (PE32/PE32+)	Size (PE32/PE32+)	Field	Description
28 / 24	4 / 8	ImageBase	Preferred address of first byte of image when loaded into memory; must be a multiple of 64K. The default for DLLs is 0x10000000. The default for Windows CE EXEs is 0x00010000. The default for Windows NT, Windows 2000, Windows XP, Windows 95, Windows 98, and Windows Me is 0x00400000.
32 / 32	4	SectionAlignment	Alignment (in bytes) of sections when loaded into memory. Must [be] greater or equal to File Alignment. Default is the page size for the architecture.
36 / 36	4	FileAlignment	Alignment factor (in bytes) used to align the raw data of sections in the image file. The value should be a power of 2 between 512 and 64K inclusive. The default is 512. If the SectionAlignment is less than the architecture's page size, then this must match the SectionAlignment.
40 / 40	2	MajorOperatingSystemVersion	Major version number of required OS.
42 / 42	2	MinorOperatingSystemVersion	Minor version number of required OS.
44 / 44	2	MajorImageVersion	Major version number of image.

Offset (PE32/PE32+)	Size (PE32/PE32+)	Field	Description
46 / 46	2	MinorImageVersion	Minor version number of image.
48 / 48	2	MajorSubsystemVersion	Major version number of sub-system.
50 / 50	2	MinorSubsystemVersion	Minor version number of sub-system.
52 / 52	4	Win32VersionValue	Reserved, must be zero.
56 / 56	4	SizeOfImage	Size, in bytes, of the image, including all headers as it is loaded in memory; must be a multiple of Section Alignment.
60 / 60	4	SizeOfHeaders	Combined size of MS-DOS stub, PE Header, and section headers rounded up to a multiple of FileAlignment.
64 / 64	4	CheckSum	Image file checksum. The algorithm for computing is incorporated into IMAGHELP.DLL. The following are checked for validation at load time: all drivers, any DLL loaded at boot time, and any DLL that ends up in the server.
68 / 68	2	Subsystem	Subsystem required to run this image. See "Windows Subsystem" below for more information.
70 / 70	2	DllCharacteristics	See "DLL Characteristics" below for more information.
72 / 72	4 / 8	SizeOfStackReserve	Size of stack to reserve. Only the Stack Commit Size is committed; the rest is made available one page at a time, until reserve size is reached.
76 / 80	4 / 8	SizeOfStackCommit	Size of stack to commit.

Offset (PE32/PE32+)	Size (PE32/PE32+)	Field	Description
80 / 88	4 / 8	SizeOfHeapReserve	Size of local heap space to reserve. Only the Heap Commit Size is committed; the rest is made available one page at a time, until reserve size is reached.
84 / 96	4 / 8	SizeOfHeapCommit	Size of local heap space to commit.
88 / 104	4	LoaderFlags	Reserved, must be zero.
92 / 108	4	NumberOfRvaAndSizes	Number of data-directory entries in the remainder of the Optional Header. Each describes a location and size.

Windows Subsystem

The following values, defined for the Subsystem field of the Optional Header, determine what, if any, Windows subsystem is required to run the image.

Constant	Value	Description
IMAGE_SUBSYSTEM_UNKNOWN	0	Unknown subsystem.
IMAGE_SUBSYSTEM_NATIVE	1	Used for device drivers and native Windows processes.
IMAGE_SUBSYSTEM_WINDOWS_GUI	2	Image runs in the Windows graphical user interface (GUI) subsystem.
IMAGE_SUBSYSTEM_WINDOWS_CUI	3	Image runs in the Windows character subsystem.
IMAGE_SUBSYSTEM_POSIX_CUI	7	Image runs in the Posix character subsystem.
IMAGE_SUBSYSTEM_WINDOWS_CE_GUI	9	Image runs in Windows CE.
IMAGE_SUBSYSTEM_EFI_APPLICATION	10	Image is an EFI (Extensible Firmware Interface) application.

Constant	Value	Description
IMAGE_SUBSYSTEM_EFI_BOOT_SERVICE_DRIVER	11	Image is an EFI driver with boot services.
IMAGE_SUBSYSTEM_EFI_RUNTIME_DRIVER	12	Image is an EFI driver with runtime services.
IMAGE_SUBSYSTEM_EFI_ROM	13	Image is an EFI ROM image.
IMAGE_SUBSYSTEM_XBOX	14	Image runs in XBOX.
IMAGE_SUBSYSTEM_NEXUS_AGENT	15	

DLL Characteristics

The following values are defined for the DllCharacteristics field of the Optional Header.

Constant	Value	Description
	0x0001	Reserved.
	0x0002	Reserved.
	0x0004	Reserved.
	0x0008	Reserved.
IMAGE_DLLCHARACTERISTICS_NO_ISOLATION	0x0200	Image understands isolation and doesn't want it.
IMAGE_DLLCHARACTERISTICS_NO_SEH	0x0400	Image does not use SEH. No SE handler may be called in this image.
IMAGE_DLLCHARACTERISTICS_NO_BIND	0x0800	Do not bind image.
	0x1000	Reserved, must be zero.
IMAGE_DLLCHARACTERISTICS_WDM_DRIVER	0x2000	Driver is a WDM Driver.
IMAGE_DLLCHARACTERISTICS_TERMINAL_SERVER_AWARE	0x8000	Image is Terminal Server aware.

3.4.3 Optional Header Data Directories (Image Only)

Each data directory gives the address and size of a table or string used by Windows. These data directory entries are all loaded into memory so that they can be used by the system at run time. A data directory is an eight-byte field that has the following declaration:

```
typedef struct _IMAGE_DATA_DIRECTORY {
    DWORD   VirtualAddress;
    DWORD   Size;
} IMAGE_DATA_DIRECTORY, *PIMAGE_DATA_DIRECTORY;
```

The first field, VirtualAddress, is actually the relative virtual address of the table. The RVA is the address of the table, when loaded, relative to the base address of the image. The second field gives the size in bytes. The data directories, which form the last part of the Optional Header, are listed below.

Note that the number of directories is not fixed. The NumberOfRvaAndSizes field in the optional header should be checked before looking for a specific directory.

Do not assume that the RVAs given in this table point to the beginning of a section or that the sections containing specific tables have specific names.

Offset (PE/PE32+)	Size	Field	Description
96/112	8	Export Table	Export Table address and size.
104/120	8	Import Table	Import Table address and size.
112/128	8	Resource Table	Resource Table address and size.
120/136	8	Exception Table	Exception Table address and size.
128/144	8	Certificate Table	Attribute Certificate Table address and size.
136/152	8	Base Relocation Table	Base Relocation Table address and size.
144/160	8	Debug	Debug data starting address and size.
152/168	8	Architecture	Architecture-specific data address and size.
160/176	8	Global Ptr	Relative virtual address of the value to be stored in the global pointer register. Size member of this structure must be set to 0.

Offset (PE/PE32+)	Size	Field	Description
168/184	8	TLS Table	Thread Local Storage (TLS) Table address and size.
176/192	8	Load Config Table	Load Configuration Table address and size.
184/200	8	Bound Import	Bound Import Table address and size.
192/208	8	IAT	Import Address Table address and size.
200/216	8	Delay Import Descriptor	Address and size of the Delay Import Descriptor.
208/224	8	clr Runtime Header	clr Runtime Header address and size.
216/232	8	Reserved	

The Certificate Table entry points to a table of attribute certificates. These certificates are ***not*** loaded into memory as part of the image. As such, the first field of this entry, which is normally an RVA, is a File Pointer instead.

4 Section Table (Section Headers)

Each row of the Section Table, in effect, is a section header. This table immediately follows the optional header, if any. This positioning is required because the file header does not contain a direct pointer to the section table; the location of the section table is determined by calculating the location of the first byte after the headers. Make sure to use the size of the optional header as specified in the file header.

The number of entries in the Section Table is given by the NumberOfSections field in the file header. Entries in the Section Table are numbered starting from one. The code and data memory section entries are in the order chosen by the linker.

In an image file, the virtual addresses for sections must be assigned by the linker such that they are in ascending order and adjacent, and they must be a multiple of the Section Align value in the optional header.

Each section header (Section Table entry) has the following format, for a total of 40 bytes per entry:

Offset	Size	Field	Description
0	8	Name	An eight-byte, null-padded UTF-8 encoded string. There is no terminating null if the string is exactly eight characters long. For longer names, this field contains a slash (/) followed by ASCII representation of a decimal number: this number is an offset into the string table. Executable images do not use a string table and do not support section names longer than eight characters. Long names in object files will be truncated if emitted to an executable file.
8	4	VirtualSize	Total size of the section when loaded into memory. If this value is greater than Size of Raw Data, the section is zero-padded. This field is valid only for executable images and should be set to 0 for object files.
12	4	VirtualAddress	For executable images this is the address of the first byte of the section, when loaded into memory, relative to the image base. For object files, this field is the address of the first byte before relocation is applied; for simplicity, compilers should set this to zero. Otherwise, it is an arbitrary value that is subtracted from offsets during relocation.
16	4	SizeOfRawData	Size of the section (object file) or size of the initialized data on disk (image files). For executable image, this must be a multiple of FileAlignment from the optional header. If this is less than VirtualSize, the remainder of the section is zero filled. Because this field is rounded while the VirtualSize field is not, it is possible for this to be greater than VirtualSize as well. When a section contains only uninitialized data, this field should be 0.
20	4	PointerToRawData	File pointer to section's first page within the COFF file. For executable images, this must be a multiple of FileAlignment from the optional header. For object files, the value should be aligned on a four-byte boundary for best performance. When a section contains only uninitialized data, this field should be 0.
24	4	PointerToRelocations	File pointer to beginning of relocation entries for the section. Set to 0 for executable images or if there are no relocations.

Offset	Size	Field	Description
28	4	PointerToLinenumbers	File pointer to beginning of line-number entries for the section. Set to 0 if there are no COFF line numbers. Should be zero for an image as COFF debugging information is deprecated.
32	2	NumberOfRelocations	Number of relocation entries for the section. Set to 0 for executable images.
34	2	NumberOfLinenumbers	Number of line-number entries for the section. Should be zero for an image as COFF debugging information is deprecated.
36	4	Characteristics	Flags describing section's characteristics. See Section 4.1, "Section Flags," for more information.

4.1 Section Flags

The Section Flags field indicates characteristics of the section.

Flag	Value	Description
	0x00000000	Reserved for future use.
	0x00000001	Reserved for future use.
	0x00000002	Reserved for future use.
	0x00000004	Reserved for future use.
IMAGE_SCN_TYPE_NO_PAD	0x00000008	Section should not be padded to next boundary. This is obsolete and replaced by IMAGE_SCN_ALIGN_1BYTES. This is valid for object files only.
	0x00000010	Reserved for future use.
IMAGE_SCN_CNT_CODE	0x00000020	Section contains executable code.
IMAGE_SCN_CNT_INITIALIZED_DATA	0x00000040	Section contains initialized data.
IMAGE_SCN_CNT_UNINITIALIZED_DATA	0x00000080	Section contains uninitialized data.

Flag	Value	Description
IMAGE_SCN_LNK_OTHER	0x00000100	Reserved for future use.
IMAGE_SCN_LNK_INFO	0x00000200	Section contains comments or other information. The .drectve section has this type. This is valid for object files only.
	0x00000400	Reserved for future use.
IMAGE_SCN_LNK_REMOVE	0x00000800	Section will not become part of the image. This is valid for object files only.
IMAGE_SCN_LNK_COMDAT	0x00001000	Section contains COMDAT data. See Section 5.5.6, "COMDAT Sections," for more information. This is valid for object files only.
IMAGE_SCN_GPREL	0x00008000	Section contains data referenced via the GP.
IMAGE_SCN_MEM_PURGEABLE	0x00020000	Reserved for future use.
IMAGE_SCN_MEM_16BIT	0x00020000	Reserved for future use.
IMAGE_SCN_MEM_LOCKED	0x00040000	Reserved for future use.
IMAGE_SCN_MEM_PRELOAD	0x00080000	Reserved for future use.
IMAGE_SCN_ALIGN_1BYTES	0x00100000	Align data on a 1 byte boundary. Valid for object files only.
IMAGE_SCN_ALIGN_2BYTES	0x00200000	Align data on a 2 byte boundary. Valid for object files only.
IMAGE_SCN_ALIGN_4BYTES	0x00300000	Align data on a 4 byte boundary. Valid for object files only.
IMAGE_SCN_ALIGN_8BYTES	0x00400000	Align data on an 8 byte boundary. Valid for object files only.
IMAGE_SCN_ALIGN_16BYTES	0x00500000	Align data on a 16 byte boundary. Valid for object files only.
IMAGE_SCN_ALIGN_32BYTES	0x00600000	Align data on a 32 byte boundary. Valid for object files only.

Flag	Value	Description
IMAGE_SCN_ALIGN_64BYTES	0x00700000	Align data on a 64 byte boundary. Valid for object files only.
IMAGE_SCN_ALIGN_128BYTES	0x00800000	Align data on a 128 byte boundary. Valid for object files only.
IMAGE_SCN_ALIGN_256BYTES	0x00900000	Align data on a 256 byte boundary. Valid for object files only.
IMAGE_SCN_ALIGN_512BYTES	0x00A00000	Align data on a 512 byte boundary. Valid for object files only.
IMAGE_SCN_ALIGN_1024BYTES	0x00B00000	Align data on a 1024 byte boundary. Valid for object files only.
IMAGE_SCN_ALIGN_2048BYTES	0x00C00000	Align data on a 2048 byte boundary. Valid for object files only.
IMAGE_SCN_ALIGN_4096BYTES	0x00D00000	Align data on a 4096 byte boundary. Valid for object files only.
IMAGE_SCN_ALIGN_8192BYTES	0x00E00000	Align data on an 8192 byte boundary. Valid for object files only.
IMAGE_SCN_LNK_NRELOC_OVFL	0x01000000	Section contains extended relocations.
IMAGE_SCN_MEM_DISCARDABLE	0x02000000	Section can be discarded as needed.
IMAGE_SCN_MEM_NOT_CACHED	0x04000000	Section cannot be cached.
IMAGE_SCN_MEM_NOT_PAGED	0x08000000	Section is not pageable.
IMAGE_SCN_MEM_SHARED	0x10000000	Section can be shared in memory.
IMAGE_SCN_MEM_EXECUTE	0x20000000	Section can be executed as code.
IMAGE_SCN_MEM_READ	0x40000000	Section can be read.
IMAGE_SCN_MEM_WRITE	0x80000000	Section can be written to.

IMAGE_SCN_LNK_NRELOC_OVFL indicates that the count of relocations for the section exceeds the 16-bits reserved for it in [the] section header. If the bit is set and the NumberOfRelocations field in the section header is 0xffff, the actual relocation count is stored in the 32-bit VirtualAddress field of the first relocation. It is an error if IMAGE_SCN_LNK_NRELOC_OVFL is set and there are fewer than 0xffff relocations in the section.

4.2 Grouped Sections (Object Only)

The "$" character (dollar sign) has a special interpretation in section names in object files.

When determining the image section that will contain the contents of an object section, the linker discards the "$" and all characters following it. Thus, an object section named **.text$X** will actually contribute to the **.text** section in the image.

However, the characters following the "$" determine the ordering of the contributions to the image section. All contributions with the same object-section name will be allocated contiguously in the image, and the blocks of contributions will be sorted in lexical order by object-section name. Therefore, everything in object files with section name **.text$X** will end up together, after the **.text$W** contributions and before the **.text$Y** contributions.

The section name in an image file will never contain a "$" character.

5 Other Contents of the File

The data structures described so far, up to and including the optional header, are all located at a fixed offset from the beginning of the file (or from the PE header if the file is an image containing an MS-DOS stub).

The remainder of a COFF object or image file contains blocks of data that are not necessarily at any specific file offset. Instead, the locations are defined by pointers in the Optional Header or a section header.

An exception is for images with a Section Alignment value (see the Optional Header description [Section 3.4]) of less than the page size of the architecture (4K for Intel x86 and for MIPS; 8K for IA64). In this case there are constraints on the file offset of the section data, as described in the next section. Another exception is that attribute certificate and debug information must be placed at the very end of an image file (with the attribute certificate table immediately preceding the debug section), because the loader does not map these into memory. The rule on attribute certificate and debug information does not apply to object files, however.

5.1 Section Data

Initialized data for a section consists of simple blocks of bytes. However, for sections containing all zeros, the section data need not be included.

The data for each section is located at the file offset given by the PointerToRawData field in the section header, and the size of this data in the file is indicated by the SizeOfRawData field. If the SizeOfRawData is less than the VirtualSize, the remainder is padded with zeros.

In an image file, the section data must be aligned on a boundary as specified by the FileAlignment field in the optional header. Section data must appear in order of the RVA values for the corresponding sections (as do the individual section headers in the Section Table).

There are additional restrictions on image files where the Section Align value in the Optional Header is less than the page size of the architecture. For such files, the location of section data in the file must match its location in memory when the image is loaded, so that the physical offset for section data is the same as the RVA.

5.2 COFF Relocations (Object Only)

Object files contain COFF relocations, which specify how the section data should be modified when placed in the image file and subsequently loaded into memory.

Image files do not contain COFF relocations, because all symbols referenced have already been assigned addresses in a flat address space. An image contains relocation information in the form of base relocations in the **.reloc** section (unless the image has the IMAGE_FILE_RELOCS_STRIPPED attribute). See Section 6.6 for more information.

For each section in an object file, there is an array of fixed-length records that are the section's COFF relocations. The position and length of the array are specified in the section header. Each element of the array has the following format:

Offset	Size	Field	Description
0	4	VirtualAddress	Address of the item to which relocation is applied; this is the offset from the beginning of the section, plus the value of the section's RVA/Offset field (see Section 4, "Section Table."). For example, if the first byte of the section has an address of 0x10, the third byte has an address of 0x12.
4	4	SymbolTableIndex	A zero-based index into the symbol table. This symbol gives the address to be used for the relocation. If the specified symbol has section storage class, then the symbol's address is the address with the first section of the same name.
8	2	Type	A value indicating what kind of relocation should be performed. Valid relocation types depend on machine type. See Section 5.2.1, "Type Indicators."

If the symbol referred to (by the SymbolTableIndex field) has storage class IMAGE_SYM_CLASS_SECTION, the symbol's address is the beginning of the section. The section is usually in the same file, except when the object file is part of an archive (library). In that case, the section may be found in any other object file in the archive that has the same archive-member name as the current object file. (The relationship with the archive-member name is used in the linking of import tables, i.e., the **.idata** section.)

5.2.1 Type Indicators

The Type field of the relocation record indicates what kind of relocation should be performed. Different relocation types are defined for each type of machine.

AMD AMD64

The following relocation type indicators are defined for AMD AMD64 and compatible processors:

Constant	Value	Description
IMAGE_REL_AMD64_ABSOLUTE	0x0000	This relocation is ignored.
IMAGE_REL_AMD64_ADDR64	0x0001	64-bit VA.
IMAGE_REL_AMD64_ADDR32	0x0002	32-bit VA.
IMAGE_REL_AMD64_ADDR32NB	0x0003	32-bit address w/o image base (RVA).
IMAGE_REL_AMD64_REL32	0x0004	32-bit relative address from byte following relocation.
IMAGE_REL_AMD64_REL32_1	0x0005	32-bit relative address from byte distance 1 from relocation.
IMAGE_REL_AMD64_REL32_2	0x0006	32-bit relative address from byte distance 2 from relocation.
IMAGE_REL_AMD64_REL32_3	0x0007	32-bit relative address from byte distance 3 from relocation.
IMAGE_REL_AMD64_REL32_4	0x0008	32-bit relative address from byte distance 4 from relocation.
IMAGE_REL_AMD64_REL32_5	0x0009	32-bit relative address from byte distance 5 from relocation.
IMAGE_REL_AMD64_SECTION	0x000A	The 16-bit section index of the section containing the target. This is used to support debugging information.
IMAGE_REL_AMD64_SECREL	0x000B	The 32-bit offset of the target from the beginning of its section. This is used to support debugging information as well as static thread local storage.

Constant	Value	Description
IMAGE_REL_AMD64_SECREL7	0x000C	7 bit unsigned offset from base of section containing target.
IMAGE_REL_AMD64_TOKEN	0x000D	clr token.
IMAGE_REL_AMD64_SREL32	0x000E	32 bit signed span-dependent value emitted into object.
IMAGE_REL_AMD64_PAIR	0x000F	
IMAGE_REL_AMD64_SSPAN32	0x0010	32 bit signed span-dependent value applied at link time.

ARM Processors

The following relocation Type indicators are defined for ARM processors:

Constant	Value	Description
IMAGE_REL_ARM_ABSOLUTE	0x0000	This relocation is ignored.
IMAGE_REL_ARM_ADDR32	0x0001	The target's 32-bit virtual address.
IMAGE_REL_ARM_ADDR32NB	0x0002	The target's 32-bit relative virtual address.
IMAGE_REL_ARM_BRANCH24	0x0003	The 24-bit relative displacement to the target.
IMAGE_REL_ARM_BRANCH11	0x0004	Reference to a subroutine call, consisting of two 16-bit instructions with 11-bit offsets.
IMAGE_REL_ARM_SECTION	0x000E	The 16-bit section index of the section containing the target. This is used to support debugging information.
IMAGE_REL_ARM_SECREL	0x000F	The 32-bit offset of the target from the beginning of its section. This is used to support debugging information as well as static thread local storage.

CEE

The following relocation type indicators are defined for CEE (clr pure object files):

Constant	Value	Description
IMAGE_REL_CEE_ABSOLUTE	0x0000	The relocation is ignored.
IMAGE_REL_CEE_ADDR32	0x0001	32-bit address (VA).
IMAGE_REL_CEE_ADDR64	0x0002	64-bit address (VA).
IMAGE_REL_CEE_ADDR32NB	0x0003	32-bit address w/o image base (RVA).
IMAGE_REL_CEE_SECTION	0x0004	The 16-bit section index of the section containing the target. This is used to support debugging information.
IMAGE_REL_CEE_SECREL	0x0005	The 32-bit offset of the target from the beginning of its section. This is used to support debugging information as well as static thread local storage.
IMAGE_REL_CEE_TOKEN	0x0006	clr token.

Hitachi SuperH Processors

The following relocation type indicators are defined for SH3 and SH4 processors. SH5 specific relocations are noted as SHM (SH Media):

Constant	Value	Description
IMAGE_REL_SH3_ABSOLUTE	0x0000	This relocation is ignored.
IMAGE_REL_SH3_DIRECT16	0x0001	Reference to the 16-bit location that contains the virtual address of the target symbol.
IMAGE_REL_SH3_DIRECT32	0x0002	The target's 32-bit virtual address.
IMAGE_REL_SH3_DIRECT8	0x0003	Reference to the 8-bit location that contains the virtual address of the target symbol.
IMAGE_REL_SH3_DIRECT8_WORD	0x0004	Reference to the 8-bit instruction that contains the effective 16 bit virtual address of the target symbol.
IMAGE_REL_SH3_DIRECT8_LONG	0x0005	Reference to the 8-bit instruction that contains the effective 32 bit virtual address of the target symbol.

Constant	Value	Description
IMAGE_REL_SH3_DIRECT4	0x0006	Reference to the 8-bit location whose low 4 bits contain the virtual address of the target symbol.
IMAGE_REL_SH3_DIRECT4_WORD	0x0007	Reference to the 8-bit instruction whose low 4 bits contain the effective 16 bit virtual address of the target symbol.
IMAGE_REL_SH3_DIRECT4_LONG	0x0008	Reference to the 8-bit instruction whose low 4 bits contain the effective 32 bit virtual address of the target symbol.
IMAGE_REL_SH3_PCREL8_WORD	0x0009	Reference to the 8-bit instruction which contains the effective 16-bit relative offset of the target symbol.
IMAGE_REL_SH3_PCREL8_LONG	0x000A	Reference to the 8-bit instruction which contains the effective 32-bit relative offset of the target symbol.
IMAGE_REL_SH3_PCREL12_WORD	0x000B	Reference to the 16-bit instruction whose low 12 bits contain the effective 16 bit relative offset of the target symbol.
IMAGE_REL_SH3_STARTOF_SECTION	0x000C	Reference to a 32-bit location that is the virtual address of the symbol's section.
IMAGE_REL_SH3_SIZEOF_SECTION	0x000D	Reference to the 32-bit location that is the size of the symbol's section.
IMAGE_REL_SH3_SECTION	0x000E	The 16-bit section index of the section containing the target. This is used to support debugging information.
IMAGE_REL_SH3_SECREL	0x000F	The 32-bit offset of the target from the beginning of its section. This is used to support debugging information as well as static thread local storage.
IMAGE_REL_SH3_DIRECT32_NB	0x0010	The target's 32-bit relative virtual address.
IMAGE_REL_SH3_GPREL4_LONG	0x0011	GP relative.
IMAGE_REL_SH3_TOKEN	0x0012	clr token.
IMAGE_REL_SHM_PCRELPT	0x0013	Offset from current instruction in longwords; if not NOMODE, insert the inverse of the low bit at bit 32 to select PTA/PTB.

Constant	Value	Description
IMAGE_REL_SHM_REFLO	0x0014	Low 16 bits of 32-bit address.
IMAGE_REL_SHM_REFHALF	0x0015	High 16 bits of 32-bit address.
IMAGE_REL_SHM_RELLO	0x0016	Low 16 bits of relative address.
IMAGE_REL_SHM_RELHALF	0x0017	High 16 bits of relative address.
IMAGE_REL_SHM_PAIR	0x0018	This relocation is only valid when it immediately follows a REFHALF, RELHALF, or RELLO relocation. Its SymbolTableIndex contains a displacement and not an index into the symbol table.
IMAGE_REL_SHM_NOMODE	0x8000	Relocation ignores section mode.

IBM PowerPC Processors

The following relocation Type indicators are defined for PowerPC processors:

Constant	Value	Description
IMAGE_REL_PPC_ABSOLUTE	0x0000	This relocation is ignored.
IMAGE_REL_PPC_ADDR64	0x0001	The target's 64-bit virtual address.
IMAGE_REL_PPC_ADDR32	0x0002	The target's 32-bit virtual address.
IMAGE_REL_PPC_ADDR24	0x0003	The low 24 bits of the target's virtual address. This is only valid when the target symbol is absolute and can be sign extended to its original value.
IMAGE_REL_PPC_ADDR16	0x0004	The low 16 bits of the target's virtual address.
IMAGE_REL_PPC_ADDR14	0x0005	The low 14 bits of the target's virtual address. This is only valid when the target symbol is absolute and can be sign extended to its original value.
IMAGE_REL_PPC_REL24	0x0006	A 24-bit PC-relative offset to the symbol's location.

Constant	Value	Description
IMAGE_REL_PPC_REL14	0x0007	A 14-bit PC-relative offset to the symbol's location.
IMAGE_REL_PPC_ADDR32NB	0x000A	The target's 32-bit relative virtual address.
IMAGE_REL_PPC_SECREL	0x000B	The 32-bit offset of the target from the beginning of its section. This is used to support debugging information as well as static thread local storage.
IMAGE_REL_PPC_SECTION	0x000C	The 16-bit section index of the section containing the target. This is used to support debugging information.
IMAGE_REL_PPC_SECREL16	0x000F	The 16-bit offset of the target from the beginning of its section. This is used to support debugging information as well as static thread local storage.
IMAGE_REL_PPC_REFHI	0x0010	The high 16 bits of the target's 32-bit virtual address. Used for the first instruction in a two-instruction sequence that loads a full address. This relocation must be immediately followed by a PAIR relocation whose SymbolTableIndex contains a signed 16 bit displacement which is added to the upper 16 bits taken from the location being relocated.
IMAGE_REL_PPC_REFLO	0x0011	The low 16 bits of the target's virtual address.
IMAGE_REL_PPC_PAIR	0x0012	This relocation is only valid when it immediately follows a REFHI or SECRELHI relocation. Its SymbolTableIndex contains a displacement and not an index into the symbol table.
IMAGE_REL_PPC_SECRELLO	0x0013	The low 16 bits of the 32-bit offset of the target from the beginning of its section.
IMAGE_REL_PPC_SECRELHI	0x0014	The high 16 bits of the 32-bit offset of the target from the beginning of its section. A PAIR relocation must immediately follow this one. The SymbolTableIndex of the PAIR relocation contains a signed 16 bit displacement which is added to the upper 16 bits taken from the location being relocated.

Constant	Value	Description
IMAGE_REL_PPC_GPREL	0x0015	16-bit signed displacement of the target relative to the Global Pointer (GP) register.
IMAGE_REL_PPC_TOKEN	0x0016	clr token.

Intel 386

The following relocation type indicators are defined for Intel386 and compatible processors:

Constant	Value	Description
IMAGE_REL_I386_ABSOLUTE	0x0000	This relocation is ignored.
IMAGE_REL_I386_DIR16	0x0001	Not supported.
IMAGE_REL_I386_REL16	0x0002	Not supported.
IMAGE_REL_I386_DIR32	0x0006	The target's 32-bit virtual address.
IMAGE_REL_I386_DIR32NB	0x0007	The target's 32-bit relative virtual address.
IMAGE_REL_I386_SEG12	0x0009	Not supported.
IMAGE_REL_I386_SECTION	0x000A	The 16-bit section index of the section containing the target. This is used to support debugging information.
IMAGE_REL_I386_SECREL	0x000B	The 32-bit offset of the target from the beginning of its section. This is used to support debugging information as well as static thread local storage.
IMAGE_REL_I386_TOKEN	0x000C	clr token.
IMAGE_REL_I386_SECREL7	0x000D	7 bit offset from base of section containing target.
IMAGE_REL_I386_REL32	0x0014	The 32-bit relative displacement to the target. This supports the x86 relative branch and call instructions.

Intel Itanium Processor Family (IPF)

The following relocation type indicators are defined for the Intel Itanium Processor Family and compatible processors. Note that relocations on *instructions* use the bundle's offset and slot number for the relocation offset:

Constant	Value	Description
IMAGE_REL_IA64_ABSOLUTE	0x0000	This relocation is ignored.
IMAGE_REL_IA64_IMM14	0x0001	This instruction relocation may be followed by an ADDEND relocation whose Value is added to the target address before it is inserted into the specified slot in the IMM14 bundle. The relocation target must be absolute or the image must be fixed.
IMAGE_REL_IA64_IMM22	0x0002	This instruction relocation may be followed by an ADDEND relocation whose Value is added to the target address before it is inserted into the specified slot in the IMM22 bundle. The relocation target must be absolute or the image must be fixed.
IMAGE_REL_IA64_IMM64	0x0003	The slot number for this relocation must be one (1). The relocation may be followed by an ADDEND relocation whose Value is added to the target address before it is stored in all three slots of the IMM64 bundle.
IMAGE_REL_IA64_DIR32	0x0004	The target's 32-bit virtual address. Supported only for /LARGEADDRESSAWARE:NO images.
IMAGE_REL_IA64_DIR64	0x0005	The target's 64-bit virtual address.
IMAGE_REL_IA64_PCREL21B	0x0006	The instruction is fixed up with the 25-bit relative displacement to the 16-bit aligned target. The low four bits of the displacement, which are zero, are not stored.
IMAGE_REL_IA64_PCREL21M	0x0007	The instruction is fixed up with the 25-bit relative displacement to the 16-bit aligned target. The low four bits of the displacement, which are zero, are not stored.

Constant	Value	Description
IMAGE_REL_IA64_PCREL21F	0x0008	The least significant bits of this relocation's offset must contain the slot number, and the rest is the bundle address. The bundle is fixed up with the 25-bit relative displacement to the 16-bit aligned target. The low four bits of the displacement, which are zero, are not stored.
IMAGE_REL_IA64_GPREL22	0x0009	This instruction relocation may be followed by an ADDEND relocation whose Value is added to the target address, and then a 22-bit GP-relative offset is calculated and applied to the GPREL22 bundle.
IMAGE_REL_IA64_LTOFF22	0x000A	The instruction is fixed up with the 22-bit GP-relative offset to the target symbol's literal table entry. The linker creates this literal table entry based on this relocation and the ADDEND relocation that may follow.
IMAGE_REL_IA64_SECTION	0x000B	The 16-bit section index of the section containing the target. This is used to support debugging information.
IMAGE_REL_IA64_SECREL22	0x000C	The instruction is fixed up with the 22-bit offset of the target from the beginning of its section. This relocation may be followed immediately by an ADDEND relocation, whose Value field contains the 32-bit unsigned offset of the target from the beginning of the section.
IMAGE_REL_IA64_SECREL64I	0x000D	The slot number for this relocation must be one (1). The instruction is fixed up with the 64-bit offset of the target from the beginning of its section. This relocation may be followed immediately by an ADDEND relocation, whose Value field contains the 32-bit unsigned offset of the target from the beginning of the section.
IMAGE_REL_IA64_SECREL32	0x000E	The address of data to be fixed up with the 32-bit offset of the target from the beginning of its section.
IMAGE_REL_IA64_DIR32NB	0x0010	The target's 32-bit relative virtual address.

Constant	Value	Description
IMAGE_REL_IA64_SREL14	0x0011	14-bit signed relative for an immediate 14 bit storage, used for the difference between two relocatable targets, information only. The linker does not apply these.
IMAGE_REL_IA64_SREL22	0x0012	22-bit signed relative for an immediate 22 bit storage, used for the difference between two relocatable targets, information only. The linker does not apply these.
IMAGE_REL_IA64_SREL32	0x0013	32-bit signed relative for an immediate 32 bit storage, used for the difference between two relocatable targets, information only. The linker does not apply these.
IMAGE_REL_IA64_UREL32	0x0014	32-bit unsigned relative for an immediate 32 bit storage, used for the difference between two relocatable targets, information only. The linker does not apply these.
IMAGE_REL_IA64_PCREL60X	0x0015	60-bit PC relative fixup that always stays as a BRL instruction in slots 1/2 of an MLX bundle.
IMAGE_REL_IA64_PCREL60B	0x0016	60-bit PC relative fixup; if target displacement fits in a signed 25-bit field, convert to MBB bundle with NOP.B in slot 1 and a 25-bit (4 lowest bits all zero and dropped) BR instruction in slot 2.
IMAGE_REL_IA64_PCREL60F	0x0017	60-bit PC relative fixup; if target displacement fits in a signed 25-bit field, convert to MFB bundle with NOP.F in slot 1 and a 25-bit (4 lowest bits all zero and dropped) BR instruction in slot 2.
IMAGE_REL_IA64_PCREL60I	0x0018	60-bit PC relative fixup; if target displacement fits in a signed 25-bit field, convert to MIB bundle with NOP.I in slot 1 and a 25-bit (4 lowest bits all zero and dropped) BR instruction in slot 2.
IMAGE_REL_IA64_PCREL60M	0x0019	60-bit PC relative fixup; if target displacement fits in a signed 25-bit field, convert to MMB bundle with NOP.M in slot 1 and a 25-bit (4 lowest bits all zero and dropped) BR instruction in slot 2.
IMAGE_REL_IA64_IMMGPREL64	0x001a	64-bit GP relative fixup.
IMAGE_REL_IA64_TOKEN	0x001b	clr token.

Appendix

Constant	Value	Description
IMAGE_REL_IA64_GPREL32	0x001c	32-bit GP relative fixup.
IMAGE_REL_IA64_ADDEND	0x001F	This relocation is only valid when it immediately follows an IMM14, IMM22, IMM64, GPREL22, LTOFF22, LTOFF64, SECREL22, SECREL64I, or SECREL32 relocation. Its Value contains the addend to apply to instructions within a bundle, not for data.

MIPS Processors

The following relocation type indicators are defined for MIPS processors:

Constant	Value	Description
IMAGE_REL_MIPS_ABSOLUTE	0x0000	This relocation is ignored.
IMAGE_REL_MIPS_REFHALF	0x0001	The high 16 bits of the target's 32-bit virtual address.
IMAGE_REL_MIPS_REFWORD	0x0002	The target's 32-bit virtual address.
IMAGE_REL_MIPS_JMPADDR	0x0003	The low 26 bits of the target's virtual address. This supports the MIPS J and JAL instructions.
IMAGE_REL_MIPS_REFHI	0x0004	The high 16 bits of the target's 32-bit virtual address. Used for the first instruction in a two-instruction sequence that loads a full address. This relocation must be immediately followed by a PAIR relocation whose SymbolTableIndex contains a signed 16 bit displacement which is added to the upper 16 bits taken from the location being relocated.
IMAGE_REL_MIPS_REFLO	0x0005	The low 16 bits of the target's virtual address.
IMAGE_REL_MIPS_GPREL	0x0006	16-bit signed displacement of the target relative to the Global Pointer (GP) register.
IMAGE_REL_MIPS_LITERAL	0x0007	Same as IMAGE_REL_MIPS_GPREL.
IMAGE_REL_MIPS_SECTION	0x000A	The 16 bit section index of the section containing the target. This is used to support debugging information.

Constant	Value	Description
IMAGE_REL_MIPS_SECREL	0x000B	The 32-bit offset of the target from the beginning of its section. This is used to support debugging information as well as static thread local storage.
IMAGE_REL_MIPS_SECRELLO	0x000C	The low 16 bits of the 32-bit offset of the target from the beginning of its section.
IMAGE_REL_MIPS_SECRELHI	0x000D	The high 16 bits of the 32-bit offset of the target from the beginning of its section. An IMAGE_REL_MIPS_PAIR relocation must immediately follow this one. The SymbolTableIndex of the PAIR relocation contains a signed 16 bit displacement which is added to the upper 16 bits taken from the location being relocated.
IMAGE_REL_MIPS_JMPADDR16	0x0010	The low 26 bits of the target's virtual address. This supports the MIPS16 JAL instruction.
IMAGE_REL_MIPS_REFWORDNB	0x0022	The target's 32-bit relative virtual address.
IMAGE_REL_MIPS_PAIR	0x0025	This relocation is only valid when it immediately follows a REFHI or SECRELHI relocation. Its SymbolTableIndex contains a displacement and not an index into the symbol table.

Mitsubishi M32R

The following relocation type indicators are defined for the Mitsubishi M32R processors:

Constant	Value	Description
IMAGE_REL_M32R_ABSOLUTE	0x0000	This relocation is ignored.
IMAGE_REL_M32R_ADDR32	0x0001	The target's 32-bit virtual address.
IMAGE_REL_M32R_ADDR32NB	0x0002	The target's 32-bit relative virtual address.
IMAGE_REL_M32R_ADDR24	0x0003	The target's 24-bit virtual address.
IMAGE_REL_M32R_GPREL16	0x0004	The target's 16-bit offset from GP (global pointer).

Constant	Value	Description
IMAGE_REL_M32R_PCREL24	0x0005	The target's 24-bit offset « 2 & sign extended from PC (program counter).
IMAGE_REL_M32R_PCREL16	0x0006	The target's 16-bit offset « 2 & sign extended from PC.
IMAGE_REL_M32R_PCREL8	0x0007	The target's 8-bit offset « 2 & sign extended from PC.
IMAGE_REL_M32R_REFHALF	0x0008	The target's 16 MSB (most significant bits) (VA).
IMAGE_REL_M32R_REFHI	0x0009	The target's 16 MSB adjusted for LSB sign extension. Used for the first instruction in a two-instruction sequence that loads a full 32-bit address. This relocation must be immediately followed by a PAIR relocation whose SymbolTableIndex contains a signed 16 bit displacement which is added to the upper 16 bits taken from the location being relocated.
IMAGE_REL_M32R_REFLO	0x000A	The target's 16 LSB (least significant bits).
IMAGE_REL_M32R_PAIR	0x000B	Must follow the REFHI relocation. Its SymbolTableIndex contains a displacement and not an index into the symbol table.
IMAGE_REL_M32R_SECTION	0x000C	The 16-bit section index of the section containing the target. This is used to support debugging information.
IMAGE_REL_M32R_SECREL	0x000D	The 32-bit offset of the target from the beginning of its section. This is used to support debugging information as well as static thread local storage.
IMAGE_REL_M32R_TOKEN	0x000E	clr token.

5.3 COFF Line Numbers

Current and future versions of Visual C++ may not create COFF line numbers due to the restrictions of the COFF system using ANSI file names in .file symbols and limitations of 16-bit line numbers without any column information. The preferred format is the new Visual C++ 8.0 files and lines. Please see the latest version of the Visual C++ Debugging Information specification in MSDN's specifications section for information on this new format of the file and line number data in object files.

COFF line numbers indicate the relationship between code and line-numbers in source files. The Microsoft format for COFF line numbers is similar to standard COFF, but it has been extended to allow a single section to relate to line numbers in multiple source files.

COFF line numbers consist of an array of fixed-length records. The location (file offset) and size of the array are specified in the section header. Each line-number record is of the following format:

Offset	Size	Field	Description
0	4	Type (*)	Union of two fields: Symbol Table Index and RVA. Whether Symbol Table Index or RVA is used depends on the value of Linenumber.
4	2	Linenumber	When nonzero, this field specifies a one-based line number. When zero, the Type field is interpreted as a Symbol Table Index for a function.

The Type field is a union of two four-byte fields: Symbol Table Index and RVA:

Offset	Size	Field	Description
0	4	SymbolTableIndex	Used when Linenumber is 0: index to symbol table entry for a function. This format is used to indicate the function that a group of line-number records refer to.
0	4	VirtualAddress	Used when Linenumber is non-zero: relative virtual address of the executable code that corresponds to the source line indicated. In an object file, this contains the virtual address within the section.

A line-number record, then, can either set the Linenumber field to 0 and point to a function definition in the Symbol Table, or else it can work as a standard line-number entry by giving a positive integer (line number) and the corresponding address in the object code.

A group of line-number entries always begins with the first format: the index of a function symbol. If this is the first line-number record in the section, then it is also the COMDAT symbol name for the function if the section's COMDAT flag is set. (See Section 5.5.6, "COMDAT Sections.") The function's auxiliary record in the Symbol Table has a Pointer to [the] Linenumbers field that points to this same line-number record.

A record identifying a function is followed by any number of line-number entries that give actual line-number information (Linenumber greater than zero). These entries are one-based, relative to the beginning of the function, and represent every source line in the function except for the first one.

For example, the first line-number record for the following example would specify the ReverseSign function (Symbol Table Index of ReverseSign, Linenumber set to 0). Then records with Linenumber values of 1, 2, and 3 would follow, corresponding to source lines as shown:

```
// some code precedes ReverseSign function
  int      ReverseSign(int i)
1:{
2:         return -1 * i;
3:}
```

5.4 COFF Symbol Table

The Symbol Table described in this section is inherited from the traditional COFF format. It is distinct from Visual C++ Debug information. A file may contain both a COFF Symbol Table and Visual C++ debug information, and the two are kept separate. Some Microsoft tools use the Symbol Table for limited but important purposes, such as communicating COMDAT information to the linker. Section names and file names, as well as code and data symbols, are listed in the Symbol Table.

The location of the Symbol Table is indicated in the COFF Header.

The Symbol Table is an array of records, each 18 bytes long. Each record is either a standard or auxiliary symbol-table record. A standard record defines a symbol or name, and has the following format:

Offset	Size	Field	Description
0	8	Name (*)	Name of the symbol, represented by union of three structures. An array of eight bytes is used if the name is not more than eight bytes long. See Section 5.4.1, "Symbol Name Representation," for more information.
8	4	Value	Value associated with the symbol. The interpretation of this field depends on Section Number and Storage Class. A typical meaning is the relocatable address.

Offset	Size	Field	Description
12	2	SectionNumber	Signed integer identifying the section, using a one-based index into the Section Table. Some values have special meaning defined in [Section 5.4.2,] "Section Number Values."
14	2	Type	A number representing type. Microsoft tools set this field to 0x20 (function) or 0x0 (not a function). See Section 5.4.3, "Type Representation," for more information.
16	1	StorageClass	Enumerated value representing storage class. See Section 5.4.4, "Storage Class," for more information.
17	1	NumberOfAuxSymbols	Number of auxiliary symbol table entries that follow this record.

Zero or more auxiliary symbol-table records immediately follow each standard symbol-table record. However, typically not more than one auxiliary symbol-table record follows a standard symbol-table record (except for **.file** records with long file names). Each auxiliary record is the same size as a standard symbol-table record (18 bytes), but rather than define a new symbol, the auxiliary record gives additional information on the last symbol defined. The choice of which of several formats to use depends on the Storage Class field. Currently defined formats for auxiliary symbol table records are shown in "Auxiliary Symbol Records."

Tools that read COFF symbol tables must ignore auxiliary symbol records whose interpretation is unknown. This allows the symbol table format to be extended to add new auxiliary records, without breaking existing tools.

5.4.1 Symbol Name Representation

The Name field in a symbol table consists of eight bytes that contain the name itself, if it is not more than eight bytes long, or else give an offset into the String Table. To determine whether the name itself or an offset is given, test the first four bytes for equality to zero.

By convention, the names are treated as zero-terminated UTF-8 encoded strings.

Offset	Size	Field	Description
0	8	Short Name	An array of eight bytes. This array is padded with nulls on the right if the name is less than eight bytes long.

Offset	Size	Field	Description
0	4	Zeroes	Set to all zeros if the name is longer than eight bytes.
4	4	Offset	Offset into the String Table.

5.4.2 Section Number Values

Normally, the Section Value field in a symbol table entry is a one-based index into the Section Table. However, this field is a signed integer and may take negative values. The following values, less than one, have special meanings:

Constant	Value	Description
IMAGE_SYM_UNDEFINED	0	Symbol record is not yet assigned a section. If the value is 0, this indicates a references to an external symbol defined elsewhere. If the value is non-zero, this is a common symbol with a size specified by the value.
IMAGE_SYM_ABSOLUTE	-1	The symbol has an absolute (non-relocatable) value and is not an address.
IMAGE_SYM_DEBUG	-2	The symbol provides general type or debugging information but does not correspond to a section. Microsoft tools use this setting along with .file records (storage class FILE).

5.4.3 Type Representation

The Type field of a symbol table entry contains two bytes, where each byte represents type information. The least-significant byte represents simple (base) data type, and the most-significant byte represents complex type, if any:

MSB	LSB
Complex type: none, pointer, function, array.	Base type: integer, floating-point, etc.

The following values are defined for base type, although Microsoft tools generally do not use this field, setting the least-significant byte to 0. Instead, Visual C++ Debug information is used to indicate types. However, the possible COFF values are listed here for completeness.

Constant	Value	Description
IMAGE_SYM_TYPE_NULL	0	No type information or unknown base type. Microsoft tools use this setting.
IMAGE_SYM_TYPE_VOID	1	No valid type; used with void pointers and functions.
IMAGE_SYM_TYPE_CHAR	2	Character (signed byte).
IMAGE_SYM_TYPE_SHORT	3	Two-byte signed integer.
IMAGE_SYM_TYPE_INT	4	Natural integer type (normally four bytes in Windows).
IMAGE_SYM_TYPE_LONG	5	Four-byte signed integer.
IMAGE_SYM_TYPE_FLOAT	6	Four-byte floating point number.
IMAGE_SYM_TYPE_DOUBLE	7	Eight-byte floating point number.
IMAGE_SYM_TYPE_STRUCT	8	Structure.
IMAGE_SYM_TYPE_UNION	9	Union.
IMAGE_SYM_TYPE_ENUM	10	Enumerated type.
IMAGE_SYM_TYPE_MOE	11	Member of enumeration (a specific value).
IMAGE_SYM_TYPE_BYTE	12	Byte; unsigned one-byte integer.
IMAGE_SYM_TYPE_WORD	13	Word; unsigned two-byte integer.
IMAGE_SYM_TYPE_UINT	14	Unsigned integer of natural size (normally, four bytes).
IMAGE_SYM_TYPE_DWORD	15	Unsigned four-byte integer.

The most significant byte specifies whether the symbol is a pointer to, function returning, or array of the base type specified in the least significant byte. Microsoft tools use this field only to indicate whether or not the symbol is a function, so that the only two resulting values are 0x0 and 0x20 for the Type field. However, other tools can use this field to communicate more information.

It is very important to specify the function attribute correctly. This information is required for incremental linking to work correctly. For some architectures, the information may be required for other purposes.

Constant	Value	Description
IMAGE_SYM_DTYPE_NULL	0	No derived type; the symbol is a simple scalar variable.
IMAGE_SYM_DTYPE_POINTER	1	Pointer to base type.
IMAGE_SYM_DTYPE_FUNCTION	2	Function returning base type.
IMAGE_SYM_DTYPE_ARRAY	3	Array of base type.

5.4.4 Storage Class

The Storage Class field of the Symbol Table indicates what kind of definition a symbol represents. The following table shows possible values. Note that the Storage Class field is an unsigned one-byte integer. The special value –1 should therefore be taken to mean its unsigned equivalent, 0xFF.

Although traditional COFF format makes use of many storage-class values, Microsoft tools rely on Visual C++ Debug format for most symbolic information and generally use only four storage-class values: EXTERNAL (2), STATIC (3), FUNCTION (101), and STATIC (103). Except in the second column heading below, "Value" should be taken to mean the Value field of the symbol record (whose interpretation depends on the number found as the storage class).

Constant	Value	Description / Interpretation of Value Field
IMAGE_SYM_CLASS_END_OF_FUNCTION	–1 (0xFF)	Special symbol representing end of function, for debugging purposes.
IMAGE_SYM_CLASS_NULL	0	No storage class assigned.
IMAGE_SYM_CLASS_AUTOMATIC	1	Automatic (stack) variable. The Value field specifies stack frame offset.

Appendix

Constant	Value	Description / Interpretation of Value Field
IMAGE_SYM_CLASS_EXTERNAL	2	Used by Microsoft tools for external symbols. The Value field indicates the size if the section number is IMAGE_SYM_UNDEFINED (0). If the section number is not 0, then the Value field specifies the offset within the section.
IMAGE_SYM_CLASS_STATIC	3	The Value field specifies the offset of the symbol within the section. If the Value is 0, then the symbol represents a section name.
IMAGE_SYM_CLASS_REGISTER	4	Register variable. The Value field specifies register number.
IMAGE_SYM_CLASS_EXTERNAL_DEF	5	Symbol is defined externally.
IMAGE_SYM_CLASS_LABEL	6	Code label defined within the module. The Value field specifies the offset of the symbol within the section.
IMAGE_SYM_CLASS_UNDEFINED_LABEL	7	Reference to a code label not defined.
IMAGE_SYM_CLASS_MEMBER_OF_STRUCT	8	Structure member. The Value field specifies n*th* member.
IMAGE_SYM_CLASS_ARGUMENT	9	Formal argument (parameter) of a function. The Value field specifies n*th* argument.
IMAGE_SYM_CLASS_STRUCT_TAG	10	Structure tag-name entry.
IMAGE_SYM_CLASS_MEMBER_OF_UNION	11	Union member. The Value field specifies n*th* member.
IMAGE_SYM_CLASS_UNION_TAG	12	Union tag-name entry.
IMAGE_SYM_CLASS_TYPE_DEFINITION	13	Typedef entry.
IMAGE_SYM_CLASS_UNDEFINED_STATIC	14	Static data declaration.
IMAGE_SYM_CLASS_ENUM_TAG	15	Enumerated type tagname entry.
IMAGE_SYM_CLASS_MEMBER_OF_ENUM	16	Member of enumeration. Value specifies n*th* member.

Constant	Value	Description / Interpretation of Value Field
IMAGE_SYM_CLASS_REGISTER_PARAM	17	Register parameter.
IMAGE_SYM_CLASS_BIT_FIELD	18	Bit-field reference. Value specifies n*th* bit in the bit field.
IMAGE_SYM_CLASS_BLOCK	100	A .bb (beginning of block) or .eb (end of block) record. Value is the relocatable address of the code location.
IMAGE_SYM_CLASS_FUNCTION	101	Used by Microsoft tools for symbol records that define the extent of a function: begin function (named .bf), end function (.ef), and lines in function (.lf). For .lf records, Value gives the number of source lines in the function. For .ef records, Value gives the size of function code.
IMAGE_SYM_CLASS_END_OF_STRUCT	102	End of structure entry.
IMAGE_SYM_CLASS_FILE	103	Used by Microsoft tools, as well as traditional COFF format, for the source-file symbol record. The symbol is followed by auxiliary records that name the file.
IMAGE_SYM_CLASS_SECTION	104	Definition of a section (Microsoft tools use STATIC storage class instead).
IMAGE_SYM_CLASS_WEAK_EXTERNAL	105	Weak external. See Section 5.5.3, "Auxiliary Format 3: Weak Externals," for more information.
IMAGE_SYM_CLASS_CLR_TOKEN	107	clr token symbol; name is ASCII string consisting of the hexadecimal value of the token. See Section 5.5.7, "clr Token Definition," for more information.

5.5 Auxiliary Symbol Records

Auxiliary Symbol Table records always follow, and apply to, some standard Symbol Table record. An auxiliary record can have any format that the tools are designed to recognize, but 18 bytes must be allocated for them so that Symbol Table is maintained as an array of regular size. Currently, Microsoft tools recognize auxiliary formats for the following kinds of records: function definitions, function begin and end symbols (**.bf** and **.ef**), weak externals, filenames, and section definitions.

The traditional COFF design also includes auxiliary-record formats for arrays and structures. Microsoft tools do not use these, instead placing that symbolic information in Visual C++ Debug format in the debug sections.

5.5.1 Auxiliary Format 1: Function Definitions

A symbol table record marks the beginning of a function definition if all of the following are true: it has storage class EXTERNAL (2), a Type value indicating it is a function (0x20), and a section number greater than zero. Note that a symbol table record that has a section number of UNDEFINED (0) does not define the function and does not have an auxiliary record. Function-definition symbol records are followed by an auxiliary record with the format described below.

Offset	Size	Field	Description
0	4	TagIndex	Symbol-table index of the corresponding .bf (begin function) symbol record.
4	4	TotalSize	Size of the executable code for the function itself. If the function is in its own section, the Size of Raw Data in the section header will be greater or equal to this field, depending on alignment considerations.
8	4	PointerToLinenumber	File offset of the first COFF line-number entry for the function, or zero if none exists. See Section 5.3, "COFF Line Numbers," for more information.
12	4	PointerToNextFunction	Symbol-table index of the record for the next function. If the function is the last in the symbol table, this field is set to zero.
16	2	Unused.	

5.5.2 Auxiliary Format 2: .bf and .ef Symbols

For each function definition in the Symbol Table, there are three items that describe the beginning, ending, and number of lines. Each of these symbols has storage class FUNCTION (101):

A symbol record named **.bf** (begin function). The Value field is unused.

A symbol record named **.lf** (lines in function). The Value field gives the number of lines in the function.

A symbol record named **.ef** (end of function). The Value field has the same number as the Total Size field in the function-definition symbol record.

The **.bf** and **.ef** symbol records (but not **.lf** records) are followed by an auxiliary record with the following format:

Offset	Size	Field	Description
0	4	Unused.	
4	2	Linenumber	Actual ordinal line number (1, 2, 3, etc.) within source file, corresponding to the .bf or .ef record.
6	6	Unused.	
12	4	PointerToNextFunction (.bf only)	Symbol-table index of the next .bf symbol record. If the function is the last in the symbol table, this field is set to zero. Not used for .ef records.
16	2	Unused.	

5.5.3 Auxiliary Format 3: Weak Externals

"Weak externals" are a mechanism for object files allowing flexibility at link time. A module can contain an unresolved external symbol (sym1), but it can also include an auxiliary record indicating that if sym1 is not present at link time, another external symbol (sym2) is used to resolve references instead.

If a definition of sym1 is linked, then an external reference to the symbol is resolved normally. If a definition of sym1 is not linked, then all references to the weak external for sym1 refer to sym2 instead. The external symbol, sym2, must always be linked; typically it is defined in the module containing the weak reference to sym1.

Weak externals are represented by a Symbol Table record with EXTERNAL storage class, UNDEF section number, and a value of 0. The weak-external symbol record is followed by an auxiliary record with the following format:

Offset	Size	Field	Description
0	4	TagIndex	Symbol-table index of sym2, the symbol to be linked if sym1 is not found.
4	4	Characteristics	A value of IMAGE_WEAK_EXTERN_SEARCH_NOLIBRARY indicates that no library search for sym1 should be performed. A value of IMAGE_WEAK_EXTERN_SEARCH_LIBRARY indicates that a library search for sym1 should be performed. A value of IMAGE_WEAK_EXTERN_SEARCH_ALIAS indicates that sym1 is an alias for sym2.
8	10	Unused.	

Note that the Characteristics field is not defined in WINNT.H; instead, the Total Size field is used.

5.5.4 Auxiliary Format 4: Files

This format follows a symbol-table record with storage class FILE (103). The symbol name itself should be **.file**, and the auxiliary record that follows it gives the name of a source-code file.

Offset	Size	Field	Description
0	18	File Name	ANSI string giving the name of the source file; padded with nulls if less than maximum length.

5.5.5 Auxiliary Format 5: Section Definitions

This format follows a symbol-table record that defines a section: such a record has a symbol name that is the name of a section (such as **.text** or **.drectve**) and has storage class STATIC (3). The auxiliary record provides information on the section referred to. Thus it duplicates some of the information in the section header.

Offset	Size	Field	Description
0	4	Length	Size of section data; same as Size of Raw Data in the section header.
4	2	NumberOfRelocations	Number of relocation entries for the section.
6	2	NumberOfLinenumbers	Number of line-number entries for the section.
8	4	Check Sum	Checksum for communal data. Applicable if the IMAGE_SCN_LNK_COMDAT flag is set in the section header. See "COMDAT Sections" below, for more information.
12	2	Number	One-based index into the Section Table for the associated section; used when the COMDAT Selection setting is 5.
14	1	Selection	COMDAT selection number. Applicable if the section is a COMDAT section.
15	3	Unused.	

5.5.6 COMDAT Sections (Object Only)

The Selection field of the Section Definition auxiliary format is applicable if the section is a COMDAT section: a section that can be defined by more than one object file. (The flag IMAGE_SCN_LNK_COMDAT is set in the Section Flags field of the section header.) The Selection field determines the way that the linker resolves the multiple definitions of COMDAT sections.

The first symbol having the section value of the COMDAT section must be the section symbol. This symbol has the name of the section, Value field equal to 0, the section number of the COMDAT section in question, Type field equal to IMAGE_SYM_TYPE_NULL, Class field equal to IMAGE_SYM_CLASS_STATIC, and one auxiliary record. The second symbol is called "the COMDAT symbol" and is used by the linker in conjunction with the Selection field.

Values for the Selection field are shown below.

Constant	Value	Description
IMAGE_COMDAT_SELECT_NODUPLICATES	1	The linker issues a multiply defined symbol error if this symbol is already defined.

Constant	Value	Description
IMAGE_COMDAT_SELECT_ANY	2	Any section defining the same COMDAT symbol may be linked; the rest are removed.
IMAGE_COMDAT_SELECT_SAME_SIZE	3	The linker chooses an arbitrary section among the definitions for this symbol. A multiply defined symbol error is issued if all definitions don't have the same size.
IMAGE_COMDAT_SELECT_EXACT_MATCH	4	The linker chooses an arbitrary section among the definitions for this symbol. A multiply defined symbol error is issued if all definitions don't match exactly.
IMAGE_COMDAT_SELECT_ASSOCIATIVE	5	The section is linked if a certain other COMDAT section is linked. This other section is indicated by the Number field of the auxiliary symbol record for the section definition. Use of this setting is useful for definitions that have components in multiple sections (for example, code in one and data in another), but where all must be linked or discarded as a set. The other section that this one is associated with must be a COMDAT and not another associative COMDAT.
IMAGE_COMDAT_SELECT_LARGEST	6	The linker chooses the largest from the definitions for this symbol. If multiple definitions have this size, the choice between them is arbitrary.

5.5.7 clr Token Definition (Object Only)

This auxiliary symbol generally follows the IMAGE_SYM_CLASS_CLR_TOKEN and is used to tie together a token to the COFF symbol table's namespace.

Offset	Size	Field	Description
0	1	bAuxType	Must be IMAGE_AUX_SYMBOL_TYPE_TOKEN_DEF (1).
1	1	bReserved	Reserved, must be zero.
2	4	SymbolTableIndex	Symbol index of the COFF symbol that this clr Token Definition refers to.

Offset	Size	Field	Description
6	12		Reserved, must be zero.

5.6 COFF String Table

Immediately following the COFF symbol table is the COFF string table. The position of this table is found by taking the symbol table address in the COFF header, and adding the number of symbols multiplied by the size of a symbol.

At the beginning of the COFF string table are 4 bytes containing the total size (in bytes) of the rest of the string table. This size includes the size field itself, so that the value in this location would be 4 if no strings were present.

Following the size are null-terminated strings pointed to by symbols in the COFF symbol table.

5.7 The Attribute Certificate Table (Image Only)

Attribute Certificates may be associated with an image by adding an Attribute Certificate Table. There are a number of different types of Attribute Certificates. The meaning and use of each certificate type is not covered in this document. For this information see the *Microsoft Distributed System Architecture, Attribute Certificate Architecture Specification.*

An Attribute Certificate Table is added at the end of the image, with only a .debug section following (if a .debug section is present). The Attribute Certificate Table contains one or more fixed length table entries that can be found via the Certificate Table field of the Optional Header Data Directories list (offset 128). Each entry of this table identifies the beginning location and length of a corresponding certificate. There is one Certificate Table entry for each certificate stored in this section. The number of entries in the certificate table can be calculated by dividing the size of the certificate table (found in offset 132) by the size of an entry in the certificate table (8). Note that the size of the certificate table includes only the table entries, not the actual certificates which the table entries, in turn, point to.

The format of each table entry is:

Offset	Size	Field	Description
0	4	Certificate Data	File pointer to the certificate data. This will always point to an address that is octaword aligned (i.e., is a multiple of 8 bytes and so the low-order 3 bits are zero).
0	4	Size of Certificate	Unsigned integer identifying the size (in bytes) of the certificate.

Appendix

Notice that certificates always start on an octaword boundary. If a certificate is not an even number of octawords long, it is zero padded to the next octaword boundary. However, the length of the certificate does ***not*** include this padding and so any certificate navigation software must be sure to round up to the next octaword to locate another certificate.

5.7.1 Certificate Data

This is the binary data representing an Attribute Certificate. The format and meaning of each certificate is defined in Attribute Certificate Architecture Specification. The certificate starting location and length is specified by an entry in the CertificateTable. Each certificate is represented by a single Certificate Table entry.

5.8 Delay-Load Import Tables (Image Only)

These tables were added to the image in order to support a uniform mechanism for applications to delay the loading of a dll until the first call into that dll. The layout of the tables matches that of the traditional import tables (see Section 6.4, "The .idata Section," for details), so only a few details will be discussed here.

5.8.1 The Delay-Load Directory Table

The Delay-Load Directory Table is the counterpart to the Import Directory Table, and can be retrieved via the Delay Import Descriptor entry in the Optional Header Data Directories list (offset 200). The Table is arranged as follows:

Offset	Size	Field	Description
0	4	Attributes	Must be zero.
4	4	Name	Relative virtual address of the name of the dll to be loaded. The name resides in the read-only data section of the image.
8	4	Module Handle	Relative virtual address of the module handle (in the data section of the image) of the dll to be delay-loaded. Used for storage by the routine supplied to manage delay-loading.
12	4	Delay Import Address Table	Relative virtual address of the delay-load import address table. See below for further details.
16	4	Delay Import Name Table	Relative virtual address of the delay-load name table, which contains the names of the imports that may need to be loaded. Matches the layout of the Import Name Table (Section 6.4.3, "Hint/Name Table").

Offset	Size	Field	Description
20	4	Bound Delay Import Table	Relative virtual address of the bound delay-load address table, if it exists.
24	4	Unload Delay Import Table	Relative virtual address of the unload delay-load address table, if it exists. This is an exact copy of the Delay Import Address Table. In the event that the caller unloads the dll, this table should be copied back over the Delay IAT such that subsequent calls to the dll continue to use the thunking mechanism correctly.
28	4	Time Stamp	Time stamp of dll to which this image has been bound.

The tables referenced in this data structure are organized and sorted just as their counterparts are for traditional imports. See Section 6.4, "The .idata Section," for details.

5.8.2 Attributes

As yet, there are no attribute flags defined. This field is currently set to zero by the linker in the image. This field can be used to extend the record by indicating the presence of new fields or for indicating behaviors to the delay and/or unload helper functions.

5.8.3 Name

The name of the DLL to be delay loaded resides in the read-only data section of the image and is referenced via the `szName` field.

5.8.4 Module Handle

The handle of the DLL to be delay loaded is located in the data section of the image and pointed to via the `phmod` field. The supplied delay load helper uses this location to store the handle to the loaded DLL.

5.8.5 Delay Import Address Table (IAT)

The delay IAT is referenced by the delay import descriptor via the pIAT field. This is the working copy of the entry point, function pointers that reside in the data section of the image and initially refer to the delay load thunks. The delay load helper is responsible for updating these pointers with the real entry points so that the thunks are no longer in the calling loop. The function pointers are accessed via the expression `pINT->u1.Function`.

5.8.6 Delay Import Name Table (INT)

The delay INT has the names of the imports that may need to be loaded. They are ordered in the same fashion as the function pointers in the IAT. They consist of the same structures as the standard INT and are accessed via the expression `pINT->u1.AddressOfData->Name[0]`.

Appendix

5.8.7 Delay Bound Import Address Table (BIAT) and Time Stamp

The delay BIAT is an optional table of `IMAGE_THUNK_DATA` items that is used along with the timestamp field by a post process binding phase.

5.8.8 Delay Unload Import Address Table (UIAT)

The delay UIAT is an optional table of IMAGE_THUNK_DATA items that is used by the unload code to handle an explicit unload request. It is initialized data in the read-only section that is an exact copy of the original IAT that referred the code to the delay load thunks. On the unload request, the library can be freed, the `*phmod` cleared, and the UIAT written over the IAT to restore everything to its pre-load state.

6 Special Sections

Typical COFF sections contain code or data that linkers and Win32 loaders process without special knowledge of the sections' contents. The contents are relevant only to the application being linked or executed.

However, some COFF sections have special meanings when found in object files and/or image files. Tools and loaders recognize these sections because they have special flags set in the section header, or because they are pointed to from special locations in the image optional header, or because the section name is "magic": that is, the name indicates a special function of the section. (Even where the section name is not magic, the name is dictated by convention, so we will refer to a name.)

The reserved sections and their attributes are described in the table below, followed by detailed descriptions for a subset of them.

Section Name	Content	Characteristics
.bss	Uninitialized data	IMAGE_SCN_CNT_UNINITIALIZED_DATA | IMAGE_SCN_MEM_READ | IMAGE_SCN_MEM_WRITE
.data	Initialized data	IMAGE_SCN_CNT_INITIALIZED_DATA | IMAGE_SCN_MEM_READ | IMAGE_SCN_MEM_WRITE
.edata	Export tables	IMAGE_SCN_CNT_INITIALIZED_DATA | IMAGE_SCN_MEM_READ
.idata	Import tables	IMAGE_SCN_CNT_INITIALIZED_DATA | IMAGE_SCN_MEM_READ | IMAGE_SCN_MEM_WRITE

Section Name	Content	Characteristics
.pdata	Exception information	IMAGE_SCN_CNT_INITIALIZED_DATA | IMAGE_SCN_MEM_READ
.rdata	Read-only initialized data	IMAGE_SCN_CNT_INITIALIZED_DATA | IMAGE_SCN_MEM_READ
.reloc	Image relocations	IMAGE_SCN_CNT_INITIALIZED_DATA | IMAGE_SCN_MEM_READ | IMAGE_SCN_MEM_DISCARDABLE
.rsrc	Resource directory	IMAGE_SCN_CNT_INITIALIZED_DATA | IMAGE_SCN_MEM_READ | IMAGE_SCN_MEM_WRITE
.sdata	GP-relative initialized data	IMAGE_SCN_CNT_INITIALIZED_DATA | IMAGE_SCN_MEM_READ | IMAGE_SCN_MEM_WRITE
.sbss	GP-relative uninitialized data	IMAGE_SCN_CNT_UNINITIALIZED_DATA | IMAGE_SCN_MEM_READ | IMAGE_SCN_MEM_WRITE
.srdata	GP-relative read-only data	IMAGE_SCN_CNT_INITIALIZED_DATA | IMAGE_SCN_MEM_READ | IMAGE _SCN_GPREL
.text	Executable code	IMAGE_SCN_CNT_CODE | IMAGE_SCN_MEM_EXECUTE | IIMAGE_SCN_MEM_READ
.tls	Thread-local storage	IMAGE_SCN_CNT_INITIALIZED_DATA | IMAGE_SCN_MEM_READ | IMAGE_SCN_MEM_WRITE
.xdata	Exception information	IMAGE_SCN_CNT_INITIALIZED_DATA | IMAGE_SCN_MEM_READ
.sxdata	Safe Exception Handler data (x86/ object only)	IMAGE_SCN_CNT_INFO Contains the symbol index of each of the exception handlers being referred to by the code in that object file. The symbol can be for an UNDEF symbol or one that is defined in that module.

Some of the sections listed here are marked "(object only)" or "(image only)" to indicate that their special semantics are relevant only for object files or image files, respectively. A section that says "(image only)" may still appear in an object file as a way of getting into the image file, but the section has no special meaning to the linker, only to the image file loader.

6.1 The .debug Section

The **.debug** section is used in object files to contain compiler-generated debug information, and in image files to contain the total debug information generated. This section describes the packaging of debug information in object and image files. The actual format of Visual C++ debug information is not described here. See the document *CV4 Symbolic Debug Information Specification*.

The next section describes the format of the debug directory, which can be anywhere in the image. Subsequent sections describe the "groups" in object files that contain debug information.

The default for the linker is that debug information is not mapped into the address space of the image. A **.debug** section exists only when debug information is mapped in the address space.

6.1.1 Debug Directory (Image Only)

Image files contain an optional "debug directory" indicating what form of debug information is present and where it is. This directory consists of an array of "debug directory entries" whose location and size are indicated in the image optional header.

The debug directory may be in a discardable **.debug** section (if one exists) or it may be included in any other section in the image file, or not in a section at all.

Each debug directory entry identifies the location and size of a block of debug information. The RVA specified may be 0 if the debug information is not covered by a section header (i.e., it resides in the image file and is not mapped into the run-time address space). If it is mapped, the RVA is its address.

Here is the format of a debug directory entry:

Offset	Size	Field	Description
0	4	Characteristics	A reserved field intended to be used for flags, set to zero for now.
4	4	TimeDateStamp	Time and date the debug data was created.
8	2	MajorVersion	Major version number of the debug data format.
10	2	MinorVersion	Minor version number of the debug data format.
12	4	Type	Format of debugging information: this field enables support of multiple debuggers. See Section 6.1.2, "Debug Type," for more information.

Offset	Size	Field	Description
16	4	SizeOfData	Size of the debug data (not including the debug directory itself).
20	4	AddressOfRawData	Address of the debug data when loaded, relative to the image base.
24	4	PointerToRawData	File pointer to the debug data.

6.1.2 Debug Type

The following values are defined for the Debug Type field of the debug directory:

Constant	Value	Description
IMAGE_DEBUG_TYPE_UNKNOWN	0	Unknown value, ignored by all tools.
IMAGE_DEBUG_TYPE_COFF	1	COFF debug information (line numbers, symbol table, and string table). This type of debug information is also pointed to by fields in the file headers.
IMAGE_DEBUG_TYPE_CODEVIEW	2	Visual C++ debug information. The format of the data block is described by the CV7 specification.
IMAGE_DEBUG_TYPE_FPO	3	Frame Pointer Omission (FPO) information. This information tells the debugger how to interpret non-standard stack frames, which use the EBP register for a purpose other than as a frame pointer.
IMAGE_DEBUG_TYPE_MISC	4	
IMAGE_DEBUG_TYPE_EXCEPTION	5	
IMAGE_DEBUG_TYPE_FIXUP	6	
IMAGE_DEBUG_TYPE_OMAP_TO_SRC	7	
IMAGE_DEBUG_TYPE_OMAP_FROM_SRC	8	
IMAGE_DEBUG_TYPE_BORLAND	9	

If Debug Type is set to IMAGE_DEBUG_TYPE_FPO, the debug raw data is an array in which each member describes the stack frame of a function. Not every function in the image file need have FPO information defined for it, even though debug type is FPO. Those functions that do not have FPO information are assumed to have normal stack frames. The format for FPO information is defined as follows:

```
#define FRAME_FPO    0
#define FRAME_TRAP   1
#define FRAME_TSS    2

typedef struct _FPO_DATA {
    DWORD       ulOffStart;          // offset 1st byte of function code
    DWORD       cbProcSize;          // # bytes in function
    DWORD       cdwLocals;           // # bytes in locals/4
    WORD        cdwParams;           // # bytes in params/4

    WORD        cbProlog : 8;        // # bytes in prolog
    WORD        cbRegs   : 3;        // # regs saved
    WORD        fHasSEH  : 1;        // TRUE if SEH in func
    WORD        fUseBP   : 1;        // TRUE if EBP has been allocated
    WORD        reserved : 1;        // reserved for future use
    WORD        cbFrame  : 2;        // frame type
} FPO_DATA;
```

6.1.3 .debug$F (Object Only)

The data in this section has been superceded in Visual C++ version 7.0 and above by a more extensive set of data that is emitted into a **.debug$S** subsection. Please see the Visual C++ 8.0 Debugging Information specification for details. There are cases where this FPO data in **.debug$F** still needs to be used, such as from hand-written assembler code.

Object files can contain **.debug$F** sections whose contents are one or more FPO_DATA records (Frame Pointer Omission information). See "IMAGE_DEBUG_TYPE_FPO" in table above.

The linker recognizes these **.debug$F** records. If debug information is being generated, the linker sorts the FPO_DATA records by procedure RVA, and generates a debug directory entry for them.

The compiler should not generate FPO records for procedures that have a standard frame format.

6.1.4 .debug$S (Object Only)

This section contains CV7 symbolic information: a stream of CV7 symbol records as described in the CV7 spec.

6.1.5 .debug$P (Object Only)

This section contains CV7 precompiled type information: a stream of CV type records as described by the CV spec. These are shared types between all of the objects that were compiled using the precompiled header that was generated with this object.

6.1.6 .debug$T (Object Only)

This section contains CV7 type information: a stream of CV7 type records as described in the CV7 spec.

6.1.7 Linker Support for Microsoft Debug Information

To support debug information, the linker:

Gathers all relevant debug data from the **.debug$F**, **debug$S**, **.debug$P**, and **.debug$T** sections.

Processes that data along with the linker-generated debugging information into the .PDB file, and creates a debug directory entry to refer to it.

6.2 The .drectve Section (Object Only)

A section is a "directive" section if it has the IMAGE_SCN_LNK_INFO flag set in the section header. By convention, such a section also has the name **.drectve**. The linker removes a **.drectve** section after processing the information, so the section does not appear in the image file being linked. Note that a section marked with IMAGE_SCN_LNK_INFO that is not named **.drectve** is ignored and discarded by the linker.

A **.drectve** section consists of a string of text which can be encoded as ANSI or UTF-8. If the UTF-8 BOM (Byte Order Marker, a three byte prefix, 0xEF, 0xBB, 0xBF) is not present, the directive string is interpreted as ANSI. This string is a series of linker options (each option containing hyphen, option name, and any appropriate attribute) separated by spaces. The **.drectve** section must not have relocations or line numbers.

6.3 The .edata Section (Image Only)

The export data section, named **.edata**, contains information about symbols that other images can access through dynamic linking. Exports are generally found in DLLs, but DLLs can import symbols as well.

An overview of the general structure of the export section is described below. The tables described are generally contiguous in the file and present in the order shown (though this is not strictly required). Only the Directory Table and Address Table are necessary for exporting symbols as ordinals. (An ordinal is an export accessed directly as an Export Address Table index.) The Name Pointer Table, Ordinal Table, and Export Name Table all exist to support use of export names.

Table Name	Description
Export Directory Table	A table with just one row (unlike the debug directory). This table indicates the locations and sizes of the other export tables.
Export Address Table	An array of RVAs of exported symbols. These are the actual addresses of the exported functions and data within the executable code and data sections. Other image files can import a symbol by using an index to this table (an ordinal) or, optionally, by using the public name that corresponds to the ordinal if one is defined.
Name Pointer Table	Array of pointers to the public export names, sorted in ascending order.
Ordinal Table	Array of the ordinals that correspond to members of the Name Pointer Table. The correspondence is by position; therefore, the Name Pointer Table and the Ordinal Table must have the same number of members. Each ordinal is an index into the Export Address Table.
Export Name Table	A series of null-terminated ASCII strings. Members of the Name Pointer Table point into this area. These names are the public names through which the symbols are imported and exported; they do not necessarily have to be the same as the private names used within the image file.

When another image file imports a symbol by name, the Name Pointer Table is searched for a matching string. If one is found, the associated ordinal is then determined by looking at the corresponding member in the Ordinal Table (that is, the member of the Ordinal Table with the same index as the string pointer found in the Name Pointer Table). The resulting ordinal is an index into the Export Address Table, which gives the actual location of the desired symbol. Every export symbol can be accessed by an ordinal.

Direct use of an ordinal is therefore more efficient, because it avoids the need to search the Name Pointer Table for a matching string. However, use of an export name is more mnemonic and does not require the user to know the table index for the symbol.

6.3.1 Export Directory Table

The export information begins with the Export Directory Table, which describes the remainder of the export information. The Export Directory Table contains address information that is used to resolve fix-up references to the entry points within this image.

Offset	Size	Field	Description
0	4	Export Flags	A reserved field, set to zero for now.
4	4	Time/Date Stamp	Time and date the export data was created.

Offset	Size	Field	Description
8	2	Major Version	Major version number. The major/minor version number can be set by the user.
10	2	Minor Version	Minor version number.
12	4	Name RVA	Address of the ASCII string containing the name of the DLL. Relative to image base.
16	4	Ordinal Base	Starting ordinal number for exports in this image. This field specifies the starting ordinal number for the Export Address Table. Usually set to 1.
20	4	Address Table Entries	Number of entries in the Export Address Table.
24	4	Number of Name Pointers	Number of entries in the Name Pointer Table (also the number of entries in the Ordinal Table).
28	4	Export Address Table RVA	Address of the Export Address Table, relative to the image base.
32	4	Name Pointer RVA	Address of the Export Name Pointer Table, relative to the image base. The table size is given by Number of Name Pointers.
36	4	Ordinal Table RVA	Address of the Ordinal Table, relative to the image base.

6.3.2 Export Address Table

The Export Address Table contains the address of exported entry points and exported data and absolutes. An ordinal number is used as an index into the Export Address Table.

Each entry in the Export Address Table is a field that uses one of two formats, as shown in the following table. If the address specified is *not* within the export section (as defined by the address and length indicated in the Optional Header), the field is an Export RVA: an actual address in code or data. Otherwise, the field is a Forwarder RVA, which names a symbol in another DLL.

Offset	Size	Field	Description
0	4	Export RVA	Address of the exported symbol when loaded into memory, relative to the image base. For example, the address of an exported function.

Offset	Size	Field	Description
0	4	Forwarder RVA	Pointer to a null-terminated ASCII string in the export section, giving the DLL name and the name of the export (for example, "MYDLL..expfunc") or the DLL name and an export (for example, "MYDLL.#27").

A Forwarder RVA exports a definition from some other image, making it appear as if it were being exported by the current image. Thus the symbol is simultaneously imported and exported.

For example, in KERNEL32.DLL in Windows 2000, the export named "HeapAlloc" is forwarded to the string "NTDLL.RtlAllocateHeap". This allows applications to use the Windows 2000-specific module "NTDLL.DLL" without actually containing import references to it. The application's import table references only "KERNEL32.DLL." Therefore, the application is not specific to Windows and can run on any Win32 system.

6.3.3 Export Name Pointer Table

The Export Name Pointer Table is an array of addresses (RVAs) into the Export Name Table. The pointers are 32 bits each and are relative to the Image Base. The pointers are ordered lexically to allow binary searches.

An export name is defined only if the Export Name Pointer Table contains a pointer to it.

6.3.4 Export Ordinal Table

The Export Ordinal Table is an array of 16-bit indexes into the Export Address Table. The ordinals are biased by the Ordinal Base field of the Export Directory Table. In other words, the Ordinal Base must be subtracted from the ordinals to obtain true indexes into the Export Address Table.

The Export Name Pointer Table and the Export Ordinal Table form two parallel arrays, separated to allow natural field alignment. These two tables, in effect, operate as one table, in which the Export Name Pointer "column" points to a public (exported) name, and the Export Ordinal "column" gives the corresponding ordinal for that public name. A member of the Export Name Pointer Table and a member of the Export Ordinal Table are associated by having the same position (index) in their respective arrays.

Thus, when the Export Name Pointer Table is searched and a matching string is found at position *i*, the algorithm for finding the symbol's address is:

```
i = Search_ExportNamePointerTable (ExportName);
ordinal = ExportOrdinalTable [i];
SymbolRVA = ExportAddressTable [ordinal - OrdinalBase];
```

6.3.5 *Export Name Table*

The Export Name Table contains the actual string data pointed to by the Export Name Pointer Table. The strings in this table are public names that can be used by other images to import the symbols; these public export names are not necessarily the same as the (private) symbol names that the symbols have in their own image file and source code, although they can be.

Every exported symbol has an ordinal value, which is just the index into the Export Address Table (plus the Ordinal Base value). Use of export names, however, is optional. Some, all, or none of the exported symbols can have export names. For those exported symbols that do have export names, corresponding entries in the Export Name Pointer Table and Export Ordinal Table work together to associate each name with an ordinal.

The structure of the Export Name Table is a series of ASCII strings, of variable length, each null terminated.

6.4 The .idata Section

All image files that import symbols, including virtually all .EXE files, have an **.idata** section. A typical file layout for the import information follows:

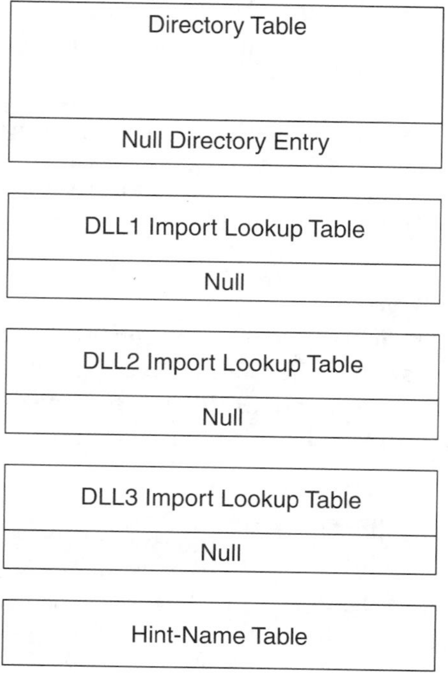

Figure A-3 Typical Import Section Layout

Appendix

6.4.1 *Import Directory Table*

The import information begins with the Import Directory Table, which describes the remainder of the import information. The Import Directory Table contains address information that is used to resolve fix-up references to the entry points within a DLL image. The Import Directory Table consists of an array of Import Directory Entries, one entry for each DLL the image references. The last directory entry is empty (filled with null values), which indicates the end of the directory table.

Each Import Directory entry has the following format:

Offset	Size	Field	Description
0	4	Import Lookup Table RVA (Characteristics)	Relative virtual address of the Import Lookup Table; this table contains a name or ordinal for each import. (The name "Characteristics" is used in WINNT.H but is no longer descriptive of this field.)
4	4	Time/Date Stamp	Set to zero until bound; then this field is set to the time/data stamp of the DLL.
8	4	Fowarder Chain	Index of first forwarder reference.
12	4	Name RVA	Address of ASCII string containing the DLL name. This address is relative to the image base.
16	4	Import Address Table RVA (Thunk Table)	Relative virtual address of the Import Address Table: this table is identical in contents to the Import Lookup Table until the image is bound.

6.4.2 *Import Lookup Table*

An Import Lookup Table is an array of 32-bit numbers for PE32, 64-bit for PE32+. Each entry uses the bit-field format (described below) in which bit 31 (63) is the most significant bit. The collection of these entries describes all imports from the image to a given DLL. The last entry is set to zero (NULL) to indicate end of the table.

Bit(s)	Size	Bit Field	Description
31 / 63	1	Ordinal/Name Flag	If bit is set, import by ordinal. Otherwise, import by name. Bit is masked as 0x80000000 for PE32, 0x8000000000000000 for PE32+.

Bit(s)	Size	Bit Field	Description
30 – 0 / 62 – 0	31 / 63	Ordinal Number	Ordinal/Name Flag is 1: import by ordinal. This field is a 31-bit (63-bit) ordinal number.
30 – 0 / 62 – 0	31 / 63	Hint/Name Table RVA	Ordinal/Name Flag is 0: import by name. This field is a 31-bit (63-bit) address of a Hint/Name Table entry, relative to image base.

In a PE32 image, the lower 31 bits can be masked as 0x7FFFFFFF. In either case, the resulting number is a 32-bit integer or pointer in which the high bit is always zero (zero extension to 32 bits). Similarly for a PE32+ image, the lower 63 bits can be masked as 0x7FFFFFFFFFFFFFFF.

6.4.3 Hint/Name Table

One Hint/Name Table suffices for the entire import section. Each entry in the Hint/Name Table has the following format:

Offset	Size	Field	Description
0	2	Hint	Index into the Export Name Pointer Table. A match is attempted first with this value. If it fails, a binary search is performed on the DLL's Export Name Pointer Table.
2	variable	Name	ASCII string containing name to import. This is the string that must be matched to the public name in the DLL. This string is case sensitive and terminated by a null byte.
*	0 or 1	Pad	A trailing zero pad byte appears after the trailing null byte, if necessary, to align the next entry on an even boundary.

6.4.4 Import Address Table

The structure and content of the Import Address Table are identical to that of the Import Lookup Table, until the file is bound. During binding, the entries in the Import Address Table are overwritten with the 32-bit (or 64-bit for PE32+) addresses of the symbols being imported: these addresses are the actual memory addresses of the symbols (although technically, they are still called "virtual addresses"). The processing of binding is typically performed by the loader.

6.5 The .pdata Section

The .pdata section contains an array of function table entries used for exception handling and is pointed to by the exception table entry in the image data directory. The entries must be sorted according to the function addresses (the first field in each structure) before being emitted into the final image. The target platform determines which of the three variations described below is used.

For 32-bit MIPS images the following structure is used:

Offset	Size	Field	Description
0	4	Begin Address	Virtual address of the corresponding function.
4	4	End Address	Virtual address of the end of the function.
8	4	Exception Handler	Pointer to the exception handler to be executed.
12	4	Handler Data	Pointer to additional information to be passed to the handler.
16	4	Prolog End Address	Virtual address of the end of the function's prolog.

For the ARM, PowerPC, SH3 and SH4 WindowsCE platforms, this function table entry format is used:

Offset	Size	Field	Description
0	4	Begin Address	Virtual address of the corresponding function.
4	8 bits	Prolog Length	Number of instructions in the function's prolog.
4	22 bits	Function Length	Number of instructions in the function.
4	1 bit	32-bit Flag	Set if the function is comprised of 32-bit instructions, cleared for a 16-bit function.
4	1 bit	Exception Flag	Set if an exception handler exists for the function.

Finally, for IA64 the pdata entry format is as follows:

Offset	Size	Field	Description
0	4	Begin Address	Relative virtual address of the corresponding function.
4	4	End Address	Relative virtual address of the end of the function.
8	4	Unwind Information	Relative virtual address of the unwind information.

6.6 The .reloc Section (Image Only)

The Fix-Up Table contains entries for all fixups in the image. The Total Fix-Up Data Size in the Optional Header is the number of bytes in the fixup table. The fixup table is broken into blocks of fixups. Each block represents the fixups for a 4K page. Each block must start on a 32-bit boundary.

Fixups that are resolved by the linker do not need to be processed by the loader, unless the load image can't be loaded at the Image Base specified in the PE Header.

6.6.1 Fixup Block

Each fixup block starts with the following structure:

Offset	Size	Field	Description
0	4	Page RVA	The image base plus the page RVA is added to each offset to create the virtual address of where the fixup needs to be applied.
4	4	Block Size	Total number of bytes in the fixup block, including the Page RVA and Block Size fields, as well as the Type/Offset fields that follow.

The Block Size field is then followed by any number of Type/Offset entries. Each entry is a word (2 bytes) and has the following structure:

Offset	Size	Field	Description
0	4 bits	Type	Stored in high 4 bits of word. Value indicating which type of fixup is to be applied. These fixups are described in "Fixup Types."
0	12 bits	Offset	Stored in remaining 12 bits of word. Offset from starting address specified in the Page RVA field for the block. This offset specifies where the fixup is to be applied.

To apply a fixup, the difference is calculated between the preferred base address, and the base where the image is actually loaded. If the image is loaded at its preferred base, the delta would be zero, and thus the fixups would not have to be applied.

6.6.2 Fixup Types

Constant	Value	Description
IMAGE_REL_BASED_ABSOLUTE	0	The fixup is skipped. This type can be used to pad a block.
IMAGE_REL_BASED_HIGH	1	The fixup adds the high 16 bits of the delta to the 16-bit field at Offset. The 16-bit field represents the high value of a 32-bit word.
IMAGE_REL_BASED_LOW	2	The fixup adds the low 16 bits of the delta to the 16-bit field at Offset. The 16-bit field represents the low half of a 32-bit word.
IMAGE_REL_BASED_HIGHLOW	3	The fixup applies the delta to the 32-bit field at Offset.
IMAGE_REL_BASED_HIGHADJ	4	The fixup adds the high 16 bits of the delta to the 16-bit field at Offset. The 16-bit field represents the high value of a 32-bit word. The low 16 bits of the 32-bit value are stored in the 16 bit word that follows this base relocation. This means that this base relocation occupies two slots.
IMAGE_REL_BASED_MIPS_JMPADDR	5	Fixup applies to a MIPS jump instruction.
	6	Reserved for future use.

Constant	Value	Description
	7	Reserved for future use.
IMAGE_REL_BASED_MIPS_JMPADDR16	9	Fixup applies to a MIPS16 jump instruction.
IMAGE_REL_BASED_DIR64	10	This fixup applies the delta to the 64-bit field at Offset.

6.7 The .tls Section

The **.tls** section provides direct PE/COFF support for static Thread Local Storage (TLS). TLS is a special storage class supported by Windows, in which a data object is not an automatic (stack) variable, yet it is local to each individual thread that runs the code. Thus, each thread can maintain a different value for a variable declared using TLS.

Note that any amount of TLS data can be supported by using the API calls **TlsAlloc**, **TlsFree**, **TlsSetValue**, and **TlsGetValue**. The PE/COFF implementation is an alternative approach to using the API, and it has the advantage of being simpler from the high-level-language programmer's point of view. This implementation enables TLS data to be defined and initialized in a manner similar to ordinary static variables in a program. For example, in Microsoft Visual C++, a static TLS variable can be defined as follows, without using the Windows API:

```
__declspec (thread) int tlsFlag = 1;
```

To support this programming construct, the PE/COFF **.tls** section specifies the following information: initialization data, callback routines for per-thread initialization and termination, and the TLS index, explained in the following discussion.

> **NOTE:**
> Statically declared TLS data objects can be used only in statically loaded image files. This fact makes it unreliable to use static TLS data in a DLL unless you know that the DLL, or anything statically linked with it, will never be loaded dynamically with the **LoadLibrary** API function.

Executable code accesses a static TLS data object through the following steps:

1. At link time, the linker sets the Address of Index field of the TLS Directory. This field points to a location where the program will expect to receive the TLS index.

The Microsoft run-time library facilitates this process by defining a memory image of the TLS Directory and giving it the special name "__tls_used" (Intel x86 platforms) or "_tls_used" (other platforms). The linker looks for this memory image and uses the data there to create the TLS Directory. Other compilers that support TLS and work with the Microsoft linker must use this same technique.

2. When a thread is created, the loader communicates the address of the thread's TLS array by placing the address of the Thread Environment Block (TEB) in the FS register. A pointer to the TLS array is at the offset of 0x2C from the beginning of TEB. This behavior is Intel x86 specific.
3. The loader assigns the value of the TLS index to the place indicated by the Address of Index field.
4. The executable code retrieves the TLS index and also the location of the TLS array.
5. The code uses the TLS index and the TLS array location (multiplying the index by four and using it as an offset to the array) to get the address of the TLS data area for the given program and module. Each thread has its own TLS data area, but this is transparent to the program, which doesn't need to know how data is allocated for individual threads.
6. An individual TLS data object is accessed as some fixed offset into the TLS data area.

The TLS array is an array of addresses that the system maintains for each thread. Each address in this array gives the location of TLS data for a given module (.EXE or DLL) within the program. The TLS index indicates which member of the array to use. The index is a number (meaningful only to the system) that identifies the module.

6.7.1 The TLS Directory

The TLS Directory has the following format:

Offset (PE32/ PE32+)	Size (PE32/ PE32+)	Field	Description
0	4/8	Raw Data Start VA (Virtual Address)	Starting address of the TLS template. The template is a block of data used to initialize TLS data. The system copies all this data each time a thread is created, so it must not be corrupted. Note that this address is not an RVA; it is an address for which there should be a base relocation in the .reloc section.

Offset (PE32/ PE32+)	Size (PE32/ PE32+)	Field	Description
4/8	4/8	Raw Data End VA	Address of the last byte of the TLS, except for the zero fill. As with the Raw Data Start VA, this is a virtual address, not an RVA.
8/16	4/8	Address of Index	Location to receive the TLS index, which the loader assigns. This location is in an ordinary data section, so it can be given a symbolic name accessible to the program.
12/24	4/8	Address of Call-backs	Pointer to an array of TLS callback functions. The array is null-terminated, so if there is no callback function supported, this field points to four bytes set to zero. The prototype for these functions is given below, in "TLS Call-back Functions."
16/32	4	Size of Zero Fill	The size in bytes of the template, beyond the initialized data delimited by Raw Data Start VA and Raw Data End VA. The total template size should be the same as the total size of TLS data in the image file. The zero fill is the amount of data that comes after the initial-ized nonzero data.
20/36	4	Characteristics	Reserved for possible future use by TLS flags.

6.7.2 TLS Callback Functions

The program can provide one or more TLS callback functions (though Microsoft compilers do not currently use this feature) to support additional initialization and termination for TLS data objects. A typical reason to use such a callback function would be to call constructors and destructors for objects.

Although there is typically no more than one callback function, a callback is implemented as an array to make it possible to add additional callback functions if desired. If there is more than one callback function, each function is called in the order its address appears in the array. A null pointer terminates the array. It is perfectly valid to have an empty list (no callback supported), in which case the callback array has exactly one member—a null pointer.

The prototype for a callback function (pointed to by a pointer of type PIMAGE_TLS_CALL-BACK) has the same parameters as a DLL entry-point function:

```
typedef VOID
(NTAPI *PIMAGE_TLS_CALLBACK) (
PVOID DllHandle,
DWORD Reason,
PVOID Reserved
    );
```

The Reserved parameter should be left set to 0. The Reason parameter can take the following values:

Setting	Value	Description
DLL_PROCESS_ATTACH	1	New process has started, including the first thread.
DLL_THREAD_ATTACH	2	New thread has been created (this notification sent for all but the first thread).
DLL_THREAD_DETACH	3	Thread is about to be terminated (this notification sent for all but the first thread).
DLL_PROCESS_DETACH	0	Process is about to terminate, including the original thread.

6.8 The Load Config Structure (Image Only)

The load_config structure was formerly used in very limited cases in the NT operating system itself to describe various features too difficult or large to describe in the file header or optional header of the image. Current versions of the Visual C++ Linker and Windows XP and above have a new version of this structure for x86 32-bit that includes the SafeSEH (Safe Structured Exception Handler) technology. This provides a list of safe SE Handlers that is used during exception dispatching by the operating system. If the handler address resides in an image's virtual address range and is marked as SAFESEH aware (see IMAGE_DLLCHARACTERISTICS_NO_SEH above), then the handler must be in the list of known, safe handlers for that image, otherwise the operating system will terminate the application. This helps prevent the "x86 exception handler hijacking" exploit that has been used in the past to take control of the operating system.

The Microsoft Linker will automatically provide a default load_config structure to include the SafeSEH data. If the user code already provides a load_config structure, it must include the new SafeSEH fields, otherwise, the linker cannot include the SafeSEH data, and hence, the image will not be marked as containing SafeSEH.

6.8.1 Load Config Directory

The data directory entry for pre-SafeSEH load_config structures needs to specify a particular size of the load_config structure, as the OS loader always expects it to be a certain value. In that regard, the size is really a version check only. For Windows XP and earlier compatibility and x86 images that must run on Windows XP and earlier, the size must be 64.

6.8.2 Load Config Layout

The Load Config structure has the following layout for 32- and 64-bit PE files:

Offset (PE32/ PE32+)	Size (PE32/ PE32+)	Field	Description
0	4	Size	The actual size of the structure, inclusive. May differ from the Size given in the data directory for Windows XP and earlier compatibility.
4	4	TimeDateStamp	Reserved, must be zero.
8	2	MajorVersion	Reserved, must be zero.
10	2	MinorVersion	Reserved, must be zero.
12	4	GlobalFlagsClear	Which global loader flags to clear for this process as the loader starts the process.
16	4	GlobalFlagsSet	Which global loader flags to set for this process as the loader starts the process.
20	4	CriticalSectionDefaultTimeout	Default timeout value to use for this process's critical sections that are abandoned.
24	4/8	DeCommitFreeBlockThreshold	
28/32	4/8	DeCommitTotalFreeThreshold	
32/40	4/8	LockPrefixTable	[x86 only] VA of a list of addresses where the LOCK prefix is used so that they can be replaced with NOP on single processor machines.
36/48	4/8	MaximumAllocationSize	

Appendix

Offset (PE32/ PE32+)	Size (PE32/ PE32+)	Field	Description
40/56	4/8	VirtualMemoryThreshold	
44/72	4	ProcessHeapFlags	
48/64	4/8	ProcessAffinityMask	
52/76	2	CSDVersion	Service pack version identifier.
54/78	2	Reserved	Must be zero.
56/80	4/8	EditList	VA.
60/88	4/8	SecurityCookie	
64/96	4/8	SEHandlerTable	[x86 only] VA of the sorted table of RVAs of each valid, unique SE Handler in the image.
68/ 104	4/8	SEHandlerCount	[x86 only] Count of unique handlers in the table.

Note that the fields ProcessHeapFlags and ProcessAffinityMask are swapped between the 32- and 64-bit versions. This was done to keep the 64-bit fields aligned properly.

6.9 The .rsrc Section

Resources are indexed by a multiple level binary-sorted tree structure. The general design can incorporate 2**31 levels. By convention, however, Windows uses three levels:

Type

Name

Language

A series of Resource Directory Tables relate all the levels in the following way: each directory table is followed by a series of directory entries, which give the name or ID for that level (Type, Name, or Language level) and an address of either a data description or another directory table. If a data description is pointed to, then the data is a leaf in the tree. If another directory table is pointed to, then that table lists directory entries at the next level down.

A leaf's Type, Name, and Language IDs are determined by the path taken, through directory tables, to reach the leaf. The first table determines Type ID, the second table (pointed to by the directory entry in the first table) determines Name ID, and the third table determines Language ID.

The general structure of the **.rsrc** section is:

Data	Description
Resource Directory Tables (and Resource Directory Entries)	A series of tables, one for each group of nodes in the tree. All top-level (Type) nodes are listed in the first table. Entries in this table point to second-level tables. Each second-level tree has the same Type identifier but different Name identifiers. Third-level trees have the same Type and Name identifiers but different Language identifiers. Each individual table is immediately followed by directory entries, in which each entry has: 1) a name or numeric identifier, and 2) a pointer to a data description or a table at the next lower level.
Resource Directory Strings	Two-byte-aligned Unicode strings, which serve as string data pointed to by directory entries.
Resource Data Description	An array of records, pointed to by tables, which describe the actual size and location of the resource data. These records are the leaves in the resource-description tree.
Resource Data	Raw data of the resource section. The size and location information in the Resource Data Descriptions delimit the individual regions of resource data.

6.9.1 Resource Directory Table

Each Resource Directory Table has the following format. This data structure should be considered the heading of a table, because the table actually consists of directory entries (see next section) as well as this structure:

Offset	Size	Field	Description
0	4	Characteristics	Resource flags, reserved for future use; currently set to zero.
4	4	Time/Date Stamp	Time the resource data was created by the resource compiler.

Appendix

Offset	Size	Field	Description
8	2	Major Version	Major version number, set by the user.
10	2	Minor Version	Minor version number.
12	2	Number of Name Entries	Number of directory entries, immediately following the table, that use strings to identify Type, Name, or Language (depending on the level of the table).
14	2	Number of ID Entries	Number of directory entries, immediately following the Name entries, that use numeric identifiers for Type, Name, or Language.

6.9.2 Resource Directory Entries

The directory entries make up the rows of a table. Each Resource Directory Entry has the following format. Note that whether the entry is a Name or ID entry is indicated by the Resource Directory Table, which indicates how many Name and ID entries follow it (remember that all the Name entries precede all the ID entries for the table). All entries for the table are sorted in ascending order: the Name entries by case-insensitive string, and the ID entries by numeric value.

Offset	Size	Field	Description
0	4	Name RVA	Address of string that gives the Type, Name, or Language identifier, depending on level of table.
0	4	Integer ID	32-bit integer that identifies Type, Name, or Language.
4	4	Data Entry RVA	High bit 0. Address of a Resource Data Entry (a leaf).
4	4	Subdirectory RVA	High bit 1. Lower 31 bits are the address of another Resource Directory Table (the next level down).

6.9.3 Resource Directory String

The Resource Directory String area consists of Unicode strings, which are word aligned. These strings are stored together after the last Resource Directory Entry and before the first Resource Data Entry. This minimizes the impact of these variable length strings on the alignment of the fixed-size directory entries. Each Resource Directory String has the following format:

Offset	Size	Field	Description
0	2	Length	Size of string, not including length field itself.
2	variable	Unicode String	Variable-length Unicode string data, word aligned.

6.9.4 Resource Data Entry

Each Resource Data Entry describes an actual unit of raw data in the Resource Data area, and has the following format:

Offset	Size	Field	Description
0	4	Data RVA	Address of a unit of resource data in the Resource Data area.
4	4	Size	Size, in bytes, of the resource data pointed to by the Data RVA field.
8	4	Codepage	Code page used to decode code point values within the resource data. Typically, the code page would be the Unicode code page.
12	4	Reserved (must be set to 0)	

6.9.5 Resource Example

The resource example shows the PE/COFF representation of the following resource data:

```
TypeId#     NameId#     Language ID   Resource Data
   1           1             0           00010001
   1           1             1           10010001
   1           2             0           00010002
   1           3             0           00010003
   2           1             0           00020001
   2           2             0           00020002
   2           3             0           00020003
   2           4             0           00020004
   9           1             0           00090001
   9           9             0           00090009
   9           9             1           10090009
   9           9             2           20090009
```

When this data is encoded, a dump of the PE/COFF Resource Directory results in the following output:

```
Offset  Data
0000:   00000000 00000000 00000000 00030000  (3 entries in this directory)
0010:   00000001 80000028    (TypeId #1, Subdirectory at offset 0x28)
0018:   00000002 80000050    (TypeId #2, Subdirectory at offset 0x50)
0020:   00000009 80000080    (TypeId #9, Subdirectory at offset 0x80)
0028:   00000000 00000000 00000000 00030000  (3 entries in this directory)
0038:   00000001 800000A0    (NameId #1, Subdirectory at offset 0xA0)
0040:   00000002 00000108    (NameId #2, data desc at offset 0x108)
0048:   00000003 00000118    (NameId #3, data desc at offset 0x118)
0050:   00000000 00000000 00000000 00040000  (4 entries in this directory)
0060:   00000001 00000128    (NameId #1, data desc at offset 0x128)
0068:   00000002 00000138    (NameId #2, data desc at offset 0x138)
0070:   00000003 00000148    (NameId #3, data desc at offset 0x148)
0078:   00000004 00000158    (NameId #4, data desc at offset 0x158)
0080:   00000000 00000000 00000000 00020000  (2 entries in this directory)
0090:   00000001 00000168    (NameId #1, data desc at offset 0x168)
0098:   00000009 800000C0    (NameId #9, Subdirectory at offset 0xC0)
00A0:   00000000 00000000 00000000 00020000  (2 entries in this directory)
00B0:   00000000 000000E8    (Language ID 0, data desc at offset 0xE8
00B8:   00000001 000000F8    (Language ID 1, data desc at offset 0xF8
00C0:   00000000 00000000 00000000 00030000  (3 entries in this directory)
00D0:   00000001 00000178    (Language ID 0, data desc at offset 0x178
00D8:   00000001 00000188    (Language ID 1, data desc at offset 0x188
00E0:   00000001 00000198    (Language ID 2, data desc at offset 0x198
00E8:   000001A8(At offset 0x1A8, for TypeId #1, NameId #1, Language id #0
        00000004(4 bytes of data)
        00000000(codepage)
        00000000(reserved)
00F8:   000001AC(At offset 0x1AC, for TypeId #1, NameId #1, Language id #1
        00000004(4 bytes of data)
        00000000(codepage)
        00000000(reserved)
0108:   000001B0(At offset 0x1B0, for TypeId #1, NameId #2,
        00000004(4 bytes of data)
        00000000(codepage)
        00000000(reserved)
0118:   000001B4(At offset 0x1B4, for TypeId #1, NameId #3,
        00000004(4 bytes of data)
        00000000(codepage)
        00000000(reserved)
0128:   000001B8(At offset 0x1B8, for TypeId #2, NameId #1,
        00000004(4 bytes of data)
        00000000(codepage)
        00000000(reserved)
0138:   000001BC(At offset 0x1BC, for TypeId #2, NameId #2,
        00000004(4 bytes of data)
        00000000(codepage)
        00000000(reserved)
0148:   000001C0(At offset 0x1C0, for TypeId #2, NameId #3,
        00000004(4 bytes of data)
        00000000(codepage)
        00000000(reserved)
```

```
0158:   000001C4(At offset 0x1C4, for TypeId #2, NameId #4,
        00000004(4 bytes of data)
        00000000(codepage)
        00000000(reserved)
0168:   000001C8(At offset 0x1C8, for TypeId #9, NameId #1,
        00000004(4 bytes of data)
        00000000(codepage)
        00000000(reserved)
0178:   000001CC(At offset 0x1CC, for TypeId #9, NameId #9, Language id #0
        00000004(4 bytes of data)
        00000000(codepage)
        00000000(reserved)
0188:   000001D0(At offset 0x1D0, for TypeId #9, NameId #9, Language id #1
        00000004(4 bytes of data)
        00000000(codepage)
        00000000(reserved)
0198:   000001D4(At offset 0x1D4, for TypeId #9, NameId #9, Language id #2
        00000004(4 bytes of data)
        00000000(codepage)
        00000000(reserved)
```

The raw data for the resources follows:

```
01A8:   00010001
01AC:   10010001
01B0:   00010002
01B4:   00010003
01B8:   00020001
01BC:   00020002
01C0:   00020003
01C4:   00020004
01C8:   00090001
01CC:   00090009
01D0:   10090009
01D4:   20090009
```

6.10 The .cormeta Section (Object Only)

Common Language Runtime (clr) metadata is stored in this section and is used as an indicator that the object file contains managed code. The format of the metadata is not documented, but can be handed to the clr interfaces for handling metadata.

7 Archive (Library) File Format

The COFF archive format provides a standard mechanism for storing collections of object files. These collections are frequently referred to as "libraries" in programming documentation.

The first eight bytes of an archive consist of the file signature. The rest of the archive consists of a series of archive members, as follows:

Appendix

1. The first and second members are "linker members." Each of these members has its own format as described in Section 8.3. Typically, a linker places information into these archive members. The linker members contain the directory of the archive.
2. The third member is the longnames member. This member consists of a series of null-terminated ASCII strings, in which each string is the name of another archive member.
3. The rest of the archive consists of standard (object-file) members. Each of these members contains the contents of one object file in its entirety.

An archive member header precedes each member. The following illustration shows the general structure of an archive:

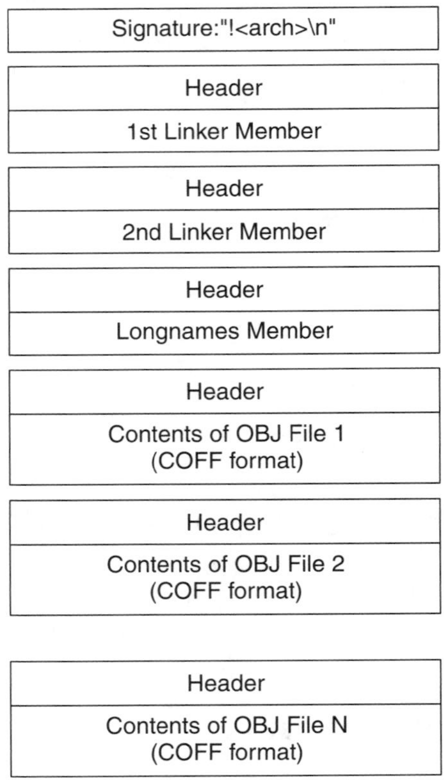

Figure A-4 Archive File Structure

7.1 Archive File Signature

The archive file signature identifies the file type. Any utility (for example, a linker) expecting an archive file as input can check the file type by reading this signature. The signature consists of the following ASCII characters, in which each character below is represented literally, except for the newline (\n) character:

```
!<arch>\n
```

7.2 Archive Member Headers

Each member (linker, longnames, or object-file member) is preceded by a header. An archive member header has the following format, in which each field is an ASCII text string that is left-justified and padded with spaces to the end of the field. There is no terminating null character in any of these fields.

Each member header starts on the first even address after the end of the previous archive member.

Offset	Size	Field	Description
0	16	Name	Name of archive member, with a slash (/) appended to terminate the name. If the *first* character is a slash, the name has a special interpretation, as described below.
16	12	Date	Date and time the archive member was created: ASCII decimal representation of the number of seconds since 1/1/1970 UCT.
28	6	User ID	ASCII decimal representation of the user ID.
34	6	Group ID	ASCII group representation of the group ID.
40	8	Mode	ASCII octal representation of the member's file mode.
48	10	Size	ASCII decimal representation of the total size of the archive member, not including the size of the header.
58	2	End of Header	The two bytes in the C string "'\n".

The Name field has one of the formats shown in the following table. As mentioned above, each of these strings is left justified and padded with trailing spaces within a field of 16 bytes:

Contents of Name Field	Description
name/	The field gives the name of the archive member directly.
/	The archive member is one of the two linker members. Both of the linker members have this name.
//	The archive member is the longname member, which consists of a series of null-terminated ASCII strings. The longnames member is the third archive member, and must always be present even if the contents are empty.
/n	The name of the archive member is located at offset n within the longnames member. The number n is the decimal representation of the offset. For example: "\26" indicates that the name of the archive member is located 26 bytes beyond the beginning of longnames member contents.

7.3 First Linker Member

The name of the first linker member is "\". The first linker member, included for backward compatibility, is not used by current linkers but its format must be correct. This linker member provides a directory of symbol names, as does the second linker member. For each symbol, the information indicates where to find the archive member that contains the symbol.

The first linker member has the following format. This information appears after the header:

Offset	Size	Field	Description
0	4	Number of Symbols	Unsigned long containing the number of symbols indexed. This number is stored in big-endian format. Each object-file member typically defines one or more external symbols.
4	4 * *n*	Offsets	Array of file offsets to archive member headers, in which *n* is equal to Number of Symbols. Each number in the array is an unsigned long stored in big-endian format. For each symbol named in the String Table, the corresponding element in the Offsets array gives the location of the archive member that contains the symbol.
*	*	String Table	Series of null-terminated strings that name all the symbols in the directory. Each string begins immediately after the null character in the previous string. The number of strings must be equal to the value of the Number of Symbols fields.

The elements in the Offsets array must be arranged in ascending order. This fact implies that the symbols listed in the String Table must be arranged according to the order of archive members. For example, all the symbols in the first object-file member would have to be listed before the symbols in the second object file.

7.4 Second Linker Member

The second linker member has the name "\" as does the first linker member. Although both the linker members provide a directory of symbols and archive members that contain them, the second linker member is used in preference to the first by all current linkers. The second linker member includes symbol names in lexical order, which enables faster searching by name.

The second linker member has the following format. This information appears after the header:

Offset	Size	Field	Description
0	4	Number of Members	Unsigned long containing the number of archive members.
4	4 * *m*	Offsets	Array of file offsets to archive member headers, arranged in ascending order. Each offset is an unsigned long. The number *m* is equal to the value of the Number of Members field.
*	4	Number of Symbols	Unsigned long containing the number of symbols indexed. Each object-file member typically defines one or more external symbols.
*	2 * *n*	Indices	Array of 1-based indices (unsigned short) which map symbol names to archive member offsets. The number *n* is equal to Number of Symbols. For each symbol named in the String Table, the corresponding element in the Indices array gives an index into the Offsets array. The Offsets array, in turn, gives the location of the archive member that contains the symbol.
*	*	String Table	Series of null-terminated strings that name all the symbols in the directory. Each string begins immediately after the null byte in the previous string. The number of strings must be equal to the value of the Number of Symbols fields. This table lists all the symbol names in ascending lexical order.

Appendix

7.5 Longnames Member

The name of the longnames member is "\\". The longnames member is a series of strings of archive member names. A name appears here only when there is insufficient room in the Name field (16 bytes). The longnames member can be empty, though its header must appear.

The strings are null-terminated. Each string begins immediately after the null byte in the previous string.

8 Import Library Format

Traditional import libraries, that is, libraries that describe the exports from one image for use by another, typically follow the layout described in Section 7, "Archive (Library) File Format." The primary difference is that import library members contain pseudo-object files instead of real ones, where each member includes the section contributions needed to build the Import Tables described in Section 6.4, "The .idata Section." The linker generates this archive while building the exporting application.

The section contributions for an import can be inferred from a small set of information. The linker can either generate the complete, verbose information into the import library for each member at the time of the library's creation, or it can write only the canonical information to the library and let the application that later uses it generate the necessary data on-the-fly.

In an import library with the long format, a single member contains the following information:

Archive member header

File header

Section headers

Data corresponding to each of the section headers

COFF symbol table

Strings

In contrast a short import library is written as follows:

Archive member header

Import header

Null-terminated import name string

Null-terminated dll name string

This is sufficient information to accurately reconstruct the entire contents of the member at the time of its use.

8.1 Import Header

The import header contains the following fields and offsets:

Offset	Size	Field	Description
0	2	Sig1	Must be IMAGE_FILE_MACHINE_UNKNOWN. See Section 3.3.1, "Machine Types," for more information.
2	2	Sig2	Must be 0xFFFF.
4	2	Version	
6	2	Machine	Number identifying type of target machine. See Section 3.3.1, "Machine Types," for more information.
8	4	Time-Date Stamp	Time and date the file was created.
12	4	Size Of Data	Size of the strings following the header.
16	2	Ordinal/Hint	Either the ordinal or the hint for the import, determined by the value in the Name Type field.
18	2 bits	Type	The import type. See Section 8.2, "Import Type," for specific values and descriptions.
	3 bits	Name Type	The Import Name Type. See Section 8.3, "Import Name Type," for specific values and descriptions.
	11 bits	Reserved	Reserved. Must be zero.

This structure is followed by two null-terminated strings describing the imported symbol's name, and the dll from which it came.

8.2 Import Type

The following values are defined for the Type field in the Import Header:

Constant	Value	Description
IMPORT_CODE	0	The import is executable code.
IMPORT_DATA	1	The import is data.
IMPORT_CONST	2	The import was specified as CONST in the .def file.

These values are used to determine which section contributions must be generated by the tool using the library if it must access that data.

8.3 Import Name Type

The null-terminated import symbol name immediately follows its associated Import Header. The following values are defined for the Name Type field in the Import Header, indicating how the name is to be used to generate the correct symbols representing the import:

Constant	Value	Description
IMPORT_ORDINAL	0	The import is by ordinal. This indicates that the value in the Ordinal/Hint field of the Import Header is the import's ordinal. If this constant is not specified, then the Ordinal/Hint field should always be interpreted as the import's hint.
IMPORT_NAME	1	The import name is identical to the public symbol name.
IMPORT_NAME_NOPREFIX	2	The import name is the public symbol name, but skipping the leading ?, @, or optionally _.
IMPORT_NAME_UNDECORATE	3	The import name is the public symbol name, but skipping the leading ?, @, or optionally _, and truncating at the first @.

Appendix: Example Object File

This section describes the PE/COFF object file produced by compiling the file HELLO2.C, which contains the following small C program:

```
main()
{
f();
```

```
}

f()
{
}
```

The commands used to compile HELLO.C (with debug information) and generate this example were the following (the -Gy option to the compiler is used, which causes each procedure to be generated as a separate COMDAT section):

```
cl -c -Zi -Gy hello2.c
link -dump -all hello2.obj >hello2.dmp
```

Here is the resulting file HELLO2.DMP: (The reader is encouraged to experiment with various other examples, in order to clarify the concepts described in this specification.)

```
Dump of file hello2.obj

File Type: COFF OBJECT

FILE HEADER VALUES
     14C machine (i386)
       7 number of sections
3436E157 time date stamp Sat Oct 04 17:37:43 1997
     2A0 file pointer to symbol table
      1E number of symbols
       0 size of optional header
       0 characteristics

SECTION HEADER #1
.drectve name
       0 physical address
       0 virtual address
      26 size of raw data
     12C file pointer to raw data
       0 file pointer to relocation table
       0 file pointer to line numbers
       0 number of relocations
       0 number of line numbers
```

Appendix

```
  100A00 flags
         Info
         Remove
         1 byte align

RAW DATA #1
00000000  2D 64 65 66 61 75 6C 74 | 6C 69 62 3A 4C 49 42 43 -default|lib:LIBC
00000010  20 2D 64 65 66 61 75 6C | 74 6C 69 62 3A 4F 4C 44  -defaul|tlib:OLD
00000020  4E 41 4D 45 53 20                                 NAMES

   Linker Directives
   -----------------
   -defaultlib:LIBC
   -defaultlib:OLDNAMES

SECTION HEADER #2
.debug$S name
       0 physical address
       0 virtual address
      5C size of raw data
     152 file pointer to raw data
       0 file pointer to relocation table
       0 file pointer to line numbers
       0 number of relocations
       0 number of line numbers
42100048 flags
         No Pad
         Initialized Data
         Discardable
         1 byte align
         Read Only

RAW DATA #2
00000000  02 00 00 00 11 00 09 00 | 00 00 00 00 0A 68 65 6C ........|.....hel
00000010  6C 6F 32 2E 6F 62 6A 43 | 00 01 00 05 00 00 00 3C lo2.objC|.......<
00000020  4D 69 63 72 6F 73 6F 66 | 74 20 28 52 29 20 33 32 Microsof|t (R) 32
```

```
00000030  2D 62 69 74 20 43 2F 43 | 2B 2B 20 4F 70 74 69 6D -bit C/C|++ Optim
00000040  69 7A 69 6E 67 20 43 6F | 6D 70 69 6C 65 72 20 56 izing Co|mpiler V
00000050  65 72 73 69 6F 6E 20 31 | 31 2E 30 30              ersion 1|1.00

SECTION HEADER #3
   .text name
       0 physical address
       0 virtual address
       A size of raw data
     1AE file pointer to raw data
     1B8 file pointer to relocation table
     1C2 file pointer to line numbers
       1 number of relocations
       3 number of line numbers
60501020 flags
         Code
         Communal; sym= _main
         16 byte align
         Execute Read

RAW DATA #3
00000000  55 8B EC E8 00 00 00 00 | 5D C3                    U‹ìè....|].

RELOCATIONS #3
                                                Symbol    Symbol
 Offset    Type              Applied To         Index     Name
 --------  ----------------  -----------------  --------  ------
 00000004  REL32                       00000000        13  _f

LINENUMBERS #3

 Symbol index:        8 Base line number:     2
 Symbol name = _main
 00000003(     3)  00000008(     4)

SECTION HEADER #4
```

```
.debug$S name
       0 physical address
       0 virtual address
      30 size of raw data
     1D4 file pointer to raw data
     204 file pointer to relocation table
       0 file pointer to line numbers
       2 number of relocations
       0 number of line numbers
42101048 flags
         No Pad
         Initialized Data
         Communal (no symbol)
         Discardable
         1 byte align
         Read Only

RAW DATA #4
00000000  2A 00 0B 10 00 00 00 00 | 00 00 00 00 00 00 00 00 *.......|........
00000010  0A 00 00 00 03 00 00 00 | 08 00 00 00 01 10 00 00 ........|........
00000020  00 00 00 00 00 00 01 04 | 6D 61 69 6E 02 00 06 00 ........|main....

RELOCATIONS #4
                                                      Symbol    Symbol
 Offset    Type                Applied To             Index     Name
 --------  ----------------   -----------------      --------  ------
 00000020  SECREL                       00000000           8  _main
 00000024  SECTION                          0000           8  _main

SECTION HEADER #5
   .text name
       0 physical address
       0 virtual address
       5 size of raw data
     218 file pointer to raw data
       0 file pointer to relocation table
```

```
     21D file pointer to line numbers
       0 number of relocations
       2 number of line numbers
60501020 flags
         Code
         Communal; sym= _f
         16 byte align
         Execute Read

RAW DATA #5
00000000  55 8B EC 5D C3                                        U‹ì].

LINENUMBERS #5

 Symbol index:       13 Base line number:     7
 Symbol name = _f
 00000003(    8)

SECTION HEADER #6
.debug$S name
       0 physical address
       0 virtual address
      2F size of raw data
     229 file pointer to raw data
     258 file pointer to relocation table
       0 file pointer to line numbers
       2 number of relocations
       0 number of line numbers
42101048 flags
         No Pad
         Initialized Data
         Communal (no symbol)
         Discardable
         1 byte align
         Read Only
```

```
RAW DATA #6
00000000  29 00 0B 10 00 00 00 00 | 00 00 00 00 00 00 00 00 ).......|........
00000010  05 00 00 00 03 00 00 00 | 03 00 00 00 01 10 00 00 ........|........
00000020  00 00 00 00 00 00 01 03 | 66 6F 6F 02 00 06 00    ........|f....

RELOCATIONS #6
                                                Symbol    Symbol
 Offset    Type              Applied To         Index     Name
 --------  ----------------  -----------------  --------  ------
 00000020  SECREL                     00000000        13  _f
 00000024  SECTION                        0000        13  _f

SECTION HEADER #7
.debug$T name
       0 physical address
       0 virtual address
      34 size of raw data
     26C file pointer to raw data
       0 file pointer to relocation table
       0 file pointer to line numbers
       0 number of relocations
       0 number of line numbers
42100048 flags
         No Pad
         Initialized Data
         Discardable
         1 byte align
         Read Only

RAW DATA #7
00000000  02 00 00 00 2E 00 16 00 | 33 E1 36 34 01 00 00 00 ........|3á64....
00000010  22 65 3A 5C 62 62 74 5C | 74 6F 6F 6C 73 5C 76 63 "e:\bbt\|tools\vc
00000020  35 30 5C 62 69 6E 5C 78 | 38 36 5C 76 63 35 30 2E 50\bin\x|86\vc50.
00000030  70 64 62 F1                                       pdb.

COFF SYMBOL TABLE
```

```
000 00000000 DEBUG  notype       Filename     | .file
    hello2.c
002 00000000 SECT1  notype       Static       | .drectve
    Section length   26, #relocs    0, #linenums    0, checksum        0
004 00000000 SECT2  notype       Static       | .debug$S
    Section length   5C, #relocs    0, #linenums    0, checksum        0
006 00000000 SECT3  notype       Static       | .text
    Section length    A, #relocs    1, #linenums    3, checksum        0, selec-
tion    1 (pick no duplicates)
008 00000000 SECT3  notype ()    External     | _main
    tag index 0000000A size 0000000A lines 000001C2 next function 00000013
00A 00000000 SECT3  notype       BeginFunction | .bf
    line# 0002 end 00000015
00C 00000003 SECT3  notype       .bf or.ef    | .lf
00D 0000000A SECT3  notype       EndFunction  | .ef
    line# 0004
00F 00000000 SECT4  notype       Static       | .debug$S
    Section length   30, #relocs    2, #linenums    0, checksum        0, selec-
tion    5 (pick associative Section 3)
011 00000000 SECT5  notype       Static       | .text
    Section length    5, #relocs    0, #linenums    2, checksum        0, selec-
tion    1 (pick no duplicates)
013 00000000 SECT5  notype ()    External     | _f
    tag index 00000015 size 00000005 lines 0000021D next function 00000000
015 00000000 SECT5  notype       BeginFunction | .bf
    line# 0007 end 00000000
017 00000002 SECT5  notype       .bf or.ef    | .lf
018 00000005 SECT5  notype       EndFunction  | .ef
    line# 0008
01A 00000000 SECT6  notype       Static       | .debug$S
    Section length   2F, #relocs    2, #linenums    0, checksum        0, selec-
tion    5 (pick associative Section 5)
01C 00000000 SECT7  notype       Static       | .debug$T
    Section length   34, #relocs    0, #linenums    0, checksum        0


String Table Size = 0x0 bytes
```

```
Summary

      BB .debug$S
      34 .debug$T
      26 .drectve
       F .text
```

Here is a hexadecimal dump of HELLO2.OBJ:

```
hello2.obj:
00000000   4c 01 07 00 57 e1 36 34 a0 02 00 00 1e 00 00 00   L...W.64........
00000010   00 00 00 00 2e 64 72 65 63 74 76 65 00 00 00 00   .....drectve....
00000020   00 00 00 00 26 00 00 00 2c 01 00 00 00 00 00 00   ....&...,.......
00000030   00 00 00 00 00 00 00 00 00 0a 10 00 2e 64 65 62   .............deb
00000040   75 67 24 53 00 00 00 00 00 00 00 00 5c 00 00 00   ug$S........\...
00000050   52 01 00 00 00 00 00 00 00 00 00 00 00 00 00 00   R...............
00000060   48 00 10 42 2e 74 65 78 74 00 00 00 00 00 00 00   H..B.text.......
00000070   00 00 00 00 0a 00 00 00 ae 01 00 00 b8 01 00 00   ................
00000080   c2 01 00 00 01 00 03 00 20 10 50 60 2e 64 65 62   ........ .P`.deb
00000090   75 67 24 53 00 00 00 00 00 00 00 00 30 00 00 00   ug$S........0...
000000a0   d4 01 00 00 04 02 00 00 00 00 00 00 02 00 00 00   ................
000000b0   48 10 10 42 2e 74 65 78 74 00 00 00 00 00 00 00   H..B.text.......
000000c0   00 00 00 00 05 00 00 00 18 02 00 00 00 00 00 00   ................
000000d0   1d 02 00 00 00 00 02 00 20 10 50 60 2e 64 65 62   ........ .P`.deb
000000e0   75 67 24 53 00 00 00 00 00 00 00 00 2f 00 00 00   ug$S......../...
000000f0   29 02 00 00 58 02 00 00 00 00 00 00 02 00 00 00   )...X...........
00000100   48 10 10 42 2e 64 65 62 75 67 24 54 00 00 00 00   H..B.debug$T....
00000110   00 00 00 00 34 00 00 00 6c 02 00 00 00 00 00 00   ....4...l.......
00000120   00 00 00 00 00 00 00 00 48 00 10 42 2d 64 65 66   ........H..B-def
00000130   61 75 6c 74 6c 69 62 3a 4c 49 42 43 20 2d 64 65   aultlib:LIBC -de
00000140   66 61 75 6c 74 6c 69 62 3a 4f 4c 44 4e 41 4d 45   faultlib:OLDNAME
00000150   53 20 02 00 00 00 11 00 09 00 00 00 00 00 0a 68   S .............h
00000160   65 6c 6c 6f 32 2e 6f 62 6a 43 00 01 00 05 00 00   ello2.objC......
00000170   00 3c 4d 69 63 72 6f 73 6f 66 74 20 28 52 29 20   .<Microsoft (R)
00000180   33 32 2d 62 69 74 20 43 2f 43 2b 2b 20 4f 70 74   32-bit C/C++ Opt
00000190   69 6d 69 7a 69 6e 67 20 43 6f 6d 70 69 6c 65 72   imizing Compiler
000001a0   20 56 65 72 73 69 6f 6e 20 31 31 2e 30 30 55 8b    Version 11.00U.
000001b0   ec e8 00 00 00 00 5d c3 04 00 00 00 13 00 00 00   ......].........
```

```
000001c0   14 00 08 00 00 00 00 00 03 00 00 00 01 00 08 00   ................
000001d0   00 00 02 00 2a 00 0b 10 00 00 00 00 00 00 00 00   ....*...........
000001e0   00 00 00 00 0a 00 00 00 03 00 00 00 08 00 00 00   ................
000001f0   01 10 00 00 00 00 00 00 00 00 01 04 6d 61 69 6e   ............main
00000200   02 00 06 00 20 00 00 00 08 00 00 00 0b 00 24 00   .... .........$.
00000210   00 00 08 00 00 00 0a 00 55 8b ec 5d c3 13 00 00   ........U..]....
00000220   00 00 00 03 00 00 00 01 00 29 00 0b 10 00 00 00   .........)......
00000230   00 00 00 00 00 00 00 00 00 05 00 00 00 03 00 00   ................
00000240   00 03 00 00 00 01 10 00 00 00 00 00 00 00 00 01   ................
00000250   03 66 6f 6f 02 00 06 00 20 00 00 00 13 00 00 00   .f.... .......
00000260   0b 00 24 00 00 00 13 00 00 00 0a 00 02 00 00 00   ..$.............
00000270   2e 00 16 00 33 e1 36 34 01 00 00 00 22 65 3a 5c   ....3.64...."e:\
00000280   62 62 74 5c 74 6f 6f 6c 73 5c 76 63 35 30 5c 62   bbt\tools\vc50\b
00000290   69 6e 5c 78 38 36 5c 76 63 35 30 2e 70 64 62 f1   in\x86\vc50.pdb.
000002a0   2e 66 69 6c 65 00 00 00 00 00 00 00 fe ff 00 00   .file...........
000002b0   67 01 68 65 6c 6c 6f 32 2e 63 00 00 00 00 00 00   g.hello2.c......
000002c0   00 00 00 00 2e 64 72 65 63 74 76 65 00 00 00 00   .....drectve....
000002d0   01 00 00 00 03 01 26 00 00 00 00 00 00 00 00 00   ......&.........
000002e0   00 00 00 00 00 00 00 00 2e 64 65 62 75 67 24 53   .........debug$S
000002f0   00 00 00 00 02 00 00 00 03 01 5c 00 00 00 00 00   ..........\.....
00000300   00 00 00 00 00 00 00 00 00 00 00 00 2e 74 65 78   .............tex
00000310   74 00 00 00 00 00 00 00 03 00 00 00 03 01 0a 00   t...............
00000320   00 00 01 00 03 00 00 00 00 00 00 00 01 00 00 00   ................
00000330   5f 6d 61 69 6e 00 00 00 00 00 00 00 03 00 20 00   _main......... .
00000340   02 01 0a 00 00 00 0a 00 00 00 c2 01 00 00 13 00   ................
00000350   00 00 00 00 2e 62 66 00 00 00 00 00 00 00 00 00   .....bf.........
00000360   03 00 00 00 65 01 00 00 00 00 02 00 00 00 00 00   ....e...........
00000370   00 00 15 00 00 00 00 00 2e 6c 66 00 00 00 00 00   .........lf.....
00000380   03 00 00 00 03 00 00 00 65 00 2e 65 66 00 00 00   ........e..ef...
00000390   00 00 0a 00 00 00 03 00 00 00 65 01 00 00 00 00   ..........e.....
000003a0   04 00 00 00 00 00 00 00 00 00 00 00 00 00 2e 64   ...............d
000003b0   65 62 75 67 24 53 00 00 00 00 04 00 00 00 03 01   ebug$S..........
000003c0   30 00 00 00 02 00 00 00 00 00 00 00 03 00 05 00   0...............
000003d0   00 00 2e 74 65 78 74 00 00 00 00 00 00 00 05 00   ...text.........
000003e0   00 00 03 01 05 00 00 00 00 00 02 00 00 00 00 00   ................
000003f0   00 00 01 00 00 00 5f 66 6f 6f 00 00 00 00 00 00   ......_f......
```

Appendix

```
00000400   00 00 05 00 20 00 02 01 15 00 00 00 05 00 00 00   .... ...........
00000410   1d 02 00 00 00 00 00 00 00 00 2e 62 66 00 00 00   ...........bf...
00000420   00 00 00 00 00 00 05 00 00 00 65 01 00 00 00 00   ..........e.....
00000430   07 00 00 00 00 00 00 00 00 00 00 00 00 00 2e 6c   ...............l
00000440   66 00 00 00 00 00 02 00 00 00 05 00 00 00 65 00   f.............e.
00000450   2e 65 66 00 00 00 00 00 05 00 00 00 05 00 00 00   .ef.............
00000460   65 01 00 00 00 00 08 00 00 00 00 00 00 00 00 00   e...............
00000470   00 00 00 00 2e 64 65 62 75 67 24 53 00 00 00 00   .....debug$S....
00000480   06 00 00 00 03 01 2f 00 00 00 02 00 00 00 00 00   ....../.........
00000490   00 00 05 00 05 00 00 00 2e 64 65 62 75 67 24 54   .........debug$T
000004a0   00 00 00 00 07 00 00 00 03 01 34 00 00 00 00 00   ..........4.....
000004b0   00 00 00 00 00 00 00 00 00 00 00 04 00 00 00 00   ................
```

Appendix: Calculating Image Message Digests

Several Attribute Certificates are expected to be used to verify the integrity of the images. That is, they will be used to ensure that a particular image file, or part of that image file, has not been altered in any way from its original form. To accomplish this task, these certificates will typically include something called a Message Digest.

Message digests are similar to a file checksum in that they produce a small value that relates to the integrity of a file. A checksum is produced by a simple algorithm and its use is primarily to detect memory failures. That is, it is used to detect whether or not a block of memory on disk has gone bad and the values stored there have become corrupted. A message digest is similar to a checksum in that it will also detect file corruption. However, unlike most checksum algorithms, a message digest also has the property that it is very difficult to modify a file such that it will have the same message digest as its original (unmodified) form. That is, a checksum is intended to detect simple memory failures leading to corruption, but a message digest may be used to detect intentional, and even crafty modifications to a file, such as those introduced by viruses, hackers, or Trojan Horse programs.

It is not desirable to include all image file data in the calculation of a message digest. In some cases it simply presents undesirable characteristics (like the file is no longer localizable without regenerating certificates) and in other cases it is simply impossible. For example, It is not possible to include all information within an image file in a message digest, then insert a certificate containing that message digest in the file, and later be able to generate an identical message digest by including all image file data in the calculation again (since the file now contains a certificate that wasn't originally there).

This specification does not attempt to architect what each Attribute Certificate may be used for, or which fields or sections of an image file must be included in a message digest.

However, this section does identify which fields you may not want to or may not include in a message digest.

In addition to knowing which fields are and are not included in the calculation of a message digest, it is important to know the order in which the contents of the image are presented to the digest algorithm. This section specifies that order.

Fields Not to Include in Digests

There are some parts of an image that you may not want to include in any message digest. This section identifies those parts, and describes why you might not want to include them in a message digest.

- Information related to Attribute Certificates – It is not possible to include a certificate in the calculation of a message digest that resides within the certificate. Since certificates can be added to or removed from an image without affecting the overall integrity of the image, this is not a problem. Therefore, it is best to leave all attribute certificates out of the image even if there are certificates already in the image at the time you are calculating your message digest. There is no guarantee those certificates will still be there later, or that other certificates won't have been added. To exclude attribute certificate information from the message digest calculation, you must exclude the following information from that calculation:
  - The Certificate Table field of the Optional Header Data Directories.
  - The Certificate Table and corresponding certificates pointed to by the Certificate Table field listed immediately above.
- Debug information – Debug information may generally be considered advisory (to debuggers) and does not affect the actual integrity of the executable program. It is quite literally possible to remove debug information from an image after a product has been delivered and not affect the functionality of the program. This is, in fact, a disk saving measure that is sometimes utilized. If you do not want to include debug information in your message digest, then you should not include the following information in your message digest calculation:
  - The Debug entry of the Data Directory in with optional header
  - The .debug section
- File Checksum field of the Windows-Specific Fields of the Optional Header – This checksum includes the entire file (including any attribute certificates included in the file) and will, in all likelihood, be different after inserting your certificate than when you were originally calculating a message digest to include in your certificate.

- Unused, or obsolete fields – There are several fields that are either unused or obsolete. The value of these fields is undefined and may change after you calculate your message digest. These fields include:
  - Reserved field of the Optional Header Windows-Specific Fields (offset 52).
  - The DLL Flags field of the Optional Header Windows-Specific Fields. This field is obsolete.
  - Loader Flags field of the Optional Header Windows-Specific Fields. This field is obsolete.
  - Reserved entries of the Data Directory in the object header.
- Resources (makes localization easier) – Depending upon the specific Attribute Certificate, it may be desirable or undesirable to include resources in the message digest. If you want to allow localization without the generation of new certificates, then you do not want to include resources in your message digest. If the values of the resources are critical to your application, then you probably do want them included in your message digest, and you will accept the overhead of generating a certificate for each localized copy of the image. If you do not want to include resources in your message digest, then you should not include the following information in the message digest calculation:
  - Resource Table entry of the Optional Header Data Directory
  - The .rsrc section

Glossary

For the purpose of this International Standard, the following definitions apply. They are collected here for ease of reference, but the definitions are presented in context elsewhere in the specification, as noted. Definitions enclosed in square brackets [ ] were not extracted from the body of the standard.

The remainder of this section and its subsections contain only informative text.

Term	Description	Pt	Section	Section Title
Abstract	Only an abstract object type is allowed to define method contracts for which the type or the VES does not also provide the implementation. Such method contracts are called abstract methods.	I	8.9.6.2	Concreteness
Accessibility of members	A type scopes all of its members, and it also specifies the accessibility rules for its members. Except where noted, accessibility is decided based only on the statically visible type of the member being referenced and the type and assembly that is making the reference. The CTS [Common Type System] supports seven different rules for accessibility: Compiler-Controlled; Private; Family; Assembly; Family-and-Assembly; Family-or-Assembly; Public.	I	8.5.3.2	Accessibility of Members

Term	Description	Pt	Section	Section Title
Aggregate data	Data items that have sub-components (arrays, structures, or object instances) but are passed by copying the value. The sub-components can include references to managed memory. Aggregate data is represented using a *value type* . . .	I	12.1.6	Aggregate Data
Application domain	A mechanism . . . to isolate applications running in the same operating system process from one another.	I	12.5	Proxies and Remoting
Array elements	The representation of a value (except for those of built-in types) can be subdivided into sub-values. These sub-values are either named, in which case they are called **fields**, or they are accessed by an indexing expression, in which case they are called **array elements.**	I	8.4.1	Fields, Array Elements, and Values
Argument	[Value of an operand to a method call.]			
Array types	Types that describe values composed of array elements are **array types**.	I	8.4.1	Fields, Array Elements, and Values
Assembly	An assembly is a configured set of loadable code modules and other resources that together implement a unit of functionality.	I	8.5.2	Assemblies and Scoping
Assembly scope	Type names are scoped by the **assembly** that contains the implementation of the type. . . . The type name is said to be in the **assembly scope** of the assembly that implements the type.	I	8.5.2	Assemblies and Scoping
Assignment compatibility	Assignment compatibility of a value (described by a type signature) to a location (described by a location signature) is defined as follows: One of the types supported by the exact type of the value is the same as the type in the location signature.	I	8.7	Assignment Compatibility
Attributes	*Attributes* of types and their members attach descriptive information to their definition.	II	5.9	Attributes and Metadata
Base Class Library	This library is part of the Kernel Profile. It is a simple runtime library for a modern programming language.	IV	5.2	Base Class Library

Term	Description	Pt	Section	Section Title
Binary operators	Binary operators take two arguments, perform some operation, and return a value. They are represented as static methods on the class that defines the type of one of their two operands or the return type.	I	10.3.2	Binary Operators
Boolean data type	A CLI [Common Language Infrastructure] Boolean type occupies 1 byte in memory. A bit pattern of all zeros denotes a value of false. A bit pattern with any bit set (analogous to a non-zero integer) denotes a value of true.	III	1.1.2	Boolean Data Type
Box	The **box** instruction is a widening (always typesafe) operation that converts a value type instance to **System.Object** by making a copy of the instance and embedding it in a newly allocated object.	I	12.1.6.2.5	Boxing and Unboxing
Boxed type	For every Value Type, the CTS [Common Type System] defines a corresponding Reference Type called the **boxed type.**	I	8.2.4	Boxing and Unboxing of Values
Boxed value	The representation of a value of a boxed type (a **boxed value**) is a location where a value of the Value Type may be stored.	I	8.2.4	Boxing and Unboxing of Values
Built-in types	Data types [that] are an integral part of the CTS [Common Type System] and are supported directly by the Virtual Execution System (VES).	I	8.2.2	Built-in Types
By-ref parameters	The **address** of the data is passed from the caller to the callee, and the type of the parameter is therefore a managed or unmanaged pointer.	I	12.4.1.5	Parameter Passing
By-value parameters	The **value** of an object is passed from the caller to the callee.	I	12.4.1.5	Parameter Passing
Calling convention	A calling convention specifies how a method expects its arguments to be passed from the caller to the called method.	II	14.3	Calling Convention

Term	Description	Pt	Section	Section Title
Casting	Since a value can be of more than one type, a use of the value needs to clearly identify which of its types is being used. Since values are read from locations that are typed, the type of the value which is used is the type of the location from which the value was read. If a different type is to be used, the value is **cast** to one of its other types.	I	8.3.3	Casting
CIL	[Common Intermediate Language]	[III]		
Class contract	A class contract specifies the representation of the values of the class type. Additionally, a class contract specifies the other contracts that the class type supports—e.g., which interfaces, methods, properties, and events shall be implemented.	I	8.6	Contracts
Class type	A complete specification of the representation of the values of the class type and all of the contracts (class, interface, method, property, and event) that are supported by the class type.	I	8.9.5	Class Type Definition
CLI	At the center of the Common Language Infrastructure (CLI) is a single type system, the Common Type System (CTS), that is shared by compilers, tools, and the CLI itself. It is the model that defines the rules the CLI follows when declaring, using, and managing types.	I	6	Overview of the Common Language Infrastructure
CLS	The Common Language Specification (CLS) is a set of conventions intended to promote language interoperability.	I	7	Common Language Specification (CLS)
CLS (consumer)	A CLS consumer is a language or tool that is designed to allow access to all of the features supplied by CLS-compliant frameworks (libraries), but not necessarily be able to produce them.	I	7	Common Language Specification (CLS)
CLS (extender)	A CLS extender is a language or tool that is designed to allow programmers to both use and extend CLS-compliant frameworks.	I	7	Common Language Specification (CLS)

Term	Description	Pt	Section	Section Title
CLS (framework)	A library consisting of CLS-compliant code is herein referred to as a "framework."	I	7	Common Language Specification (CLS)
Code labels	Code labels are followed by a colon (":") and represent the address of an instruction to be executed.	II	5.4	Labels and Lists of Labels
Coercion	Coercion takes a value of a particular type and a desired type and attempts to create a value of the desired type that has equivalent meaning to the original value.	I	8.3.2	Coercion
Common Language Specification (CLS)	The Common Language Specification (CLS) is a set of conventions intended to promote language interoperability.	I	7	Common Language Specification (CLS)
Common Type System (CTS)	The Common Type System (CTS) provides a rich type system that supports the types and operations found in many programming languages.	I	8	Common Type System
Compiler-controlled accessibility	Accessible only through use of a definition, not a reference, hence only accessible from within a single compilation unit and under the control of the compiler.	I	8.5.3.2	Accessibility of Members
Compound types	Types that describe values composed of fields are **compound types**.	I	8.4.1	Fields, Array Elements, and Values
Computed destinations	The destination of a method call may be either encoded directly in the CIL instruction stream (the **call** and **jmp** instructions) or computed (the **callvirt** and **calli** instructions).	I	12.4.1.3	Computed Destinations
Concrete	An object type that is not marked **abstract** is by definition **concrete**.	I	8.9.6.2	Concreteness
Conformance	A system claiming conformance to this International Standard shall implement all the mandatory requirements of this standard, and shall specify the profile that it implements.	I	2	Conformance

Term	Description	Pt	Section	Section Title
Contracts	**Contracts** are named. They are the shared assumptions on a set of **signatures** . . . between all implementers and all users of the contract.	I	8.6	Contracts
Conversion operators	Conversion operators are unary operations that allow conversion from one type to another. The operator method shall be defined as a static method on either the operand or the return type.	I	10.3.3	Conversion Operators
Custom attributes	Custom attributes add user-defined annotations to the metadata. Custom attributes allow an instance of a type to be stored with any element of the metadata.	II	20	Custom Attributes
Custom modifiers	Custom modifiers, defined using **modreq** ("required modifier") and **modopt** ("optional modifier"), are similar to custom attributes . . . except that modifiers are part of a signature rather than attached to a declaration. Each modifer associates a type reference with an item in the signature.	II	7.1.1	modreq and modopt
Data labels	Data labels specify the location of a piece of data.	II	5.4	Labels and Lists of Labels
Delegates	**Delegates** are the object-oriented equivalent of function pointers. Delegates are created by defining a class that derives from the base type `System.Delegate`.	I	8.9.3	Delegates
Derived type	A derived type guarantees support for all of the type contracts of its base type. A type derives directly from its specified base type(s), and indirectly from their base type(s).	I	8.9.8	Type Inheritance
Enums	An **enum**, short for "enumeration," defines a set of symbols that all have the same type.	II	13.3	Enums

Term	Description	Pt	Section	Section Title
Equality	For value types, the equality operator is part of the definition of the exact type. Definitions of equality should obey the following rules: • Equality should be an equivalence operator, as defined above. • Identity should imply equality, as stated earlier. • If either (or both) operand is a boxed value, equality should be computed by ▪ First unboxing any boxed operand(s), and then ▪ Applying the usual rules for equality on the resulting values.	I	8.2.5.2	Equality
Equality of values	The values stored in the variables are **equal** if the sequences of characters are the same.	I	8.2.5	Identity and Equality of Values
Evaluation stack	Associated with each method state is an evaluation stack. . . . The evaluation stack is made up of slots that can hold any data type, including an unboxed instance of a value type.	I	12.3.2.1	The Evaluation Stack
Event contract	An event contract is specified with an event definition. There is an extensible set of operations for managing a named event, which includes three standard methods (register interest in an event, revoke interest in an event, fire the event). An event contract specifies method contracts for all of the operations that shall be implemented by any type that supports the event contract.	I	8.6	Contracts
Event definitions	The CTS [Common Type System] supports events in precisely the same way that it supports properties. . . . The conventional methods, however, are different and include means for subscribing and unsubscribing to events as well as for firing the event.	I	8.11.4	Event Definitions
Exception handling	Exception handling is supported in the CLI through exception objects and protected blocks of code	I	12.4.2	Exception Handling

Glossary

Term	Description	Pt	Section	Section Title
Extended Array Library	This Library is not part of any Profile, but can be supplied as part of any CLI implementation. It provides support for non-vector arrays.	IV	5.7	Extended Array Library
Extended Numerics Library	The Extended Numerics Library is not part of any Profile, but can be supplied as part of any CLI implementation. It provides the support for floating point (`System.Float`, `System.Double`) and extended-precision (`System.Decimal`) data types.	IV	5.6	Extended Numerics Library
Family accessibility	Accessible to referents that support the same type—i.e., an exact type and all of the types that inherit from it.	I	8.5.3.2	Accessibility of Members
Family-and-assembly accessibilty	Accessible only to referents that qualify for both family and assembly access.	I	8.5.3.2	Accessibility of Members
Family-or-assembly accessibility	Accessible only to referents that qualify for either family or assembly access.	I	8.5.3.2	Accessibility of Members
Field definitions	Field definitions [are composed of a] name and a location signature.	I	8.11.2	Field Definitions
Field inheritance	A derived object type inherits all of the non-static fields of its base object type.	I	8.10.1	Field Inheritance
Fields	Fields are typed memory locations that store the data of a program.	II	15	Defining and Referencing Fields
File names	A file name is like any other name where "." is considered a normal constituent character. The specific syntax for file names follows the specifications of the underlying operating system.	II	5.8	File Names
Finalizers	A class definition that creates an object type may supply an instance method to be called when an instance of the class is no longer accessible.	I	8.9.6.7	Finalizers
Getter method	By convention, properties define a **getter** method (for accessing the current value of the property).	I	8.11.3	Property Definitions

Term	Description	Pt	Section	Section Title
Global fields	In addition to types with static members, many languages have the notion of data and methods that are not part of a type at all. These are referred to as *global* fields and methods.	II	9.8	Global Fields and Methods
Global methods	In addition to types with static members, many languages have the notion of data and methods that are not part of a type at all. These are referred to as *global* fields and methods.	II	9.8	Global Fields and Methods
Global state	The CLI manages multiple concurrent threads of control . . . , multiple managed heaps, and a shared memory address space.	I	12.3.1	The Global State
GUID	[A unique identification string used with remote procedure calls.]	II	23	
hide-by-name	The introduction of a name in a given type hides all inherited members of the same kind (method or field) with the same name.	II	8.3	Hiding
hide-by-name-and-sig	The introduction of a name in a given type hides any inherited member of the same kind but with precisely the same type (for fields) or signature (for methods, properties, and events).	II	8.3	Hiding
Hiding	Hiding controls which method names inherited from a base type are available for compile-time name binding.	II	8	Visibility, Accessibility, and Hiding
Homes	The **home** of a data value is where it is stored for possible reuse.	I	12.1.6.1	Homes for Values
Identifiers	**Identifiers** are used to name entities	II	5.3	Identifiers

Term	Description	Pt	Section	Section Title
Identity	The identity operator is defined by the CTS as follows. • If the values have different exact types, then they are not identical. • Otherwise, if their exact type is a Value Type, then they are identical if and only if the bit sequences of the values are the same, bit by bit. • Otherwise, if their exact type is a Reference Type, then they are identical if and only if the locations of the values are the same.	I	8.2.5.1	Identity
Identity of values	The values of the variables are **identical** if the locations of the sequences of characters are the same—i.e., there is in fact only one string in memory.	I	8.2.5	Identity and Equality of Values
ilasm	An assembler language for CIL.	II	2	Overview
Inheritance demand	When attached to a type, an inheritance demand requires that any type that wishes to inherit from this type shall have the specified security permission. When attached to a non-final virtual method, it requires that any type that wishes to override this method shall have the specified permission.	I	8.5.3.3	Security Permissions
Instance methods	Instance methods are associated with an instance of a type: within the body of an instance method it is possible to reference the particular instance on which the method is operating (via the *this pointer*).	II	14.2	Static, Instance, and Virtual Methods
Instruction pointer (IP)	An instruction pointer (**IP**) points to the next CIL instruction to be executed by the CLI in the present method.	I	12.3.2	Method State
Interface contract	Interface contracts specify which other contracts the interface supports—e.g., which interfaces, methods, properties and events shall be implemented.	I	8.6	Contracts

Term	Description	Pt	Section	Section Title
Interface type definition	An **interface definition** defines an interface type. An interface type is a named group of methods, locations, and other contracts that shall be implemented by any object type that supports the interface contract of the same name.	I	8.9.4	Interface Type Definition
Interface type inheritance	Interface types may inherit from multiple interface types; i.e., an interface contract may list other interface contracts that shall also be supported.	I	8.9.8.3	Interface Type Inheritance
Interface types	Interface types describe a subset of the operations and none of the representation, and hence, cannot be an exact type of any value.	I	8.2.3	Classes, Interfaces, and Objects
Interfaces	Interfaces . . . define a contract that other types may implement.	II	11	Semantics of Interfaces
Kernel Profile	This profile is the minimal possible conforming implementation of the CLI.	IV	3.1	The Kernel Profile
Labels	Provided as a programming convenience; they represent a number that is encoded in the metadata. The value represented by a label is typically an offset in bytes from the beginning of the current method, although the precise encoding differs depending on where in the logical metadata structure or CIL stream the label occurs.	II	5.4	Labels and Lists of Labels
Libraries	To a programmer a Library is a self-consistent set of types (classes, interfaces, and value types) that provide a useful set of functionality.	IV	2.1	Libraries
Local memory pool	The local memory pool is used to allocate objects whose type or size is not known at compile time and which the programmer does not wish to allocate in the managed heap.	I	12.3.2.4	Local Memory Pool
Local signatures	A **local signature** specifies the contract on a local variable allocated during the running of a method.	I	8.6.1.3	Local Signatures

Term	Description	Pt	Section	Section Title
Location signatures	All locations are typed. This means that all locations have a **location signature**, which defines constraints on the location, its usage, and on the usage of the values stored in the location.	I	8.6.1.2	Location Signatures
Locations	Values are stored in **locations.** A location can hold a single value at a time. All locations are typed. The type of the location embodies the requirements that shall be met by values that are stored in the location.	I	8.3	Locations
Machine state	One of the design goals of the CLI is to hide the details of a method call frame from the CIL code generator. The machine state definitions . . . reflect these design choices, where machine state consists primarily of global state and method state.	I	12.3	Machine State
Managed code	Managed code is simply code that provides enough information to allow the CLI to provide a set of core services, including • Given an address inside the code for a method, locate the metadata describing the method • Walk the stack • Handle exceptions • Store and retrieve security information	I	6.2.1	Managed Code
Managed data	**Managed data** is data that is allocated and released automatically by the CLI, through a process called **garbage collection**. Only managed code can access managed data, but programs that are written in managed code can access both managed and unmanaged data.	I	6.2.2	Managed Data
Managed pointer types	[The **O** and **&**] data types represent an object reference that is managed by the CLI.	I	12.1.1.2	Managed Pointer Types: O and &

Term	Description	Pt	Section	Section Title
Managed pointers	Managed pointers (&) may point to a field of an object, a field of a value type, an element of an array, or the address where an element just past the end of an array would be stored (for pointer indexes into managed arrays).	II	13.4.2	Managed Pointers
Manifest	An **assembly** is a set of one or more files deployed as a unit. Every assembly has a **manifest** that declares what files make up the assembly, what types are exported, and what other assemblies are required to resolve type references within the assembly.	II	6	Assemblies, Manifests, and Modules
Marshalling descriptors	A marshalling descriptor is like a signature—it's a "blob" of binary data. It describes how a field or parameter (which, as usual, covers the method return, as parameter number 0) should be marshalled when calling to or from unmanaged coded via PInvoke dispatch or IJW ("It Just Works") thunking.	II	22.4	Marshalling Descriptors
Member	Fields, array elements, and methods are called **members** of the type. Properties and events are also members of the type.	I	8.4	Type Members
Member inheritance	Only object types may inherit implementations, hence only object types may inherit members.	I	8.10	Member Inheritance
Memory store	By "memory store" we mean the regular process memory that the CLI operates within. Conceptually, this store is simply an array of bytes.	I	12.6.1	The Memory Store
Metadata	The CLI uses metadata to describe and reference the types defined by the Common Type System. Metadata is stored ("persisted") in a way that is independent of any particular programming language. Thus, metadata provides a common interchange mechanism for use between tools that manipulate programs (compilers, debuggers, etc.) as well as between these tools and the Virtual Execution System.	I	9	Overview of the Common Language Infrastructure

Term	Description	Pt	Section	Section Title
Metadata token	This is a 4-byte value that specifies a row in a metadata table, or a starting byte offset in the Userstring heap.	III	1.9	Metadata Tokens
Method	A **method** describes an operation that may be performed on values of an exact type.	I	8.2.3	Classes, Interfaces, and Objects
Method contract	A method contract is specified with a method definition. A method contract is a named operation that specifies the contract between the implementation(s) of the method and the callers of the method.	I	8.6	Contracts
Method definitions	Method definitions are composed of a name, a method signature, and optionally an implementation of the method.	I	8.11.1	Method Definitions
Method inheritance	A derived object type inherits all of the instance and virtual methods of its base object type. It does not inherit constructors or static methods.	I	8.10.2	Method Inheritance
Method pointers	Variables of type **method** pointer shall store the address of the entry point to a method with compatible signature.	II	13.5	Method Pointers
Method signatures	**Method signatures** are composed of • A calling convention, • A list of zero or more parameter signatures, one for each parameter of the method, • And a type signature for the result value if one is produced.	I	8.6.1.5	Method Signatures
Method state	Method state describes the environment within which a method executes. (In conventional compiler terminology, it corresponds to a superset of the information captured in the "invocation stack frame.")	I	12.3.2	Method State
methodInfo handle	This . . . holds the signature of the method, the types of its local variables, and data about its exception handlers.	I	12.3.2	Method State
Module	A single file containing executable content.	II	6	Assemblies, Manifests, and Modules

Term	Description	Pt	Section	Section Title
Name Mangling	The platform may use name-mangling rules that force the name as it appears to a managed program to differ from the name as seen in the native implementation (this is common, for example, when the native code is generated by a C++ compiler).	II	14.5.2	Platform Invoke
Native data types	Some implementations of the CLI will be hosted on top of existing operating systems or runtime platforms that specify data types required to perform certain functions. The metadata allows interaction with these **native data types** by specifying how the built-in and user-defined types of the CLI are to be marshalled to and from native data types.	II	7.4	Native Data Types
Native size types	The native-size, or generic, types (native int, native unsigned int, O, and &) are a mechanism in the CLI for deferring the choice of a value's size.	I	12.1.1	Native Size: native int, native unsigned int, O, and &
Nested type definitions	A nested type definition is identical to a top-level type definition, with one exception: a top-level type has a visibility attribute, while the visibility of a nested type is the same as the visibility of the enclosing type.	I	8.11.5	Nested Type Definitions
Nested types	A type (called a nested type) can be a member of an enclosing type.	I	8.5.3.4	Nested Types
Network Library	This Library is part of the Compact Profile. It provides simple networking services, including direct access to network ports as well as HTTP support.	IV	5.3	Network Library
OOP	[Object-Oriented Programming]			
Object type	The object type describes the physical structure of the instance and the operations that are allowed on it.	I	8.9.6	Object Type Definitions

Term	Description	Pt	Section	Section Title
Object type inheritance	With the sole exception of `System.Object`, which does not inherit from any other object type, all object types shall either explicitly or implicitly declare support for (inherit from) exactly one other object type.	I	8.9.8.1	Object Type Inheritance
Objects	[Instances of a class.] Each object is self-typing; that is, its type is explicitly stored in its representation. It has an identity that distinguishes it from all other objects, and it has slots that store other entities (which may be either objects or values). While the contents of its slots may be changed, the identity of an object never changes.	I	8	Common Type System
Opaque classes	Some languages provide multi-byte data structures whose contents are manipulated directly by address arithmetic and indirection operations. To support this feature, the CLI allows value types to be created with a specified size but no information about their data members.	I	12.1.6.3	Opaque Classes
Overloading	Within a single scope, a given name may refer to any number of methods, provided they differ in any of the following: • Number of parameters • Type of each argument	I	10.2	Overloading
Overriding	Overriding deals with object layout and is applicable only to instance fields and virtual methods. The CTS provides two forms of member overriding, **new slot** and **expect existing slot**.	I	8.10.4	Hiding, Overriding, and Layout
Parameter	[Name used within the body of a method to refer to the corresponding argument of the method.]			
Parameter passing	The CLI supports three kinds of parameter passing, all indicated in metadata as part of the signature of the method. Each parameter to a method has its own passing convention (e.g., the first parameter may be passed by value while all others are passed by ref).	I	12.4.1.5	Parameter Passing

Term	Description	Pt	Section	Section Title
Parameter signatures	**Parameter signatures** define constraints on how an individual value is passed as part of a method invocation.	I	8.6.1.4	Parameter Signatures
Pinned	While a method with a pinned local variable is executing, the VES shall not relocate the object to which the local refers.	II	7.1.2	Pinned
PInvoke	Methods defined in native code may be invoked using the *platform invoke* (also know as PInvoke or p/invoke) functionality of the CLI.	II	14.5.2	Platform Invoke
Pointer type	A **pointer type** is a compile-time description of a value whose representation is a machine address of a location.	I	8.2.1	Value Types and Reference Types
Pointers	*Pointers* may contain the address of a field (of an object or value type) or an element of an array.	II	13.4	Pointer Types
Private accessibility	Accessible only to referents in the implementation of the exact type that defines the member.	I	8.5.3.2	Accessibility of Members
Profiles	A Profile is simply a set of Libraries, grouped together to form a consistent whole that provides a fixed level of functionality.	IV	2.2	Profiles
Properties	Propert[ies] define named groups of accessor method definitions that implement the named event or property behavior.	I	8.11	Member Definitions
Property contract	A property contract is specified with a property definition. There is an extensible set of operations for handling a named value, which includes a standard pair for reading the value and changing the value [typically get and set]. A property contract specifies method contracts for the subset of these operations that shall be implemented by any type that supports the property contract.	I	8.6	Contracts
Property definitions	A property definition defines a named value and the methods that access the value. A property definition defines the accessing contracts on that value.	I	8.11.3	Property Definitions

Term	Description	Pt	Section	Section Title
Public accessibility	Accessible to all referents.	I	8.5.3.2	Accessibility of Members
Qualified name	Consider a compound type `Point` that has a field named `x`. The name "field `x`" by itself does not uniquely identify the named field, but the **qualified name** "field x in type `Point`" does.	I	8.5.2	Assemblies and Scoping
Rank	The **rank** of an array is the number of dimensions.	II	13.2	Arrays
Reference demand	Any attempt to resolve a reference to the marked item shall have specified security permission.	I	8.5.3.3	Security Permissions
Reference types	**Reference Types** describe values that are represented as the location of a sequence of bits. There are four kinds of Reference Types: • Object types • Interface types • Pointer types • Built-in types	I	8.2.1	Value Types and Reference Types
Reflection Library	This Library is part of the Compact Profile. It provides the ability to examine the structure of types, create instances of types, and invoke methods on types, all based on a description of the type.	IV	5.4	Reflection Library
Remoting boundary	A **remoting boundary** exists if it is not possible to share the identity of an object directly across the boundary. For example, if two objects exist on physically separate machines that do not share a common address space, then a remoting boundary will exist between them.	I	12.5	Proxies and Remoting
Return state handle	This handle is used to restore the method state on return from the current method.	I	12.3.2	Method State
Runtime Infrastructure Library	This Library is part of the Kernel Profile. It provides the services needed by a compiler to target the CLI and the facilities needed to dynamically load types from a stream in the file format.	IV	5.1	Runtime Infrastructure Library

Term	Description	Pt	Section	Section Title
Scopes	Names are collected into groupings called **scopes**.	I	8.5.2	Assemblies and Scoping
Sealed	Specifies that a type shall not have subclasses.	II	9.1.4	Inheritance Attributes
Sealed type	An object type declares it shall not be used as a base type (be inherited from) by declaring that it is a **sealed type**.	I	8.9.8.1	Object Type Inheritance
Security descriptor	This descriptor is not directly accessible to managed code but is used by the CLI security system to record security overrides (**assert**, **permit-only**, and **deny**).	I	12.3.2	Method State
Security permissions	Access to members is also controlled by security demands that may be attached to an assembly, type, method, property, or event.	I	8.5.3.3	Security Permissions
Serializable fields	A field that is marked **serializable** is to be serialized as part of the persistent state of a value of the type.	I	8.11.2	Field Definitions
Setter method	By convention, properties define . . . optionally a **setter** method (for modifying the current value of the property).	I	8.11.3	Property Definitions
Signatures	**Signatures** are the part of a contract that can be checked and automatically enforced. Signatures are formed by adding constraints to types and other signatures.	I	8.6.1	Signatures
Simple labels	A simple label is a special name that represents an address.	II	5.4	Labels and Lists of Labels
Special members	There are three special members, all methods, that can be defined as part of a type: instance constructors, instance finalizers, and type initializers.	II	9.5	Special Members
Special types	Special Types are those that are referenced from CIL, but for which no definition is supplied: the VES supplies the definitions automatically based on information available from the reference.	II	13	Semantics of Special Types

Term	Description	Pt	Section	Section Title
Standard profiles	There are two Standard Profiles. The smallest conforming implementation of the CLI is the Kernel Profile, while the Compact Profile contains additional features useful for applications targeting a more resource-rich set of devices.	IV	3	The Standard Profiles
Static fields	Types may declare locations that are associated with the type rather than any particular value of the type. Such locations are **static fields** of the type.	I	8.4.3	Static Fields and Static Methods
Static methods	Types may also declare methods that are associated with the type rather than with values of the type. Such methods are **static methods** of the type.	I	8.4.3	Static Fields and Static Methods
Super calls	In some cases, it may be desirable to reuse code defined in the base type. For example, an overriding virtual method may want to call its previous version. This kind of reuse is called a *super call*, since the overridden method of the base type is called.			
This	When they are invoked, instance and virtual methods are passed the value on which this invocation is to operate (known as **this** or a **this pointer**).	I	8.4.2	Methods
Thunk	A (typically) small piece of code used to provide a transition between two pieces of code where special handling is required.			
try block	In the CLI, a method may define a range of CIL instructions that are said to be *protected*. This is called the "try block."	II	18	Exception Handling
Type	Types describe values and specify a contract . . . that all values of that type shall support.	I	8	Common Type System
Type definers	Type definers construct a new type from existing types.	I	8.9	Type Definers

Term	Description	Pt	Section	Section Title
Type definition	The **type definition**: • Defines a name for the type being defined—i.e., the **type name**—and specifies a scope in which that name will be found. • Defines a **member scope** in which the names of the different kinds of members (fields, methods, events, and properties) are bound. The tuple of (member name, member kind, and member signature) is unique within a member scope of a type. • Implicitly assigns the type to the assembly scope of the assembly that contains the type definition.	I	8.5.2	Assemblies and Scoping
Type inheritance	Inheritance of types is another way of saying that the derived type guarantees support for all of the type contracts of the base type. In addition, the derived type usually provides additional functionality or specialized behavior.	I	8.9.8	Type Inheritance
Type members	Object type definitions include member definitions for all of the members of the type. Briefly, members of a type include fields into which values are stored, methods that may be invoked, properties that are available, and events that may be raised.	I	8.9.6.3	Type Members
Type safety	An implementation that lives up to the enforceable part of the contract (the named signatures) is said to be **typesafe**.	I	8.8	Type Safety and Verification
Type signatures	Type signatures define the constraints on a value and its usage.	I	8.6.1.1	Type Signatures
Typed reference parameters	A runtime representation of the data type is passed along with the address of the data, and the type of the parameter is therefore one specially supplied for this purpose.	I	12.4.1.5	Parameter Passing

Term	Description	Pt	Section	Section Title
Types	Types describe values. All places where values are stored, passed, or operated upon have a type—e.g., all variables, parameters, evaluation stack locations, and method results. The type defines the allowable values and the allowable operations supported by the values of the type. All operators and functions have expected types for each of the values accessed or used.	I	8.2	Values and Types
Unary operators	Unary operators take one argument, perform some operation on it, and return the result. They are represented as static methods on the class that defines the type of their one operand or their return type.	I	10.3.1	Unary Operators
Unbox	**Unbox** is a narrowing (runtime exception may be generated) operation that converts a `System.Object` (whose runtime type is a value type) to a value type instance.	I	12.1.6.2.5	Boxing and Unboxing
Unmanaged code	[Code that does not require the runtime for execution. This code may not use the Common Type System or other features of the runtime. Traditional native code (before the CLI) is considered unmanaged.]			
Unmanaged pointer types	An **unmanaged pointer type** (also known simply as a "pointer type") is defined by specifying a location signature for the location the pointer references. Any signature of a pointer type includes this location signature.	I	8.9.2	Unmanaged Pointer Types
Validation	**Validation** refers to a set of tests that can be performed on any file to check that the file format, metadata, and CIL are self-consistent.	II	3	Validation and Verification
Value type inheritance	Value Types, in their unboxed form, do not inherit from any type.	I	8.9.8.2	Value Type Inheritance
Value types	In contrast to classes, value types (see Partition I) are not accessed by using a reference but are stored directly in the location of that type.	II	12	Semantics of Value Types

Term	Description	Pt	Section	Section Title
Values	The representation of a value (except for those of built-in types) can be subdivided into sub-values. These sub-values are either named, in which case they are called **fields,** or they are accessed by an indexing expression, in which case they are called **array elements.**	I	8.4.1	Fields, Array Elements, and Values
Vararg methods	vararg methods accept a variable number of arguments.	II	14.4.5	vararg Methods
Variable [-length] argument lists	The CLI works in conjunction with the class library to implement methods that accept argument lists of unknown length and type ("varargs methods").	I	12.3.2.3	Variable [-Length] Argument Lists
Vectors	Vectors are single-dimension arrays with a zero lower bound.	II	13.1	Vectors
Verifiability	Memory safety is a property that ensures programs running in the same address space are correctly isolated from one another . . . Thus, it is desirable to test whether programs are memory-safe prior to running them. Unfortunately, it is provably impossible to do this with 100% accuracy. Instead, the CLI can test a stronger restriction, called **verifiability.**	III	1.8	Verifiability
Verification	**Verification** refers to a check of both CIL and its related metadata to ensure that the CIL code sequences do not permit any access to memory outside the program's logical address space.	II	3	Validation and Verification
Version number	The version number of the assembly is specified as four 32-bit integers.	II	6.2.1.4	Version Numbers
Virtual call	A virtual method may be invoked by a special mechanism (a **virtual call**) that chooses the implementation based on the dynamically detected type of the instance used to make the virtual call rather than the type statically known at compile time.	I	8.4.4	Virtual Methods
Virtual calling convention	The CIL provides a "virtual calling convention" that is converted by an interpreter or JIT compiler into a native calling convention.	I	12.4.1.4	Virtual Calling Convention

Term	Description	Pt	Section	Section Title
Virtual Execution System	The Virtual Execution System (VES) provides an environment for executing managed code. It provides direct support for a set of built-in data types, defines a hypothetical machine with an associated machine model and state, a set of control flow constructs, and an exception handling model.	I	12	Virtual Execution System
Virtual methods	Virtual methods are associated with an instance of a type in much the same way as for instance methods. However, unlike instance methods, it is possible to call a virtual method in such a way that the implementation of the method shall be chosen at runtime by the VES depends upon the type of object used for the **this** pointer.	II	14.2	Static, Instance, and Virtual Methods
Visibility	Visibility is attached only to top-level types, and there are only two possibilities: visible to types within the same assembly, or visible to types regardless of assembly.	II	8.1	Visibility of Top-Level Types and Accessibility of Nested Types
Widen	If a type overrides an inherited method, it may *widen*, but it shall not *narrow*, the accessibility of that method.	II	9.3.3	Accessibility and Overriding
XML Library	This Library is part of the Compact Profile. It provides a simple "pull-style" parser for XML. It is designed for resource-constrained devices, yet provides a simple user model.	IV	5.5	XML Library

End informative text

References

(Note that many of these references are cited in the XML description of the class libraries and in the *.NET Framework Standard Library Annotated Reference.*)

Extensible Markup Language (XML) 1.0 (Second Edition), 2000 October 6, http://www.w3.org/TR/2000/REC-xml-20001006.

Federal Information Processing Standard (FIPS 180-1), *Secure Hash Standard (SHA-1)*, 1995 April.

IEC 60559:1989, *Binary Floating-Point Arithmetic for Microprocessor Systems* (previously designated IEC 559:1989).

ISO 639:1988, *Codes for the Representation of Names of Languages.*

ISO 3166:1988, *Codes for the Representation of Names of Countries.*

ISO/IEC 646:1991, *ISO 7-Bit Coded Character Set for Information Interchange.*

ISO/IEC 9899:1990, *Programming Languages—C.*

ISO/IEC 10646 (all parts), *Universal Multiple-Octet Coded Character Set (UCS).*

ISO/IEC 11578:1996 (E), *Open Systems Interconnection—Remote Procedure Call (RPC), Annex A: Universal Unique Identifier.*

ISO/IEC 14882:1998, *Programming Languages—C++.*

ISO/IEC 23270:2002, *Programming Languages—C#.*

RFC-768, *User Datagram Protocol.* J. Postel. 1980 August. http://www.ietf.org/rfc/rfc768.txt.

RFC-791, *Internet Protocol, DARPA Internet Program Protocol Specification.* 1981 September. http://www.ietf.org/rfc/rfc791.txt.

RFC-792, *Internet Control Message Protocol, DARPA Internet Program Protocol Specification*. Network Working Group. J. Postel. 1981 September. http://www.ietf.org/rfc/rfc792.txt.

RFC-793, *Transmission Control Protocol, DARPA Internet Program Protocol Specification*. J. Postel. 1981 September. http://www.ietf.org/rfc/rfc793.txt.

RFC-919, *Broadcasting Internet Datagrams*. Network Working Group. J. Mogul. 1984 October. http://www.ietf.org/rfc/rfc919.txt.

RFC-922, *Broadcasting Internet Datagrams in the Presence of Subnets*. Network Working Group. J. Mogul. 1984 October. http://www.ietf.org/rfc/rfc922.txt.

RFC-1035, *Domain Names—Implementation and Specification*. Network Working Group. P. Mockapetris. 1987 November. http://www.ietf.org/rfc/rfc1035.txt.

RFC-1036, *Standard for Interchange of USENET Messages*, Network Working Group. M. Horton and R. Adams. 1987 December. http://www.ietf.org/rfc/rfc1036.txt.

RFC-1112, *Host Extensions for IP Multicasting*. Network Working Group. S. Deering. 1989 August. http://www.ietf.org/rfc/rfc1112.txt.

RFC-1222, *Advancing the NSFNET Routing Architecture.* Network Working Group. H.-W. Braun and Y. Rekhter. 1991 May. http://www.ietf.org/rfc/rfc1222.txt.

RFC-1510, *The Kerberos Network Authentication Service (V5)*. Network Working Group. J. Kohl and C. Neuman. 1993 September. http://www.ietf.org/rfc/rfc1510.txt.

RFC-1741, *MIME Content Type for BinHex Encoded Files*. Network Working Group. P. Faltstrom, D. Crocker, and E. Fair. 1994 December. http://www.ietf.org/rfc/rfc1741.txt.

RFC-1764, *The PPP XNS IDP Control Protocol (XNSCP)*. Network Working Group. S. Senum. 1995 March. http://www.ietf.org/rfc/rfc1764.txt.

RFC-1766, *Tags for the Identification of Languages*. Network Working Group. H. Alvestrand. 1995 March. http://www.ietf.org/rfc/rfc1766.txt.

RFC-1792, *TCP/IPX Connection Mib Specification*. Network Working Group. T. Sung. 1995 April. http://www.ietf.org/rfc/rfc1792.txt.

RFC-2236, *Internet Group Management Protocol, Version 2*. Network Working Group. W. Fenner. 1997 November. http://www.ietf.org/rfc/rfc2236.txt.

RFC-2045, *Multipurpose Internet Mail Extensions (MIME) Part One: Format of Internet Message Bodies*. Network Working Group. N. Freed. 1996 November. http://www.ietf.org/rfc/rfc2045.txt.

RFC-2068, *Hypertext Transfer Protocol—HTTP/1.1*, Network Working Group. R. Fielding, J. Gettys, J. Mogul, H. Frystyk, and T. Berners-Lee. 1997 January. http://www.ietf. org/rfc/rfc2068.txt.

RFC-2396, Uniform Resource Identifiers (URI): Generic Syntax. Internet Engineering Task Force. T. Berners-Lee, R. Fielding, and L. Masinter. 1998 August. http://www.ietf.org/rfc/rfc2396.txt.

RFC-2616, *Hypertext Transfer Protocol—HTTP/1.1.* Network Working Group. R. Fielding, J. Gettys, J. Mogul, H. Frystyk, L. Masinter, P. Leach, and T. Berners-Lee. 1999 June. http://www.ietf.org/rfc/rfc2616.txt.

RFC-2617, *HTTP Authentication: Basic and Digest Access Authentication.* Network Working Group. J. Franks, P. Hallam-Baker, J. Hostetler, S. Lawrence, P. Leach, A. Luotonen, and L. Stewart. 1999 June. http://www.ietf.org/rfc/rfc2617.txt.

The Unicode Consortium. The Unicode Standard, Version 3.0, defined by: *The Unicode Standard, Version 3.0* (Reading, MA, Addison-Wesley, 2000. ISBN 0-201-61633-5), and Unicode Technical Report #15: *Unicode Normalization Forms.*

Index

B

C

E

F

G

H

I

J

N

O

S

T

Microsoft .NET Development Series

0321113594

0201734117

0321160770

0321154916

0321228391

0321228960

0321154932

0201760401

0201760398

0201734958

0321116208

0321125193

0201770180

0201745682

For more information go to www.awprofessional.com/msdotnetseries/

Register Your Book

at www.awprofessional.com/register

You may be eligible to receive:

- Advance notice of forthcoming editions of the book
- Related book recommendations
- Chapter excerpts and supplements of forthcoming titles
- Information about special contests and promotions throughout the year
- Notices and reminders about author appearances, tradeshows, and online chats with special guests

Contact us

If you are interested in writing a book or reviewing manuscripts prior to publication, please write to us at:

Editorial Department
Addison-Wesley Professional
75 Arlington Street, Suite 300
Boston, MA 02116 USA
Email: AWPro@aw.com

Addison-Wesley

Visit us on the Web: http://www.awprofessional.com